DEREK ROLLINSON

Organisational Behaviour and Analysis

An Integrated Approach

FOURTH EDITION

Prentice Hall
FINANCIAL TIMES

An imprint of **Pearson Education**
Harlow, England • London • New York • Boston • San Francisco • Toronto • Sydney • Singapore • Hong Kong
Tokyo • Seoul • Taipei • New Delhi • Cape Town • Madrid • Mexico City • Amsterdam • Munich • Paris • Milan

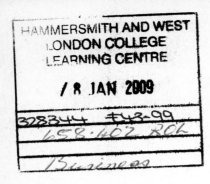
Pearson Education Limited
Edinburgh Gate
Harlow
Essex CM20 2JE
England

and Associated Companies throughout the world

Visit us on the World Wide Web at:
www.pearsoned.co.uk

First published 1998
Second edition published 2002
Third edition published 2005
Fourth edition published 2008

© Pearson Education Limited 1998, 2008

ISBN 978-0-273-71114-8

British Library Cataloguing-in-Publication Data
A catalogue record for this book is available from the British Library

Library of Congress Cataloging in Publication Data
Rollinson, Derek.
    Organisational behaviour and analysis : an integrated approach / Derek Rollinson – 4th ed.
        p. cm.
    Includes bibliographical references and index.
    ISBN 978-0-273-71114-8
    1. Organizational behavior.   I. Title.
    HD58.7. R654 2008
    158.7—dc22

                                                                    2008017067

10 9 8 7 6 5 4 3 2
12   11   10   09   08

Typeset by 35 in 9.5/12 pt Sabon
Printed and bound by Ashford Colour Press, Gosport

The publisher's policy is to use paper manufactured from sustainable forests.

To my wife Victoria, whose tolerance and help enabled this book to be written, and my daughter Sara, who kept my feet on the floor.

Brief Contents

Contents

Supporting resources

Visit www.pearsoned.co.uk/rollinson to find valuable online resources

Companion Website for students
- Comprehensive learning objectives and key concepts for each chapter
- Multiple choice questions – revise the key points of each chapter
- Links to further useful information on the web
- Additional case studies and OB in Action examples

For instructors
- Instructor's Manual – includes activity and case study notes, answers to the exercises in the book and additional discussion, essay and exam questions
- Test-bank – enables you to check your students have covered the basics
- PowerPoint slides – edited and updated for this edition

Also: The Companion Website provides the following features:

- Search tool to help locate specific items of content
- E-mail results and profile tools to send results of quizzes to instructors
- Online help and support to assist with website usage and troubleshooting

For more information please contact your local Pearson Education sales representative or visit
www.pearsoned.co.uk/rollinson

Further reading
Annotated
further reading
encourages you to
read more widely
around the subject
and provides a
shortlist of
recommendations

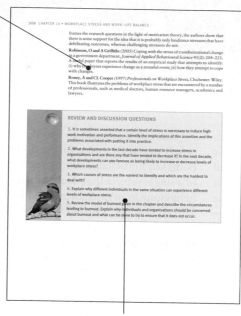

308 CHAPTER 10 • WORKPLACE STRESS AND WORK–LIFE BALANCE

frames the research questions in the light of motivation theory, the authors show that there is some support for the idea that it is probably only hindrance stressors that have debilitating outcomes, whereas challenging stressors do not.

Robinson, O and A Griffiths (2005) Coping with the stress of transformational change in a government department, *Journal of Applied Behavioural Science* 41(2): 204–221. A useful paper that reports the results of an empirical study that attempts to identify: (i) why employees experience change as a stressful event; (ii) how they attempt to cope with changes.

Roney, A and CL Cooper (1997) *Professionals on Workplace Stress*, Chichester: Wiley. This book illustrates the problems of workplace stress that are encountered by a number of professionals, such as medical doctors, human resource managers, academics and lawyers.

REVIEW AND DISCUSSION QUESTIONS

1. It is sometimes asserted that a certain level of stress is necessary to induce high work motivation and performance. Identify the implications of this assertion and the problems associated with putting it into practice.

2. What developments in the last decade have tended to increase stress in organisations and are there any that have tended to decrease it? In the next decade, what developments can you foresee as being likely to increase or decrease levels of workplace stress?

3. Which causes of stress are the easiest to identify and which are the hardest to deal with?

4. Explain why different individuals in the same situation can experience different levels of workplace stress.

5. Review the model of burnout given in the chapter and describe the circumstances leading to burnout. Explain why individuals and organisations should be concerned about burnout and what can be done to try to ensure that it does not occur.

Review and Discussion Questions
Encourage critical reflection on the main
topics and issues covered in each chapter,
either individually or in a group.

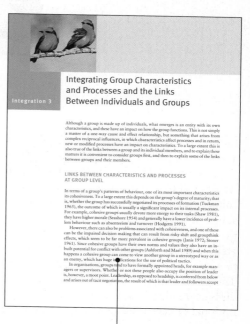

Integration 3

Integrating Group Characteristics and Processes and the Links Between Individuals and Groups

Although a group is made up of individuals, what emerges is an entity with its own characteristics, and these have an impact on how the group functions. This is not simply a matter of a one-way cause and effect relationship, but something that arises from complex reciprocal influences, in which characteristics affect processes and in return, new or modified processes have an impact on characteristics. To a large extent this is also true of the links between a group and its individual members, and to explain these matters it is convenient to consider groups first, and then to explain some of the links between groups and their members.

LINKS BETWEEN CHARACTERISTICS AND PROCESSES AT GROUP LEVEL

In terms of a group's patterns of behaviour, one of its most important characteristics its cohesiveness. To a large extent this depends on the group's degree of maturity; that is, whether the group has successfully negotiated its processes of formation (Tuckman 1965), the outcome of which is usually a significant impact on its internal processes. For example, cohesive groups usually devote more energy to their tasks (Shaw 1981), they have higher morale (Seashore 1954) and generally have a lower incidence of problem behaviour such as absenteeism and turnover (Hodgetts 1991).

However, there can also be problems associated with cohesiveness, and one of these can be the impaired decision making that can result from risky shift and groupthink effects, which seem to be far more prevalent in cohesive groups (Janis 1972; Stoner 1961). Since cohesive groups have their own norms and values they also have an in-built potential for conflict with other groups (Ashforth and Mael 1989) and when this happens a cohesive group can come to view another group in a stereotyped way or as an enemy, which has huge implications for the use of political tactics.

In organisations, groups tend to have formally appointed heads, for example managers or supervisors. Whether or not these people also occupy the position of leader is, however, a moot point. Leadership, as opposed to headship, is conferred from below and arises out of tacit negotiation, the result of which is that leader and followers accept

Integration
Five integrating sections enable
you to establish links between
topics and chapters.

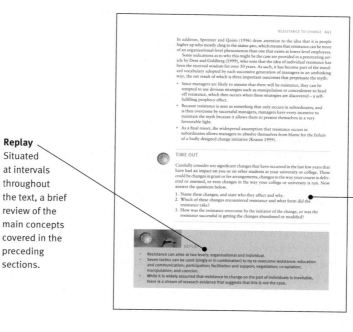

RESISTANCE TO CHANGE 641

In addition, Spreitzer and Quinn (1996) draw attention to the idea that it is people higher up who mostly cling to the *status quo*, which means that resistance can be more of an organisational-level phenomenon than one that exists in lower-level employees.

Some indications as to why this might be the case are provided in a penetrating article by Dent and Goldberg (1999), who note that the idea of individual resistance has been the received wisdom for over 50 years. As such, it has become part of the standard vocabulary adopted by each successive generation of managers in an unthinking way, the net result of which is three important outcomes that perpetuate the myth:

* Since managers are likely to assume that there will be resistance, they can be tempted to use devious strategies such as manipulation or concealment to head off resistance, which then occurs when these strategies are discovered – a self-fulfilling prophecy effect.

* Because resistance is seen as something that only occurs in subordinates, and is then overcome by successful managers, managers have every incentive to maintain the myth because it allows them to present themselves in a very favourable light.

* As a final resort, the widespread assumption that resistance occurs in subordinates allows managers to absolve themselves from blame for the failure of a badly designed change initiative (Krantz 1999).

TIME OUT

Carefully consider any significant changes that have occurred in the last few years that have had an impact on you or on other students at your university or college. These could be changes in grant or fee arrangements, changes to the way your course is delivered or assessed, or even changes in the way your college or university is run. Now answer the questions below.

1. Name these changes, and state who they affect and why.
2. Which of these changes encountered resistance and what form did the resistance take?
3. How was the resistance overcome by the initiator of the change, or was the resistance successful in getting the changes abandoned or modified?

REPLAY

* Resistance can arise at two levels: organisational and individual.
* Seven tactics can be used (singly or in combination) to try to overcome resistance: education and communication; participation; facilitation and support; negotiation; co-optation; manipulation; and coercion.
* While it is widely assumed that resistance to change on the part of individuals is inevitable, there is a stream of research evidence that suggests that this is not the case.

Replay
Situated
at intervals
throughout
the text, a brief
review of the
main concepts
covered in the
preceding
sections.

Time Out
Exercises enable
you to draw
on your own
experiences to
apply a concept
or theory.

Like previous editions of the book, this one provides a comprehensive introduction to the study of Organisational Behaviour (OB) and Organisational Analysis (OA), and it has been written to make it suitable for students with no prior exposure to these subjects. Nevertheless, it also gives an initial exposure to some of the more advanced knowledge in the area, and this makes it of use to those who wish to commence studying the subjects at a higher level. The text is primarily designed for undergraduate and diploma students for whom OB and OA are core or optional subjects, and also for postgraduate and post-experience students, where an exposure to knowledge of human behaviour in organisations is an essential part of their programme of studies.

Organisational Behaviour and Organisational Analysis are both subjects that deal with the behaviour of people in organisations, and together they contain a wealth of knowledge about this matter. Nevertheless, each one has a somewhat different focus. The traditional concern of OB is at the micro level of organisation and so it normally has a heavy, if not exclusive focus on the characteristics and processes of individuals and groups. Conversely, OA is much more heavily focused on the organisation as a whole and deals with characteristics such as structure, effectiveness, goals and culture, and also with processes such as control, communication and change.

To some extent this is a matter of academic convenience. It allows what is a broad and extensive body of knowledge to be broken down into two manageable parts for the purposes of instruction. In addition, because OB is sometimes considered an essential prerequisite to the study of OA, it is also a matter of necessity. However, it can result in two unfortunate tendencies. First, OB is often regarded as a less advanced topic than OA and, second, the two bodies of knowledge can come to be regarded as discrete and separate; indeed, they are often taught by different people, using totally unrelated teaching materials.

This book sets out to avoid these pitfalls. It purposely avoids treating OB and OA as two separate bodies of knowledge. Both are regarded as two parts of a single subject that deals with the matter of human behaviour in organisations and how that behaviour affects, and is affected by, the behaviour of the organisation as a whole. The rationale for adopting this approach is quite simple. In practice, the two levels do not exist in isolation and they are in continuous interaction. The behaviour of individuals and groups in an organisation is inevitably affected by the organisational context within which the behaviour occurs and if we wish to understand why individuals and groups behave as they do, account needs to be taken of the influence of these wider organisational factors. Similarly, the behaviour of a whole organisation is strongly influenced by the actions of its individuals and groups, which means that account has to be taken of lower-level factors to understand the behaviour of an organisation as a whole. In summary, therefore, understanding behaviour at either the macro or the micro level requires an integrative approach, where attention is directed at the effects of one level on the other.

This does not mean that OB and OA cannot be taught separately, or in a sequence in which one follows the other. Indeed, because of time constraints in many institutions, together with the extensive nature of both subjects, this will probably continue to be a matter of necessity. Nevertheless, it still remains important that students of OB are made aware that OB is only part of the story, and the same is true for OA. For this reason both subjects need to be taught in a way that demonstrates the complementary nature of their respective concerns, rather than as separate subjects in which the body of knowledge in one is allowed to override or contradict that in the other.

This can be difficult to achieve when teaching the subjects from two separate textbooks. For example, many OB texts tend to focus exclusively on micro level issues, or pay lip service to the existence of OA. In the same way, texts in OA frequently ignore the body of knowledge in OB. The remedy adopted here has been to produce a text in which both subjects are brought within the same cover. Therefore, if OB and OA are taught separately for the sake of convenience, integration is made easier because both are covered in a similar way and with integration in mind.

Another feature of either OB or OA texts that this book seeks to avoid is the way that topics within each subject are sometimes treated as discrete parcels of knowledge. Most books cover different topics in different chapters in order to break down the subject into manageable parts that can be easily digested by the reader. However, this is sometimes done in a way that leaves the reader with an impression that they are unrelated topics. Clearly this is not the case, and for this reason the book purposely cross-links the different topics in OB or OA, as well as integrating OB and OA with each other.

Like most texts, this book also has its own philosophical approach to dealing with the subject matter. For example, in most American texts a strongly managerialist stance is adopted and this is also the case with several British books. These texts are addressed primarily at a management (or would-be management) audience, and the subject matter of OB and OA is put over as being part of the managerial tool-kit that helps managers to remain 'in control'. While OB and OA are subjects that are often included in courses taken by people who see themselves as managers, or the managers of the future, this book is at pains to avoid a managerialist perspective. Indeed, the underlying philosophy is that both subjects are, or should be, neutral. Thus, the approach adopted is that of informing the reader rather than trying to equip him or her with the knowledge to manipulate or control others.

DEVELOPMENTS FROM THE THIRD EDITION

Readers familiar with the third edition, published in 2005, will notice a number of changes to the text. For the most part these differences between the third and fourth editions are a matter of progressive refinement, rather than a fundamental change in direction. In deciding what these should be, the author has been greatly aided by many helpful comments and suggestions from reviewers, colleagues and numerous other lecturers and students. The aim has been to retain features from the third edition that people found particularly useful and to add (or re-locate) features and content that these people felt would improve the utility of the book. Examples of the former are: the comprehensive nature of the book; specific learning objectives; margin notes; self-study exercises; summary points and further readings. One of the features that has been amplified is to strengthen the integrative message of the book by providing integrative case studies at the end of parts 2, 3, 4 and 5 of the book. Another change from the previous edition has been change in the way that cross-national or cross-cultural matters are covered. In the previous edition a separate chapter covering these matters was provided at the end of the book. In this edition, however, the subject material is dispersed across virtually all other chapters of the book. For example, different types of cross-national organisation tend to have distinct structures and so these features are explained in Chapter 17 (Organisational Structure) and Chapter 18 (Organisational Design). Similarly, there is often a necessity for different styles of leadership or management behaviour to be used according to the characteristics of the national culture in which an overseas subsidiary of a firm is located. Thus, the cross-cultural implications of leadership are covered in Chapters 12 and 13 (Leadership). Other features that have been amplified are: an increased emphasis on the practical applications of OB and OA; and a certain amount of case material set in a non-British context. To summarise, while the format of the book remains much the same as the third edition, all chapters have been updated and some have been extensively revised.

Derek Rollinson
April 2008

THE STRUCTURE OF THE BOOK

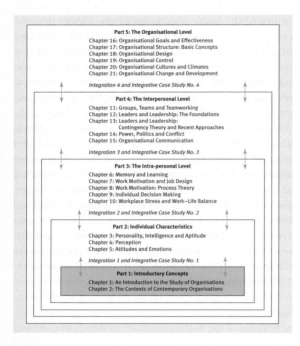

The above diagram, which indicates the contents of the book, has two main uses. First, it is a conceptual model that stresses the need to integrate the subjects of Organisational Behaviour (OB) and Organisational Analysis (OA). As will be explained in greater detail in Chapter 1, although these subjects are often taught separately, there are powerful arguments that they are just two halves of a single, bigger subject. Therefore, a full understanding of human behaviour in organisations only comes from taking account of both bodies of knowledge.

The model divides an organisation into different levels, and the important point to note is that straddling the boundaries of each level there are a pair of double-headed arrows. This reflects the idea that whatever the issue or topic on which a particular chapter is focused, it is necessary recognise that the topic is affected by matters at the levels above, and the levels above are affected by this topic in return.

The second use for the model is as an navigational aid that helps the reader steer him or herself through the book. For this reason it will reappear in a slightly modified form in the short introductions that precede the five sections into which the book is divided. Each of these sections deals with topics that are focused at a particular level of organisation and are briefly described in what follows.

Section 1: Introductory Concepts

This section contains two chapters that are introductory in nature. The first gives a general introduction to the subjects of Organisational Behaviour and Organisational Analysis, based on the assumption that the reader has no prior exposure to either of them. The second chapter further amplifies an important point made in Chapter 1. Organisations are not sealed-off from their surrounding environment, but are in continuous interaction with their contexts. By definition, these contexts are not under the direct control of organisations, and firms have very little choice but to respond to environmental factors. This need to respond to environment is likely to result in considerable challenges for firms in the years ahead, three are discussed further before closing the chapter.

Section 2: Individual Differences

This section commences the study of the micro aspects of human behaviour in organisations and all three chapters focus on the way that people differ as individuals. Chapter 3 covers personality, intelligence and aptitude, Chapter 4 deals with perception and Chapter 5 attitudes and emotions. At the end of the section there is a short integrative sub-section, which is shown on the model as Integration 1. This traces links between the three characteristics covered in the preceding chapters and is followed by an integrative case study, which gives students the opportunity to apply the integrative principles in a practical way.

Section 3: The Intrapersonal Level

The five chapters in this section also deal with matters at an individual level, but since they cover processes that occur within (intra) people, they have a more dynamic focus. Chapter 6 deals with the processes of memory and learning and Chapters 7 and 8 cover work motivation. Chapter 9 deals with the matter of individual decision making and Chapter 10 with stress, work–life balance and stress management. Again an integrative sub-section (Integration 2) is given, which traces links between the topics covered in the preceding five chapters. It also explains how the individual characteristics covered in section 1 of the book are related to the individual processes covered in this section and this is followed by an integrative case study, which gives students the opportunity to apply the integrative principles in a practical way.

Section 4: The Interpersonal Level

In the five chapters included in this section the focus moves to the level of the group. These chapters deal with some of the visible social aspects of organisational life, which are important in their own right, but also as a bridge with the chapters in section 5, which will be outlined presently. Chapter 11 covers the topic of groups; why they are important, their functioning, characteristics and processes. The next two chapters (12 and 13) address the matter of leadership and the processes involved. In Chapter 14, the focus widens to consider three important intra- and inter-group processes: power, politics and conflict, and, finally, Chapter 15 deals with the topic of organisational communication. The integrative sub-section (Integration 3) that comes after these chapters traces links between the topics covered in each one and shows how group level matters are related to the matters covered in Integration 2. Once again this is followed by an integrative case study.

Section 5: The Organisational Level

Although it is much more difficult to distinguish between characteristics and processes at this level of an organisation, an arbitrary distinction can be made by treating the first three chapters in the section as characteristics and the remaining three as processes. Chapter 16 covers the apparently simple (but in reality complex) issues of organisational goals and effectiveness, and in Chapters 17 and 18 the focus moves respectively to organisational structure and organisational design.

The remaining three chapters all deal with macro organisational processes. The first of these, Chapter 19, addresses the matter of organisational control, which is purposely located here because control systems are often part of an organisation's structural design. Depending on the way they are viewed, the topics of culture and climate, which are the subject of Chapter 20, could either be viewed as characteristics or processes. However, Chapter 21, which covers change and development, is very firmly process-orientated.

As with other sections of the book, integration is also covered at the end of this one: first, by tracing links between the characteristics and processes covered in Chapters 16 to 21; and, second, by briefly tracing links between all the different levels of organisation covered in the book. This is followed by the final integrative case study in the book, which gives students the opportunity to apply the integrative principles in a practical way.

HOW TO USE THE BOOK

General

Lecturers vary considerably in terms of the theories and concepts that they consider to be the necessary minimum when providing instruction on a particular topic. They also differ in terms of the amount of time they have available for instruction. Therefore, in the interests of providing a text that can be used by the widest possible number of lecturers, it has purposely been made comprehensive in terms of the coverage of each topic. This means that in some cases there could be more information in some chapters than a lecturer wishes to use. For this reason the chapters have been written in a way that permits some of the material to be omitted (where this is necessary) and lecturers should not hesitate to be selective about the concepts and theories they use from each chapter.

Each chapter in the book deals with a separate topic and, since each one has a clear set of learning outcomes that can be met by covering its contents, it is not vital to use the chapters in the order in which they appear in the book.

The material reflects teaching styles that have now become more common in higher education in Great Britain. These have a focus on *learning* rather than teaching, which tends to mean that there is less emphasis on formal, in-class instruction, and students are required to take an increased level of responsibility for their own learning outside the classroom. For this reason, instruction periods often have a stronger focus on checking that learning has taken place, and applying the concepts in exercises and/or case studies. To facilitate this, the book has been written as a complete vehicle of instruction in its own right, rather than just background reading. Each chapter contains a full explanation of the concepts and theories it contains, together with associated exercises and/or case studies that can be used to apply the material. There are two main reasons for doing this. First, to produce a text in which students and instructors have confidence. Second, the aim has been to *eliminate the need for an additional workbook to support the text*. This latter point reflects the difficulty of persuading students to buy *any* book, let alone an additional one, at a time when their income has been progressively reduced by cutbacks in funding.

Activities Featured in the Text

> LEARNING OUTCOMES
>
> After studying this chapter you should be able to:
>
> - define organisations and name the five key features that distinguish an entity as an organisation
> - explain why it is important to study organisations
> - define Organisational Behaviour (OB) and Organisational Analysis (OA) and briefly trace their origins
> - understand the traditional differences in approach to the study of organisations adopted by OB and OA and the case for their integration
> - compare and contrast different conceptualisations used for the study of organisations (metaphors) and contrast them with the postmodernist perspective
> - describe the characteristics of contemporary Organisational Behaviour and Analysis, together with the approach towards the

A set of **Learning Outcomes** is given at the start of each chapter, and these tell the reader what he or she should be able to understand or to accomplish after covering the chapter's contents. To some extent,

these can also be used by readers to measure their progress.

> TIME OUT
>
> 1. Think about a university or college as an organisation. Describe ways in which it qualifies as an organisation in terms of the five characteristics given above. That is: is it an artifact?; does it have goals and what do you feel that they are?; are there many people involved and who are they?; does it have a structure and coordinating mechanisms and, if so, what are the signs that these exist?; can you place nominal boundaries on the institution and, if so, where would you place them?
> 2. Now do the same for your immediate family; how easy is it to conceptualise this as an organisation?

A small number of **Time Out** exercises are included in each chapter. These are very short exercises that confront the reader with questions that encourage the application of concepts and theories covered in the text, but in a way that prompts the person to draw on his or her own experience. While these are primarily designed to be an aid to learning, which allows students to complete exercises outside the classroom, they can, if required, be used in the classroom as discussion topics or as illustrative exercises. Students are also provided with **Margin Notes**, which define new concepts as they are introduced and are also brought together at the end of the book in a **Glossary**.

> **CASE STUDY 6.1: Knowledge management at British Petroleum**
>
> The practice of knowledge management arose in the early 1990s, when companies attempted to harness their under-used knowledge and intellectual capital. Nearly a decade later, it has not delivered on that promise, but has become narrowly focused on databases and other electronic means. While these have their uses they are not far-reaching; in part because they do not alter employees' attitudes to sharing and using knowledge. To do this, knowledge management needs to tackle something more fundamental – the design of a collaborative organisation.
>
> British Petroleum (BP) provides a good example of this new approach. Over the past decade it has transformed the company from a collection of individual management fiefdoms and independent business units, into a collaborative business, thereby cutting costs, improving efficiency and lifting revenues. It has changed the resource allocation process so that a group of peers – business unit heads who run similar businesses – has become responsible for the allocation of capital expenditure to that group; effectively forcing it to work together to maximise allocations to the group, rather than to each individual. It has also developed the techniques of 'peer assist' and 'peer challenge' processes, in which managers and engineers in a business unit receive help from other units. Engineers in a typical business unit now spend about 5 per cent of their time on peer assists in other units, and BP has developed several electronic knowledge management systems and used video technology to aid with peer assists.
>
> Promotion and reward systems have also changed. Managers now receive a '360-degree' review, and those who do not collaborate effectively across the organisation are excluded from more senior management positions. In addition, 30–50 per cent of the bonuses of senior managers depend on the performance of the company as a whole, and these changes go well beyond simply being electronic tools. They have altered the organisation and management principles of the company, which has led to enhanced levels of collaborative behaviour in the organisation; a lateral way of managing across units that complements the traditional hierarchy. Nevertheless, although most managers acknowledge the value of a 'collaborative culture', few know how to build one. To this end BP has identified a few simple techniques that can help instil the right types of behaviour. Because each organisation is different, however,

From Chapter 2 onwards, each chapter contains short **Case Studies**, which give students the opportunity to apply a single concept or theory. In addition, the companion Instructor's Manual and associated Student Website contain a longer, supplementary case study for each chapter, which brings together several concepts or theories.

The integrative cases located after the integrative material at the end of each section of the book are of a special type. These are all linked to each other, and are of the 'unfolding/rolling scenario' type, in which the second case in the book (e.g. Integrative Case Study No. 2) builds on information given in the first one (Integrative Case Study No. 1), and so on. This removes the necessity to examine a new situation from scratch for each case, and allows the student to focus on answering the case questions of these rolling scenarios, thus saving valuable time for students and lecturers.

Most cases are drawn from real-life situations, some from the author's own experience of encountering these conditions within an organisational context, perhaps when collecting research data. Others were reported to the author by students or colleagues and were subsequently written-up into cases.

Although primarily intended for in-class use, the cases can also be used as material around which assignments or examination questions can be based. Because case studies will sometimes be a new learning vehicle for students, a guide to using cases has been provided in the companion website to this book.

OB IN ACTION: British Petroleum's green credentials

Over the last decade, British Petroleum (BP), the world's second largest oil company, has burnished its green credentials. In 1996, the company withdrew from the Global Climate Coalition, the anti-global warming body backed by the oil industry, and in 2000, it re-branded itself as an energy company, 'Beyond Petroleum', stressing its commitment to environmentalism. Indeed, in 2005 the company said it would spend $8bn on solar, wind and hydrogen energy over ten years. 'No one should be able to use the environment without restoring it,' stated the company's group chief executive officer, Lord (John) Browne.

But does BP have a dark side? In 2006 the company halted production at Prudhoe Bay, the USA's biggest oilfield on Alaska's North Slope, after it found severe corrosion inside 16 miles of transit lines, which help feed crude oil from 2,200 wells into the Trans-Alaska Pipeline, although production has since resumed in Prudhoe Bay's western section. This problem surfaced when BP inspected feeder pipes following a 270,000-gallon spill – Prudhoe Bay's worst – in March. Whereas BP had run external tests on pipes, the insides had not been electronically inspected since 1992, as there was no legal requirement to do so. Prudhoe Bay opened in 1977 and was exploited by BP in a joint venture with Exxon Mobil and Conoco-Phillips. This is an old field and production has steadily declined since the late 1980s, and sludge had built up inside feeder lines, preventing inhibitor chemicals from reaching the corrosion.

So why hadn't eco-friendly BP anticipated this problem? To the company's critics, it is part of a disturbing pattern that they claim gives the lie to BP's green credentials. Last month the company closed 57 wells 'that exhibited problems with surface leakage' and said 37 remain 'shut in' as they 'did not meet the company's operating criteria'. Earlier another BP line ruptured on the North Slope and the same month the company was fined $2.4m for safety problems at a facility in Ohio. In March 2005, following a refinery explosion that killed 15 workers and inured 170

OB in Action boxes will also be found dispersed throughout the text in most chapters. These are not case studies in the accepted meaning of the expression, although they can be used to illustrate a point or to stimulate discussion. Rather, they are real-world examples of the application of concepts or theories

covered in the text. Sometimes they supplement a point already made in the chapter. Their main use, however, is to bring home the idea that the theories and concepts in OB and OA are not abstract pieces of knowledge constructed for the amusement of academics, but things that find real-world applications in organisations.

REPLAY

- Organisational Behaviour and Organisational Analysis originate from two different sources that were focused respectively on micro and macro level aspects of organisations.
- While not in itself Organisational Behaviour, there are assumptions about factors that influence micro level aspects of behaviour contained in scientific management theories. However, the more identifiable origins of Organisational Behaviour lie in the findings of the Hawthorne experiments that gave rise to the human relations movement.
- Organisational Analysis traces its roots to the classical management school of theorists, who attempted to formulate universal principles for the design and functioning of organisations.

Replay lists will also be found at the end of each major section of a chapter. Each one consists of a list of bulleted summary points that re-emphasise concepts, theories, ideas and themes contained in the section.

At the end of each chapter there is a block of **Review and Discussion Questions**. These can be used for a final review of its contents, or to re-emphasise its major points. They can also be used for separate tutorials, or as a check on learning. Finally, for those who may wish to delve deeper into a particular topic or issue, each chapter also contains a short list of **Further Reading** at its end.

Supporting Materials

The book is supported by its own dedicated website www.booksites.net/rollinson and an **Instructor's Manual**. The website, which is organised chapter by chapter and is freely accessible to students provides:

- a short summary of the major points covered in a chapter
- definitions of new concepts introduced in the chapter
- hints for completing Time Out exercises
- the supplementary case study associated with the chapter
- a short battery of multiple-choice questions, which can be used by students for self-assessment purposes
- answers for the multiple-choice questions

- a list of potentially useful additional literature references, over and above those given in the main text
- a list of potentially useful websites that provide additional information.

The Instructor's Manual, access to which is restricted to lecturers who adopt the book, provides in addition:

- session running guides for each chapter
- model answers to the cases and exercises in the book
- additional tutorial questions and answers
- specimen assignment and examination questions
- a short battery of multiple-choice test questions and answers for each chapter
- OHP slide masters for the diagrams in the book.

Introductory Concepts

The diagram, which was first introduced on page xx, tells you that this section of the book contains two chapters. Both of these are introductory in nature and the first introduces the subjects of Organisational Behaviour and Organisational Analysis. Chapter 2 is rather different. It makes the point that organisations are not sealed-off from their environments, but are strongly affected by the different contextual circumstances that surround them.

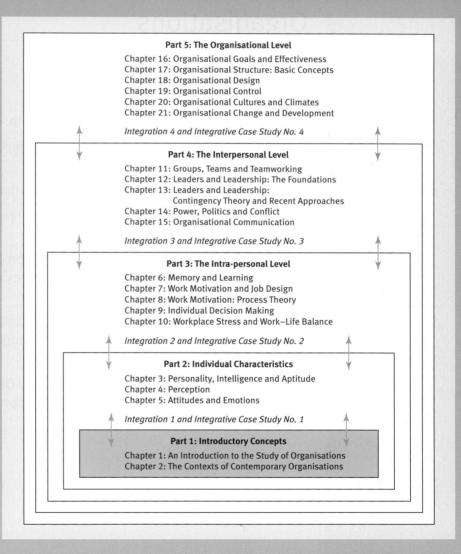

Part 5: The Organisational Level

Chapter 16: Organisational Goals and Effectiveness
Chapter 17: Organisational Structure: Basic Concepts
Chapter 18: Organisational Design
Chapter 19: Organisational Control
Chapter 20: Organisational Cultures and Climates
Chapter 21: Organisational Change and Development

Integration 4 and Integrative Case Study No. 4

Part 4: The Interpersonal Level

Chapter 11: Groups, Teams and Teamworking
Chapter 12: Leaders and Leadership: The Foundations
Chapter 13: Leaders and Leadership:
            Contingency Theory and Recent Approaches
Chapter 14: Power, Politics and Conflict
Chapter 15: Organisational Communication

Integration 3 and Integrative Case Study No. 3

Part 3: The Intra-personal Level

Chapter 6: Memory and Learning
Chapter 7: Work Motivation and Job Design
Chapter 8: Work Motivation: Process Theory
Chapter 9: Individual Decision Making
Chapter 10: Workplace Stress and Work–Life Balance

Integration 2 and Integrative Case Study No. 2

Part 2: Individual Characteristics

Chapter 3: Personality, Intelligence and Aptitude
Chapter 4: Perception
Chapter 5: Attitudes and Emotions

Integration 1 and Integrative Case Study No. 1

Part 1: Introductory Concepts

Chapter 1: An Introduction to the Study of Organisations
Chapter 2: The Contexts of Contemporary Organisations

Chapter 1

An Introduction to the Study of Organisations

LEARNING OUTCOMES

After studying this chapter you should be able to:

- define organisations and name the five key features that distinguish an entity as an organisation

- explain why it is important to study organisations

- define Organisational Behaviour (OB) and Organisational Analysis (OA) and briefly trace their origins

- understand the traditional differences in approach to the study of organisations adopted by OB and OA and the case for their integration

- compare and contrast different conceptualisations used for the study of organisations (metaphors) and contrast them with the postmodernist perspective

- describe the characteristics of contemporary Organisational Behaviour and Analysis, together with the approach towards the subjects adopted in this book

INTRODUCTION

This chapter has two purposes: first, to introduce organisations as a field of study; and, second, to explain how this book will deal with the subject. Because the word organisation is often used in a very loose way that means different things to different people, the chapter starts by defining how the word is used in this book. The next section of the chapter deals with the subjects of Organisational Behaviour (OB) and Organisational Analysis (OA).

Traditionally, OB and OA have tended to focus on different levels of organisation. For the most part OB deals with the micro level, which has a focus on the behaviour of individuals and groups within organisations, whereas OA has focused on the macro level and deals with the behaviour of whole organisations. Since the book covers both levels of organisation, OB and OA are defined, their respective approaches to understanding behaviour in organisations and by organisations are compared, and their origins are described. The chapter then argues that while the distinction between macro and micro levels has some convenience, it is artificial. That is, fully understanding behaviour at the micro level requires that we take account of factors at the macro level, a corollary of which is that understanding the behaviour of a whole organisation requires that due account is taken of how individuals and groups behave at the micro level. The chapter then sets out a number of different perspectives that are frequently used as ways of conceptualising an organisation, and it closes with a description of the characteristics of contemporary Organisational Behaviour and Organisational Analysis, together with a statement of the approach towards the study of organisations adopted in this book.

WHAT IS AN ORGANISATION?

Although our lives are dominated by organisations, like many things we take them for granted. Since this book deals with the behaviour of organisations and the people in them, before entering the subject matter it is necessary to define the entities on which it is focused. As will be seen later in the chapter, there are several ways of conceptualising an organisation but here a simpler approach will be used to illustrate that organisations have a number of important features, which are set out in the following list:

- **Organisations are artifacts** They do not exist in nature but are brought into existence by humans.
- **Goal directed** Organisations are created to serve some purpose. However, this does not mean that everyone in a particular organisation has the same common goal and neither does it follow that everybody is aware of the goals pursued by the organisation.
- **Social entities** Organisations usually consist of more than one person and although a one-person business (such as the corner shop) can be conceived of as an organisation, and in legal terms it might well be classified as one, this is not normally what we mean by the word.
- **Structured activity** Achieving the purpose or goals for an organisation normally requires that human activity be deliberately structured and coordinated in some way, thus there will usually be identifiable parts or activities.

- **Nominal boundaries**   It is usually possible to identify nominal boundaries for an organisation, which give a degree of consensus about who or what is part of the organisation and who or what belongs elsewhere. However, this does not mean that the organisation is, or can be, completely sealed off from what is outside.

With these features in mind, a basic definition which would encompass all major conceptualisations of an organisation is:

> **social entities brought into existence and sustained in an ongoing way by humans to serve some purpose, from which it follows that human activities in the entity are normally structured and coordinated towards achieving some purpose or goals.**

TIME OUT

1. Think about a university or college as an organisation. Describe ways in which it qualifies as an organisation in terms of the five characteristics given above. That is: is it an artifact?; does it have goals and what do you feel that they are?; are there many people involved and who are they?; does it have a structure and coordinating mechanisms and, if so, what are the signs that these exist?; can you place nominal boundaries on the institution and, if so, where would you place them?

2. Now do the same for your immediate family; how easy is it to conceptualise this as an organisation?

WHY STUDY BEHAVIOUR IN ORGANISATIONS?

Although organisations are extremely complex entities that are not easily understood without conscious effort, this in itself is no reason why they should be studied. Nevertheless, there are two important reasons why an understanding of organisations and the behaviour of people in them is, or should be, of concern to us all.

First, it takes but a moment's thought to realise that, in one form or another, organisations are the dominant institution in the modern world. The nature of society is shaped (some would assert badly shaped) by them, and in return they are shaped by the world in which they exist. Some things in life can only be accomplished if people come together to apply collective physical and mental effort, and in many cases this enables tasks to be completed in a more effective way. Although organisations exist in many forms, for the last 400 years they have tended to become larger, more complex and more specialised in what they do. The days have long gone when a family could itself do all that needed to be done to remain self-sufficient, and most people today would be incapable of performing all these activities because they have been taken over by organisations. Thus we all occupy specialist niches in a huge jigsaw of roles that makes up a modern society, in which organisations have become the institutions that shape the conditions under which we live. In addition, they have huge amounts of power. Their decisions about where to locate and the activities in which they engage have a huge impact on individuals, communities and even nation states.

They wield immense power with governments, and in certain cases there is more than a suspicion that they control government decisions. Therefore, the life of everyone in modern society is affected by the existence and behaviour of organisations, and this alone is sufficient reason to try to understand them better.

Second, throughout our lives we are inevitably involved in organisations of some sort. In our early years we are members of an immediate family (a special type of organisation), and from then on we are members of other organisations for the remainder of our lives. We are educated by organisations and our livelihoods depend on them, as does a large part of our social contact with other people, and when we approach the end of our lifespan and can no longer care for ourselves, we gyrate to other organisations to live out our remaining years. This book is mainly concerned with work organisations, in which we probably spend well over half of our lives. For most of this time we try to come to terms with how an organisation functions, how it affects our behaviour and how, in turn, we affect the behaviour of others. To understand this context is part of understanding the world in which we live, and this is also sufficient reason for knowing about the behaviour of organisations and the people in them.

In addition to these two reasons, which apply to everyone, there is a third, which applies to a smaller population: those who manage, or even aspire to manage, organisations or parts of them. For these people, a vital part of performing their roles effectively is to understand the behaviour of humans in an organisational context. Organisations are social collectivities and whatever is done in or by them is ultimately the result of human action. Even in the abstract, robotic world of science fiction, it is humans who decide to create and switch on the robot, and so even machine activity is ultimately traceable to some human action. Therefore, if we are concerned about the effective functioning of organisations, or whether they should become a force for good rather than evil, the human element must be considered. In this sense, understanding the behaviour of organisations and the people in them goes to the very heart of the process of management. However, it must be stated at the outset, and this is a theme that pervades the whole book, these subjects are not lessons in how to manage. Neither do they seek to show managers how to manipulate others, or to bend them to their will. This cannot be emphasised too strongly because there is a regrettable tendency to treat these subjects as part of a tool-kit that equips the manager to 'be in charge'. This view can be detected in some European texts, but is much stronger in those published in America, and is probably linked with the American view of organisations, which is highly functionalist and instrumental. That is, organisations are not seen as social entities but, in terms of tasks that need to be completed, functions that need to be performed and objectives that must be achieved. This view gives rise to a strong managerialist perspective, in which managers are seen to have an almost divine right to decide the goals and objectives of other people and, perhaps more significantly, a right to be obeyed. Thus, anything that is official in organisational terms, or is laid down by a manager, is that which is correct, and while American texts are full of platitudes about the need to understand human behaviour, they leave a strong impression that the main purpose of understanding is to enable managers to get their own way.

However, the managerialist perspective is not one that is universally held. Neither is the belief that human behaviour can be easily controlled by the use of structures and rules. Over 40 years ago Philip Selznick (1957) drew attention to the idea that an organisation is first and foremost a collection of human beings. Therefore, while organisations do have formal and officially sanctioned structures, these can never account for the full range of human behaviour. In practice, individuals interact as people who bring their personalities, problems and interests with them into the work situation, and this influences how well they fit into the neat set of boxes that we call work roles.

REPLAY

The main reasons for studying organisations and the behaviour of people in them are:

- everyone in modern society is affected by the existence and behaviour of organisations
- we are all members of organisations of one sort or another for most of our lives
- since all that happens in organisations is ultimately traceable to human action, those who manage organisations need to take account of those factors that affect human behaviour; not, however, to control or manipulate humans but to better understand their behaviour.

TIME OUT

Reflect on an organisation of which you are or have been a member, preferably not your family or the university or college at which you study, but perhaps one where you have worked. Now re-examine the three reasons given in the Replay section for studying organisations and try to answer the questions below.

1. In what ways did the organisation or the people in it affect your behaviour? How did you feel about this?
2. In what ways did you affect the behaviour of the organisation or that part of it in which you were located? How did you feel about this?
3. If you aspire to manage an organisation or a part thereof, how could the conclusions you have drawn by answering questions 1 and 2 be useful to you in the future?

ORGANISATIONAL BEHAVIOUR AND ANALYSIS

Opening Definitions

Since the terms were first coined, a number of competing definitions for Organisational Behaviour and Organisational Analysis have existed. While this book argues that this is somewhat unreal, because both are really part of a wider subject concerned with understanding human behaviour in organisations and the behaviour of organisations themselves, it is necessary to understand how this state of affairs came about. To some extent it is because, in practice, there has always been some tendency for organisations to be studied at one or other of two levels, which itself creates an impression that there are two different subjects: one called Organisational Behaviour and the other Organisational Analysis.

Organisational Behaviour can most succinctly be defined as:

the study of individuals and groups in organisations.

(Schermerhorn *et al.* 2000, p 3)

This subject is primarily concerned with examining organisations at the micro level and deals with the cognitive and emotional differences between individuals and how individuals interact with each other. To a large extent the subject relies on knowledge drawn from individual psychology, social psychology and, to a far lesser extent, sociology, and in this book this is dealt with in Chapters 3 to 14, and to some extent Chapter 15.

Organisational Analysis is much harder to define, mainly because it is still an evolving subject in which there is an ongoing debate about what an organisation is, how it can most appropriately be viewed, and what methods should be used to study organisations. The reader should also be aware that some authors in this subject do not even use the title Organisational Analysis, but instead prefer the older expression Organisation Theory. This can be defined as:

the macro level examination of organisations, which uses the whole organisation as the unit of analysis.

(Daft 1996, p 26)

The subject is primarily concerned with differences in structure and behaviour at this level of analysis. Since it views the organisation itself (rather than its component parts) as the social system to be examined, it draws heavily on sociological work. This perhaps is the reason for the ongoing debate about what the nature of the subject should be: different schools of sociology can be notorious in 'going their own ways' and distancing themselves from others who approach a phenomenon from a different perspective. In this book, Chapters 16–21 cover topics that would normally be considered part of Organisational Analysis.

THE EVOLUTION OF ORGANISATIONAL BEHAVIOUR AND ANALYSIS

While humans have worked together in organisations for thousands of years, the serious study of behaviour in organisations is less than 100 years old, and what we know today is just one stage in an evolving body of knowledge. Until the 1940s, Organisational Behaviour and Organisational Analysis tended to be regarded as part of a somewhat ill-defined subject, variously called Industrial Administration or Administrative Studies, and, while the subject was almost exclusively focused on formal aspects of organisations, it had a strong influence on thinking about behaviour in them. However, some of the theories that have evolved and which have had an abiding influence on the subject are much older than this. Therefore, it is convenient to trace the historic emergence of OB and OA as occurring in a number of phases: first, early formative work; second, for OB and OA separately, a precursor phase followed by a maturity phase; and, finally, for OB and OA together, the current phase. This is shown in outline in Figure 1.1 and for convenience the account that follows will deal with matters in this historical order.

Early Formative Work

Long before people began to focus explicitly on the study of organisations and the behaviour of people in them, scholars working in different places and at different times

Figure 1.1 An outline
of the evolution of
contemporary
Organisational
Behaviour and
Analysis

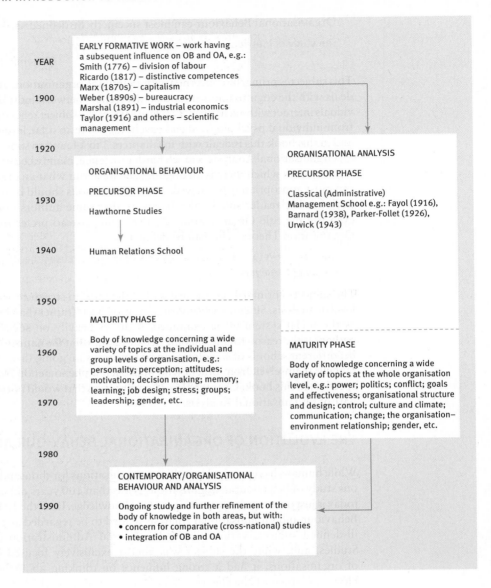

had addressed topics that subsequently shaped the thinking of later workers. The list
of these people is almost endless and space precludes mentioning more than a few of
the most influential scholars. Among the earliest was an economist, Adam Smith (1776),
whose classic description of pin making in Redditch illustrated the effects of specialisation of labour on the economic efficiency of production and this had a lasting impact
on theories of organisational structure and the design of jobs. A little later, another
economist, David Ricardo (1817), expanded on the work of Smith and developed the
concept of 'distinctive competencies', that is, the skills and capabilities that an organisation has over and above its competitors. Later still, another economist, Alfred Marshall
(1891) developed Ricardo's ideas even further to explore the competitive advantages
of organisations under different market conditions and shortly before this, Karl Marx

(1894) had explained how organisational structure and work design were used as primary mechanisms for subjugating and exploiting workers.

In addition to economic theories, there were early social scientists whose work had a lasting impact on thinking about organisations. One who had a great influence on the next (precursor) phase in the development of OA was the German sociologist Max Weber (1948), who documented the characteristics and workings of bureaucracy, which was influential in later thinking about organisational structure.

All the above work originated from academic sources but, in terms of its enduring impact, the most significant set of ideas came from another source altogether. This appeared early in the twentieth century and, since its effects are still very much in evidence, it deserves a more lengthy description.

Scientific Management

Well before the turn of the nineteenth century, the increasing size and complexity of industrial organisations started to make it more difficult to organise human effort in an effective and efficient way. A diverse but informal collection of American industrial managers, the so-called 'systematic management movement', was formed, which reached the conclusion that the (then) current methods of organising large-scale production were no longer appropriate. The most influential set of ideas to emerge from this movement became known as *scientific management*, a term coined by Frederick Winslow Taylor (1911), but it is also associated with others who later developed his ideas.

Scientific management: a set of techniques for organising work methods to give managers greater control over the labour process, i.e. the exchange of effort for rewards

Scientific management is very different from anything that we would now call Organisational Behaviour. Strictly speaking it is a technique for organising or re-organising work methods to give managers greater control over the labour process; that is, the exchange of effort for rewards. Nevertheless, in management circles, Taylor's ideas were, and still are, very influential, and his work contains a number of behaviourial assumptions. Taylor was an engineer and, to judge from his writings, he had a limitless faith in the application of the principles of physical science and engineering to identify the 'one best way' for an organisation to function. As applied to the matter of obtaining maximum productive effort, this was enshrined in his four key principles: that managers should:

1. Gather together all of the traditional knowledge (the essence of skills, techniques, etc.) which had been acquired and held by workmen in their minds, record and tabulate this information and, wherever possible, reduce it to laws, rules, or even mathematical formulae.

2. Scientifically select workpeople and progressively train and develop them to do the jobs that are required.

3. Bring the scientifically designed job and the scientifically selected workers together.

4. Divide up the actual work of the organisation between management and workers (according to their capabilities and training).

Soldiering: working at a much slower pace than the one of which a person is capable

Taylor had an obsession with combating *soldiering* – the practice of working at a much slower pace than the one of which a person is capable – and he reasoned that there were two basic ways to address this issue. Either close and constant supervision could be given (which adds to the cost of the job), or some incentive to work faster could be provided. The second of these was his preferred option, and his proposed solution is reflected in the first of his four principles, which removes all responsibility for the design and planning of work from the hands of those who perform it, and allows work to be designed by managers to extract the maximum amount of effort from the worker. Taylor recognised that this did not necessarily mean continuous effort, for example obtaining the best effort for a full day would mean that rest pauses would be needed, to permit a measure of recuperation. However, this brought into play the second of his four principles. He openly acknowledged that maximum effort would result in boring and repetitive tasks, which in turn required careful selection of operators with the required physical attributes, but a corresponding lack of aspiration for anything more mentally stimulating. More significantly, he stressed that the most effective way to induce people to follow the laid-down design was to make payment contingent on output. Thus, in basic terms, his theory rests on the assumption that high pay is the main (and perhaps only) thing that people seek to obtain from work.

Taylor's ideas contain a great deal that would be considered controversial, if not downright patronising today. For instance, he asserted that everyone is first class at something, and that being less than first class could only arise for one of two reasons: either the person had been badly selected or trained for the task, or the person was just plain lazy. He also reasoned that since some people are better endowed with mental abilities, and others with physical attributes, efficiency required the separation of 'thinking' from 'doing', with each task allocated to the appropriate people. In Taylor's view, since managers were the (superior) thinking part of an organisation they should provide the mental effort, with the operatives performing the (more menial) physical tasks. Taylor could also be accused of being naive in his thinking. He was convinced that because both parties get the rewards they most desire – for workers, more pay, and for managers a more productive and efficient workforce – scientific management would bring huge benefits to both parties, and lead to a community of interest with an in-built force for cooperation. The truth, of course, turned out to be somewhat different. Managers tended to use the techniques to grind the last ounce of effort from employees and, later, when applied to mass production, they simplified and deskilled work so that cheaper labour could be used. Thus it is not surprising that trade unions saw scientific management as a device to denigrate workers and hasten a return to 'sweated labour' conditions and, as a result, in 1911 there was a wave of strikes against its use in America. Nevertheless, by the 1920s the principles were in widespread use on both sides of the Atlantic and it has become the most widely used set of general principles for organising production.

Although scientific management is a long way from having the same concerns as either Organisational Behaviour or Organisational Analysis, it became the starting point for many fruitful lines of enquiry. For example, it contains an implicit if somewhat oversimplified and crude theory of motivation, an issue which is important in Organisational Behaviour. In the emphasis on task specialisation it also has an outline prescription for the structural design of organisations and this is an important topic in both Organisational Behaviour and Analysis.

Organisational Behaviour

The Precursor Phase: The Hawthorne Studies and Human Relations

Scientific management has attracted a measure of criticism from quite early on, mainly because it seemed to result in an element of dehumanised working conditions, together with physical and psychological strain. A study that did much to highlight its shortcomings, and which became a major turning point in thinking about people in organisations, emerged from a series of investigations in the late 1920s and early 1930s in the Hawthorne plant of West Electric Company in America. This work, which subsequently become known as the Hawthorne Studies, can be thought of as the first, founding step in Organisational Behaviour, and it also gave rise to a new school of management thought, the *human relations movement*.

The original work, undertaken by industrial engineers in the company, started in the early 1920s and studied female employees engaged in light assembly work, with the aim of uncovering the intensity of lighting conditions that gave the highest level of output. Workers were divided into two groups: an 'experimental' group, where lighting conditions were systematically varied, and a comparison 'control' group, where no changes took place. The experiments took place over a two-year period and resulted in two major findings. First, whenever the intensity of lighting was changed output increased in the experimental group, even when conditions were restored to those pertaining at the start. Second, and perhaps more puzzling, although lighting conditions were only changed for the experimental group, whenever they were changed, output rose in both groups. From this it was concluded that it was probably the change rather than the actual amount of light that influenced output. Moreover, since the control group also responded to the change, it was obviously not the lighting conditions alone that caused the rise in output. There had to be some other factor. Word of these results soon came to the attention of a group of industrial psychologists at Harvard University who, together with employee relations research staff at Hawthorne, conducted experiments for several more years (Mayo 1933; Roethlisberger and Dickson 1939). Since the work is far too extensive to be covered in full, two major experiments, from which significant conclusions were drawn, will be described.

The first is what is now known as the **Relay Assembly Test Room (RATR) Experiments,** in which six female workers engaged in assembling relays for telephone switchboards first had their baseline output accurately measured on the production line, and then were moved into a specially constructed experimental room. The studies on this group took place over a five-year period, and a large number of changes to working conditions was introduced, either singly or in combination. For example, changes were made to working hours, rest periods and physical conditions such as temperature and lighting and also the use of a group financial incentive scheme. These workers were also allowed to make suggestions about conditions in the experimental room, in which a member of the research team was located permanently as an observer, and who virtually took on the role of their supervisor.

Over the five years, output rose to its highest ever recorded level: a 30 per cent increase on the baseline. However, other significant changes were observed in the group. Since the people had much more freedom to control the way that work was done and could interact socially, they welded together as a social entity with its own standards of behaviour and a strong team ethos. Two general conclusions were drawn from this experiment. First, that work satisfaction is strongly dependent on informal social factors, for example friendliness, cooperation between group members, the feeling they were doing something worthwhile and, importantly, relations with the supervisor. Second, that these social factors had a far greater impact on output than physical conditions.

The second set of experiments is generally referred to as the **Bank Wiring Observation Room (BWOR) Studies,** in which 14 men engaged in wiring, soldering and inspecting banks of telephone switchgear, were subject to detailed observation. In time, the men came to ignore the observer, who was able record several interesting features about the group, one of the most important of which was the existence of a distinct group structure. In practice, there were two sub-groups or cliques: one at the back of the room and one at the front, and each had slightly different patterns of behaviour. In addition, there was a certain amount of rivalry between the groups, with the one at the front considering itself to be of slightly higher status, because it was engaged in more difficult work. However, as a whole the 14 men had developed a code of conduct, which was enforced by workers putting pressure on each other, and the most significant item in the code seemed to be a norm about the level of output. No matter what management and supervision deemed to be the required output, the group had established its own criteria for what it considered to be a 'fair day's work'. Therefore, even though management introduced a payment-by-results bonus scheme to boost output, the group made no attempt to maximise production, but aimed for the figure that they had decided was fair. If by chance they did overproduce, this was kept secret from management and used to restore the balance on some future day when there was underproduction. Moreover, this output norm was actively policed by group members, who exerted pressure to conform on the 'chisellers' (those who underproduced), or those who overproduced (the 'rate busters'). This pressure usually took the form of unpleasant but not harmful physical blows, which the men called 'bingeing', together with mild social isolation of the offending colleague. However, the pressure was clearly experienced as significant by those concerned, because there were cases of individuals asking to be transferred to other work.

Output restriction of this type is not unknown and so the Bank Wiring Room results are important in drawing attention to one of the limitations of scientific management. In theory, it is possible to create a formal system of work in which jobs are carefully designed to eliminate non-productive effort. However, alongside, or even as part of, the formal system there exists an informal organisation, which has its own norms, values and expectations, and these informal codes of conduct are sometimes more influential on day-to-day behaviour than the formal rules.

TIME OUT

Look closely at the conclusions drawn by the Hawthorne researchers and compare these with the major assumptions associated with scientific management.

1. To what extent are the two sets of ideas compatible, or does one contradict the other?
2. Can you identify an organisation or an industry in which the principles of scientific management could still be in use?

While the results and conclusions of the Hawthorne Studies have been criticised in terms of the rigour of the research (Yorks and Whitsett 1985), they have had a major impact on the understanding of behaviour in organisations. The most important inference is that people have social needs to be satisfied at work, which can be equally as important as monetary needs. This, it can be noted, is a direct contradiction of one of the tenets of scientific management. Ideas such as this gave rise to the **human relations** school of thought that heralded the emergence of what has eventually become the subject of Organisational Behaviour. As will be seen in Chapters 7 and 8, some of the assumptions of human relations theory have a strong influence on certain theories of work motivation. Human relations theory also gave rise to much of the work on groups and leadership, which will be covered in Chapters 11 to 13.

The Maturity Phase of Organisational Behaviour

From the 1950s onwards, OB rapidy emerged as a mature field of study in its own right. Psychologists were the first in the field, but shortly after this other academic disciplines became involved and it is probably true to say that virtually every aspect of human behaviour in organisations has received some attention, often from several different disciplinary perspectives. Since a great deal of this work is covered in the different chapters of this book, it would be inappropriate to single out any one in particular here.

Organisational Analysis

The Precursors: Classical Organisation Theory

Classical organisation theory: a diverse group of theories which sets out to derive universal rules and guidelines for the design and functioning of organisations

Shortly after scientific management came into widespread use, a complementary set of ideas began to emerge, which subsequently became known as *classical organisation theory*. While scientific management initially focused on the micro level issue of job design, organisation theory attempted to lay down guiding principles for the design and functioning of a whole organisation. In some respects the ideas that emerged are similar to those put forward by the German sociologist Max Weber (1948), whose classic study of bureaucracy laid the foundations for the serious scientific study of formal organisation (see Chapter 18). However, unlike Weber, whose ideas were based on empirical investigation and focused on the large public sector bureaucracies of Germany, classical management theorists were largely practising managers, who derived their ideas from the practical experience of running large industrial organisations, and who set out what they believed to be guides to good practice. Although these writers differ in detail, they are remarkably similar in terms of basic approach. All give highly prescriptive guidelines, which they claimed were universally applicable. Perhaps the best known is Henri Fayol (1916) who derived a set of 14 principles of organising. Because these will be considered in Chapter 17, details need not concern us here. Suffice it to say that these guidelines set out a highly prescriptive recipe for the design of organisational structures that Fayol claimed was universally applicable, and for this reason the whole approach has been much criticised. For example, it takes no account of interactions between people and, because it underestimates their mental capacities, it has a very naive view of the way they think; in addition it understates the potential for conflict in organisations (March and Simon 1958). Indeed, so prescriptive and mechanical is the approach that it has been called a description of 'organisations without people' (Bennis 1959). Nevertheless, the ideas give a very clear and unambiguous set of guidelines that is easy to understand and apply, and the approach is remarkably resilient in management circles; dressed up in different words it is still common to find the ideas espoused in current management textbooks. So far as current thinking is concerned, the strongest criticism of this school is the assumption that a valid set of universally applicable design principles can be derived from it.

The Maturity Phase of Organisational Analysis

Shortly after OB entered its maturity phase, what has now become known as OA began to emerge as a mature field of study, although the term Organisational Analysis was coined somewhat later. For the most part the first workers in the field were essentially management theorists, many of whom were dissatisfied with the prescriptions of classical management theory with respect to structure and organisational design. As such they abandoned the search for universal prescriptions and, instead, sought to locate structural forms that best fit the specific circumstances of an organisation. In addition, scholars from other academic backgrounds entered the area and, if anything, OA emerged as a more eclectic field than OB. Nevertheless, it is relevant to point out that some of these developments, particularly in terms of work that originated in the USA, are somewhat controversial. Until the early 1960s, the development of organisation theory was mainly located in sociology departments of universities, but from then on in America it was increasingly concentrated in business schools. When this occurred, the purer concerns of social science tended to be replaced by highly managerialist concerns that were almost exclusively focused on promoting the design of more effective, efficient (and sometimes harsher and more exploitative) organisations. As such, many interesting and vital lines of enquiry about the nature and functioning of organisations had a tendency to be regarded as irrelevant (Hinings and Greenwood 2002). This, it can be noted, parallels an earlier change that had occurred in OB, in which the Harvard Business School had effectively hijacked the findings and conclusions of the Hawthorne Studies, to evolve an equally managerialist (and exploitative) version of Human Relations Theory (O'Connor 1999). Once again, since much of this work is covered in later chapters of this book, it would not be appropriate to single out anything for a special mention here.

REPLAY

- Organisational Behaviour and Organisational Analysis originate from two different sources that were focused respectively on micro and macro level aspects of organisations.

- While not in itself Organisational Behaviour, there are assumptions about factors that influence micro level aspects of behaviour contained in scientific management theories. However, the more identifiable origins of Organisational Behaviour lie in the findings of the Hawthorne experiments that gave rise to the human relations movement.

- Organisational Analysis traces its roots to the classical management school of theorists, who attempted to formulate universal principles for the design and functioning of organisations.

The Case for Integration

At first sight it would be all too easy to conclude that Organisational Behaviour and Organisational Analysis are two completely unconnected subjects. They have different names, they are often taught and researched by two different sets of people, who barely communicate with each other. Nevertheless, since both subjects deal with the behaviour of people in organisations, the author of this book views the distinction as more apparent than real. Why then is the distinction so frequently made? To some extent, it is the result of different academic disciplines imposing their own definitions of the most important features of organisations that should be studied. When applied to organisations and the people in them, the word behaviour can refer to a number of different levels:

Level 1: Individual: where the focus is on matters such as values, attitudes, beliefs, aptitudes, intelligence and motivation that influence how people behave as individuals.

Level 2: Group: which is more concerned with social and interactive features such as group dynamics and leadership.

Level 3: Organisational: where the main concern is with the behaviour of an organisation as a whole, for example its relationship with environment and its structure, culture and processes.

This rather arbitrary classification is only possible because different academic disciplines focus their efforts at these different levels. For instance, level 1 exists because this is what individual psychologists do; level 2 exists because this is where social psychologists and, to a lesser extent, sociologists focus their endeavours; and level 3 because this is the area of interest to writers on management, sociologists and economists. This has regrettably led to two distinct views of organisations: the **macro** (level 3) view and the **micro** (levels 1 and 2) view. However, the separation could be very unreal and even downright misleading.

Academically, placing micro level features in one box and calling it Organisational Behaviour and macro level matters into another box and calling it Organisational Analysis is very convenient. It permits the whole body of knowledge to be cut up into manageable chunks and written down as syllabi for courses. Problematically, it also permits different academic disciplines to claim territorial rights over the boxes and sometimes results in an element of unhealthy criticism between the disciplines, and the net result is that there is almost an in-built force that conspires to treat Organisational Behaviour and Organisational Analysis as different bodies of knowledge. However, if we examine one of the first attempts to define the subject of Organisational Behaviour – which, despite its age, is more in keeping with the arguments expressed in this book – we can see that this was never intended:

> the study of the structure, functioning and performance of organisations and the behaviour of groups and individuals within them.   (Pugh 1971, p 9)

Note that, in addition to the behaviour of people in organisations at the micro level, it also refers to the behaviour of an organisation as a whole. However, it is important to sound a note of caution here. While people regularly speak of the behaviour of an organisation, organisations can never be said to behave in the same sense that people behave. The word organisation refers to something that is an abstract phenomenon. Therefore, to refer to the behaviour of a person and an organisation in the same sense is *reification*; that is, it treats an abstract idea as something that actually exists. Nevertheless, because this is part of the way that people normally conceive the world, they customarily talk of organisations 'behaving', and to some extent it is meaningful to do so. For example, an organisation behaves as a whole towards its environment, and although this is usually the result of a decision by an individual or group

Reification: to treat an abstract idea as something that actually exists

of individuals, since what behaves is a social collectivity, it is meaningful to speak of the behaviour of the collectivity as a whole. Thus, in this case, reification of the organisation has been argued to be one of organisation theory's most essential and useful tools (Koza and Thoenig 2003). Moreover, it amply justifies why Organisational Behaviour and Organisational Analysis cannot sensibly be considered to be two separate areas of study. Without behaviour by people within an organisation there would be no behaviour of the organisation as a whole. Thus, we need to understand how the behaviour of people influences its actions. Similarly, if we want to know why people behave as they do, we not only need to understand how individual and group factors shape behaviour, but also how the organisation and its interactions with the outside world result in pressures for people to behave in certain ways. Indeed, a review article by Porter (1996) notes that the single most significant failure of Organisational Behaviour (OB) over the last 40 years is to ignore the 'O', and overemphasise the 'B', which tends to result in paying insufficient attention to the impact of the organisational context on the behaviour of individuals and groups. For this reason it is worthwhile examining certain features that the two approaches have in common, and this is considered next.

CONTEMPORARY ORGANISATIONAL BEHAVIOUR AND ANALYSIS

As noted, until comparatively recently, Organisational Behaviour and Organisational Analysis have largely remained apart. However, it is now more widely recognised that they are two aspects of the same overall subject, which can be illustrated by examining some of the characteristics that they have in common.

The Use of Concepts and Theories from Social Science

Both subjects deal with the human element in organisations, with the aim of understanding and explaining the behaviour of organisations and people within them. To do this they draw heavily on concepts and theories from the social sciences and apply them in an organisational setting.

A Multidisciplinary Focus

There are a number of different social science disciplines, which all tend to focus on slightly different aspects of the social world. Therefore, the same phenomenon is sometimes studied by people from more than one discipline, and each one brings its own unique concepts and theories. Thus, there are often several competing explanations of the same phenomenon. However, this does not mean that the findings and explanations stay separate in discrete compartments. Sometimes, scholars working in the same area integrate the work, to produce a more comprehensive explanation and, occasionally, something will be studied by a cross-disciplinary team. The major disciplines involved and their primary areas of focus are shown in Table 1.1.

Theoretical Orientations with Practical Implications

While the whole area uses theory to understand organisational phenomena, this is seldom a matter of 'knowledge for knowledge's sake'. Usually the aim is to inform a

Table 1.1 The major social science disciplines involved in Organisational Behaviour and Analysis

Social science discipline	Typical organisational phenomena of interest
Individual psychology	Individual differences, intelligence, personality, aptitude, motivation, learning, perception
Social psychology	Group dynamics, attitudes, leadership
Sociology	The organisation as a social system, socialisation of organisational members, structures, cultures, communication
Social anthropology	Culture and its effects on behaviour
Politics	Power, decision making, conflict, the behaviour of interest groups, coalitions, control
Economics	Labour markets, product markets and their influence as part of organisational environment

wider audience so that its members will better understand what goes on in organisations. This audience includes other scholars and teachers in the area, and specialist staff and managers in organisations. However, it is important to note that this knowledge is not targeted at any one group in particular. The subject is more frequently taught to students of business and management than to anyone else, and the intention in this is that those who want to make their careers in organisations should better understand the complexities of human behaviour. Having said this, there are differences in approach that reflect the use of the various social sciences, the most notable of which are those that are commonly held in Great Britain and in the USA.

The British position is one that attempts to maintain a neutral and unbiased stance in terms of the uses to which new knowledge are put. At the risk of overstating the position, this broadly entails undertaking research with a view to promoting further understanding and knowledge. Thus, it most definitely is *not* the aim that any new knowledge that is uncovered, should become the sole property of managers so that they become better equipped to control or manipulate the actions of others in a way that takes away their freedom or dignity. One by-product of this is that British academics can be highly critical of management, and their research results feel no compunction to report only the good news, but will often be written in a 'warts and all' style. In the US, however, OB and OA tend to be approached from a very different perspective. Both subjects tend to be far more managerialist in their focus and many books and research papers in the area are unashamedly devoted to providing a toolkit that facilitates the perpetuation of managerial control over others.

Nevertheless, in both countries, the very nature of the work undertaken tends to produces a situation in which knowledge gives rise to technologies; that is, pure knowledge (science) results in a technology for applying the scientific knowledge. At the risk of giving a rather oversimplified picture, Figure 1.2 shows the relationship.

Note that all four cells in Figure 1.2 are connected, which means that the theories connect with practice. Starting with the macro level, organisational development is an organisation-wide strategy for change, which is covered in Chapter 21 and will not therefore be discussed here.

At the micro level, a great deal of the knowledge that emerges gets incorporated into what is now known as human resource management. However, to speak of a 'human

Figure 1.2 Relation of
macro and micro level
of theory and practice

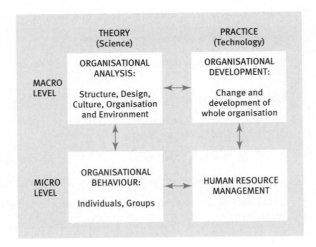

resource manager' is somewhat confusing. Most managers deal with human resources
and they need to know something about human behaviour. Nevertheless, in many organisations there are specialists in this area who advise and guide functional managers.

Open Systems Perspectives

Open systems: a
system not sealed off
from its environment
and, therefore,
subject to the
intrusion of
environmental
influences

Either consciously or unconsciously, both OB and OA adopt an *open systems*
perspective.

This a way of thinking about organisations which contains a recognition that anything on which we focus exists in an environment, by which it can be affected. In its
simplest form, an open system can be portrayed, as in Figure 1.3, and the basic principle can be translated into something that is more easily recognised as a commercial
organisation in Figure 1.4.

Complex systems have a host of interdependent parts, which contribute to the well-
being and survival of the whole. The important point about anything that can be classified
as a 'system' is that it exists in an environment, to which it must adapt in order to be
able to survive. An organisation as a system can often be thought of as a set of sub-
systems, all of which interact with each other, and the whole exists in an environment
with which it interacts. This is shown in Figure 1.5, where the sub-systems labelled
groups A–D can be thought of as departments or functions, although, for convenience,
they are simply called groups here. Also note that each group is made up of sub-
sub-systems, which can be regarded as individuals.

The first and most obvious point that can be made relates to the focus and concerns of OB and OA as two levels of study. At the micro level the main focus is on

Figure 1.3 Basic open
systems model

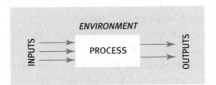

Figure 1.4 Simplified open systems model of a commercial organisation

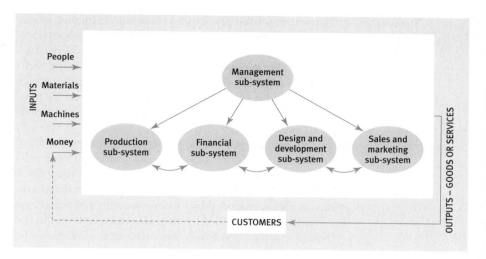

Figure 1.5 The organisation as a system of sub-systems and sub-sub-systems

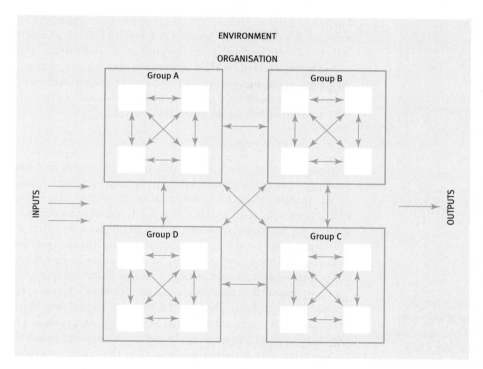

parts (or sub-systems) of an organisation, and so the unit of analysis is the individual or group. The macro level perspective has a focus on the organisation as a whole, that is, the total system made up of all the sub-systems.

A second highly important point that emerges from Figure 1.5 is the idea of system, sub-system and sub-sub-system. At any level, a feature or process that is under consideration can usually be viewed as a system in its own right. Each of the groups in Figure 1.5 is a sub-system made up of individuals that interact with each other, so its characteristics and properties are not simply the sum of its parts; it will have emergent properties that only arise because the individuals interact. Thus, if we reduce one of the groups from four people to three, it would behave differently. Therefore, an individual in one of the groups is affected by being part of the sub-system, and the behaviour of the sub-system is affected by his or her presence, and the sub-system will be affected if he or she leaves. This principle can be applied in the same way at the next level upwards. The system itself (organisation) is made up of interacting sub-systems, and some of its characteristics only exist because sub-systems A–D interact. Moreover, each one is affected by being part of the system, the system is affected because it is there, and the system's characteristics and behaviour will change if it is removed.

The final point concerns environments. Each of the individuals in groups A – D is surrounded by an environment: the other people in the group. Moreover, each of the groups is also surrounded by an environment; and the groups, and the organisation as a whole, are surrounded by an environment external to the firm.

This is a rather elementary use of systems principles. Nevertheless, it illustrates the idea that if we wish to gain a fuller understanding of the behaviour of people in organisations, or the behaviour of an organisation as a whole, there is a need to integrate micro and macro approaches. To some extent, the behaviour of component sub-systems and sub-sub-systems is a result of being part of a bigger system; therefore, to comprehend behaviour of groups and individuals, account needs to be taken of the forces exerted on these systems by the organisation as a whole. Similarly, the behaviour of the organisation as a whole is dependent on the way individuals and groups behave and we can only understand the behaviour of the whole organisation if we take account of behaviour at the lower level.

Contingency Perspectives

Although the precursors of Organisational Behaviour and Analysis sought universal principles and often tried to identify the 'one best way' of addressing problems, this is only possible if there is absolute certainty about what influences a particular piece of behaviour. To some extent this is possible in the physical sciences because they deal with things rather than people. For example, we know that if we heat an iron bar it will expand and so, if we carefully measure its length before it is heated, then raise its temperature by a known amount, we can determine its expansion per degree celsius. From then on we can with certainty assume that if the temperature of the bar is raised by a given number of degrees we can predict its exact length. However, human beings are not like iron bars. They react differently to the same factor and what motivates one individual might not have the same effect on another. For this reason it can be very hard to predict behaviour. Therefore, almost all current work abandons any pretext of being able to derive universal rules that apply everywhere. It usually adopts a *contingency perspective*, which acknowledges that the solution to a problem has to fit the situation in which the problem exists. This, in turn, requires very careful examination of the situation to see what factors are at work, and an equally careful selection of a solution that addresses these factors.

Contingency perspective: an approach to problem solving which assumes that there is no universally applicable solution to a particular type of problem and so remedies have to be tailored to the situation in which the problem exists

Research Orientated and Unprescriptive

Concepts and theories in Organisational Behaviour and Analysis invariably arise out of extensive research. Although this does not mean that students of the subjects need to be experienced researchers, to grasp the strengths and weaknesses of a theory it is sometimes necessary to have an elementary knowledge of the research process. For those who wish to look a little deeper into this matter, the associated website to the book gives a very brief outline of the nature and methods of organisational research, and for the present it is sufficient to note that there are two important features of the theories that result.

First, as theories, they are much more descriptive than predictive. The function of a theory in social science is usually to specify whether there is a relationship between two or more variables and, if possible, to explain the nature of this relationship. However, this does not mean that we can predict with any degree of certainty what change will take place in one variable if there is a change in another. The subject is rich in results that tell us a great deal about the complex nature of behaviour in organisations and also alerts us to the idea that, if one variable should change, changes can be expected in others. In some cases it also provides highly plausible explanations of why these changes occur, but the explanations are seldom strong enough to enable us to predict behaviour with certainty.

Second, although the subject provides information that gives us a better understanding of human behaviour in organisations, in British OB and OA no attempt is made to say what that behaviour should be. This is often a source of acute frustration to students of the subject, particularly if they are managers who feel that they should be able to obtain precise remedies for problems. However, reluctance to be prescriptive does not mean that scholars in the area are evasive, or that they have no opinions. Social scientists are only too painfully aware that when someone asks for prescriptive advice it is because he or she has a reason. All too often this reason is connected with the person's desire to manipulate the behaviour of others to his or her own advantage. Quite simply, British social scientists do not see their purpose in life as serving a particular constituency of interests in this way, and they can be highly critical of those of their number who do. In addition, it is part of a social scientist's training to recognise that he or she has values and to be on guard, lest they influence the way that a social situation is perceived. A natural extension of this is to avoid making prescriptions, because these are almost bound to reflect what the prescriber thinks is right, rather than give an unbiased picture.

Cross-national Perspectives

Organisational Behaviour and Analysis both orginated in the USA and, while considerable contributions have been made by scholars from European nations and elsewhere, overall there has traditionally been a strong bias towards the Anglo-American conceptualisation of organisations and their employees. In recent years, however, perhaps because of the growing prominence of internationalised organisations, there has been a growing awareness that the body of knowledge based on American and British studies should not be regarded as the last word on matters. That is, whatever the body of knowledge tells us about human behaviour in organisations, it might be necessary to accept that matters could be different in other countries. Therefore, wherever possible, there is an increasing tendency to try to incorporate an element of comparative work into topics that are studied, and a cross-cultural perspective is fast becoming an important dimension of the subject in its own right. However, much of this work is still in its infancy and a great deal remains to be uncovered. To a large extent this is because it is much more difficult to undertake comparative work than to study matters in a single country. To start with, the costs incurred in replicating a study of the same phenomenon in several different countries can be significant. In addition, unless the work can be undertaken as a collaborative venture, for example by several universities around the world, the sheer volume of work for a single research team is prohibitive.

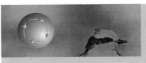

REPLAY

- Contemporary Organisational Behaviour and Analysis reflect a trend towards integrating the two subjects, which is based upon the premise that micro and macro levels are so strongly interconnected that events and behaviour at one level cannot be understood without taking account of matters at the other level.

- Organisational Behaviour and Analysis both use concepts and theories from social science; they usually take an interdisciplinary perspective, have strong practical implications, use open systems perspectives, adopt a contingency (rather than 'one best way') approach and are research orientated and unprescriptive.

DIFFERENT PERSPECTIVES ON ORGANISATIONS

The definition of an organisation given at the start of this chapter is a very general one that purposely avoids singling out anything as the most important characteristic of an organisation. This is only one way of viewing matters and it is often the case that the perspective used to view a particular organisational phenomenon depends on what the person investigating the phenomenon considers to be the most appropriate way to view an organisation. For this reason it is important to make the reader aware that there is no single right way of conceptualising an organisation. Rather, the conceptualisation used tends to depend on what are considered to be the most important characteristics of an organisation, or the reasons for examining a particular phenomenon.

Metaphor: a figure of speech in which a term is transferred from an object it ordinarily designates to another object it can designate by implicit analogy

Morgan (1989) draws attention to the idea that there are a number of competing metaphors for organisations. A *metaphor* is a figure of speech in which a term is transferred from the object it ordinarily designates to another object it can designate by an implicit analogy. For example, to refer to the world of business as a jungle implies that it operates on the basis of Kipling's first law of the jungle: 'kill or be killed'. Because metaphors provide a distinct way of perceiving an object and make us aware that some features are considered more important than others, they can be very useful devices. However, because each metaphor provides a different and sometimes competing insight or perspective, none of them is inherently right or wrong. Each one is only a partial view that draws attention to those features of organisations that the user of the metaphor considers to be the most important or interesting. Nevertheless, they can be useful and the four metaphors described by Morgan (he calls them different images of organisations) are: the machine metaphor; the organism metaphor; the (political) systems metaphor and the cultures metaphor. Each of these is now discussed separately.

The Machine Metaphor

Machines are constructed to do something specific, for example, a kettle turns cold water into hot water. Thus the *machine metaphor* focuses on the purpose and goals of an organisation and how these are achieved by combining its component parts. This view draws attention to such matters as:

- **Purpose or goals**: what is to be achieved.
- **Organisational design**: how the overall task is split down into a set of structured sub-tasks and how these are coordinated.
- **Methods, rules and procedures**: what is done, what behaviour is permitted and what is prohibited.
- **Effectiveness and efficiency**: whether goals are achieved and whether this is done in a way that is economic in the use of resources.

If it is inappropriate for the job, or when a part malfunctions, a machine can fail to serve its purpose. Thus the metaphor is useful if the main reason for studying an organisation is to define what it does and how well it does it. Nevertheless, this view has its shortcomings. Everything is evaluated in terms of technical efficiency and only the functional aspects of organisations are considered. Indeed, people tend to be viewed as merely components of the total machine, which contains two implicit assumptions: that people have a common purpose; and that they should all behave in a predictable way. Since both of these are highly questionable, the metaphor tends to ignore the complexity and diversity of motives that underlie human behaviour.

The Organism Metaphor

Organisms are living entities and so the *organism metaphor* is based on a biological analogy. It also makes use of a concept which in one form or another has come to dominate most current views of organisations – the organisation as a system, which draws attention to:

- **Interaction with environment**: that an organisation exists in, interacts with and is affected by its environment.
- **Sub-systems**: organisations are systems made up of sub-systems.
- **Interconnectedness**: the way that all parts of an organisation are connected, either directly or indirectly.
- **Human element**: implicit recogition that humans are an important organisational component.

The word system is familiar to everyone and most of us use it almost every day. However, it also refers to a whole way of thinking about the world, which originated in biology. Together with Physics, Biology shares the distinction of being highly *reductionist*, because it advances knowledge by studying progressively smaller components of an organism to examine how they work. For example, by progressing from organs down to cells and, these days, down to the fundamental building blocks such as DNA and RNA. This is an extremely powerful approach, but in the 1930s a rather different way of thinking began to emerge in Biology. This was the *holistic* perspective which, expressed in the simplest way, pointed out that cells do not exist in isolation but as parts of organisms. Thus, to understand how cells work in an organism

---

Machine metaphor: organisations regarded as analogous to a machine that is designed for a purpose

Organism metaphor: organisations regarded as analogous to biological organisms

Reductionist: the belief that complex systems can be understood completely by understanding their constituent parts

Holistic: the belief that reality is made up of unified wholes that are greater than the simple sum of their parts

or, indeed, how the organism itself affects the functioning of cells, it is necessary to think in wholes.

Providing certain criteria are met, almost anything can be regarded as a system. For example, we can think of the human body as a total system composed of many sub-systems, all of which interact together: the digestive system, the respiratory system, the nervous system, to name just three. Many people would assert that 'all' systems are open systems, which interact with their environments by taking in inputs and transforming them into outputs. For instance, the human body takes in food and transforms this into usable energy to maintain the body and also exports waste products. Deciduous trees take in nutrients from the ground and their leaves convert sunlight into energy; they also shed their leaves in the autumn and shut down for the winter. The fallen leaves decay, which provides food for a host of smaller organisms that convert the leaves into nutrients so that they can be reingested by the plant. A parallel can be drawn with organisations. Just as a tree absorbs water, nutrients and the sun's energy, organisations take in inputs and use them to survive; and just as a tree sheds its leaves in autumn to protect itself against the harsh winter, an organisation must be managed and controlled to enable it to respond to its environment in an appropriate way. An example of the use of this conceptualisation is given earlier in the chapter where it was used to explain the case for integration of micro and macro level perspectives on organisations.

Since the organism metaphor accepts that all the parts of an organisation are interconnected and have to function in a way that contributes to the whole, it recognises the importance of the human element. However, it still tends to assume that all the component parts of an organisation have a unified, common purpose and, so far as the human element is concerned, this is an oversimplification.

The (Political) Systems Metaphor

Political systems metaphor: organisations regarded as analogous to a political system composed of diverse groups, all of which have their own objectives

The *political systems metaphor* marks a fundamental break with an assumption held by those described above, and draws attention to:

- **Sub-system aims and objectives**: recognition that different parts of an organisation can have their own aims and objectives that they seek to fulfil, rather than all of them subscribing to a single set of organisational goals.
- **Potential for conflict**: the possibility of competition or conflict between sub-systems is acknowledged.

The machine and organisms metaphors both assume that an organisation has a common purpose or goal, whereas this perspective draws attention to the idea that organisations consist of diverse groups that pursue their own aims, some of which are common to all groups, but others can be unique to a particular group. This means that there is always some potential for conflict. However, it does not mean that the metaphor endorses the idea of conflict, merely that a hierarchy of authority and a structure that brings people together into departments and functions will result in groups that have different viewpoints and interests, some of which can give rise to a degree of competition or even conflict. The perspective also focuses on how conflicts are pursued.

The great strength of this metaphor is its recognition of the complex nature of human behaviour in organisations. Instead of assuming a common purpose for everybody, it regards this state of affairs as something that occurs for very special reasons. It also recognises that conflict is not always pursued in an open way, and so political behaviour is regarded as a natural part of organisational life, not just an aberration. Nevertheless, it has its limitations. It all too easily overplays the conflictual aspects of organisations and neglects the idea that if the circumstances are appropriate there is also potential for cooperation.

Organisations as Cultural Systems

Cultural systems metaphor: organisations regarded as analogous to cultural systems in which members have common beliefs, values and shared assumptions

The *cultural systems metaphor* also takes a systemic perspective, but this time the focus is on one of the less tangible features of an organisation: its culture. This metaphor draws attention to such features as:

- **Values and beliefs:** that organisational members usually share a number of values and beliefs that they use to make sense of the world.
- **Effects of culture on behaviour:** the ways in which deep-rooted and largely unstated patterns of belief and values have a pervasive influence on behaviour in an organisation.

In broad terms, a culture is a system of values and beliefs shared by a group of people, and their culture has a very pervasive effect on behaviour. For instance, it helps them to understand why they do certain things and establishes desired patterns of behaviour. Few of us would deny the existence of different national cultures and their influence on behaviour, and, in much the same way, different organisations can also have distinctive cultures. Indeed, in some ways, exploring the culture of a firm can involve viewing it as a society in miniature. However, to identify a culture and its effects it is usually necessary to delve well beneath the surface to try to uncover the social significance that procedures and practices have for organisational members.

In terms of explaining behaviour this can be a very penetrating perspective, but for those not used to this way of thought it has its problems. To start with, each of the three previous metaphors has its own logic or rationality, which is applied to explain organisational activities. For example, the machine analogy uses an engineering logic to decide whether sensible rules have been followed to design and maintain an effective and efficient organisation. The organism metaphor applies its own criteria of rationality to examine whether an organisation is able to adapt internally, to adjust to changing environmental conditions. Finally, the political systems metaphor seeks to explain behaviour by applying the logic of competition for scarce resources. Therefore, if we accept that any of these metaphors is a useful tool for its intended purpose, with practice we can see how each one can be used to explain how certain actions can lead to certain outcomes. However, the cultural metaphor has no overarching rationality, and it casts doubt on whether the word rational can be used to explain human behaviour. It holds that if a person behaves in a certain way because this is the normal way to behave in a certain context, he or she may not even be aware of behaving in that way. Thus, there are probably no universal criteria that can be used to evaluate whether the culturally induced patterns of behaviour are more appropriate in one organisation than another. Indeed, to analyse an organisation it is usually necessary to accept the culture as what it is, and simply try to identify how it affects behaviour.

A second problem stems from the use of the word 'organisational' in conjunction with the word 'culture'. This is sometimes used to imply that everybody in an organisation has the same set of cultural norms. However, different parts of an organisation usually have some differences in outlook, and it is these differences and their behavioural outcomes that give rise to the political systems metaphor. Thus, rather than view an organisation as a cultural system, it might make more sense to think of it as a system of sub-cultures. Finally, as will be seen in Chapter 20, which explores culture in greater depth, although the concept started out as a penetrating way of examining the nature of organisations, certain popular writings have trivialised and watered it down to the extent that in some ways it has become almost worthless.

In summary, each of the four metaphors has its distinctive uses, strengths and weaknesses, and for comparative purposes these are shown in Table 1.2.

Table 1.2 Comparison of organisational metaphors

Metaphor	Analogy	Main focus	Strengths	Weaknesses
Machine Metaphor	Organisation as a machine that is designed to serve a specific purpose	Technical efficiency or fitness for purpose	Strong focus on organisation as a whole and how efficiently it functions	Neglects the human element
Biological System	Organisation as an organism existing in, interacting with and influenced by its environment	Relationship with environment Interrelation of sub-systems in organisation and influence this has on the behaviour of the organisation as a whole	Acknowledges that organisations have a wide variety of component parts (including the human element) which have to play their respective parts if the whole organism is to function well	Tends to assume that all the component parts have a common purpose
Political System	Organisation as a system composed of diverse sub-systems, all of which have their own aims and objectives	Conflict and competition between sub-systems	Accepts that organisations contain different groups whose interests need to be reconciled. Thus conflict and competition are everyday features of organisational life	Some tendency to focus on conflict to the exclusion of all else, and underplay the idea that there are also cooperative features of organisations
Cultural System	Organisations as cultures	Beliefs, values and shared meanings of organisational members and how these result in identifiable patterns of behaviour	Goes well beneath the surface to try to uncover some of the less tangible features of organisations, and their effects on human behaviour	Has a tendency to regard culture as the most important factor, which underplays the impact of other factors external to the person

TIME OUT

Think about the organisation where you work. If you are not in employment, think about your own university or college as an organisation. Identify those aspects and features of the organisation (and the way that it functions) that you would focus on if you were to examine the institution by using:

the machine metaphor
the organism metaphor
the political systems metaphor
the cultural systems metaphor.

A More Recent Development: The Postmodernist Perspective

Postmodernist:
either (i) a new
era in which the
fundamental nature
of organisations will
be different from
hitherto, or (ii) a
philosophical stance
which questions
current assumptions
of the nature of
reality

Epistemology: a
branch of philosophy
dealing with the
nature and origins of
knowledge

Over the last 15 years a more radical view of organisations has emerged: the so-called *postmodernist* perspective. However, the word is used in two very distinct ways. The first defines a new era in which there will be a radical change in the fundamental nature of organisations (Cooper and Burrell 1988), and this will be considered briefly in Chapter 2. The second use of the word involves epistemological considerations. *Epistemology* is a branch of philosophy dealing with the nature and origins of knowledge. Postmodernist thought goes to the very root of how an organisation and its activities are conceived, and this results in something much more radical than a new metaphor. Postmodernists are highly critical of conventional ways of conceiving organisations and they would probably reject all four of the metaphors described above as unreal and false. In essence, they argue that current thinking is based on a false notion of scientific rationality, which emphasises rigorous investigation and communication of results to expand the boundaries of knowledge. This is said to hinge on the practice of viewing the world as a set of static, discrete entities and trying to identify causal links between them. For example, phenomena such as individuals, organisations and structures are treated as things which can be separated from the rest of the world, and conventional thought tends to focus on such questions as 'is there a link between culture and structure?', or 'is culture caused by structure or vice versa?' Postmodernists point out that because nothing is static features such as culture and structure have no reality, but are merely temporary states that are treated as fixed and static. This ignores the most important matter of all: the social processes that result in the movement from one state to another. Some postmodernists, for example Bauman (1992), argue that this search for causality is a futile endeavour, based on the false assumption that reality exists and consists of certainty about entities, or what Whitehead (1985) calls the 'fallacy of misplaced concreteness'. Thus the key idea is that everything is in motion, and that what traditional thought views as an object or an entity is only a transitional state, which means that anything that seeks to establish the ultimate truth about entities is a search for the impossible.

Postmodernists argue that to pretend that there is a truth about anything is to deny the essential nature of the world. Their remedy is to regard everything as being in a state of motion, and to reject the idea that anything is real and tangible. So far as studying organisations is concerned, they believe we should shed the intellectual tyranny of thinking in terms of objects, and direct our attention to more important issues. Indeed, they argue that the very term 'organisation' is problematic, because it is not a real entity, simply a label we attach to a very fluid and mobile social configuration (Chia 1995).

These, of course, are very deep philosophical questions, but for anyone who aspires to do more than retreat into a cave and contemplate his or her own navel they are full of problems. For someone who is trying to grasp what makes an organisation tick, postmodernist thought results in more paradoxes than helpful insights. For instance, if nothing is concrete, people can only describe things to each other in terms of their own experience, but postmodernism also asserts that meaning is so personal that it cannot really be communicated. Taken together, these points lead to the inevitable conclusion that it is simply not worth conducting enquiries to try to understand organisations, because we cannot communicate our findings. Therefore, what is portrayed as the leading edge of analytical thought can all too easily start to look like the long discredited doctrine of *nihilism*: that nothing exists, is knowledgeable or can be communicated.

Nihilism: a now discredited doctrine that nothing really exists and thus there can be no knowledge of anything and hence knowledge cannot be communicated

Perhaps the greatest problem is the postmodernist conception of scholarship. Many self-proclaimed postmodernists reject the value of empirical work, favouring instead a seemingly endless stream of *post-hoc* criticism of the empirical work of others. This is a rather particular definition of scholarship, which is less concerned with explanation and verification than with vilifying the explanations produced by other people. Thus postmodernists probably spend more time convincing other postmodernists of the correctness and sanctity of postmodernism than they do in advancing the frontiers of knowledge (Brown 1990). Indeed, one observer has remarked that 'postmodernism' may well end up being nothing more than writers who write about other writers, and address what they write to even more writers: a rather dangerous approach that comes near to turning social science into literary criticism rather than empirical enquiry (Alvesson 1995).

REPLAY

- The machine metaphor likens an organisation to a machine that is designed to serve a specific purpose.
- The organism metaphor likens an organisation to a biological system that exists in conjunction with and must adapt to its environment.
- The political systems metaphor views an organisation as a system of sub-systems, all of which have their own aims and goals, which means that there is always some potential for conflict between sub-systems.
- The cultural systems metaphor views an organisation primarily as a system of values, beliefs and understandings that guide the behaviour of its members.
- The postmodernist perspective is not a metaphor but a philosophical standpoint that strongly questions current assumptions about the nature of organisations.

Although the above critique has some validity, postmodernist thought has matured considerably since the days when early theorists tended to avoid empirical enquiry. Indeed, these days the major focus in the area is in developing new ways of looking at organisations and in this respect postmodernism has made a significant contribution in giving new insights on phenomena that have long been of central concern to OB and OA. To a large extent this has come about through the application of certain concepts that are central to postmodernist analysis, first the concept of *discourse*, which is usually coupled with the allied technique of *deconstruction*.

The very idea of *discourse* alerts us to the idea that language is much more than a useful tool of communication; it can sometimes contain elements (what is said and how it is said) to portray what can be made to seem the essential truth of how things are. This has the effect of limiting the discussion along the lines that the speaker considers legitimate, and disarms any challenges that the listeners might advance to this way of thinking. This can also suppress alternative meanings, by supporting a particular interpretation or conclusions drawn from the discussion. For example, if I state that in the face of the globalisation, all organisations have to be prepared to change to survive. This looks like a statement of common sense wisdom, which on the face of it cannot be challenged.

However, the technique of *deconstruction* could then be applied to this statement to reveal its underlying assumptions about what at first sight appears to be common sense. For instance that:

- there is such a thing as the globalised economy
- it is all powerful and that organisations have to subordinate themselves to these powerful forces
- one of the effects of this is that the organisation must be constantly ready (and able) to change in the way that globalised markets dictate
- failure to do this would be to condemn the organisation to failure
- thus all members of the organisation should willingly embrace change.

The deconstruction can then be taken one stage further to reveal what my motives might be in portraying things in this way, which prompts a whole series of questions about my likely motives for giving this message.

These are very powerful tools of analysis that go well beyond simply trying to uncover the finer nuances of communication. They contain an implicit recognition that communication is almost always underpinned by an agenda, which reflects how the message sender wants her or his audience to interpret the world, so that the audience reacts in a predictable way. For those who might wish to explore the topic further, some suggestions are included in the list of further reading at the end of the chapter.

Discourse: the idea that language is more than just a useful tool of communication because what is said can convey what is seemingly the essential truth about how things are, which has the effect of challenges to an argument, suppressing alternative meanings and supporting particular interpretations or conclusions

Deconstruction: a method used in postmodernist analysis to reveal underlying assumptions in a discourse and challenge them with counter-arguments or alternative interpretations

CONCLUSIONS AND PREVIEW

Summary

From their early beginnings approximately 80 years ago Organisational Behaviour and Organisational Analysis have developed into subjects that contain a wealth of knowledge that seeks to explain the behaviour of humans in an organisational context, and the behaviour of organisations themselves. Although the two subjects have evolved separately, one dealing with micro-level aspects of organisations and the other with macro-level factors, there is now a wider recognition that a more complete understanding of the behaviour of people in organisations, or indeed, the organisation itself is more likely to be obtainable by integrating the two approaches.

The Approach of this Book

There are several ways that could be used to write a text that seeks to explain the behaviour of people in organisations. For instance, it could be written from the perspective of any one of the social science disciplines shown earlier in Table 1.1. Alternatively, it could seek to explain matters by using one of the metaphors contrasted in Table 1.2, or even from a postmodernist perspective. However, since it only draws on these disciplinary and metaphoric approaches where it is felt that it will be helpful for the reader's understanding, perhaps the most appropriate way to describe the general approach is to start by explaining what it is not.

Unlike many books these days, it is not written with the aim of serving the interests of any particular constituency or group in an organisation, either employees or managers. Thus it is most definitely not a textbook on management, nor is it a managerial tool-kit that is designed to give managers the upper hand in bringing employee behaviour under their control. Nevertheless, managers are far from being excluded from the audience at which the book is addressed, if only because as Pfeffer and Sutton (2005) point out, a great deal of management practice is based on very dangerous half-truths promoted by so-called management gurus, and this sometimes results in a host of unintended consequences in organisations. For this reason, although it is hoped that the book will be read by managers, they are not regarded as the primary audience at which it is directed. Rather, there are two reasons why reading the book could have some utility to managers: first, to keep themselves informed, and, second, to encourage them to look critically at some of the ideas they espouse, particularly those that fly in the face of other evidence about factors that affect human behaviour in organisations.

To the extent that it is possible for an individual author to be completely free from his own values and prejudices, the book purposely takes a neutral stance in examining a wide range of factors that impact on humans in an organisational context. These include individual characteristics and processes, because people normally work in settings that are as much social as operational. The book also seeks to be comprehensive by covering topics that are important at all levels, up to that of the whole organisation. For the most part it adopts a critical perspective by seeking to uncover what a particular theory or concept can usefully tell us about human behaviour and, where necessary, to highlight instances where it could have a lack of practical utility. As such, the main aim is describe and explain particular concepts and theories, and at the same time encourage a similarly critical perspective in the reader.

To do this, the book draws extensively on theories and concepts from the social sciences; that is, individual psychology, social psychology, sociology, and more rarely from social anthropology, politics and economics. Some of the theories and concepts that will be explored date from the early, formative stages of development of OB and OA, which involves describing strands of work that are, by now, quite elderly. However, since the book has been written to make it accessible to readers with no prior exposure to the subject, there is no escape from this, because sometimes an understanding of current approaches can crucially depend on understanding the weaknesses in prior work.

Finally, and in keeping with what is said earlier in this chapter, it is considered vital that the reader should never lose sight of the idea that the various chapters in the book are not discrete parcels of knowledge that are divorced from each other. Rather, they are but part of a whole, more complex story and this is particularly true of the need integrate knowledge from Organisational Behaviour and Organisational Analysis.

FURTHER READING

Appignanesi, R and C Garratt (1995) *Postmodernism for Beginners*, Cambridge: Icon Books. An informative, but difficult-to-read book that contains a useful commentary on the use of language to describe what is apparent reality.

Bauman, Z (1992) *Intimations of Postmodernism*, London: Routledge. Not an easy book to read, but an essential text for those wishing to explore postmodernist thought.

Carey, A (1967) The Hawthorne studies: a radical criticism, *American Sociological Review* 32(2): 403–416. As the title suggests, a critique of the findings and conclusions that were drawn from the Hawthorne studies.

Hatch, MJ (1997) *Organisation Theory, Symbolic and Postmodern Perspectives*, Oxford: Oxford University Press. An interesting and clear guide to organisation theory that explores and contrasts three perspectives on organisations: modernist, social constructivist and postmodern.

Hinings, CR and R Greenwood (2002) Disconnects and consequences in organisation theory, *Administrative Science Quarterly* 47(3): 411–421. A review article that traces the origins of organisation theory and how it has been coopted by American business schools in a way that serves managerial ends.

Kvale, S (ed.) (1992) *Psychology and Postmodernism*, London: Sage. A book of readings that explores the implications of postmodernist thought for psychology.

Mayo, E (1933) *The Human Problems of Industrial Civilization*, New York: Macmillan. A work by one of the founding fathers of Organisational Behaviour, which contains ideas that by now read as highly patronising and full of elitism.

Morgan, G (1997) *Images of Organisation*, London: Sage. A very readable book that develops and fully explains the different metaphors for organisations.

O'Connor, ES (1999) The politics of management thought: a case study of the Harvard Business School and the Human Relations School, *Academy of Management Review* 24(1): 117–131. Gives a useful insight describing how early developments in Human Relations theory were hijacked by the Harvard Business School, to serve managerialist ends.

Storey, J, G Salaman and K Platman (2005) Living with enterprise in an enterprise economy: freelance and contract workers in the media, *Human Relations* 58(8): 1033–1054. An interesting paper that illustrates how discourse analysis (a postmodern approach) can be applied in a research study to illustrate how freelance and short-term contract workers can be induced to accept their changed working conditions as normality.

Whitehead, AN (1985) *Science and the Modern World*, London: Free Association Books. An essential, but rather technical, text for those wishing to explore postmodernist thought.

REVIEW AND DISCUSSION QUESTIONS

1. Explain what you take the word 'organisation' to mean and compare your answer with the five key features (given at the beginning of the chapter) which qualify an entity as an organisation.

2. Explain the case for integrating knowledge from OB and OA. To what extent do you feel that failing to integrate knowledge from both areas can result in an incomplete or inaccurate explanation of behaviour in and by organisations?

3. Debate the following statement and state whether, in your collective view, the assertion is a valid one.

> Social science seldom, if ever, produces definitive, irrefutable laws that enable behaviour to be predicted with certainty. Therefore, it is highly questionable whether Organisational Behaviour and Analysis can add much to our understanding of organisations, and even more questionable whether they can provide information that is useful in making organisations more effective.

4. Compare and contrast the main foci and strengths and weaknesses of the following organisational metaphors: the machine metaphor; the organism metaphor; the political systems metaphor; and the cultural systems metaphor. Compare the use of these metaphors with the 'postmodernist' approach to organisations. What do you feel is the practical utility of the postmodernist approach?

Chapter 2

The Contexts of Contemporary Organisations

LEARNING OUTCOMES

After studying this chapter you should be able to:

- identify the contextual factors that influence organisations
- describe the main effects of political-legal, economic, socio-ideological and technological changes emanating from the contexts of organisations
- trace the impact of environmental contexts on British organisations
- describe effects of three significant challenges that are likely to confront organisations in the foreseeable future.

INTRODUCTION

At the press of a button a financial institution in Hong Kong could move billions of dollars around the world, the consequences of which could impact on the fortunes of hundreds of different organisations worldwide. Although this is a rather dramatic example of the way that events outside an organisation could have an impact on its interior, these days these effects are all too common. However, it can sometimes be difficult to trace these connections, if only because some of the external factors at work can be rather unspecific in terms of their effects. Some, for example, can act in combination with others, and some of them can have indirect effects that are hard to quantify.

Unfortunately, there has been a regrettable tendency for OB and to some extent OA to ignore the impact of environment, but as Capelli and Sherer (1991) point out, in the same way that individuals and groups are affected by their surrounding contexts, the external environment has an impact on the behaviour of a whole organisation. This, it will be recalled, is one of the fundamental principles of the open systems approach, which was briefly described in the previous chapter. Therefore, since this book deals with all levels of an organisation, it is fitting that it should include some mention of the effects that their environments have on them.

To explain these matters the chapter commences by presenting an explanatory model that identifies a number of broad contextual factors that can influence the nature of organisations. These can be likened to a set of forces or pressures to which a firm must respond in an appropriate way if it is to survive and prosper. The model is then applied to Great Britain to explain how changes in contextual circumstances have shaped the nature of organisations in the last three decades. In the final section of the chapter three prominent challenges that are likely to affect organisations for the foreseeable future are discussed, and the chapter closes with an overview section that integrates its main points.

THE CONTEXTS OF ORGANISATIONS: AN EXPLANATORY MODEL

Environment: issues, events and pressures that arise externally to an organisation, and which present opportunities for it to survive and prosper, but also put constraints on its behaviour and the behaviour of people in a firm

Political-legal context: the extent to which the state intervenes in organisations, either directly and/or indirectly

In total, the environment of an organisation consists of a host of issues, events and pressures that can affect the interior of a firm, and one way of examining these broad influences is to use the PEST framework shown in Figure 2.1. Before doing so, however, it is important to sound a cautionary note. The model given is only a very simplified representation of a far more complex reality, and the reader is urged to remember this and bear in mind that while models of this type can aid understanding they are, of necessity, incomplete, and can never fully capture the richness and complexity of the real world situation.

Clearly, although *environment* is something external to a firm, it is more than simply 'everything out there'. Some parts of it are of greater significance than others and, to structure the discussion, Figure 2.1 shows four environmental contexts, all of which can have effects on an organisation: the *political-legal context*, the *economic context*, the *socio-ideological context* and the *technological context*.

The Political-legal Context

The *political-legal context* refers to the extent to which the state intervenes in organisations and the ways in which they conduct their activities. This can occur in one of

Figure 2.1 Contextual influences on organisations

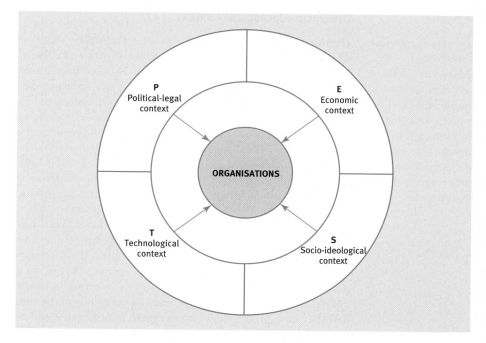

two ways. Where *direct intervention* takes place, the government or one of its agencies plays an active and ongoing role in determining certain aspects of their conduct as commercial organisations. For example, there is legislation in the various Companies Acts that sets out the duties and obligations of directors of companies, and this is largely designed to protect shareholders and other investors from fraud and malpractice. In addition, legislation was introduced in the 1980s and 1990s to privatise a number of organisations in the public sector, with the aim of introducing the use of free market principles. Direct legal intervention also includes employment laws that require the parties (employers, employees and trade unions) to modify their relationship to conform with certain standards, such as health and safety obligations and laws covering the national minimum wage and statutory trade union recognition.

Indirect intervention is rather different. It occurs when the state seeks to promote a particular public policy objective. Examples include the government's work–life balance objective, which encourages companies to adopt more family-friendly policies for employees. In addition there have been attempts to promote more cooperative employment relations policies, through union-management partnerships and there is now a designated partnership fund administered by the Department of Trade and Employment (DTI) to help promote public policy in this direction.

Economic context: the overall state of the economy in which an organisation operates, for example whether it is buoyant or recessionary

The Economic Context

The *economic context* is used to denote the key characteristics of a country's economy, such as whether it is buoyant or recessionary. Key economic indicators include global economic pressures, international currency fluctuations, labour market conditions such as employment and unemployment, wage costs, and changes to consumer tastes and demands.

The Socio-ideological Context

The socio-ideological context: the behavioural norms and cultural values prevalent in a society, which can, for example, influence the nature of the relationship between a firm and its employees

The third wider environmental context in Figure 2.1 is the *socio-ideological context*, which describes the dominant behavioural norms and cultural values in a society. As will be seen later in the book (see Chapter 13), four important characteristics of social cultures that affect organisations are: (i) *power-distance*, the extent to which deference to authority is considered a normal way to behave; (ii) *uncertainty-avoidance*, the extent to which aversion to risk-taking is considered a normal way to behave; (iii) *individualism vs. collectivist*, the extent to which people derive their sense of identity from being individualistic rather than part of a group; (iv) *masculine vs. feminine*, the extent to which being aggressive and 'macho' is part of peoples' psychological make-up. These cultural characteristics can vary significantly from one country to another, and to some extent between one firm and the next. For instance, in Great Britain and the USA, people are low in their deference to authority, but in other countries, such as Japan, they are more tolerant of power-distance. The need to accommodate ourselves to different social values by changing our behaviour can sometimes become very obvious if we travel outside our native country. It is also important to note that the effects of wider social cultures can be pervasive. That is, the culture of an organisation needs to be compatible with the culture or region in which it is located, otherwise people can find that expected patterns of behaviour in the enterprise clash with those that they have been brought up to regard as acceptable and normal.

The Technological Context

Technological context: the choices made by firms about the technology that they use in their activities, which affects employee job tasks, skills and competences

The *technological context* reflects the state of technical development in the environment within which the firm is located, and it is from this context that the firm makes its choices about which technologies it uses in its activities. This can have very far-reaching effects, because technology influences not only *what* tasks employees perform, but also *how* they perform them (Child 1972). For instance, on one hand technological innovation can make some jobs redundant, and provide management with new and more sophisticated forms of employee control and surveillance. On the other hand, however, it can create new jobs that require additional employee skills and competences. For these reasons, the technological context has significant implications for the social relations that shape an organisation's relationship with its employees.

TIME OUT

Using the PEST contextual factors described above (political-legal, economic, socio-ideological and technological) list what you feel could be the main influences on the university or college at which you study.

THE CHANGING CONTEXTS OF ORGANISATIONS IN GREAT BRITAIN

The Political-legal Context

The government is the only institution that has the capability to make new laws or abolish old ones and, in so doing, it effectively establishes the rules of the game for many organisations. As such, this context has had a significant affect on firms in Great Britain and to explain why it is necessary to trace some of the changes that have taken place across three last decades.

From 1979 onwards, the government abandoned prior principles of non-intervention in organisations and radically changed employment law to reform employment relations. In the following two decades successive Conservative governments adopted a strongly anti-union stance and, on average, introduced an item of statutory legislation every two years, much of which was aimed at curbing trade union activities (Ackers *et al.* 1996). The net effect of this was that the balance of power was firmly shifted into the hands of employers, on the grounds that these steps were necessary to weaken trade unions in order to free the market and promote a more individualistic (rather than collective) dimension in employment relations. Indeed, the government even banned trade union membership for workers employed at the Government Communications Headquarters (GCHQ) (McLoughlin and Gourlay 1994).

With the election of a 'new Labour' government in 1997 there was a radical change in state philosophies. Faced with the unpalatable extreme of Thatcherism, the newly elected Blair government offered a new approach based on the so-called *Third Way* (Giddens 2000). In general, while this eschewed a return to 'old' labour values of nationalisation, public spending and high taxation, it also avoided a continuance of Thatcherite free market policies. Therefore, while any definition is bound to be imprecise, the *Third Way* project broadly embraced five core pillars: competitive markets, innovation, skills, fairness and equity (Blyton and Turnbull 2004). Having said this, there is considerable debate about the efficacy of the Third Way. For some commentators it is little more than a continuation of Thatcherite neo-liberal free market principles (Callinicos 2001). For example, 'new labour' has continued the sell-off of elements of the public sector and nationalised industries, the labour market remains fundamentally unequal for many women, part-time workers and for millions who are subject to precarious forms of employment. In addition, while there is a raft of associated legal rights that protect individual workers – for example, family-friendly workplace policies and minimum wage protection – the restrictions on trade union behaviour remain on the statute book.

In addition, many of the changes in the political and legal context since 1997 have arisen from developments at the European Union (EU) level (Green 2001). In this respect *European Social Policy* has established regulations on a host of matters such as working hours, equal pay, redundancy, employee protection during company takeovers and transfers, maternity and paternity leave, and consultation rights. These matters are enshrined in the Social Chapter of the Maastricht treaty, from which the Conservative government obtained an opt-out in 1991. However, in 1997 the newly elected Labour government adopted an obligation to conform to the Social Chapter, and since then it has become an increasingly significant way in which the political-legal context has affected organisations. Indeed, the government argues that many of the individual worker laws, such as the national minimum wage and rights for part-time workers, serve to rectify the injustices of a previous political era. However, European legislation also has its critics. For example, many British employers argue that these European-led laws are restrictive and burdensome, and that they impose severe constraints on management's 'right to manage'.

The Third Way: a political ideology in which government charts a path between state regulation and free market forces; its core values include support for: competitive markets, innovation, skills, fairness and equity

European Social Policy: a set of regulations that provide rights for workers which are comparable across EU Member States, and which incorporates rights on working hours, employee voice, redundancy, health and safety, maternity and paternity leave

- The political-legal context has changed considerably in the last three decades.

- After 1980, Conservative governments were extremely hostile to trade unionism and as result the balance of power in employment relationship was shifted firmly into the hands of employers, and away from workers and unions.

- Since 1997 the Labour government has continued with many free market principles such as privatisation, but at the same time has introduced several important worker rights and protections. As a result, there are now many important legal interventions that affect organisations such as minimum wage protection and trade union recognition rights.

- European Social Policy has been at the vanguard of new rights and worker protections. The objective being to create a more even playing field across EU member states.

The Economic Context

The economic context has undergone far reaching changes, all of which can influence the nature of organisations. Following World War II, while full employment resulted in rising affluence and aspirations in the working population, there were certain fundamental weaknesses in the British economy: notably, declining competitiveness that fuelled a growing skills deficit compared with other market economies. By the 1980s, decline had firmly set in, and manufacturing industry was particularly hard hit with many regions in the UK plagued with high unemployment. While these recessionary effects have had a lasting impact in Great Britain, economic growth since 1997 has largely exceeded most forecasts. For example, inflation has remained relatively low and, with the growth of a new service sector, unemployment has declined. Two particularly important contextual changes that have an effect on organisations are *globalisation* and the changing *composition of the workforce*. The first of these will be covered later in the chapter as one of the significant challenges facing most British firms and so discussion will largely be confined to the second.

With respect to the *changing composition of the workforce*, one of the more visible economic changes is evident in changes that have occurred in its structure and composition. Across the last century the proportion of women who are part of the workforce has increased substantially from 29 per cent to 46 per cent (Lindsay 2003). In addition, average weekly hours worked has fallen from 53 hours per week to 42 hours and many of these changes have occurred because of wider economic pressures. For instance, there has been a sharp increase in service sector jobs, with a significant reduction in manufacturing employment. However, when viewed in more detail, the labour market remains highly segmented. For example, compared to most male occupations, many of the jobs taken by women tend to be part-time and of a temporary nature. In addition, women in full-time employment only earn about 80 per cent of the salary of men in equivalent full-time occupations (Office for National Statistics 2004). About half of all women work in service sector jobs, such as catering, cleaning and personal contract services, and these are often lower paid and lower skilled occupations. For example, according to the Low Pay Commission (2005), the main beneficiaries of any increase in the National Minimum Wage are women, part-time workers, some minority ethnic groups and younger workers. Thus, reference to the female participation rate on its own can hide other important labour market changes, many of which reflect a disproportionate distribution of the quality and security of work for millions of women (Grimshaw and Rubery 2003).

TIME OUT

Consider the changes in the composition of the workforce in Great Britain. To what extent do you feel that these are likely to have had an impact on the college or university at which you study?

In part, explanations for the increased participation of women in employment can be accounted for by wider changes in the economy (Millward *et al.* 2000). For example, the proportion of jobs in manufacturing industry has fallen substantially. Indeed, over the course of the twentieth century, employment in manufacturing industry has decreased from 28 to 14 per cent of all employees (Lindsay 2003). In the 1950s, only about 9 million people worked in service sector occupations and the current figure is now over 20 million (Labour Market trends 2004). Moreover, there are one-third fewer workers employed in the public services than there were in the early 1980s. This reduction illustrates the connections between economic changes and political developments, because it can mostly be explained by the privatisation of whole industries, such as gas and telecommunications, together with the outsourcing of other public sector functions to private enterprises (Millward *et al.* 2000).

REPLAY

- The economic context has undergone significant change and, in particular, two developments have been influential: *globalisation* and *labour market composition*.
- Service sector employment has increased significantly, while the number of manufacturing jobs has declined.
- The composition of the labour market in Britain has become segmented, with many women employed in lower paid and lower skilled jobs.

The Socio-Ideological Context

In broad terms, while Great Britain is a capitalist democracy, in the aftermath of World War II there was a strong belief that stronger members of a society should protect the weak. For this reason the government of the day constructed the welfare state, which included the National Health Service (NHS), and it also nationalised key industries so that they operated as enterprises that produced public goods, rather than existing for private profit. In response to widespread public demand, the government also widened access to education and social welfare provision. In addition, post-war full employment and the growth of trade union membership largely saw the demise of the deferential society, which resulted in aspirations of security, affluence and basic living standards.

However, throughout the 1980s and 1990s, the economic and political changes described above negated many of the social developments of earlier decades, and increased the gap between the 'have's and have-not's'. Thus, the 18 years of neo-liberal economic policies under Conservative rule resulted in an ethos in which the ideological values of private profit and entrepreneurship are more prevalent in Britain than they were two decades ago. Moreover, many organisations are now small businesses, in which employers adopt either a hostile or neutral response to the idea of unionisation. Changes to broad social values also tend to be reflected in government policy, and 'new Labour' continues to promote greater market choice and flexibility, albeit with important individual worker protections built-in to the social and economic fabric of society. As such, in the twenty-first century, Britain is (theoretically at least) a *meritocracy* that is guided by those who perceive that the basic principles of a free market society are superior to its alternatives.

Meritocracy: a social and economic system in which advancement is based on ability or achievement

REPLAY

- Social and ideological values are strongly connected to changes in the economic and political-legal contexts.
- Broader social values and norms are also reflected in individual attitudes; for example, whether workers embrace values such as entrepreneurship.
- Social norms can also reflect employer ideologies and hostility towards employee collective representation.

The Technological Context

There is a strong connection between technology and some of the economic changes described above, and it is no coincidence that the decline in manufacturing industry has occurred during periods of rapid technological innovation (Towers 2003). Indeed, technology in general, and in particular the use of Information and Communication Technologies (ICT), have transformed almost every aspect of employment.

As explained earlier, the word technology can be used to embrace not only *what* tasks employees perform, but also *how* these tasks are undertaken. In addition, the use of various technologies denotes the choices that employers make about how people are managed. Significantly, therefore, technology in the workplace is seldom a matter of new hardware or software alone, but tends to be part and parcel of new ways of managing people, such as Total Quality Management, or more flexible organisational structures. In many situations, technological change has streamlined workers' tasks, increased productivity and in some cases empowered employees in their jobs. It has also altered the way employees are managed, with increasingly more invasive forms of surveillance and control over almost every part of a worker's job.

Thus it is fair to say that technological change of one sort or another has affected practically all sectors of economic activity, from manufacturing, finance and banking to the way that McDonald's makes its burgers. Indeed, most people are touched by technology in some way in their everyday lives, both as customers and workers, and some of these technological developments have had an impact on health and safety at work. For example, the amount of time workers spend in front of computer screens or using various computer-aided technologies can have adverse health effects. Indeed, it was the adverse health effects of increased computer usage that prompted trade unions to campaign for improved safety conditions, which eventually led to the introduction of the 1992 European Display Screen Regulations.

REPLAY

- The technological context not only affects the tasks workers perform but also how they perform them.
- This provides employers with a greater degree of control over what and how employee tasks are performed.
- Technology has also affected workplace health, safety and well-being, particularly in terms of the increased use of computer-related work activities.

THE IMPACT OF CONTEXTS ON ORGANISATIONS

The changing nature of organisations has been vastly influenced by changes in the contexts of the wider environment. However, it is seldom the case that internal changes can be directly attributed to something that has occurred in one of the contexts alone. Rather, an organisation usually feels an imperative to respond to environment because of interconnected changes that occur in several contexts together. In what follows, some indication will be given of the particular contexts that have been most influential in prompting changes.

Market-prompted Changes

Because an organisation is strongly influenced by the demand for its products or services, many of the changes in this area have been in response to pressures from the *economic context*. Three general trends with respect to markets and competitive pressures can be detected and, since these are conceptually different, they will be described separately.

First, there has been a fairly high level of retrenchment in British firms, which started as long ago as the early 1980s. While new names such as *downsizing*, *rightsizing*, *delayering*, or even simply cutbacks have been invented to gloss over what occurred, the results were remarkably similar. Plant closures, redundancies, wage cuts, capacity reductions and the replacement of people with machines were all commonplace, and, while some firms survived and even regained a competitive position, this resulted in a great deal of unemployment. When an initiative of this type is in progress, people are understandably apprehensive and so commitment and loyalty are inevitably lowered (Savery *et al.* 1998). In addition, for those who are not made redundant, working life is frequently more stressful, insecure and more physically demanding, due to longer hours. As such conditions have been described by one author as 'working with pain' (Berggren 1993), and the survivors were sometimes so demotivated and dispirited that they lack a sense of security, and their loyalty to an employer is severely reduced because they feel that they work for an organisation that treats people as a commodity, rather than as humans who deserve consideration (Cooper 1998). One of the most strongly affected groups of survivors consisted of managers who, because they had to make people redundant, developed subliminal fears that what they did to others could be done to themselves (Kets de Vries and Balazs 1997). The need to address these psychological effects on those who remain has only recently been recognised (Doherty and Horsted 1995) and research in some of these slimmed-down organisations has revealed that organisational commitment can be much lower and the intention to leave much higher (Allen *et al.* 2001) than before.

Second, there has been considerable change prompted by what is now often called the 'quality revolution'. These days, quality tends to be viewed as a whole bundle of attributes that ensures that the needs of customers are satisfied, and, in the last two decades, the greater degree of competition for business is often said to have led to consumers becoming much more demanding (Grey and Mitev 1995). However, price has not been totally eclipsed by quality as the basis of competition and, where there are two substitute products of equal quality, customers will usually buy the cheaper one. Thus it is usually important to achieve high quality while keeping the price low and *productivity* – which can be defined as the quantity of outputs obtained from a given level of inputs – is a very important consideration. For this reason, the aim these days is to build-in quality during the production process.

A number of approaches to this issue have been put forward, one of which is *Total Quality Management* (TQM), which theoretically consists of an organisation-wide strategy that focuses on achieving or exceeding customer expectations. Most texts on TQM argue that realising its promised advantages is crucially dependent on using human resources in an appropriate way (Hodson and Roscigro 2004). Here there is very strong evidence that the firms who get the best from TQM are those that also have a compatible set of human resource practices, such as empowering the workforce and eliciting its cooperation and commitment (Datta *et al.* 2005; Wright *et al.* 2005). However, there is also evidence that the use of TQM often sets up a number of workplace tensions. For instance, work is sometimes deliberately organised to put pressure on employees to produce for every second, and worker autonomy is actually reduced because people are forced to achieve tight work targets. In addition, people are usually organised in teams, in which they have to cover for an absent colleague, which results in peer pressure being used as an instrument of management control to minimise absence (Parker *et al.* 1993) and, needless to say, employees are not blind to these effects (McCabe 1996).

Finally, one effect of a globalised marketplace is that products and services can rapidly become obsolete, and this means that the markets for many products become more volatile, more competitive and product life-cycles tend to be shorter. A response to this phenomenon in the search for competitive advantage is the use by management of a ruthless pursuit of new methods of cutting the costs of labour. To some extent this is associated with the fallacy fostered in the media that countries such as Taiwan, Malaysia, China and some of the new EU accession states have a cheap and abundant supply of labour. Thus, labour costs in these countries become the benchmark for what managers try to achieve in Great Britain. In reality, however, Great Britain is also a low wage economy relative to other advanced economic nations. For example, of all the original G7 nations (Great Britain, Germany, Japan, America, France, Canada, Italy), Britain is ranked sixth in terms of its relative wage levels – Italy is seventh (Blyton and Turnbull 2004).

TIME OUT

Consider the market-prompted changes that have taken place in organisations. How are these likely to have an impact on you and your fellow students in terms of the future careers that you pursue when you leave university?

Organisational Inputs

Turning now to the inputs to organisations, two phenomena in particular are worthy of discussion: *suppliers of capital* and *employees*, both of which have been affected by changes in the *economic context* of the wider environment. With respect to *suppliers of capital* in spite of government attempts to use the privatisation of state enterprises to bring about much wider share ownership, the share capital of large organisations is increasingly in the hands of large financial institutions (Blackhurst 1996) that regard themselves as having only one duty: to produce the highest possible return. As such, they have no loyalty to the firms whose shares they hold and this puts heavy pressure on these firms to produce high short-term returns, which sometimes means that they have to forego long-term opportunities (Hutton 1995).

Private equity funds: funds put together and raised on the stock exchange by (nominally) private investors, usually to engineer the acquisition or takeover of a large, publicly quoted organisation

This trend alone can make life difficult enough for firms, but a more recent and somewhat insidious turn of events has now arisen: the activities of *private equity funds* (see OB In Action Box following). These companies are rapidly acquiring an unenviable reputation for their ruthless and exploitative approach to business. Typically, after having acquired control of a large company, they install their own management team, who ruthlessly prune-down the firm by asset stripping, and increasing its financial leverage to give a rapid increase in profits. This, of course, tends to elevate share prices and so the time soon becomes ripe for the equity fund to return the shares to the open market, where they can be sold at a vast profit. By now employee morale and sense of security could be rock bottom, which means that the longer-term future of the company is at best perceived as doubtful.

The number of large firms subject to this treatment is growing daily. For example, a consortium bought the car rental firm Hertz, which in 2005 was re-structured into a number of blocks that could be sold-on. The retail group Debenhams was bought and its property portfolio of owned stores was sold-off and leased back, and, eventually, the company was re-sold on the stock market. The latest candidate, at time of writing, is the supermarket group Sainsbury's, which is reputedly being stalked by a consortium of four private equity firms (Hutton 2007).

 OB IN ACTION: Private Equity Companies

Six months ago, very few outside the City had come across the idea of private equity, but today, as Sainsbury's is stalked by a club of four private equity firms and the GMB (General, Municipal and Boilermakers) has ignited a campaign against job losses incurred in private equity restructurings, it is even becoming an issue in the contest for the deputy leadership of the Labour party.

Private equity is now the dominant element in the stock market. According to the Financial Services Authority, in the first six months of 2006 private equity firms raised £11.2bn in capital on the London Stock Exchange, whereas ordinary firms raised £10.4bn. So many public companies are being taken over by private equity companies, or retiring their own shares to head off the risk, that the London stock market, despite rising average share prices, shrank by nearly £50bn in the same period.

However, the story that private equity companies tell of themselves is that by taking public companies out of the public arena of accountability, regular reporting and scrutiny, they can instead enjoy the benefits of engaged, committed ownership. Too many companies, they allege, are just not trying hard enough to maximise their profits, and that they need the managerial alchemy of private equity investors who, by aiming to make 'life transforming' money for themselves, will give them the necessary managerial and strategic shock treatment. Nevertheless, one truth about private equity shines out: the extravagant management fees and annual 'carry' (the share in profits) certainly means life-changing fortunes. Researchers at Manchester University's ESRC Centre for Socio-cultural Change recently got hold of the internal management accounts of one fund with up to £8bn of funds under management. After five years, 30 full partners expected to make between £25m and £50m each. Moreover, the rest of the industry's claims about creating jobs, investment and exports do not bear close scrutiny. Much of the alleged managerial alchemy is no more than old-fashioned engineering – leveraging up returns by incurring lots of debt. Indeed, one study by Citigroup showed that if pension funds and insurance firms had borrowed money themselves and invested in a basket of companies in which private equity groups invested, they would have made higher returns than even the best-performing private equity firms.

Mortgaging the future to capture gains for personal gain in the present is easy and, as one chief executive of a well-known public company reported recently, the task of the good manager is to resist it. Managers have to balance the interests of today's shareholders with tomorrow's shareholders and private equity drives a coach and horses through the proposition. As Paul Myners, the former chairman of Marks & Spencer and chairman of Guardian Media Group, has remarked: 'The one party that is not rewarded is the employees, who generally speaking suffer an erosion of job security and a loss of benefits.'

Currently, other public companies, including ICI, Amec and EMI, are being stalked, and having to adjust their strategies accordingly. The shadow of private equity falls everywhere, making the gamut of British business hyper-short-termist.

The foundation of a durable business, as James Collin and Jerry Porras argued in their famous book, *Built to Last*, requires vision, values, leadership and purpose

around an organisation's 'reason to be'. So, if we want companies like this, shareholders have to give managers room for manoeuvre and back long-term business strategies. The problem is that British shareholders are not required by law to take their ownership responsibilities seriously. Nor are British companies required to give them the range and quality of information that might help them to do so. As a result, British shareholders are extraordinarily neglectful of their ownership responsibilities. Pension funds and insurance companies are myopic and short-term enough, but, because takeover is so easy in Britain, private equity has been able to carry short-termism to new extremes. While this is said to raise productivity and performance, the opposite could be argued. The chief reason British business remains at the bottom of the international league tables for innovation, research and development, and productivity growth is because there is too much takeover, and too much private equity.

The answer is obvious. Private equity cannot be outlawed; in any case it can do a good job. Rather, the perverse incentives in Britain that favour takeover need to be removed. We need to defend the public company and create conditions in which it can prosper. But who is going to do that? Not the Conservative party, which is in thrall to private equity, and not, judging by its legislative record, the government. Our politicians are confused and there is much more to wealth creation than constructing a plutocracy of private equity partners.

Source:

Adapted from Hutton, W (2007) Private equity is casting a plutocratic shadow over British business, *Guardian*, 23 February, p 39

Since this book deals with the behaviour of people in organisations, it is important to trace the effects of some of the changes mentioned above on the human element (employees) of organisations. From the 1980s onwards, Great Britain endured severe recessionary conditions, and redundancies, restructuring, re-equipping and re-design of jobs were all commonplace. Since then, life in organisations has become much harder and more stressful for almost everyone, and there are a number of legacies of this. To start with there is a psychological legacy in the minds of many employees who have lived through prior recessionary periods. According to a survey conducted by the Economic and Social Research Council (ESRC 2002) there is more than a hint that the working population of Great Britain is extremely dispirited and pessimistic about the future. This seems to apply to people who are back in employment after prior periods of recession, as well as those who have so far managed to avoid becoming unemployed. These feelings appear to affect almost anybody touched by the recession (Donnelly and Scholarios 1998), and this pessimism also has its effects on managers of organisations, many of whom are reluctant to expand capacities in order to take advantage of any economic upturn.

Second, since many of the 'new' jobs in organisations make use of part-time and/or contract workers, people seem to have little faith that things will get better. To many people the notion of a career is very important. It implies that hard work, diligence and loyalty can lead to rewards later, and gives people hope for the future. Research shows that in many organisations this hope is fast disappearing and is being replaced by strong feelings of demoralisation and frustration (Holbeche 1995).

Third, many jobs now exist in organisations where jobs have been re-designed to contain elements of teamworking and empowerment. For some years, empowerment has been a buzz word in management circles and, as Claydon and Doyle (1996) point out, much of its appeal to organisational managers lies in two features:

* it seems to offer a way of obtaining a higher level of performance from employees without the use of strict supervision and control
* its rhetoric is humanistic, which allows managers to feel that they are doing the right thing by giving employees autonomy and opportunities for self-development and personal growth.

Theoretically, empowerment gives people the authority to make decisions in their own area of operations, without getting the approval of someone above and, although this sounds much the same as delegation, it is much more. Since empowerment is results-orientated, people are not just allowed to make decisions, they are encouraged to use their initiative and given the necessary resources to implement their decisions. This, however, is empowerment in theory and saying that employees have been empowered is one thing, empowering them in practice is another.

Almost inevitably, empowerment occurs in a delayered or downsized organisation and, although there is often initial enthusiasm among employees (because they see work as becoming more interesting and responsible), it can quickly turn to disillusionment when they start to ask where all this is leading. For example, because managers tend to assume that more interesting work is sufficient reward in itself, employees find themselves working much harder for the same remuneration (Cunningham *et al.* 1996). Moreover, many of the things that employees hoped for in the future, such as promotion and security, become far less accessible.

CURRENT AND FUTURE ORGANISATIONAL CHALLENGES

From what has been described earlier, across the last three decades organisations have had to adapt to increasingly turbulent environments and, for the future, it is inconceivable that this need for adaptation will do other than continue. To bring matters to a close, this final section of the chapter examines three prominent organisational challenges that are likely to require ongoing adaptation by organisations. However, predicting what the future may bring is a somewhat hazardous occupation and, with this in mind, the challenges identified are all those where the phenomenon is already with us. There are already signs that future adaptation might be required: these are the challenge of globalisation; the challenge of ethics and social responsibility; and the challenge of catering for an increasingly more diverse workforce.

THE CHALLENGE OF GLOBALISATION

Whether or not a firm operates internationally by competing in a ***globalised (one-world) economy***, the effects of globalisation are so significant that henceforth the phenomenon will affect almost everyone. Large business organisations increasingly see their markets as international rather than purely domestic and this represents a way of thinking in which the world is perceived as a smaller place, and new business strategies are required (Bartlett and Ghoshal 1991). This did not come about overnight and, as things now stand, there are three very large trading regions: the so-called golden triangle of North America, which embraces the USA, Canada and Mexico; the Pacific Rim countries of Japan, which include South Korea, Taiwan, Singapore, Hong Kong and Australasia; and the European Union, which at present embraces 25 west European nations. Moreover, the position is fluid and other countries are likely to emerge as part of one of these regions in the near future. For example, countries such as China, Malaysia, Indonesia and Thailand are industrialising rapidly, and are likely to become part of the Pacific Rim group. Some of the Latin American countries are also making great strides in industrialisation and, in addition, the former Soviet command economies have all more or less embraced a free market system and are lining up to join an enlarged EU.

THE GROWTH OF INTERNATIONAL BUSINESS

Factors Facilitating the Growth of International Business

Except for a few rare cases, there were no really large cross-national organisations prior to World War II; they only started to appear in the 1970s and, although this was helped along by the gradual appearance of the three major trading regions identified above, Bedeian and Zammuto (1991) argue that there have been four main developments that prompted the increase in international trade, and these made the emergence of globalised markets virtually inevitable.

Industrialisation

With the exception of Japan, prior to World War II the major industrialised countries were all located in the northern hemisphere and, after the war, most of them quickly sought to re-establish their export trades. Although an exporting country largely keeps its expertise at home and merely sells its goods abroad, its prosperity and power are visible to the rest of the world, and this provides an incentive for every non-industrialised country to industrialise. Thus, other countries, many of which had previously been colonial outposts of a European nation, pursued conscious policies of industrialisation with the aim of becoming just as prosperous and powerful.

Rising Living Standards

In the two decades following the end of the World War II, living standards rose tremendously in Western countries, but more rapidly in the industrialising nations of the Far East. In the West, national markets were fairly mature and Western firms tended to see countries in the East as extremely attractive export markets because they had higher rates of economic growth. Since these countries were rapidly developing an industrial base, they also had an incentive to export, sometimes to the less developed countries of South East Asia but increasingly to the northern hemisphere.

Rapid Technological Change

Rising living standards bring changes in consumer tastes and these days tastes change quite rapidly. This shortens product life-cycles and increases the proportion of profits that needs to be ploughed back into development. It also means that the length of time in which development costs can be recouped is shorter and, for this reason, firms everywhere seek to sell their outputs in the widest possible range of markets.

Improvements in Global Transport and Communication

Since the 1960s, the declining cost of foreign travel has enabled people to experience other countries first hand. In addition, mass communication brings increased familiarity with lifestyles and customs in other parts of the world, and, to some extent, this also prompts a convergence in consumer tastes, which, although not identical everywhere, are often similar enough to enable a basic product to be adapted in minor ways so that it caters for local tastes. Rapid developments in communications technology have removed many of the barriers to operating internationally; satellite telephone gives easy access to remote locations and fax machines and e-mail enable complicated documents to be transmitted in seconds.

PRESSURES TO ENGAGE IN CROSS-NATIONAL ACTIVITY

The facilitating factors given above greatly ease the problems of international trade. However, there are more specific motives that apply to individual organisations and prompt them to look abroad.

Access to Resources

For reasons of cost and security of supply, many organisations, particularly those in the manufacturing industry, tend to feel a need to be close to their sources of supply of vital raw materials (Mendenhall *et al.* 1995). While this usually results in small subsidiaries that deal only with the supply of resources, if organisations also see market opportunities close to these sources, they may also engage in manufacturing abroad.

Economic and Political Changes

In the three very large trading regions mentioned earlier, countries are often bound together by political treaties that influence cross-border trade. For instance, while the European Union (EU) permits free movement of goods and labour between its member states, it has tariff barriers to the rest of the world and, to some extent, the same is true with most major trading blocs. To do business in these areas can sometimes mean becoming more deeply integrated with the area in question. A case in point is the EU, which has a requirement that goods are only free of import duties if a minimum percentage of the product is manufactured within the EU. Japanese and American manufacturers cannot afford to ignore the potential for sales in the EU, which prompted them to set-up manufacturing facilities in Europe (notably in Great Britain) to ensure access to European markets.

Product Markets

The most important single factor prompting an organisation to internationalise is the quest for new markets. An outstanding example of this is Nestlé, the Swiss confectionery manufacturer. Switzerland has far too small a population to sustain the growth that Nestlé has been able to achieve through international trading.

Lower Costs of Production and Distribution

Capital tends to migrate to the cheapest centre of production, and since the EU consists of some nations where wage rates are high and others where they are very low, there was a fear that there would be a tendency for this to happen within its member states. For this reason it constructed the Social Chapter, which seeks to harmonise employment legislation in all its members, so that the difference between countries would eventually disappear (Marginson *et al.* 1995). Nevertheless, large organisations always seem to be on the lookout for cheaper centres of production and this is a strong motivation for engaging in overseas activities.

Competitor Activity

As more and more organisations enter the international marketplace, it becomes increasingly difficult for other companies to insulate themselves from foreign competition. Indeed, a company can wake up one morning to find that what it thought was a competitor in an overseas country, is now a competitor on its own doorstep. A study by Martin *et al.* (1998) shows just how sensitive firms are to the activities of their competitors. For example, if a firm is a major supplier to another firm in its home country and this customer sets up an overseas facility, there is a strong impetus to do likewise for fear that an overseas competitor will acquire the business.

These facilitators and pressures for cross-national business activity are summarised in Figure 2.2.

Figure 2.2 Facilitators of, and pressures to engage in, cross-national business activity

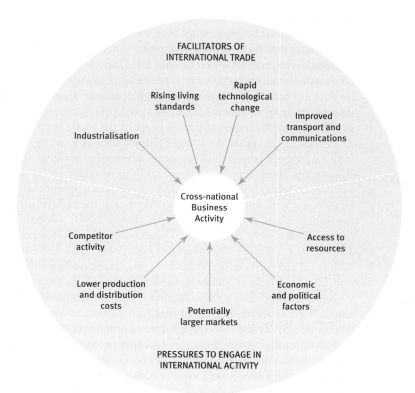

FACILITATORS OF
INTERNATIONAL TRADE

Rising living
standards

Rapid
technological
change

Improved
transport and
communications

Industrialisation

Cross-national
Business
Activity

Competitor
activity

Access to
resources

Lower production
and distribution
costs

Economic
and political
factors

Potentially
larger markets

PRESSURES TO ENGAGE IN
INTERNATIONAL ACTIVITY

The Effects of Globalisation

Globalisation has had a dramatic effect on organisations, and this can be illustrated by considering the USA, a country relatively unaffected by foreign competition until the 1970s. By 1980, 70 per cent of the goods and services produced by American firms faced competition from imported products (Astley and Braham 1989). In terms of relative size, American firms also ceased to dominate the world. In 1960, 70 of the world's 100 largest firms were American, but by 1985 the number had dropped to 45 and by 1990 it was down to 33.

Large firms sometimes often have no choice but to adopt a global perspective. To target only the home market is to compete against larger firms that can draw on global finances and that often have better design, competencies and technologies, from which come production advantages. The moral is stark and simple: compete on the same basis or lose the ability to compete at all. Indeed, it has been powerfully argued that it was the lack of competitive pressure within the USA that made it an easy target for Japanese firms (Porter 1990).

In Great Britain, globalisation has had a huge effect on the nation's manufacturing base. Rather than manufacture something themselves, many smaller firms simply sell foreign products. Moreover, an increasingly large proportion of British industry is foreign owned, often by Japanese or American companies. In addition, some large British companies are now seeking to become global organisations. For instance, until the late 1980s British Gas was a nationalised industry almost exclusively concerned with providing fuel and services in Great Britain, but it now derives an increasingly large proportion of its revenues from foreign operations. Changes like this immeasurably alter the face of an organisation, if only because it has to learn to deal with a more diverse and heterogeneous customer base.

It should also be remembered that it is often employees who feel the most impact of global economic changes (Ghoshal 2005) and some changes have significant effects on the way we all conduct our everyday lives. For example, many banking and finance services are now available over the internet, and are accessible from almost anywhere, no matter where the bank is actually located. Similarly, thousands of people are employed in call centres situated in different parts of the globe, irrespective of the customers' exact location. In addition, budget airlines such as Ryanair purposely utilise technology and agency labour in different countries to provide what they regard as a rapid, flexible and cheap service. Moreover, it is quite common for designer clothing manufacturers, such as Nike and The Gap, to produce many of their products in low wage economies, with subsequent employment and unemployment consequences in both the domestic and host country market (Eaton 2000). Globalisation can even impact on the employment conditions of workers employed in local supermarkets. For example, the US retailer Wal-Mart has taken over Asda, the German-owned Lidel and Aldi retail chains have significantly increased the number of outlets in Great Britain, and Tesco has now established stores in several other European countries.

As such, the effects of global economic factors on organisations should not be underrated. With an increasing use of new technologies and new ways of working, global economic activity can shape the fabric of employment for millions of people. These things can strongly affect the sense of security or insecurity of a workforce, which makes it much harder to satisfy employee expectations and provide them with meaningful roles to perform Moreover, now the phenomenon of globalisation is with us, it is not likely to go away, which makes it one of the most significant challenges faced by contemporary organisations.

TIME OUT

Bearing in mind what you have read about the globalised economy and, in particular, the nature of the globalised company:

1. Identify the likely effects on the working population of an industrialised country.
2. What do you feel would be the effect on a small or medium-sized company that is not large enough to contemplate becoming a globalised organisation?
3. What do you feel would be the major differences in working for a globalised organisation compared with one that is not globalised?

REPLAY

- In the last three decades markets have become far more globalised and three very large trading regions have emerged: North America; the Pacific Rim countries; and the European Union (EU) and these will almost certainly grow in the future.
- Globalised organisations tend to have significant competitive advantages and so large organisations have little alternative but to move in this direction, which poses a strong challenge for all organisations, irrespective of whether they are large enough to contemplate this step.

THE CHALLENGE OF ETHICS AND SOCIAL RESPONSIBILITY

The study of ethics and the social responsibilities of organisations are both fairly recent additions to Organisational Behaviour and Analysis, and modules on ethics are now offered by some universities and colleges as part of a Business Studies curriculum. Strictly speaking, there is a sense in which they cannot be divorced but, because they concern behaviour at different organisational levels, here they will be considered separately.

The scope of the topic of *ethics* has been described as:

> dealing with moral issues and choices and concerning an individual's beliefs about what is right or wrong and good or bad.   (Garrett and Klonoski 1992)

Social responsibility:
an organisation's
obligation to
contribute to,
or protect, the
environment of
which it is a part

Social responsibility is somewhat harder to define, but with respect to organisations it can be described as:

> concerning the relationship of an organisation to its social environment and the obligation to protect or contribute to that environment of which it is a part.
> (Donaldson and Preston 1995, p 67)

Thus, strictly speaking, ethics is essentially an individual matter, whereas social responsibility is a macro level concept. Nevertheless, any judgement about whether an organisation behaves in a socially responsible way inevitably involves a consideration of whether it behaves ethically and, in the eyes of the world, being socially responsible means behaving ethically.

Ethics

Standards of behaviour in organisations, and in particular the behaviour of those who own or manage them, have been a matter of public concern since the industrial 'robber barons' of the nineteenth century first attracted public criticism, because they were widely perceived to have amassed vast personal fortunes at the expense of the public and to be ruthless and corrupt in their dealings with anyone who stood in their way. Much of the current attention to *ethics* in business has been prompted by a resurfacing of similar concerns; for instance, the 'fat cats' scandal in which senior executives of companies are widely perceived to be in receipt of exorbitant remuneration packages, including overgenerous severance terms. Another issue which hit the headlines was the unauthorised futures dealings of the Singapore-based broker Nick Leeson, which resulted in the collapse of Barings merchant bank. Although these are very dramatic examples, it has been argued that ethical dilemmas arise in business more frequently than it is convenient to recognise (Walton 1988). Moreover, ethical standards are relative, not absolute; they vary from place to place and change with time (Carlisle and Manning 1996). Thus, it is important to recognise that there are a large number of factors that influence a person's behaviour, some of which are not always conducive to the individual behaving in a way that is ethical in a particular organisational context. These are outlined in Figure 2.3.

Ethics: an individual's moral beliefs about what is right or wrong, or good or bad, and provides a guide to his or her behaviour

Figure 2.3 Factors influencing individual behaviour

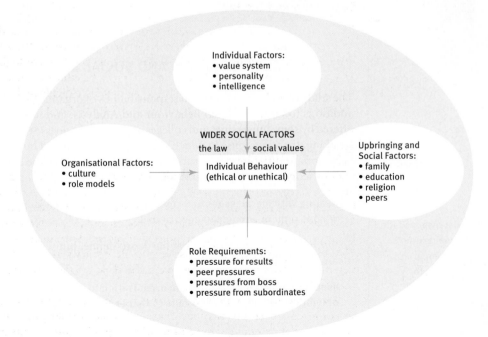

Individual Factors

Personal characteristics such as personality, intelligence and values play a part in the ethics of individual behaviour. However, for the present it is sufficient to note that they have a bearing on what individuals with these characteristics consider to be the acceptable limits of behaviour.

Upbringing and Social Background

Socialisation has a huge influence on a person's ethical standards, and what he or she learns through early family experiences, at school, and in church or peer groups can have dramatic effects later in life. As will be seen in the next chapter, Freudian theory (Freud 1940) stresses that an individual's superego (an aspect of personality that can loosely be equated with conscience) is acquired as part of his or her upbringing. In addition, the work of Kohlberg (1968) and Wright (1971) show that moral responsibility is strongly influenced by early social experience.

Role Requirements

As will be seen in Chapter 11, a person's work role often results in pressures to behave in certain ways, and most of us are subject to a number of these competing pressures; for instance, from the boss, from peers, from subordinates, and pressures to produce results. All of these can exert an influence on the person to deviate from standards that are part of his or her personality, or those that have been learned outside the organisation.

Organisational Factors

Most organisations expect certain patterns of behaviour from their members and an organisation's culture usually gives clear signals about the behaviour expected. For example, a culture in which senior figures clearly have high ethical standards and act as role models can help an individual to be ethical, whereas one in which the individual's own ethical code is subject to constant ridicule makes it much harder for him or her to behave ethically (Trevino and Bart 1992).

Wider Social Factors

A number of factors in the outside world also directly impinge on organisational life, and have a bearing on individual behaviour. Certain standards are enshrined in law, and some originate in the basic values of society. In certain parts of the world, for example in Arab states, business is conducted in a different way from the West. Hiring relatives in preference to others, using family contacts to influence and expedite events and paying money for favours do not have the unethical connotations of nepotism or bribery that most people in the West would associate with these practices (Muna 1980).

All of these groups of factors interact and, because the demands of a particular situation can overwhelm other considerations, people can sometimes act out of character. For example, if the culture of an organisation permits people to be treated harshly in a time of crisis, someone who is normally humane and considerate can behave in a highly cavalier fashion towards others.

Social Responsibility: The Organisation's Relationship with Environment

An organisation's relationship with its environment often poses a considerable number of ethical dilemmas but, until comparatively recently, the dominant view has been that a profit-making organisation's responsibility to its shareholders should be set above all other responsibilities. However, in the last half-century, British governments have introduced an increasing amount of legislation to emphasise organisational responsibilities to wider society and three examples are: the Companies Acts from 1948 onwards; Consumer Protection legislation from the 1960s onwards; and the Health and Safety at Work Act 1974. While opinion is still divided on this matter, a consensus has emerged across the last two decades that business owes some form of duty to a wider set of interests than those of shareholders. To some extent this has been prompted by a number of corporate scandals such as the demise of giant US corporations such as Enron and WorldCom, together with the activities of Shell (the Brent Spar episode), Union Carbide (the Bhopal disaster) and Monsanto. For this reason the expression corporate social responsibility (CSR) is now familiar in most boardrooms and it is one that has also attracted a great deal of public attention. However, it is always difficult to tell whether a business that behaves ethically towards its environment is prompted by altruism or something else. The skeptical view expressed by writers such as Roberts (2003), Parker (2003), Arthur (2003) and Doane (2003) is that talk of ethics in CSR is talk and little else: a cheap and easy way for the corporation to manufacture an image of its own goodness. Conversely, there are others who point out that the pressures to improve CSR performance are real, albeit prompted by self-interest as much as anything else (see Vogel 2005). For example, it could be a matter of sound business sense because a host of groups such as customers, employees and shareholders have developed tendencies to disassociate themselves from companies that fail to behave responsibly. This begs the question of how organisations could (or should) approach the matter of CSR. Since this of necessity involves considering the interests of a wide variety of internal and external groups, the most convenient perspective to adopt is that of the 'stakeholder organisation', which is considered next.

The Stakeholder Organisation

In the last decade the word *stakeholder* has attracted an increasing amount of attention when discussing organisations. No one who followed the run-up to the 1997 General Election in Great Britain (and how could anyone avoid it!), could help becoming aware that new Labour had adopted the concept of a *stakeholder economy* in its manifesto, within which it also embraced the idea of the stakeholder organisation. In organisational terms, stakeholders can be defined as:

> **people or groups with an interest in the activities of an organisation and the outcomes of those activities . . . they are identified as people who have an interest in the organisation, whether or not the organisation has an interest in them.**
>
> **(Donaldson and Preston 1995, p 67)**

Stakeholder: people or groups with an interest in the activities of an organisation and the outcomes of those activities, whether or not the organisation has an interest in them

Stakeholder economy: an economy which is theoretically run for the benefit of all participants who have an interest in the performance of the economy

TIME OUT

Bearing in mind that all organisations have stakeholders:

1. Who would you identify as the different stakeholder groups of a university or college?
2. What are your grounds for stating that the groups you have identified are relevant stakeholders?
3. What are the interests of these stakeholder groups?
4. Are the interests of the different stakeholder groups compatible; that is, is it possible to satisfy them all or are the interests so opposed that if one group is satisfied some other group could not be satisfied, and what would be your suggested remedy to this situation?

There is nothing new about the idea that organisations have stakeholders and in academic circles the term has been in use for some time. Donaldson and Preston (1995) point out that the word has been used in three different ways. First, descriptively, to advance the idea that there are many groups of people that have a vested interest in the actions of an organisation. This has clearly had some effect because there is strong evidence that even managers now view matters in this way (Merrick 1997). Second, in an instrumental way, mainly by academic researchers who have explored the idea that there is a link between organisational performance and considering the interests of a wide constituency of stakeholders; for example, there is said to be strong evidence that successful firms adopt a multiple-stakeholder perspective (Greenley and Foxall 1997). Finally, there is what Donaldson and Preston call the normative use, which is essentially a moral and philosophical argument that firms should be managed in a way that takes due account of the interests of all stakeholders.

Currently the normative use of the word dominates the debate, and this is in sharp contrast to the traditional view that, since shareholders are the owners of the business, the primary (if not sole) consideration should be to maximise their return. However, Donaldson and Preston argue that the traditional view is morally untenable, if only because society now demands that organisations should adopt a wider perspective of their responsibilities; that is, one in which each group of stakeholders merits consideration for its own sake.

An early visible sign that this view is taking root in Britain was the appearance in 1995 of a report entitled *Tomorrow's Company* (RSA 1995). This strongly advocates a style of corporate governance that is fast becoming known as a *stakeholder management perspective*, the key attribute of which is a simultaneous attention to the legitimate interests of all appropriate stakeholders. While a strong rearguard action is being fought by traditionalists, there are encouraging signs that the report had some impact. For instance, to explore ways of implementing the report's proposals, a permanent 'think tank', The Centre for Tomorrow's Companies, was set up. In addition, in 1996, Kleinwort Benson Investment Management launched its 'Investment in Tomorrow's Companies' fund, which invests only in companies that take an inclusive approach to business relationships. Moreover, in late 1996, British Telecom announced that it was

Stakeholder management perspective: simultaneous attention to the legitimate interests of all the appropriate stakeholders of an organisation

Figure 2.4 Areas of
social responsibility
for organisations

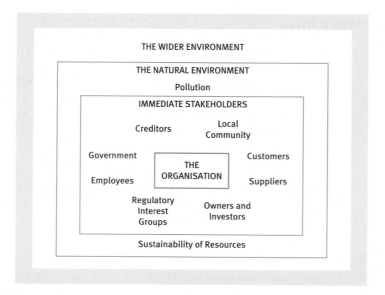

Figure 2.4 Areas of social responsibility for organisations

well on the way to becoming the first large, mainstream, commercial organisation in the UK to undergo a regular, independent social audit of how it treats stakeholder groups (Cowe 1996).

Nevertheless, the stakeholder approach is not without difficulties. In legal terms, the directors of a company owe a primary duty to protect shareholders' interests and, while this does not prevent other interests being considered as well, it still leaves the problem of defining whose interests should legitimately be considered (see Mitchell *et al.* 1997). The most interesting and comprehensive approach to this matter is to adopt what could be described as the *potential harms and benefits approach*, that is, to define relevant stakeholders as 'those who potentially benefit or are potentially harmed by the actions of an organisation' (Donaldson and Preston 1995). With this in mind, Figure 2.4 portrays stakeholder constituencies to whom this duty of consideration could be argued to be held.

Potential harms and benefits approach: a way of identifying the relevant stakeholders of an organisation as those who potentially benefit or are potentially harmed by its actions

Immediate Stakeholders

Immediate stakeholders are groups of people or organisations that are directly affected by the actions of a firm and to some extent who they are speaks for itself.

The Natural Environment

Responsibility to the natural environment is an area of increasing concern, and there are two particular issues. The first is pollution, which here is taken to include pollution of the upper atmosphere, which leads to global warming. In the past, the record of commercial undertakings has been abysmal in this respect and, although there is legislation to outlaw pollution, this does not stop it happening, largely because doing so costs money, which affects profits. Those who create the pollution seldom have to live with its consequences, for example atmospheric pollution creates acid rain, but this tends to fall on another country. Another obvious example is the depletion of the ozone layer and the resultant global warming, the results of which are more likely to be felt by subsequent generations. However, there is now widespread acceptance of where the blame lies for these things and, in their own interests, large companies now tend to be more vigilant in this matter (see OB in Action Box following).

The second area of concern is the depletion of the world's natural resources, where there is much debate about moving towards development that is sustainable and which avoids exploiting natural resources that provide a fast stream of income that rapidly withers as resources disappear. One example is the problem of deforestation, which is proceeding at an alarming rate in some tropical countries. Trees take a long time to grow and cannot be replaced quickly, even where replanting takes place (which is all too rarely the case). Moreover, the felling of trees reduces the planet's capability to absorb carbon dioxide, a greenhouse gas which contributes considerably to global warming.

 OB IN ACTION: British Petroleum's green credentials

Over the last decade, British Petroleum (BP), the world's second largest oil company, has burnished its green credentials. In 1996, the company withdrew from the Global Climate Coalition, the anti-global warming body backed by the oil industry, and in 2000, it re-branded itself as an energy company, 'Beyond Petroleum', stressing its commitment to environmentalism. Indeed, in 2005 the company said it would spend $8bn on solar, wind and hydrogen energy over ten years. 'No one should be able to use the environment without restoring it,' stated the company's group chief executive officer, Lord (John) Browne.

But does BP have a dark side? In 2006 the company halted production at Prudhoe Bay, the USA's biggest oilfield on Alaska's North Slope, after it found severe corrosion inside 16 miles of transit lines, which help feed crude oil from 2,200 wells into the Trans-Alaska Pipeline, although production has since resumed in Prudhoe Bay's western section. This problem surfaced when BP inspected feeder pipes following a 270,000-gallon spill – Prudhoe Bay's worst – in March. Whereas BP had run external tests on pipes, the insides had not been electronically inspected since 1992, as there was no legal requirement to do so. Prudhoe Bay opened in 1977 and was exploited by BP in a joint venture with Exxon Mobil and Conoco-Phillips. This is an old field and production has steadily declined since the late 1980s, and sludge had built up inside feeder lines, preventing inhibitor chemicals from reaching the corrosion.

So why hadn't eco-friendly BP anticipated this problem? To the company's critics, it is part of a disturbing pattern that they claim gives the lie to BP's green credentials. Last month the company closed 57 wells 'that exhibited problems with surface leakage' and said 37 remain 'shut in' as they 'did not meet the company's operating criteria'. Earlier another BP line ruptured on the North Slope and the same month the company was fined $2.4m for safety problems at a facility in Ohio. In March 2005, following a refinery explosion that killed 15 workers and inured 170 in Texas, BP was fined $421.4m and, a few days earlier, the company agreed to an $81m settlement following charges that it had released toxic gases from a refinery in California. 'It's the tip of an iceberg,' says Melanie Duchin, a Greenpeace energy specialist, of the latest shutdown. 'What other ugly surprises are out there?' So, are BP's eco concerns genuine? It depends on your perspective. 'You can't be a green oil company – it's like being a healthy tobacco company', says Duchin. 'Oil is dirty. There are direct impacts to the environment in terms of spills, leaks and toxic messes. When you burn the stuff, it causes global warming.' There are some 400 spills at Prudhoe Bay and on the Trans-Alaska Pipeline each year. And climate change is alarmingly obvious in the Arctic – three to five times the global average, as the trundra melts and sea ice thins, drowning polar bears. Nonetheless, BP did acknowledge global warming when other oil companies assiduously denied its existence. It also pulled out of Arctic Power, the lobby group that wants to drill in the Arctic National Wildlife Refuge. Confronted by a BP disaster when the pipe corrosion scandal surfaced, the company has stressed its commitment to alternatives. These include a project to provide clean energy to 250,000 California homes by separating hydrogen from natural gas. Natural gas is a central plank of BP's Beyond Petroleum vision, the next stage in a 'journey of many steps', from oil to alternatives. Along with Exxon and Conoco, BP wants to build a $20bn pipeline to ship gas from Prudhoe Bay to the Lower 48. But environmentalists complain that the gas released carbon emissions, fuelling climate change.

Greenpeace wants BP to close its field at Prudhoe Bay. 'That's a radical position', says Duchin. 'But we need to take this debate beyond oil', which would send a signal that BP was accelerating its journey towards alternative energies. Yet reacting to demand is different from leading the market. BP's website stresses its search for 'sustainable supplies of oil and gas for decades to come', even as it acknowledges 'precautionary action is necessary', to curb global warming. It is a tricky dilemma. How to reconcile oil and gas extraction with green stewardship?

Source:

Adapted from Huck, P (2006) Burning questions, *Guardian*, 23 August, p 8

The Wider Environment

Theoretically, this takes in the whole world and, in the past, this has been regarded as the preserve of the government. However, there are now suggestions that firms should look beyond their immediate environments, a trend which started in the 1980s, when a number of organisations in America and Europe withdrew from all activities in South Africa as a protest against apartheid. Shortly afterwards the British charity Oxfam urged retailers to band together and sign up to a code of practice that would preclude them buying from highly exploitative, overseas producers, many of whom use child labour, and some of Europe's biggest companies have now formed the European Business Network for Social Cohesion and pledged themselves to such measures as bringing socially disadvantaged people into the labour market, creating new jobs and promoting social integration. More recently, the retailing chain Littlewoods announced that in future it will require all of its international suppliers (and their sub-contractors) to guarantee that they adopt ethical human resource practices.

An important associated challenge for firms, that concerns both ethics and social responsibility, is the issue of so-called *whistleblowers*. Many firms that like to think of themselves as ethical and socially responsible also have employee 'gagging' clauses as a condition of employment. Procedures that allow employees to bring ethical issues to the surface internally are also fairly uncommon and this places employees in an impossible position. While an employee who discovers something unethical can ignore the matter and keep silent, this makes a mockery of having a policy on ethics in the first place. Alternatively, he or she can try to highlight the concern internally, which raises the risk of being considered a troublemaker. In the last resort, if the person makes the matter public outside the organisation, he or she risks dismissal (Smith 2002). However, legislation, in the form of the Public Interest Disclosure Act (1998), now gives employees some safeguards in this respect. For instance, in appropriate circumstances it gives a victimised 'whistleblower' the right to claim unfair dismissal and compensation (Williams 1999). However, by this time an employee would have been dismissed, which begs the question of whether legislation can ever adequately protect people who inform on their employers in this way. Evidence from America, which has had laws to protect whistleblowers in the public sector for several years, would suggest otherwise (Miceli *et al.* 1999). For example, although legislation seems to have encouraged people to 'blow the whistle' if they actually observe wrongdoing, the numbers who say that they have observed something worth reporting tend to have declined. In addition, the number of whistleblowers who report that they have been subjected to a degree of employer retaliation has increased significantly, as has the number who say they are only prepared to inform on their employer if their anonymity can be protected (Rothschild and Miethe 1999). For these reasons Kenyon (2003) argues that genuinely progressive firms – those that wish to put ethical policies into practice – should welcome whistleblowers rather than treat them as criminals.

THE CHALLENGE OF WORKFORCE DIVERSITY

Historically, people in any given workplace tended to have strong similarities, but in the last four decades a number of changes has altered these patterns. Traditional industries that were largely staffed along gender lines have declined and changed technologies and production methods now allow jobs that were once physically arduous to be undertaken by women. Wider access to further and higher education has also resulted in a larger number of women who are well qualified, and the population now contains an increased number of well-educated people from diverse ethnic origins, who (rightfully) seek equality of opportunity with other citizens. Declining birthrates and longer life expectancies have also produced a population where people have longer active lives, and some of them have no desire to leave the world of work early. The net result of all this is a heterogeneous working population, which for most firms results in a potentially more diverse workforce, and this gives rise to a challenge of considerable proportions.

One issue that can arise is that of avoiding the sensitive, unpleasant and potentially volatile behaviour that occurs when groups or individuals who differ in some respect

Whistleblowers: people (usually employed by an organisation) who make public unethical or questionable activities of an organisation

come into close contact. Individuals have the same prejudices, stereotypes and value systems at work that they have outside, which can lead to some people being singled out or even persecuted for being different, One example, that currently attracts attention, is the matter of ageism. Until comparatively recently it was not illegal to discriminate on the basis of age in Great Britain. Indeed, survey evidence has consistently shown that approximately one-third of all employees report some experience of this phenomenon (MacLachlan 1996) and it is not hard to see why. Because older employees may have been awarded high pay rises in earlier periods of high inflation, they can be more expensive than new recruits, and thus become the first targets in a redundancy situation (Rowlinson 1996).

Theoretically, there are two distinct approaches to the tackling discrimination of this type. The first, which originates in America, is the *diversity management* approach. This seeks to give equality of opportunity to all groups by taking steps to promote a positive image of workforce diversity, together with the use of proactive measures to affect the composition of a workforce so that it reflects the degree of diversity in wider society (Thomas 1990). To ensure equal treatment for underrepresented groups organisations set targets for including minority groups in the workforce, together with an element of positive discrimination in their favour.

Laudable as it appears at first sight, there are significant problems with this approach. In Great Britain positive discrimination would be of dubious legality and even in America, where it is lawful, it tends to result in a high degree of understandable resentment (Nemetz and Christensen 1996), because discriminating in favour of one group automatically results in discrimination against another. Indeed, those who benefit from positive discrimination are sometimes branded as not having been appointed or promoted on merit, and feel stigmatised or patronised. In addition, training to support or promote diversity is often badly received and invites accusations of political correctness and white-male bashing (*ibid.*).

In Great Britain a rather different approach has been adopted, the aim of which is to ensure equality of treatment. This is known as the *equal opportunities* approach, which is underpinned by extensive legislation outlawing unfair discrimination on the basis of gender, race, religion, ethnic origin, age, sexual orientation and, to some extent, physical disability. Although there is no requirement in law to train people in equal opportunities, it is difficult to provide equality of opportunity unless the idea is actively promoted. Thus many firms find it prudent to give such training to create awareness of how easily unintentional discrimination can occur.

Clearly the equal opportunities approach is very different from diversity management. Legally its aim is to provide equality of opportunity and this means just what it says: eliminating discrimination for or against a person on a number of grounds, unless there are very sound reasons for doing so. In the USA, discriminating is seen as perfectly legitimate, in the interests of achieving proportional representation of the different groups, but in Britain the legal framework virtually ensures that the equal opportunities approach is the dominant one. However, there are some firms that have made attempts to go beyond equality of opportunity, and have adopted a uniquely British version of diversity management. Broadly speaking this is based on a business case for greater workforce diversity, rather than a moral imperative to be fair by promoting equality of treatment (Gangon and Cornelius 2000). The rationale for this is that recognising people's differences can deliver considerable human resource and

Diversity management: a systematic, proactive approach aimed at promoting the positive image of workforce diversity, which usually involves steps to affect the composition of a workforce so that it reflects the degree of diversity in wider society

Equal opportunities: a systematic approach to ensuring there is no unjustifiable discrimination for appointment or promotion on the basis of gender, race, religion, ethnic origin and, more recently, disability

market-related benefits, because it helps maximise the available pool of talent and creates business opportunities by drawing on wider perspectives that give a firm the capability to thrive in different cultures (Robinson and Dechant 1997). A notable example of this approach is the DIY retailer B&Q, which employs considerable numbers of older workers, who are perceived to be more skilled at giving DIY advice to customers than are younger staff (B&Q 2004).

However, using an equal opportunities approach is still a legal requirement in Great Britain, and unfortunately this has led to problems in a number of organisations, some of which were revealed in a study by Foster and Harris (2005). For example, it was noted that middle managers, who had to implement the new approach, were bewildered by what was expected of them. On one hand they were expected to abide by the law by giving equality of opportunity, but at the same time found themselves being encouraged to promote an approach that had a strong emphasis on what they saw as diversity for diversity's sake. To reconcile this dilemma they developed strong tendencies to 'play it safe' by sticking to equal opportunities principles.

In summary, therefore, although significant steps have been taken in Great Britain to provide legal safeguards against the discrimination that can still be rife in some organisations, there is a strong case for the newer diversity management approach and finding a compromise set of practices that reconcile both approaches is likely to be one of the most significant challenges facing organisations in the future.

CONCLUSIONS

There are two overriding themes of this chapter. First, organisations are not sealed-off from the rest of the world, but are subject to a host of forces that emanate in their environments. Second, that since an organisation cannot exert control over its environment, it has little choice but to respond by adapting itself to changing contextual circumstances.

The chapter commenced by setting-out a simplified model that identifies four major groups of contextual factors that influence and shape the general nature of organisations: the *political-legal context*, the *economic context*, the *socio-ideological context* and the *technological context*. The model was then used to review some of the main changes in the wider environment of Great Britain across the last four decades, and traced the impact on matters within organisations, commenting on how these factors have affected both employees and managers within firms. Needless to say, what happens in the environment does not necessarily impact on all organisations in the same way, or to the same extent. Certain issues are likely to be more significant in some firms than in others, and so firms tend to respond in their own individualised ways.

Finally, to illustrate the point that environment itself is seldom, if ever, static, three future challenges for organisations were discussed. These are all in areas where past movements in one or more environmental contexts have required organisations to adapt and change, and where future developments of one sort or another can be expected. As such, they are all areas in which organisations are likely to have to respond with further changes in the future.

FURTHER READING

Cannon, T (1994) *Corporate Responsibility*, London: Pitman. A serious but readable text on business ethics and the corporate social responsibilities of organisations.

Doyle, C (2003) *Work and Organisational Psychology: An Introduction with Attitude*, Hove: Psychology Press. An interesting, easily digested text that examines (often critically) current trends and likely future developments in organisations.

Dunning, JN (1993) *The Globalisation of Business*, London: Thomson. Globalisation and its development is explained in an easy-to-read way, together with informed speculation about possible future trends.

Greener, I (2006) 'Nick Leeson and the collapse of Barings Bank: socio-technical networks and the "rogue trader"', *Organisation* 13(3): 319–343. A very interesting paper that examines the unethical behaviour of Nick Leeson, whose unauthorised futures trading eventually led to the collapse of Barings Bank.

Hutton, W (1995) *The State We're In*, London: Vintage. A penetrating account of economic and political developments over the last three decades, which gives a good background to many of the challenges facing organisations.

Johns, G (2006) 'The essential impact of context on organisational behaviour', *Academy of Management Review* 31(2): 386–408. A very useful paper giving a well stated rationale for the consideration of the effects of environments in OB and OA research.

Levine, DP (2005) 'The corrupt organisation', *Human Relations* 58(6): 723–740. A penetrating examination of ethics. It explains why individuals fail to become attached to moral principles and the role that this plays in certain key features of corruption. The article uses the case of Enron to explain matters.

Sahdev, K (2003) 'Survivors' reactions to downsizing: the importance of contextual factors', *Human Resource Management Journal* 13(4): 56–74. Reports the results of an empirical study of what has been an increasingly popular way for organisations to survive across the last two decades. It comments on what turned out to be both positive and negative outcomes of the exercise.

Stein, H (2001) *Nothing Personal, Just Business: A Guided Journey Into Organisational Darkness*, Westport, CT: Quorum Books. Although a difficult read in places, a penetrating book that exposes the interior of many current organisations to reveal how they operate on the assumption that everyone is made disposable in the name of organisational survival.

Vogel, DJ (2005) 'Is there a market for virtue? The business case for corporate social responsibility', *California Management Review* 47(4): 19–45. A useful and extensive review of the evidence about whether CSR has a payoff for organisations. While acknowledging that this idea is both attractive and appealing, the author concludes that there is very little evidence that socially responsible firms are more profitable.

REVIEW AND DISCUSSION QUESTIONS

1. Identify the four components of the PEST model of the external environment of an organisation, and explain what elements of environment are covered by each context.

2. Explain how the organisational size reductions that took place in the 1980s and 1990s have resulted in changed conditions in organisations, the repercussions of which could continue to have an impact in the future.

3. Explain why the phenomenon of globalisation tends to be regarded as an inevitable development, and comment on what you perceive to be the main outcomes of a globalised economy.

4. Define ethics and social responsibility and explain why there is likely to be an overlap between ethics and social responsibility on the part of an organisation. Illustrate your conclusions by explaining how ethical considerations apply to other areas in addition to the interests of immediate stakeholders.

5. Distinguish between diversity management and the equal opportunities approach. Why is it that the adoption of a diversity management approach can be a problematic step in Great Britain?

Section 2 Individual Characteristics

As the diagram indicates, this part of the book consists of three chapters, all of which deal with important ways in which people can be distinguished as individuals. These characteristics have a bearing on a person's behaviour in an organisation and, among other things, they are likely to have a strong impact on whether the individual is more suitable for some roles rather than others. Nevertheless, it is important to realise that although these characteristics are present in everyone, they are merely abstract constructs used as 'expressions of convenience' to summarise what are presumed to be certain mental attributes. Thus, while they all have different names, they are not 'stand alone' characteristics, and the short integrative section following Chapter 5 traces links between them.

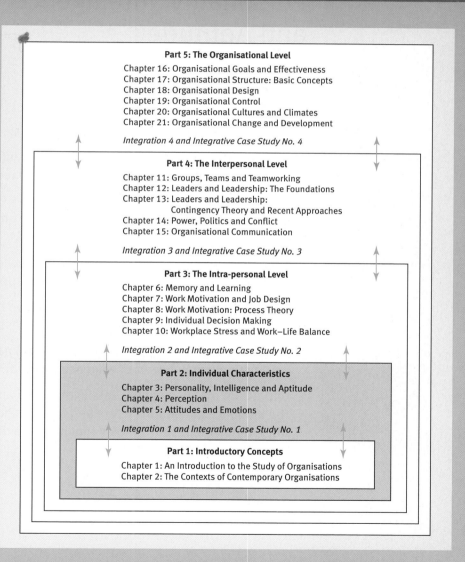

Part 5: The Organisational Level

Chapter 16: Organisational Goals and Effectiveness
Chapter 17: Organisational Structure: Basic Concepts
Chapter 18: Organisational Design
Chapter 19: Organisational Control
Chapter 20: Organisational Cultures and Climates
Chapter 21: Organisational Change and Development

Integration 4 and Integrative Case Study No. 4

Part 4: The Interpersonal Level

Chapter 11: Groups, Teams and Teamworking
Chapter 12: Leaders and Leadership: The Foundations
Chapter 13: Leaders and Leadership:
            Contingency Theory and Recent Approaches
Chapter 14: Power, Politics and Conflict
Chapter 15: Organisational Communication

Integration 3 and Integrative Case Study No. 3

Part 3: The Intra-personal Level

Chapter 6: Memory and Learning
Chapter 7: Work Motivation and Job Design
Chapter 8: Work Motivation: Process Theory
Chapter 9: Individual Decision Making
Chapter 10: Workplace Stress and Work–Life Balance

Integration 2 and Integrative Case Study No. 2

Part 2: Individual Characteristics

Chapter 3: Personality, Intelligence and Aptitude
Chapter 4: Perception
Chapter 5: Attitudes and Emotions

Integration 1 and Integrative Case Study No. 1

Part 1: Introductory Concepts

Chapter 1: An Introduction to the Study of Organisations
Chapter 2: The Contexts of Contemporary Organisations

Personality, Intelligence and Aptitude

LEARNING OUTCOMES

After studying this chapter you should be able to:

- define personality, describe the factors that influence personality differences and explain the relationship between personality and behaviour

- explain the differences between idiographic an nomothetic approaches to personality

- explain in outline the basic principles of psychodynamic theory and contrast psychodynamic and interpersonal approaches

- describe, compare and contrast trait and type theories of personality and explain how personality is normally assessed

- define intelligence, explain the controversial nature of the concept and distinguish between intelligence, aptitude and ability

- appreciate that personality, intelligence and aptitude can reflect the influence of cultural factors and that this has implications for interpreting the results of tests that measure these characteristics

INTRODUCTION

By definition, all individuals are different and two ways that are commonly used to distinguish between them are their personalities and their intelligence. Starting with personality this chapter deals with these differences. The concept is defined and the two major approaches to the study of human personality are briefly explained. Some of the factors that can shape personality are then considered, followed by an explanation of several major personality theories. Finally, the significance of personality characteristics in the work context are examined, together with ways in which personality can be assessed.

Intelligence, which is the next topic to be considered, is one of the most controversial subjects in the field of psychology and, for this reason, the meaning of the concept is discussed at some length. The major theory concerning the structure of human intelligence is explained and its measurement discussed. To consider its practical implications in a work context, the chapter briefly explores two concepts closely allied to intelligence: aptitude and ability. Finally, the interactions between personality and intelligence are explored, together with a brief exploration of the effects of national cultures on personality and intelligence.

PERSONALITY

The Importance of Personality

Just as individuals can be distinguished in terms of physical characteristics, they think in slightly different ways. Thus, most of us routinely use words to distinguish people in terms of their mental characteristics, saying, for example, that someone is moody, lively, morose or bookish. These words describe what we see as the essence of a person's mental make-up or, to put it another way, his or her personality. These descriptions are also used to predict the behaviour of people, and at some time we have all probably said something like: 'Of course he does that; what do you expect? He's that type of person.' However, these are only implicit personality theories and, in psychology, personality has a much more rigorous meaning. It is an all-embracing concept that reflects how individuals interpret and react to the world, and this goes to the very heart of the way that people differ as individuals. Although there are many different psychological theories of personality, for the purposes of discussion the definition used here is:

> those relatively stable and enduring aspects of an individual that distinguish him/her from other people and at the same time form a basis for our predictions concerning his/her future behaviour.
> (Wright *et al.* 1970)

This represents the mainstream view in psychology and, although there is debate about the stability and permanence of a person's characteristics, it has two important implications:

- stability and permanence imply a capability to identify an individual's personality characteristics, and
- their use implies an ability to predict the person's behaviour.

The Origins of Personality

Personality is probably one of the most misused terms in the English language (Terborg 1981). For instance, evaluations are often made without any real evidence, and people have a tendency to describe other people by what they believe is his or her most important characteristic. Considerably more evidence than this is required to fully describe an individual's personality, and in scientific psychology there are two main approaches: the **nomothetic** approach, which is mainly concerned with identifying the basic dimensions of human personality and devising ways to measure it; and the **idiographic** approach, which focuses on the uniqueness of the individual and treats him or her as an integrated whole. One way in which these two approaches differ is the extent to which an individual's personality is regarded as fixed and this is a reflection of an even more fundamental controversy in psychology: the *nature vs. nurture debate*.

Naturists hold that mental and physical characteristics are largely determined by genetic make-up, whereas the nurture school regards mental characteristics as arising from an interaction with environment, for example in upbringing and the experience of mixing with others.

Although there are extreme positions in either school, these days most psychologists adopt a middle ground, *interactionist perspective*, by assuming that while mental characteristics predispose us to behave in set ways, our environments also exert a considerable influence, which brings about slight adjustments to our psychological characteristics.

Within this general viewpoint there is a bewildering array of theories that explain personality. However, here discussion will centre on the general factors that can shape the personality of all people. These fall into the four groups shown in Figure 3.1.

Genetic Factors

Our inherited genes play some part in the formation and development of many of our mental characteristics, including that of personality. For example, children of the same family tend to have some aspects of temperament in common and identical twins (who are identical in genetic make-up) have even stronger similarities. Moreover, the incidence of schizophrenia tends to be much higher in children of schizoid parents (Gottesman and Shields 1972) and, in addition to these direct effects, genetics could

Nature vs. nurture debate: the question of whether hereditary factors or the environment have most effect on behaviour

Interactionist perspective: that hereditary factors and environment interact to determine behaviour

Genetic factors: inherited factors that influence physical and mental characteristics

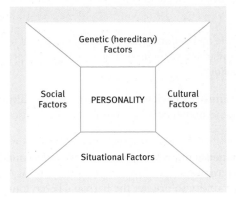

Figure 3.1 Sources of personality

have an indirect influence on personality. [Height, build and physical attractiveness are all genetically determined and these things affect how others behave towards us in social settings, which can influence how we view ourselves.]

A very extreme theory of genetic determinism is that of Sheldon (1954), who associated three body shapes with personality types:

- The **endomorphic** person who has a soft, round, stocky body, with a large trunk and short legs is said to have a relaxed, easy-going and sociable temperament.
- **Ectomorphic** people who have a delicate, slender build, tend to be aesthetic, inhibited and socially withdrawn.
- The **mesomorph**, who is the muscular, athletic type is said to be highly energetic, assertive, boisterous and possibly aggressive.

Ideas such as these are now regarded as naive and simplistic and, although most psychologists acknowledge that personality has a genetic component, the idea that it is totally determined by genes has largely been discounted (Pervin 1980; Plomin 1994).

Social Factors

Social factors: factors that influence personality that arise from interaction with other people

Since humans are social animals, their psychological characteristics are, in part, a reflection of their interactions with other members of the species. Therefore early *socialisation*, which includes interaction with parents, siblings and peers, has an effect on personality and behaviour in later life. Indeed, the *behaviourism* school of psychology, which views all human behaviour as environmentally determined, regards personality as little more than a set of accumulated learning experiences (Skinner 1974). Moreover, the literature on socialisation strongly supports the idea that early experiences carry over into adult life and so to some extent we are probably socialised and resocialised throughout our lives (Wanous *et al.* 1984).

Socialisation: the process of being taught how to behave and how to feel by other (influential) people within a specific social setting

Behaviourism: the branch of psychology which holds that all human behaviour is determined by factors outside the person

Cultural Factors

Cultural factors: wider social beliefs, values and motives that are absorbed by an individual and guide behaviour towards that which is acceptable within a particular social context

In many ways, *cultural factors* are an extension of socialisation. Culture gives us beliefs, values and motives acceptable to a particular society, which gives individuals a general set of predispositions to behave in certain set ways. However, what is acceptable can vary dramatically between different cultures. In Western society, for example, a high value is placed on individualism and achieving worldly success and this has been powerfully argued to result in a socially induced personality trait, the 'need to achieve' (McClelland 1967). Conversely, in Japan individualism takes second place to being a good team player and the success of the group comes first (Hofstede 1980). Although it would be an exaggeration to state that there is something as far-reaching as a Japanese or American personality, these value differences are almost bound to have some effect on the personalities of people in each country.

Situational Factors

Situational factors: the effect of a specific experience or situation on a person's feelings and behaviour

Different experiences also affect personality. For example
ent or a loved one can sometimes change a person in a dra
certain situations can bring out hitherto unrecognised aspec
have been repressed in the past.

TIME OUT

Try to take a dispassionate look at what you perceive to be your own personality characteristics by answering the questions below.

1. Using single words or short expressions try to think of six characteristics that accurately reflect your own personality.
2. To what extent do you feel that these characteristics are similar to those of your parents?
3. To what extent do you feel that these characteristics have been influenced by your upbringing?
4. Do your personality characteristics always show through whatever the situation, or are there some situations in which they remain largely hidden?

The Stability of Personality and Behaviour

As can be seen from the above, several factors play a part in shaping personality and, to some extent, personality development is an ongoing process. For this reason an important issue is whether personality characteristics are stable and unchanging, because if they are not it would be difficult to evaluate personality and any measures that we develop would be of little use in predicting behaviour. Although the evidence suggests that after 30 years of age the adult personality is relatively stable and unchanging (McCrae and Costa 1990), it is by no means an infallible guide to a person's behaviour. Epstein (1980), for example, points out that because personality characteristics are only a *predisposition* to behave in a certain way, they can sometimes be overwhelmed by situational factors. For this reason, Mischel (1977) cautions that there is a need to take account of these effects by distinguishing between two types of situation that affect the predictive value of a personality measure:

Strong situations: those where personality characteristics are good predictors of behaviour

Weak situations: those where personality characteristics are poorer predictors of behaviour

- *Strong situations* give people discernible cues about what behaviour is appropriate in that situation. Because these are usually interpreted in the same way by most people, the incentive to behave in a predictable way is very strong and the situation itself is likely to overcome any minor personality differences, and in these circumstances personality measures are likely to be good predictors of behaviour.

- *Weak situations* provide only ambiguous cues about an appropriate response and people are likely to have different interpretations of the circumstances, which means that it is much harder for someone to draw on prior learning as a guide to what is appropriate. Thus there is a much weaker incentive to behave in a predictable way and in these circumstances the finer nuances of personality can take over and personality measures can become poor predictors of behaviour.

For these reasons the stability of personality (and its effects on behaviour) can be portrayed as shown in Figure 3.2, in which personality can be likened to the skin of an onion; something that is made up of an infinite number of layers. On the surface are those aspects of personality which are most amenable to change, but as we get deeper we reach those aspects that are much more likely to be fixed and unchanging.

Figure 3.2 Stability of personality characteristics (adapted from Mischel 1977)

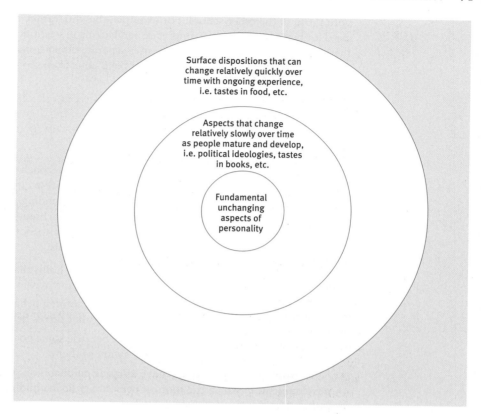

Surface dispositions that can change relatively quickly over time with ongoing experience, i.e. tastes in food, etc.

Aspects that change relatively slowly over time as people mature and develop, i.e. political ideologies, tastes in books, etc.

Fundamental unchanging aspects of personality

Theories of Personality

Idiographic vs. Nomothetic Approaches

Idiographic: theories which describe personality in terms that are unique to the person

Nomothetic: theories which describe personality in terms of set dimensions that could be applied to all people

Earlier it was noted that a distinction can be drawn between two major approaches to the study of personality: idiographic and nomothetic. *Idiographic* theories view personality as an integrated whole and attempt to capture the essence of an individual's total personality, drawing inferences about how the person will react in different situations. These theories avoid the assumption that personality is fixed, but focus on how it develops and changes as a result of ongoing experience. Therefore, they seldom categorise people according to fixed personality dimensions, but produce a description of an individual's personality that is highly idiosyncratic. In contrast, the *nomothetic* approach is concerned with identifying basic personality characteristics that are common to all people, but which can vary in degree from person to person. They are based on an assumption that personality is relatively fixed and resistant to change and use schemes that describe personality along a number of dimensions (or as a number of types).

Because they approach personality with different sets of underlying assumptions, neither approach is inherently right or wrong. Assessment and description of personality is also undertaken in different ways and, usually, the information obtained is put to a different use. Needless to say, adherents of either approach often conflict strongly with those of the other school. For example, the idiographic approach is often criticised for being too subjective, imprecise and lacking in scientific rigor, while the nomothetic approach probably overemphasises separate dimensions, and sometimes draws rather glib conclusions about subsequent behaviour from scores on a personality test (Lazarus 1971).

Idiographic Personality Theories

The Psychodynamic Perspective

Although most people associate the psychodynamic approach with Freud, it is a much wider body of knowledge that has only some assumptions in common and distinct differences on others. Nevertheless, Freud was the founding father of the approach and, since his name is better known than many others, Freudian theory will be outlined here. However, before doing so it is important to note that psychodynamic theories all embrace a number of common assumptions:

- **Psychological determination of behaviour**, which holds that all human physical behaviour is preceded by mental activity.
- **The unconscious** has a prominent role in determining behaviour; it is constantly at work and is the dynamic source of energy that drives behaviour.
- All behaviour is **goal directed**. However, because some goals are located in the unconscious, humans are not always aware of them.
- Most psychodynamic theories have a strong emphasis on **personality development**, in which the roots of personality lie in childhood experiences; thus, rather than simply seeking to describe and measure personality, the approach seeks to explain in a detailed way how an individual's personality comes to be what it is.

Id: the biologically driven component of personality that consists of inherited drives etc. and which demands immediate gratification of its pleasure-seeking drives

Ego: a component of personality that grows out of the id and which strives to reconcile the demands of the id, superego and the realities of the outside world

The Freudian Conception of Personality Structure and Dynamics
In Freud's (1901a) theory, a person's psyche consists of three components. These develop from birth onwards, but are not associated with any physical parts of the brain. Rather they are abstract concepts, used to describe the driving forces behind behaviour, which reside at different levels of depth in the mind. This idea is portrayed diagrammatically in Figure 3.3.

The ultimate driving force of all behaviour is the *id*. This is present at birth and consists of the biologically driven element of personality containing all our inherited instinctual drives, desires and urges. Since the id is irrational, impulsive and demands immediate gratification, it makes no distinction between right or wrong, but acts as a powerful driving force to seek pleasurable experiences no matter what the consequences.

Ego is absent at birth and eventually develops out of the id. In early development the infantile ego is narcissistic and seeks to gratify the demands of the id by taking from the outside world. However, on progressing into early childhood, it recognises the immense power of the outside world, and that, if the id is given a free rein, conflict with the outside world will become inevitable. For this reason, ego develops into that part of the mind that tries to protect the person from the potentially destructive forces of the id, by attempting to balance the id's demands against the reality of the external world; thus becoming the force that holds the individual together as a whole.

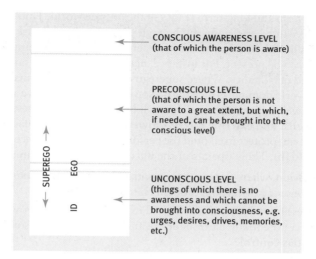

Figure 3.3 Freud's conceptualisation of the structure of personality

Superego: a component of personality that reflects the learned rules of society which are absorbed in upbringing

The *superego* consists of the learned values and demands of society, which are absorbed in childhood as part of a person's upbringing. Superego eventually gives rise to two psychological sub-structures: the **ego ideal,** which informs the person of behaviour that is appropriate, and **conscience,** which allows a person to recognise that certain behaviour is not permitted.

In Freudian theory, adult personality dynamics are viewed as a three-cornered conflict between id, ego and superego, as shown in Figure 3.4.

In a normal, well-adjusted person, effective functioning occurs when these conflicts are resolved by the ego. The id will always seek to drive the person to gratify instinctive desires without regard for the consequences but, at the same time, superego works in the opposite direction to restrict gratification. Moreover, the person is confronted with the external reality of the situation, which can tip the scales in favour of either id or superego, and since neither id nor superego are parts of the psyche that have any inclination to compromise, because external reality is all powerful, any resulting behaviour is likely to have longer-term consequences. This is because ego has to absorb the demands of both id and superego, and find a compromise solution that matches

Figure 3.4 Freud's concept of the conflictual dynamics of personality

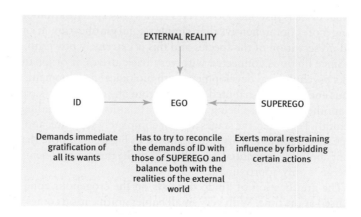

the short-term and long-term reality of the outside world. Thus, to the extent that ego is well developed and powerful enough to undertake this task, the person is said to be well adjusted, but if either id or superego is more dominant than ego, permanent anxieties can be present. For instance, **neurotic anxieties** are said to result from an id-dominated personality. Where superego dominates, **moral anxieties** arise, and if the external world dominates then the person experiences **objective anxieties** (Freud 1940).

In the well-adjusted person, ego will be able to resolve these conflicts by coordinating internal and external forces. However, if the conflict places severe demands on the ego, it can protect itself (and the person) by bringing defence mechanisms into play (Freud 1901b). These operate at the unconscious level and are:

- **Repression**, where the ego protects itself by denying the existence of a problem and removing disturbing thoughts into the unconscious.

- **Suppression**, which occurs when id exerts an extremely powerful demand to satiate a potentially harmful desire and ego urges the person to exercise conscious control.

- **Projection**, where to protect him or herself from uncomfortable feelings, a person attributes the motive, giving rise to the feelings to another person; for example, a person who has a subconscious desire to steal can become acutely suspicious about the honesty of others.

- **Fixation**, which occurs where the prospect of doing something creates anxiety, and ego protects itself by finding a reason for not doing it.

- **Regression** is said to occur when ego is confronted with a threat, which it resolves by adopting a form of behaviour that was successful earlier in life; for example, when told off for a minor misdemeanour, such as being late, a person might break down into tears.

- **Reaction formation** occurs when ego copes with an undesirable, id-driven impulse or desire by doing the exact opposite. For example, a person who enjoys staying in bed and has a tendency to want to arrive late for work may go out of his or her way to be the first one into the office in the morning.

Freud's Theory of Psychosexual Development

The three components of personality – id, ego and superego – are said to develop sequentially. In Freud's view all interactions in the psyche involve energy, and the only source of energy available is *libido*, which is associated with instinctual drives, of which the sexual drive is just one. However, Freud's conceptualisation of the sex drive is something more comprehensive than simple sexual gratification. It embraces the life instinct and preservation of the species and this is extremely powerful.

Libido: the source of all psychological energy, including the sex drive

Since libido is connected with very basic drives, it originates in the id and Freud links psychological development with biological development, which occurs as libidinous energy is redistributed in stages from one erogenous (sexually stimulating) zone to another; the zones being mouth (oral), anus (anal), phallus (phallic) and genitals (genital). However, the stages are not completely separate, and none of them ever disappears completely. This idea is shown in Figure 3.5; note that while there is agreement about the sequential development of the three components, the age at which they emerge is only approximate.

The gratification of libido depends on the erogenous zone on which attention is focused at the time. With very small babies gratification comes via the mouth through

Figure 3.5
Developmental
aspects of Freud's
theory

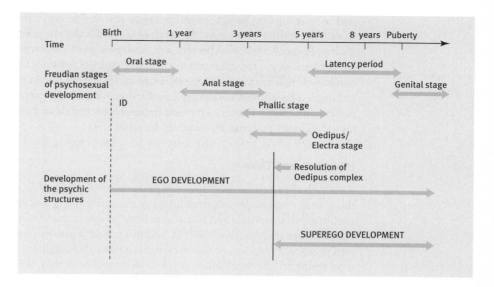

feeding and suckling, but later on other zones become more prominent. While these changes in focus are partly determined by physical development, shifts in the focus of gratification can also be prompted by external factors, such as social relationships, and events in early life handled in a way that is disturbing to the child can have an emotional impact later on; for example, an over-severe emphasis on toilet training is said to give rise to id domination in adult life.

It is important to note that while other psychodynamic theorists agree with the idea of staged development, there are many who strongly disagree with Freud's belief that personality development is sexually driven. Jung (1960), for example, while accepting that development takes place in stages, considered Freud's emphasis on the sexual influence far too strong. Similarly, Adler (1928), another disciple of Freud, while broadly endorsing the idea of sequential development, focused on how, in development, infants overcome their feelings of powerlessness and inferiority. In addition, another psychodynamic theorist, Eric Fromm (1942), placed a much stronger emphasis on the effects of the social context as a determinant of behaviour, which to some extent acknowledges cultural influences.

Psychodynamic Theory: An Overview

For the most part, psychodynamic theory is little used outside clinical settings and, with the exception of Jung's work, which has been applied to derive a scheme of personality types, it is neither used nor well known in organisations. Nevertheless, Freud's theories have been used to penetrating effect to analyse neurotic behaviourial styles in managers (Kets de Vries and Miller 1984) and there have been arguments that it would be an extremely powerful tool for exploring unconscious processes that affect behaviour in organisations (Amado 1995). One problem is, however, that the psychodynamic approach is very different from the vast majority of most current schools of psychology, which leads to criticisms by nomothetic personality theorists such as Eysenck (1970) that it is unscientific and untestable, because some of the concepts such as id, ego and superego are near impossible to define in terms of observable behaviour and so it is hard to design experiments to test the theory. Having said this, Freud's work is currently enjoying something of a renaissance in psychology, with workers such as Power (2000) and Brewin and Andrews (2000) pointing out that it is consistent with many current theories in cognitive psychology and, in particular, those that explore certain memory processes. Thus the psychodynamic analysis of personality, although a highly specialised area, is not dead yet. Moreover, it is the only branch of personality theory that goes beyond descriptive schemes and attempts to explain how an individual's personality comes to be what it is.

Interpersonal Theory

Although the interpersonal theory of personality is idiographic, it is very different from those in the psychodynamic tradition. It primarily maps perceptions rather than personality characteristics and focuses on how people respond to what they believe to be the objective reality of their world, and this can be a powerful way of gaining insights into personality. Although theories of this nature also originate in clinical work, rather than trying to uncover hidden or repressed emotions, they are more sharply focused on the everyday implications of personality.

Kelly's Personal Construct Theory

Kelly's (1955) view of the human personality assumes that, in order to be able to function on a day-to-day basis, people need to be able to anticipate events; not just react to them. As such, they seek to bring meaning and order into their lives by using a set of criteria (constructs) to interpret the world. However, constructs are only usable in a practical way if they provide a person with accurate and useful guides to action. Thus people revise their constructs in the light of experience.

Two important points should be noted about Kelly's use of the word constructs: first, they are assumed to be bipolar and thus have extremes; for example, a person might use a certain construct to evaluate other people, the extremes of which are:

EASY TO ——————————————— DIFFICULT TO
WORK FOR   TO WORK FOR

Second, there are no universal constructs; people develop their own and use those that are meaningful distinctions between outside objects (people being considered as one class of outside objects).

Each construct is a dimension along which objects are evaluated and each dimension is bipolar. Thus one extreme is the opposite of the other. A person's constructs are not universally applicable to all events, objects or people, and each one has what Kelly calls a range of convenience. Some can be applied quite widely, for example tall or short could be applied to people, buildings or trees. Most, however, can only be used selectively, for instance evergreen or deciduous can only be applied to trees. Therefore, constructs are often nested together hierarchically, which means that if we spot one characteristic of a person, this can lead us to making evaluations at a more general level (Bannister 1970). This is illustrated in Figure 3.6, which shows a set of hierarchically arranged constructs that a person might use to evaluate his or her supervisor.

THIS WILL NOT BE USED

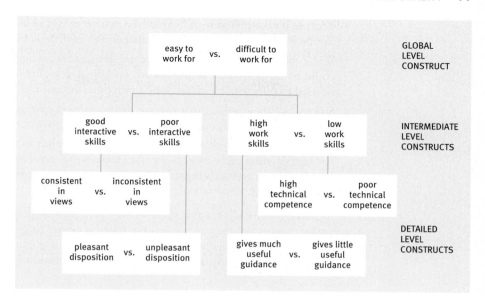

Figure 3.6
Hierarchical
arrangement of
bipolar constructs

Kelly explicitly assumes that people often have to revise their personal construct systems in the light of experience and so one way to view a person's construct system is as a set of working hypotheses. Like hypotheses, they are tested and if found valid are retained, but if shown to be false they are modified or discarded. In addition, Kelly acknowledges that because construct systems are part of personality, they can give rise to behaviourial problems. For example, when an individual's personal construct system is applied to events that have never been encountered before, it might turn out to be inadequate and the person becomes racked with anxiety. Similarly, if a construct system is used to evaluate another person and the evaluation turns out to be totally inaccurate, hostility can occur. For example, I might use a particular set of constructs to predict that a job applicant will fit nicely into my work team but subsequently find that he or she does not. Instead of revising my construct system I could become hostile and aggressive towards the person and try to coerce the individual into fitting in. As such, people can feel threatened if they discover that their construct systems do not work accurately.

The Idiographic Approach: Concluding Comments

The idiographic approach takes a highly idiosyncratic view of personality. It seeks to understand the uniqueness of individuals and to capture the essence of their personalities, which has a number of advantages. Because people are accepted as unique, the approach is relatively free of preconceived notions of how personality can be most appropriately described, and this is likely to produce a very rich picture of individual characteristics. In addition, the approach directly links personality and behaviour, and so it fits well with other psychological constructs such as attitudes and perceptions that have behaviourial implications. Notwithstanding these advantages, there are criticisms of the approach:

- Because it takes a highly individualistic perspective, it ignores situations where it can be important to compare the personalities of different individuals.
- While the approach infers that there are dimensions along which personality could be categorised, it stops short of actually developing measures that could be used to differentiate individuals along these dimensions.
- Since most idiographic theories have their origins in clinical work, they have a tendency to be more concerned with the abnormal than the normal.
- In particular, the psychodynamic view has been subject to much criticism because its ideas and concepts are not amenable to experimental investigation and many psychologists regard it as implausible, unscientific and unverifiable mumbo-jumbo.

In summary, while idiographic theories are useful in explaining poor adjustment to everyday conditions, they are of less use when it comes to describing personality in a way that can be applied to a wider range of day-to-day situations. This requires a completely different approach and it is to this that attention is now directed.

The Nomothetic Approach

Theories adopting this approach seek to identify regular, measurable aspects of personality and relate them to human behaviour. They are based on the assumption that people have relatively stable and unchanging personality characteristics, and the theories fall into two main groups: trait theories, which describe people in terms of a number of personality dimensions; and type theories, which place people into one of a number of personality types.

Traits: individual characteristics of thought or feeling that result in tendencies to behave in specific ways

Surface traits: those that are directly observable in behaviour

Source traits: those that cannot be observed directly and whose existence can only be inferred

Primary factors: the factors which, in Cattell's personality theory, are the fundamental building blocks of personality

Trait Theories

Traits are individual characteristics of thought or feeling that give rise to predispositions to act or react in certain ways (Drever 1964). For example, conscientious people are not simply conscientious because they persevere in what they do; rather, they persevere because their behaviour is driven by a mental characteristic (personality trait) of conscientiousness.

There are many different types of trait: for instance motive traits that guide behaviour; ability traits, which relate to specific skills and abilities; temperament traits, that refer to mood, etc. However, in personality theory the most important distinction is between surface traits and source traits. *Surface traits*, such as assertiveness, can be observed in behaviour, while *source traits* such as self-discipline, can only be inferred. Theories in this tradition all use traits in a very similar way: as a scheme of psychological universals that all people have in some degree. These are then used to classify people according to their combination of trait strengths, and how these traits are organised to give a person a unique personality (Allport 1961).

Cattell's Sixteen Personality Factor Scheme

Cattell (1965) distinguishes between patterns of observable behaviour (surface traits) and source traits, which he calls *primary factors*; the former being what he claims are the fundamental building blocks that make up personality.

In Cattell's original work, 12 primary factors (source traits) were identified and these were said to be the fundamental dimensions of personality, from which all visible behaviourial tendencies (surface traits) originate. Subsequent work led to an upward revision and currently the most widely used scheme has 16 factors, which form the basis of the Cattell Sixteen Personality Factor Questionnaire (16 PF for short). These are shown in Figure 3.7.

Figure 3.7 Cattell's 16 personality factors

Low score description	Factor	High score description
Reserved, detached, critical, aloof *sizothymia*	A	**Outgoing**, warmhearted easygoing, participating *affectothymia, formerly cyclothymia*
Less intelligent, concrete thinking *lower scholastic mental capacity*	B	**More intelligent**, abstract thinking, bright *higher scholastic mental capacity*
Affected by feelings, emotionally less stable, easily upset *lower ego strength*	C	**Emotionally stable**, faces reality, calm, mature *higher ego strength*
Humble, mild accommodating conforming *submissiveness*	E	**Assertive**, aggressive, stubborn, competitive *dominance*
Sober, prudent, serious, taciturn *desurgency*	F	**Happy-go-lucky**, impulsively lively, gay, enthusiastic *surgency*
Expedient, disregards rules, feels few obligations *weaker superego strength*	G	**Conscientious**, persevering, staid, moralistic *stronger superego strength*
Shy, restrained, timid, threat sensitive *threctia*	H	**Venturesome**, socially bold, uninhibited, spontaneous *parmia*
Tough minded, self-reliant, realistic, no-nonsense *harria*	I	**Tender-minded**, clinging, over-protected, sensitive *premsia*
Trusting, adaptable, free of jealousy, easy to get along with *alaxia*	L	**Suspicious**, self-opinionated, hard to fool *protension*
Practical, careful, conventional, regulated by external realities, proper *praxernia*	M	**Imaginative**, wrapped up in inner urgencies, careless of practical matters, bohemian *autia*
Forthright, natural, artless, unpretentious *artlessness*	N	**Shrewd**, calculating, worldly, penetrating *shrewdness*
Self-assured, confident, serene *untroubled adequacy*	O	**Apprehensive**, self-reproaching, worrying, troubled *guilt proneness*
Conservative, respecting established ideas, tolerant of traditional difficulties *conservatism*	Q_1	**Experimenting**, liberal, analytical, free thinking *radicalism*
Group dependent, a 'joiner' and sound follower *group adherence*	Q_2	**Self-sufficient**, prefers own decisions, resourceful *self-sufficiency*
Undisciplined self-conflict, follows own urges, careless of protocol *low integration*	Q_3	**Controlled**, socially precise, following self-image *high self-concept control*
Relaxed, tranquil, unfrustrated *low ergic tension*	Q_4	**Tense**, frustrated, driven, overwrought, *high ergic tension*

Although at first sight some of these factors might appear to overlap, Cattell's view is that they do not and are independent dimensions. Also note that the 16 factors are bipolar, and although a person can be located somewhere between Reserved and Outgoing, these are two opposing characteristics, not a scale which measures how reserved or outgoing the person is. It is possible to reduce Cattell's 16 primary dimensions to a smaller number (five) of second-order factors, but since Cattell believes these can only influence behaviour through the source traits, they will not be considered further here.

As noted earlier, Cattell claims to have identified the fundamental building blocks of personality. While this is a highly controversial claim and one that has been disputed by others, Cattell's theory is extremely robust. It has stood the test of time and the 16 PF test, which has been revised and refined a number of times, is widely used in organisational settings. Indeed, psychometric testing for selection and other purposes has now found its way into the field of professional football (see OB in Action Box following).

 OB IN ACTION: AC Milan on the ball in personality testing

Bruno Demichelis, AC Milan's sports scientist, believes footballers need to be mentally and emotionally assessed and developed as well as physically trained.

He argues that football teams have been experimenting with psychology for some time, yet our goal was to find a way of analysing both individuals and the team dynamic and mirrored the techniques used by big companies. Saville Holdsworth Limited's (SHL) occupational personality questionnaire (OPQ) provides a measurable, objective analysis of players' behavioural styles, he says.

In the past few months, the club has been using psychological profiling not only to better understand the players, but also to look at succession planning, and according to Gary Smith, head of European business at SHL, the OPQ will be fundamental in selecting the next captain. As well as using it to assess whether potential new players will complement the existing team, the club has found it valuable off the pitch for branding purposes. This is where the club looks at the personalities of individuals and the traits the club wants to portray, deciding on the best fit for various sponsorship activities, says Smith. On that basis, Brazilian player Kaka was used to promote Armani jeans.

Demichelis is also using the information to encourage 'groupship', a term originated by himself, which explores how they can work better as a team. The club has exceptional individual performers, but it also needs exceptional team players if it is going to achieve Berlusconi's dream goal. The club has also started to look into links between the personalities of players and recovery times from possible injury. Depending on the personality type, individuals respond to different things for a faster recovery says Smith. So we are helping the club to develop recovery plans that are tailored to individual needs.

Adapted from: *People Management* (2005) 13 January, p 40

Type Theories

Type theories place people into predetermined categories (personality types) on the basis of characteristics that are said to give rise to certain patterns of behaviour, and since most type theories use a very small number of categories into which people must be slotted, people seldom fit neatly into one type or another. Thus, one criticism is that the theories oversimplify matters. Nevertheless, some type theories are quite sophisticated and two that are well known are described in the followings.

Jung's Type Theory

The starting point of Jung's theory (1971) is that people have psychological preferences for extroversion or intraversion. However, a simple dichotomy such as this is unlikely to give a scheme that is extensive enough to be able to accommodate the huge variations in human behaviour. Thus he introduces four additional mental functions that describe how people relate to their external worlds. The *sensing* function expresses the extent to which the person relies on his or her senses to become aware of external phenomena and process information on them. The *thinking* function captures the extent to which the individual attempts to identify and understand something; the *feeling* function describes the extent that the person reacts emotionally to something and regards it as either acceptable or unacceptable; while the *intuitive* function describes whether the individual goes beyond feeling, to develop hunches or subjective evaluations, even in the absence of concrete information. These variables result in the four basic personality types shown in Figure 3.8.

Figure 3.8 Jung's personality types

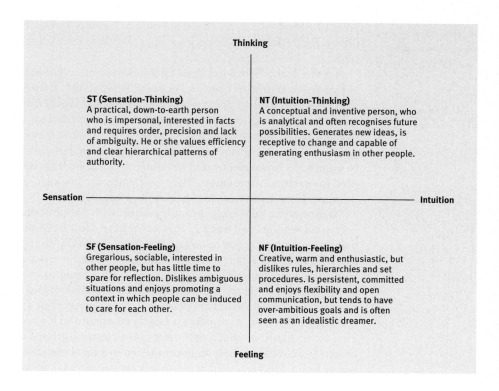

A development of Jung's theory is the Myers–Briggs Type Indicator (MBTI) (Myers and McCauly 1985), which classifies individuals into one of 16 personality types, each of which is known by its associated letter code that gives a synopsis of the associated personality characteristics, four of which are shown in Figure 3.8. For instance, ENTJ, which falls in the top right-hand quadrant is *extrovert, intuition, thinking, judging*. ISTP, which falls in the top left-hand quadrant corresponds to *introvert, sensation, thinking, perceiving*. The MBTI is a widely used personality assessment tool, that has been used for a wide variety of applications in organisations, such as selection, management development, counselling, evaluating decision-making styles and even ensuring that there are complimentary role incumbents in groups and teams (see Chapter 11).

Eysenck's Type Theory

Like Cattell, Eysenck's theory is based on extensive empirical work. In its original form, it uses one of the basic distinctions used by Jung – that between extrovert and introvert – to which he adds another to give two fundamental dimensions of personality: *extroversion–introversion* and *neuroticism–stability* (Eysenck 1947). This results in four general personality types:

(emotionally) stable extroverts
(emotionally) unstable extroverts
(emotionally) stable introverts
(emotionally) unstable introverts.

However, it is rare to find that someone is an extreme example of any single type. Moreover, each type is associated with a number of specific personality traits, which gives his theory the appearance of being a 'halfway house' between trait and type theory. Figure 3.9 shows Eysenck's well-known diagram relating traits to the personality types.

A great deal of work has been undertaken to identify the behaviourial correlates of extroversion–introversion and neuroticism–stability. **Extroverts** are usually found to be tough-minded, impulsive, quick-tempered and visibly emotional. They are often aggressive, crave strong external stimulation and excitement and are sociable, carefree and active. Since extroverts like to be the centre of attention and are fond of social occasions, they prefer not to do things on their own, but also have some tendency to be unreliable. **Introverts** tend to be tender-minded, strongly emotional and with little need for external stimulation. They are frequently 'bookish', are fond of order, tend to suppress their emotions and to be somewhat pessimistic.

Neurotics are inherently unstable people, who are emotional, anxious, obsessive, over-conscientious and finicky. They often have a low opinion of themselves and feel that they are unattractive failures. Thus they are usually disappointed with their lives and tend to be persistent worriers. They are also easily upset when things go wrong, tend to be annoyed by a lack of order and easily submit to those with greater formal power. **Stable** people are the well adjusted, self-confident and are usually optimistic. They tend to be self-reliant and have few regrets about their past.

In Eysenck's view, personality is largely inherited and is associated with the physiology of the brain, in which the lower brain contains groups of cells that have been shown by research to have an important role in regulating the level of arousal of the higher brain. He suggests that introverts are people who are generally over-aroused,

Extroversion–introversion: one of the two fundamental dimensions of personality used in Eysenck's type theory

Neuroticism–stability: the second fundamental dimensions of personality used in Eysenck's type theory

Figure 3.9 'Eysenck's personality types'

Source: Eysenck, HJ (1965) *Fact and Fiction in Psychology* (pub Penguin Books Ltd), copyright © HJ Eysenck 1965

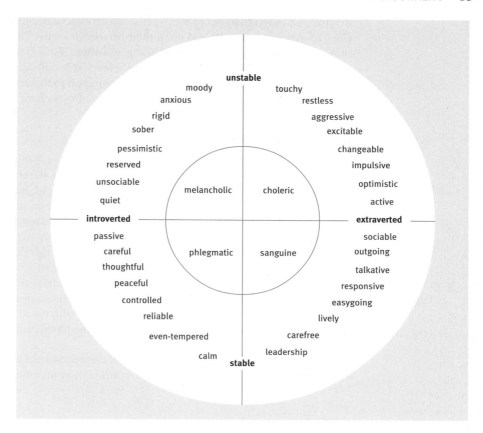

which results in the level of excitation in the upper brain centres as being high. To correct this imbalance they tend to avoid all possible outside stimulation, which accounts for their behaviourial characteristics. Conversely, extroverts are under-aroused and so they seek out all that they can possibly obtain in terms of additional outside stimulation.

Traits vs. Types: Cattell and Eysenck Compared

Since traits play a part in the theories of both Eysenck and Cattell it is sometimes difficult to grasp the difference between trait and type theories. However, the matter is really very simple and depends on whether traits are seen as the determining factors in personality. In Cattell's theory there are 16 bipolar source traits, of which any combination is theoretically possible. Thus it is the way they combine that gives an individual his or her personality. With Eysenck's theory, personality is said to fall into one of a number of types, and certain traits flow automatically from being a particular type. Thus it is the type which defines a person's personality, and traits are just visible manifestations of the type.

There is also a difference between Eysenck and Cattell in terms of the role that heredity plays in determining personality. Eysenck believes that while people become more diverse and individualistic as they gain a wider experience of the world, their reactions to the experience depend upon their personality type. Therefore hereditary factors are assumed to have a strong enduring influence. While Cattell also acknowledges that genetic inheritance shapes traits, he believes that socialisation and experience play a more prominent role in determining the position on each particular trait dimension. Thus he leans more towards the idea that personality is changeable, albeit slowly.

A Recent Development: The 'Big Five'

In one form or another, personality assessment has always relied heavily on the trait concept and the debate has seldom been about whether the trait or type approach is most appropriate, but about how traits are structured and, in particular, how many traits are needed to give a comprehensive description of an individual's personality. Eysenck (1991) expresses a strong preference for four personality types, from which clusters of traits flow automatically, and Catttell remains strongly committed to 16 source traits, of which one is intelligence. The winner in this debate has now emerged as a five-factor structure; the so-called 'Big Five' (Digman 1990; Costa and McCrae 1992). This expresses what are said to be the five core dimensions of personality, which are expressed along five dimensions, each of which consists of six traits, giving the use of 30 traits in total. These are shown in Table 3.1, where a degree of practical applicability is introduced by giving an indication of the particular roles that people with these traits are most suited for.

Note, however, that the five dimensions are not personality types. Rather, they are clusters of personality traits. Also note that while there are positive and negative signs

Table 3.1 The Big Five personality dimensions and associated traits

Dimension	Traits	
Openness	**Explorers** (O+) traits creativity, aesthetic, open-minded Useful to: entrepreneurs, architects, visual arts	**Preserver** (O−) traits unimaginative, detached, narrow-minded Useful to: financial managers, performing arts, project managers
Conscientiousness	**Focused** (C+) traits competence, achievement-orientated, self-disciplined Useful to: leaders, senior executives	**Flexible** (C−) traits frivolous, carefree, disorganised Useful to: research workers, management consultants
Extraversion	**Extrovert** (E+) traits gregarious, warmth, positive-minded Useful to: salesmen, politicians, the arts	**Introvert** (E−) traits quiet, reserved shy Useful to: engineers, scientists
Agreeableness	**Adapter** (A+) traits trusting, straightforward, compliant Useful to: teachers, social workers, caring professions	**Challenger** (A−) traits quarrelsome, oppositional, unfeeling Useful to: managers, military officers
Negative emotionality	**Reactive** (N+) traits anxious, depressed, self-conscious Useful to: social scientists, academics, customer-service	**Resilient** (N−) traits calm, contented, self-assured Useful to: airline pilots, accountants, planners

indicated for the traits given, each dimension has a double-headed arrow between its extremes and it is not at all uncommon to find that an individual is at neither extreme. Neither should it be inferred that the positive and negative signs mean that a trait cluster – say Explorers – are superior in some way to Preservers; merely that their personality traits are likely to make them more suitable for some roles rather than others.

A robust assessment of personality is only obtained from the Big Five if a rather long (240 questions) test is taken, which gives scores for all five dimensions. However, this produces a profile that is easier to read than many other tests and, importantly, evidence suggests that the profiles derived integrate well with older theories (Barrick *et al.* 2003; Lord and Rust 2003). Perhaps the most visible sign that the Big Five framework has now come into its own as a reliable and valid instrument that permits a rigorous measurement of personality is that it is now widely used for serious empirical work (see, for example, Bamberger and Bacharach 2006; Mount *et al.* 2005; Mount *et al.* 2006; Wallace and Chen 2006).

PERSONALITY IN THE WORKPLACE

The definition of personality given above assumes that an individual's personality will result in predictable patterns of behaviour, and it is this that makes the concept a significant one for organisations. Since jobs are likely to differ in terms of the personal characteristics they require, an individual's personality could have an impact on his or her suitability for certain roles. In a selection situation this gives rise to two important considerations: the key personality characteristics that make someone best fitted for a particular organisational role; and how to determine whether a person has these characteristics. In practice these are closely connected but, for the sake of convenience, each will be considered separately.

The Issue of Key Characteristics

When selecting a new employee for a particular vacancy, sound recruitment practice dictates that an organisation should derive a *person specification* for the individual who will occupy the role. This would identify those attributes that it is felt are most closely associated with successful performance in the job. If personality characteristics are part of this specification, and, providing a large number of existing incumbents are already in this role, in theory it is a comparatively straightforward matter to identify these characteristics. For example, we could get all of them to take a psychological test that determines their characteristics, and obtain job performance ratings on incumbents from their supervisors or managers. By comparing personality scores with job performance scores, we could then evaluate the extent to which a personality test predicts job success. However, this is a somewhat ideal situation and in the real world things are seldom this simple.

For example, there might not be a large, captive pool of existing employees on whom we could conduct this exercise. The job could well be a new one that has not existed until this point, in which case specifying personality characteristics could well become a rather subjective exercise, which could perhaps be approached by seeking the opinions of the manager to whom the incumbent will report, and this is where the problems start to appear. To start with, the manager might be unfamiliar with the jargon used by psychologists to identify personality traits and, even where this is not a problem, a manager might have his or her own personal preferences about the weight that should be given to certain characteristics. Thus the whole exercise could come down to little more than an educated guess about what is necessary. Worst of all, if we ask managers in today's fast moving organisations what they consider to be the most valuable characteristic for a new employee, in good faith they might well answer with a single word – 'flexibility'; a catch-all attribute that is unlikely to mean the same thing to everybody, and one that is notoriously hard to identify.

Having said these things, the problems are not insurmountable and there is no reason why an accurate specification cannot be derived. For example, there are schemes of job analysis that facilitate the reduction of jobs to their micro-components, and to some extent these allow identification of elements that are associated with personality characteristics. The important thing is that, whatever test is used, it should be capable of assessing all of the attributes that are relevant for successful job performance, and avoid assessing those that are irrelevant (Bartram 2005). It should also be borne in mind that psychological testing is not always the most appropriate way of determining whether a person has the attributes that are required, a matter that receives further consideration next.

The Issue of Assessing Personality

Where personality is a factor that could significantly influence job performance, there could be an advantage in having this information available when making selection or promotion decisions. In addition, knowledge of an individual's personality can sometimes be useful for vocational guidance purposes.

A number of tests that assess personality are available. These are usually based on the nomothetic approach, and most are self-completed, pencil-and-paper questionnaires, in which the person responds 'Yes' or 'No' to a forced choice statement that describes him or herself. Although some of these tests are widely used in organisations, their use has been criticised on the grounds that they are prone to giving an inaccurate picture of personality, and this is not necessarily because the tests themselves are at fault. There is a regrettable tendency on the part of those completing the tests to lie to themselves, by ticking boxes in a way that is more indicative of what they would like to be, rather than what they are (Furnham 1990). Although it is possible to overcome this to some extent by incorporating lie scales into the questionnaire, it is virtually impossible to eliminate it altogether.

Reliability: whether a test produces the same results when applied to the same person on two separate occasions

To be useful as a method of assessing personality, a test requires a number of features. First, it must possess what is technically known as *reliability*; that is, there should be little possibility of getting different personality profiles if a person takes the test on two successive occasions. Because they have been subjected to extensive investigation to produce standardised score profiles, reputable personality tests are extremely reliable. Tests also need to possess the property of **validity** and, in the context discussed here, the essential requirement is for *predictive validity*, which means that the personality of the individual, as revealed by the test, should be a good predictor of performance in a specific role. For selection purposes, the most widely used personality tests measure traits (Deary and Matthews 1993); for them to be useful in this role there should be some evidence that a certain trait profile will result in a predictable job performance.

Predictive validity: whether tests scores are good predictors of behaviour or job performance

Great care is needed in selecting a personality test. Developing an instrument of this type is a complex and expensive business, and the investment of time and money in this process could run into several hundreds of thousand pounds. Other things being equal, the longer is a test the more reliable and valid will be the results it produces (Bartram 2005) and the tests described in this chapter are all in excess of 240 questions. Nevertheless, users of tests prefer them to be kept as short as possible and, unfortunately, some of the less scrupulous test developers have responded to this requirement by developing tests that are as short as 25 questions, which they claim will give an accurate profile of a person's personality: a highly debatable contention. Another interesting development is for tests to be available via the internet. This does not necessarily mean that access to the tests is completely open, because test publishers usually restrict access of both tests and scoring details to psychologists qualified to use them. However, given certain safeguards, internet access to test materials makes for a great deal of convenience for test users, and one of the most important precautions that needs to be applied is how the test is actually taken. Here the significant difference is between what are technically described as un-proctored and proctored situations. In the *un-proctored situation*, web-based testing can take place at any location that has internet access, and without the supervision of a test administrator. In *proctored situations*, however, the person must take the test in the presence of a test administrator, usually at a specified location. A recent study by Ployhart *et al.* (2003) shows that as long as proctored conditions are used, web-based tests are as safe and reliable as their pencil and paper equivalents.

Although personality tests are increasingly in vogue as a selection tool, particularly for management jobs, one problem is that there is little evidence that they accurately predict future job behaviour (Epstein 1980; Gray 2003; Monson *et al.* 1982; Robertson 2001). This can be most easily understood by reference back to two types of situation distinguished by Mischel (1977), described earlier in the chapter. These days many jobs, particularly management jobs, consist of dealing with uncertainty. Because there are no cues about what is the right thing to do, the person needs to be able to 'think on the hoof' in order to act in an appropriate way and, in these circumstances, this is usually what is meant by good job performance. However, these circumstances are what Mischel also describes as a 'weak situation', and good job performance might well require the individual to act in a way that goes against the grain of his or her personality. Thus, personality could well be a very poor predictor of job performance.

This is not to say that personality tests have no role in selection. To this end it is worth examining the predictive validity of a number of different employee assessment methods, which is shown in Table 3.2.

As can be seen, personality assessments have a fairly low validity coefficient (1.0 would be equivalent to 100 per cent validity) but if used in combination with other techniques such as interviews, exercises and role play, which provide information on behaviour in a wider variety of situations, they can help to provide a well-rounded picture of a person. This is generally referred to as the **assessment centre** method, which has long been a growing trend in selection. There is, however, a more worrying feature, and this is one that applies to psychometric tests of all types. There is no such thing as a culturally neutral test and so, unless great care is taken, psychometric tests can introduce an element of unfair discrimination into a selection or assessment procedure. Since this applies to intelligence and aptitude tests as well as those that assess personality, it is more convenient to defer further discussion until later in the chapter.

Un-proctored situation: web-based testing can occur at any location that has internet access, and without the supervision of a test administrator

Proctored situation: web-based testing occurs in the presence of a test administrator, usually at a specified location

Table 3.2 The predictive validity of selected employee selection methods

Measure	Predictive validity
Graphology	0.0
References	0.13
Unstructured interviews	0.31
Personality assessments	0.38
Biodata	0.40
Ability tests	0.54
Work samples	0.55
Structured interviews	0.62
Assessment centres – promotion (decisions)	0.68

Adapted from Anderson, N and V Shackleton (1993) *Successful Selection Interviewing*, Oxford: Blackwell.

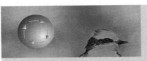

REPLAY

- An individual's personality characteristics are influenced by four main groups of factors: genetic, social, cultural and situational (experience).
- The connection between personality characteristics and behaviour is influenced by the situation in which behaviour occurs.
- Idiographic personality theories deal with the individual as an integral whole and are of two main types: psychodynamic theories, which focus on the development of personality, and interpersonal theories, both of which are more concerned with mapping the personality of the individual as it is.
- Nomothetic theories of personality focus on the description and assessment of personality in terms that could be applied to all people, either by describing personality along a number of dimensions (trait theory), or by personality types.
- Most personality assessment in organisations is conducted using a nomothetic approach.

INTELLIGENCE

Many topics in psychology are controversial but the concept of intelligence, and in particular the testing and measurement of intelligence, is so controversial that it tends to arouse quite passionate feelings. Some scholars, such as Hernstein (1973), hold that the measurement of intelligence is psychology's most telling accomplishment to date. Others point out that while intelligence testing is often portrayed as a highly rigorous branch of psychological science, it is so riddled with circularities and inconsistencies that it would embarrass any respectable scientist (Heather 1976). There are those who go even further and claim that intelligence testing has adverse social consequences, which make the practice unethical (Kamin 1977). Much of this debate arises from what is meant by the expression intelligence, a word that tends to be used in an ill-defined way, even by some psychologists (Miles 1957). As such, the first step must be to explore the meaning of the word and to define how it will be used in this chapter.

TIME OUT

Think of a number of people you know well. Try to identify some you would classify as intelligent and some who are less intelligent. What evidence have you used to classify the people in this way?

The Concept of Intelligence

Like many psychological concepts, intelligence is an abstract construct based on the tenet that mental activity of some sort precedes all physical behaviour. In common with other constructs, it is plagued by our inability to see mental activity directly, and so the only indication of intelligence is observable behaviour. In a broad sense, intelligence is revealed by adaptation to environment and, since humans are the most adaptable species in the animal kingdom, it is generally accepted that we are the most intelligent animal of all. No other species has yet been able to bridge the quantum gap that exists between itself and humans. Thus it is fair to assume that there must be an inherited component in intelligence, which means that, in simple terms, it can be defined as 'an innate, general, cognitive ability' (Burt 1955).

The idea of a genetic component to intelligence is much older than Burt's definition, and disputes about the size of the component are still very much alive today. In an attempt to sidestep this controversy and progress towards a more precise definition it is important to note that Hebb (1949) distinguished between two meanings that can be attached to the word. Vernon (1955) later added a third, and all three will be used hereafter. They are:

- **IA**   the potential intelligence of an individual as determined by his or her genetic make-up, which is neither observable nor measurable directly.

- **IB**   the level of ability an individual actually shows in his or her behaviour in everyday life (quickness and depth of thought, understanding, insight, practical judgement, etc.), which is a product of the interplay between genetic potential and the stimulation provided by environment.

- **IC**   an expression of a person's intelligence as measured by standardised tests which attempt to give a sample expression of the skills involved in intelligent behaviour.

The three uses of the word neatly distinguish between what is measurable and what is not and a move from IA to IC gets further and further away from a pure expression of intelligence towards its assessment and measurement, and this contains inherent problems. By definition, IA is not measurable, and to get a true evaluation of IB it would be necessary to know the individual's reactions to every experience that he or she has encountered – a difficult, if not impossible, task. This leaves IC, which relies on 'sampling' from what it is hoped is the whole repertoire of a person's intelligent behaviour, which contains a risk that something important will be omitted from the sample of repertoires chosen, with the corresponding risk that an individual's potential will be wrongly estimated.

Moreover, intelligence IB acknowledges an interaction between environmental experience and genetic potential, and so anything measured in IC could be partly the result of learning. For example, if there are two people with the same level of intelligence IA, and one has wider experiences of the world than the other, they will almost certainly be different in terms of intelligence IB. Since intelligence IC only takes a sample of IB, if both people are compared, in all likelihood, one will be evaluated as more intelligent than the other, whereas in fact both have the same potential.

Since IA cannot be observed or measured directly, any definition of intelligence is bound to be controversial, which is why all three definitions are given. All this poses difficult problems for organisations and, unfortunately, there are no easy answers. Clearly, intelligent behaviour is important in employees, but what do we mean by intelligence and how can we tell whether a potential recruit is intelligent? Leaving aside the actual testing of intelligence IC, which will be considered presently, by definition, IA cannot be evaluated and so, at best, an organisation can try to assess intelligence IB in job applicants. In most cases this comes down to judging them in terms of qualifications and other attainments. However, this has its own problems. Some people might have had better teachers than others and might have worked harder at school or university, although arguably this could be taken as a sign of intelligent behaviour in terms of adapting to the academic environment. With lower-level qualifications (those below first degree level) there could also be the problem of social background. For instance, some people could have been sent to a boarding school by their parents, where classes are smaller and there are fewer distractions. On their own these problems are bad enough, but there is the additional matter of the other indicators that selectors use to evaluate intelligence, which will be considered later.

The Genetic Component of Intelligence

The three-part definition given above alerts us to the idea that there is a strong genetic component in intelligence, the evidence for which is overwhelming. For example, the incidence of retarded children born to retarded parents is much higher than with non-retarded parents (Reed and Reed 1964). However, it is much more difficult to be precise about the degree of genetic influence, both in terms of size and the effects that it has. The most thorough work to date is derived from studies of identical twins. One such study used standardised tests to compare the intelligence of identical and non-identical twins, either reared together since birth or reared apart. From this it was estimated that somewhere between 60 and 80 per cent of intelligence is associated with genetic factors (Erlenmeyer-Kimling and Jarvik 1963). Although this was a very rigorous study, there are still problems in generalising too widely from the results. One problem is that we know environment has some effect and child-rearing practices vary between the social classes. For instance, middle- and upper-class children tend to be brought up in environments where, in their early years, they receive a great deal of stimulation and attention from their parents, and the work cited above gives evidence of these effects: identical twins in socially advantaged families have much closer intelligence levels than those of non-identical twins or siblings. However, when children from disadvantaged families are compared, the intelligence of identical twins is not much closer than that of non-identical twins or other siblings. Thus, while genetics play a considerable part in intelligence, environmental factors such as child-rearing practices also have an important effect. For this reason it is safer to assume that genetics merely sets a limit on a person's intelligence, and whether the individual ever comes near to realising his or her full potential depends on environmental effects. Indeed, the interaction between genetics and environment is extremely complex, so complex that it is nearly impossible to unravel. While it is probably safe to assume that 60–80 per cent of a person's intelligence is genetically determined, it is impossible to be precise about which 60–80 per cent this is.

Models of Human Intelligence

The controversy over the testing and measurement of intelligence has its counterpart in the debate about how the structure of intelligence can best be described. Most tests are based on Spearman's (1904) theory, in which *general intelligence (g)* is determined by two major subsidiary factors: *verbal:educational intelligence (V:Ed)* and *kinaesthetic:motor intelligence (K:M)*, and these in turn are determined by minor specific 's' factors, which are the skills associated with each type of intelligence. This is shown in Figure 3.10.

The real foundations of modern intelligence testing can be traced to the work of Alfred Binet (Binet and Simon 1908), who in 1904 was appointed by the French Minister for Public Instruction to a commission which examined the problems associated with teaching retarded children. The first problem confronting the commission was how

General intelligence (g): an individual's overall intelligence level as measured by a test

Verbal:educational intelligence (V:Ed): that part of an intelligence test which assesses verbal, numeric and educational skills and abilities

Kinaesthetic:motor intelligence (K:M): that part of an intelligence test which assesses practical, mechanical and spatial skills and abilities

Figure 3.10 Spearman's hierarchical conceptualisation of the structure of intelligence

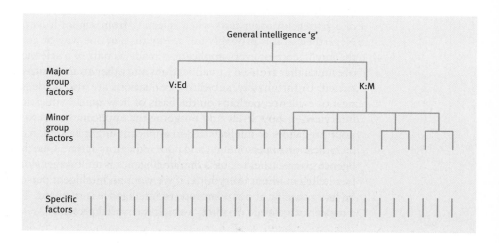

to classify and measure the ability levels of these children. Binet's approach was to evolve a number of test items that children between the ages of three and 12 ought to be able to complete successfully, such as being able to name objects in pictures correctly, or drawing simple designs from memory. To allow for the probability that older children could have greater capabilities than younger ones, each one of these test items contained a number of tasks of graded difficulty. In an extensive series of investigations, Binet identified items that the 'average' child of a given age could answer correctly; as expected, younger children were less proficient in addressing these tasks. He then asked teachers to select their brightest, average and dullest pupils. The tests were then completed by these samples, from which Binet identified the questions and tasks that best distinguished between proficient and less proficient children. This gave a robust series of test items that could be used to compare mental abilities.

A later revision of his scale, which appeared in 1908, included an innovative (some people would say infamous) feature. This was a method for calculating a child's mental age, the *intelligence quotient* (*IQ*), which is defined as:

Intelligence quotient (IQ): mental age (as indicated by an intelligence test) divided by actual (chronological) age

$$\frac{\text{mental age}}{\text{chronological age}}$$

Using this measure, a child of six who can correctly answer the same items (and achieve the same score) as the average child of eight has an IQ of 133.3, i.e. $\frac{8 \times 100}{6}$.

After the Binet–Simon scale was translated into English in 1910, the testing of intelligence grew rapidly in popularity. The tests that resulted were individually applied and required the services of a trained and qualified practitioner. This means that they are somewhat inconvenient and expensive in mass-testing situations, and the main growth area in intelligence testing has therefore been in the use of group tests, usually self-administered 'pen-and-paper' tests. The best known in the UK are the AH2 to AH6 series devised by Alice Heim, which are based on (or at least expressed in terms of) Spearman's model of intelligence.

Although 'pure' tests of this type are sometimes applied in organisations, they are by no means used for all job applicants. They would probably be used most as part of a battery of other tests when selecting from school-leavers for trainee positions. Nevertheless, it is probably fair to say that, in one way or another, an evaluation of the intelligence of every applicant is made as part of a selection process, and one set of criteria that are used – qualifications and other attainments – has already been mentioned. Unfortunately, subjective evaluations are also made, sometimes on the flimsiest of evidence, perhaps on the basis of how quickly questions are answered in an interview, or how lively and outgoing the applicant seems to be. Not only are these poor predictors of intelligence (an applicant might be shy), if anything they are more an indication of personality, and poor indicators at that. One thing the models of intelligence given earlier tell us is that intelligence is multidimensional. Since few of us can be intelligent about everything, if we want an intelligent person for a job we have to be more specific about what type of intelligence is required. To a large extent, this is a matter of aptitude or ability, which is covered presently.

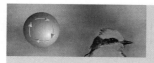

- There is no single valid definition of intelligence and, in the interests of accuracy, three separate definitions are required: intelligence IA – potential intelligence as determined by genetic factors; intelligence IB – intelligence as displayed in everyday life which arises from the interplay between genetic potential and experience; intelligence IC – intelligence as measured by standardised tests.
- Structural models of intelligence usually adopt Spearman's two-factor theory, which portrays general intelligence as made up of two primary factors: V:Ed and K:M.

Emotional Intelligence: A Recent Development

Emotional Intelligence: ability or competence in managing one's own feelings and recognising (and dealing effectively with) other peoples' feelings

A concept that has recently enjoyed considerable popularity, (or according to the viewpoint adopted, notoriety) is that of *Emotional Intelligence* (EI). Daniel Goleman (1998) who did much to popularise EI in America, describes the emotionally intelligent person as someone who recognises, understands and manages his or her own feelings, and the feelings of other people. Goleman states that EI is far more important to career success than technical skills or rational intelligence, and argues that it gives a person huge advantages at work and is a vital element in the success of people in senior management positions.

Dulewicz and Higgs (1999), who are the foremost British proponents of EI, argue that it can be measured in a valid and reliable way, and it consists of three components, each of which is associated with a number of traits:

Drivers (motivation and decisiveness) are traits that energise people and give them the motive force to achieve their goals (people high in EI normally set themselves fairly high goals).

Constrainers (conscientiousness, integrity and emotional resilience) are traits that curb the excesses of drivers.

Enablers (sensitivity, influence and self-awareness) are traits that enable people to perform well and achieve their goals.

All of these traits are what would normally be regarded as dimensions of personality and, for this reason, the word 'intelligence' needs to be interpreted with some caution. For instance, using the word intelligence might be little more than a re-packing of personality theory into a more easily marketable form, which makes it attractive because it appears to be new (Woodrufe 2000, 2001; Chapman 2001). However, there is an increasing number of consultants that offer development in EI and, largely due to the assertion that it can be developed by appropriate training, there seems to be no shortage of organisations eager to embrace the idea. Problematically, however, there is something questionable in Goleman's assertion that a hallmark of high EI is the ability to manage the feelings of other people. While this might well be a trait that is vital for success in organisations, it smacks of manipulation and in the long-run, when people recognise that they have been manipulated, a great deal of resentment can arise.

Nevertheless, empirical work in the area tends to show that it could be a very promising concept. For instance, a study by Dulewicz and Higgs (1999) clearly shows that a combination of IQ and EI can be a highly effective way of predicting the job performance of individuals. In addition, a longitudinal study using abstracted data collected across a 50 year time span, which included personality and IQ measures, shows that there is an enduring relationship between personality traits, general intelligence and career success (Judge *et al.* 1999), and similar results over a shorter time span are also revealed in a study of de DeFruyt and Mervielde (1999). Although work of this type is still in its infancy, the organisational implications are highly significant. For example, by using appropriate personality and intelligence measures in combination, it might be possible to inject a higher degree of accuracy into selection decisions.

APTITUDE AND ABILITY

Aptitude: the facility or potential to be able to do something (the latent ability)

While the only practical way of assessing intelligence is with reference to observable behaviour, structural models of intelligence reveal a host of different skills and abilities that could be used to do this. However, one of the things that makes intelligence testing controversial is that, although intelligence has a genetic component, most abilities are the result of an interaction between innate factors and experience. Thus, intelligence IA gives someone an *aptitude* (latent ability) to do something, but the actual skills to do it are acquired through *learning* (experience).

Learning: a relatively permanent change in behaviour, or potential behaviour, that results from experience

Unfortunately, many people have a limited range of experiences and so, in an organisational context, tests that reveal what a person can do or even what he or she would be able to do given appropriate training, can sometimes be of more interest. In this situation tests of achievement or aptitude come into their own, but there is a difference between them. *Achievement tests* are designed to reveal what a person can do now, whereas *aptitude tests* give an indication of what a person should be able to do with training. However, both are very similar in terms of the questions or problems they use and the real difference is in the way that the resulting answers or scores are interpreted (Atkinson *et al.* 1987).

Achievement tests: tests that assess what a person can currently do

Aptitude tests: tests that assess what a person will be able to do if given the required training

Depending upon the circumstances, either type of test has a potential use in employee selection. Most jobs require a range of connected skills, and one way to assess a person's suitability is to use tests that are representative of the requirements of the job. For example, a keyboard operator could be given a practical achievement test, which assesses speed and accuracy. Alternatively, an aptitude test could be used to determine whether a person has the manual dexterity and hand–eye coordination to become a proficient keyboard operator. Since the ability and aptitude approaches to testing are not mutually exclusive, in some situations both can be used together. This is sometimes done in selecting management trainees, where it can be reasoned that managerial aptitude consists of a complex combination of mental and analytical skills, accompanied by a personal ability to express oneself lucidly. So far as more specific skills are concerned, a wide range of tests has been developed and some of the more important areas in which aptitudes can be assessed are given below.

- **Manual dexterity**   This covers abilities such as hand–eye coordination, which could be vital in a number of manual jobs. With greater use of computers and keyboards this is also increasingly important for white-collar work.

- **Numeric ability**   In its simplest form, numeric ability means that arithmetic calculations can be completed accurately. However, at a more advanced level, there are also tests of this type which assess the potential for more abstract mathematical manipulations.

- **Spatial and diagrammatic ability**   These can be extremely important in creative or design work, for example being able to mentally rotate an object and imagine what it would look like from a different position.

- **Verbal ability**   This is important in a number of jobs. At a basic level, comprehension and word meaning tests can be used to assess suitability of people for clerical work. For higher organisational levels, more advanced tests that involve critical features of vocabulary and reasoning can be applied to management candidates.

THE INTERACTION OF PERSONALITY AND INTELLIGENCE

Like many things in psychology, personality and intelligence have some things in common and some that are different. In terms of similarities, they are both psychological constructs that deal with human cognitive processes and they both acknowledge that people are unique. They are also abstract concepts involving mental activity that cannot be observed directly, and so personality and intelligence can only be inferred from visible behaviour. Finally, personality and intelligence both deal with aspects of behaviour that reflect a person's reactions or responses to the external world. Alongside these similarities, however, there is an important difference. Personality is a more global concept than intelligence and while it embraces some facets of intellectual activity, it essentially expresses a person's reactions and responses to the social world, whereas intelligence is more often used to describe responses to the world of objects, things and abstract thoughts. Nevertheless, there is still a degree of overlap between the two concepts, and it could be asked whether they actually deal with distinctly different aspects of mental functioning, or whether both are simply different perspectives on the same thing.

The danger of giving different names to abstract concepts is that they can come to be seen as separate entities and in the case of personality and intelligence this might well be very misleading. Like many other psychological constructs, they are simply words of convenience that are used to explain different aspects of a person's behaviour and, although something is known about those parts of the brain that control certain aspects of behaviour, our knowledge of the way the brain functions is not extensive enough to say that some parts of the brain deal only with what we call personality while others affect intellect. What we do know is that if certain parts of the brain are damaged, both personality and intelligence are affected. In addition, some psychologists have noted that the trait approach to personality is extremely close to the usual method of measuring intelligence (Phares 1987). Thus, personality and intelligence might just be different but connected aspects of cognitive functioning.

If this is the case, why then do we bother to have different concepts at all? So far as the majority of people in the world are concerned (and this applies to this book) the answer is simple – because it is convenient to do so. If our aim is to understand the behaviour of people in organisations, it is more convenient to take personality and intelligence as reflections of two different types of behaviour: personality as a convenient way of describing some aspects of behaviour in *social* situations; while intelligence describes the physical and intellectual skills and abilities that are more concerned with *task performance*. While a knowledge of both aspects of behaviour can be highly relevant to organisations, having knowledge is one thing, knowing how to interpret it is another.

PERSONALITY AND INTELLIGENCE: AN INTERNATIONAL PERSPECTIVE

Earlier in the chapter it was noted that social and cultural factors can have a considerable influence on the development of an individual's personality and this is also true of intelligence, or at least of intelligence or aptitude as it is measured by tests. Thus it is possible that personality and intelligence might have a culturally induced component and, if this is true, and it almost certainly is, certain personality characteristics could be more prevalent in some cultures than in others. In addition, what is regarded as intelligent behaviour could also vary between different contexts. Because the effects of different cultures can have important implications for international organisations, it is important to briefly mention some of these sources of variation.

A very broad description of culture is:

> a pattern of social, emotional and mental behaviours that is derived from a set of deeply ingrained beliefs and values held by people who exist within a particular environmental context.

A considerable overlap often exists between racial and cultural groupings of people. In terms of its historic development, a race usually occurs because different groups of people are geographically separated and, because this results in a restricted gene pool, it sometimes gives rise to identifiable differences in inherent physical characteristics. However, isolation also results in social differences, and there is considerable debate on whether genetic or cultural differences are most responsible for intellectual and personality development.

So far as intellectual capacities are concerned, although roughly 80 per cent of what we refer to as intelligence is genetically determined, it is near impossible to be precise about the cognitive abilities that are affected in this way. Nevertheless, there is a wealth of evidence, some of which has existed for many years, to show that there are systematic differences in the psychological characteristics of members of different cultures, three of which will be considered here.

- **Perceptions** The mechanisms of perception are generally thought of as the same for all people and, as will be seen in the next chapter, the essence of perception is interpretation. There is a considerable body of evidence to show that there are widespread, culturally-induced habits that result in the same phenomena being interpreted in different ways in different cultures (see, for example, Segall *et al.* 1966).

- **Socialisation** How we are brought-up has huge affects on what people are taught to believe is an acceptable way to behave and there is a well-documented stream of evidence to show that how people are socialized has an abiding influence on what they come to accept as appropriate or inappropriate ways of thinking, speaking and behaving (Berry 1969).

- **Language and proxemics** While language is a very different thing from culture, language and the way it is used can often reflect dominant cultural values. Our native language has a huge influence on the way that we think. It acts as a filter, through which our thoughts pass, and dictates the way in which we organise, analyse and interpret our external world. Therefore, two groups of people whose languages differ widely in terms of lexicon (vocabulary) and grammar usually go well beyond using different labels for the same phenomena – they tend to hold fundamental differences in the way they view the world (Whorf 1940). One of the most significant ways in which this happens is in terms of unspoken signs, or non-verbal communication. A significant example here is the matter of proxemics. In the West we tend to regard a distance of between 18 inches and 4 feet as the appropriate one to conduct a normal conversation. Anything above this is regarded as impersonal and lacking in intimacy, whereas anything less is an invasion of a person's personal space. The important point to note here is that proxemics set standards about what is considered to be polite behaviour in different parts of the world. People from northern Europe tend to feel very uncomfortable when someone comes too close, and in those cultures where closeness is the norm, to stand too far away tends to be regarded as aloofness.

The points discussed above are very powerful forces and when taken together, they often result in some cultures placing a higher value on certain skills and behaviour than others. Thus cultures usually develop practices to foster what they regard as the most important skills and behaviour in their members, and in this way a culture becomes something that tells its members what is acceptable and what is not acceptable. Since what is acceptable in one culture may be highly inappropriate in another, it is only to be expected that there can be differences in the personality characteristics of members of different cultures. The same is true of patterns of aptitude and skills and some of these differences are underpinned by deeper mental characteristics. Nevertheless, it would be very inaccurate to suggest that there is anything so all-embracing as a Japanese or French personality, and it would be just as wrong to suggest that any culture produces a better personality profile, or more intelligent people, than others; they are simply different and nothing more.

An employer is entitled to employ staff whose characteristics give a reasonable assurance that they will perform well in a job, or at least be able to benefit from training. Problematically, when it comes to comparing the personalities or aptitudes of people from different cultures for these purposes, there can be significant problems. People from different cultural groups are likely to have had different opportunities to build up the mental frameworks called for by a personality or aptitude tests and, since a test only samples from a whole range of skills and abilities, there is a danger that a test constructed for one cultural group only samples the skills and behaviour valued in that person's native culture. In other words, the test could be culturally biased. Psychological testing is a particularly Western invention and older personality tests often have a distinct gender bias and tests of specific abilities or aptitudes can discriminate against some ethnic minorities, albeit unwittingly. There is probably no such thing as a culturally unbiased test. The best we can hope for is that a test is culturally fair, and this is often a function of the test situation; that is, the test itself and the people who are tested. Unfortunately, it is all too easy to incorporate items in a test that unwittingly discriminate against certain ethnic gender or groups. Vernon (1969) gives an example to illustrate this by pointing out that intelligence, aptitude and some personality tests often make use of pictures or drawings of humans. This is quite acceptable in most Western cultures, but, in the Moslem religion, pictorial representation of the human form is discouraged. Thus, even allowing for the unfamiliarity of these pictures to an Arab, a test item could inhibit the person from recognising the principle that the picture sets out to illustrate.

TIME OUT

Carefully consider the impact that different national cultures can have on the behaviour of people within a country. Identify a foreign country that you have visited, perhaps on holiday. Based on your experience of that country, try to identify its culture and how it is different from the culture of your home country. If you have never visited a foreign country, compare the cultures of different parts of your home country with which you may be familiar; for example, north and south, rural and city-dwelling. Now answer the questions below.

1. In what ways do the two cultures differ?
2. Do these differences result in different patterns of behaviour in the people in the two cultures?
3. Are there any ways in which you might need to change your own behaviour if you moved from one culture to the other and, if so, why would you need to do this?

REPLAY

- While aptitude and ability are two concepts that are allied to intelligence, they are more strongly focused on the measurement of intelligent behaviour in terms of usable skills.
- Aptitude reflects a person's potential to be able to do something and aptitude tests assess a person's capability to do something if given the necessary training.
- Ability is a product of aptitude and learning and ability tests measure what a person can do at the current time.
- Allowance should be made for the effects of cultural factors when comparing scores of individuals on tests of intelligence, aptitude and ability.

OVERVIEW AND CONCLUSIONS

To close this chapter it is important to draw attention to two organisational implications of personality and intelligence. First, people are unique in both respects and this is what makes the two concepts potentially useful in organisational terms. Where appropriate, differences between individuals can be distinguished, and the effectiveness of some organisational processes can be considerably improved; for example, selection, appointment, placement, promotion, counselling and even vocational guidance. In all of these the aim is either to select the most appropriate person for a particular job or to improve the performance of an existing role occupant. While personality and/or intelligence tests could have a part to play in these activities, if either is to make a useful contribution we have to be sure, beyond reasonable doubt, that some aspect of personality or intelligence is a determinant of successful job performance. Unfortunately there is some tendency to use these measures without having first established whether this is the case. Psychological tests are sometimes used because it is fashionable to do so (Newton 1994) and, when this is the case, they often turn out to be very poor predictors. With personality tests it is also important to remember that the effects of a situation are sometimes so powerful that they override an individual's personality characteristics and a similar degree of caution needs to be exercised with respect to intelligence testing. Because what a person can do is partly the result of prior experience, it is necessary to be quite clear about whether it is achievement or aptitude that needs to be examined.

Second, even where personality and/or intelligence can be shown to be important correlates of job performance, personal characteristics should never be evaluated on an implicit basis. Regrettably, some managers have an almost evangelical faith in their own ability to spot the most suitable person as he or she 'comes through the door', and this sometimes extends to evaluations of personality or intelligence. Needless to say there is a need to guard against any inclinations to make snap judgements and to realise that it is impossible to obtain an accurate picture of a person's personality or intelligence from a 20-minute interview and since there are a number of well-validated tests to examine these characteristics there is no excuse for doing so. However, measuring the characteristics and making inferences about behaviour from test scores are not tasks for untrained people. Although administering a test can often be a straightforward procedure, interpreting the results can be far more difficult, and it is usually a job for someone with psychological training.

FURTHER READING

Barrick, MR and AM Ryan (eds) (2002) *Personality and Work. Reconsidering the Role of Personality in Organisations*, San Francisco, CA: Josey-Bass. A broad but comprehensive examination of the topic of personality at work, that gives a state-of-the-art overview of the subject.

Blinkhorn, S and C Johnson (1990) The insignificance of personality testing, *Nature* 34(8): 671–682. A brief but penetrating article that takes a critical view of the use (and overuses) of personality testing.

Cook, M and B Cripps (2004) *Psychological Assessment in the Workplace*, Chichester: Wiley. A useful book that draws on recent research to give a critical review of psychological assessment techniques.

Goldberg, LR (1993) The structure of phenotypic personality traits, *American Psychologist* 48(1): 26–34. An article that critically examines trait theories of personality.

Goleman, D (1998) *Working with Emotional Intelligence*, London: Bloomsbury. A best-selling book that probably turned the concept of EI into what has become one of most recent best-selling organisational fads. Very easy to read, but it is probably as well to remember that the book is essentially an advertisement for EI.

Jackson, C (1996) *Understanding Psychological Testing*, Leicester: BPS Books. An easy-to-read introductory text that explains all aspects of the construction, uses, advantages and limitations of psychological tests.

Pervin, A and OP John (1996) *Personality: Theories and Research*, 7th edn, Chichester: Wiley. A comprehensive text, giving unbiased coverage of all major approaches to personality theory.

Phillips, A (ed.) (2005) *The Penguin Freud Reader*, Harmonsworth: Penguin. A very readable account of Freud and his work, that cuts through some of the myths and misunderstandings about Freud.

Smith, M and P Smith (2004) *Testing People at Work*, Oxford: Blackwell. A comprehensive guide to psychometric testing, that emphasises the importance of using tests in a socially responsible way.

Spector, P (1995) *Industrial and Organisational Psychology: Research and Practice*, Chichester: Wiley. The book contains an interesting overview of personality and intelligence as psychological concepts.

Toplis, J, V Dulewicz and C Fletcher (2004) Psychological Testing, 4th edn, Maidenhead: CIPD Publishing/McGraw-Hill. A clear and very practical guide to psychological testing.

Warr, PB (1996) *Psychology at Work*, 4th edn, Harmondsworth: Penguin. An easily read, broad introduction to the psychological aspects of work and work organisations.

CASE STUDY 3.1: Psychometric testing and redundancy

During the mid-1990s, occupational psychologists made their first tentative attempts to use psychometric testing to select people for redundancy. However, the move created an uproar both inside and outside the testing industry and both Southwark Council and Anglian Water, who introduced these measures, attracted strong criticism from trade unions and some psychologists. In the face of this reaction, the occupational psychologists backed away from the controversy and the consensus seemed to be that testing people for redundancy was a bad idea.

Nevertheless, behind the scenes, some companies continued to explore the use of testing as part of the process they used to decide who should stay and who should go, particularly with respect to groups of employees whose job responsibilities would change markedly in post-merger reorganisations. For the first time in about ten years, these processes came out into the open during a debate at the British Psychological Society's recent annual conference of occupational psychologists in 2005. At the centre of the debate was the use of objective assessment, including psychometric tests, in reorganisation programmes at the Royal Mail Group, where some 34,000 jobs have been shed in the past three years.

The job-shedding followed the appointment of Allan Leighton as chairman in 2002, who inherited an organisation that was losing about £1.25m a day; today it is making profits of about £1.25m a day. The turnround is all the more remarkable for the way that restructuring appears to have been achieved with relatively little dissent among staff, no compulsory redundancies and no industrial tribunal cases. The Royal Mail reorganisation required urgent measures. The state-owned business was barely solvent and services would need to be reorganised,with the disappearance of thousands of jobs and creation of others.

A team of assessors and occupational psychologists headed by David Thompson, chief psychologist, needed to act quickly but where to start? The appraisal system, which might have been seen as a reliable source of employee information, was nothing of the sort. Staff appraisals were characterised by inconsistent application and manager bias and although some appraisals may have rated people on the basis of clear and measurable objectives, others were compiled in a more subjective way. Mr Thompson commented that the HR department files them away and no-one ever looks at them. Thus, with 200,000 people, a big problem was actually finding all the appraisals. Moreover, he added that he had yet to come across an organisation that was confident about its employee performance data, except for those with sales forces and they tend to be measured to death.

An alternative route was to gather new sets of data using psychometric testing, interviews and role simulations. For one of the larger exercises, Royal Mail turned to a personality test published by Saville Holdworth Limited (SHL), the UK human resources group. James Bywater, SHL's product group manager, understood the sensitivity surrounding testing: tests were being used in such exercises, but organisations were pushing the issue under the carpet because they found tests uncomfortable, he says. The biggest objection, he decided, covered the use of assessment in directly choosing individuals for redundancy. We were not in favour of that. but a more considered approach that brought-in objective assessment to see who would be best fitted for new and often quite different roles, we thought had some advantages. One advantage, he says, is the way that the inclusion of neutral assessors and formal assessment can help avoid decisions based on favouritism or old antagonisms between managers and staff. The view was that any kind of process that was seen to be objective had to be a good thing, he says.

Royal Mail did not use tests for all its redundancies. For instance, none of the unionised frontline staff was subject to assessment because large staffing volumes and natural wastage made this unnecessary. Moreover, among managerial staff where psychometrics were used, some staff volunteered for immediate redundancy and overall, testing or other forms of objective assessment were used in about a third of the redundancies.

Some of the most drastic job cutting involved the human resources department, which was asked to remove £50m from its cost base, which represented about 85 per cent of staff. People had to decide whether they would rather accept redeployment or leave and for many who were redeployed, the move amounted to a demotion. In those cases salaries were not reduced but were held on a 'mark time' basis, in which people working under this arrangement do not get automatic pay rises until their pay had come in to line with their lower job grade.

Looking back at press reports of the Southwark and Anglian Water cases in the 1990s, it is clear that most of the criticism appeared to centre on the way that tests were being used. There were also questions of relevance. One of the Southwark council employees, for example, revealed that she was asked to give her views on religion, her relationship with her parents and her attitude to dirty jokes. Even psychologists at SHL were raising concerns about the use of tests. In a redundancy situation, you will already have data on an employee's job performance; you don't need a prediction, said one of its psychologists. Another insisted that tests should not be used in isolation. These comments, however, do not apply to the Royal Mail experience. Its psychologists took care to select tests for their relevance and melded them with other

▶

forms of assessment. Moreover, they used tests precisely because of the inconsistency of existing performance data.

A more difficult issue when the possibility of redundancy may be looming at the back of such assessment exercises, is what become known as the *ultra high stakes* phenomenon, which occurs when, because of a potential job loss, some candidates may be less than candid in the way they complete their tests. Therefore, cross-referencing at interviews or in other support exercises, played a crucial role, says Mr Bywater. Where interviews involve an experienced operational manager and a consultant psychologists, they can take the candidate through their profile and look for evidence of the behaviours that emerge, he says. Perhaps the most valuable outcome of the Royal Mail assessments has been a set of *top tips* that would make excellent guidelines for similar assessment exercises in future. These include ensuring that past performance, in most cases, is given more weight than potential performance and that the exercise is balanced to avoid an overload of information that is costly and time-consuming to process. Just as important is a reminder that any process should be legally defensible lto those involved and to the scrutiny of the press.

Questions

1. What are your views on the use of psychometric testing for something so potentially controversial as selecting people for redundancy?

2. In terms of the situation at Royal Mail, do you feel that the company had sufficiently 'grasped the nettle' with respect to the shortcomings in the appraisal of its own employees?

3. In terms of its aim of using only 'objective' evidence to choose those employees who might be made redundant, do you feel that the procedures used by Royal Mail to show 'fairness' to employees were satisfactory?

4. In your estimation, would the procedures used by Royal Mail be likely to result in employees being convinced that the company had handled redundancy in a fair and honest way, or would the redundancy exercise have degenerated into a long, drawn-out process in which the firm had to handle a glut of individual grievances?

Adapted from: Donkin, R (2005) Appointments: the proper place for psychometric testing, *Financial Times*, 25 February

REVIEW AND DISCUSSION QUESTIONS

1. Giving examples to illustrate your answer, explain the factors that are influential in shaping an individual's personality.

2. It is sometimes said that personality traits, as revealed by a personality test, can be very poor predictors of a person's behaviour. Explain why this might be the case.

3. What is the idiographic approach to personality and how does this differ from the nomothetic approach?

4. What three meanings can be attributed to the word intelligence and what are the main implications of these different definitions?

5. To what extent and in what circumstances do you feel that the concept of intelligence is one that is useful for organisations? Justify your conclusion by citing examples where a measure of the intelligence of an individual employee might (or might not) be useful in predicting the person's future behaviour.

Chapter 4

Perception

LEARNING OUTCOMES

After studying this chapter you should be able to:

- define perception

- in outline, describe the perceptual process

- explain perceptual selectivity and attention, perceptual organisation and object recognition, and perceptual interpretation and inference

- explain some of the problems associated with social perception, including stereotyping, halo effects and self-fulfilling prophecy effects

- define attributions and describe how attributions can influence the processes used for dealing with poor employee performance

INTRODUCTION

This chapter deals with perception; another important way in which people differ as individuals. Since perception results in people having highly individualised ways of exeriencing their surroundings, it can mean that two people could perceive the same situation differently, and behave towards it in different ways; something that has strong implications for organisations.

The chapter commences with a brief explanation of human sensory processes and culminates in a definition of perception. Because perception is a very complex matter, the first step in exploring the process is to consider it in its simplest form, the perception of static objects. This is followed by a consideration of a more complex version of the process that relates directly to organisational life: the perception of people and social situations. Differences in perceptual ability and accuracy are then considered and this is followed by an explanation of some of the outcomes of social perception: the self-fulfilling prophecy, and the way that managers' attributions influence the way that they deal with poor employee performance. A brief consideration of cross-cultural differences in perceptions is given and the chapter closes with a short overview section that brings together its contents.

THE HUMAN SENSORY PROCESS

Sensor organs: organs that detect information about stimuli in the environment, i.e. the eye for visual information

To function in the world, we all have to take in information from our surroundings and use it to regulate our behaviour. This is done through the five traditional senses of hearing, sight, touch, smell and taste, plus two more that are now currently accepted: pain and proprioception – our sense of body and limb position. Each is a different channel for importing information about 'what is out there', and has its own *sensor organs*, (the eye for visual data and the ear for auditory information), but there are limits on what a receptor can sense. After having sensed something, the information is transmitted to the brain via the appropriate nervous pathways and, although a certain amount of pre-processing takes place, the major and most important processing functions are performed in the appropriate cortex of the brain.

Perception: a mental process involving the selection, organisation, structuring and interpretation of information in order to make inferences and give meaning to the information

In everyday life most situations are so rich in information that there is probably too much to handle. Therefore, we attend to some features and not to others and this can happen with any of the receptor channels. Moreover, the process is highly individualised, and two or more people confronted with the same external situation can experience matters in different ways. Thus humans seldom see or hear reality; they infer or construct personalised versions of reality from the stimuli to which they are exposed. While a simplistic and very naive view of this is that some people are more observant than others, this assumes that people are simply passive recipients of information. However, the reality is that we all process information in an active way and with this in mind, *perception* is defined as:

> an active mental process which involves the selection, organisation, structuring and interpretation of information in order to make inferences and give meaning to the information.

In organisations our perceptions are usually of people, and we make judgements about them and how they respond on the basis of our perception. However, since our perceptions are inferences rather than a faithful reproduction of what is there, before dealing with the extremely complex matter of social perception it is important to understand something of the limitations that the perceptual process places on us by considering it in a basic way: the perception of static objects.

THE PERCEPTUAL PROCESS

In what follows, the discussion will deal mainly with visual perception. However, it is important to recognise that we use all our senses to perceive, and so other channels have their own equivalents of many of the phenomena that will be described.

The Basic Perceptual Model

Although perceiving something depends on the stimuli that register on a particular sensor, perception is more than simply sensing 'what is out there'. The idea that perception is just a one-way, data-driven process will be referred to here as the *bottom-up processing* conception, which is now regarded as a rather simplistic. For example, it implies that identifying something such as a triangle simply means that information about external stimuli is passed to the brain, where it is processed and matched up with some sort of stored template, with the label triangle attached to it. However, triangles come in all shapes and sizes, and we are able to recognise them all as triangles. Therefore, perception is more than recognising distinctive shapes and, because we can identify all three-sided figures in which the sides connect as triangles, it must also involve the use of concepts. Thus, higher-order brain processes are at work and a certain amount of *top-down processing* occurs as well. Without going into detail, it is known that incoming sensory data is refined a great deal along the nervous pathways and, in all probability, the brain instructs the pathways how to process the data. One way to portray the idea that bottom-up and top-down processes are at work together is by using the simplified model shown in Figure 4.1. Somewhat artificially, the model divides the perceptual process into three stages, in which incoming sensory data is gradually transformed into a perception. For convenience, the process will be described in three main stages and each one will be explained separately.

Bottom-up processing: perceptual processes driven by incoming data imported through sensor organs

Top-down processing: perceptual processes driven by the higher brain

Stage 1: Attention and Selection

People are often confronted with more stimuli than they can comprehend at the same time. Some are outside the range of their sensory apparatus and some are screened out to enable attention to be focused on others. This is not a random event. People usually attend to stimuli that are the most salient (noteworthy) at that point in time. In general terms, two sets of factors influence salience: first, the characteristics of the stimulus itself, which are registered via bottom-up processes and, second, internal, higher-order mental processes, which come into play through top-down aspects of processing.

Attention and selection: the tendency to acknowledge some stimuli and ignore or mask out others

Figure 4.1 The basic
perceptual process

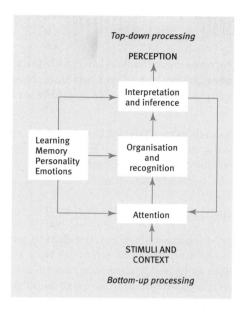

External (Bottom-up) Factors

All other things being equal, the **size** of a stimulus, its **intensity** and the **contrast** between stimulus and background all influence the degree of attention. An example of contrast is given in Figure 4.2: even though both of the dark, inner circles are the same size, the one on the right probably seems slightly larger.

People also attend more to an object in **motion** than to one that is static and within limits; **repetition** or repeated exposure to a stimulus has the same effect. An allied principle is that of **novelty** and **familiarity**, in which new objects in a familiar setting attract our attention.

These characteristics of the perceptual process are well known and used by the advertising industry. Monster advertisements on a hoarding, for example, attract our attention more than small fly-posters on a wall. Bright colours in an advertisement are likely to grab the attention more than those that are drab, particularly if there is a strong element of contrast between a focal object and its background. In addition, novelty is also used in advertisements to make them eye-catching, for example the medieval lord sitting down to a banquet with a bottle of tomato ketchup on the table.

Figure 4.2 The contrast principle

Source: *Organizational Behavior*, 5th Edn by D Hellriegal, JW Slocum and RW Woodman, © 1989. Reprinted with permission of South-Western College Publishing, a division of Thomas Learning

TIME OUT

Try to think of a 'still' advertisement that you can readily bring to mind that you have seen recently in a magazine, newspaper or on a hoarding. Now try to analyse what it is about the advertisement that caught your eye and made it memorable. Was it:

intensity of colours
contrast between the focal object and the background
an impression of **motion** in the scene
the **novelty** of a familiar object in an unusual setting?

Internal (Top-down) Factors

Personality variables predispose people to pay attention to certain stimuli more than others. **Motivations** also have an impact on attention. Since an unsatisfied need has a motivating effect, people can be highly sensitive to stimuli that offer a route to needs satisfaction. For instance, a picture of a refreshing drink in an advertisement would probably attract the attention of someone who was thirsty. Because prior **learning** and **experience** create expectancies that some things are more important than others, these also influence attention. For instance, a policeman's experience and training could make him sensitive to an open window on the ground floor of a house because it is an easy access point for a burglar. Finally, a person's **perceptual set**, that is, the mental pre-dispositions that make some stimuli more interesting than others, can also play an important role in selective attention; if you know that you have to let your boss have a particularly important item of information, the very presence of a computer on your desk might attract your attention because e-mail is a means of conveying the message.

Stage 2: Stimulus Organisation and Recognition

After certain features of a stimulus have attracted attention, they are organised into meaningful 'wholes', and the basic principles of what goes on here were uncovered many years ago.

The *figure-to-ground effect* is the most basic form of perceptual organisation, which simply means that figures are always seen against a background. For example, in this text what registers on your eyes is a set of irregular black and white shapes, but your mind organises these into recognisable black figures (letters, words and punctuation marks) on a white background. However, things are not always as simple as this. In some situations figure and ground can seem to switch. In Figure 4.3, what do you see; a white vase against a dark background, or two faces silhouetted against a white background?

The figure-to-ground effect is actively used in organisations to make people more aware of particularly important pieces of equipment by painting them in bright colours to increase the figure-to-ground effect. For example, fire alarm switches are normally painted bright red.

Grouping effects reflect the principle that we tend to organise stimuli into meaningful groups and patterns, by either closure, proximity, continuity or similarity. In *closure*, top-down processes fill in any gaps in the incoming sensory stimuli, and

Stimulus organisation and recognition: the organisation of stimulus information into meaningful patterns that form identifiable wholes

Figure-to-ground effect: the tendency to organise data so that all figures are seen as existing against a background

Grouping effects: the tendency to organise data into meaningful groups or patterns

Closure principle: gaps between stimuli are filled in so that discrete stimuli are perceived as connected

Figure 4.3 Figure-to-ground effect

Proximity principle: objects are perceived as related because of their closeness

Continuity principle: the existence of missing stimuli is inferred, resulting in a perception of links between unconnected stimuli

Similarity principle: the tendency to infer that two objects alike in some respects are alike in other ways

a meaningful whole is inferred where one does not exist. An example of closure is shown in Figure 4.4, where the blobs are usually interpreted as the number 5 or the letter 'S'.

The *proximity principle* results in a group of objects being perceived as related because of their physical closeness to each other. For instance, in Figure 4.5 some people find it more meaningful to perceive the three groups of blocks in (b) as a larger group of nine (as shown in (a)). In addition, it is probably easier to recognise that a string of digits that you have written down is a telephone number if it is presented as 0161 729785, rather than 0161729785.

The *continuity principle* is similar but not quite the same. Because the mind has a tendency to disregard changes in shape or direction, missing stimuli are supplied where none exist, to result in the perception of a continuous line. An example of this is shown in Figure 4.6, where a number of separate lines tend to be seen as one that traces an irregular shape.

With the *similarity principle*, an object, that is alike in some way to another one, is perceived as being identical in several other respects. An example of this is given

Figure 4.4 Closure principle

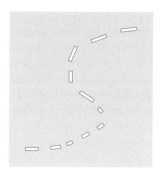

Figure 4.5 Perceptual grouping

Figure 4.6 Continuity principle

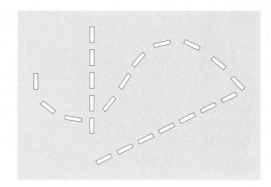

Figure 4.7 Similarity principle

DOB102
BOD2O3
AOX33O

in Figure 4.7, where the first line contains the capital letters 'D', 'O', 'B', followed by the digits one, zero, two. Here, there is usually a tendency to see the digits in the second and third lines as also containing zeros, but they actually contain the capital letter O.

Constancy effect: the perceiver is able to make adjustments for distance, etc., so that the object is experienced as the same size irrespective of its distance

The *constancy effect* enables us to organise incoming stimuli in a highly sophistic-ated way. In much the same way that the size of a photographic image depends on distance between camera and object, the size of an image on the retina depends on the distance between the object and the eye. Thus, if someone walks towards us the retinal image gets larger and so we could expect to see the person increasing in size. However, we do not experience things in this way because, somehow, top-down pro-cessing compensates for the size of the retinal image.

Context effect: the use of information from the context of the object to infer its identity

The *context effect* also has an effect on recognition because the features surround-ing a stimulus can have a profound effect on the way that incoming information is organised, which also involves top-down processing, in which the deeper recesses of memory are used to make sense of the stimuli. For example, in Figure 4.8(a), the object might possibly be interpreted as a badly drawn letter 'T', but compare this with Figure 4.8(b), where a context of diagonal hatching has been superimposed. This makes it much easier to infer that the object could be an umbrella.

Figure 4.8 The effect of context

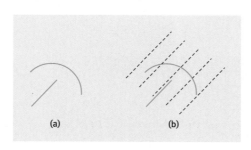

(a)   (b)

Again, context effects are found in organisations where furniture is sometimes arranged to make it easier to locate certain people. For example, sections or departments can have their desks laid out in a triangle arrangement, in which the section leader or head is always located at the apex of the triangle.

Finally, *perceptual defence*, which reflects our accumulated inhibitions to acknowledging certain stimuli, can occur. For instance, McGinnies (1949) notes that people can have a strong emotional resistance to the recognition of critical, taboo words, or even to certain preconceived ideas. Defences such as these can be strongly related to the phenomena of stereotyping, which will be discussed in greater depth later in the chapter.

Perceptual defence: the resistance to acknowledging a stimulus because doing so would contradict a person's deeply held values or what he or she already believes

Stage 3: Interpretation and Inference

In the two prior stages certain stimuli receive attention while others are largely ignored, and those that are accepted are organised into meaningful patterns. However, a perception does not take place until a decision is made that the pattern means something and this is a more significant phenomenon. The philosopher Wittgenstein (1953) observes that all seeing is 'seeing as'. We do not just observe shapes and sounds, but see the shapes as recognisable objects, and thus an identity and nature is imputed. Since sensory data are usually insufficient to provide unequivocal evidence about identity, we make a *perceptual inference*. That is, we reach a conclusion about something based on incomplete evidence, and make assumptions about what the missing evidence is. In short, we bring together the various pieces of evidence we have collected so far to infer that something is out there, and that it has an identity. To do this we all probably make use of *schema* of some sort. These are structured mental representations of what the world is like, or what it contains, and we use them to bring the evidence together and draw conclusions about an object's identity. Look at the line drawings in Figures 4.9(a), (b) and (c). What objects do they represent?

Perceptual inference: a conclusion about an object is reached on the basis of incomplete evidence

Schema: a structured mental representation of what the world is like or what it contains

As you have probably spotted, each picture could represent two objects: Figure 4.9(a) is either a duck or a rabbit; Figure 4.9(b) is an old crone or a sophisticated young woman; and Figure 4.9(c) is a kneeling woman or a man's face. With practice you can possibly switch between the two interpretations, but note that it is impossible to see both together. Thus, at any point in time, the information has to be structured in a particular way to infer what the object is, and this is related to a mental picture (schema) of how an object of this type should look. This is a very important idea. Schema tell us

Figure 4.9 Ambiguous shapes

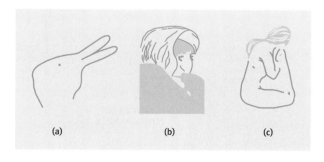

(a) (b) (c)

Figure 4.10 An
impossible shape

what to expect, and are vital in recognising that something is impossible. Now look closely at the object shown in Figure 4.10. What do you notice?

Clearly the object in Figure 4.10 is a triangle, but a very odd one. If you look closely, you will see that it could never exist in practice, because a flat surface cannot be both behind and in front of another flat surface at the same time. Very complex mental processes are at work in recognising this and, unless we assume that schema of some sort exist, it is difficult to see how we could do it. While schema tell us what to expect, where do they come from and, more importantly, how do we use them? Our accumulated knowledge and expectations probably provide the schema, and how they are used is addressed by Neisser's (1976) *analysis by synthesis* model, which is shown in Figure 4.11.

Neisser suggests that there is a self-adjusting cycle, which starts when receptor cells and nervous pathways give a preliminary representation of the stimulus on the basis of its properties such as figure-to-ground relationships and proximity. At this point the person is not actually attending to the stimulus but nevertheless extracts some of its important features. If this results in an initial indication that the stimulus could be salient, attention is triggered, followed by a preliminary best guess or working hypothesis about what the stimulus could be. At this point other top-down processes are activated. An appropriate schema is selected and compared with the bottom-up sensory input and, if there is a match, the cycle is repeated to search for additional confirmatory evidence. Where there is no match, an alternative working hypothesis is constructed and this prompts a further search until a match is found.

Analysis by synthesis: a self-adjusting cycle in which an estimate of the identity of an object is derived from incoming sensory data. This is compared with a schema for the object and if the initial inference is confirmed, a search for confirmatory information is made

Figure 4.11 Analysis by synthesis (adapted from Neisser 1976)

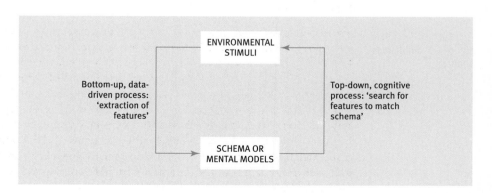

SOCIAL PERCEPTION

Perception in social situations follows the general flow of basic processes described in Figure 4.1. However, it is a vastly more complicated process and there are at least four significant differences between perceiving objects and perceiving social scenes.

To start with, in object perception the stimuli are relatively unchanging. If you look at the ambiguous objects in Figures 4.9(a), (b) and (c), because the drawings will not have changed, your perceptions are likely to be the same tomorrow. In social situations, however, the stimuli keep changing and the ground shifts under the perceiver's feet. Thus he or she probably needs to make constant revisions and refinements.

Second, in social perception the stimulus is another person or people. We do not just perceive other people, we interact with them, and our perceptions influence our interactions, because how I experience somebody else is often a function of how he or she experiences me. For example, individuals who perceive that they have a good relationship with their immediate superior often put increased effort into doing their work well to cement this relationship. Effectively this rewards the supervisor and so he or she also tends to put more into the relationship and it is likely to become even stronger (Wayne *et al.* 1997).

Third, social perception involves the use of several sensory systems together and processing centres in the brain have to try to integrate these different messages. Problematically, contradictory signals can be received, which require an inference to be made about which one is correct; for example, people might tell us that they are trustworthy, but something about their posture or facial expression conveys the impression that this is not true.

Finally, and allied to the previous point, we tend to make inferences about abstract properties of the stimulus. In object perception we seldom go beyond deciding 'what it is', but in perceiving people our perceptions often involve inferences about their mental and emotional characteristics such as their intelligence, personality and motives. For example, if members of a self-managed team come to perceive that the team is mature, well developed and competent, they are prone to developing a highly positive self-image, which in turn seems to result in the team becoming a more effective unit (Neck *et al.* 1999). However, in social perception we often have to deal with a great deal of ambiguity, which can result in our inbuilt inhibitions coming into play.

Perceiving People

Social perception plays an important part in almost every aspect of Organisational Behaviour. Thus, to the extent that we are accurate in our perceptions of other people and what prompts their behaviour, we are likely to relate well to them and have productive relationships at work. Some people are immensely proud of what they believe is their ability to make accurate judgements about others, and the assumption that some individuals have special skills of this type is quite widespread. Ideas such as this have long fascinated psychologists, and they give rise to two separate but interconnected questions. First, do people differ in terms of their abilities to perceive the characteristics and attributes of others? Second, to what extent are people able to make accurate assessments of other people? Since both are important, they will be considered separately.

Differences in Perceptual Abilities

In object perception, a factor that can influence whether a stimulus attracts a person's attention is its salience. Therefore one explanation of differences in perceptual abilities could lie in the salience of another person's characteristics. Tagiuri (1969) suggests that the impressions we form fall into basic classes, each of which represents a group of attributes of other people, such as their:

• intentions	• attitudes	• emotions
• ideas	• abilities	• purposes
• traits	• thoughts	• memories

Each of these basic classes splits down further, to give more specific dimensions along which we make perceptual judgements about other people. For example, the dimensions for abilities might include:

• creativity	• imagination	• intelligence
• physical	• musical	• literary, etc.

TIME OUT

Look closely at Tagiuri's (1969) nine basic classes for evaluating other people. For each of these classes write down two or three dimensions that you would use to evaluate other people. For example, in what three ways do you evaluate their emotions?

We also know from object perception that people differ in what they attend to, and in social situations it is possible that they differ in terms of the dimensions that attract their attention. For instance, consider two people: Jane and Fred. While both of them tend to focus on the abilities of other people, creativity and intelligence attract Jane's attention, while Fred notices musical and literary abilities. What, then, makes some dimensions more salient than others? Tajfel (1969) suggests that an individual's most salient dimensions are those that have the highest *functional significance*, that is, those that the person finds most useful in ordering and making sense of his or her particular perceptual world; for example, to a clothes designer the physical attributes of a person might be all important but, for a busy manager, a person's reliability and initiative could be the most salient.

One of the most important things we know about the use of categories is that people differ in terms of the size of their repertoires of dimensions. This is known as a person's *cognitive complexity*, which reflects his or her degree of sophistication in perceiving the world, usually the number of **independent dimensions** the person employs. For instance, if I evaluate someone as happy because he or she is outgoing, I am not differentiating between happiness and being outgoing as two independent dimensions; whereas if I work on the assumption that the two things are not the same, I would be using a more complex system of dimensions.

A word of caution is necessary about the concept of cognitive complexity. Although people with high cognitive complexity find it easier to make sense of apparently conflicting information about others (Little 1969), there is no relationship between cognitive

Functional significance: the dimensions of evaluation used by a person because they are useful in making sense of the world

Cognitive complexity: the number of independent dimensions used by a person to evaluate objects and people

complexity and intelligence (Cook 1971). Nevertheless, people with complex systems of categorisation are much less likely to make the 'stereotyping' or 'halo effect' errors that will be discussed shortly.

It is also important to remember that context plays a significant part in social perception. If someone is wearing a white coat in a laboratory setting we might well assume that he or she is a scientist and make favourable inferences about intelligence and skills, whereas the same person in the same white coat emerging from the back room of a restaurant could attract a far less complementary judgement.

TIME OUT

Try to think of someone you know, or have known in the past, about whom your initial evaluation turned out to be incomplete, misleading or inaccurate when you came to know the person better. Now try to analyse why there were differences between your initial impression and the more accurate one you built up over time. Was this because you:

assumed that the person had certain attributes or qualities because he or she fell into a certain class of person that you believe normally has those attributes, or

was it because you assumed that since the person had a certain characteristic he or she automatically had other definable attributes?

Accuracy in Perceptions of Others

Although the perceptual process results in inferences rather than in a faithful reproduction of reality, the idea of perceptual accuracy implies that some people produce more faithful representations than others. A great deal of research has been carried out in this area and, while people differ in their evaluation of others, the idea that this is connected with the accuracy of their evaluations is an oversimplification.

The current view is that while people differ in the way that they perceive others, this is not linked to accuracy. Rather, some people are good at perceiving some attributes but not so good at perceiving others, and nobody is likely to be perfect at perceiving everything (Cook 1971). For instance, person 'A' could be an accurate judge of 'impulsiveness' in others, but a poor judge of 'kindliness', and the reverse could be true of person 'B'. Thus accuracy could come down to whether the most appropriate person is asked to make the judgement. One way of guarding against perceptual errors of this type is by having different individuals evaluate whether or not a particular person has certain attributes. This is a widely adopted practice in organisations in the selection process, where an interview panel made up of several different people, each one of which is looking for something different, is used to assess the suitability of applicants for a job.

So, what conclusions can we draw about the accuracy of peoples' perceptions of others. Surprisingly, although most of us are by no means perfect at perceiving others, neither are we so bad at it that we are completely useless. A great deal seems to depend on the effort and skill we devote to the task, and this in turn seems to depend on our aims. When we need to be accurate, most of us have the skills and resources available to do so, even if it takes some of us more time than others. It is only when we are rushed, or when we consider that our opinions do not matter that we tend to make a large number of mistakes (Fiske 1993). Moreover, since making a mistake can alert us to the idea that our person perceptions are fallible, most of us are capable of learning from the experience (Higgins and Bargh 1987). Having noted this, however, while our perceptions of others show a reasonably high level of competence and accuracy, the same cannot be said of our self-perceptions. Thus Dunning (2006) notes that our self-perceptions of competence and character are frequently so full of bias, misconceptions and illusions, that they have only a very modest relationship to reality. Importantly, because an organisation is a context in which individuals perceive other individuals all the time, and their perceptions are likely to influence the nature of their interactions, we must always be concerned about anything that impairs the perceptual process, and two phenomena that can do this are considered in what follows.

Stereotyping

Stereotyping: attributing a person with qualities assumed to be typical of members of a particular category (e.g. age, sex, etc.) because the person falls into that category

A stereotype is a convenient, pre-assembled block of text used by printers because that particular combination of words occurs frequently. The word is also used in perception to describe:

> the general inclination to place a person in some category according to an easy and quickly identifiable characteristic such as age, sex, ethnic membership, nationality or occupation, and then attribute the person as having qualities believed to be typical of members of that category.   (Tagiuri 1969)

Almost any characteristics can be used to make stereotyped judgements, for instance: age – older people are resistant to change; gender – women are too swayed by their emotions; nationality – Scots are mean about money; occupation – all engineers are good at maths; physical appearance – blondes are dumb; social background – upper-class people are all snobs; interests – artistic people are badly organised.

People make stereotyped evaluations on very limited information and their use is thought to be derived from a need to establish a mental map of their social world in which identity is defined in terms of the group to which a person belongs. Thus when the perceiver evaluates someone, that person is grouped together with others, on basis of a restricted framework that assumes that some attributes go hand-in-hand. Since all individuals are unique, this can result in wildly inaccurate generalisations and, although not all stereotypes are negative, research into stereotyping has usually focused on its negative side, often in the study and analysis of prejudice.

Much of our knowledge of stereotyping is derived from *social identity theory* (Tajfel and Turner 1985), which holds that in creating cognitive maps of their social worlds people seek to uphold the values of their own social groups (relative to other groups) and this in turn leads to a gross overestimation of the differences between their own group and other groups (Krueger 1991). Thus one of the outcomes of stereotyping can be severe conflicts between workgroups. This was examined in a study by Ashforth and Mael (1989), who uncovered strong evidence that inter-group conflict can be much stronger where groups evaluate each other through stereotyped frameworks. Moreover, there are other harmful effects that can be prompted by the use of stereotypes.

To start with, we know that, once formed, stereotypes can be highly resistant to change (Hill *et al.* 1990). Because using a stereotyped image saves someone the trouble of searching for a better developed picture of another person, they are economical in the use of time. Thus they tend to be brought into play when people are under time pressures (Heaton and Kruglanski 1991). Thus their use is probably most prevalent where people feel overworked or stressed – which describes most organisations these days – and the inevitable consequence could be even more impairment of personal relationships and poor work performance.

In most organisations, however, perhaps the greatest danger is that something important about a person will be overlooked. For example, in the selection situation, incorrect assumptions can be made about candidates, which result in an inadequate exploration of their skills and abilities. The same point could be made about the performance appraisal process, which not only wastes an organisation's resources, but can also result in unfair and unjust evaluations about people that run foul of the law on racial or sexual discrimination. This can be tremendously important when we stop to consider that for years gender stereotypes have held women back from achieving the highest levels in organisations. To a large extent these were based on a stereotype, which attributed women with characteristics that were very different from men. It is therefore both surprising and pleasing to find that recent research reports a significant change in these views. Women now appear to be perceived as no different from men in their innate characteristics and the most significant thing about these perceptions seems to be that it is men who have revised their attitudes (Duehr and Bono 2006).

The Halo Effect

This occurs when a person who has one behaviourial trait is automatically credited with having other traits. At first sight this might seem to be the same as stereotyping and, in the final analysis, the end result is often the same: an inaccurate evaluation of a person. However, in stereotyping the judgement is made because all people in a certain category are assumed to have common characteristics, whereas with the *halo effect* a single trait is taken to be evidence that a person also has a number of other traits and this can lead to generalisations that are either positive or negative. For instance, a cooperative subordinate who is receptive to a manager's ideas could be evaluated as perceptive and intelligent, whereas one who is not so cooperative might be condemned as blinkered and unintelligent. In reality, of course, the first person might just be trying to ingratiate him or herself with the manager, while the second has genuinely spotted a flaw in the manager's ideas.

The most worrying thing about the halo effect is its seemingly all-pervasive nature. This is well illustrated in an early study by Asch (1946), in which subjects were shown lists describing the personality traits of two imaginary people. Only one word was different on the lists: person 'A' was described as warm and person 'B' as cold. However, the subjects seemed blind to all other words but warm and cold and inferred that 'A' and 'B' had completely different personalities.

Two areas of organisational activity in which the halo effect can have potentially adverse consequences are selection and performance appraisal. While it has been known for some time that the phenomenon is commonplace and, despite all the effort that is put into training interviewers and appraisers, the problems are still very much in evidence. Indeed, a review of the literature indicates that it is still an extremely common problem in performance appraisal (Murphy *et al.* 1993).

Halo effect: the assumption that because a person has a certain trait he or she automatically has other traits

THE OUTCOMES OF SOCIAL PERCEPTIONS

One of the most important things about social perception is that it influences the way that people interact with each other. In organisations almost everything that takes place involves human interaction, which means that the effectiveness of organisational processes can be strongly influenced by perceptions. To illustrate this point, in addition to stereotyping and the halo effect, there is another area worthy of particular attention: the self-fulfilling prophecy effect.

The Self-fulfilling Prophecy

Self-fulfilling prophecy: a prophecy that comes true solely because it has been made

Merton (1957) is usually credited with inventing the term '*self-fulfilling prophecy*', which broadly means a prophecy which comes true solely because it has been made. It is now widely accepted that it is a common feature of all social interaction, and in Organisational Behaviour it is important because our perceptions of other people can unwittingly influence their behaviour and their perceptions of themselves.

The best-known account of the phenomenon is a study conducted in an elementary school in the USA (Rosenthal and Jacobsen 1968). Over a 12-month period the school used psychological tests that were said to be able to predict intellectual growth in pupils and while the fine details of the study are interesting, they are less important than the results and conclusions drawn by the researchers.

Early in the academic year, the researchers selected the names of a number of children randomly, and teachers were told that these children would be academic 'fast developers'. By the end of the year, teachers reported that the selected children had, as predicted, 'bloomed', but that other children, (who had actually developed as much, or even more), were reported on in far less favorable terms.

Rosenthal and Jacobsen largely attributed these differences to the way that teachers had behaved towards the children during the year. Those who had been predicted to show intellectual growth were treated in a way that encouraged them to grow intellectually; for example, if one of them raised a query, the teacher tended to answer in a way that gave the child the impression that he or she had asked a profound or intelligent question. Conversely, a pupil branded as less intellectual who asked the same question might receive an answer that conveyed the impression that the teacher viewed the child as rather backward. As a result, the predicted bloomer was rewarded and the other child punished. Teachers also tended to reward fast-track children in other ways; for instance by giving them more time and attention, or asking them questions that allowed them to shine.

There is much support for the existence of the self-fulfilling prophecy effect, and it has been widely documented in organisational settings (see OB in Action Box opposite). Indeed, an early study by Word *et al.* (1974) provides convincing evidence that in job interviews black candidates get fewer encouraging non-verbal signs of approval from white interviewers than do white candidates. Therefore they tend to give less confident answers to questions and have a poorer interview performance. It is not hard to extrapolate these findings to many situations in organisations, and a process something like the one shown in Figure 4.12 could be at work.

To illustrate the model, assume that a manager has just appointed three new employees 'A', 'B' and 'C', who joined his department directly from university. In the selection process he gained an impression that 'A' is the sharpest, most enthusiastic

Figure 4.12 Model of
self-fulfilling prophecy
effect

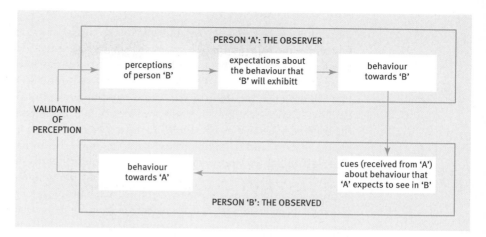

and ambitious. After a short assimilation period he starts to take 'A' under his personal wing, perhaps by giving him special instructions, accurate feedback and jobs that allow the person to fully grasp the intricacies of the work and show his best capabilities. Unless 'B' and 'C' have been lucky enough to attract the attention of someone else who gives them similar advantages, 'A' will probably soon outstrip them. Indeed, even if they do progress to a similar extent, this may not be recognised by the manager because he will be far more familiar with 'A' than with the other two.

 OB IN ACTION: Think the worst and it will happen

Most of the story of modern management is a quixotic struggle to substitute numbers for judgement. According to strategy guru Igor Ansoff, managers start off trying to manage what they want, and finish up wanting what they can measure and the proof is the 'self-fulfilling prophecy'. First described in the 1940s by sociologist Robert Merton, the mechanism by which belief creates its own reality is unique to social science. In the physical sciences, human attitudes have no effect on reality but in human affairs, however, where even if a proposition is 'wrong' to start with, if enough people believe and act on it, it becomes 'right'.

Management writers Jeffery Pfeffer and Robert Sutton have identified 500 research studies on the self-fulfilling prophecy. They show that, to a remarkable degree, performance depends on expectation; whether or not it is objectively justified. 'Irrespective of other factors,' writes Sutton, 'when leaders believe their subordinates will perform well, positive expectations lead to better performance, and the converse holds for poor performance.' Thus mangers' theories about performance and ability are self-fulfilling. One effect of this is to turn the company into a battleground between two rival views of human nature. For example, suppose managers assume that employees are basically lazy and self-interested, and must be coerced

into doing a good job. They will then use hierarchy, supervision and incentives and punishments to make employees comply. But the research evidence is that the more people are treated as naughty children the worse they behave, and this justifies even more repressive methods. The circle is not only self-fulfilling but vicious. A company built on assumptions of self-interest and opportunism progressively recasts employees in its own misshapen image. Meanwhile, a company that functions on the basis of trust and co-operation creates a system in which honest, co-operating people flourish and the more it flourishes, the more the norm is reinforced. Thus the self-fulfilling prophecy makes the company quite literally into a force for good.

Another example is the use of incentives. They are ubiquitous, but be careful, because incentives work most powerfully to teach people to expect them. One snag is that people who join the firm for incentives leave for better ones, and so the ratchet moves ever upward. The inexorable rise of chief executive pay is an awesome example of double self-fulfilling prophecy; incentive expectations are compounded by learnt self-interest – which is why nothing seems to be able to slow their growth.

Another problem with incentives occurs all over the public sector As with the new GP contracts, to get people to concentrate on a few headline measures, the government sets targets and incentives for reaching them. This has two effects: doctors find ways of meeting the targets, so payments go through the roof; but also by definition their motivation changes. (Extrinsic) incentives drive out (intrinsic) professionalism: but which doctor would you rather go to, one who is motivated by money, or by a good medical job? No wonder patients are dissatisfied and doctors conflicted.

Some dilemmas raised by the power of expectation are less clear cut. In his provocative book *Weird Ideas That Work*, Sutton suggest that one good way to approach innovation is to decide to do something that will almost certainly fail, then convince yourself and everyone else it is bound to succeed. You can probably see what's coming. Statistically, almost all innovations flop, but telling the truth will make failure certain. Conversely, the one thing you can do to change the odds at least slightly in your favour is to ignore the evidence and persuade yourself and others that it will be a triumph.

Source:

Caulkin, S (2006) Rule one: think the worst and it will happen, *The Observer*, 5 November, p 8

PERCEPTION AND ATTRIBUTIONS

Attribution: imputing a cause for an observed action

Attributions can be thought of as a special class of perceptions that we use to make sense of our own and other people's behaviour. When we perceive a certain action we seldom leave matters at that, but subconsciously impute a reason for it. In the original formulation of attribution theory (Heider 1958) the person who observes a particular piece of behaviour in someone else will attribute its cause to factors

Internal attribution: the cause of a person's behaviour is assumed to be connected with his or her psychological characteristics, e.g. attitudes, personality, etc.

External attribution: the cause of a person's behaviour is assumed to be connected with a factor in his or her environment

Behaviourial consistency: whether a piece of behaviour is typical of the way that the person normally behaves

Behaviourial consensus: whether a person's behaviour in a particular situation is typical of other people in the same situation

Behaviourial distinctiveness: whether a person behaves in the same way in several different circumstances

Fundamental attribution error: the tendency automatically to attribute internal causes for behaviour

associated with one or other of two sources: those internal to the person who behaves in a certain way (his or her abilities, attitudes, intentions etc.) or those external to the person (task-related factors, luck, environment, etc.).

This distinction, which is fundamental in attribution theory, has some important implications for judgements made about other people. An *internal attribution* contains an assumption that the person's behaviour is under his or her control, whereas in an *external attribution* it is assumed that the person is under the influence of circumstances beyond his or her control. For instance, if I make an internal attribution about one of my colleagues who is persistently late for work, I might infer a lack of self-discipline, but an external attribution could involve an assumption that the lateness is due to a poor bus service.

What then prompts us to make an internal or external attribution? Kelley (1967) suggests that we observe a person's behaviour within a particular context and that three factors influence the type of attribution that is made. These are shown in Figure 4.13.

In everyday language, *behaviourial consistency* means that a particular piece of behaviour is 'in character' for the person, because this is the way that he or she normally behaves in the same situation. The more consistent the person's behaviour, the more likely is an internal attribution.

Behaviourial consensus is the extent to which other people behave in the same way within a particular context. The more a person's behaviour is in line with that of other people, the more likely is an external attribution.

Behaviourial distinctiveness concerns whether the person tends to behave in the same way in several different situations. The more a person's behaviour is unique to one context, the more likely we are to assume that the behaviour is a result of the specific circumstances and to make an external attribution.

The problem is that to use these factors we need prior knowledge of the person's behaviour. So what happens when we do not have this? A great deal of evidence suggests that people make what is known as the *fundamental attribution error* (Ross 1977) and impute an internal cause, particularly where the other person's behaviour has an impact on the beholder (Chaikin and Cooper 1973). However, when people attribute a cause to their own behaviour, they take a much more charitable view and display a pervasive tendency to attribute their own actions to situational factors; and attribute the cause of the same behaviour in another person to his or her personal disposition (Jones and Nisbett 1972). This is fraught with problems and is at the root of many difficulties between subordinate and superior in organisations, one of which is considered next.

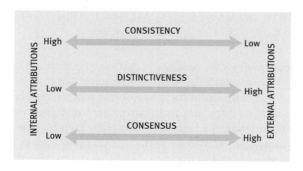

Figure 4.13 Criteria for inferring causes of behaviour

Perception, Attributions and Dealing with Poor Performance

There are times when a manager or supervisor has to deal with poor subordinate performance, or with a subordinate who has broken an organisational rule. Matters of this type often come within the confines of the disciplinary process and, almost inevitably, manager and supervisor perceptions and attributions are at work; notably, perceptions about guilt and attributions about the causes of behaviour. Using Kelley's (1967) attributional model, a study of disciplinary judgments by Mitchell *et al.* (1981) revealed some interesting outcomes. Using the criterion of **consistency**, their results strongly suggest that an employee who has transgressed in the past is much more likely to have his or her behaviour attributed to an internal characteristic, for instance low ability or lack of effort. Similarly, using the criterion of **consensus**, the results show that an employee whose behaviour is dissimilar to that of other workers is also more likely to attract an internal attribution. A number of studies has shown that other factors also affect whether an internal or external attribution is made. External attributions are more likely if the manager has personal experience of a subordinate's job (Mitchell and Kalb 1982) and also where the person about whom the judgement is made holds a senior position (Rosen and Jerdee 1974). Internal attributions are more likely if the supervisor or manager is personally affected by the employee's transgression (Greenberg 1996) and, in addition, female subordinates are much more likely than males to attract an internal attribution for the same transgression (Larwood *et al.* 1979). Moreover, because an internal attribution contains an assumption that the person concerned has acted 'in character', it is hardly surprising that these attributions are associated with disciplinary sanctions that are much more severe (Mitchell and Wood 1980).

These features of the disciplinary situation can have a huge impact on subsequent employee behaviour. In discipline, sanctions can be taken against an employee and so it would be hoped that managers would err on the side of caution in making attributions about the causes of poor performance or rule breaking. However, the evidence suggests that is not always the case. The fundamental attribution error seems to be just as commonplace in discipline as in other situations and, if a manager has pre-judged matters in some, the outcome of imposing the sanction is likely to be the exact opposite of encouraging acceptable behaviour in the future. For example, a study by Rollinson *et al.* (1997) shows that where the disciplined subordinate has perceptions and attributions of this type, there is a strong tendency for the employee to rationalise him or herself as a victim. This in turn has the rather predictable consequence that the tendency to flout the rule in the in the future is increased rather than lowered.

IMPRESSION MANAGEMENT: MANIPULATING PERCEPTIONS OF OTHERS

It is all too easy to draw the conclusion that social perception is so full of inbuilt biases that the perceiver cannot help but draw inaccurate conclusions about the person perceived. However, suppose for the moment that you are the object of another person's perceptions and you purposely want him or her to receive a far more complementary impression of you than you believe you normally convey; how likely is it that you will be able to manipulate or manage that perceivers impressions in some way? In broad terms, so long as you realise that you are setting out to deceive, and that the person is not an expert at spotting attempted deceptions, and that you avoid the obvious trap of trying to be 'all things to all people', the possibility of deceiving the perceiver can be very high. Indeed, it is remarkable just how far these deceptions can extend. For example, a recent study by Wiseman and Greening (2005) provides fairly conclusive evidence that people with alleged psychokinetic abilities (those who lay claim to being able to bend metal objects such a spoons by mental effort) are able to convince observers of their ability to do so by making relatively slight suggestions that serve to shape the observer's perceptions.

Impression management: a process in which people seek to control the image that other people have of them

In an organisational context it has long been recognised that many people attempt to convey highly complementary impressions of themselves to other people. The term used to describe these activities is *impression management*. In essence, this is a conscious attempt to send cues to other people (either verbally and/or non-verbally) with the aim of promoting an enhanced perceptual inference, so that the image projected is firmly under the control of the person playing the impression management game. One way of viewing this is as a form of organisational dramatics or play-acting, in which certain people take on roles that are purposely intended to deceive other people. Clearly, to the extent that they are able to do this, they are likely to accrue considerable advantages in an organisation. Moreover, no matter how much we might wish to condemn behaviour like this, we should recognise that it is widely practiced, particularly in management circles. For example, Dale Carnegie's book *How to Win Friends and Influence People*, which was first published nearly 70 years ago and since then has constantly been near to the top of the list of 'management best-sellers', actively promotes these principles. Some idea of the behaviour and techniques advocated in impression management can be seen in Table 4.1.

Table 4.1 Techniques of impression management (adapted from Feldman and Klich 1991, Rosenfeld *et al.* 1995)

Behaviour involved	Techniques of implementation	Desired effect on the perceiver
Ingratiation	Agree with the person you wish to influence	To increase the target person's liking for yourself
	Flatter the person you wish to influence by telling them good things about themself	To increase the target person's liking for yourself
	Do favours for the person you wish to influence by (appearing to) 'put yourself out' for the person	To increase the target person's liking for yourself
Intimidation	Convey an impression that you alone know about a potential hazard for the for the person you wish to influence	To turn a person who is a potential barrier to your advancement into an ally
Promote one's own image	Embellish one's own accomplishments or overstate own abilities	To convey an image of self as highly motivated and competent
Playing it safe	Avoid situations where you might appear in an unfavourable light	To maintain an impression of never making mistakes
Playing it dumb	Pretend you are unable to undertake certain tasks	To ensure that you have time available to do what you do well
Cite experts	Use the opinions of high status people to support own position	To create an impression of expertise and being well connected

CROSS-CULTURAL EFFECTS ON PERCEPTION: A BRIEF NOTE

The perceptual process is a highly individualised one and, since it is invisible, it is near impossible to draw hard-and-fast conclusions about how it could be influenced by cross-cultural factors. Nevertheless, in the previous chapter it was pointed out that personalities can be shaped by the beliefs and values inherent in the cultures in which people are reared. In addition, there are almost certainly differences between cultures in terms of what are taken to be the signs of 'intelligent' behaviour. For these reasons there are strong grounds for suspecting that the three stages of the perceptual process – attention and selection, organisation and recognition, interpretation and inference – are all influenced by cultural factors. One way to understand these potential effects is by applying Tagiuri's (1969) explanation of perceptual dimensions given earlier.

Different cultures are likely to place greater value on certain dimensions of a particular class of attributes than others, because people reared in a particular culture are taught as part of their upbringing that certain attributes and behaviours are more acceptable than others, and become highly sensitised to their presence or absence. There is nothing inherently right or wrong with this. Indeed, since people are prisoners of the culture in which they are reared, the behaviour that results seems normal to other people. However, there can be significant differences between cultures and so, in this respect, stereotyped images of people in cultures other than our own can be all too common, and a fairly obvious example of this the extent that a culture permits people to express their emotions.

In Great Britain people tend to be rather reserved and taciturn, and many of them are reared with a caution of 'not showing their feelings'. In other cultures, however, notably in some of the Latin countries such as Italy and France, there is far less inhibition about giving a visible display of emotion. An unfortunate side-effect of this is that people in one culture can develop stereotyped images of the characteristics of people in other cultures, and also make attributional judgements about what causes these characteristics. People in Latin countries can sometimes interpret British reserve as being prompted by 'aloofness' or 'coldness' and, in return, British people are sometimes wont to regard Latin emotional expression as 'volatility' or 'lack of self control'. Needless to say there is often insufficient evidence to come to these conclusions, and it is only when we come to know people from other cultures better that we find that the conclusions can be highly inaccurate. What is perhaps more disturbing is that these judgements have a habit of resulting in self-fulfilling prophecy effects. Because British people have a tendency to regard Latin people as somewhat volatile, they keep their distance in interactions. This probably exasperates Latin people, and perhaps prompts them to try to be warmer and more demonstrative. However, this only confirms the British view that Latins are volatile and makes them keep their distance even more, which further strengthens the Latin opinion that the British are cold and reserved.

This has important implications for organisations. As pointed out in Chapter 1, international organisations are becoming far more common, and there is an increasing need for people from different cultural backgrounds to work with each other. Even where an organisation does not operate on an international basis, its members probably come into contact with people from other cultures far more frequently these days. Thus, unless people can make allowance for and, if necessary, guard against cultural influences on their perceptions, their interpersonal interactions can be impaired.

- Perception is an active mental process in which features of the environment are selected as a focus of attention and the incoming information about these features is organised to make inferences and give meaning to what is there.

- Because perception involves both data-driven, bottom-up processes and higher brain functions (top-down processing) that guide selection and inference, it is much more than simply being observant.

- Object perception can take place through any of the five senses, but it is normally studied through one sense in isolation to reveal basic laws. For example, in visual perception the effects of size and intensity on stimulus selection and attention, and figure-to-ground relationships on object recognition.

- Social perception – the perception of people in social situations – follows the same basic process as object perception, but is a much more complex phenomenon. All five senses are usually at work together and individuals not only perceive characteristics of other people, they behave towards those people according to what is perceived. Therefore the process is highly dynamic and how we behave towards other people shapes their perceptions of us.

- In organisations, social perception has the added hazard of having a potential for impaired interactions or misjudgements about people. Therefore, it is important to remember that judgements about people are based on perceptions and perceptions are not necessarily the reality of a situation; merely a personal inference about what reality is.

OVERVIEW AND CONCLUSIONS

Perception is an important way in which people differ as individuals and can influence the way that they behave in organisations. It is a complex mental process in which we filter out some of the incoming information from the environment and attend to only part of what is available. Information is then organised into meaningful patterns and recognisable wholes, which allows us to make an inference about what is there. The factors affecting this are external (the nature of the object perceived and its surrounding context) and internal (our higher mental processes and personalities). These processes are also at work in perceiving people and social situations, but matters often go one stage further. We not only perceive people and what they do, but also attribute reasons for their behaviour. Judgements such as these often contain errors and misunderstandings, and so some account needs to be taken of the idea that our evaluations of others are seldom based on hard facts, but on what we perceive to be the facts. Perhaps most important of all, it is necessary to recognise that in a social situation perceptions give rise to chain effects in behaviour. How we perceive people has a strong influence on how we behave towards them and this, in turn, has a strong effect on how they behave towards us. For this reason we need to guard against snap judgements which can give rise to halo effects and self-fulfilling prophecies.

FURTHER READING

Goldstein, E (1998) *Sensation and Perception*, San Francisco, CA: Brooks Cole. A very comprehensive, but easy to read introduction to the psychology of perception and sensations.

Gordon, IE (1997) *Theories of Visual Perception*, 2nd edn, Chichester: Wiley. A comprehensive text which fully explores the seven major approaches to understanding visual perception.

Hewstone, M (1989) *Causal Attribution: From Cognitive Processes to Collective Beliefs*, Oxford Blackwell. A rather technical and scholarly book, but nevertheless one that is easy to read and gives a comprehensive introduction to attribution theory.

Laing, RD (1972) *Knots*, Harmondsworth: Penguin. A rather old but nevertheless penetrating description of the way that we interact with others and how this can be influenced by our perceptions and attributions.

Rosenfeld, P, RA Giacalone and CA Riordan (1995) *Impression Management in Organisations*, London: Routledge. A scholarly but straightforward and entertaining account of how people in the workplace are able to manipulate the judgements that others make of them.

CASE STUDY 4.1: In terrorism it's perceptions that count

Companies are rarely faced with counsel as diverse and contradictory as that on terrorism risk management. For instance, the Organisation for Economic Cooperation and Development (OECD) thinks the danger is so great that insurance should be mandatory, while others say it is so small that action does not even merit a cost–benefit analysis. As such, it is possible that the issue has little to do with actual risk, and much more to do with the perception of risk.

After all, although it may not seem like it, terrorism is waning and according to the US terrorism Country Report, international terrorism has been in decline since 1987, with fewer than half as many incidents in 2005 than annually during the peak years of the mid-1980s. Moreover, in spite of the horrific events of September 11 2001, in New York, fewer people were killed by acts of international terrorism in that year than in 1998. What has changed, however, has been the emergence of the once-sheltered US business sector as a target for international terrorism. Businesses are now more likely to be attacked than other targets, including diplomatic, government and military facilities and two-thirds of those attacks invariably use bombs, not in the Middle East, but in South America and Asia. For this reason it can be argued that business needs to catch up on the lessons of terrorism management, long-since applied in diplomatic and military circles.

After September 11 2001, the new focus on terrorism in companies saw all eyes turn to insurance and, thanks to a US state reinsurance scheme, four years later, 44 per cent of US businesses are covered against terrorism. In the heavy lobbying that preceded this move, it was assumed that insurance was unquestionably desirable in the face of terrorism risks, and the OECD went so far as to call for mandatory terrorism insurance. However, the OECD's conclusions were rooted in an analysis of September 11, and it argued that a similar event now would prove even more costly, making the paucity of insurance alarming.

This begs the question of whether businesses should be prepared for more attacks along the lines of September 11. According to Justin Priestley, director of the crisis management division at risk managers Aon: 'It will be years before another such attack.' The war on terror has knocked back the expertise, commanders and financing of al-Qaeda and the foreseeable terrorism risk is now of the home-grown variety, on soft targets, he says. The attacks in London on 7 July 2005 were typical of this under-resourced, 'brand terrorism'. While this was the deadliest single terrorism event in London, with the most explosions, one study by the Victoria Transport Policy Institute argues, that when commuters view public transport as dangerous and switch to cars, traffic accidents kill and maim more people than terrorism, and this makes it vital to manage perceptions of risk. Thus public transport and companies too must be seen to be exercising a duty of care if they are to continue business as normal. Moreover, being a visibly soft target is a poor management strategy, whether or not you are in a terrorism-target city.

In the US, 2 per cent of disasters that befall companies are the result of malicious acts and so there are very few are acts of terrorism; disgruntled staff are a far greater threat. Indeed, in food production or the chemical industry, the potential for malicious damage makes the security of production facilities a corporate duty and the same element of responsibility applies to contingency planning. For example, a recent survey by insurer Royal & SunAlliance found that, since the London attacks, just one in seven British businesses had reviewed their contingency plans for terrorist attacks, although in London one-third had. Yet across all potential business disasters, including fire, avian flu, flooding and hurricanes, the consequences of terrorism are similar to those of other risks; premises can be destroyed, staff killed and communication temporarily destroyed.

Essentially, poor preparation for terror attacks reflects weak risk management. In the past two years, vanguard companies have grasped this and begun turning to specialist advisers to ensure they are better prepared. For example, security experts can train staff at entrances to spot a reconnaissance operation and advise on the design of buildings, says Mark Cooper, a director at security consultancy C2i International. In concentrating resources on security and contingency planning, companies can also reduce terrorism insurance premiums and this is particularly important once terrorism insurance is needed, says Graham Heale, underwriting director at Royal & SunAlliance. Through the Pool-Re system, UK companies have access to terrorism cover across all their properties. But often, companies seek insurance only for a trophy building or new buildings where financiers require such cover. This has caused the stand-alone market, which allows for bespoke terrorism insurance to grow to a capacity in 2006 of $1.3bn, says Aon. Thus companies are becoming more sophisticated in their response to terrorism risk.

The best are improving their security and contingency planning and buying targeted insurance policies. But many more have yet to see that the business consequences of terrorism resemble those of many other possible disasters, which can, and should, be prepared for.

Questions

1. What are your views on the risks facing British business from international and domestisc terrorism?

2. Do you feel that business takes these risks seriously enough and, from what you have read in the chapter about the process of perception, how do you account for the apparent lack of attention focused on this matter?

3. What, in your view, should be the approach of British businesses to the potential threats from international and domestic terrorism, and what practical steps could firms take to protect their employees and customers to risks of this type?

Source: Luesby, J (2006) Terrorism: it is perception that counts, *Financial Times*, 25 April

REVIEW AND DISCUSSION QUESTIONS

1. Define perception, distinguish between 'bottom-up' and 'top-down' processing and explain the significance of these for the assertion that perception is an 'active' mental process.

2. To what extent is it useful to divide the perceptual process into three distinct stages for the purposes of explanation and what misconceptions can arise from using this three-stage model?

3. Explain the ways in which social perception differs from the perceiving of simple objects. What are the implications of these differences for the accuracy of perceptions of people?

4. What is meant by the term 'cognitive complexity', what is its significance in perceiving other people and is it true that some people are much more accurate than others in their perceptions of other people?

5. Explain two prevalent perceptual errors that people can make, and also how the self-fulfilling prophecy effect can influence the perception of people.

6. What is an attribution, what is the difference between an external and an internal attribution and explain the three factors that influence whether a particular piece of behaviour by a person will attract an internal or external attribution?

Chapter 5 Attitudes and Emotions

After studying this chapter you should be able to:

- define attitudes, distinguish between attitudes, beliefs and values, and describe the three components of an attitude

- explain the functions of attitudes, describe factors that influence their formation and discuss the principles of attitude change

- explain the association between attitudes and behaviour, define the conditions under which attitudes are good predictors of behaviour, and discuss the nature of the work-related attitudes of job satisfaction and organisational commitment

- define emotions, distinguish between emotions and moods, and, in outline, describe the stages of the emotion process

- explain the significance of the psychological contract for the occurrence of emotional issues in the work situation

- explain the role of factors that can moderate the effects of emotions

INTRODUCTION

This chapter deals with two further ways in which people can differ as individuals: their attitudes and their emotions. We all have attitudes of some sort and, since our actions towards objects and people are influenced by how positively or negatively we feel about them, attitudes affect our behaviour. To consider these matters, the chapter commences by distinguishing between attitudes and two associated constructs: beliefs and values. Attitudes are then discussed further and their components described. Discussion then turns to the functions of attitudes, how they are formed, and the link between attitudes and behaviour, and this is followed by a consideration of attitude change. Techniques of attitude measurement are briefly described and, to close, two important work-related attitudes are discussed: job satisfaction and organisational commitment.

The next topic to be considered is human emotion. Emotions are defined and, to trace the onset of an emotion episode, a working model of the emotion process is given. The first stage in this model is the occurrence of an event that elicits the emotion. People, in a work situation, tend to have expectations about how they will be treated by other people, and to explain how this can result in a situation in which emotions come to the fore, an explanation of the psychological contract is given. This is followed by a description of the internal dynamics of the emotion process, and the chapter closes with a short summary of its contents.

ATTITUDES

Associated Constructs

To avoid confusion in the remainder of the chapter, it is important to explain something of two associated constructs that have an important role in the formation of attitudes. These are beliefs and values.

Beliefs

Beliefs: assumptions that something exists and that it has certain characteristics

Beliefs are assumptions about the probability that some object or event exists, that it has certain characteristics or that it is related in certain ways to other objects or events; for example, that there is such a thing as the sky and that it is blue, or that there is a God, who is all-powerful. Importantly, because beliefs do not involve an emotional reaction to the object, they do not determine behaviour, but merely indicate what the holder of the belief thinks is true.

Values

Values: what a person wants to be true

Values on the other hand tell us what we want to be true. They are not concerned with a desire for objects, but whether objects are considered desirable. Thus they have a strong judgemental element and this acts as a benchmark of desirability (George and Jones 1997). The most important thing to note is that, whereas beliefs have little direct influence on behaviour, values always have a behaviourial impact.

Attitudes Defined

Attitudes: a mental state of readiness, organised through experience to behave in a characteristic way towards the object of the attitude

In addition to beliefs and values, people also have positive or negative feelings about objects. These are their *attitudes* and, for the purposes of discussion, an attitude is defined as:

> **a mental and neural state of readiness, organised through experience, exerting a directive or dynamic influence upon the individual's response to all objects and situations with which it is related.**   **(Allport 1954a, p 45)**

Several important implications flow from this definition:

- attitudes are held towards something specific that is part of the world of the attitude holder, for example, a job, another person or an organisation
- they reflect the attitude holder's experience, feelings and evaluation of that aspect of his or her world, for instance liking or disliking the job
- to a large extent they are learned from experience, are relatively enduring, and since they involve feeling and evaluation, they have a bearing on how the individual reacts to the object
- because attitudes involve mental processes, they are not tangible objects that can be observed directly; their existence can only be inferred.

Cognitive component: the perceptions and beliefs about an attitude object

An attitude can be thought of as the combined effect of a belief and a value, which gives a feeling about a particular object. This forms the basis of a very powerful theory that links attitudes and behaviour, which will be described later. Current theories hinge on the idea that an attitude has the three basic components, given below (Breckler 1984). All three are related, and the more they are consistent with each other the more stable is the attitude.

Affective component: emotional feelings (likes or dislikes) about the attitude object

The *cognitive component* consists of our thoughts, perceptions, beliefs and evaluations about an attitude object. For example, it could result in us having a positive attitude towards the policies of a particular political party, because we believe that these will result in a better-ordered society.

The *affective component* gives an emotional or feeling aspect to the attitude, which results in an object being liked or disliked – in the example of the political party, whether we feel a warmth or liking for it.

Behaviourial component: the tendency to act towards the attitude object in a consistent and characteristic way

The *behaviourial component* refers to the tendency to act towards the object in a consistent and characteristic way; for instance in the case of the political party, to cast a vote in its favour, or to work actively on its behalf.

THE FUNCTIONS OF ATTITUDES

Functional approach: the assumption that attitudes are held because they serve a useful purpose for the holder

Unlike other individual differences, which have some genetic component, attitudes are man-made, and attitude theory adopts a distinctly *functional approach*, which assumes that attitudes serve a useful purpose for the attitude holder. The most widely used framework for expressing this idea is the one developed by Katz (1960), which identifies four functions served by attitudes.

The Adjustment Function

Adjustment function: helps the person adjust to his or her world

The *adjustment function* is sometimes referred to as the instrumental or utilitarian function, because it helps the individual to adjust to the realities of his or her world.

It explains, for example, why most people have positive attitudes to objects they experience as rewarding and negative attitudes towards punishing objects.

The Ego-defensive Function

Ego-defensive function: helps the person to defend his or her self-image

The *ego-defensive function* helps people to defend their self-image, which explains why individuals who feel that their abilities are unrecognised sometimes develop positive attitudes towards status symbols to bolster their self-image.

The Value-expressive Function

Value-expressive function: allows the person to derive satisfaction from expressing attitudes that reflect his or her central values

The *value-expressive function* allows people to derive satisfaction from expressing attitudes that reflect their central values and concept of self, and this goes much deeper than the two previous functions. For example, it allows them to express to the world that they are what they believe themselves to be.

The Knowledge Function

Knowledge function: helps the person mentally to structure and organise his or her world so that it is more understandable

Katz points out that most people want to be able to understand events that impinge on them, and the *knowledge function* helps them to do this, by organising and structuring their worlds, so that they are more understandable. For example, managers and union officials often express negative attitudes towards each other: the union official because he is wary of managers who might try to withdraw hard-won concessions; and managers because they are wary of union officials who try to extract new concessions. Although their attitudes are probably stereotyped to some extent, they enable them to cast the other person in an anticipated role, and thus help them both make sense of the task in hand.

ATTITUDE FORMATION

Attitudes take shape as part of our mental and emotional development, and they result from our experience of life. This means that there are a number of potential sources from which we derive our attitudes, the most prominent of which are given below.

Direct Experience

There is a saying 'that only fools fail to learn from their experiences'. Thus, peoples' direct experiences of objects and events are the most easily understood sources of their attitudes. Indeed, we usually have much more confidence in opinions we form in this way, than in those that we gain from hearsay or second-hand information (Fazio and Zanna 1978).

Exposure to Objects

Because familiarity gives a degree of assumed predictability, most of us are more positively disposed towards familiar objects or events than towards those that are unfamiliar (Moreland and Zajonc 1979). However, this usually has a somewhat weaker effect than direct experience.

Socialisation and Social Learning

Many of our basic values and beliefs are acquired during our upbringing (Halaby 2003). Since beliefs and values are the basic building blocks of attitudes (Fishbein and Ajzen 1975), it is not surprising that they can have potent effects later in our lives. For instance, someone brought up to condemn swearing and bad language might have real difficulties in adjusting to life on the shop floor of a factory, where these things can be commonplace.

Self-image

This usually has an indirect but powerful influence on our attitudes. As noted above, one of the prime functions of an attitude is to give a measure of protection from information that potentially threatens our concept of self (Katz 1960) and, to protect our egos, we sometimes develop attitudes that legitimise behaviour that seemingly contradicts our values. For instance, some males feel that women are inferior to men and, to justify discriminating against them for promotion, rationalise an attitude of 'women have a lot of good qualities, but not those necessary to make a good manager'.

Value-expression

In some respects, this is the reverse of self-image. Instead of developing attitudes that shield us from the true nature of our values and beliefs, we sometimes need to give open expression to our core values (Katz 1960). Academics, for example, place a high value on advancing knowledge through scholarship. Thus they tend to develop positive attitudes towards reasoned argument and rigorous testing through empirical investigation, which become benchmarks for evaluating the work of colleagues and students.

Cross-cultural Influences on Attitude Formation

The functional approach tells us that we develop attitudes because it is convenient for us to do so; largely because it helps us to cope with events on a day-to-day basis. Moreover, the attitudes that we develop are strongly influenced by direct exposure to objects and the socialisation process, which tells us what to regard as normal and acceptable in our environment.

These are extremely powerful forces that have a huge influence on the attitudes that we come to hold. However, because different societies have different ingrained value systems, we should not expect people in all countries to have similarly positive or negative attitudes towards the same thing. For example, in some countries people will be brought up to be highly deferential to authority figures and elsewhere it could be far less culturally acceptable for people to behave in this way.

Another way in which culture can have an influence on attitudes is in terms of individuality. In some cultures a very high value is placed on individuality, whereas in others keeping one's individuality in check and being a good, loyal group member is considered to be more praiseworthy. Finally, being highly materialistic is quite acceptable in some cultures, while in others there is a much stronger emphasis on having a stronger and more spiritual aspect to one's character.

Differences such as these can have a very real effect on attitude formation and they can result in people from different cultures reacting to the same organisational circumstances in different ways. Thus, rather than viewing the attitudes of someone from a different cultural background as 'abnormal', we should perhaps expect him or her to have attitudes that are different from our own.

TIME OUT

Try to think of an attitude that you strongly hold. Perhaps the easiest way to do this is to think of two objects (two very similar people, two similar organisations, or two similar situations), the mere thought of which arouses strong feelings of like or dislike on your part. Now identify what it is about the objects that you strongly like or dislike and you will have an approximate idea of your attitude to the object.

Now try to identify how you could have formed this attitude. Was it:

from direct experience of the objects?
from being brought up to like or dislike these objects?
because the object threatens or confirms your concept of self?
because liking or disliking the object allows you to express your central values?

REPLAY

- Attitudes are held towards specific situations and objects (people being a special class of object) and they reflect how the attitude holder experiences and reacts to that part of his or her world.
- While attitudes are related to a person's beliefs and values, they are not the same thing.
- Attitudes are formed as a result of experiences of objects, people and social situations and have three component parts: cognitive, affective and behavioural.
- They also have a number of functional purposes for their holders, all of which relate to the holder's world.
- Attitude formation takes place as part of a person's mental and emotional development, which is affected by his or her direct experience, exposure to objects, socialisation and social learning, development of self-image and the need to express values.

ATTITUDE CHANGE

So far as the holder of an attitude is concerned he or she changes an attitude for much the same reasons that is was formed: because it is useful to do so. Nevertheless, there are many situations in which attempts are made to change the attitudes of an individual or a whole group and this is usually because a manager perceives that the attitudes held by a particular person stand in the way of the manager achieving goals

Consistency principle: that people attempt to maintain consistency between the three components of an attitude: affective, behaviourial, cognitive

or objectives that he or she considers important. In general terms, the prevailing view is that attitude change conforms to the *consistency principle*, in which people strive to maintain a consistency between the affective, behaviourial and cognitive components of their attitudes. In practice, this means that if one of these components changes, it gives rise to feelings of inconsistency between the three components, which leaves a person with two alternatives:

* to reverse the change; or
* change the other components to fall in line.

The best-known example of a consistency theory this type is Festinger's (1957) theory of *cognitive dissonance*, which assumes that consistency is sought between a consciously-held attitude, and the behaviour towards an object. Festinger's basic propositions are:

Cognitive dissonance: the unpleasant mental feeling that arises when behaviour towards an object is not consistent with the attitude towards the object

* if inconsistencies exist between attitude and behaviour, an individual will develop a feeling of dissonance, i.e. that something is not quite correct
* the experience of dissonance is unpleasant and so the person is strongly motivated to remove or avoid it, and the stronger the dissonance the greater the urge to do so
* where dissonance is present, as well as attempting to reduce it, the person will actively try to avoid situations and information that create awareness that dissonance exists.

To give a simple example of how this works, suppose that I am so fond of dogs that I try to make friends with them in the street, but I do this once too often and get badly bitten. Naturally I tend to be more wary in future, but this is inconsistent with my liking for dogs and, to remove inconsistency, my attitude changes, perhaps by rationalising that dogs are nice but also unpredictable. So if I now see a dog in the street, I avoid the inconsistency of liking them but being wary at the same time by crossing over to the other side of the road.

The consistency principle underpins most serious attempts to change attitudes and, as noted earlier, in organisations there are many occasions when attitude change is considered desirable; often as part of a change initiative. Organisational change is covered in detail in Chapter 21 and here it is sufficient to note that most attitude change initiatives rely on techniques of persuasion to create dissonance, in the belief that that if dissonance occurs, behaviourial change will follow. For this reason, it is important to examine factors that influence the effectiveness of the persuasive process.

The Source of the Message

This has a huge impact on the persuasive process. Credible sources – those that we admire, respect and trust – are much more influential than those that lack credibility. Thus, in organisations, it is clearly advantageous if managers who convey these messages have a high degree of credibility, perhaps because their expertise is highly regarded by subordinates. However, it must be remembered that persuasion can be seriously undermined if a manager is not trusted, or the person's motives are suspect.

The Nature of the Message

If a message is perceived to be balanced and unbiased, it reinforces the sender's credibility, because he or she is seen to be someone who does not underrate the intelligence of the audience (Murphy and Davey 2002) but, where the message is seen to be biased and one-sided, the reverse is often the case. In addition, the evidence suggests that because it arouses strong emotions that stiffen defences to the message, attempts to use fear can be counter-productive (Janis and Feshback 1953).

The Recipients

People vary in their receptiveness to persuasive arguments: those low in self-esteem seem to be highly susceptible to persuasive messages, while those who hold stronger attitude positions tend to have a great deal of resistance. Any discrepancy between a person's current attitude position and the one advocated by the message can also have an effect. A small difference will often mean that the message is interpreted as concordant with the person's current attitudes, but where the difference is wide the recipient can exaggerate the gap even more, which reduces the credibility of the source.

The Boomerang Effect

An attempt to change attitudes can sometimes result in a change that is opposite to the one desired. One explanation is that where people are confronted by a message that threatens their personal freedom, they become aroused to take steps to maintain the freedom (Brehm 1972). Therefore, if the persuasiveness of the message is low compared to the importance of the freedom, the person is likely to do the reverse of what has been requested. This also explains why attempts to change attitudes that are central to a person's concept of self are often met with a fierce reassertion of individuality and strong resistance to change (see OB in Action Box below). Nobody likes to feel easily manipulated, and if a great deal of visible pressure is put on us to change our attitudes we are likely to exert pressure in return, perhaps by doing the opposite (Heller *et al.* 1973).

The possibility of a boomerang effect, which can include increased antagonism towards the source of the message, raises the question of whether attitude change should be attempted, or even whether it is possible. Although persuasive messages might prompt people to think about their attitudes, they are only changed if there is a good reason to do so. Ultimately, the only person who can change an attitude is the attitude holder, and this seldom happens because artful manipulation or quick-fix communication exercises have been used.

ATTITUDES AND BEHAVIOUR

The most extensive exploration of the link between attitudes and behaviour is given in a theory developed by Fishbein and Ajzen (1975), which summarises matters in the general equation:

$$A_o = \sum_{i=1}^{n} b_i e_i \quad \text{where:} \quad \begin{aligned} &A_o \quad \text{is the attitude towards some object 'o'} \\ &b_i \quad \text{is the belief that i is an attribute of 'o'} \\ &e_i \quad \text{is the evaluation of attribute i} \\ &n \quad \text{is the number of beliefs about 'o'} \end{aligned}$$

In essence, this equation simply means that an attitude is the sum of the positive and negative feelings about the different attributes of an object. To give an example, suppose that we want to identify an individual's attitude towards cars and determine that he has five identifiable beliefs about them, i.e. that cars:

- are a convenient means of personal transport
- pollute the air
- are dangerous
- are costly
- make their owners lazy

Since it is unlikely that the person believes that all of these attributes are equally true, a subjective probability of something between 0 (untrue) and 1 (true) can be placed against each one. In terms of evaluations, 'e' represents the general goodness or badness of an attribute, which is usually estimated as somewhere between +3 (good) and −3 (bad). This gives us the attitude shown in Table 5.1, which overall is a weak negative attitude.

Table 5.1 Calculation of attitudes to cars

Beliefs that cars are:	'b' subjective probability that belief is true	'e' goodness or badness of attribute	b × e
Convenient	0.9	+3	2.7
Pollutants	0.7	−2	−1.4
Dangerous	0.5	−1	−0.5
Costly	0.6	−1	−0.6
Make owners lazy	0.3	−2	−0.6
		Total	−0.4

TIME OUT

Think about the experience of your life at college or university. Using the Fishbein and Ajzen method illustrated above, do the following:

1. Set down your beliefs about university life and estimate your subjective probabilities that these are true.
2. Set down the goodness or badness of each one of these beliefs.
3. Now calculate your overall attitude to university life.

Two important points can be noted about this conceptualisation of attitudes:

1. It acknowledges that a person can have positive and negative feelings about an attitude object at the same time. This would have an effect on the behavioural outcome of the attitude (a point that will be explained shortly).

2. To obtain an accurate picture of a person's attitude to an object, it is also necessary to know a person's most important beliefs about the object, and these are bound to vary in some degree between individuals. For instance, I might consider the most important attribute of cars is their convenience, while someone else could view their polluting effect as the most important attribute. This clearly has strong implications for constructing measures of attitudes that can be applied to a wide number of people.

The Fishbein and Ajzen theory has found its most significant use in tracing the link between attitudes and behaviour. This was originally expressed as the theory of behaviourial intentions, but more recently has emerged as the revised theory of 'planned behaviour' (Ajzen 1991), a diagrammatic representation of which is given in Figure 5.1.

The main idea underpinning the model is that behaviour is more predictable if we focus on the specific behaviourial intentions rather than attitudes in isolation. In general terms, a positive attitude results in a predisposition to behave towards an object in a positive way, while a negative attitude gives a predisposition to behave negatively. This is shown in the model as the **attitude to the behaviour**, which broadly corresponds to the person's predisposition to behave towards the attitude object in a particular way. However, this attitude is influenced by **beliefs about the outcome of the behaviour**; that is, people tend to feel more positive about acting in a way that they believe will help them achieve their goals, and are negatively disposed towards acting in a way that blocks goal achievement (Rosenberg 1960). Thus, the stronger is the attitude, the stronger the intention to behave in a certain way. Nevertheless, peoples' intentions can also be strongly affected by **subjective norms**: the socially-accepted rules of behaviour within the person's group or context. If these conflict with the attitude to the behaviour, the intention to behave in the way it suggests will be weakened, but where the norms support the attitude the behaviourial intention is strengthened. Similarly,

Figure 5.1 The theory of planned behaviour (adapted from Ajzen 1988)

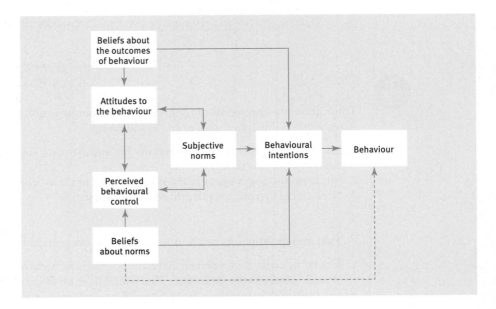

a person's actions are influenced by his or her degree of **perceived behaviourial control**. This is a subjective estimate of how easy or difficult it will be to behave in a particular way, which arises from past experience and also reflects a view of current impediments or obstacles to behaving as intended (Orbell 2003). As can be seen, this is also influenced by **beliefs about norms,** which reflect the person's perceptions of how other people expect him or her to behave – a very powerful set of constraints on most people.

All these variables interact and, where they support acting in a certain way, the stronger is the intention to do so and, the greater is the probability that this way of behaving will be selected. Conversely, where norms and perceived control work in opposition to attitudes, intentions are weakened and the tendency to act in a certain way is reduced.

Using the theory, it is possible to state general propositions about the strength of the attitude–behaviour link.

- **Attitudes to an object do not predict behaviour as well as they predict the intention to behave in a certain way towards it**

- **General attitudes will seldom predict specific behaviours accurately** Since people can have negative and positive feelings about an object at the same time, behaviour depends on which belief is uppermost in a person's mind at the time. For instance, a negative attitude towards cars could result in a resolve to use the car as little as possible, but, if someone gets out of bed late one morning, a belief in the convenience of cars will probably take over, and the car will be used.

- **Attitudes only predict behaviour where the situation does not limit the freedom to behave as the attitude indicates** For example, someone who has a highly unfavourable view of a work colleague, but also knows that the boss has a high regard for this person, will probably keeps his or her mouth shut.

- **Un-activated attitudes can remain latent** Until confronted with the object of an attitude, the attitude probably remains at a subconscious level. For instance, a person could have a strong attitude about racial or sexual discrimination, but if he or she works in an environment where there is no discrimination, the person may not even be aware of holding the attitude.

The theory of planned behaviour has been extensively tested in empirical studies, which has revealed that it is capable of predicting a wide range of intentions and behaviour (Conner and Armitage 1998; Sheeran *et al.* 2003; Webb and Sheeran 2006; Fife-Schaw *et al.* 2007). However, current work in the area mostly focuses on refining the model. For example, Armitage and Conner (1999) suggest that *self-efficacy*, which can broadly be described as a person's belief in his or her ability to act in a certain way (see discussion in Chapter 10), is a readily available way of evaluating a person's 'perceived behavioural control'. In addition, Terry *et al.* (1999) suggest that the 'subjective norms' variable in the model needs to take account of self-identity, because the behaviour of some people is much more strongly influenced by their own self-images, than the views of their peers.

The great value of a theory such as this, is that if it is applied carefully to tap people's attitudes, it gives a useful way of predicting how they will behave. Thus the theory finds widespread application in certain aspects of organisational life, such as market research and employee opinion surveys. For this reason it is necessary to explain something of how attitudes can be measured, which is covered next.

Self-efficacy: a person's belief in his or her ability to act in a certain way

ATTITUDE MEASUREMENT

Since attitudes play an important part in explaining behaviour, a great deal of time and effort has been devoted to developing ways of measuring them. While this could be done by simply asking someone a question, this is seldom reliable because single questions tell us very little about the strength of an attitude. The usual way to resolve this is to develop a multiple-item, pencil-and-paper test that attitude holders complete themselves, which gives a scale that reflects the strength of the attitude. The most widely used scaling technique used at present is the Likert scale, which is briefly described next.

Likert Scales

This method (Likert 1932) is very widely used and results in a usable scale that requires considerably less development time and effort than earlier methods. Space precludes an extensive description of the methods used to design scales of this type but, for those who wish to know more, suggestions are made in the Further Reading section at the end of the chapter.

An example of the first six items of a scale developed by the author to examine attitudes to work for public sector employees is shown in Figure 5.2, and the figures in circles at the top of the scale are the scores used for each column.

Figure 5.2 An example of a Likert scale

SECTION A: VIEWS ON WORK

GIVEN BELOW ARE A NUMBER OF STATEMENTS OF OPINION ABOUT WORK, SOME ARE CONCERNED GENERALLY WITH WHITE-COLLAR WORK – THAT IS SALARIED STAFF OR NON-MANUAL OCCUPATIONS; OTHERS REFER MORE SPECIFICALLY TO FEELINGS THAT COULD EXIST ABOUT DOING A PARTICULAR JOB OR WORKING FOR A SPECIFIC EMPLOYER. PLEASE INDICATE HOW MUCH YOU AGREE WITH EACH ONE BY TICKING THE APPROPRIATE BOX.

	⑤ I definitely agree	④ On balance I agree	③ Neither agree nor disagree	② On balance I disagree	① I strongly disagree
1. I would always want to stay in the white-collar field because of its better promotion opportunities.					
2. So far as I can see manual jobs are now far better paid than white-collar work.					
3. I would be quite happy to remain in this organisation for the rest of my working life.					
4. Here the only people who get promoted are those who toe the line and don't make waves.					
5. You can't really supervise people in white-collar work too tightly because the jobs vary so much.					
6. Management and supervisors here are very bad at dealing with the people beneath them.					

EMPLOYEE OPINION SURVEYS

Employee opinion surveys are widely used to assess employee attitudes and perceptions about work-related issues (Edwards 1997). For reasons of convenience, speed, economy and ease of analysis the usual way to do this is with pencil-and-paper questionnaires, which are completed by a sample, or even all of a particular workforce. Most questionnaires use the Likert format to tap opinions (see Figure 5.2), and this has the advantage of allowing the person completing the questionnaire to express a degree of agreement or disagreement with the statements.

Where scales of this type are well designed and have been thoroughly pilot tested before use, they are capable of providing a great deal of useful information about employee attitudes. However, there are inherent (but not insurmountable) difficulties in using attitude questionnaires for this purpose. To start with, designing an attitude questionnaire may look simple, but it is full of pitfalls for the unwary. For this reason, organisations often seek expert help, perhaps by importing the services of a consultant occupational psychologist on a temporary basis and, to some extent, this can also help acquire the expertise to interpret the results. Nevertheless, one error that is commonplace even with experts, is the treatment of 'non-responses', that is, people who have been asked to complete the questionnaire but have not done so.

To give an example, suppose that we want to evaluate the levels of job satisfaction and commitment among employees in a firm. Well-validated, published scales are obtainable to tap these attitudes, and this solves the design problem. To obtain a well-rounded picture of these attitudes everybody in the organisation (say 500 people) is given a questionnaire to complete but, despite appeals and reminders, only 300 are completed and returned. This is only 60 per cent of the workforce and in surveys of this type, even lower response rates are commonplace. In order to obtain frank and honest responses to questions, the questionnaire would almost certainly have been designed to protect the anonymity of individuals. Thus there is no way of identifying the people who failed to complete the instrument and we would probably have to accept that a 60 per cent sample is the best we can obtain.

What usually happens in this situation is that an assumption is made that those who failed to respond have broadly similar attitudes to those who did. Thus the 60 per cent of employees whose attitudes we have successfully tapped would be treated as representative of all the employees in the organisation. Problematically, evidence suggests that there is often something very distinctive about people who choose not to take part in an employee opinion survey, particularly where it seeks to tap attitudes such as job satisfaction or commitment. Thus a very misleading picture of attitudes is likely to emerge. This information comes from a study reported by Rogelberg *et al.* (2000), who deliberately set out to compare the attitudes of people who complete an employee survey questionnaire with those who do not. Those who 'opted out' were found to be much lower in all aspects of job satisfaction and commitment to the organisation and, despite any assurances they were given, they had very negative and suspicious beliefs about how the survey data would be used. This raises the possibility that those who do not respond are often disaffected in some way, and that they fail to take part as a way of not cooperating with the organisation. Therefore, an allowance for this needs to be made in any decisions that are based on the survey evidence.

WORK-RELATED ATTITUDES

There are many work-related attitudes that could be of interest to an organisation. While some are highly specific, for example attitudes towards a particular process or a technology, there is usually more interest in generalised attitude patterns, two of which – job satisfaction and organisational commitment – are explored here.

Job Satisfaction

Job satisfaction can be defined as:

> **a pleasurable or positive emotional state resulting from the appraisal of one's job or job experience.** (Locke 1976, p 1300)

For many years this was viewed as a single, unified concept (i.e. general job satisfaction). These days, however, it is widely recognised that it comprises a more complex cluster of attitudes towards different aspects of a job, which arise from a person's expectations of work and his or her actual experiences (Clark 1996). Since people differ widely in what they expect, this is likely to be a highly individualised attitude cluster, but research suggests that it has five major dimensions, all of which reflect affective responses to particular job aspects.

Job satisfaction: a pleasurable or positive emotional state resulting from a person's appraisal of his or her job or job experience

The Antecedents of Job Satisfaction

The Work Itself

This reflects the match between expectations and experience in terms of whether the job provides interesting tasks, a measure of responsibility and opportunities for learning. To the extent that there is a good match, this aspect of the job is likely to be rated positively.

Pay

There seem to be two connections between pay and satisfaction; first, whether the financial reward for a job is regarded as adequate; and, second, whether it is considered to be equitable compared to what other people receive. However, although most people need a certain minimum level of income on which to live, the relationship between pay and satisfaction is a very complex one. To some people pay is a reflection of how much their efforts are recognised, which means that it has an intrinsic component as well as the purely extrinsic effect of cash in hand. In addition, many other rewards have a financial equivalent, for example fringe benefits such as medical insurance and pensions.

Promotion

To some extent this speaks for itself and reflects the perceived possibility of an increase in status. However, promotion is not desired by everybody, and so satisfaction in this respect is very strongly influenced by the match between expectations and receipts. Indeed, since promotion usually brings an increase in pay, for some people this is the major satisfaction it provides, while for others it is more connected with self-image and ego.

Supervision

This dimension reflects the extent to which a person derives satisfaction from the relationship with his or her immediate superior. As will be explained in Chapters 12 and 13, satisfaction with supervision is usually connected to two aspects of supervisor behaviour:

- **interpersonal support**   the supervisor's interest in the person's welfare
- **technical support**   the extent to which the supervisor provides technical and task-related help and guidance.

Again satisfaction tends to be a highly personalised matter and not everybody welcomes a close personal interest. Indeed, some people interpret this as a sign that the supervisor has a lack of trust in their work.

Co-workers

Satisfaction in this respect has similar effects to supervision and reflects the extent that members of an individual's workgroup are perceived to be socially supportive and competent in their own tasks. Once again, this can acutely depend on the match between expectations and receipts. While most people find group membership is psychologically rewarding, they also vary in their sociability and the need for peer support.

The Outcomes of Job Satisfaction

The interest in job satisfaction dates from **human relations theory**, a basic assumption of which is that a satisfied worker is automatically an effective and productive one. However, since the relationship between job satisfaction and performance is now acknowledged to be much more complex (Staw and Barsade 1993), it is important to examine what the research evidence tells us about the potential effects of satisfaction.

Employee Turnover

There is convincing evidence that where job satisfaction is high, labour turnover is reduced (Tett and Meyer 1993). However, because there are many other things that affect turnover, it is unwise to draw a conclusion that this is a direct relationship. For instance, the longer a person stays with a firm, the greater is the wrench involved in leaving and in a recession, when jobs are harder to find, people tend to stay where they are. Therefore job satisfaction is probably one of those experiences of work that make it less likely that someone will think about leaving, even if there are available opportunities. However, if it is absent and the opportunities to quit are there, turnover could well increase.

Employee Absenteeism

The effects of satisfaction on absenteeism seem to be much stronger. When job satisfaction falls absenteeism tends to rise (Steel and Rentsch 1995), and since absenteeism is an alternative to leaving when the possibility of finding a suitable job elsewhere is low, this is understandable. As such, satisfaction probably has a similar influence on absenteeism as that which it has on quitting.

Employee Productivity

There has long been a debate about whether satisfaction leads to high performance. The idea that it does has a great deal of intuitive appeal to managers, because it implies that rewards play a relatively minor part in obtaining productivity. However, a review of a large number of studies indicates that, if a relationship exists at all, it is a rather weak one (Iffaldano and Muchinsky 1985). What seems more likely is that rewards have a far more important effect on productivity than was once thought, and that satisfaction only has a mediating role; that is, rewards result in satisfaction, which then leads to greater effort (Podsakoff and Williams 1986). It should also be noted that there is an ongoing but as yet unresolved debate about whether satisfaction leads to good performance, or whether good performance leads to satisfaction.

Organisational Commitment

Organisational commitment: an attitude towards the organisation as a whole, reflecting the individual's acceptance of its goals and values, his or her willingness to expend effort on its behalf and an intention to remain with the organisation

Whereas job satisfaction refers to attitudes to specific aspects of a job, *organisational commitment* is normally regarded as a global attitude to the organisation as a whole. Nevertheless, there is a connection between the two concepts in that people who have job satisfaction are often found to have higher levels of commitment (Eaton 2003; Mulinge 2001). The original definition of commitment was set out by Mowday *et al.* (1979) as 'the relative strength of an individual's identification with and involvement in an organisation', manifested in three specific ways:

- belief in and acceptance of the goals and values of the organisation
- willingness to exert effort on behalf of the organisation
- desire to maintain membership in the organisation.

These days, however, a more recent refinement of the concept by Allen and Meyer (1990) is used, which distinguishes between three different aspects of commitment:

Affective Commitment: a person's emotional attachment to the organisation.
Continuance Commitment: a person's perception of the costs and risks associated with leaving the organisation, which breaks down into two aspects (the personal sacrifice that leaving would entail, and the lack of alternatives available to the person).
Normative Commitment: a moral dimension based on the person's felt obligation and responsibility to the employer.

These three forms of commitment have received strong support from the empirical work of Dunham *et al.* (1994) and Blau and Holladay (2006). Interestingly, it can be noted that these three dimensions correspond very closely to the three components of an attitude (*cognitive, affective* and *behaviourial*) that were given earlier.

While there is no hard evidence to support the contention, the outcomes of commitment are widely assumed to be the same as for job satisfaction: increased employee effort and lowered tendencies to undesirable behaviour such as absenteeism and quitting (Mathieu and Zanjoc 1990). However, it should also be noted that the whole concept of commitment has attracted a great deal of criticism in recent years; largely because in the way that it is conceived of by managers, it turns out to be a very one-sided affair. That is, what employers seem to mean when they use the word commitment is employees who are totally committed to an organisation to the extent that they are willing to be exploited and cast aside as soon as they have served a useful purpose (Hirsh *et al.* 1995). Indeed, there is some confusion about how and why employees would want to engage in a committed relationship with an employer. The current view is that if such a relationship emerges at all, it would emerge from a process of social exchange (Morris *et al.* 1993) and, to illustrate this, imagine that you have just joined an organisation. In all probability your subjective feelings about your future relationship with it will be something like the following:

- I expect that the relationship will result in rewards for myself, specifically something near to the combination of intrinsic and extrinsic rewards that I desire.
- In return I expect that the relationship will cost me something in terms of the effort I expend and the inconvenience of not having complete freedom of choice over what I do.
- This gives me a ratio of costs to benefits, and so long as my benefits at least equal my costs the exchange will be a fair one.
- If this ratio is maintained in the future, the organisation is being fair with me and I will be fair in return.

TIME OUT

Using the four statements of subjective feelings about a social exchange relationship given above apply them to the relationship between yourself and the organisation you work for. If you have no direct experience of paid employment, complete the exercise for the relationship between you and your college or university.

1. What rewards do you expect to obtain from the relationship, i.e. how do you expect to be treated?
2. What costs do you expect to incur to obtain these rewards, i.e. how do you expect to treat the organisation?

These expectations give rise to three crucial points about any future relationship:

- unless people feel that there is some commitment to satisfying their needs and meeting their expectations, they are unlikely to be committed in return
- where commitment exists, it is because it has grown out of the relationship and is only likely to be obtained if steps have been taken to win this attachment from an employee; for this reason it would be impossible to select new entrants in advance, who are already committed
- perhaps most important of all, it is doubtful whether sentiments of this type are held towards an organisation as a whole and it is much more likely that, in time, people could develop these feelings about the immediate context in which they work. Thus any commitment (if it exists) will be expressed towards departments and sub-units, rather than a whole organisation (Becker *et al.* 1996; Cohen 2000; Belanger *et al.* 2003).

Taken together, these points lead to the inevitable conclusion that there are two huge paradoxes in current management thinking about employee commitment. The first of these revolves around the management assumption that commitment consists solely of something that employees give to the organisation. As can be seen, this is only one side of the exchange, and something has to be given in return. The second is connected with the part that commitment can play in formulating human resource strategies (Iverson and Buttigieg 1999; Wood and Albanese 1995). These days it is widely assumed that in the light of the fast-moving business environment it is desirable, if not essential, to have committed employees, because commitment results in creativity and flexibility. However, flexibility and creativity tend to be products of the diversity of views and perspectives that arise in different organisational sub-units. Problematically however, managers tend to view it as something that is given to the organisation as a whole, but as noted above, it is unlikely that people are committed to the whole organisation; if anything, they are committed to their immediate workgroups.

This almost certainly means that there is a great deal of extremely muddled thinking about commitment. While it is easy to see why the concept appeals to managers, commitment is not an attitude that people bring into the organisation when they join. It is something that they acquire from their experience of the exchange between organisation and employee, and this begs the question of whether employee commitment can be managed. One argument is that commitment, like any other attitude, is amenable to change, which, as was explained earlier, is normally attempted by communication initiatives. However, because it actually arises out of what is exchanged, rather than what is said, it is unlikely to be an attitude that is amenable to easy modification using persuasive communication. Indeed, as Guest (1992) notes, the very idea of managing commitment is based on the assumption that employees are passive recipients of a manager's attempts to manipulate their feelings. Needless to say they are not, and they almost certainly resent being told what to think.

REPLAY

- Theories of attitude change are usually based on the assumption that people strive to maintain consistency between the three components of an attitude, and methods of attempting to bring about change usually rely on creating inconsistency by using techniques of persuasive communication.

- While attitudes have a strong impact on the intention to behave in a characteristic and consistent way towards an attitude object, the existence of an attitude is not an infallible guide to the behaviour that will occur.

- Attitudes are usually measured by the use of self-administered, multiple-item attitude scales, the most commonly used technique being the Likert scale.

- Because of the behaviourial implications of attitudes, work-related attitudes are of some interest to managers in organisations and the two that are currently of greatest interest are job satisfaction and organisational commitment.

EMOTIONS

The topic of emotions is a comparatively recent addition to Organisational Behaviour and Analysis; a rather belated development if we stop to consider that psychology has long acknowledged the influence of emotions as a strong driving force in human behaviour. Nevertheless, emotions are now firmly on the OB agenda and, as a first step, consider the OB in Action Box below.

 OB IN ACTION: New hope for the addicted?

A brain lesion could possibly cure a person of bad habits, according to a new study that appears in this week's issue of the journal *Science*. Researchers have found that smokers with a damaged insula – a region in the brain associated with emotion and feelings – are able to quit smoking easily, although nobody knows exactly why. The study is the first of its kind to use brain lesions to examine a drug addiction in humans.

According to scientists at the Brain and Creativity Institute at the University of Southern California, who conducted the study, the findings raise the question of whether damage to the insula could cause a person to quit other addictive behaviours, such as alcohol abuse and overeating.

The discovery of the insula's role in addiction could also open new directions for therapies, according to Antoine Bechara, one of the authors of the study. There is a lot of potential for pharmacological developments, he said, adding that any treatment would need to preserve the beneficial functions of the insula. But Bechara noted that the region appeared to be involved, especially in learned behaviours as opposed to the basic drives necessary for survival. As a result, it might be possible to aim at one without disturbing the other.

Source:

Knight, R (2007) *Financial Times*, 26 January

 ## TIME OUT

Carefully examine the OB in Action Box above. What would be your likely emotional reactions if you were invited to have brain surgery, albeit minor surgery, to enable you to give up smoking?

EMOTIONS: TOWARDS A DEFINITION

As with many other constructs in psychology, emotions can be hard to define. However, Lazurus (1991) defines an emotion as 'an affective experience that unfolds over a short period of time', and Parkinson (1995) gives some indication of what could be involved in the unfolding of an emotion by noting that four sub-processes seem to be at work: *cognitive appraisal of a situation*; *a change in the individual's action tendencies*; *physical reactions, such as heart rate, pulse, etc.*; and *expressive changes such as facial expression, posture, etc.* Note, however, that while some of these could occur almost immediately, it is by no means certain that they all appear together. With this in mind and for the purposes of this chapter, an *emotion* is defined as:

> **a specific affective experience which is relatively intense and of short duration that occurs in response to a particular event.**

It is also important to point out that an emotion is not the same thing as a mood, which is an allied construct that is more indicative of what we could broadly categorise as a 'state of mind'. To this end, Parkinson (1996) distinguishes between moods and emotions in terms of the six characteristics shown in Table 5.2.

Emotion: a specific affective experience which is relatively intense and of short duration that occurs in response to a particular event

Table 5.2 Moods compared to emotions

	Mood	Emotion
Duration	Long-term impact on the individual	Short-term impact
Onset period	Slow	Rapid
Intensity	Weak	Strong
Antecedents	General causality	Usually caused by a specific event
Function	Not situation specific	Situation specific
Directness	Not usually focused on a specific object	Focused on a specific object

THE EMOTION PROCESS: A WORKING MODEL

Emotions are highly idiosyncratic and so an event that evokes an emotional episode in one person might have no apparent effect in someone else. Moreover, even where an emotional reaction occurs, some people can be remarkably adept at concealing the visibility of their emotions, and for this reason it is necessary to describe the emotion process in a very general way. To structure the discussion, the process is portrayed in Figure 5.3 as one that has three main stages, which in outline are:

- an event occurs which evokes the emotion
- the development of the emotion leading to it being experienced by an individual
- further mental processing, in which moderators can affect the way in which the emotion is expressed.

Before discussing the model, a word of warning is necessary. The problem with compartmentalised models, such as this, is that they can convey the impression that the

Figure 5.3 A working model of the emotion process

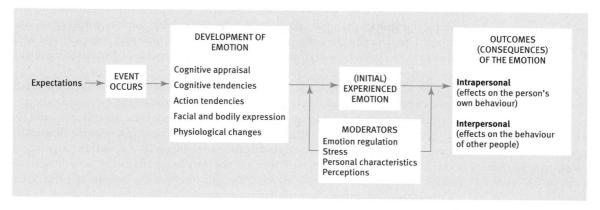

emotion process is a long, drawn-out affair, whereas the whole process can unfold fairly rapidly. Strictly speaking, the first stage consists of an event that evokes the emotion but, in organisations, there are factors at work which have occurred before the event and these give rise to expectations that are likely to play a part in shaping the nature of the emotion that arises.

Expectations and the Event

Two highly important characteristics of humans are that they:

- they have a sense of self
- hold expectations about the way they will be treated by others in their social milieu.

Therefore, since the event that evokes an emotion is often concerned with the actions of other people, there is almost always a social dimension to emotions that arise in a work situation (Manstead 2005). A useful concept for exploring the role of these expectations and events in the emotion process is that of the 'psychological contract', which is considered next.

The Psychological Contract

The expression 'psychological contract' has its roots in a branch of social psychology known as 'social exchange theory' (Blau 1964). The concept of the psychological contract can be traced to ideas put forward by Argyris (1960). It was later articulated in a more explicit way by Schein (1980) and more recently, there has been a significant reawakening of interest in these ideas (Guest and Conway 2002; Rousseau and Parks 1993). Space precludes an extensive explanation of this work, but the first thing we should note is that the psychological contract, or rather breaches of it, have a strong potential to give rise to emotional reactions.

Schein draws attention to the point that there are three types of contract at work in the employment relationship. The *formal contract*, largely reflects the economic aspects of the exchange, which are normally embraced by the legal conception of a contract of employment. In addition there is always an *informal contract*, some of

Formal contract: the formally agreed terms of the employment relationship, i.e. the legal concept as reflected in the 'contract of employment'

Informal contract: a less formal expression of the employment relationship, which reflects a degree of give and take between the parties the components of which are derived from wider social norms about how people should treat each other, while others are more specific to a particular organisation; for example, how much give and take there will be about things such as timekeeping and working late. Usually the contents of both formal and informal contracts are well understood by employer and employees, who are quite capable of discussing the terms in an open way.

Psychological contract: an (unvoiced) set of expectations that the parties have of each other and obligations that they feel towards each other

The third type of contract, the *psychological contract*, has contents that are seldom, if ever, explicitly stated or discussed. These largely consist of the unvoiced expectations that a party to the employment relationship holds of the organisation and its managers, together with the obligations that he/she feels in return towards the organisation. Since these expectations and obligations are unvoiced and neither party might be consciously aware of them until they are not met, its details can be very difficult to specify. Nevertheless, some idea of what it might embrace can be seen in Table 5.3.

Importantly, all three contracts have an impact on the nature and shape of the relationship between an employer and employees. For the relationship to come into existence the formal contract has to be seen by both parties as acceptable. By putting in place convenient variations through which the parties accommodate to each other, the informal contract then acts as a lubricant to the formal one. Finally, the psychological contract goes to the very heart of the exchange by expressing emotional aspects of the relationship such as fairness and trust. Should either party perceive that the other one is failing to honour his or her part of the implied bargain, it is likely that a *breach of contract* will be perceived to exist, and in these circumstances the exchange is likely to be seen as unequal and weighted in favour of the other party. Since nobody likes to feel that they are being cheated, there can be strong emotional reactions to this perceived breach, and these include feelings of betrayal, anger, and wrongful treatment because a highly salient promise remains unfulfilled. Thus, at the very least, the outcome could be that the relationship will deteriorate, which might mean, for example,

Table 5.3 The psychological contract – possible expectations of employees and employers

Employee expectations (of employer)	Employer expectations (of employees)
Working conditions will be safe and as pleasant as possible	Acceptance of the main values of the organisation
Jobs will be interesting and satisfying	Recognition that diligence and conscientiousness in pursuit of objectives are important to the organisation
Reasonable efforts to provide job security	To avoid abusing the trust and goodwill of superiors
Involvement or consultation in decisions that affect them	To have concern for the reputation of the organisation
Equality of opportunity and fairness in selection and promotion	Loyalty and willingness to tolerate a degree of inconvenience for the good of the organisation
Opportunities for personal development and progression	Trustworthiness and honesty
To be treated with consideration and respect	To conform to the accepted norms of behaviour in the organisation
Fair and equitable remuneration	Consideration for others

that the other party will no longer be treated with consideration and, in a severe case, there will probably be no desire for the relationship to continue (Lambert *et al.* 2003).

This is not to say that breaches of the psychological contract will inevitably occur. Nevertheless, it is important to recognise that the work situation is one in which people have expectations that become benchmarks, against which comparisons are made with what actually happens. As such, the whole situation is fertile ground for the occurrence of emotional reactions.

TIME OUT

In an earlier Time Out exercise, on page 145, you were asked to compare your expectations of university in terms of the costs and rewards that you obtain. What similarities do you feel that this has with a psychological contract?

DEVELOPMENT OF THE EMOTION

As can be seen from Figure 5.3, development of the emotion consists of a number of sub-processes, which are described in what follows.

Cognitive Appraisal

When a personally relevant event occurs, the first thing that usually happens is *cognitive appraisal*. In this people evaluate the event and its potential affect on themselves in terms of:

- its causality – is it caused by the circumstances, another person, or self
- its potential consequences – are these threatening, harmful, or benign?

As will be seen later in Chapter 10 (Stress) while cognitive appraisal actually takes place in two stages, it is the first one that has by far the greatest impact on the emotion experienced. For instance, unpleasant events, particularly those perceived to be caused by another person, often elicit the emotion of anger (Roseman 2001). However, whether or not a strong emotion is elicited at this stage depends on other initial responses that occur.

Cognitive Tendencies
These are initial dispositions to process information in certain ways. For example, a potentially hostile event perceived to be caused by another person might prompt the individual to adopt a more jaundiced view of this other person.

Action Tendencies
These are initial dispositions to engage in certain behaviour; for instance, to tackle the person who is perceived to be responsible for the event or, alternatively, to remain cool and collected while waiting for further developments.

Facial and Bodily Expressions
These are initial public displays of increased emotional activity, such as embarrassment, anger or pleasure.

Physiological Changes

These can vary widely from increased heart rate or blood pressure in the case of a potentially threatening event, to elation and smiling to one that is perceived to be rewarding.

Note that while all of these sub-processes can occur together, some of them might take longer to develop and others can actually subside. What eventually happens, however, is that they all come together in a cumulative way, as an emotion that is experienced by the person concerned.

THE OUTCOMES (CONSEQUENCES) OF THE EMOTION

While emotions can manifest themselves in several ways, in terms of their consequences it is important to distinguish between two primary effects: **intrapersonal consequences** (the effects that the emotion has on the individual's own behaviour); and **interpersonal consequences** (the effects that emotional expression has on the behaviour of other people). Clearly, the particular form that an act of emotional expression takes will depend greatly on:

- the importance of the event
- what the person concerned expects to achieve by engaging in a public show of emotion.

Here it is important to recognise that emotions are sometimes made public because of the anticipated impact that a public show will have on the behaviour of other people.

THE MODERATORS OF EMOTION

There is a number of factors that can moderate the effects of emotions, either in terms of how they are experienced or in how they are displayed. In some cases these effects are well documented, but for others the evidence is relatively sparse and is only just beginning to be explored. It should also be noted that while they are all described separately here, some of them are likely to be connected and act in combination.

Emotion Regulation

When discussing the emotion process above it was noted that cognitive tendencies and action tendencies are only *initial dispositions* to either act or think in certain ways, and to some extent the same is true for facial expressions and physiological changes. For this reason, immediate action might never occur, because the emotionally charged person engages in cognitive re-appraisal before anything actually happens. Gross (1999) defines *emotion regulation* as 'a person's efforts to increase, maintain, or decrease one or more of the components of an emotion'. Although this could be something that a person does instinctually, in the light of the way it is defined by Gross (1999) it will be treated here as something that he/she does as a matter of conscious choice.

Theoretically, emotion regulation can occur at any point during the emotion process, e.g. either from early on, when a person is still evaluating the potential effects of

Emotion regulation: a person's efforts to increase, maintain, or decrease one or more of the components of an emotion

an event, to later on, when certain of the physical signs of emotional arousal have already started to appear. A number of scholars such as Gross (1999) and Hochschild (1983) distinguish between two forms of emotion regulation: deep acting and surface acting. *Deep acting* is antecedant-focused and involves manipulating the components of an emotion before it is fully in progress. This is likely to change the way that an emotion is experienced, and also the way it is displayed in public. It might, for example, occur if someone re-evaluated an event as not being threatening after all, which could reduce tendencies to display signs such as fear or dislike. *Surface acting* however, is response-focused. While this still involves attempting to manipulate the components of the emotion, it does not happen until the emotion is well into its development and, although it could result in a change to the public display of emotion, it is unlikely to affect the way the emotion is experienced internally.

It is also important to recognise that there can be two intended directions of emotion regulation. *Emotion amplification* consists of initiating, or enhancing the public display of an emotion. Note, however, that this is not always a concerted attempt to regulate emotions, but can sometimes be used for reasons that are more concerned with impression management (see Chapter 4). The other intended direction is what is known as *emotion suppression*, which consists of trying to reduce or eliminate public displays of emotion; something that can be near impossible with certain emotions.

Combining the two forms of emotion regulation (deep and surface acting) with the two intended directions of regulation (amplification and suppression) gives a 2 × 2 matrix of regulation strategies, which is shown in Figure 5.4.

Deep acting: an antecedent-focused emotion regulation strategy that involves manipulating the components of an emotion before the emotion is fully in progress

Surface acting: a response-focused emotion regulation strategy that involves manipulating the components of an emotion after it is well into its development

TIME OUT

Think carefully about emotion regulation and, in particular, about the four strategies shown in Figure 5.4. In terms of what a person might desire to achieve by emotion regulation, what are the potential strengths and weaknesses of these strategies?

Emotion amplification: initiating or enhancing the public displays of emotion

Emotion suppression: attempts to reduce or eliminate public displays of emotion

There are important implications for the eventual handling of emotional issues contained in Figure 5.4, both for the emotionally charged person and for other people in his or her surroundings. In the top left-hand quadrant, because the person winds-up with more intensely experienced emotions as well as a more public display of them, this is only an appropriate state of affairs if he or she wants to give a public demonstration of his or her indignation, while not wanting to retreat. Thus a successful resolution of the issue will depend on those who have to handle the matter having sufficient sensitivity and willingness to give ground.

In the top right-hand quadrant, while the emotionally charged person avoids experiencing the emotion more intensely, the emotion is more firmly revealed to public view and as far as the rest of the world is concerned, the issue is still a 'live' one. Thus, the person probably needs to make up his or her mind fairly quickly about further steps that could be taken to resolve the matter.

The bottom (left and right) quadrants are probably ones where cognitive reappraisal has resulted in the person feeling, on reflection, that his or her initial stance has subsided. Theoretically, while this means that matters could be left as they are, it would

Figure 5.4
Implications of
emotion regulation

	Timing of emotion regulation	
	Antecedent-focused	Response-focused
Emotion amplification	**DEEP ACTING** Heightens internal experience of emotion and increases public display of emotion	**SURFACE ACTING** Leaves internal experience of emotion untouched but increases public display of emotion
Emotion suppression	**DEEP ACTING** Reduces internal experience of emotion and reduces public display of emotion	**SURFACE ACTING** Reduces public display of emotion but leaves internal experience of emotion untouched

Direction of emotion regulation

probably be far better for the future if the person met with his or her manager to discuss matters.

Organisational Stress Levels

Stress will be considered in detail in a later chapter of the book (Chapter 10). Nevertheless, it can be noted that a frequently cited reason given for the neglect of emotion as a subject is that a great deal of the relevant information is assumed to have been revealed in research on stress (Briner 1999). Here, two important points can be made. First, the signs that stressful conditions are widespread in an organisation can be remarkably similar to those that indicate that its some of its members are confronted with emotional issues. This makes it difficult to identify whether a broader set of organisational conditions are at work (as in stress), or whether an emotional matter that might have a more specific personal cause is in progress. Whichever is the case, it is important to remember that if employees have to cope with conditions that make the organisation inherently more stressful, the resources they have available to handle emotional issues will be depleted.

Second, stress tends to have less immediate effects than emotion. Indeed, stress is something that could have built-up over months or even years, and the conditions responsible could have become progressively more deeply ingrained into the practices and processes of an organisation. This, of course, is no reason why they should be allowed to persist, but by the time stress appears it could mean that the practices have become so 'taken for granted' that nobody questions their existence. This can be a highly important point because, if anything, there is a tendency for inherent stressfulness to increase in many organisations rather than decrease. Moreover, many of the 'stress management' initiatives currently used in organisations seem to be less concerned with eradicating stressful conditions, than attempting to enable employees to function in what will be ever more stressful environments (Cooper and Sadri 1991). A great deal of the blame for this situation can be placed firmly at the feet of organisational job design practices, one of which, in particular, can be expected to give rise to stress or an increased number of emotional issues.

The Emotional Labour Effect

One of the features that we need to recognise about many organisations these days is that there are many jobs in which the incumbent is made responsible for controlling the visible signs of his or her emotional state. While this has always been the case for certain types of employee such as sales staff – i.e. the so-called 'service-with-a-smile' pattern of behaviour – the requirement has now been extended to a far larger number of people. In modern organisations people are now required to be much more flex-ible in the duties they undertake and, in the vastly enlarged service sector, direct contact with customers is more commonplace for almost all employees. An example that can be cited is staff in call centres, where over one million people are employed in Great Britain. In the interests of pacifying what can sometimes be irate customers, people in these jobs are expected to create an impression of being blissfully happy in their work, which has now become a criterion of good performance against which they are appraised and eventually rewarded. Hochschild (1983) has dubbed this situation *emotional labour*, because the employee is expected to manage his or her own feelings and emotions in the interests of somehow persuading the customer to love the product and the enterprise (Bolton 2000). So important has this pattern of behaviour become to employers, that in many cases it has become an explicit job require-ment. Indeed, some employers argue that the job is not being done effectively unless employees display these outward signs.

Problematically, this gives rise to a number of problems for people who are called-on to behave in this way. To start with the design of jobs in customer service occupa-tions and call centres gives a work experience that is highly routine and tedious, which can itself give rise to a situation where emotions can all too easily erupt. Second, people clearly vary in their volatility, to say nothing of their capabilities to 'manage' their emotions should the need arise. Therefore, it is hardly surprising to find that staff turnover in these firms can be as high as 40 per cent each year. Moreover, for those who do not move on, the requirement of having to 'manage' their emotions can become a highly stressful experience, which can ultimately result in 'burnout' due to the emo-tional costs and frustrations of having to live-out their working lives in this way (Grandey *et al.* 2005). Therefore Hochschild (1983) argues that there are a number of associated negative effects on psychological functioning such as depersonalization, emotional numb-ness and difficulties with emotional relationships beyond the work situation.

OVERVIEW AND CONCLUSIONS

Attitudes are patterns of feeling and emotion towards objects, persons, ideas and events that give rise to persistent tendencies to behave in characteristic ways. They have three components (emotional, cognitive and behaviourial) and have positive functions for the attitude holder in that they facilitate adjustment to what people encounter, allow them to define and confirm their own self-images, express their basic values and react

Emotional labour: work in which an employee is required to manage his or her own feelings and emotions in the interests of maintaining a sympathetic and friendly relationship with the customer

to the world in a consistent way. However, while attitudes have some stability over time, they are not infallible guides to a person's behaviour because although an attitude usually gives rise to an intention to behave in a particular way, many other factors can influence actual behaviour. Work-related attitudes are of importance to many organisations and, because they have potential outcomes that could be beneficial, the two that are usually considered the most significant are job satisfaction and organisational commitment.

Emotions, which until recently have been much neglected in Organisational Behaviour, are specific affective experiences to a particular event, which are relatively intense and short-lived. However, they are not the same as moods or dispositions, which are more indicative of a 'state of mind'.

The emotion process usually starts with cognitive appraisal of the event that elicits the emotion, and perceptions of the event can be affected by prior expectations associated with the psychological contract. Other activities taking place in the emotion process are: development of other cognitive and action tendencies; appearance of facial and bodily expressions; and physiological changes, all of which can temper the emotion experienced. The consequences of an emotion, which are some combination of intrapersonal and interpersonal behaviour, follow from the experienced emotion. However, in-between experiencing the emotion and the onset of its consequences, it can be moderated to some extent, especially where the person concerned attempts emotion regulation.

FURTHER READING

Ajzen, I (1988) *Attitudes, Personality and Behaviour*, Milton Keynes: Open University Press. An interesting introduction to the subject of attitudes, which examines the link between attitudes and behaviour and sets out the theory of planned behaviour.

Cohen, A (2000) The relationship between commitment forms and work outcomes; a comparison of three models, *Human Relations* 53(3): 387–417. While a somewhat technical paper in places, the article is an interesting study that explores different approaches to explaining the relationship between commitment and its likely outcomes.

Edwards, JE (1997) *How to Conduct Organisational Surveys*, Thousand Oaks, CA: Sage. A good overview of the techniques involved in designing and using employee opinion surveys.

Fife-Schaw, C, P Sheeran and P Norman (2007) Simulating behaviour change interventions based on the theory of planned behaviour: impact on intention and action, *British Journal of Social Psychology* 46(1): 393–401. An interesting example of ongoing work to refine Ajzen's Theory of Planned Behavior.

Grandey, AA, GM Fisk and DD Steiner (2005) Must 'service with a smile' be stressful? The moderating role of personal control for American and French employees, *Journal of Applied Psychology* 90(5): 893–904. An interesting paper reporting an empirical study of emotional labour, and whether having a degree of personal control of work circumstances helps employees cope with the inherent strains of the job.

Hochschild, AR (1983) *The Managed Heart: Commercialisation of Human Feeling*, Berkley, CA: University of California Press. The classic work which first exposed the phenomenon of emotional labour. Well worth a read.

Meyer, JP and NJ Allen (1997) *Commitment in the Workplace: Theory, Research and Application*, London: Sage. An extensive exploration of what is probably considered to be a highly important attitude in most organisations. The text gives a thorough examination of the potential link between commitment and employee behaviour.

Parkinson, B (1995) *Ideas and Realities of Emotion*, London: Routledge. A well written and informative explanation of the emotion process.

Payne, RL and C Cooper (eds) (2001) *Emotions at Work*, Chichester: Wiley. An extensive exploration of how people's emotions have a strong impact on their overt behaviour, both in and away from the work situation.

Rousseau, DM and J Parks (1993) The contracts of individuals and organisations, *Organisational Behaviour* 15(1): 1–43. A very well argued explanation of the concept of the psychological (and other) contracts and their effects on the work situation.

CASE STUDY 5.1: Attitudes to McJobs

Stefan Stern, a journalist working for the *Financial Times* reports receiving an indignant letter from David Fairhurst, senior vice-president and chief people officer in northern Europe for McDonald's, the global fast-food chain. It invites its recipients to sign a petition as part of a new campaign to get publishers to change the current dictionary definition of the word 'McJob'. Open your dictionary today and you will probably find a McJob defined as 'an unstimulating, low-wage job with few benefits, espcially in a service industry'; or 'a McJob requires little skill, is often temporary, and offers minimal or no benefits or opportunity for promotion'.

In the light of this you can understand Mr Fairhurst's objections because, in the UK at least, McDonald's has established a pretty solid reputation as a decent employer. It features regularly in most of the main *good employer* league tables, and recently won *The Caterer and Hotelkeeper* magazine's *Best Place to Work in Hospitality* award. Eighty per cent of McDonald's UK branch managers joined the company as hourly paid crew members, as did half the company's executive team and, compared to some other companies in the service sector, McDonald's is serious about training and development. It is also more female-friendly than most: 40 per cent of managers and 25 per cent of the company's executives are women. So here's the paradox: you can get a hamburger and milkshake at your local McDonald's but, on this evidence, you will probably look in vain for a McJob.

People based in the US may think that this curious semantic battle sounds a bit familiar, and they would be right. In 2003 Jim Cantalupo, McDonald's then-chief executive, lambasted the 11th edition of America's distinguished Merriam-Webster's Collegiate dictionary for publishing another downbeat definition of the McJob, and there were even threats of legal action, which came to nothing. One aspect of McDonald's complaint was that they actually had a scheme called 'McJobs' – a training programme for disabled people. Nevertheless, the word and its unsavoury definition remain in English-language dictionaries to this day.

Attempting to turn back a linguistic tide is futile. Dictionaries reflect contemporary usage – they describe rather than prescribe, and as Dennis Baron, a professor at the University of Illinois at

▶

Urbana-Champaign, said in 2003: 'if lexicographers allowed individuals or pressure groups to dictate definitions, then our language would be reduced to mere McWords'.

The American psychologist Frederick Herzberg once said: 'If you want someone to do a good job, give them a good job to do.' However, that is not always easy in an era of automation and efficiency, where employers deliberately seek – often unwisely – to simplify and de-skill certain jobs.

But what should managers do about their front-line, customer-facing staff if they want to avoid the disgruntlement and disillusion of those condemned to carry out repetitive tasks? Lyn Etherington, a director of Cape Consulting, which advises businesses on their customer service, says that some companies go wrong at the recruitment stage.

She argues that you should 'recruit for attitude, train for skills', as Archie Norman [former chairman of the supermarket group Asda] put it. There are some people who will never be suited to a customer-facing role, but if you want to beat the competition by offering superior customer service, it is no use management over-designing people's jobs, which minimises the opportunity for staff to respond to the individual customer's needs. She then argues that there are 5 key conditions for achieving good customer service.

1. clarity within the business as to what the customer experience is supposed to be; do senior managers, middle-managers and front-line staff all share the same clarity of purpose?
2. is that purpose regularly reinforced by managers, at daily briefings and team meetings?
3. is good customer service measured and rewarded; people notice who gets promoted and 'who gets on' Ms Etherington says?
4. does the idea of customer service fit in with other organisational priorities; if all the talk is of cutting costs, don't expect customer delight?
5. does the business present itself to customers in a seamless way; hard to achieve when technological advances (and cost savings) tend to fragment the organisation?

However, it can be argued that McDonald's must be getting something right. In January it reported its best results in 30 years, with fourth quarter net profits more than double those that were achieved 12 months earlier. Moreover, the company has managed 44 consecutive months of sales growth, and is pulling in 4m more customers a day than it was four years ago. Nevertheless, McDonald's seems to be doomed to be controversial, and questions will always be asked about its management style and working conditions. Jerry Newman, a professor at the University of Buffalo, who has just published *My Secret Life on the McJob*, his account of 14 months spent undercover as a fast-food industry employee, concludes that the McJob isn't McEasy. There are good managers in this sector, but also a lot of toxic and destructive ones.

Questions

1. What are your attitudes to the likely nature of work at McDonald's or similar firms (some of you might actually have worked for firms like this)?

2. In your view (or experience) is McDonald's the excellent place to work at that is claimed for it in the case material, or does it have characteristics that are nearer to those claimed for it in dictionaries?

3. If there is a difference between the picture portayed in the dictionaries and your own views or experience, why and how do you feel that the firm acquired its unsavoury reputation?

4. Carefully examine the five key conditions for achieving good customer service set-out by Ms Etherinton in the case material. Do you feel that observing these will make a firm a more pleasant place to work, or are they simply geared to ensuring that it is more profitable?

5. Do you feel that McDonald's could have achieved the commercial success reported for it without having at least some of the characteristics set out in dictionary definitions of McJobs?

Source: Stern S. (2007) *Financial Times*, 20 March

REVIEW AND DISCUSSION QUESTIONS

1. Explain what is meant by the 'functional' approach to the study of attitudes and state the purposes that attitudes serve for people.

2. Describe the most pronounced sources from which people derive their attitudes.

3. Using Fishbein and Ajzen's theory of planned behaviour, explain why attitudes are far more likely to predict behavioural intentions than actual behaviour.

4. Explain what is meant by the expression 'job satisfaction'. According to the research evidence what aspects of employee behaviour are most likely to be affected by job satisfaction?

5. Explain what is meant by the expression 'organisational commitment'. To what extent is organisational commitment likely to have a positive impact on employee behaviour and explain why it is unlikely that an organisation would be able to recruit committed employees?

6. In outline, describe the emotion process.

7. What is meant by the expression 'emotion regulation'; why might an emotionally aroused person attempt to regulate his or her emotions?

8. Distinguish between 'deep acting' and 'surface acting' in emotion regulation and also emotion amplification and emotion suppression.

Integrating Individual Characteristics

The previous three chapters all dealt with characteristics that distinguish between people as individuals, and for convenience they were all covered separately. However, they are not discrete attributes that appear in isolation, but are interconnected in a way that has a bearing on how people:

- experience and make sense of their surroundings
- behave towards their work milieu.

This section of the book traces some of the ways in which individual characteristics have an impact on each other, and to explain matters, it is convenient to consider these characteristics in pairs.

PERSONALITY AND INTELLIGENCE

As was pointed out in Chapter 3, so far as understanding individual behaviour is concerned, distinguishing between personality and intelligence is a matter of convenience; personality describes behaviour in social situations, whereas intelligence describes the physical and intellectual skills that are necessary to behave in certain ways. Thus there are almost certainly close links between these two characteristics, and there is a school of thought that argues that intelligence might well turn out to be just another dimension of personality (Phares 1987). For instance, both characteristics have a strong genetic component (Erlenmeyer-Kimling and Jarvick 1963; Pervin 1980) and both are influenced by socialisation. For example, Wanous et al. (1984) argue that early childhood socialisation has an influence on personality in a general way and more specifically McClelland (1967) has advanced the argument that the strength of the need to achieve (NAch) is influenced by child-rearing practices. Moreover, intelligence, at least in the way that it is normally measured, can be argued to be a matter of stored knowledge as much as anything else, and this is also a reflection of the type and range of socialisation experiences to which a person has been exposed.

PERSONALITY AND ATTITUDES

Personality also has links with a person's attitudes and emotional make-up. For instance, personal construct theory (Kelly 1955) informs us that how an individual views the world, using a set of personal evaluative dimensions is strongly connected to how the person behaves towards objects in the world (Orbell 2003). Attitudes are also evaluative frames of reference that influence how people behave towards objects and one of their most important functions is to protect an individual from information that contradicts his/her self-image (Katz 1960). Self-image, it should be noted, is a fundamental part of personality, and its defence by an attitude means there are also connections between personality and object recognition in perception. Indeed, there is evidence to show that people erect strong mental barriers against recognising objects or symbols that are threatening to the concept of self (Bruner and Postman 1947; Haire and Grunes 1950; McGinnies 1949).

PERCEPTION AND ATTITUDES

There is almost bound to be a strong connection between attitudes and perception and some hint of this is given above. Although attitudes only reflect the way that people feel about their surroundings, whether a person likes or dislikes an object, person or event that he or she encounters is virtually certain to impact on the way that it is perceived, which in turn can influence behaviour towards the object.

PERSONALITY, PERCEPTION AND ATTITUDES

Since perceptions attitudes and emotions all have behavioural implications, each one probably has some connection with personality. It should be remembered, however, that unlike personality and intelligence, both of which are widely acknowledged to have a direct hereditary component, perceptions and attitudes are much more the result of social, cultural and developmental experiences. Nevertheless, this raises the possibility (although it is probably very slight) that ultimately, there is a genetic influence on perception and attitudes.

In summary, therefore, personality seems to have a pervasive link with all other individual characteristics. However, because personality is unique to the individual and, by definition, there are as many personalities as there are people, this means that personality is not a foolproof way of predicting a person's intelligence, perceptions or attitudes; they are all merely connected. These links are shown in Figure I1, the first integrative diagram in the book and this is just the first of several building blocks that will be used throughout the book to integrate its contents. As you progress through the different sections of the book you will encounter further integrative sub-sections that make links between the topics covered in a particular section, and between different book sections.

Figure I1 Interactions between individual characteristics

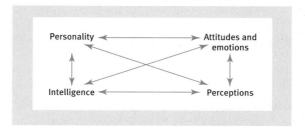

INTEGRATIVE CASE STUDY No. 1: David Orton plc

In early 2004, the Orton Group, a major British food retailer, set-out to acquire one of its major rivals, by making a public offer for the shares of Costwise, another large supermarket group. This immediately prompted a number of counter-bids from other large retailing groups and it was not until mid 2005 that the Orton Group and Costwise merged under the banner of David Orton plc. Events in the case study that follow largely focus on the staff in Costwise during the 15 months leading-up to the formal merger. Subsequent cases will deal with events after mid-2005.

Although the senior management of Costwise was favourably disposed towards Orton's bid, they recognised that it could take some time before the two companies would be able to merge physically. To a large extent this was because when the takeover bid was launched, the Competition Commision (CC) had expressed reservations about a merger between two retailing groups who were already very large in their own rights. For instance, if allowed to go ahead as a simple takeover, it might well result in the new company having a near-monopoly position in certain geographical areas. For this reason it was thought likely that the CC might insist on the new group divesting itself of a number of retail outlets, in order for permission to merge to be granted. At the time that Orton made its bid, however, the CC could not be specific about whether this requirement would be imposed. Neither was it able to state unequivocally which stores it would wish the new group to dispose of; that is, whether it would wish them to be drawn from Orton's sites, Costwise's stores, or a mixture of both. Indeed, about the only information about which the Costwise management group had any inkling in this area had emerged from earlier, informal discussion between Orton and Costwise. Unlike other large food retailers, Orton had chosen not to move into the smaller, 'convenience store' sector, which was likely to mean that its primary interest in acquiring Costwise premises was its desire to expand in the larger (25,000 sq ft and above) sector. This would fit-well with its focus on 'superstores'. Thus, if it had any choice in the matter it would probably opt to divest itself of Costwise's smaller 'compact stores', probably by selling them as going concerns to rival supermarket chains. All this, of course, would build a delay into any merger timetable, and it also gave rise to significant problems. Until the eventual size and structure of the merged group was identified, management and staff at both companies would probably feel that a degree of uncertainty had been introduced into their futures, and this was felt to be particularly the case for staff at Costwise, which would be likely to wind-up as the junior partner in the combined organisation. As such there could be significant problems in maintaining the morale of staff in the interim period.

In retailing, staff attitudes can have important effects on the performance of an organisation. Thus, in the interests of remaining an attractive merger partner, the senior management of Costwise decided to hold a meeting to review the strengths and weaknesses of the firm as revealed by staff feelings. The following are summary notes that were taken at the meeting.

Current Situation

The meeting opened with the chairman summarising the present situation to those present. They were asked to note that until the Competition Commission had completed its deliberations, the size and structure of the combined organisation was still very much a matter of conjecture. As such, although this was likely to be a piece of information about which everybody wanted an answer, at this stage no definitive answer could be given.

Current Trading Performance

The chairman noted that it was nice to be able to report that this was holding-up surprisingly well, considering the amount of uncertainty and ambiguity in the firm.

Employee Morale

He then asked the Human Resources Manager whether the organisation was experiencing a higher than usual level of staff turnover. The manager's answer to this was 'surprisingly not'. To expand on this the HRM manager noted that pay levels at Costwise had traditionally not been high, and at the present any consideration of a general organisation-wide increase was being held in abeyance, pending further discussions about the merger. Nevertheless, he noted that while in the past there had been a pretty constant tendency for staff at all levels to complain about pay, this seemed to have subsided recently; perhaps because people had more important things to think about. Another thing that seems to have occurred was what he felt tempted to call an increased sense of loyalty to the firm, although, on reflection, it could probably be better described as a heightened spirit of camaraderie among employees. Here he noted that evidence from prior employee opinion surveys had always tended to show that staff have a strong sense of loyalty to each other and, even with the moaning about pay that had occurred in the past, to some extent he had always suspected that staff stayed out of loyalty to their colleagues. In summary, therefore, although he regarded it as possible that morale problems might eventually occur, and it could be dangerous to assume that things will never get worse, at the moment there were no obvious problems.

Discussion then turned to positive steps that could be taken to try to ensure that staff attitudes remain positive. Since this was a matter that required further thought, it was agreed to close the meeting and reconvene it at a later date to review any suggestions that had emerged.

Questions

1. From the evidence that has emerged so far, how would you characterise staff morale at Costwise?

2. What do you feel is the state of the psychological contract at Costwise?

3. What issues do you feel might be of concern to staff at Costwise at the present time?

4. What perceptions are the staff at Coswise likely to have of employees at Ortons and what attitudes are they likely hold towards these people?

5. What practical steps could the management of Costwise take to try to ensure that staff morale does not deteriorate?

The Intrapersonal Level (Individual Processes)

As indicated by the diagram, this section of the book consists of five chapters, all of which deal with important individual processes. These processes exercise a strong influence on the way that people behave, and have an impact on whether they are likely to be considered more suitable for some organisational roles than others. Because a person's behaviour is a reflection of his or her mental characteristics, there is clearly a connection between this part of the book and the one that precedes it. For this reason, the integrative sub-section that follows Chapter 10, not only traces the links between processes, it also traces links between individual characteristics and processes.

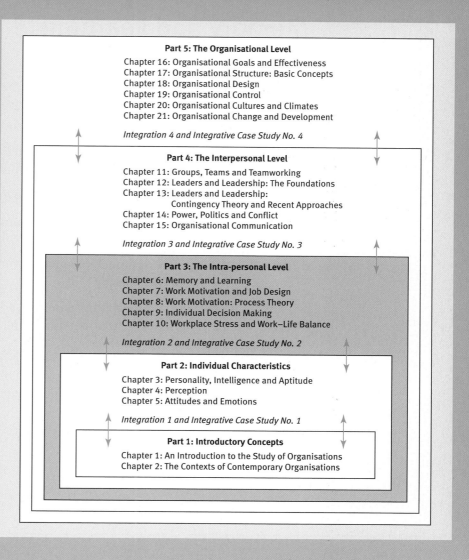

Part 5: The Organisational Level

Chapter 16: Organisational Goals and Effectiveness
Chapter 17: Organisational Structure: Basic Concepts
Chapter 18: Organisational Design
Chapter 19: Organisational Control
Chapter 20: Organisational Cultures and Climates
Chapter 21: Organisational Change and Development

Integration 4 and Integrative Case Study No. 4

Part 4: The Interpersonal Level

Chapter 11: Groups, Teams and Teamworking
Chapter 12: Leaders and Leadership: The Foundations
Chapter 13: Leaders and Leadership:
          Contingency Theory and Recent Approaches
Chapter 14: Power, Politics and Conflict
Chapter 15: Organisational Communication

Integration 3 and Integrative Case Study No. 3

Part 3: The Intra-personal Level

Chapter 6: Memory and Learning
Chapter 7: Work Motivation and Job Design
Chapter 8: Work Motivation: Process Theory
Chapter 9: Individual Decision Making
Chapter 10: Workplace Stress and Work–Life Balance

Integration 2 and Integrative Case Study No. 2

Part 2: Individual Characteristics

Chapter 3: Personality, Intelligence and Aptitude
Chapter 4: Perception
Chapter 5: Attitudes and Emotions

Integration 1 and Integrative Case Study No. 1

Part 1: Introductory Concepts

Chapter 1: An Introduction to the Study of Organisations
Chapter 2: The Contexts of Contemporary Organisations

Chapter 6

Memory and Learning

LEARNING OUTCOMES

After studying this chapter you should be able to:

- define memory, understand its importance in the learning process and, in outline, explain the 'two-store' model of memory

- define learning and explain the concept of 'levels of learning'

- distinguish between classical and operant conditioning and understand the limitations of behaviourist explanations of learning

- describe the cognitive approach to learning and explain the major tenets of Social Learning Theory

- explain the concept of experiental learning, the concepts of learning cycle and learning styles, and understand their significance for organisations

INTRODUCTION

This chapter deals with memory and learning; mental processes that are used by everyone and, since all human behaviour is influenced by them, they have a strong impact on the way people function in organisations. However, although they are complementary processes, they are usually treated as separate topics in psychology.

The chapter commences by considering the topic of memory. A definition is given and this is followed by a description of what has come to be the most widely accepted model of human memory; the 'two-store' theory.

The remainder of the chapter deals with the subject of learning. This opens with a definition and an overview of the different approaches that have been used to try to explain the learning process. This is followed by descriptions of the three main theoretical approaches to understanding learning: behaviourist theory, cognitive theory and experiential learning theory. These are brought together to compare and contrast the different approaches, and the chapter closes with an overview section that integrates the topics of memory and learning.

MEMORY

Memory: the ability of an organism to retain information internally and demonstrate this retention through behaviour

Memory performs many functions and it is involved in virtually every aspect of our lives. Nevertheless, it is something we take for granted, and we are usually more aware of forgetting things than remembering them. All that we do or experience involves a contribution from memory and we interpret what is new in relation to past experiences.

There are many definitions of memory, but here it is defined in a general way as:

the ability of an organism to retain information internally and to demonstrate this retention through behaviour.

Two important points can be noted from this definition, both of which imply a connection between learning and memory:

- to retain information it is necessary to be exposed to it and acknowledge its existence
- the acid test of memory is whether retention of information can be demonstrated by behaving in a certain way.

As will be seen, a potential change in behaviour is also the acid test of whether something has been learned. Nevertheless, the reader needs to be aware that learning and memory are regarded as two separate topics in psychology, and they address two different questions. With learning the question is 'How and why an organism learns?' and memory research asks 'How, when something has been learned, is the information represented, stored and retrieved?'

The academic study of memory is a very complex area. It comprises many different theoretical approaches and it would be impossible to cover them all in a book such as this. Many of the basic principles were uncovered nearly 50 years ago and since then work in the area has become increasingly more specialised and complex. Thus, the study of memory is near to becoming a branch of psychology in its own right, and this poses a problem for an introductory text such as this. Grasping the implications of recent developments requires an understanding of basic models and principles, which is difficult enough for students of pure psychology. Thus, because this is not a book on pure psychology, the chapter is confined to covering only the basic principles of memory, and explanations that are given mostly draw on older, more basic studies.

A Model of Human Memory

The naive view of memory is that it is simply a repository for storing information. However, since memory plays an important part in the way we experience the world, and the basic question addressed in memory research is 'In order for it to be remembered and recalled when required, what happens to information as it arrives from the outside world?' This results in what can broadly be described as the 'information processing' approach to memory, in which the most widely accepted model is 'two-store theory'. In some respects, however, the expression 'two-store' is misleading. While the name reflects the idea that the overwhelming body of evidence suggests that humans have two memory stores, it glosses-over the equally important point that there are several separate and important processes associated with each store. However, before setting-out this theory it is important to sound a notion of caution. The two-store model is a theory derived from experimental evidence, and it explains how memory *could* work and nothing more. It is not a model of the physical parts of the brain and it portrays different memory stores that have different functions, which do not work in isolation but are strongly interdependent. A simplified model of the two-store theory is shown in Figure 6.1, and its different stages are described in what follows.

Sensory registration: the memory stage in which environmental stimuli are first registered for onward transmission into memory

Stage 1: Sensory Registration

For material to get into the memory, it must be sensed in the organism's environment and its presence registered. This is clearly connected with the perceptual process described in Chapter 4 and, since this is a fleeting process, it is more convenient to describe the stage as one that uses a register, rather than a store.

The information is encoded to travel along neural pathways in a pathway-specific form, using visual coding for visual signals and acoustic coding for acoustic signals

Figure 6.1 The 'two-store' model of memory

(Coleheart *et al.* 1974). However, the information is not retained in a mode-specific way in the register, but is just registered 'as there'. The capacity of the register is very limited and once information is registered, it fades rapidly. For instance, Sperling (1960) shows that the capacity of the register is only about nine characters for visually encoded information and, although all nine can usually be recalled immediately, the number that a person is able to recall reduces drastically if recall is delayed for as little as one second. Because people are exposed to many different signals at the same time in a work situation, this can sometimes pose problems. Thus, if we want to make sure that a particularly important piece of information is registered so that it will pass onwards into memory, it is often necessary to try to get a person to focus on that signal and nothing else. For example, in a process in which an article is heat-treated in a furnace, there will probably be a gauge that indicates the temperature and, in addition, a flashing light that draws attention to the temperature if it exceeds a safe level.

Stage 2: Short-term (Working) Memory

Short-term (working) memory: the stage in which information from the sensory register enters a short-term memory store

From the sensory register, information is passed to a short-term memory store (STS), which also has a fairly limited capacity, but a slightly longer duration of retention. Miller (1956), for example, suggests that it can hold about seven chunks of information (names, words, etc.) and that these are retained for something between six and 12 seconds for the average person. However, there is a crucial difference between the sensory register and short-term memory. The short-term store is not just a simple repository for information, but a functioning component of memory that undertakes a host of tasks. For this reason, some psychologists (i.e. Baddeley 1976; Logie 1999) refer to the STS as 'working memory'. It is the centre of a control system that directs the flow of information and probably attaches additional information that helps with retrieval from long-term memory. Thus, information in the short-term store is almost certainly re-coded after it leaves the sensory register.

Short-term memory seems to use an abstract, verbalised code (Conrad 1964) and one of the more interesting control functions performed in the short-term store is rehearsal – the repetition of information to retain it in the STS – for eventual onward transmission into long-term memory. Most of us find it necessary to engage in rehearsal at times; for example, if I look up a number in a telephone I tend to repeat it to myself.

Stage 3: Long-term Memory

Long-term memory: the relatively permanent store in which information and knowledge is retained

This is the (relatively) permanent memory store, the capacity and duration of which is theoretically limitless. So far as we know the information stored in *long-term memory* is different from that in the STS. Thus, further encoding or re-coding must take place between the two stores. Indeed, Tulving (1974) suggests that there are two types of long-term memory, which are connected with how the information is stored, and also with how it has been acquired.

Episodic memory: a memory store containing information about episodes and past events in our lives

The first of these, *episodic memory*, receives and stores information about past episodes and events in our lives, which allows us to draw on experience; for instance, it facilitates recall of such details as procedures for evacuating the building if the fire alarm bell rings (which I acquired at a safety drill some six months ago). One way that information of this type can be stored is by the use of schema. These were described in Chapter 4 and they are structured to organise incoming information in relation to previous experience. Another way is by the use of scripts, which can be thought of as elaborate schema, which in a single word or phrase gives a repertoire of behaviour appropriate to a particular situation (Gleitman 1991). For example, the 'going to the cinema' script could be: buy ticket, buy popcorn between the kiosk to the auditorium, locate a suitable seat in the auditorium, relax and wait for the film to start.

Semantic memory:
a memory store recording information of an abstract, conceptual nature

The second type of memory, *semantic memory*, is much more abstract and contains our accumulated knowledge about things we may never have experienced first-hand but nevertheless know, or believe that we know; for instance, that there are 100 centimetres in a metre, or knowing the meaning of the word 'aggressive'.

Collins and Quillian (1969) suggest that we store this information in hierarchical taxonomies of ideas or concepts, that we are able to relate to each other. An example of such a taxonomy relating to the animal kingdom is given in Figure 6.2. Note, however, that this does not mean that we have a picture similar to Figure 6.2 stored in the memory. Rather that we recognise that birds and fishes are both part of the animal kingdom and that canaries and ostriches are both types of bird, with their own distinctive characteristics.

Stage 4: Retrieval

Retrieval: the processes used to recall information or knowledge from the long- (or sometimes short-) term memory store

Strictly speaking this is not part of a memory store but is a process. However, unless we can retrieve information and demonstrate this in behaviour, it is hard to show that the material has been assimilated and retained in memory. Although most of the discussion here centres on retrieval from long-term memory, it is important to recognise that we also retrieve from the short-term store.

Problematically, there are few cast-iron explanations of how the retrieval process works, because most of the experimental evidence deals with forgetting – the inability to remember. One explanation of failure to remember is the 'levels of processing hypothesis' (Craik and Lockheart 1972), which argues that retention is a function of the level at which information processing occurs; for example, that superficial processing only leads to a shallow, short-term retention and a high level of forgetting. However,

Figure 6.2
Simplified example of a hierarchical semantic taxonomy (adapted from Collins and Quillian 1969)

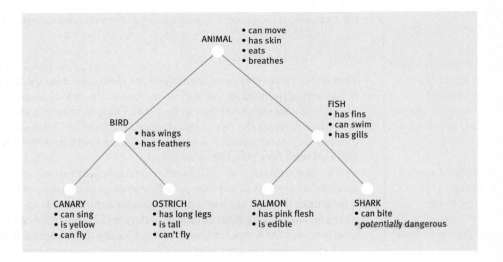

Taylor *et al.* (1979) argue that retention is connected with processing effort. For instance, if, fairly soon after having learned something, we retrieve the information from the long-term store and re-learn it, we are more likely to fix it in memory.

Theoretically, there could be a number of reasons why we forget information: inefficient search procedures in long-term memory; a poor storage system for information; poor retrieval cues; or a decayed memory trace. However, the strongest evidence is for a phenomenon known as interference (Waugh and Norman 1965). This can occur in two ways. The first is *retroactive interference*, in which material that is learned later interferes with the recall of something learned earlier. For example, suppose you have an important meeting at work tomorrow and rehearse what you need to say at the meeting immediately before falling asleep. This gives you a greater likelihood of remembering it, because while you are asleep there is no new incoming material to interfere with what has been learned; that is, unless you dream (Ekstrand 1972). The second type of interference is *proactive interference*, in which material learned earlier interferes with attempts to recall subsequent material. To use the meeting example again, although you have memorised what you need to say, someone might give you some important additional facts just before the meeting starts and this message is swamped out by the earlier material. However, it is also possible that there are other reasons why we forget things. We could have repressed the information, because we have a subconscious desire to avoid retrieving something associated with an unpleasant event; for instance, it can sometimes be convenient to forget a dental appointment. Similarly, emotions could render retrieval processes ineffective, for example nervousness in examinations.

Retroactive interference: the most recent material learned interferes with recall of material that has been learned earlier

Proactive interference: recall of material learned earlier interferes with recall of material that has been learned later

---

TIME OUT

Make a list of all the things that you did last Saturday, from the time you got out of bed in the morning until the time you went to bed that night.

1. How complete is your memory of the whole day? Are there any parts of the day where, although you are generally aware of doing something, you cannot recall the full details? Why do you think this is the case?
2. Now, from what you can recall, try to analyse the different ways in which doing all these things involved you in drawing on your memory.
3. In which of these activities was memory essential to its completion?
4. Was there any time at which your inability to recall something from memory made an activity more difficult?

Memory: Concluding Comments

Memory plays an important role in our day-to-day, minute-by-minute functioning. It is much more than a crude, static repository for information, but is a set of at least three highly active mental processes: *input processes*, which provide appropriate encoded representations of environmental stimuli; *retention processes* that maintain information in the store; and, finally, *retrieval processes* that seek out information from the store as and when it is needed.

These processes do not store information at random and, like any efficient storage system, there is a place for everything and everything has its place. Moreover, the mind actively associates new inputs with knowledge already stored, so that new material is integrated into a framework that already exists. Therefore, enlarging the memory is rather like expanding a well-designed filing system.

REPLAY

- Current approaches to understanding memory adopt an information-processing perspective.
- The 'two-store' model dominates current explanations of the memory process.
- Memory consists of three interconnected sets of processes: input processes to sense and register environmental stimuli; retention processes to store information about stimuli; retrieval processes to re-activate information from memory stores.

LEARNING

Learning: a relatively permanent change in behaviour, or potential behaviour, that results from experience

Although there are many definitions of *learning*, it is defined here as:

> a relatively permanent change in behaviour, or potential behaviour, that results from experience
> (Hulse *et al.* 1980)

A number of important points flow from this definition:

- It excludes changes in behaviour that result purely from maturation.
- Learning cannot be observed directly but only inferred from behaviour.
- Because a person is unlikely to perform better until he or she has learned to do so, there is clearly a relationship between performance and behaviour, but a lack of performance is not an infallible sign that no learning has taken place. This is emphasised in the definition by use of the phrase 'potential behaviour'.
- For the behaviour that provides evidence that learning has taken place to be exhibited, there often has to be a motivation or incentive to do so.

As with memory, the principles of some of the older theories of learning were laid-down many years ago and since then they have not substantially changed. Thus, in the interests of simplicity, with these theories reference is made to the original work. Although these theories can explain some aspects of learning, they cannot explain everything, and so other theories that clarify other facets of the learning process have evolved, and these will be presented in the order in which they appeared.

Learning is a complex process that could take place in many ways and the four points made above imply that it is not a discrete process, but has connections with other mental activities. Bruner (1973) draws attention to the idea that, to understand learning, account needs to be taken of the three important groups of variables that are shown in Figure 6.3.

Figure 6.3 The three sets of factors that affect learning (adapted from Bruner 1973)

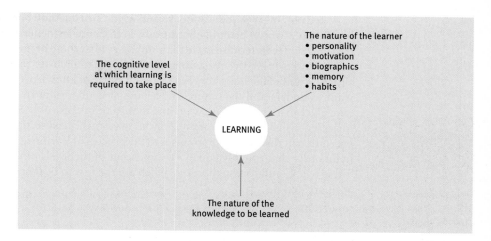

The cognitive level at which learning is required to take place

The nature of the learner
• personality
• motivation
• biographics
• memory
• habits

LEARNING

The nature of the knowledge to be learned

We will return to two of these factors later but, for the present, it is more important to focus on just one of them: the nature of the knowledge to be learned.

Unfortunately, there is no all-encompassing theory that embraces all types of learning. However, Bloom (1956) identifies six levels at which learning can take place and these are given in Table 6.1. Note that, as the hierarchy is ascended, the nature of what is to be learned gets progressively more complex and so the mental activities involved also increase in complexity. It should also be noted that learning at any level subsumes the use of all lower levels. That is, learning at level 4 also involves learning at levels 1

Table 6.1 Levels of learning and their associated behavioural outcomes (adapted after Bloom 1956)

Level	Cognitive domain	Example
6	Evaluation	The ability to judge the value of the material using explicit, coherent criteria. For example, that if we have a set amount of voltage available, delivered at a set current, we can derive the maximum resistance that the circuit must have in order to be able to deliver the voltage along an electrical conductor, which would enable us to select appropriate material to construct the circuit.
5	Synthesis	To be able to re-assemble the parts into new and meaningful relationships forming new wholes. That is, to be able to transform the equation above into $R = V$ divided by I, which tells us what the resistance of the circuit is when the voltage and current are known.
4	Analysis	The ability to break down the material into its constituent parts and see the relationship between them. That is, if the resistance of the circuit and the current are known, the voltage that needs to be available to drive electricity around the circuit can be ascertained.
3	Application	The ability to apply the knowledge. That is, to calculate V if I and R are known.
2	Comprehension	Understanding the meaning of the knowledge. That is, that V represents power in Volts, I is current in Amperes, R is Resistance in Ohms.
1	Knowledge	Simple knowledge of facts in terms of theories, actions, etc. That is, that Ohm's law for an electrical circuit is $V = I \times R$.

to 3. Indeed, most psychologists would argue that methods of learning suitable for levels 1 to 3 would be unlikely to result in learning at the levels above this, because these higher levels require more than simply rote learning of information produced by other people. It involve reasoning, or the ability to uncover the underlying logic in a situation and make links between different items of knowledge. For this reason, if we want to understand the nature of learning, it is important to understand that it can take place in many different ways and that some of these only facilitate learning at the lower levels in Bloom's hierarchy. For this reason, the next section of the chapter examines different theoretical approaches to the process of learning, and these are presented in an order that roughly equates to an ascent of the levels of the hierarchy shown in Table 6.1. Conditioning theories, which are the first to be described, explain learning at up to level 3.

THEORIES OF LEARNING

Behaviourist (Conditioning) Theories

Classical Conditioning

Unconditioned stimulus: a naturally occurring stimulus to which there is an inbuilt response in an organism's nervous system

Unconditioned response: a reflex response built into the nervous system of an organism

Neutral stimulus: a stimulus which does not evoke a reflex response on the part of an organism

Conditioned stimulus: a relatively artificial trigger to the production of a reflex response in an organism

Conditioned response: a reflex behaviour elicited by pairing a neutral stimulus with an unconditioned response

Classical conditioning evolved from the work of Ivan Pavlov (1927), who uncovered the concept of the conditioned reflex. A reflex is a predictable, unlearned, involuntary response to a stimulus. However, it is not a response that occurs as a result of a conscious decision to do something, but usually has the function of protecting the organism in some way, or helping it to adapt to its environment; for instance, if someone waves a fist in my face, I blink automatically to protect my eyes. A reflex of this type is known as an unconditioned reflex (UR) and Pavlov's work showed that it is possible to condition a reflex so that it is elicited by a new and completely different stimulus. Perhaps the easiest way to explain this is to describe Pavlov's experiment, the main stages of which are shown in Figure 6.4.

In Figure 6.4(a) the *unconditioned stimulus* (US) is the sight of food, which elicits an *unconditioned response* (UR) of salivation by the dog. This is a natural, automatic response on the part of the animal and, if a *neutral stimulus* (NS), in this case the sound of a bell, appears on its own, as in Figure 6.4(b), the dog does not salivate. However, if the bell is rung in the presence of food, as in Figure 6.4(c), once again the dog continues to produce the unconditioned response of salivation, and if Figure 6.4(c) is repeated enough times, the animal builds up an association between the NS and the US and the two stimuli become 'paired' in its mind. This permits moving to the final stage shown in Figure 6.4(d), where the sound of the bell alone is sufficient to excite the nervous system of the animal. The bell becomes a *conditioned stimulus* (CS), that is, it elicits salivation and salivation is now a *conditioned response* (CR).

In classical conditioning, learning has occurred when the conditioned stimulus becomes paired with the unconditioned response and, for this to happen, there must first be an association between the unconditioned stimulus and the unconditioned response. However, once the pairing has taken place, it is possible to substitute a new neutral stimulus and turn it into a conditioned stimulus. For example, with the animal that has learned to salivate in response to the sound of the bell, a flashing light could be paired with the bell and eventually the dog will salivate in response to the

Figure 6.4 Classical
conditioning

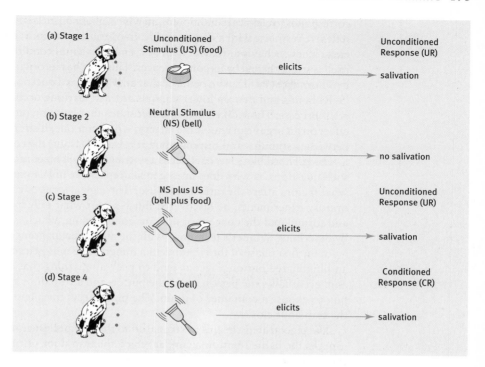

light. When an animal is conditioned in this way the association can remain intact for
a considerable period but, gradually, some deterioration tends to occur; for example,
the dog might continue to salivate, but less saliva would be produced. Indeed, the conditioned response can be removed altogether by introducing an inhibitory force to induce
extinction. For instance, if the bell is rung enough times and the dog never receives
food in its presence, it will eventually cease to salivate at the sound of the bell.

While classical conditioning can only explain reflexive or passive learning, it still
has a number of applications in everyday life. It is quite widely used in advertising;
for example, in advertisements that convey the message that using a particular brand
of aftershave results in a man becoming more attractive to beautiful women. Here the
unconditioned stimulus is probably an imagined liaison with the highly attractive woman,
which produces the unconditioned response of a degree of sexual arousal and paring
the use of aftershave with the unconditioned stimulus eventually produces the same
effect. However, as an explanation of learning it has its limitations. Although it explains
how we learn to associate a new stimulus with a reflex response, it cannot explain how
behaviours that are not already built into the nervous system are learned. The next
theory to be covered gives an insight into this matter and, although this still involves
conditioning, it is a very different type of conditioning.

Operant Conditioning

Skinner (1974), the originator of the term 'operant conditioning', distinguishes
between the two types of behaviour: respondent and operant. Respondent behaviour

corresponds to classical conditioning, in which an organism learns to associate an innate, reflexive response with a new stimulus. In operant behaviour, however, the organism emits a new behaviour to deal with new environmental conditions and the behaviour itself is strengthened by its consequences. This idea has its origins in much earlier work by Thorndike (1911), who believed that all learning is a question of stimulus–response (S–R) bonds and that, in lower animals at least, learning occurs through a trial-and-error process. Thorndike's law of effect states that learning only occurs if it has some effect on an organism and, if the effect is a pleasant one, it strengthens the connection between a stimulus and response but, if it is unpleasant, the connection is weakened.

Using Thorndike's law of effect as a starting point, Skinner proceeded to try to answer such questions as why does an organism repeat (or not) a particular behaviour and what factors affect the rate of response? Through a series of carefully controlled laboratory experiments, he discovered much about what influences operant behaviour and formulated the concept of operant conditioning, which is most easily explained by describing Skinner's technique with the aid of the diagram shown in Figure 6.5.

In the first phase of the experiment a hungry pigeon is placed in a box that contains an illuminated button. Pigeons tend to peck at anything that attracts their attention and, eventually, the pigeon pecks the button and a trap door opens in the wall of the box to expose a container of grain. The pigeon eats for a few moments, after which the trap door closes.

The pigeon again begins to strut around the box pecking randomly and eventually it pecks the lighted button again, at which the trap door opens for a brief while and it eats. As time goes by, the pigeon will cease to strut and peck in a random way, and will peck the button more often. Eventually, each time the trap door closes, it will immediately peck the lighted button to open the trap door again. Note that what has happened in this experiment is that the pigeon has learned to peck at a button to obtain food. Moreover, access to the food container has been reinforced (made more likely) by the behaviour of pecking the button. Thus, access to the food makes it much more

Figure 6.5 Operant conditioning

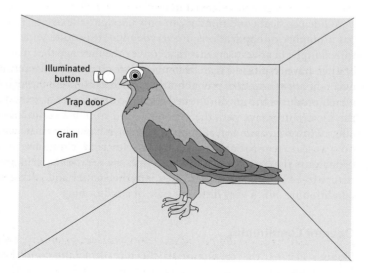

likely that the button-pecking behaviour will be repeated on future occasions. The important point is that, unless the organism emits the correct response, no reward is forthcoming. Therefore, the reward, which is only given after the desired response, becomes contingent on the occurrence of the response.

This is a very simple example, but a wide variety of behaviour can be shaped in this way. For example, pigeons have been taught to knock skittles down by bowling a ball and, in the USA the technique has been widely employed in organisations in behaviour modification techniques, which are described in Chapter 8. To understand how this is possible, it is necessary to know a little more of the principles of using reinforcement.

Reinforcement

A reinforcer is only a reinforcer if it increases the probability that the organism will respond in the desired way. For this reason operant conditioning is sometimes called 'instrumental' conditioning. In *positive reinforcement* the organism is rewarded for a particular piece of behaviour (a response). However, positive reinforcers can be of two types: primary and secondary. Primary reinforcers satisfy a primary need such as hunger or thirst, and their rewarding properties are automatic and do not have to be learned. Secondary reinforcers, however, acquire their reinforcing value through learning, often because they have become paired with a primary reinforcer. An obvious example is money, which gives us the ability to acquire a primary reinforcement. Indeed, behaviourists argue that there can be whole chains of secondary reinforcement. For example, praise or con-gratulations from the boss can have a positive reinforcing effect because it engenders a hope that promotion and/or higher pay will eventually be forthcoming.

Negative reinforcement refers to a situation in which the removal of an aversive stimulus increases the likelihood of a particular behaviour. For example, if I start a new job, I may be told that the first six months' service is a probationary period and a permanent appointment is contingent on good performance in this period. This creates a situation of uncertainty, which for most people is an aversive stimulus. However, the uncertainty can be removed by performing well.

Punishment

This is often confused with negative reinforcement, but they are quite different. *Punishment* is intended to eliminate a particular behaviour, whereas a negative rein-forcement aims to strengthen a behaviour by removing an aversive stimulus. Punishment can be applied in two ways. *Punishment by application* consists of using an aversive stimulus immediately following a particular act of behaviour, for instance spanking a child for misbehaviour. Another way of applying punishment is *punishment by removal*, which occurs when a positive reinforcement is removed after a particular behaviour. An example here could be the loss of certain privileges for persistent lateness at work.

Schedules of Reinforcement

If they are to have the desired effects in operant conditioning, rewards and/or punish-ments should not be used in a haphazard way. Reinforcement can be given in a

Positive reinforcement: an outcome occurring after a behaviour that tends to maintain repetition of the behaviour

Negative reinforcement: the removal of an aversive stimulus as a result of an organism exhibiting a desired behaviour

Punishment: the application of an aversive stimulus (or removal of a positive reinforcement) after a response by an organism that reduces the probability of a repetition of the response

Punishment by application: an aversive stimulus is applied immediately following an act of behaviour that is to be eliminated

Punishment by removal: a positive reinforcement is removed after behaviour which is to be eliminated has occurred

Continuous reinforcement: a reward is given each time the desired behaviour occurs

Intermittent reinforcement: a reinforcer is not given every time the desired response occurs

Fixed interval schedule: reinforcement delivered at fixed time intervals

Variable interval schedule: reinforcement delivered at non-uniform time intervals

Fixed ratio schedule: reinforcement delivered after a fixed number of desired responses

Variable ratio schedule: reinforcements which are delivered after a random number of desired responses

Extinction: a decrease in the occurrence of a behaviour arising from its non-reinforcement

continuous or intermittent way. In *continuous reinforcement* a reward is given each time the desired behaviour occurs. This is a useful technique in the early stages of the conditioning procedure because it quickly establishes a strong link between the desired behaviour and the reinforcing stimulus. However, the person who is conditioned only by continuous reinforcement tends to have a low tolerance to frustration on the task and low perseverance when things go wrong. *Intermittent reinforcement* occurs when a reinforcer is not given every time the desired response occurs. It has a variety of forms and each one has its own associated behavioural outcomes.

In a *fixed interval schedule*, reinforcement is given at regular, fixed intervals of time. For instance, reinforcement can be given once per minute, hour or day, irrespective of how often the desired behaviour occurs. Problematically, the organism soon seems to learn how often the reinforcement arrives and adjusts its own rate of exhibiting the desired behaviour accordingly.

A *variable interval schedule* makes the reinforcement available in a less predictable way, sometimes after a short interval and sometimes after long intervals. Because the organism is less able to predict when the reward will occur, this leads to a certain degree of persistence in exhibiting the behaviour. That is, because reinforcement can occur at any time, it becomes worthwhile for the organism to exhibit the desired behaviour continuously and this is probably one of the most useful forms of reinforcement to maintain a behaviour once it has been learned.

In a *fixed ratio schedule*, reinforcement occurs when a single reinforcement is given for a fixed number of desired responses, for example 1 in 10, or 1 in 20 and so on. To some extent the organism can predict when reinforcement will be given and so this tends to result in a pause in activity immediately after reinforcement, followed by a rapid burst of activity leading up to the next reinforcement. Perhaps the most readily available organisational example of this schedule is the use of piecework payment systems, in which pay is contingent on the amount of work done. Thus, a machine operator can see how much bonus (the reward) has been earned by simply counting the number of pieces of work he or she has completed. However, with this payment system people can slow down as soon as they have earned as much reward as they desire, and so, instead of maximising output, people might work very hard in the morning and take things easy in the afternoon.

A *variable ratio schedule* is the most difficult one for the organism to predict. Sometimes reinforcement occurs after a few responses and sometimes after many. Because the organism can never accurately judge when the reward will be given, this tends to result in a more continuous level of persistence in behaviour. This perhaps explains why people show persistence when playing gambling games, for instance, fruit machines or roulette.

Extinction

Withdrawing reinforcement usually has the result of extinguishing the behaviour, which, paradoxically, occurs much faster if continuous reinforcement has been used to shape the behaviour than where it has been shaped with intermittent reinforcement. It is easy to see why this is the case if we imagine ourselves using two vending machines. The first one, machine A, produces what we desire (say a cup of coffee) every time we insert the correct money. Machine B is far less reliable and sometimes it produces nothing. If, on a particular day, both machines are broken down, it is far more likely that we

Table 6.2 Classical and operant conditioning compared

Characteristic	Classical conditioning	Operant conditioning
Behaviour involved	Involuntary, reflex behaviour	Voluntary behaviour
How behaviour obtained	Elicited (drawn-out) by use of relevant stimulus	Emitted by organism for instrumental reasons, i.e. to obtain rewards, or to avoid aversive stimuli
Procedures used	Organism passive, with no control over US or CS	Organism active. It cannot obtain reward or avoid aversive stimulus until it emits desired behaviour, and can obtain repeated rewards for doing so
Selection of desired behaviour	Only innate responses can be selected for conditioning	Any natural behaviour emitted by the organism can be selected for conditioning
Changes in behaviour possible	Only to the extent that an innate response is made to occur to different stimuli	Since organism learns that certain behaviours result in it obtaining reinforcement, whole new repertoires of behaviour can be learned
Reinforcement	Reinforcement not contingent on response. Reinforcement elicits the response, i.e. $S \longrightarrow R$	Reinforcement contingent on response, i.e. $R \longrightarrow S$

would persevere longer with trying to obtain coffee from machine B than machine A. Why? Probably because machine B is less predictable than machine A, and so we would have to try to use it many more times before we realised that it was broken.

A Comparison of Classical and Operant Conditioning

Although they can both be classified as conditioning techniques, classical and operant conditioning are quite different. This can be seen in Table 6.2.

The Limitations of Behaviourist Theories of Learning

While behaviourists tend to explain all human behaviour in terms of stimulus and response links, it is difficult to see how this can explain all types of learning. For instance, if you look at Table 6.1 it is quite likely that with sufficient patience, levels 1 to 3 (factual knowledge, comprehension and application) could be learned with some form of operant conditioning. For instance, the material to be learned could be broken down into small increments, and appropriate reinforcements used to reward successful learning. Indeed, this is the way new staff are trained in some call centres using computer-based techniques (Whitehead 1999). In addition, there is strong evidence that conditioning can be used to ensure that people adopt patterns of behaviour, such as consistent attendance that is desired by organisations (Stajkovic and Luthans 1997).

However, these examples only require people to exhibit fairly simple behaviour, which involves learning at low levels. Beyond these levels learning requires more than mere knowledge of what is or is not acceptable and, for anything above level 3 in Table 6.1, higher brain processes, such as memory and reasoning, are required. For example, Adam (1972) shows that it is relatively easy to condition people to produce a certain quantity of output, but it is much harder to get them to pay attention to quality, simply because quantity only requires the learner to count, whereas quality is a much more abstract concept that involves learning to analyse and evaluate. Thus, useful as they are in explaining some learning, behaviourist theories cannot deal with the ways in which we learn some of the complex knowledge that helps us to cope with daily life. For this reason, the next section considers some of the approaches that take a more complex view of learning.

TIME OUT

Carefully consider the subjects you study at university or college. If you examine matters closely, you will probably be aware that lecturers attempt to get you to behave in certain ways and dissuade you from other patterns of behaviour. Focus on just one of the subjects you study and answer the questions below.

1. What is the pattern of behaviour that the lecturer seems to want you to adopt?
2. What specific behaviours does the lecturer seem to want to discourage?
3. Does the lecturer use inducements of some sort to try to get you to behave as he or she wants and, in particular, are there any reinforcements that he or she gives when you or others behave in this way?
4. Does the lecturer use particular methods of dissuading you from behaving in certain ways and, in particular, does he or she use punishments (either by application or withdrawal) to induce you to avoid these behaviours?

REPLAY

- Classical conditioning theory explains how an organism can be induced to learn to emit a reflex response to a new environmental stimulus.

- Operant conditioning theory explains how an organism can be induced to learn how to behave in a set way by reinforcing (rewarding) the desired behaviour after it has been emitted and/or extinguishing undesired behaviour using punishment, after it has been emitted.

- The different schedules of reinforcement and/or punishment that can be used in operant conditioning have different behavioural outcomes in terms of the learning process. Thus different schedules each have their own uses at different stages in the process of shaping behaviour.

- Conditioning theories only explain relatively simple levels of learning, beyond which account needs to be taken of the role played by cognitive processes in learning.

The Cognitive Approach to Learning

A revolt against the behaviourist explanation of learning had started to occur even in the heyday of behaviourism. Hebb (1949), for example, who was himself a behaviourist, argued that it is impossible to describe behaviour as simply an interaction between sensory processes and motor processes and that central brain processes, such as thinking, must also be at work.

The cognitive approach has a strong emphasis on change in what a learner knows, rather than simply what he or she does. Most work in this area assumes that people participate actively and consciously in order to learn; for example by drawing on past experience to make decisions about the present. These ideas were first put forward by other behaviourists (Tolman *et al.* 1946), who conducted a series of experiments in which rats were allowed to wander at random around a laboratory maze, in order to find a roundabout route to gain access to food. Tolman and his colleagues noted that when the most obvious route to the food was blocked off, the rats seemed to know their way around the maze and quickly located an alternative pathway. From this it was concluded that the rats had probably developed some sort of cognitive map of the maze in their earlier explorations, which means that central brain processes, including memory, could be at work.

More recent cognitive theories all expand and develop these ideas and there are two broad strands in work of this type. The first, the latent learning approach, emphasises the use of what has been learned on a prior occasion (sometimes without realising it) and using the knowledge later. The work of Tolman *et al.* (1946), described above, is an example of this and another development in this tradition will be explained presently. The second strand is the 'learning by insight' approach. This has an emphasis on the organism understanding what it has learned and thinking about it, so that the learning can be generalised to cope with new situations. Work in this tradition will also be described presently when dealing with experiential learning.

Social Learning Theory

While social learning theory (SLT) has its roots in behaviourism, it uses behaviourist terms in a revised and more liberated way. In general it holds that a vast amount of human behaviour is learned in interpersonal situations. Although it does not deny the effect of classical and operant conditioning, it holds that these processes cannot adequately account for every aspect of behaviour, particularly the use of appropriate behaviour in novel situations that have never before been encountered.

In SLT, prominence is given to two main ways of learning from social situations: observation and imitation, both of which can result in learning without the learner setting out to learn something. For example, Bandura *et al.* (1961) show that, to some extent, aggression is a behaviour that can be learned by imitation. However, not all behaviour is learned by imitating others and there is a difference between learning from others and directly imitating them. For instance, people can learn and absorb the behaviour of others, but not display a behaviour until it is rewarding for them to do so (Bandura and Walters 1963). This is sometimes called vicarious learning, because it involves learning a pattern of behaviour without actually doing it. It can also result in learning to avoid the mistakes that other people make. For example, if we see someone behaving in a certain way and he or she is punished for this act, we can learn not to replicate the person's behaviour (Manz and Simms 1981).

Perhaps the most interesting development in SLT is the use of the concept of *self-efficacy*. This is a person's belief in his or her ability to act in a certain way and Bandura (1982) describes it as perception of self, in which a person evaluates how well he or she has coped with a task. People high in self-efficacy tend to persevere and perform better without becoming stressed than those low in self-efficacy (Gist and Mitchell 1992), and there is a stream of research work that shows a strong relationship between high self-efficacy and high work performance. Social learning theory shows that, as well as

Self-efficacy: a person's belief in his or her ability to act in a certain way

learning by responding to external reinforcement, people also develop new patterns of behaviour acquired through self-reinforcement and, to some extent, this explains why people with high self-efficacy perform well. They could well reward (reinforce) themselves for high performance, which leads to greater perseverance to continue to do well.

 OB IN ACTION: On-the-job training

Almost half of on-the-job training has been branded a failure by the most recent annual report of the Adult Learning Inspectorate, which found that 46 per cent of schemes were failing – although this represented an improvement on the 60 per cent found to be failing in the previous year. Some 40 per cent of organisations that provided training at work, in prisons, for the unemployed and in adult education were 'blighted' by poor leadership and management, said David Sherlock, chief inspector of adult learning. 'Too many unlucky learners unknowingly join an organisation which is never going to give them the teaching and support that they deserve.' His report also criticised 'a confusing array of syllabuses, awards and awarding bodies' and called for the government to devise a simpler system.

Sixth form colleges were singled out for 'impressively high' standards, and the report said Learn Direct and the University for Industry had 'almost eliminated poor provision'. However, 95 of the providers of work-based learning for young people, or contractors for Jobcentre Plus were awarded the lowest grades by inspectors – 'a matter of real concern', according to Mr Sherlock. The Learning and Skills Council, the agency charged with delivering the government's £8bn skills strategy, was praised for withdrawing contracts from providers who were not delivering high standards.

Source:

Green, M (2003) Half of on-the-job training fails, say inspectors, *Financial Times*, 18 November

Experiential Learning

With the exception of social learning theory, the approaches covered so far only explain how learning in its simpler forms takes place. This is not to deny that learning by conditioning is a significant influence on behaviour, although it can only explain the acquisition of very basic knowledge and its associated behaviour, but not some of the more abstract facets of learning, such as how people learn in an ongoing way by building on experience, or are able to generalise from one situation to another to generate solutions to problems that they have never before encountered (see OB in Action Box above). This aspect of learning can be particularly important in organisations, where people are expected to be able to learn from their day-to-day experiences.

Senge (1994) distinguishes between two types of learning: adaptive and generative. **Adaptive learning** involves ongoing development of understanding and a capacity to cope with new situations. This can be done by people reflecting and analysing what has been done in the past, with a view to improving ways of dealing with fairly familiar situations; for example, by asking themselves such questions as:

- What did I do then?
- Did it work?
- What could I have done better?
- How could it help solve the current problem?

Almost everybody does this in some degree and it is the mode of learning that will be dealt with here.

The second form of learning, **generative learning**, is a different process, which consists of developing new ways of viewing the world. Since this is an approach that receives a great deal of attention when considering organisational change and development, discussion will be deferred until Chapter 21. In the meantime, because it applies to most adults, it is more important to consider adaptive learning and to do this we must return to two of the groups of factors that affect learning, and which were shown in Figure 6.3: the nature of the learner and the nature of the learning process.

The nature of the learner

Here there are many factors that could influence whether effective learning takes place. For example, if people are wracked with *anxiety*, this can inhibit the learning process. Conversely, if they can see that the knowledge has a practical use in achieving their goals, people who are *highly motivated* tend to learn easily. To some extent, *age* also has a bearing on effective learning. Very young children tend to have difficulties in handling abstract concepts, but, in organisations, learners are usually adults and by this stage of their development most people can deal with abstract information in some degree. A person's *memory* is another factor that can affect his or her learning process. For instance, the more a person can recall from past experience, the more likely it is that he or she will use this recollection for integrating new knowledge.

The nature of the learning process

Gangé (1974) suggests that the act of learning involves a chain of seven events, some of which are internal to the learner and some are external. He further argues that if any of the six links shown in Figure 6.6 do not operate effectively, there will be a failure to learn. This whole sequence of seven steps is highly dependent on relating the past to the present and so the model specifically acknowledges that higher order brain processes, such as motivation, perception and memory, are involved.

Here it can be noted that individuals tend to have their own cognitive styles, that is, preferred ways of organising information to give it meaning. As part of his or her cognitive style, an individual will also have a learning style or a learning strategy, which is used by the person to integrate new knowledge with that which has already been acquired, and to develop strategies for putting the knowledge to use, if and when it is required. There are two useful models for describing the effects and implications of these ideas, and these will be considered in turn.

Figure 6.6 The sequence of events in learning (adapted from Gangé 1974)

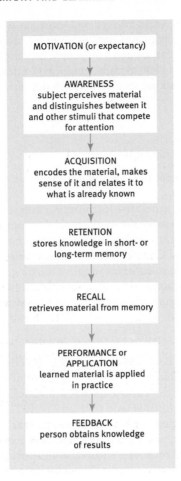

The Kolb and Fry Learning Cycle

Kolb and Fry (1975) argue that learning, and for that matter personal development, occur through an integrated process. This is based firmly on experience and its four stages are shown in Figure 6.7.

A **concrete experience** occurs when a person encounters something new and (perhaps subconsciously) collects information on the phenomenon. If, for example, I have heard of something called a 'ratchet screwdriver', but as yet have never seen one, the first time that I encounter this tool I might note that it is like any other screwdriver, except that it has a 'slide switch' just below the handle.

In the **reflective observation** stage, the person moves beyond merely collecting information and begins to analyse its implications. With the screwdriver, for example, I might reason that the switch on the screwdriver must have a purpose, probably that of locking the handle, according to whether I want to turn a screw, clockwise or anti-clockwise.

Abstract conceptualisation involves reflecting even further; with the screwdriver, I already know that if I turn a screw clockwise, it screws into a piece of wood, and if I turn it anti-clockwise the screw comes out of the wood. From this I conceptualise a

Figure 6.7 The Kolb
and Fry learning cycle

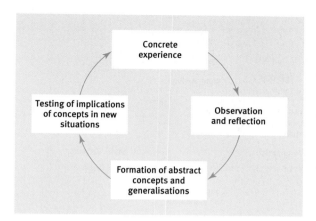

situation where I only need one hand and not two (one to steady the screwdriver and one to turn it) to tighten or loosen a screw.

In the **active experimentation** stage the abstract model I have developed is tested and, lo and behold, the ratchet screwdriver works with only one hand.

There are two very important implications of the Kolb and Fry model:

- It views learning as a cyclical process, in which the end of each cycle becomes the start of a new one. For example, I might think of other jobs where a 'ratchet' tool would be useful, for instance a 'ratchet spanner'.
- The model firmly places learning within the context of our everyday experience of life, not something that only occurs in formal learning or training sessions.

Kolb and Fry (1975) further argue that individuals vary in their preferences for using one of the stages in the cycle – usually the one with which they are most 'at ease'. While a person's style can be modified over time with a great deal of persistence and effort, he or she has a natural inclination to use the dominant style in preference to others. Indeed, people can find that trying to learn in the style that corresponds to another stage in the cycle is difficult, stressful or even unpleasant.

A practical outcome of Kolb and Fry's ideas is a questionnaire, the 'Learning Styles Inventory', which can be used to identify an individual's dominant learning style. However, this has been criticised on statistical and methodological grounds (see Allinson and Hayes 1988) and research into learning styles now tends to centre on a broadly similar typology, which is considered next.

The Honey and Mumford Model

Like Kolb and Fry, Honey and Mumford (1992) also identify four learning styles, each of which is associated with a preference for a particular stage of a learning cycle which is shown in Figure 6.8. While Honey and Mumford argue that none of the stages is fully effective on its own (and so all styles are needed), they also acknowledge that people tend to be more at ease with, and focus more strongly on, one style rather than others. However, their ideas differ from those of Kolb and Fry in one important respect. They do not regard it as inevitable that after a person has completed the cycle, he or she will revisit the stages to improve learning on the current issue. That is, the person

Figure 6.8 The Honey
and Mumford learning
cycle and associated
learning styles

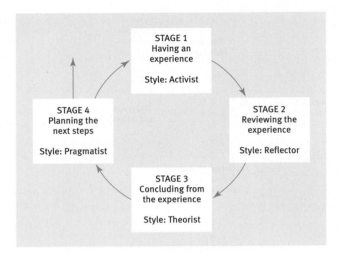

might veer away from a straightforward repeat of the cycle and enter a completely new learning activity. Honey and Mumford also describe the patterns of behaviour that are associated with each style, summary descriptions of which are given in what follows.

Activists are people who enjoy the here and now. They throw themselves into immediate experiences and are open minded, which tends to make them enthusiastic about anything new. Because they will try anything once, they tend to act first and consider the consequences afterwards. However, as soon as the excitement from one activity has died down, they look for the next. As such, they thrive on the challenge of new experiences, but are bored with implementation and longer-term routine.

Reflectors prefer to stand back and ponder experiences. Thorough collection and analysis of data about experiences and events is all important to them, and so they try to observe experiences from many different perspectives. Because they are thoughtful and introspective, they try to consider all possible implications before making a move, and tend to postpone reaching definite conclusions for as long as possible. They prefer to take a back seat in meetings and discussions and enjoy observing other people in action and listening to their views. Thus when they act, they adopt a low profile, consider the past as well as the present, and take other people's knowledge into account.

Theorists adapt and integrate their observations into complex but logical theories. They think problems through in a step-by-step way and assimilate disparate facts into coherent theories. However, they tend to be perfectionists who prefer to analyse and synthesise. Above all, they prize rationality and logic and are dedicated to rational objectivity rather than anything subjective or ambiguous. They prefer to maximise certainty and feel uncomfortable with subjective judgements, lateral thinking and anything flippant.

Pragmatists are keen to try out ideas, theories or techniques to see whether they work. They search out new ideas and take all available opportunities to experiment and get involved with the application of ideas they find attractive. As such, they respond to problems and opportunities as challenges and are often impatient with long, open-ended discussions. They are essentially practical people, who like making practical decisions and solving problems.

TIME OUT

Carefully examine the outline descriptions of Honey and Mumford's four learning styles.

1. Which of these do you feel most closely resembles your own dominant style and what evidence can you offer that this is the case?

2. What do you feel are the main implications of this learning style for successfully studying the subjects that you take at university or college? For example, do you find that some subjects seem easier for you to learn than others? Could this be because the methods that need to be used to acquire knowledge in the subject fit well with your dominant learning style?

3. To what extent do you feel that you complete the full learning cycle when studying something new in this subject? Or do you seem to get locked into one stage in the cycle? What implications does this have for your proficiency in the subject?

The Implications of Learning Styles

One of the most important implications of learning styles is that they influence how people prefer to learn, and this is likely to have a huge impact on how well individuals work with each other. For instance, a person whose natural style is that of a pragmatist, will probably be impatient with discussions about possibilities and options. Indeed, such people may well find these activities irrelevant and frustrating. They also have a need for clear guidelines and prefer to avoid the ambiguity inherent in some tasks. If they are subject to training or re-training, they will probably prefer a conventional mode of instruction where they are 'talked at', rather than working in a group that reaches conclusions through discussion. In contrast, the very nature of activists is that they are gregarious people. While they enjoy social contact and have few problems in interacting with others, they can sometimes try to centre all activity on themselves. Thus, while pragmatists and activists are both 'activity orientated', they are different enough for them to clash if they are both members of the same team. As will be seen in Chapter 11, this might not be a huge problem in a permanent group, where people learn to keep some of their natural tendencies in check to preserve group harmony. However, as is often the case these days, when forming teams and groups on a temporary basis, some account needs to be taken of different learning styles of people in the group so that they work well together.

Another important implication of experiential learning is in terms of organisational change and development. While this is considered in detail in Chapter 21, it can be noted here that these days, this places a strong emphasis on a firm transforming itself into what will be identified in Chapter 21 as a 'learning organisation'; one that continually learns from its environment. While this is normally taken to mean that the organisation itself learns, it is impossible to conceive of this unless there is a high degree of learning by individuals, and this gives rise to two interconnected issues.

First, individuals are likely to be far more comfortable with their own natural learning styles and in most firms there will probably be a fair degree of accommodation to people who have different styles. However, this also means that there is little incentive for people to break away from relying on their single dominant style to become employees who complete each stage of the learning cycle with equal ease. Nevertheless, this might be vital in a 'learning organisation', and so the first problem to resolve is to devise ways of encouraging people to shed reliance on a single style, and to become individuals for whom completing the full cycle becomes second nature.

The second matter, which is strongly connected with the first, is that individuals are affected by the nature of the organisations in which they are located. They can either be helped or hindered in their efforts to become complete learners by the cultures and climates of the organisations in which they work. In a conventional firm, the person who has a theorist learning style is probably likely to be considered, at best, as a time-wasting perfectionist and, at worst, an oddball or a maverick. Therefore, considerable attention might need to be devoted to changing cultures and climates, or at least develop a tolerance to theorists.

REPLAY

- Cognitive theories of learning, which first arose as a reaction to the restrictions of behaviourism, emphasise changes in what the learner knows, rather than simply what the learner does.
- In the cognitive approach to learning, account is taken of the role of brain processes, including perception, memory and reasoning.
- Social learning theory, which had its origins as an application of behaviourist principles, has now emerged as part of the cognitive approach and lays stress on the (sometimes unconscious) learning that takes place in social situations, through the process of modelling.
- Experiential theories stress the idea that people differ in the ways that they learn, that is, in terms of their dominant styles of learning.
- Experiential learning theories also stress that effective learning of something involves the completion of a sequence of learning activities, in which the learner uses all of the different learning styles in turn.

KNOWLEDGE MANAGEMENT

Knowledge management: a process or practice of creating, acquiring, capturing sharing and using knowledge, wherever it resides, to enhance learning and performance in organisations

As noted earlier, learning at an individual level has strong implications for learning by a whole organisation. For instance, if an organisation is able to learn it will probably be better equipped to cope with the fast-moving nature of the globalised economy. Here the burning question seems to be can it do this or, to put matters another way, how does it take advantage of individual learning and translate it into something that gives competitive advantage? In the eyes of many people the answer is to install a system of *knowledge management*, which is loosely defined by Scarbrough and Swan (1999) as 'a process or practice of creating, acquiring, capturing sharing and using knowledge wherever it resides, to enhance learning and performance in organisations'.

In many respects, knowledge management has acquired the status of the latest 'must have' in many organisations, and its popularity relies as much as anything else on the belief in some quarters that the one thing that an organisation cannot have too much of is management.

Explicit knowledge:
knowledge available
to everybody which
is easy to codify,
articulate and
express

Tacit knowledge:
individualised
personal knowledge
and understanding,
which although
understood by the
person is difficult to
describe, articulate
and disseminate
because it embraces
the person's
experience and
intuitions

Problematically, however, knowledge itself is tremendously hard to define. Nonaka and Takeuchi (1995) draw an important distinction here between two types of knowledge: explicit and tacit. *Explicit knowledge* is knowledge which is easily communicated, codified and expressed and is available to anyone within a particular context. This, for example, is the type of knowledge and understanding that most people in organisations have about the procedures and practices that need to be followed in order to do their jobs. *Tacit knowledge*, however, is much more personal and individualised. It is difficult to articulate and communicate to others because it is part of a person's experience and know-how. Thus it includes his or her intuitions and insights, or what he or she has found is a something that works, even when not explicitly specified. For example, if you are particularly good at a sport such as soccer, this is probably what enables you to send the ball just where you want it to go; however, just try explaining how you do this to somebody else.

According to Nonaka and Takeuchi, both explicit and tacit knowledge, complement each other and, if an organisation is to be creative and innovative, they are both required. Taken together, they are the accumulated wisdom of the organisation or, to put matters another way, what could be described of as part of its intellectual assets. Thus an organisation that knows how and when to use both types of knowledge is likely to have a significant competitive edge. For this reason, steps are being taken in many organisations to capture knowledge of both types, often by using information technology to develop databases of organisational specialists (and their prospective expertise) which can be used as and when necessary (Rajan *et al.* 1999). However, installing a system of knowledge management which attempts to ensure that people's knowledge is made available to everybody can be fraught with problems. To start with, knowledge and expertise are what give an individual his or her personal market value, and this can prompt people to self-censor any creative ideas that they might have (Williams 2002). Second, it can be noted that one of the fundamental principles of scientific management is that managers should try to make themselves the central repository for all knowledge in organisations (see Chapter 1). To a large extent, managers have been unsuccessful in this, simply because employees are not naive and quickly become aware that an invitation to share knowledge and expertise can become the fast route to redundancy. As such, there are grave reservations in some quarters about the extent to which knowledge can actually be managed (Harrison 2000).

OVERVIEW AND CONCLUSIONS

Memory and learning are both crucial processes in everyday life. For most people, the world changes from day to day, albeit in very small increments. Thus, most of us encounter something that is new in our personal environments at fairly frequent intervals, and it is through the learning processes that we adjust to what is new and discover how to cope with it. Without a memory where we can store this information until it is needed again, there would probably be little point in learning, and this is as true of our lives outside the workplace as it is about our time at work. For this reason, the first and perhaps most important conclusion that can be drawn is that the processes of memory and learning are highly interdependent and in constant interaction. The second major conclusion that can be drawn is that learning can take place at several levels. At one extreme it can consist of a simple awareness that a new phenomenon exists and, at the other, a sophisticated understanding of what phenomenon means, and how this knowledge can be put to practical use. This is made clear in the discussion of Bloom's (1956) levels of learning, explored earlier in the chapter.

The third conclusion is allied to the previous one. Just as there are different levels of learning, so there are many explanations of how learning takes place. These range from the simpler, behaviourist explanations of learning by conditioning, to much more sophisticated accounts of the cognitive processes at work contained in the theories of experiential learning cycles. Because behaviourist theories take no account of cognitive processes such as perception and memory, they give a somewhat mechanical explanation of learning, which ignores the role of meaning in what the learner learns. To explain learning of more complex information and, in particular, how we make sense of what we learn and we can apply it to new situations, cognitive approaches to learning are required. These theories all acknowledge the importance of higher order brain processes such as perception and memory, and for this reason, recent developments that focus on experiential learning are probably those that have most to offer to organisations.

FURTHER READING

Argyris, C (1982) *Reasoned Learning and Action*, San Francisco, CA: Jossey-Bass. By now this has come to be regarded as a classic book about the nature of individual and organizational learning.

Bandura, A (ed.) (1997) *Self-efficacy in Changing Societies*, Cambridge: Cambridge University Press. A book of readings, most of which use a social learning theory perspective to analyse the diverse ways in which beliefs of personal efficacy shape life events. It contains interesting perspectives on the influence of cross-cultural factors.

Dixon, NM (2000) *Common Knowledge: How Companies Thrive by Sharing What They Know*, Boson, MA: Harvard Business School Press. The book effectively argues for the use of knowledge management techniques. It advances the idea that organisations need to deal with different types of knowledge each of which needs to be managed in a different way, otherwise people will not share the knowledge.

Honey, P and A Mumford (1992) *The Manual of Learning Styles*, Maidenhead: Peter Honey. The definitive text on experiental learning, which contains an extended description of different individual learning styles and their implications.

Pedler, M, J Burgoyne and T Boydell (1997) *The Learning Company: A Strategy for Sustainable Development*, 2nd edn. London: McGraw-Hill. Although having a very strong managerialist stance, the book gives a well rounded if somewhat theoretical account of the learning organisation.

Rubin, DC (1995) *Remembering Our Past: Studies in Autobiographical Memory*, Cambridge: Cambridge University Press. A scholarly but readable account of cognitive theories of memory.

CASE STUDY 6.1: Knowledge management at British Petroleum

The practice of knowledge management arose in the early 1990s, when companies attempted to harness their under-used knowledge and intellectual capital. Nearly a decade later, it has not delivered on that promise, but has become narrowly focused on databases and other electronic means. While these have their uses they are not far-reaching; in part because they do not alter employees' attitudes to sharing and using knowledge. To do this, knowledge management needs to tackle something more fundamental – the design of a collaborative organisation.

British Petroleum (BP) provides a good example of this new approach. Over the past decade it has transformed the company from a collection of individual management fiefdoms and independent business units, into a collaborative business, thereby cutting costs, improving efficiency and lifting revenues. It has changed the resource allocation process so that a group of peers – business unit heads who run similar businesses – has become responsible for the allocation of capital expenditure to that group; effectively forcing it to work together to maximise allocations to the group, rather than to each individual. It has also developed the techniques of 'peer assist' and 'peer challenge' processes, in which managers and engineers in a business unit receive help from other units. Engineers in a typical business unit now spend about 5 per cent of their time on peer assists in other units, and BP has developed several electronic knowledge management systems and used video technology to aid with peer assists.

Promotion and reward systems have also changed. Managers now receive a '360-degree' review, and those who do not collaborate effectively across the organisation are excluded from more senior management positions. In addition, 30–50 per cent of the bonuses of senior managers depend on the performance of the company as a whole, and these changes go well beyond simply being electronic tools. They have altered the organisation and management principles of the company, which has led to enhanced levels of collaborative behaviour in the organisation; a lateral way of managing across units that complements the traditional hierarchy. Nevertheless, although most managers acknowledge the value of a 'collaborative culture', few know how to build one. To this end BP has identified a few simple techniques that can help instil the right types of behaviour. Because each organisation is different, however, executives first need to understand why people in the firm are failing to collaborate and share as much as they should. Here there are four obstacles that must be overcome.

Unwillingness to seek advice and learn from others. Employees may not want to seek advice across the organisation, either because they believe they cannot learn anything, or because there is a prevailing norm that people ought to solve their own problems. Electronic knowledge management systems cannot fix this problem and simply making documentary links to experts available does not help if employees do not want input from others. To address this BP uses peer pressure to make sure people seek advice and learn from others. Senior managers keep a close eye on the extent to which a business unit manager asks for assistance from peers and will intervene if he or she seeks too little. A peer challenge is an even more direct form: peers, not superiors, will go directly to a business unit, challenge it and help it improve in areas in which it is under-performing.

The inability to find expertise. There is often someone who knows the answer to a problem, but it may be nearly impossible to connect this person to the one who needs help. Clearly, databases and electronic search engines serve a useful role here, but more in the capacity of being 'electronic yellow pages', than as self-sufficient electronic repositories. However, technology has its limits. Expert directories can quickly get out of date, and fail to capture what each person knows. More importantly, they do not allow for a creative combination of ideas and individuals. Therefore, companies need to cultivate people who know where experts and ideas reside. These 'connectors' tend to be long-serving employees who have worked in many different areas in the company and thus have an extensive personal network. They see opportunities for new value creation based on the combination of talent, ideas and expertise in different units.

The unwillingness to help. Employees may be willing to seek advice, but others are sometimes reluctant to share it. The growing emphasis on performance management has fuelled this problem: people no longer have the time to help others, and some do not care because they are only asked to deliver on their own targets. While performance is important, executives also need to develop incentives to help others and cultivate a shared identity among employees.

The inability to work well together. A 'chemistry' problem can sometimes prevent people working well together, even if they want to and are part of a project team. It is a very different problem from the other three obstacles and requires different responses, including training sessions on teamwork, coaching people as they try to work together, and the development of strong relations between people from different units.

Managers need to respond to each of these obstacles in different ways. For example, developing an electronic knowledge management system will not help if the underlying problem is that employees hoard knowledge and will not seek help; it might even make people more cynical about collaboration. Likewise, making promotion contingent on the extent to which people seek advice from others will not help if there is no way of identifying experts. Thus all four obstacles need to be overcome for effective collaboration to occur and, if the problem is a lack of willingness to seek advice and share it, there are several effective responses. Leaders should urge the importance of collaboration and its value should be incorporated into the company's value statement. If the problem is an inability to find expertise, then the company should cultivate informal networks of experts to be used by those searching for particular expertise. Electronic yellow pages should be set up to identify the company's various experts and benchmark systems established to allow staff to identify the company's best practices.

If the problem is an inability to work together, managers should develop regular, structured interactions between relevant sets of employees, such as the peer groups at BP. Those who need to work across the organisation should be given coaching and training where necessary.

One pitfall of collaboration is that it can easily be overdone. Before you know it, people participate in meetings without getting anything done, leading to ineffective collaboration that undermines overall performance. Levers to create a collaborative organisation must therefore be counterbalanced by clear performance management of each individual and business unit, including a specification of who is responsible for what.

Companies that achieve this balance break one of the most ingrained compromises in corporations – that between decentralisation and centralisation. Decentralising responsibility by giving each manager a clear performance mandate leads to better local decisions, but at the same time, companies also reap economic gains from working together across decentralised business units. This in turn creates managers who transcend parochial self-interests, and can see the whole while delivering their own part.

Source: Hansen, M (2002) Turning the lone star into a real team player, *Financial Times*, 8 August

Questions

1. Who, in your view, did BP hold most responsible for the lack of success in its prior knowledge management system: the senior executives of BP; its managers; or its employees?

2. What particular advantages for the company would you envisage from adopting collaborative working?

3. To what extent do you feel that the measures BP adopted would be likely to bring about collaborative working?

4. Can you identify anything that BP has failed to do, the absence of which which might might stand in the way of achieving collaborative working?

REVIEW AND DISCUSSION QUESTIONS

1. For the purposes of study, learning and memory are regarded as two specialist areas in psychology. Explain the limitations of this perspective in terms of gaining a practical understanding of the learning process.

2. Using practical examples from work or your place of study to illustrate your answers explain the role of the following in learning:

- positive reinforcement
- negative reinforcement
- punishment by application
- punishment by withdrawal.

3. While it has its roots in behaviourist psychology, social learning theory (SLT) has a very different conception of the process of learning. Using practical examples to illustrate your answer, explain what SLT tells us about the learning process that is not explained by behaviourist ideas.

4. Critically examine the idea that 'an understanding of his or her own learning style can help a person become a more effective learner'.

Chapter 7

Work Motivation and Job Design

LEARNING OUTCOMES

After studying this chapter you should be able to:

- define motivation and describe the basic motivational process
- understand the role of needs and expectations of work in the motivational process, together with some of the barriers to work motivation
- describe the origins of motivation theory, and understand, discuss and integrate four major content theories of work motivation
- understand and describe the implications of individual job design for work motivation

INTRODUCTION

Humans seldom passively accept their surroundings, but seek to make use of contextual circumstances to pursue their aims and objectives. For this reason work motivation is a topic of enduring interest in the field of Organisational Behaviour because motivation theory seeks to explain how hard people strive to undertake their work tasks.

This chapter deals with basic theories of motivation. It commences by examining the importance of motivation in an organisational context, and gives a general description of the motivational process. This is followed by a consideration of some of the barriers to work motivation, together with human reactions to the barriers. Since needs and expectations play a fundamental part in all motivation theories, the discussion then considers human needs and expectations of work, and explains four 'content' theories that deal with human needs and their role in work motivation.

The nature of the jobs that people do has a strong impact on work motivation. This is considered in the next section of the chapter, which deals with the design of individual jobs and its motivational implications. As a prelude to the next chapter, which deals with more advanced theories of work motivation, this one closes with a short overview section.

MOTIVATION IN A WORK CONTEXT

Although motivation is fascinating to social scientists as an abstract topic, it has a much stronger practical significance to managers. Ultimately everything achieved in or by an organisation depends on human activity, and managers want subordinates who willingly channel their energies into their allotted tasks (Child 1984). However, people usually join an organisation for their own reasons, which means that they can be more interested in achieving their own personal aims than the objectives laid down by a manager. For this reason, the management interest in motivation is usually highly instrumental and by understanding what motivates people, managers hope to be able to control their work performance so that they work harder and more willingly. However, performance does not depend on motivation alone, and Vroom (1964) argues that task performance is a function of the three factors given in the following symbolic equation:

$P = f(E, A, M)$ – where:

Performance (P) is how well the task is performed
Environment (E) is the context of equipment, etc., in which the task is to be performed
Ability (A) is the skills and knowledge to perform the task well
Motivation (M) is the motivation to perform the task.

Here it should be noted that:

- managers have direct control over the selection process, which has some influence on employees' skills and knowledge
- in addition, skills and knowledge can be improved with training and development, which is also under management's control
- however, motivation comes from inside an employee, it is unobservable and cannot be altered at will by a manager.

One of the most enduring myths about motivation, however, is that managers 'motivate' their subordinates, and it is commonplace to hear them refer to it as if it is some sort of medicine that can be dispensed in variable quantities to those who need it most. This is an impossibility, and Vroom's equation also draws attention to several highly important points:

- by inference, motivation is an invisible process and the nearest a manager is likely to come to being able to motivate people is to control the circumstances surrounding them, so that they find the situation psychologically stimulating
- in itself this is a difficult task, because people must be equipped with appropriate skills and abilities, and placed in surroundings that offer a prospect of some of their most important needs and wants being satisfied
- only then will they want to use their skills in a willing way that also achieves some of the manager's aims.

MOTIVATION: A DEFINITION AND EXPLANATION

The first step in understanding how these points can be satisfied is to examine the motivational process in a very basic way. However, it can be very difficult to find a universally acceptable definition of motivation, and so in this chapter the word is taken to mean:

> a state arising in processes that are internal and external to the individual, in which the person perceives that it is appropriate to pursue a certain course of action (or actions) directed at achieving a specified outcome (or outcomes) and in which the person chooses to pursue those outcomes with a degree of vigour and persistence.

In psychology, motivation is a word used to explain why a person behaves in a certain way, and describes three components of behaviour that have an impact on performance:

- **the direction** of behaviour, which is greatly influenced by what a person most desires to do
- **the intensity** of behaviour, which roughly equates to how hard the individual strives to go in that direction
- **persistence**, which consists of the individual's willingness to stay with the direction when obstacles are encountered.

The Basic Motivation Process

Conception of self: a person's view of what he or she is

Needs: experienced deficiencies between what someone is or has and what he or she wants to be or have, which result in a desire to remove the deficiency

Figure 7.1 shows the basic process of motivation and expresses the idea that there is a driving force within individuals that prompts them to achieve a goal of some sort. This is triggered by comparison between **self** and **ideal self**. All humans have a self-identity (Rogers 1961) which consists of their view of what they are in terms of such things as: strengths and weaknesses, abilities, beliefs and feelings. An individual also has a *conception of self* – the person he or she would like to be. This is usually somewhat different from the actual self and even small differences usually give rise to a desire to bring actual and ideal selves into closer alignment (Leonard *et al*. 1999) and this has strong motivational implications.

Needs are the experienced differences (deficiencies) between ideal or actual self. For example, a person can perceive a difference between the skills and abilities that

Figure 7.1 Basic
motivation process

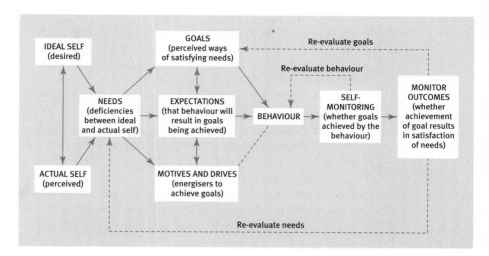

Goals: milestones
that are perceived to
lead to satisfaction of
needs

Expectations: an
anticipation that
certain behaviours
will result in
achieving goals

Motives and drives:
subconscious
processes that
provide the energy to
engage in the goal-
directed behaviour

Behaviour: activity
directed at achieving
something

Self-monitoring:
examining one's own
behaviour to see
whether it has had
the desired result

**Monitoring of
outcomes:** examining
whether the
behaviour used has
resulted in needs
satisfaction

he or she has and those that other people acknowledge. This can give rise to a need for recognition, which prompts the next stage in the model.

Goals are milestones that a person believes will lead to remedying these deficiencies. *Expectations* also come into play, because humans have a strong tendency to anticipate that certain behaviours will result in predicable outcomes; that is, achieving the goals. *Motives and drives* are the energisers of action to achieve the goal. In the example given earlier, there could be an expectation that a position of higher status would be a mark of recognition, and so promotion could become a goal. This might suggest to the person that he or she displays a pattern of behaviour that induces other people to see him or her as suitable for promotion and one again this results in the next stage of the model.

Behaviour is directed at achieving the goal and in the example used here the person could be expected to engage in actions calculated to show superiors that he or she is capable of things beyond the present role and, because these acts are intended to achieve something, the person will normally engage in the next stage, *self-monitoring*, in which he or she evaluates whether the desired outcome has been achieved; for example, whether the new pattern of behaviour actually impresses the boss. For this reason there is a feedback loop shown in Figure 7.1, which indicates that behaviour can be modified if necessary.

Monitoring of outcomes enables the person to evaluate whether the behaviour originally perceived as appropriate achieved the intended outcome, in this case whether recognition is reflected in promotion. This is one of the main ways in which humans learn appropriate repertoires of future behaviour, because achieving a goal reinforces similar behaviour in the future. In some cases, however, it leads to the person re-evaluating the goal itself, and in the example used so far, the person could find that promotion is not achieved and the goal might be seen as no longer seen as attainable. Thus the person will probably search for another one to satisfy the need. As will be seen later, the idea that there is an almost unlimited reservoir of needs just waiting to be awakened is embodied in at least one significant theory of work motivation. It is therefore important to examine needs and expectations in the work context.

 OB IN ACTION: The public sector – still an attractive destination for needs fulfillment

In recent years the civil service has been assaulted externally by private sector contractors and consultants over its contracting skills, and internally by everyone from the prime minister downwards. Moreover, it has been subjected to endless bouts of 'reform'. Nevertheless, it remains a top destination for graduates, and is repeatedly ranked as an 'employer of choice', among Britain's brightest university graduates.

According to Sir Gus O'Donnell, the new Cabinet Secretary, the reasons are not hard to see. One of its big motivators, he said, was the ability for someone to go home at the end of the day feeling that he or she had made a real difference to other people's lives. Sir Gus might have added that, these days, even though it is under some pressure, there is also the public sector pension to consider: defined benefit schemes that remain generous at a time when they are fast disappearing in the private sector. This is also true of places other than the civil service. For example, the boom in spending on the NHS, education and much else, also seems to reflect a perception that government plainly believes in public services, and this has probably boosted the public sector as a destination for top graduates. Indeed, the NHS is ranked fifth in a recent *Times* poll, and the police force which can be through its 'fast track' scheme' is also attractive to graduates.

However, these days, those joining the public sector are entering a changing world that is arguably becoming more challenging: a change that, for some at least, may make it even more attractive. More work is being contracted out, which requires procurement and market management skills that the public sector has long been short of, and these skills equally valued in the private sector. Furthermore, there is growing pressure on civil servants who want to get to the very top to take a so-called 'delivery' post on the way up, so that practical skills are added to policy ones. This offers broader experience, marketable in places other than the public sector, and eases transfer from other parts of the public sector.

Source:

Timmins, N (2005) *Financial Times*, 14 October

NEEDS AND EXPECTATIONS OF WORK

Work is not the only place where a person can engage in activities that satisfy needs and, although being an employee normally involves exchanging labour for rewards, humans usually have more needs than money (see OB in Action Box above). They come to expect that at least some of these will be satisfied in the work situation and so it is useful to have a way of classifying the various ways in which rewards can be obtained.

Extrinsic rewards: rewards conferred from outside the individual

Intrinsic rewards: psychological rewards that come from inside the person

Social rewards: psychological rewards obtained through interaction with other people

- *Extrinsic rewards* are those tangible benefits such as pay, fringe benefits, pensions, conditions of work and security that individuals receive in return for their efforts. Because these are provided by the organisation, how much is received is largely beyond the control of the individual.

- *Intrinsic rewards* are the psychological rewards that come from the experience of work, or from being part of an organisation; for example, having an opportunity to use skills and abilities, having a sense of challenge or achievement, or having one's efforts recognised and appreciated. These rewards come from inside the person and are given by people to themselves, which can only occur if the conditions they experience allow them to feel this way.

- *Social rewards*, which are obtained by being with other people, often by having a sense of common purpose with them and obtaining reassurance or confirmation of identity. These also have a substantial psychological content.

Humans have very strong social impulses. As will be seen in Chapter 11, a large part of the human 'sense of self' comes from being able to test our ideas of who and what we are on other people, and from obtaining some confirmation that we are correct: the so-called 'looking-glass self' (Cooley 1964).

Whether or not something at work is experienced as rewarding and, if it is, how it rewards a person, is a highly individualised matter. What is seen as an extrinsic reward by one person can sometimes be an intrinsic reward for someone else and, while people vary enormously in the relative mix they expect, most individuals expect rewards of all three types, which is portrayed diagrammatically in Figure 7.2.

Since the motivation to engage in a particular piece of behaviour is triggered by the expectation that the behaviour will lead to a reward that satisfies a need of some sort, it is important to note the following:

- extrinsic motivation comes from an expectation of receiving an extrinsic reward and intrinsic motivation from the expectation of obtaining an intrinsic reward

Figure 7.2 Rewards and satisfaction of needs and expectations

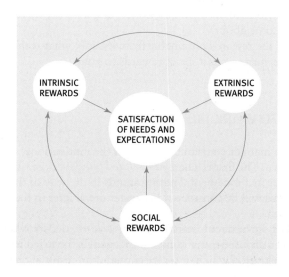

- because social rewards emanate from outside the person, but their rewarding effects are largely psychological, they are a combination of extrinsic and intrinsic factors
- in practice it is very difficult to ensure that people receive some types of reward rather than others; for instance, the opportunity for people to interact can be provided, but nobody can make people give and receive social rewards
- because intrinsic motivation is generally assumed to be a more powerful driving force, most managers focus on intrinsic and extrinsic rewards
- since motivation is a highly personalised process that depends on a person's desired mix of extrinsic, intrinsic and social rewards, providing intrinsically motivating circumstances requires a good understanding of an individual's pattern of needs, but for a variety of reasons this is seldom convenient or possible
- thus there is often a general reliance on extrinsic motivators.

However, relying on extrinsic motivators alone seldom results in motivated employees. It tends to make people feel that their behaviour is primarily driven by external factors rather than their own motives, and evidence suggests that too high a level of extrinsic rewards tends to damp down intrinsic motivation (Jordan 1986).

TIME OUT

Carefully consider the experience of your job to date and try to answer the questions below. If you are in full-time or part-time employment, this should be your present job. If you have never been an employee, answer the questions in terms of your experience of university or college life.

1. What do you feel were your needs, goals, expectancies, motives and drives when you started the job?
2. What do you feel are your needs, goals, expectancies, motives and drives now?
3. Is there a difference between questions 1 and 2? If so, why and how did this difference come about?
4. In terms of the rewards obtainable from the job, what is the relative importance of extrinsic, intrinsic and social rewards to you?

Job-related barriers: features of the job that remove the likelihood that it can satisfy a person's needs

Goal blocking: a state where motivations are aroused but goal attainment is thwarted

BARRIERS TO WORK MOTIVATION

There are two main circumstances in which the motivational chain described earlier can break down. The first is where *job-related barriers* exist – where something about the job itself or its fundamental nature stands in the way of the individual becoming motivated. This will be considered in greater detail later in the chapter when dealing with job design.

The second set of circumstances, *goal blocking*, occurs when a person's motivations have been aroused but attainment of a goal is thwarted in some way. This tends to result in **frustration** which, if severe enough, can result in one or other of two basic reactions, which will be described here as *adaptive behaviour*, or *non-adaptive behaviour*. The first alternative is to engage in *adaptive behaviour* of some sort. One way to do this is for the person to try to remove or circumvent the barrier. Someone with a strong need for recognition of a job well done could, for example, make a definite request for feedback.

Non-adaptive behaviours are the other possible reaction. They are a way of shutting out the goal-blocking conditions and most of them, such as repression, suppression, projection, fixation, regression and reaction formation, were described in Chapter 3 when discussing Freud's (1901b) explanation of defence mechanisms.

Because there are usually several factors at work when goal blocking occurs, it is often extremely difficult to predict whether a person's behaviour will be adaptive or non-adaptive. The individual's personality, the strength of his or her needs, how firmly the person is attached to a particular goal, the strength of the motivational force and whether he or she perceives that the barrier can be circumvented, can all be pertinent. Where only one of these is involved, things are not too complicated, but it is far more likely that there will be several, and this results in a highly complex situation, the remedies for which are well beyond the scope of this book.

Adaptive behaviour: that aimed at removing or circumventing a situation where goal blocking occurs

Non-adaptive behaviour: that which is directed at shutting out the realisation that goal attainment is blocked

REPLAY

- Motivation is an inner mental state that prompts a direction, intensity and persistence in behaviour.
- It is triggered by a desire to bring the actual self closer to the ideal self, which results in needs, goals, expectancies, motives and drives, which result in motivated behaviour.
- Needs and expectations of work are highly individualistic and consist of the desire to obtain some combination of extrinsic, intrinsic and social rewards.
- Barriers to motivated behaviour can exist in the work situation and these can be classified as two main types: job-related barriers and barriers that block individual goal attainment.

THEORIES OF WORK MOTIVATION

The Precursors of Work Motivation Theory

All motivation theories make assumptions about what is popularly called 'human nature' – the idea that all people have inner driving forces that prompt them to do certain things. This is a very old idea, in use long before the appearance of what we now call theories of motivation. The beginnings of motivation theory as we know it today can most easily be traced to the work of Frederick W Taylor (1911), the originator of **scientific management**, whose work and its assumptions were described in Chapter 1.

While scientific management is not a theory of work motivation, but a technique for obtaining more efficient use of labour, it is highly influential with managers and contains assumptions that have strong motivational implications. The most important of these is the assumption that the main (and perhaps only) thing that people seek to obtain from work is high pay. This ignores situations where people exhibit highly motivated behaviour where economic rewards are low and the next major development took a different perspective.

This was the **Hawthorne Studies** (Roethlisberger and Dickson 1939) (described in greater detail in Chapter 1), which gave rise to a new school of management thinking: the **human relations movement**. This left its own mark on ideas about work motivation, the most important of which is that people have social needs that are as important as the economic imperative. As will be seen presently, the assumptions inherent in human relations theory have had a strong influence on the major group of motivation theories which were the next development in the area. To put them into context, however, it is important to stress that work motivation theory has tended to split into two major streams, each of which deals with a different aspect of the subject.

Content theories: focus on the needs of people as the prime impetus for motivated behaviour

The group covered in this chapter is generically known as *content theories*. These theories focus on the needs, wants and desires of people, which are taken to be the main impetus for motivated behaviour. The second group, which is covered in the next chapter, is called *process theories*. These theories do not discount the importance of needs as a driving force and explicitly acknowledge that it is the compulsion to satisfy a need at any given time that provides the motivational impetus. However, theories of this type recognise that needs are highly personalised and can vary for each individual over time. As such, there is a much stronger focus on matters that influence the strength of the motive force and the ways in which a need gets translated into a particular pattern of behaviour.

Process theories: focus on mental processes which transform the motive force into particular patterns of behaviour

CONTENT (NEEDS) THEORIES OF MOTIVATION

Theories of this type assume that people strive to satisfy a range of deep-rooted needs. While they differ in terms of their assumptions about the relative importance of different needs, it is the desire to satisfy them that is said to energise behaviour.

Maslow's Needs Theory

Maslow's work (1954) dates from the late 1940s, and assumes that human needs are virtually inexhaustible and that as one set of needs is satisfied, another arises in its place. Thus needs are arranged in a hierarchy, which is usually portrayed as a pyramid of five levels. This is shown in Figure 7.3, where the bottom three levels comprise basic needs and the top two are the so-called higher order needs.

- **Physiological needs** are the most basic of all and arise from internal physical imbalances such as hunger, thirst, warmth and shelter; they need to be satisfied at fairly frequent intervals.
- **Security needs** are at the next level and consist of security, freedom from pain or harm, emotional security and well-being, fairness, predictability and order.
- **Affiliation needs** are prompted by the strongly social nature of humans. Most people enjoy feelings of belonging, friendship or being loved, which can only be satisfied through social interaction. Needs of this type provide the motivation to be part of a group, an experience that gives us the opportunity to form meaningful relationships and to gain (and give) support from (and to) others.

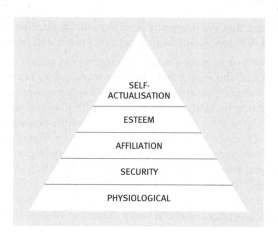

Figure 7.3 Maslow's needs hierarchy (adapted from Figure 'Hierarchy of needs' in *Motivation and Personality,* 2nd edn by AH Maslow. Reprinted by permission of Pearson Education, Inc., Upper Saddle River, NJ)

- **Esteem needs,** which are sometimes called 'ego' needs, are located at the next level upwards and are often split down into two sub-types. Needs for **self-esteem** concern an individual's view of him or herself, for instance having a sense of self-respect, self-confidence or of doing something that is meaningful and worthwhile in a competent way. **Esteem by others** is needed because a considerable part of our self-concept is obtained from signals about ourselves that we get from other people (Cooley 1964). If other people indicate that their view of us is as favourable as the one that we hold of ourselves, it is a highly rewarding experience.

- The topmost level consists of the so-called **self-actualisation needs.** These are virtually inexhaustible and are concerned with a person's need to realise his or her full potential, and it is these that are said to drive humans to do things that have never been done before.

Maslow's theory contains a number of highly important assumptions, two of which have significant implications for work motivation:

- He argues that the different levels of need are universally addressed sequentially. This means that needs at one level will not normally play a significant part in motivation until those at the level immediately below have been satisfied. However, in rare cases an individual will bypass one or more levels altogether. For example, if someone is deprived of love and affection in childhood, the person will sometimes lack affiliation needs later in life. Similarly, there are people with very high moral ideals who willingly forgo satisfaction of everything else to concentrate on self-actualisation.

- Maslow assumes that needs which are satisfied no longer have a motivational effect.

Although the theory has a strong intuitive appeal, there are a number of strong criticisms:

- First, in terms of the values it expresses, the theory is arguably patronising and elitist; for example, the idea that some needs are primitive and some are more advanced (Lazarus 1971).

- Second, the idea that the hierarchy is universally applicable takes no account of cross-cultural differences, and a return to this point will be made later.

- Third, Maslow's ideas have a mystic, metaphysical quality. They are largely the result of armchair theorising and often contradicted by research evidence. For example, the hierarchical structure of needs has been contradicted by a five-year longitudinal study by Hall and Nougain (1968) who examined changes in the needs of a group of people. In addition, there is little empirical support for his explanation of the way that different levels of needs trigger different motivations; for example, that satisfied needs no longer have a motivational effect. Empirical work by Whahaba and Bridewell (1976) has failed to find any evidence for this idea and an investigation by Alderfer (1972), which explored the relative importance of several needs for over 2,000 managers, showed quite clearly that unless people were actually conscious of non-fulfilled lower-level needs, those at the very highest level were always considered the most important.

- Perhaps most damning of all is that the basic assumptions underpinning Maslow's ideas are seriously flawed. These were derived from armchair theorising in his early anthropological studies of dominance in groups of monkeys, where he not only assumed that it is safe to generalise across species, (in itself a highly questionable assumption) but the generalisations were based on animals held in captive conditions, who behave in far less subtle ways than those existing in the wild (Cullen 1997).

In the light of this evidence there must be grave doubts about the practical utility of Maslow's theory, and it might well be far too simplified and imprecise to be useful as a way of influencing employee motivation. However, this is not to say that it has no value at all. It gives a general framework for categorising needs of different types, and if nothing else, it makes an important contribution as a descriptive tool.

TIME OUT

Carefully reflect on your life to date and, using the description of needs at each level in Maslow's hierarchy, try to answer the questions below.

1. What level of needs satisfaction do you feel you have reached?
2. Is it true that in reaching this level you have satisfied all of your needs at the levels below? If not, what needs remain unsatisfied?
3. Assuming that needs at the next level upwards are now your motivators, what are your particular goals at this level and how does this affect your behaviour in terms of its direction, intensity and persistence?
4. Now try to repeat questions 1 and 3 for someone else that you know well, for example a friend or parent.

Alderfer's ERG Theory

Alderfer (1972) also uses the idea of hierarchical ordering, but this has only three levels: Existence (**E**), Relatedness (**R**) and Growth (**G**), from which comes the theory's name.

- **Existence needs** are those necessary for human survival and are roughly equivalent to Maslow's bottom two levels.
- **Relatedness needs** are concerned with needs to interact with others and approximate to Maslow's affiliation category, together with some of his esteem needs.
- **Growth needs** are at the highest level and take in some of the esteem needs in the Maslow scheme, plus self-actualisation.

While there is some similarity between the Maslow and Alderfer models, the categories do not match up exactly and there are also other very important differences:

- in Alderfer's scheme the different levels are viewed more as a continuum than as discrete categories
- Alderfer does not assume a sequential progression up the hierarchy, but allows for more than one level (or even all levels) to be active at the same time
- although he suggests that satisfaction of needs at one level will normally lead to someone seeking satisfaction at the level above, he also deals with the important issue of what happens when needs are not satisfied.

In Maslow's theory it is assumed that a person remains at one level until all needs are satisfied, whereas Alderfer argues that continued frustration of satisfaction at one level can result in a person regressing to the level below and refocusing attention there. This is shown schematically in Figure 7.4.

Unfortunately, Alderfer's theory has received little empirical testing beyond that done by its author. Despite this, he argues that the theory could be a more powerful, but simpler explanation of the effects of needs than Maslow's ideas (Alderfer 1972). In some academic circles the theory has been well received and is considered to be an

Figure 7.4 Alderfer's ERG theory

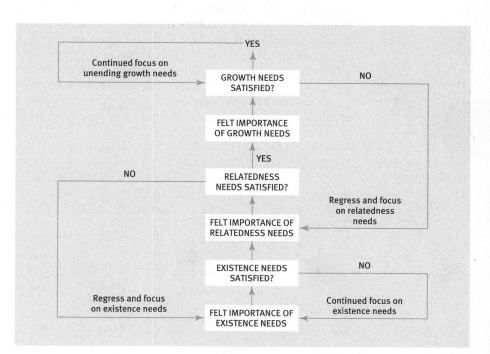

important contribution to needs theory because it gives a plausible explanation of a person's likely reactions when needs are not satisfied (Hodgetts 1991).

Herzberg's Two-factor Theory

A departure from the idea of hierarchically ordered needs is given in the theory of Frederick Herzberg and his co-workers (1959), which hinges on the idea that people are motivated by things that make them feel good about work, but have aversions to things that make them feel bad. Herzberg avoids using the word 'need' and, instead, divides features of the work environment into two major groups: hygiene factors and motivators. Motivators are the factors that produce good feelings about work, while hygiene factors, if not present, can result in feelings that the work situation is unsatisfactory. However, it is important to note that the two sets of factors are not opposites. They have different roles and in Herzberg's view, these are equally important, as shown in Figure 7.5.

Hygiene factors are features of the work environment rather than the work itself, for example working conditions, status, company procedures, quality of supervision and interpersonal relations. The word 'hygiene' indicates that they have a role similar to preventative medicine; that is, they stop illness (in this case dissatisfaction) from occurring. However, their presence do not motivate because the absence of dissatisfaction is not satisfaction. All the hygiene factors do is ensure that a state of **no dissatisfaction** exists.

Nevertheless, unless this is the case, the other set of factors cannot come into play. These are the *motivators*, which are mainly intrinsic in nature, for instance a sense of achievement, recognition, responsibility, the nature of the work itself and prospects of growth and advancement. Once again, if the motivators are absent, this will not actually result in dissatisfaction, so long as the hygiene factors are adequate, because the opposite of satisfaction is not dissatisfaction, it is merely **no satisfaction**.

Herzberg's original study has been replicated many times, both by himself (1974) and by others (Hodgetts and Luthans 1991). While the results usually support his original findings there are still some worrying criticisms of the theory.

Almost inevitably there are criticisms of his research methodology, which used what is technically known as a 'critical incident' technique, in which people were asked to

Hygiene factors: features of the work environment which, if present, help avoid dissatisfaction with work

Motivators: features of the job itself that people find enjoyable and that have a motivational effect

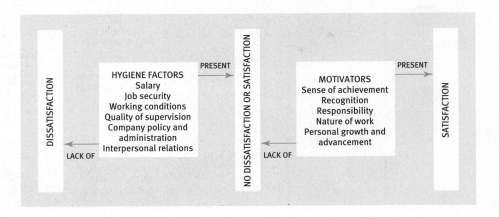

Figure 7.5 Herzberg's two-factor theory

recount incidents that had made them feel exceptionally good or bad about their jobs. Criticisms here are that:

- Answers to this type of question are all too easily contaminated by respondent self-images, for instance people commonly attribute something that made them feel good to their own behaviour and shift the blame for feeling bad on to the organisation. Thus hygiene factors and motivators could be incorrectly classified.

- There is always some tendency for the answer to a question to depend on how the question is put, which means that researcher biases can enter the data collection process, and these can be reinforced in the way that the researcher interprets the answers.

- The technique also tends to push things into bipolar (good or bad) categories of evaluation and this takes no account of a situation where someone dislikes one aspect of a job but, overall, likes the job a great deal.

While these criticisms do not really detract from the idea that satisfaction and dissatisfaction could be different dimensions of the work experience, people are unique. Thus motivators for one person could well be hygiene factors for another.

A second set of criticisms centres on the way that Herzberg classifies organisational features of the work situation as hygiene factors or motivators, and even more controversial is his assertion that the two sets of factors have distinctly different functions. A replication study by Wernimont (1966), for example, indicated that both motivators and hygiene factors are capable of giving feelings of satisfaction or dissatisfaction. Indeed, House and Wigdor (1967) argue that the theory grossly oversimplifies the sources of job satisfaction and dissatisfaction and this could be particularly true if the potential effects of different national cultures are considered. Just as Maslow's theory can be criticised for its assumption of universal applicability, so can Herzberg's work. What are hygiene factors in one culture could be motivators in another and vice versa.

The theory has also been criticised in terms of its very limited range of application. Herzberg's original work and a great many of the replication studies have been conducted on samples of professional or quasi-professional employees; people who tend to regard job interest and enrichment as the most important features of work. In other jobs, for instance unskilled manual work, there is usually far less scope to enlarge the task and provide the motivators that Herzberg considers so essential (Schneider and Locke 1971). Moreover, there is evidence to suggest that not everyone wants highly challenging work. A study of car assembly line workers in the 1960s (Goldthorpe *et al.* 1968) revealed a considerable number of employees who had what the researchers identified as an instrumental orientation to work. That is, their central life interests lay outside the firm, and work was merely a means to an end but seldom seen as a route to satisfying higher order needs, so long as it provided the remuneration to support the lifestyles they desired.

Nevertheless, in the face of all these criticisms, Herzberg's theory has remained highly popular with managers. Despite a number of weaknesses it has the virtue of giving a fairly refined way of thinking about satisfaction and dissatisfaction at work, and also draws attention to the all-important topic of job design as a way of providing conditions that are potentially motivating.

TIME OUT

Reflect on your experience as an employee in your current job (either full-time or part-time) and answer the questions below. If you have never been an employee, answer the questions in terms of your experience of the university or college. Using Herzberg's two-factor theory:

1. Identify what you consider to be the hygiene factors that are present in your work situation.
2. Identify any important hygiene factors that you consider to be absent.
3. From questions 1 and 2, what do you consider to be the overall balance with respect to hygiene factors?
4. Now repeat questions 1–3 for the motivators.
5. Overall, to what extent do you feel that work or university/college is a situation that you experience as motivating?

McClelland's Theory of Learned Needs

McClelland's (1967) theory assumes that certain individual needs are a reflection of society's cultural values and are acquired in childhood, which makes the behaviour associated with satisfying needs in adult life something akin to a culturally induced personality trait. Three very powerful needs are acknowledged by McClelland, each of which will be described in turn.

The Need for Achievement (N.Ach.)

Need for achievement (N.Ach.): the need to succeed or excel in areas of significance to the person

This prompts a person to try to succeed or excel in areas that have significance to the individual. McClelland (1971) cites evidence that themes in children's literature, together with other child-rearing practices in a particular country, promote high levels of N.Ach., and that these correlate strongly with the economic prosperity of a particular nation. A theory as bold as this clearly has strong implications for selecting people to fill organisational roles. Therefore, a great deal of research (e.g. Cassidy and Lynn 1989) has been devoted to identifying the characteristics of people with a high need for achievement. In general terms this has revealed that high N.Ach. people:

- have a major preoccupation with succeeding in whatever they do
- find the prospects of failing highly depressing, and so they tend to choose tasks of only moderate difficulty with clear but attainable goals, because with goals that are too ambitious there is a risk of failure and too modest a goal gives no sense of accomplishment
- tend to prefer to work on their own so that they take full responsibility for what they do
- like to receive regular, clear and unambiguous feedback
- tend not to value money for itself, but more as a symbol of success.

In the light of these characteristics it is not surprising to find that people high in N. Ach. are more frequently found in some occupations than in others. Entrepreneurs, for example, tend to have high N.Ach. scores, whereas scientists' scores are low. However, although people high in N.Ach. are often successful (because the behaviour of trying to achieve probably helps them to rise fairly rapidly to a certain level), very senior organisational roles often require very different attributes. For instance, delegating work to others is not likely to appeal to someone high in N.Ach., but senior executives who do not learn to delegate and avoid personal involvement can quickly collapse under the strain. Moreover, top managers tend to be involved in long-term decision making about the future, a situation in which the risks are high and there is little prospect of clear and immediate feedback, which could be distasteful to the high-N.Ach. person. A more controversial research finding is that women generally have lower N.Ach. levels than men, one explanation being that women are said to have a fear of success because it is largely incompatible with traditional female roles (Horner 1970). Although whether this is still true today, when woman have a far greater tendency to take control of their own lives, is a highly debatable point. Since the needs which a person acquires are not necessarily connected with work, McClelland has also suggested ways in which adults can be retrained to increase their N.Ach. levels, and he claims a great deal of success for these methods.

The Need for Power (N.Pow.)

Because power is almost inevitably associated with prestige and social standing, people who have this need and are able to satisfy it probably obtain a sense of psychological fulfilment which boosts their self-concept. Indeed he argues that for managers in large, modern organisations, the need for power is a more important attribute than N.Ach. and his research indicates that successful managers tend to have moderately high levels of N.Pow., coupled with low needs for affiliation (McClelland and Boyatzis 1982).

The Need for Affiliation (N.Affil.)

This results in a tendency for the person to want reassurance and approval from others. People high in N.Affil. frequently seek work that has a strong element of interpersonal contact. They are strongly influenced by what they perceive other people want them to be and tend to accommodate themselves to the will of other people.

Although McClelland's theory is generally accepted as valid, there are some criticisms. McClelland's assertion that adults can be easily retrained to have higher levels of N.Ach. is debatable. For this to occur, a fairly radical shift in personality would need to take place and the idea that this is easily done flies in the face of a wealth of contrary psychological evidence. To some extent it also contradicts McClelland's own argument that traits such as N.Arch. are permanently acquired in early childhood. Personality characteristics are relatively fixed by the time a person becomes an adult and so, while intensive training could have a short-term effect, there are strong reservations about effecting permanent changes (Stahl and Harrell 1982).

CONTENT THEORIES: INTEGRATION AND OVERVIEW

All content theories assume that motivation is best understood by focusing on the structure of innate or learned needs. However, each theory explains matters in a slightly different way, and has its own view about which needs are most important. To the

Need for power (N.Pow.): the need to control the activities of other people

Need for affiliation (N.Affil.): the need to interact with, and be liked by, other people

uninitiated this can be perplexing and raises questions about which theory is correct. The simple answer is that none of them is inherently right or wrong. None should be regarded as a definitive picture of human needs and neither should any one, on its own, be used as the sole basis for explaining behaviour. Thus the theories do not contradict each other, and since each one emphasises a different pattern of needs it is more appropriate to view them as complimentary. This idea is reflected in Figure 7.6, which compares the theories.

As can be seen:

- The Maslow and Alderfer theories have a strong affinity: both view needs as structured hierarchically and where they differ is that Maslow sees the order of needs as fixed, while Alderfer views them in a much more flexible and dynamic way.

- In Herzberg's work hygiene factors roughly correspond to Maslow's physiological, safety and affiliation needs (existence and relatedness in the ERG scheme), and Herzberg's motivators are roughly equivalent to Maslow's esteem and self-actualisation needs (growth in ERG theory).

- McClelland's theory does not take specific account of lower order needs, but the need for affiliation embraces some of Herzberg's hygiene factors, which means that it has some correspondence to the security and relatedness categories in Maslow and Alderfer schemes.

- Similarly, N.Pow. is strongly related to Herzberg's recognition factor and thus to Maslow's esteem needs.

Figure 7.6
Relationship between content theory categories

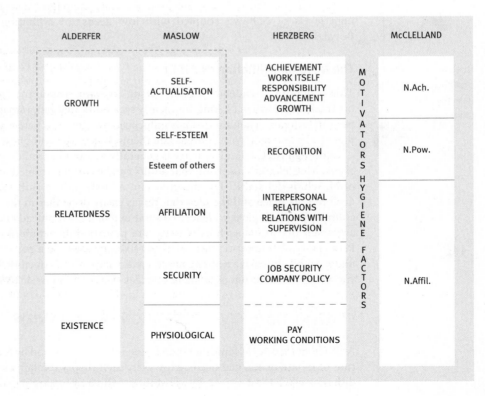

- Finally, the need for achievement has some similarity to Maslow's self-actualisation needs and Alderfer's growth needs.

To some extent all of the theories are known and have an appeal to managers (Hollyforde and Whiddett 2002). However, their popularity probably rests on the fact that they are simple and easy to understand, which tends to confirm the no-nonsense, commonsense folk wisdom that managers use to explain employee behaviour (Salancik and Pfeffer 1977). Indeed, managers often feel distinctly uncomfortable, suspicious and possibly insecure about explanations that are too obviously the output of social science research (Staw *et al.* 1986). Therefore, Maslow's theory, which is the simplest of all, is probably the best known because it is very easy to grasp and probably gives managers a feeling of 'being in control' by knowing how to motivate employees.

If Maslow's theory is the most popular, Herzberg's work comes a close second. Again, it is easy to understand, explains things in terms managers are likely to find intuitively appealing, and offers something they probably feel that they can apply. McClelland's work tends to be far less widely known, at least among managers in the UK.

Despite their appeal, none of the theories is above criticism, but most of their weaknesses are conveniently ignored by managers. They all ignore some potentially important features of human motivation, for example:

- Maslow ignores individual differences and the effect of a change in needs.
- Alderfer's model could well simplify the structure of needs far too much.
- Herzberg's use of hygiene factors and motivators tends to assume that everybody has similar needs to be satisfied.
- McClelland's assertion that needs can be permanently changed by training is far from proven.

The theories all adopt a psychologically universal view, which assumes that everyone has a common set of needs and conveys the impression that people are predictable in terms of what motivates them. However, it is important to remember that, for many people, work is essentially a means to an end, and just one of many ways that they can use to satisfy their needs. Moreover, the theories mostly ignore the crucial issue of individual differences, and also the potentially powerful effects of different national and organisational cultures as factors that can shape human needs, and this is addressed next.

CONTENT THEORIES: A CROSS-CULTURAL PERSPECTIVE

These days many firms seek to extend their sphere of operations into the international arena. To successfully do this they often need to make allowance for the variability of humans and, in particular, the factors that result in motivated behaviour by people. All content theories have their origins in America and this section of the chapter briefly examines whether the information provided by these theories about human needs in the workplace hold good throughout the world.

Orientations to Work

In broad terms, peoples' orientations to work reflect their perceptions of the purpose and meaning of work, for example whether it is seen simply as a means to an end, or

Figure 7.7 Relative importance of different functions of work for selected countries (adapted from Ronen 1986)

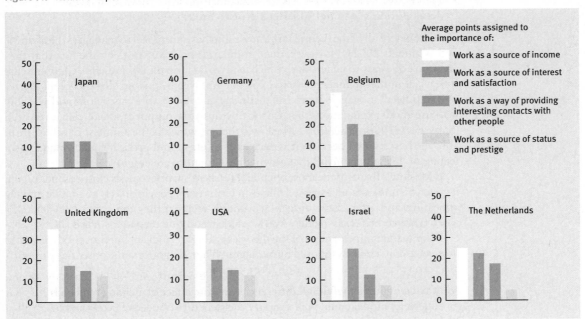

whether work is a dominant and significant part of their lives. These are important because they provide insights into what motivates people in different cultures.

People the world over go to work to earn a living, but there is also a number of intrinsic and social rewards that people get from work which may (or may not) have the same relative importance everywhere. Ronen (1986) offers some insights into this by citing results from a wide-ranging international study on the meaning of work, a summary of which is given in graphic form in Figure 7.7.

As can be seen, while income is rated as the most important function of work in all countries, there are considerable differences in terms of the relative importance of other factors. In Japan, for example, income is much more important than in the UK, the USA, Israel and the Netherlands. However, in Israel and the Netherlands, interesting and satisfying work is almost equal in importance to money, which implies that in these two countries, it would be unwise to rely too heavily on financial incentives to motivate people.

Motivation

Adler (1997) draws attention to the idea that while motivation theories are widely assumed to be universally applicable, they consistently fail to provide useful explanations outside their country of origin. The vast majority of cross-cultural research in this area uses content theories and there is evidence that these are not applicable in the same way everywhere. To use Maslow as an example, although it appears to be true that most people have a hierarchy of needs, the order of priority of these needs varies considerably in different cultures. For instance, in Peru, India, Mexico, the Middle East and Canada it is broadly the same as those set-out by Maslow's theory (Adler

1997). However, in countries such as Japan and Greece safety needs tend to be more important and in Scandinavian countries social needs dominate (Adler *et al.* 1986). Similarly, while all cultures have hygiene factors and motivators as suggested by Herzberg, hygiene factors in one culture can be motivators in another and vice versa. What this means is that we cannot expect people to be motivated by the same things in different cultural contexts. Evidence on this comes from a study by Black (1999) who addressed the matter of whether 'high-commitment management' (HCM) techniques are likely to work as well in other countries as they do in the USA. High-commitment management is normally associated with the use of a number of key practices such as:

- employee involvement and participation using teamworking, team briefings and quality circles
- employee autonomy achieved through jobs that are designed to give added responsibility and flexibility
- job security, and opportunities for advancement
- recruitment practices aimed at obtaining committed employees whose skills can be developed
- good relations between employees and management.

Using a classification of cultures developed by Hofstede (1980), Black examined whether HCM is equally effective in motivational terms in different cultures and his major conclusion is that this varies considerably from country to country. For instance, in what Hofstede calls 'high-individualism' cultures, these techniques have a reasonably high motivational effect because people are culturally acclimatised to value opportunities that enable them to stand out as individuals. Similarly, in 'low-uncertainty avoidance' cultures they are likely to motivate individuals because people have been culturally conditioned to taking risks and being assertive. However, where these values are not part of the wider social culture, HCM techniques will probably not have the same motivational effects, and may even be demotivating. This conclusion is not really surprising in the light of a more recent study by Gibson and Zellmer-Bruhn (2001) that clearly shows that conceptions of what constitutes 'teamworking' can vary widely according to differences in national culture.

REPLAY

- Maslow's and Alderfer's theories assume that needs are structured in a hierarchy and are addressed in ascending order.
- Herzberg's theory describes two groups of needs, hygiene factors and motivators, which have different roles in motivation.
- McClelland identifies three important needs that are said to be culturally induced.
- While needs theories, particularly those of Maslow and Herzberg, are well known by managers in organisations, at best they tell us about needs that could trigger motivation, but nothing about the process of motivation itself.
- Cross-cultural studies indicate that the satisfaction of human needs is by no means as straightforward and universally applicable as traditional content theories suggest.

JOB DESIGN AND MOTIVATION

As noted earlier, the management interest in motivation is likely to be prompted by a hope that if managers understand something of what motivates people, employees can be induced to work harder. Using a content theory approach this implies that if jobs are designed to satisfy important employee needs (extrinsic, intrinsic and social) this will result in a situation in which people become more highly motivated to give of their best (Griffin and McMahan 1994). Job design (or re-design) can be defined as:

> a set of activities that involve alteration of specific jobs or interdependent systems of jobs with the aim of improving the quality of employee job experience and on-the-job productivity. (Bowditch and Buono 1985, p 210)

Much of the thinking and research into job design has focused on how jobs can be made more intrinsically rewarding, and this will be the main concern of what is covered here. However, social rewards are also important and in recognition of this, some of the more recent ideas about job design are focused at group, rather than individual, level. Since these are more easily grasped if the reader has some appreciation of the internal dynamics of groups and teams, which is covered in Chapter 11, consideration of these initiatives will be deferred until then.

The Traditional Approach to Job Design

Job simplification: the breaking down of a job into its simpler constituent elements

Traditionally, this has relied heavily on *job simplification*, where the overall task is broken down into combinations of its smallest possible elements, and these become the jobs of individual people. This does not necessarily mean that each person only completes a single element, such as putting a nut in place, while someone else tightens the nut. Using work study techniques, the details of which need not concern us here, the aim is usually to identify the optimum degree of simplification so that the overall task can be completed in the cheapest way. Nevertheless, this usually results in a whole task being broken down into a set of much simpler sub-tasks, which are completed in a set order. This is illustrated in Figure 7.8(a).

The most widespread application of this approach is found in mass production industries, for example in the manufacture of cars. However, its use is not confined to manufacturing and if you visit a fast-food restaurant such as McDonald's you can observe the principles in action. The task of serving customers is broken down into taking the order, grilling the burgers, putting them in rolls, adding condiments and wrapping, all of which are completed on a form of assembly line.

Job simplification has significant economic advantages and its most important advantages for an employer are:

- a significant increase in productive efficiency and economy when compared to multi-task methods
- because job occupants are only required to master a very limited range of skills, training costs are low
- job occupants work faster because they do not have to stop doing one thing to focus on something else
- special purpose machines that speed up the operation can be used
- unskilled labour, which is cheaper and more easily replaced, can be used
- the operation is more predictable and easily controlled.

Figure 7.8 (a) Job simplification; (b) Job enlargement; (c) Job rotation

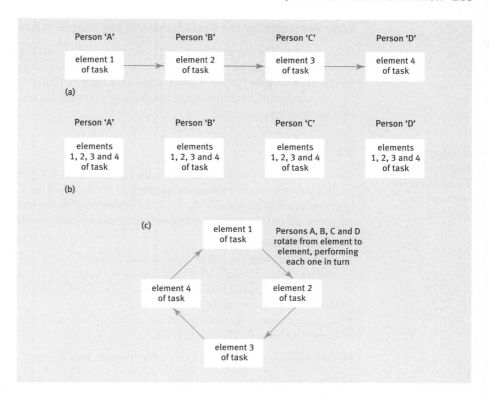

However, nothing in this world is for free, and a number of disadvantages have been identified:

- employees often experience the jobs as monotonous, boring and repetitive
- employees tend to have no feelings of accomplishing anything meaningful
- many types of problem behaviour tend to appear, for example carelessness, low quality, absenteeism, high turnover, industrial unrest and occasionally sabotage.

Probably the best documented account of the dysfunctional effects of job specialisation comes from a study of car manufacture by Walker and Guest (1957), who identified that while workers were reasonably satisfied with pay and non-monetary benefits, they were extremely dissatisfied with the work itself. In particular there were six aspects of work that gave rise to discontent:

- the machine-paced nature of jobs
- lack of control over how the job was done
- low skill requirements
- the repetitive nature of jobs
- the meaninglessness of jobs – workers could not see how their efforts related to the whole
- few opportunities for social interaction.

In summary, it is possible that job simplification might only create an illusion of efficiency. Its drawbacks could mean that the theoretical advantages of lower costs and increased productivity are not fully realised.

Early Remedies for the Dysfunctions of Job Simplification

It is doubtful whether any firm could completely abandon the economic advantages of job simplification. Nevertheless, when taken too far, it has its problems and, prompted by research such as that of Walker and Guest (1957), there was a search for alternatives to counter the demotivating conditions it creates, three of which are described in what follows.

Job Enlargement

By horizontally expanding a person's job and introducing a greater range of tasks, this technique aims to alter the scope of work. This is shown in outline in Figure 7.8(b), where instead of persons A, B, C and D performing separate elements, each of them performs all four tasks. This has the theoretical advantages of:

- greater task variety
- workers are more versatile in what they can undertake, which can be useful in coping with temporary absences due to sickness
- it can be used as the first step in a move towards obtaining a wider degree of flexibility in the workforce
- to some extent it results in a greater degree of job satisfaction
- work motivation could be greater.

Nevertheless, job enlargement can have its own drawbacks:

- it sacrifices some of the advantages (e.g. speed) obtainable from simplification
- since the workforce is more versatile, workers could ask for more pay
- except in the very short run, it does little to increase motivation and satisfaction because a large boring job is no less boring than four small boring jobs
- workers can feel threatened and vulnerable by the new arrangements because versatility could make them easier to replace.

Job Rotation

Job rotation also consists of increasing the scope of a job by using horizontal enlargement. This time, however, it is done by systematically moving people between different elements in a cycle, as shown in Figure 7.8(c). This tends to have the same advantages and disadvantages as job enlargement.

Job Enrichment

It is generally assumed that motivation is sustained by the job itself and in particular, the level of intrinsic rewards it provides. Note that this is the main argument that underpins Herzberg's two-factor theory explained earlier, and he argues that raising motivation requires a lot more than simply expanding a job by horizontal enlargement – it requires the job to be 'enriched'. In this sense the technique of *job enrichment* is a direct outcome of Herzberg's work and it results in something quite different from either job enlargement or job rotation, both of which only expand a job horizontally. That is, it also involves a measure of vertical expansion so that the person has some authority over the planning, execution and control of the work. This, Herzberg

---

Job enlargement: horizontal expansion of a job to provide variety for the individual

Job rotation: the systematic rotation of workers from one job to another to reduce boredom

Job enrichment: enlargement of a job both horizontally and vertically to give the employee more responsibility and control over how the job is performed

Figure 7.9 The
principles of job
enrichment (adapted
from Herzberg 1968)

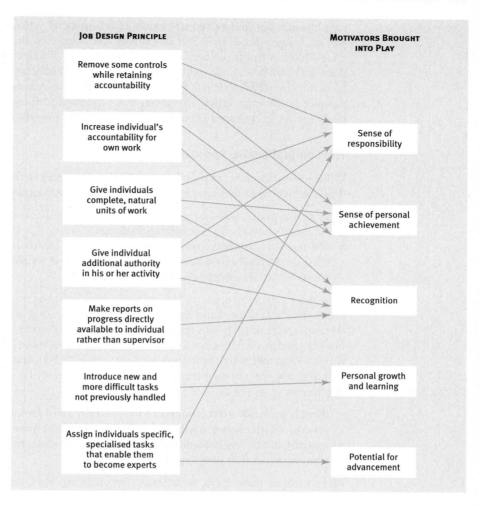

(1968) argues, will bring into play the more powerful intrinsic motivators. His
recommendations about how this can be achieved are shown in Figure 7.9.

Theoretically the advantages of job enrichment are:

- it is easy to apply; that is, by simply enlarging the job vertically as well as
  horizontally
- it is broadly in line with currently fashionable ideas about empowerment
- it almost certainly increases job satisfaction
- adding task complexity and responsibility should have a positive effect on work
  motivation.

Notwithstanding these arguments, the research evidence on job enrichment is
extremely mixed. Some firms have embraced the idea and report enthusiastically on
the effects, whereas others have tried it and withdrawn very quickly. While there is
little doubt that this results in higher levels of job satisfaction, managers might expect
to see something additional; for example increased productivity. In this respect job

enrichment is something of an act of faith. Herzberg merely assumes that a more satisfied worker is more productive and this is also an assumption that is present in most of the evaluation studies of enrichment (see House and Wigdor 1967). For this reason there may well be an important limiting condition that affects whether job enrichment gives improvements that satisfy both managers and employees. That is, it might only produce results that satisfy everybody if it is applied to those employees who positively value the increased autonomy that results. Not everybody does.

The Comprehensive Approach to Job Design

While job enrichment, as proposed by Herzberg, is a step in the right direction, it is a 'broad brush' approach that has a number of inherent problems:

- since it is underpinned by a universalistic (content) theory of motivation, it has an equally universal approach to job design
- it defines enrichment purely in terms of providing Herzberg's motivators
- it assumes everybody wants an enriched job in these terms, and that everyone wants his or her job enriched in the same way.

Like the content theories on which it is based, it takes no account of individual differences and these could be crucial. For instance, some people might only want certain aspects of their jobs enriched and others might prefer mundane jobs that are not enriched at all. There have been attempts to address these issues, the first of which was a pioneering study by Turner and Lawrence (1965), the results of which show that different types of people respond to different aspects of complexity and challenge in different ways. Thus:

- there is probably no such thing as a universally valid prescription for enriched jobs, to which everyone will respond in an equally positive way
- individual differences could be an important determinant of the job characteristics that people prefer.

Ideas such as these have been tested by other workers, for example Blood and Hulin (1967) drew the conclusion that individual differences could be an important moderator of the way that people respond to the design of jobs. This led to a search for ways of allowing for these differences, and gave rise to what is generally acknowledged to be the most successful comprehensive theory of job design. This is Job Characteristics Theory (Hackman and Oldham 1980), the essentials of which are shown in Figure 7.10.

The job characteristics model sets out to identify two important causal links:

- the connection between the key features of a job (its core characteristics, which are shown in the left-hand column of Figure 7.10) and the way that a person doing the job experiences these characteristics (shown in the middle column)
- the link between these experiences and the probable outcomes in terms of intrinsic motivation, satisfaction and work performance (shown in the right-hand column).

The five core job characteristics are:

1. *Skill variety*: the extent to which the job requires a mix of skills, the exercise of which is valued by the job holder.

Figure 7.10 The job characteristics model (adapted from Hackman and Oldham 1980)

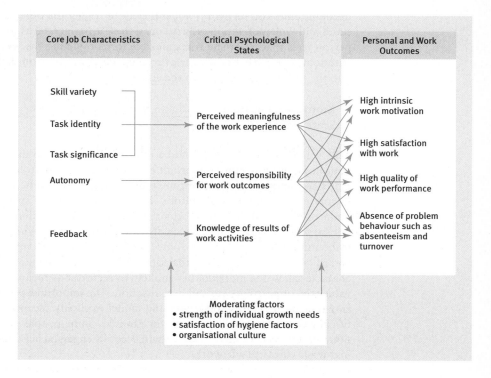

2. *Task identity*: the extent to which the job is a 'whole' one; that is, it has a beginning and an end, and results in completion of a tangible, identifiable outcome.
3. *Task significance*: the extent to which the job occupant perceives that the job 'matters', in terms of affecting the work or lives of other people inside or outside the organisation.
4. *Autonomy*: the extent to which the job gives its occupant the freedom and discretion to plan the work and decide how it is carried out.
5. *Feedback*: the extent to which doing the job gives its occupant clear information about the effectiveness of his or her efforts.

To the extent that these features exist, they are said to influence the critical psychological states that are shown in the central column of the model. These arise from the persons' perceptions of:

- *Meaningfulness*: the degree to which the person experiences the job as one that makes a valuable and worthwhile contribution.
- *Responsibility*: the extent to which the person perceives that he or she is personally responsible for the successful completion of the work.
- *Knowledge of results*: the extent to which the person has clear understanding and evidence of how effectively he or she performs the job.

It is important to note that different core characteristics trigger different psychological states. For instance, it is skill variety, task identity and significance that result in the job being experienced as meaningful. However, according to Hackman and Oldham, meaningfulness on its own is not sufficient to trigger the other critical psychological states and high motivation only occurs if these are triggered as well. That is, when the person feels that he or she is responsible for completing the work (triggered by job autonomy), and has knowledge of results, which comes from having feedback built into the job. This is reflected in the equation:

$$\textbf{Motivating Potential Score (MPS)} = \frac{(\text{Variety} + \text{Identity} + \text{Significance})}{3} \times \text{Autonomy} \times \text{Feedback}$$

MPS is fairly easy to measure and a return will be made to this shortly. For the present, however, it is more important to note that at the bottom of the model there is a box containing three moderators: individual growth needs, satisfaction of hygiene factors and organisational culture. The presence of these spells out that there are limits on the extent to which the core job characteristics will necessarily result in the critical psychological states, which also limits the extent to which the states will result in the attitudinal and behavioural outcomes shown. The need for personal growth broadly corresponds to Maslow's self-actualisation needs and, even if the job has the three required characteristics, the individual is unlikely to regard it as meaningful unless he or she values the opportunity for self-actualisation. The important point here is that, so far as work motivation is concerned, the model explicitly recognises that the presence of growth needs cannot be taken for granted. Some people prefer boring jobs and others might seek to satisfy their growth needs by engaging in (what are to them) meaningful activities outside work.

Even if this condition exists and the person has high growth needs, the second moderator, hygiene factors, is important because Herzberg's two-factor theory tell us that motivators only come into play if hygiene factors are satisfied. Finally, certain organisational cultures can give rise to contextual circumstances that are not supportive of the causal chain suggested by the model. For example, a highly bureaucratic culture that has a strong emphasis on rules and formal procedures would probably result in a situation where people experienced some of the core job characteristics, such as increased autonomy, as highly 'unnatural'.

Returning now to the motivating potential score, this can fairly easily be measured by using a questionnaire called the Job Diagnostic Survey developed by Hackman and Oldham (1975). This taps employee perceptions of the characteristics of the job, employee psychological states and personal work outcomes. Therefore, as well as being a theory, the job characteristic approach has a great deal of practical applicability. For instance, it would enable an organisation to estimate whether a job has the potential to be intrinsically motivating and, if not, whether conditions are favourable for a redesign initiative.

In general terms there is a great deal of empirical support for the Hackman and Oldham model. This indicates that people who score high on the Job Diagnostic Survey are more highly motivated, have higher job satisfaction and perform better than those who score low (Glick *et al.* 1986; Renn and Vandberg 1995). Note, however, that there are no universals in terms of designing jobs with the required characteristics – the people who do these jobs have to be asked how they experience things.

Like most theories, there are also criticisms of the Hackman and Oldham model. Some studies, for example, suggest that the critical psychological states are in serious need of refinement and revision (Kelly 1992). In addition, there are some doubts about whether the job characteristics actually predict the critical psychological states and whether the psychological states faithfully predict the personal and work outcomes (Algera 1983). Nevertheless, the model is not so easily dismissed. The balance of evidence is in its favour, and this shows that people who work in jobs that contain core dimensions that are thoughtfully designed are usually more highly motivated, satisfied and productive.

The Work Context and Motivation

The most important feature of Herzberg's two-factor theory is the distinction between hygiene factors and motivators, which is acknowledged in the Hackman and Oldham model by including hygiene factors as a moderating variable. In effect this tells us that job redesign can be a futile exercise unless attention is paid to satisfaction of hygiene factors. Since some of these factors can be part of the job itself, it is important to consider those that can be influential. These are shown in Figure 7.11 and are described in what follows.

The Physical Working Environment

Any student who has tried to concentrate in an ill-ventilated, overheated examination room, or attempted to study in a library where other users persist in chattering, will understand the demotivating effects of poor physical working conditions. Four in particular (temperature, noise, lighting and air quality) can be powerful sources of discomfort and reduced motivation (Bell *et al.* 1990).

Temperature can have a noticeable effect on motivation and performance, although the tolerance to either low or high temperature varies considerably between individuals.

In terms of *noise*, the human auditory system is fairly limited in its capabilities. Although noise levels of up to about 85 decibels can be tolerated so long as the noise level is fairly constant, unpredictable variations in pitch or level can seriously interfere

Figure 7.11
Contextual factors
affecting work
motivation

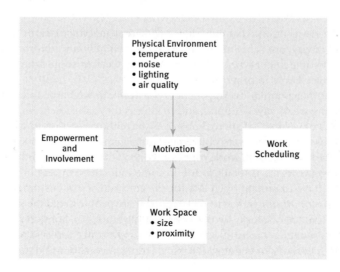

with concentration, and reduce job satisfaction and motivation (Baron 1994; Bell *et al.* 1990).

The intensity of *lighting* required for work to take place depends heavily on the task to be undertaken; for example, on the degree of accuracy and precision that is required (Baron 1994). Insufficient illumination puts a strain on the eyes and can result in tension, headaches and the long-term deterioration of sight, and the same is true of extremely harsh lighting.

Air quality sometimes has unseen effects. To function well we all need to breathe, and breathing polluted air can have long-term effects on health. However, while people seem to adjust to air contamination without actually being aware of it, their performance deteriorates.

Work Space

Unfortunately the strongest correlate of the *size* of a person's work space is not what he or she needs to do the job, but status. Here we should note that highly visible differences of this type can have a demoralising effect on people, particularly where they have insufficient 'elbow room' to do their jobs effectively.

Proximity refers to the distance between people in a work situation and how far they are from the facilities necessary to do their jobs. We all need some degree of personal space, but if people are too distant from each other social contact becomes difficult. Thus the layout of a workplace can have either a motivating or demotivating effect. Because it permits them to complete complex, demanding tasks that require concentration, many people also need a degree of privacy (Baron 1994) and if this is absent it can sometimes lead to frustrations and de-motivation.

Work Scheduling

Irrespective of the content of a job, there are a number of ways that work can be scheduled. Some of these have strong implications for motivation because they allow people to achieve a more convenient balance between home and work life (Curran 2003). It is important to note, however, that operational considerations often mean that few of them can be used everywhere.

In organisations that experience wide seasonal fluctuations in the volume of business activity, one scheduling alternative is *annual hours contracts*. Under this arrangement people might work a shorter working week at some times of the year, balanced by longer hours in other seasons.

Another popular arrangement is *flexitime*, in which people attend for a standard working week (say 37 hours), and so long as they are present for a specified core period in each day (often 10 am to 3 pm), they have the discretion to start early or finish late. Clearly this can be a very convenient arrangement for employees who have a need to balance home life with work, for example people with young children. However, flexitime arrangements are difficult to use in some industries; in retailing, for example, where stores have to remain open late for the convenience of customers.

Telecommuting refers to a situation where people avoid the physical journey to and from a place of work, by performing their duties at home on a computer, with the results sent electronically to the firm. This was once forecast to be the fastest area of growth in terms of changed working arrangements, but to date any increase has been relatively modest. While those who work at home often appreciate the convenience and lack of interruption that this brings, it can be a lonely life. Thus it is probably not for those people to whom the social interaction opportunities of conventional working arrangements are important. In addition, homeworkers can come to realise that there are hidden costs, for example the heating and lighting expenses that are normally borne by the employer are shifted onto the homeworker.

Empowerment and Involvement

If implemented in an appropriate way, and unfortunately it seldom is, these are methods of providing some degree of enrichment to jobs, by giving employees more autonomy, discretion and responsibility.

In today's conditions, where competing in globalised markets means that a fast response to changing conditions is needed, it can be argued that something that not only harnesses the talents and skills of employees, but also their commitment can be vital. One way to do this is to allow people a greater say in making decisions that affect their daily working lives, and where they are used properly both empowerment and involvement seek to do this.

REPLAY

- The work motivation of individuals is influenced by the nature of their jobs and the traditional approach to designing jobs relied on job simplification techniques.
- While job simplification has significant economic advantages, it tends to result in a number of human problems.
- Early remedies for these dysfunctions were the introduction of variety into jobs, using designs that expanded job content horizontally, i.e. job enlargement and/or job rotation.
- These initiatives had limited impact and were superseded in some firms by attempts to introduce an additional measure of vertical expansion using job enrichment.
- More recently, comprehensive theories of job design have appeared that take account of individual differences, for example Hackman and Oldham's Job Characteristics Model.
- Job satisfaction and motivation are not only affected by the design of jobs, but also by a host of contextual factors that can influence whether the needs of the employee, as well as those of the employer, are satisfied.

OVERVIEW AND CONCLUSIONS

The content theories covered in this chapter have all had a strong influence on the body of knowledge concerned with the motivation of people at work. Two of these theories are well known in management circles and this is testament to their influential, if somewhat simplistic ideas. However, while the theories tell us something about work-related factors that could trigger motivation, they have nothing to say about the mechanisms of motivation itself. For example, they cannot explain why two people with identical needs could pursue them with different degrees of intensity and persistence. For this reason, they only tell us something about needs that could give rise to motivated behaviour, but are silent about the actual mechanisms of motivation itself (Arnold *et al.* 1998). This is the province of process theories, which are considered in the next chapter.

FURTHER READING

Kanfer, R (1992) Work motivation: new directions in theory and research. In I Robertson and CL Cooper (eds) *International Review of Industrial and Organisational Psychology*, Vol. 74, Chichester: Wiley. An interesting, but rather technical account of the ongoing development of motivation theory.

Petri, HL (1996) *Motivation: Theory, Research and Application*, London: Thompson. A specialist but nevertheless readable text that gives a comprehensive coverage of all the major approaches to motivation theory.

Pfeffer, J (1996) *Competitive Advantage Through People: Unleashing the Power of the Work Force*, Boston, MA: Harvard Business School Press. The book gives a damning critique of scientific management and goes on to explain a range of techniques for increasing employee motivation and enhancing employee performance.

Spector, P (1995) *Industrial and Organisational Psychology: Research and Practice*, Chichester: Wiley. A wide-ranging text that has good coverage of motivation, and discusses it within in a wider psychological context.

Robertson, I, M Smith and D Cooper (1992) *Motivation: Strategies, Theory and Practice*, 2nd edn, London: IPD. A very easily read analysis of the strengths and weaknesses of theories of work motivation.

Weiner, B (1992) *Human Motivation: Metaphors, Theories and Research*, London: Sage. A comprehensive book that gives an interesting integration of the different theoretical perspectives on motivation.

CASE STUDY 7.1: The battery chicken workers

According to the General, Municipal and Boilermakers' Union (GMB), distribution workers who supply high street supermarkets and shops are being treated like battery farm chickens as a result of new technology that links sales computers directly to devices worn on employees' bodies. The technology, which is used to supply customers such as Tesco, Sainsbury, Marks and Spencer, Boots and B&Q, can also monitor the movements of distribution workers, control what breaks they take, and even how much time they take to go to the toilet, said the union.

Paul Kenny, acting general secretary of the union noted that this technology, which involves the electronic tagging of workers, has been imported into Britain from the USA, and that while the GMB is not a Luddite organisation, it could not stand idly by to see its members reduced to automatons. Paul Campbell, a union national officer, said that at least two companies in London were considering using similar devices to direct their billboard walkers and noted that the technology could be used by all kinds of industries to monitor workers. He estimated that 5,000–10,000 workers could already be using the new devices, which had been introduced by a number of distributors over the past six months.

A study for the union by Michael Blakemore, of Durham University, said that devices worn on the arms or fingers of warehouse workers were linked to local area radio networks and to global positioning satellite systems. The GMB reported that this enabled orders to be beamed to workers to tell them which goods to pick in different parts of the warehouse for dispatch to top up the shelves in a store and added that the only role for the worker is to do as the computer requires. This, said Professor Blakemore is bringing the concept of prison surveillance into the workplace, and raises the possibility of a new series of industrial injuries, because workers have to hold their arms at a certain angle to read information.

The GMB said it was not seeking to ban new technology that increased efficiency, but wanted to reach common agreements with employers to ensure that it was introduced safely, and took account of the human needs of employees.

Source: Taylor, A. (2005) *Financial Times*, 7 June

Questions

1. What are your feelings about the use of the technologies reported in the material above?

2. Using an appropriate theory of motivation, assess what you feel could be the likely effects on the motivations of the workers involved.

3. Why do you feel that employees are likely to have these reactions?

4. In your view, would this be a 'reasonable' reaction on the part of employees?

5. What alternative and non-controversial way could the employer have used to introduce the new technology?

REVIEW AND DISCUSSION QUESTIONS

1. Explain the difference between Needs, Goals, Expectations, Motives and Drives and their respective roles in the process of motivation.

2. In outline terms, describe Maslow's theory of human needs. What are the two major assumptions that underpin Maslow's theory and what implications do these have for work motivation?

3. Since Herzberg does not use the word 'needs' in his two-factor theory, to what extent can it be regarded as a content theory and what are the respective functions of hygiene factors and motivators in the theory?

4. Describe the three needs dealt with in McClelland's work and state his assumptions about the way that humans acquire their needs.

5. What do you feel are the particular strengths vs. weaknesses and advantages vs. disadvantages of content theories of motivation?

Chapter 8

Work Motivation:
Process Theories

LEARNING OUTCOMES

After studying this chapter you should be able to:

- distinguish between content and process theories of work motivation

- understand and discuss two alternative expectancy theories of work motivation

- understand and discuss the equity theory of work motivation

- understand and discuss the goal-setting theory of work motivation

- understand and discuss the concept of Organisational Behaviour Modification and how it differs from motivation theory

INTRODUCTION

At the end of the previous chapter it was pointed out that while content theories have a great deal to say about human needs that could give rise to motivated behaviour, they tell us virtually nothing about the actual process of motivation. Knowledge of this type is the province of cognitive psychology and theories that deal with motivation in this way are known as process theories. Rather than simply cataloguing what people do, these theories focus on variables that account for the direction, intensity and persistence of behaviour. An important feature of them all is that they recognise that most individuals have preferences for certain outcomes rather than others, and so motivated behaviour is usually a result of conscious choices.

The chapter presents four of the best-known and most highly developed process theories. These are presented separately, after which there is a short section that compares and integrates them. This is followed by a consideration of Behaviour Modification, which in some American texts is portrayed as another theory of motivation. As will be seen, however, it is not and can more accurately be described as an application of operant conditioning (see Chapter 6). A brief consideration of how motivation is assessed in organisations is then given and the chapter closes with an overview of motivation theories given in this and the previous chapter.

EXPECTANCY THEORY

In academic circles, this is currently the most influential process theory. However, it is not a single theory, but a group of theories all of which have three common assumptions:

- that in choosing between different courses of action, people are influenced by their expectations of whether the action will result in a favourable outcome for themselves
- they are capable of weighing up the odds about whether acting in a certain way will result in a favourable outcome
- other things being equal, people will try to behave in a way that gives the maximum return to themselves.

To set the scene, assume that an employee has been asked to take on a new and unfamiliar task by his or her manager, who infers that if the task is done well the employee will benefit in some way, perhaps by being promoted. Applying the three assumptions above, the employee will then evaluate:

- whether he or she values the prospect of promotion enough to make it a desirable end
- what is involved in being able to successfully perform the new task
- whether successfully performing the new task is likely to improve his or her promotion prospects.

The basic principle underlying expectancy theories is that the motivation to take on the task will only be strong where the employee values promotion and promotion is seen as the likely outcome of performing well. There are, however, different ways of

Figure 8.1 Vroom's valence–expectancy model

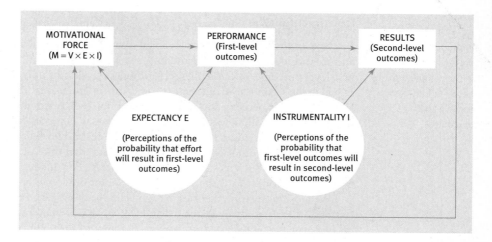

explaining the strength of the motivation and the way that the motivated state arises, and these in turn depend on which expectancy theory is used.

Vroom's Valence–Expectancy (VIE) Model

Vroom (1964) is usually credited with the first articulation of expectancy theory and his ideas are shown diagrammatically in Figure 8.1. To understand the model, it is necessary to explain the terms used.

Valence

Valence: the strength of preference for a particular outcome

Valence is the strength of an individual's preference for a particular outcome, which can be positive or negative. In the example given above, if the employee desired promotion it would have positive valence, and if promotion was not wanted it would be negative. Valence only expresses the feelings about the outcome and Vroom's theory allows for values (say from −10 to +10) to be put on valence.

Outcomes

Outcomes are the things that result from behaviour and can be expressed at two levels:

First-level outcomes: the immediate results of behaviour

- *First-level outcomes* are the immediate results of behaviour. In the example given earlier, the first-level outcome would be performing the new task (hopefully in a successful way).

Second-level outcomes: those that flow in the longer term from first-level outcomes

- *Second-level outcomes* are those that flow from the first-level – for example, gaining promotion.

Expectancy

This is the person's perception that his or her behaviour will result in the first-level outcome – in this instance, whether he or she will be able to perform the new task successfully. Note that the word 'perception' is used. Since the event has not yet occurred, a person's expectancy can only ever be a subjective estimate.

Instrumentality

Instrumentality: the perceived strength of the connection between first- and second-level outcomes

Instrumentality consists of the perceived strength of the connection between first-level and second-level outcomes. Again, note the word 'perception'. Any preference for the first-level outcome (successfully performing the task) not only depends on the extent to which the second-level outcome (promotion) is valued, but also on whether the first-level outcome is perceived to lead to the second-level outcome; that is, the likelihood that promotion will be forthcoming if the new task is successfully performed.

Vroom acknowledges that outcomes at the second level are usually multiple. For example, while promotion can be valued for its own sake, it normally brings other valued outcomes such as status and higher salary. For this reason, what Vroom calls 'motive force' or effort is the sum of the different outcomes and their valences.

Like most motivation theories, Vroom's has been subjected to a degree of empirical testing. An early study by Pritchard and DeLeo (1973) demonstrated powerful effects on performance when conditions were changed to those where instrumentality was higher. Nevertheless, like most innovative theories, the original model is open to some criticism, in this case because it can be very hard to apply in a practical way. However, the concept of expectancy is generally considered to be too useful to discard, and this has led to further developments, the best known of which is considered next.

TIME OUT

Using the instructions below, apply Vroom's model by working out your own 'motive force' for working hard on an assignment in order to pass this module with flying colours.

1. Work out your Valence (V) for getting a good final mark for the module. Assuming that this will always have a positive value, give valence a score between 0 (you don't care whether or not you get a good mark for the module) to 10 (it is very important for you to get a good mark).

2. Now give a score for Expectancy (E), your estimate of the probability that if you work hard for the assignment this will result in a good grade. This should be between 0 (there is no connection between working hard and getting a good assignment mark) and 1.0 (there is a very strong connection between working hard and getting a good assignment mark).

   Note: the assignment mark corresponds to the first-level outcome in Vroom's model.

3. Now work out your Instrumentality (I) score, that is your estimate of the probability that if you get a good mark for the assignment this will result in you getting a good mark for the module as a whole. This should also be 0 (no probability) and 1.0 (high probability).

   Note: the mark for the module as a whole corresponds to the second-level outcome in Vroom's model.

4. Now work out your motive force by using the formula $M = V \times E \times I$. This should be somewhere between 0 and 10.

5. What conclusions do you draw from your motive force score?

The Porter and Lawler Expectancy Model

This model (Porter and Lawler 1968) is a development of Vroom's ideas and has a number of important additional features that enhance the explanatory power of the expectancy concept. The most significant development is Porter and Lawler's treatment of Vroom's 'motive force'. Porter and Lawler note that a criticism of Vroom's model is that, even where the valence of second-level outcomes and instrumentality are both high, other factors can influence the success of a person's actions. Figure 8.2 shows the Porter and Lawler model and the terms are explained below.

Value of reward (1) is the extent to which a person values an outcome; it has a similar role to valence in Vroom's model. However, Porter and Lawler note that value is highly individualised, so an outcome valued by one person might have no value to someone else. They also note that the value placed on an outcome can be strongly influenced by prior experiences, for example whether a reward obtained on an earlier occasion was experienced as satisfying. This is indicated by the feedback loop to value from another variable (9) further on in the model, about which more will be said presently.

Perceived *effort to reward probability* (2) is almost identical to Vroom's expectancy concept and is the perceived likelihood that rewards will follow from successful performance.

Effort on task (3) indicates something rather different from Vroom's use of the word. It is not a motive force, but simply how hard someone tries to perform the task and, important as it is, effort alone does not ensure successful task performance because two other variables are likely to have mediating effects:

- **personal attributes and traits** (4), which are the skills, aptitudes and mental dispositions of the person, which facilitate or inhibit task performance
- **the fit between perceptions of role and demands of performance** (5), which corresponds to the person's views about whether performing the task is

Value of reward: the extent that a person values a reward

Effort to reward probability: the perceived likelihood that a reward will follow successful task performance

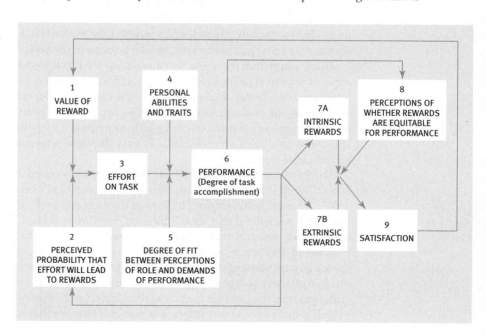

Figure 8.2 The Porter and Lawler expectancy model (source: Porter and Lawler 1968)

compatible with his or her current role. For instance, if the new task requires dealing with more ambiguous situations and decisions have to be made on incomplete information, this might make the task more stressful, or even distasteful.

Performance (6) is the final outcome of engaging in the task and includes whether it is successfully accomplished or not.

Rewards are the outcomes for the person performing the task and they fall into two groups:

- **intrinsic rewards** (7A) are the inner feelings of accomplishment and sense of challenge
- **extrinsic rewards** (7B) are tangible items such as pay and promotion.

Note that there is a connection between both types of reward so they must be considered together. Porter and Lawler stress that it should not be assumed that doing a job well is a reward in its own right, particularly if special efforts have been made to perform it. Nor should it be assumed that extrinsic rewards are the ones most desired, because extrinsic incentives can merely serve to incentivise people to demand even more extrinsic incentives (Caulkin 2005). Also note the feedback loop from the reward variables to variable 2. This reflects the idea that, on a future occasion, a person's perception of whether it will be worthwhile expending effort is likely to be affected by the rewards that he or she receives now.

Perception of equitable rewards (8) equates to the person's judgement about whether the intrinsic and extrinsic rewards obtained on this occasion are fair and just in terms of the successful performance that has been delivered.

Satisfaction (9) is influenced by intrinsic and extrinsic rewards, largely the extent to which they are perceived as equitable, and this is one of the most significant features of the Porter and Lawler theory. Merely giving rewards does not ensure job satisfaction. This is crucially dependent on whether the rewards are perceived as equitable for the effort that has been expended in performing the task.

Finally, note that there is a very important feedback loop from satisfaction (9) to value of reward (1) which reflects the point made earlier – what happens now is likely to influence the future. In the example of the employee who has been asked to take on a new task, the manager inferred that this could lead to promotion. If the employee finds that promotion turns out to be little more than a job with greater responsibility and a new title but with no increase in pay, the word promotion is unlikely to act as an inducement in the future.

The Porter and Lawler model has been extensively tested, both by its authors and others. While it stands up well to the rigours of empirical examination (Wanous *et al.* 1983), there are still criticisms. It is one of the most comprehensive models yet devised, but this is something of a mixed blessing, because it is hard to apply in a practical way. It also assumes that people make decisions in a rational, objective and well-considered way when, in practice, they are sometimes more intuitive. Finally, the theory ignores some of the more unpleasant features of organisational life, which still result in effective task performance; for example coercion and insecurity. Despite these criticisms, and the fact that outside academic circles the theory is less well known than others, it makes some very important points. These are that it:

- draws attention to the important point that extrinsic and intrinsic rewards are not substitutes for each other; both need to be provided
- directs attention to the importance of employee traits, skills and abilities, particularly those which are needed in order to be able to perform well
- draws attention to the idea that incentives for good performance only have a practical use if they are valued by employees
- stresses that employees need to be able to see that rewards are realistically obtainable.

EQUITY THEORY

Equity: the fairness of treatment of a person compared to the way that another person is treated

The concept of *equity* has a long pedigree in social science as a factor that affects work attitudes and behaviour (Runciman 1966). It has a pivotal role in social exchange theory, which acknowledges that, since there are no absolute criteria of fairness, people normally evaluate how fairly they are treated by making comparisons with others in similar circumstances (Blau 1964). The equity theory of motivation (Adams 1965) uses these principles and incorporates a very simple idea: that an individual's motivation to put effort into a task will be influenced by perceptions of whether the rewards obtained are fair in comparison to those received by other people. To explain the theory, the process involved is shown in Figure 8.3.

Figure 8.3   Equity theory

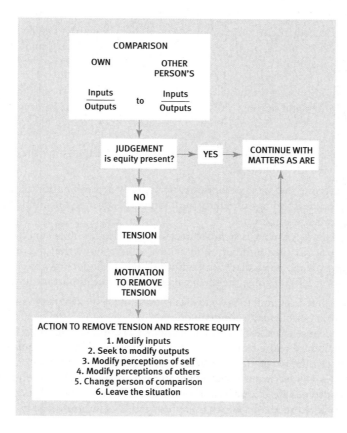

The process starts with a **comparison** stage, in which someone evaluates the inputs and outputs associated with performing a task, and these are compared with the inputs and outputs of another person's task. This is usually someone in close proximity, with whom a direct comparison can be made because he or she does similar work. Inputs are the things that a person brings to the job, such as education, skill, experience and effort. Outputs are the rewards received for the job, such as pay, promotion, praise, etc. Inputs can be viewed as costs, and outputs as benefits and, to make a comparison, a person mentally constructs two subjective cost–benefit ratios: one for him or herself, and one for the other person. Although these comparisons are almost bound to contain a high element of subjectivity, they are nevertheless the 'reality' of the situation to the person concerned, and this brings the next stage of the model into play.

A **judgement** is made about whether the person's own ratio is the same or near to that of the 'comparison other'. If it is, then all is probably well, but if it is not, feelings of inequity can arise and this triggers the next stage in the process.

Tensions, or feelings of psychological discomfort, arise from perceived inequity. For example, someone who perceives that he or she brings more skill and experience to a job than the other person can feel that inequity exists until pay is raised above the other person's level. The greater the degree of tension, the greater is the motivation to do something that eases it.

This results in **action** to lessen the tension, invariably by restoring equity to the situation. Here Adams lists six basic options for action:

- modifying inputs; for example where a person feels under-rewarded effort can be reduced, and in the case of perceived over-reward it can be increased
- seek to modify outputs, perhaps by demanding more pay if there is a feeling of being under-rewarded, although it is hard to see how a person would deal with a situation of perceived over-reward
- modify perceptions of self; for example, the person could re-evaluate his or her inputs and outputs and come to the conclusion that equity does exist after all
- modify perceptions of the 'comparison other', which has much the same result as the previous option
- change the person or persons used as the 'comparison other'
- leave the situation.

Exercising one of these options (or possibly a combination of them) is said to result in restored feelings of equity and, when this occurs, tension is eased and the person accepts the situation.

Adams's theory is straightforward, and elegant in its simplicity. It has been tested empirically on a number of occasions, which shows that the theory has good predictive powers, particularly in conditions where under-reward could exist (Cosier and Dalton 1983). Thus, the theory has a number of important implications:

- when designing jobs and reward systems, it is extremely important to recognise that people make comparisons
- because these comparisons are subjective and seldom precise, care should be taken to relate similar jobs in terms of the inputs they require and outputs they provide, particularly if they are in close proximity
- if managers want to avoid inaccurate conclusions about equity, it is necessary to keep people informed about the basis on which rewards are made, particularly where the quality of what is produced is as important as its quantity.

TIME OUT

Carefully reflect on your own work situation, on the job you do and on those of two other people you work with who do similar jobs to yourself. If you are not in employment, either part-time or full-time, reflect on your own situation and that of fellow students you know well and with whose work you are familiar. Now answer the questions below.

1. What inputs do you bring to work (e.g. skills, knowledge, diligence, persistence, extent of private study outside the classroom, care in assignments and contribution in class)? How many of these things do the other people bring as inputs?
2. What outputs do you receive for your efforts (e.g. pay, praise, understanding, good grades, etc.)? How do these compare with the outputs received by the other people?
3. Do you feel there is equity of treatment compared to these other people and, if not, do you feel under-rewarded or over-rewarded? Why?
4. If you feel there is inequity, go back and carefully check that you have not omitted an important input or output for yourself or the other people.
5. If you still feel there is inequity, do you feel inclined to take steps to restore the equity balance? What steps will you take?

GOAL-SETTING THEORY

Most people have goals or objectives of some sort and the idea that motivated behaviour is a function of a person's conscious goals and intentions is the basis of Locke's (1968) goal-setting theory. His major concern is the way that performance is affected by the process of setting goals and, for this reason, he acknowledges that his model, which is shown in Figure 8.4, is more a motivational technique than a theory of motivation.

Figure 8.4 Goal setting (source: Latham and Locke 1979)

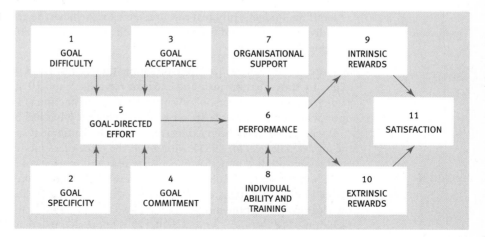

Two basic features of goals are said to be highly important:

Goal difficulty: how challenging and demanding the goal is

- *goal difficulty* (1), which is the extent to which a goal is challenging and demanding. Up to a certain point, motivated effort rises as goal difficulty increases. However, a very modest goal will not challenge the person enough, while one that is too difficult can cease to have a motivational effect because it is seen as frustrating and unattainable (Locke *et al.* 1981).

Goal specificity: how clear and explicit the goal is

- *goal specificity* (2) is the clarity and explicitness of the performance target. In Locke's view, goals with specific outcomes lead to greater effort and the best way to be specific is to express the goal quantitatively, because this allows the person to evaluate how close he or she comes to achieving it (Locke 1968; Locke *et al.* 1981).

In the model, goals give rise to **goal-directed effort** (5). However, this is influenced by two additional factors:

- **goal acceptance** (3), the extent to which a goal is accepted as a legitimate and appropriate;
- **goal commitment** (4), which is a person's vested interest in achieving the goal

Neither acceptance nor commitment happen by themselves, and it is important to recognise that they can be influenced by a number of other factors. First, the person must be able to see that achieving the goal will lead to the receipt of valued rewards (Latham and Steele 1983). Here it can be noted that if a person participates in selecting the goals, this often leads to higher commitment to achieving them (Arnold *et al.* 1991; Erez *et al.* 1985). Having said this, it should be noted that the evidence on whether participating in goal setting actually leads to better performance is very mixed. However, to enhance future commitment, Locke considers it important to give people accurate feedback on performance (Latham and Locke 1979). which is said to increase a person's sense of achievement and accomplishment as well as indicating that his or her efforts have been noticed (Latham and Locke 1979).

Performance (6) is an indication of whether, and to what extent, the goal is actually achieved, and the theory recognises that this can be strongly influenced by two additional factors:

- **organisational support** (7), whether the person receives adequate resources (staffing, budgets, physical resources, etc.) to achieve the goal
- **individual ability and training** (8), which also need to be commensurate with achieving the goal.

Where goals are achieved, the person should then be rewarded and, like Vroom, Locke explicitly states that **intrinsic** and **extrinsic rewards** (9 and 10) are both important. He also recognises that a person's eventual level of **satisfaction** (11) will crucially depend upon whether the rewards are seen as equitable for what has been achieved.

Locke's ideas have been extensively researched and most studies strongly support the model (Locke *et al.* 1981). Moreover, the principles embodied in the theory have been widely applied in performance appraisal and schemes of management by objectives, both of which are dealt with elsewhere in this book. Like all theories, however, Locke's ideas have attracted a number of criticisms. One of these is related to Locke's own admission that the model is not really a theory of motivation but a motivational technique. For instance, Arnold *et al.* (1991) note that its greatest deficiency is that it simply accepts that goals are motivators, but fails to explain why they should have such a pronounced effect. In addition, Austin and Bobko (1985) note that there are circumstances where the effects are much more uncertain than those predicted. First, they note that the quality of a person's performance is often as important as quantity of output but, unless this can somehow be translated into a quantitative measure, the theory tends to break down. Second, organisations increasingly emphasise group effort by using techniques such as team working, which runs counter to Locke's basic theory that goals and responsibility for achieving them should be assigned to individuals. Third, rather than having one goal to achieve, an individual usually has several, which inevitably results in a degree of conflict between goals, and could mean that one goal probably has to be sacrificed to achieve the others (Yearta *et al.* 1995). Finally, it has been noted that as well as giving a degree of motivation to achieve a goal, goal setting has been shown to result in an impetus to behave unethically; for example, by grossly overstating goal achievement (Schweitzer *et al.* 2004).

 OB IN ACTION: Motivation? Just fix the happiness factor

What keeps you committed at work? Is it the pay, the job itself, or something to do with your boss or colleagues? A recent study by Capital Incentives and Motivation, a Chester-based incentives business which surveyed 2,000 people across the UK, found that fair treatment in the workplace and having good relationships with colleagues were regarded as the two most important factors in keeping people committed to their jobs, but also noted that pay and job security are now moving up the league table compared to previous years.

This suggests that, although some issues retain their importance over time, the strength of other factors fluctuates, depending perhaps on economic circumstances. This year, for example, UK interest rates are increasing, suggesting that finances are going to be under increasing pressure in some households. Financial pressures and a tight labour market tend to make employees risk averse. On the other hand, as confidence grows and companies begin to recruit again, we can expect the market to slacken as people begin to think about moving jobs. In this event, fears about job security would be likely to subside.

Other variables influencing the degrees of employee motivation include the age and career progress of respective employees. Young employees and those in mid-career are more likely to move than those approaching the end of their careers. However, variables aside, there appears to be an enduring set of factors underpinning job commitment that have emerged time and again in successive studies over the past 80 years. The late Frederick Herzberg defined motivational factors such as recognition, personal responsibility and the scope for personal achievement, while other issues such as pay, working conditions and management policy were described as hygiene factors. While the first set of qualities related to improved morale and

▶

aspirations, the second group could generate high levels of dissatisfaction if they were misapplied. Even a pay rise, he noted, could prove divisive if an employee regarded it as unfair when compared with others' treatment. The poor application of a merit system, therefore, could influence the sense of fair treatment and relations among colleagues regarded as prime factors in maintaining commitment.

Herzberg's theories suggest that those issues that tend to create demotivated and disillusioned workforces may be more significant than the idea of building motivation. So instead of trying to motivate employees, managers would be better served by concentrating on maintaining the working conditions that keep people happy. As an illustration of the way staff relations can go awry, look how professional services firms have actually created dissatisfaction among young staff, by trying to squeeze ever greater levels of productivity from people by concentrating on working hours.

Source:

Donkin, R (2004) *Financial Times*, 24 June

PROCESS THEORIES: AN INTEGRATION AND OVERVIEW

While all process theories have certain similarities, they also differ in terms of:

- the degree of importance they attach to factors internal or external to the individual
- the role that rewards play in the motivational process.

Nevertheless, they can all be reconciled to some extent. For example, it has been suggested that goal-setting and equity approaches are both capable of being integrated into a more comprehensive version of expectancy theory (Mitchell 1982). As such there are three important points that emerge from these theories:

1. All process theories stress the need to establish clear links between performance and rewards.
2. They all show that, if motivation is to be aroused, it is important to pay attention to work environments; for example, employees need to feel that work organisation and group sentiments are not barriers to successful performance.
3. Since the theories all acknowledge that successful performance can crucially depend on individual attributes, there is a clear need to match employees with their jobs.

Therefore, what emerges from these points is a highly significant general implication. People bring a whole range of skills and abilities to a job and, in this respect, equity theory has a particularly significant point to make. Even when the job only calls for some skills to be used, individuals are still likely to build all of their skills into evaluations of equity. The moral of this is all too clear: it is important to use the full range of talents of each employee and reward the person accordingly.

REPLAY

- Process theories focus on the cognitive processes at work that account for the direction, intensity and persistence of motivated behaviour.
- Expectancy theories are based on the assumption that people choose between different courses of action according to which one results in the most favourable outcome for themselves.
- Equity theory focuses on the way that people are motivated to adjust their behaviour, according to their perceptions of the fairness of their own inputs and receipts from performing a task compared to the inputs and receipts of other people performing comparable tasks.
- Goal-setting theory assumes that the goals set for a person are the source of motivation rather than the needs that prompt people to derive their own goals. As such, it is more a motivational technique than a theory of motivation.

ASSESSING MOTIVATION AND DEALING WITH MOTIVATIONAL PROBLEMS

Since high motivation results in people having a direction, intensity and persistence of behaviour, there are clear advantages for an organisation if it has employees who are highly motivated to perform their tasks. This gives rise to two important questions:

- How can it be determined whether (or not) motivation is at a high level?
- Where it is not, how can it be raised?

Any answers to these questions are bound to be connected but, for convenience, the issues will be examined separately.

The Issue of Evaluating Motivational States

Any evaluation of motivation involves making a judgement about a person's inner psychological state. Fortunately, there are psychological tools to do this, one of which is Hackman and Oldham's (1980) Job Diagnostic Survey questionnaire, which was described in Chapter 7. Another method is to use a well-designed attitude question-naire (see Chapter 5). However, these are more often used to conduct employee opinion surveys, where, in the interests of obtaining frank responses to questions, respondents usually remain anonymous, which tends to rule-out their use for assess-ing individuals. Nevertheless, they can be useful in identifying general trends in a work-force, for example whether people are conscious of features of the organisation such as poor hygiene factors that could stand in the way of high motivation.

An opportunity to evaluate individual motivation also occurs in many organisations in the form of the annual 'performance appraisal' interview. However, making an accur-ate assessment of motivation in these circumstances requires special skills, that go beyond simply asking appropriate questions; they also have to be asked in an appropriate way. Thus, unless they have received special training, managers can draw highly inaccurate conclusions about subordinates. This is not to say that these evaluations are never made, but the problem is that most managers evaluate motivation in a very subjective way and draw conclusions that are based on the flimsiest of evidence. This is often done on the basis of evaluating an isolated incident of a subordinate's behaviour, and making a judgement about whether the individual concerned shows the signs of what the manager believes to be the signs of a satisfied or committed employee. There are huge problems here. To start with there is the matter of fairness. For example, should an isolated incident be used as evidence of an employee's motivational state across a whole year?

Second, many managers incorrectly assume that motivation is something they directly bring about in subordinates, and few managers would want to admit that they could have failed in this respect. Thus there can be a high element of self-deception in any evaluation that a manager makes about the motivational state of an employee. Even where this is not the case and the manager is scrupulously honest with him or herself, there is still a strong possibility that the actions of employees can result in inaccurate evaluations. For instance, if an employee wants to safeguard his or her future prospects, it is not in the person's interests to make it obvious that his or her work motivations are low, and this can result in a great deal of behaviour designed to demonstrate keenness, enthusiasm and commitment.

Addressing Motivational Problems

As noted in the previous chapter, management's main interest in motivation is in the prospects it offers for bringing employee behaviour under tighter control. Thus, what interests managers most is not the process of motivation but employee behaviour. However, managers can hardly be blamed for believing that motivation theory offers this opportunity, because content and process theories both imply that if we know a person's needs, the person can be motivated (Hancock 1999).

Nevertheless, when dealing with performance that does not reach the level that a manager requires, there is an inbuilt tendency to assume that motivation is the culprit and, in the absence of concrete evidence to the contrary, managers have a tendency to make a 'fundamental attribution error' (see Chapter 5). That is, the manager explains poor performance as something that is prompted by an internal factor (such as lack of motivation), rather than seeking an explanation in the surrounding circumstances (external attribution). Needless to say, if this error is to be avoided, the first place to look for a remedy to poor performance should always be in the context of a task.

Nevertheless, to address low motivation, the most common approach for the last four decades has been through job-redesign. Where this is used there are often strong tendencies to search for a universal solution that raises the motivation of everybody; often by relying exclusively on content theories. Here it should always be remembered that motivation is an individual matter. Thus, it is often necessary to search for individual solutions using process theories. For example, Ganzach (1998) convincingly demonstrates that there is an interaction between intelligence and the jobs that people find satisfying. Thus not everybody wants a complex, challenging job.

BEHAVIOUR MODIFICATION: AN ALTERNATIVE TO USING MOTIVATION THEORY

So far, motivation has been discussed in a rather detached way and it has been noted that the appeal of motivation theory to managers it is because it is seen as a way of increasing control over employee behaviour. Using motivation theory to achieve this end is just one way of applying behavioural science knowledge, and is a uniquely

European way of looking at things. European social scientists are somewhat wary of being seen to serve managerial interests too closely, whereas their counterparts in the USA seldom have these inhibitions and they are far less reluctant to advocate practices that serve management aims. A case in point is Behaviour Modification, which is often described in American textbooks as a theory of motivation but, as will be seen, is nothing of the sort. Rather, it is an application of one of the theories of learning described in Chapter 6. Nevertheless, it has some capability to shape employee behaviour (at least in the short-run) and for this reason managers can make use of it to achieve control over employee behaviour.

In essence, Behaviour Modification – the full title is Organisational Behaviour Modification (OB Mod.) – is a form of the Skinnerian operant conditioning described in Chapter 6, and the technique is applied to humans in work situations with the aim of shaping and fixing behaviour into a pattern that is desired by a manager. In technical terms, it has been defined as:

> the systematic reinforcement of desirable organisational behaviour and non-reinforcement of unwanted organisational behaviour.
>
> (Luthans and Kreitner 1985, p 303)

In this definition lies the crucial difference to motivation theories. Whereas motivation is concerned with internal factors that influence behaviour, reinforcement principles are concerned solely with external causes. Conditioning theory assumes that the primary determinant of an organism's behaviour is the consequence (for the organism) of behaving in a certain way. Therefore OB Mod. is only concerned with shaping, and any psychological causes of behaviour have little significance.

In theory, although not necessarily in practice, the principles applied are very simple. The fundamental idea is that behaviour can be learned, shaped and maintained by the judicious use of rewards and punishments. Before describing how the techniques are used, you may wish to briefly refresh your memory of the principles of operant conditioning given in Chapter 6.

When the principles of operant conditioning are incorporated into a well-designed, systematically applied plan in a work organisation, the process is known as OB Mod. (Luthans and Kreitner 1985). Figure 8.5 gives a simplified model of the steps involved and a description of the method follows.

To illustrate the method, assume that a bank wishes to engender loyalty in customers by getting them to feel that the bank really cares about them and considers them important. Customer opinions have been researched and this has revealed that the two features most associated with a caring attitude by the bank are the friendliness and helpfulness of counter staff.

Step 1: identify the employee behaviours that need to be changed Here, assume that the research has identified that customers are conscious of three behaviours on the part of counter staff associated with friendliness and helpfulness. These behaviours are for counter staff to: (i) greet customers in a cheerful way; (ii) serve them and answer queries promptly; (iii) wish customers a cheerful goodbye as they leave.

Step 2: take baseline performance measures for the three behaviours indentified
Here the aim is to establish the current frequency of these behaviours for each member of counter staff, together with the current frequency of undesirable behaviour. This is a vital step and, as will be seen presently, the information is used later to evaluate whether the behaviour shaping intervention has been a success.

Figure 8.5 Simplified model of behaviour modification process

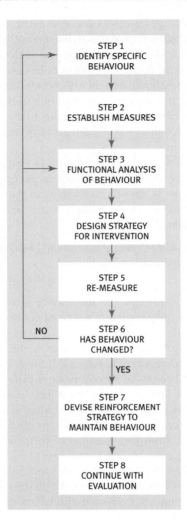

Step 1
IDENTIFY SPECIFIC
BEHAVIOUR

Step 2
ESTABLISH MEASURES

Step 3
FUNCTIONAL ANALYSIS
OF BEHAVIOUR

Step 4
DESIGN STRATEGY
FOR INTERVENTION

Step 5
RE-MEASURE

Step 6
HAS BEHAVIOUR
CHANGED?

NO

YES

Step 7
DEVISE REINFORCEMENT
STRATEGY TO
MAINTAIN BEHAVIOUR

Step 8
CONTINUE WITH
EVALUATION

Step 3: functional analysis   In this step it is established whether employees know how management wants them to behave, whether there are impediments to them behaving in this way and what outcomes (such as rewards and punishments) can be used to reinforce the desired behaviours and eliminate those that are undesirable.

Step 4: devise methods to shape employee behaviour into the desired patterns   To do this, two matters need to be addressed:

- to choose the range of rewards that are available to reinforce desired behaviour
- to select those that will be used, together with punishments that will be applied for undesirable behaviour.

To establish a basis for applying rewards and punishments, the bank might get counter staff to give customers a very short questionnaire or checklist that evaluates friendliness and helpfulness. This has a code number on it somewhere, which identifies the member of staff who dealt with the customer, and the questionnaire is deposited in a box as the customer leaves. Thus, a weekly or monthly customer evaluation of each member of staff is obtained and this is translated into a number of points scored by each individual staff member. Points can be accrued over time and traded for rewards such as a cash bonus, or additional holiday days. Staff who get adverse ratings from customers are admonished. In addition, schedules of reinforcement can be selected to reward or punish staff behaviour. Since it is much harder to use punishment as a conditioning stimulus than to use positive reinforcement, wherever possible, positive reinforcement is used.

Step 5: re-measure the frequency of desired and undesirable employee behaviours
Strictly speaking, in this example this would be unnecessary because behaviour is measured continuously by using data from customer questionnaires. However, this is not always possible, and sometimes a distinct re-measurement stage is required.

Step 6: evaluate the success of the intervention   If there has been little or no improvement, it may then be necessary to return to step 1, and possibly step 3, to re-design the intervention strategy. Where success has been obtained, matters proceed to steps 7 and 8.

Step 7: devise ongoing strategy to maintain the desired patterns of behaviour   This would be done by selecting methods of reinforcement that would be used in the long term, and since no system of rewards has an indefinite shelf life, this leads to step 8.

Step 8: ongoing re-evaluation

What then is the potential usefulness of OB Mod.? As noted above, it is not a motivation theory, or even an application of one. In Great Britain it tends to be considered a highly controversial technique, not least because it has unpleasant connotations of Orwell's 'Big Brother' watching everybody. Thus, advocates of motivation theory are likely to condemn these methods strongly and argue that people are far too complex to be treated like white rats in a laboratory experiment. Indeed, to many psychologists operant conditioning does not even qualify as psychology, but should rightfully be classified as a mere technique; Behaviourists, of course, argue otherwise. Nevertheless, the research evidence suggests that OB Mod. can be effective in shaping behaviour, at least in the short term (Stajkovic and Luthans 1997).

As usual, however, there are criticisms, and these cannot be ignored. Locke (1977), for example, considers that the effects are likely to be too short-lived to be useful, because the effects quickly wear off. Indeed, even if steps are taken to maintain the behaviours, in the long run these can quickly come to be regarded by employees as a routine part of the organisation's rewards package.

Other criticisms focus on the idea that OB Mod. takes no account of individual differences in personality. What is a reinforcer for one person is not for another and this makes it hard to identify rewards that are likely to have the same effect on all employees. Yet another criticism is that OB Mod. takes no account of whether group norms and peer pressures run counter to the behaviours that managers want to obtain.

Perhaps the most significant criticisms of all centre on the ethical considerations alluded to above. Most British psychologists would be reluctant to use techniques that give managers even more power over employees. To do so is to subscribe to the idea that managers are infallible and have an unquestioned right to exercise control over everything. However, since psychology likes to consider itself an ethical discipline, it is possible that these feelings are more connected to psychologists' self-images than anything else. Their objection is not so much to OB Mod. itself but to the uses to which it can be put, for example to induce a slavish following of management instructions. Paradoxically, few people (and this includes psychologists) would find anything reprehensible about conditioning employees to avoid accidents by working more safely. This, after all, is doing good and can easily be reconciled with our self-images. Moreover, almost everybody is conditioned to some extent during their upbringing and most managers probably use crude conditioning techniques on a day-to-day basis without realising it. For the present, however, OB Mod. is, and will probably continue to be, a relatively unused technique in Great Britain.

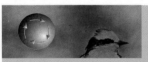

REPLAY

- OB Mod. is not, as it is sometimes portrayed, a theory of motivation that explains the process which results in motivated behaviour.
- It is an application of operant conditioning techniques in a workplace setting that aims to induce workers to behave as managers want them to behave.
- As such, OB Mod. is an alternative to using motivation theory.

OVERVIEW AND CONCLUSIONS

Since there are strong connections between this chapter and the one that precedes it, this section will review the contents of both. The major approaches covered in the two chapters focus on different aspects of motivation, and it might appear that there is an element of contradiction in what they say. However, they are complementary rather than opposed. Content theories deal with the needs that give rise to motivated behaviour, but perhaps oversimplify matters because they tend to portray human beings as having a homogeneous set of needs. Nevertheless, as long as due allowance is made for individual differences, this does not detract from their potential usefulness. Process theories have a different emphasis: they seek to explain the dynamics of the motivation process and so much greater account is taken of individual differences. Problematically, this results in theories that are more complex, which means that they are more difficult to apply in practice. Although Behaviour Modification is not a motivation theory, it is potentially useful to explain how motivation can be sustained once a person has become motivated. Thus, while none of the theories should be regarded as the whole story, when taken together they all have something useful to offer. Therefore, it is fitting to conclude by highlighting a number of important conclusions that can be drawn from the motivation theories covered in this and the previous chapter:

- When an employee becomes motivated this is the outcome of a psychological process.
- It is not possible directly to observe this process at work, nor can managers supply motivation directly to employees.

- Nevertheless, it is still possible to influence an employee's level of motivation to some extent, by creating conditions that the individual finds stimulating and encouraging.

- It is unlikely that stimulation and encouragement can be provided for all employees in an identical way and so there is a need to be sensitive to variations in individual needs, goals, preferences and abilities (Lucas 2003).

- Conditions can change, both inside and outside an organisation, which means that the needs of individuals can change and so can the organisation's capability to meet them. For this reason the provision of a stimulating and encouraging work environment should never be taken for granted, nor should it be regarded as a once-and-for-all exercise, but rather as a matter which should be kept under constant review.

- It is important to recognise that work is not the only vehicle that individuals can use to satisfy their needs and wants.

- Nevertheless, if work has the capability to result in outcomes that are highly valued by employees, the first and perhaps most important step in the motivational process has been taken.

- The people most likely to be able to ensure that this step is taken are the managers of an organisation, and this can be done in two ways: by seeking to discover what conditions are required by individuals in order to satisfy their needs, and by providing a work experience that gives sufficient diversity, opportunity and challenge to satisfy the needs.

FURTHER READING

Locke, EA and GP Latham (1990) *A Theory of Goal Setting and Task Performance*, New York: Prentice Hall. A comprehensive account of the authors' views, which, by their own admission, are more a technique for applying motivation theory, rather than a new theory of motivation.

Furnham, A and T Booth (2005) *Just For The Money? What Really Motivates Us At Work*, London: Cyan Books. A critical examination of the (apparently) dominant role that money plays in motivating people at work.

Petri, HL (1996) *Motivation: Theory, Research and Application*, London: Thomson. A specialist, but nevertheless readable, text that gives a comprehensive coverage of all the major approaches to motivation theory.

Porter, LW and EE Lawler (1968) *Managerial Attitudes and Performance*, Homewood Il: Irwin. A very clear explanation of the authors' expectancy theory that is widely cited in academic circles.

Sarafino, EP (1997) *Principles of Behaviour Change*, Chichester: Wiley. Again a specialist book, but one that gives an up-to-date coverage of Behaviour Modification techniques and practices.

Spector, P (1995) *Industrial and Organisational Psychology: Research and Practice*, Chichester: Wiley. A wide-ranging text that has good coverage of motivation, and discusses it within in a wider psychological context.

Steers, R, RT Mowday and DL Shapiro (2004) The future of work motivation theory, *Academy of Management Review* 29(3): 379–387. A useful overview of the history of work motivation theory is given, together with a number of suggestions made by scholars active in this area for future directions in research on work motivation.

Steers, R and Porter L (1991) *Motivation and Work Behaviour*, New York: McGraw-Hill. The book gives a very detailed but highly managerialist view on the application of motivation theory from an American perspective.

Weiner, B (1992) *Human Motivation: Metaphors, Theories and Research*, London: Sage. A comprehensive book that gives an interesting integration of the different theoretical perspectives on motivation.

CASE STUDY 8.1: Corporate social responsibility (CSR) and motivation

Note Before addressing this case you may find it helpful to examine the section in Chapter 2 of this book that discusses CSR.

Today, there are few self-respecting companies that do not have a corporate responsibility programme or mission statement, but many have struggled to establish a tangible business case for the investment in these programmes. However, in recent years, it has become clear that staff motivation is a powerful bottom-line benefit of corporate responsibility, and Robert Davies, chief executive of the International Business Leaders Forum, which works with corporations to promote responsible business practices, argues that the employee audience has become a major driver of CSR. For instance, according to a report published by the research company Ipsos MORI, evidence is emerging that staff are concerned about the ethical behaviour of the companies for whom they work and 86 per cent of British workers believe it is important that their employer should be responsible to society and the environment.

In the UK, the push by retailers to meet the demands of a growing number of ethical shoppers has raised the profile of the ethical practices of businesses. Marks and Spencer, for example, is inviting shoppers to 'look behind the label' at the sustainability of its products, as well as its labour, fair trade and animal welfare practices. Moreover, as global warming has taken centre stage, companies have implemented carbon reduction programmes. Tesco, for example, has embarked on an ambitious labelling initiative that will eventually let shoppers compare all its products on their carbon emissions levels and people want to see similar practices in action, not only in the supermarket aisle but also in the workplace.

People are in search of meaning at work, says Linda Holbeche, director of leadership and consultancy at the Work Foundation, and they are conscious of the ways in which organisations 'walk the talk' on things such as CSR. In addition, the activities of leading business figures such as Bill Gates – whose foundation is tackling global health problems such as the spread of HIV/Aids – have also increased the desire on the part of workers to see their employers take action on some of the world's social and health problems.

Indeed, the opportunity for staff to participate in community initiatives has now become important. To this end KPMG, winner in this year's 'best workplace' corporate responsibility category, offers staff the chance to volunteer. In 2006, for instance, 31 per cent of its workforce volunteered, contributing 32,000 hours to community projects, and the company has recognised that such commitments are what help it attract and retain top talent, both from executives and graduates. Thus if you want to be a great place to work, it is not just about base salary and benefits, says Mike Kelly, UK head of corporate social responsibility at KPMG. While people expect leading companies to provide leading remuneration packages and expect the best in training and development, increasingly they also expect to work in an environment where they can contribute to the community.

Source: Murray, S (2007) *Financial Times*, 2 May

Questions

1. To what extent do you feel that the motivations of employees are likely to be affected by the CSR activities (or lack of) of the firms that they work for?

2. Using an appropriate motivation theory state how you would classify CSR (or lack of it) in terms of being a motivator?

3. Assume that you have just finished the final year of your degree and are about to be interviewed for your first full-time job. List your priorities for the things that you would be looking for in a job that would make you feel good about the job.

4. Now rank these things in terms of importance starting from 1 for the most important of them.

5. List the things that you would most want to avoid in any job that you take.

6. Now rank these starting from minus 1 downwards.

7. Are positive CSR policies on the part of a potential employer anywhere on your list?

REVIEW AND DISCUSSION QUESTIONS

1. Define the terms 'valence', 'expectancy' and 'first-level outcomes' as used in Vroom's (VIE) expectancy model. Explain how these are connected to demonstrate a person's motive force.

2. Describe any important additional features that the Porter and Lawler model has beyond those contained in Vroom's version of expectancy theory. Explain whether, in your view, these additional features result in a more plausible explanation of the process of motivation, which is of practical utility to people in organisations.

3. In equity theory, what is assumed to be the factor that most influences a person's motivation to expend effort on a task? Explain in outline the basic sequence of mental processes that is said to influence motivation.

4. To what extent are goal-setting and Organisational Behaviour Modification (OB Mod.) theories of motivation?

5. What do you feel are the advantages and shortcomings of OB Mod., and explain the extent to which you feel that it is a technique that can be practically applied by managers?

Chapter 9 **Individual Decision Making**

LEARNING OUTCOMES

After studying this chapter you should be able to:

- define decision making and distinguish between decision making and problem solving

- distinguish between bounded and unbounded problems, and trace the implications of each type for the nature of the decision making process

- compare and contrast the three decision making models described in the chapter: rational choice, bounded rationality and the garbage can model

- describe the phenomenon of escalation of commitment to a failing course of action and the factors that explain its existence

- describe the three main groups of factors that influence the way in which decisions are made by individuals in organisations

INTRODUCTION

The decision making process has long been of interest to Organisational Behaviour and Organisational Analysis and it is usually studied at one of three levels. First, strategic decision making. This affects the whole organisation and is concerned with decisions that establish an appropriate relationship between the organisation and its environment, but, since this is the major concern of the subject of Business Policy, it is beyond the scope of this book.

Second, decision making by groups, which usually focuses on the internal dynamics of the decision process and how this has an influence on the way that decisions are made. To understand this it is first necessary to understand something of how groups function and, since this is covered in Chapter 11, the topic will be deferred until then. Finally, decision making by individuals, which is the focus of this chapter. Here the aim is to understand how individuals handle information in order to select alternative courses of action.

To address this matter the chapter commences with a definition of decision making and how it relates to the broader process of problem solving. To set the scene for what follows, two types of problem that can be encountered by people in organisations are contrasted – bounded problems and unbounded problems – each of which normally requires its own approach to decision making. The remainder of the chapter then explores a number of models of decision making and the first to be considered is the 'rational choice' model, which is a theoretical prescription for how decisions *should* be made. Since this model is based on a number of underlying assumptions and these mean that in its pure form the use of the model is comparatively rare, the next model to be considered is the theory of 'bounded rationality', which gives a more realistic description of how decisions are made in practice. The last model to be covered is the theory of 'garbage can' decision making, which presents a picture of how decisions are made in more ambiguous circumstances.

The next section of the chapter considers the matter of post-decision behaviour. This is explored by considering the phenomenon of 'commitment to a failing course of action', in which a decision maker persists in implementing a decision in the face of evidence that the decision is inappropriate. This is followed by a section that pulls together the material covered in the chapter into a model of the three main groups of factors that can shape the behaviour of decision makers, and the chapter closes with an overview section that reviews its contents.

DECISION MAKING IN PERSPECTIVE

Decision making: the process of making a choice between alternatives

Problem solving: the process of producing a solution to a recognised problem

Decision making is widely defined as 'choosing between alternatives', which reflects the idea that if there is only one alternative to choose from, there is no decision to take. However, the term is sometimes used synonymously with the expression *problem solving*, and some authors (e.g. Lang *et al.* 1978) refer to problem solving as part of the decision making process. In practice, while problem solving can never be completely isolated from making a decision, at a conceptual level the two things are different. This can be seen in Simon's (1960) conceptualisation of the decision making processes as something consisting of the three main activities (Figure 9.1).

Figure 9.1 The three basic activities involved in decision making (adapted from Simon 1960)

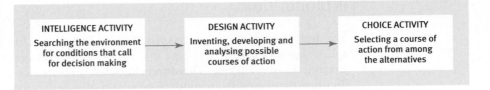

Strictly speaking, only the final activity in Figure 9.1 involves making a decision, but the first two are necessary prerequisites for the third and can rightly be considered part of the process. However, taking the third step does not necessarily mean that a problem has been solved. The decision might only be one of a series that all contribute to solving the problem and, even where only a single decision is involved, the chosen alternative might be incorrect and another needs to be tried. As such, problem solving embraces other activities, for example implementing the decision and monitoring its appropriateness. Since these take place after a decision has been made, the essence of a decision is that a number of alternatives are considered before one is chosen. Note, however, that evaluation of alternatives on its own is not decision making, which only happens when a choice is made. For these reasons, decision making is taken to be an activity that focuses on the central issue of choosing between alternative courses of action, and problem solving is a much broader process, of which decision making is a part (Cook and Slack 1991).

TYPES OF DECISION

Not all decisions are the same. Some are relatively simple and others involve a more complex range of considerations. For example, even though they can be extremely complex, engineering problems often involve only hard, tangible considerations, whereas if human factors are concerned, decisions may involve softer, intangible aspects of organisational life. Some writers, for example Cook and Slack (1991), suggest that it is possible to distinguish betweens decision in terms of 'good' and 'bad'. This however is misleading, if only because what is perceived to be good by one person can just as easily be perceived by someone else as bad. For this reason decisions will be distinguished in terms of their 'effectiveness', which ultimately comes down to whether a decision is focused on the matter about which a decision is required. Decisions are usually made in the hope that they will solve problems and, to decide whether a decision is effective in this sense, it is necessary to consider the nature of the problem on which it is focused.

Bounded problems: problems that can be more easily defined and treated as separate from the context in which they exist

As with many things, problem types cannot be distinguished on the basis of a single criterion and so a multidimensional perspective is required. These dimensions can be brought together, to distinguish between what will be referred to here as *bounded* and *unbounded problems*, the major characteristics of which are shown in Table 9.1.

Unbounded problems: ambiguous problems that are harder to define and which cannot easily be separated from the context in which they exist

To illustrate a bounded problem, imagine the case of an organisation considering the purchase of a new machine. Because this is a one-off issue of whether to replace a single machine, its implications are small and although the existing machine probably requires an increased level of maintenance, it is not completely defunct. Thus, the decision could be put off and, in terms of time scale, it is a short-term problem that is not really serious. The relative costs and benefits of replacement can easily be determined and, since these give a clear set of priorities to guide decision making, it is clear

Table 9.1 Bounded and unbounded problems

Characteristics	Bounded problems	Unbounded problems
Scale of problem	Usually small, or can be broken down into a series of smaller discrete problems	Large and if there are multiple problems they usually need to be solved simultaneously
Implications of problem	Usually less serious	Serious implications
Time scale	Usually exists over a limited time scale	Longer and uncertain time scales
Clarity of problem	It is usually clear what the problem is	Uncertainty about what the problem is; there are often several candidates
Potential solution	Even though the actual solution to a problem has not yet been identified, it is known what a solution would be	There is, as yet, no known solution to the problem
Priorities	Clear priorities exist to determine a satisfactory solution	Priorities are uncertain
Knowledge	A solution to the problem is known, which means that relevant information can be collected	It is not certain what information needs to be obtained to solve the problem
Discreteness	The problem can be divorced from the context in which it exists and solved separately	The problem is part and parcel of the context in which it exists
People	Usually few people are involved	Often many people are involved

what information needs to be obtained to make the decision. Finally, the problem can be treated as discrete from any others in the firm, and it has few associated human implications.

Compare this with the highly unbounded problem of a firm that has some worries about its ageing product line. The scale of the problem is much larger, it has potentially serious implications for the whole organisation and these stretch well into the future. However, although the firm has apprehensions about the age of its products, there is little clarity about whether a problem actually exists, or what its nature might be. Neither is there a clear solution, merely a realisation that, at some time in the future, a replacement range of products will be needed, but not, however, what the products will need to be. As such, priorities are very unclear. For instance, the cost, sales and production implications are not known and, at this stage, the firm does not know what its information requirements are in order to solve the problem. Neither can it treat the problem as discrete from a host of other problems. For example, what are its competitors doing about the future and are customer tastes changing? Perhaps most worrying of all, as well as the people in the firm who may be affected, external stakeholders are likely to be concerned, for example shareholders, customers and banks.

The nature of each of these problems is quite different. It is not just the size of the issue that is significant. What makes life difficult with an unbounded problem is the degree of inherent risk, uncertainty and ambiguity. For this reason, each type of problem needs to be handled in a different way. If, for example, a bounded problem is treated as one that is unbounded, a great deal of time and effort could be wasted in searching for solutions. Even worse, if the complexities of an unbounded problem are not recognised and it is treated as one that is bounded, the range of possible solutions developed could be inadequate.

TIME OUT

Looking to the future, carefully consider what you feel your ideal job would be when you eventually leave university or college. Try to list your preferences for particular types of work, your goals in terms of salary, location and so on, and what you estimate to be your chances of obtaining the sort of job that you want.

Now look at the characteristics of bounded and unbounded problems given in Table 9.1. Is the matter of making a decision about your future career at this point in time a bounded problem or one that is unbounded?

REPLAY

- Decision making, which can be defined as 'choosing between alternatives', is part of the wider process of problem solving.
- The complexity of a problem that requires a decision can be expressed by the extent to which it is either bounded or unbounded.
- Decisions associated with unbounded problems tend to require a different approach from those that are bounded.

MODELS OF DECISION MAKING

Decision making models fall into two broad categories: normative (prescriptive) models and descriptive models. Normative models express how decisions 'should' be made, whereas descriptive models set out to explain how decisions are made in practice. Most normative models have a heavy emphasis on rationality, and in decision making this hinges on knowing the link between doing something (cause) and what happens when we do something (effect). In many organisational situations this link is tenuous, to say the least, and we will return to this point later. For the present, however, it is more important to set out the first model – the model of rational choice.

> **Rational choice:** the assumption that decisions are taken with full knowledge of all the relevant facts and that the option chosen maximises expected utility

Rational choice: decision making as it is supposed to be

The *rational choice* approach to decision making is firmly in the normative category. It gives a prescriptive set of steps that describe what decision makers should do if they behave in a rational, detached way. Its origins lie in the economic theory of expected utility (Von Neuman and Morgenstern 1947), which is underpinned by the idea that a rational economic decision maker will always seek the optimal solution to a problem. Here 'optimal' is defined as the solution with the greatest economic utility. The model has a number of assumptions. That:

- the decision maker recognises and has knowledge of all the possible alternative solutions to a problem
- he or she has complete knowledge of the consequences of each of these alternatives
- the decision maker has a well-developed and perfectly organised set of preferences for outcomes, so that the alternatives can be evaluated
- he or she will have unlimited resources, including the skills and abilities to process data to compare the utilities of these outcomes and to determine the one that is optimal.

The model gives a logical set of steps that should be followed in order to arrive at the optimal decision. These are shown in Figure 9.2.

Step 'A': Problem identification and definition
Normally a problem is acknowledged when there is a shortfall between a planned or desired state of affairs and what happens in practice. After this the model splits into two parallel sets of activities, which can occur simultaneously, or as a set of four steps in sequence.

Step 'C1': Goal formulation
In this step, clear goals are established, the achievement of which will result in removal of the problem. This usually consists of identifying why there is a gap between targets or goals and the actual state of affairs.

Step 'C2': Devise criteria to evaluate alternatives
Since the aim is to maximise expected economic utility, the most common criterion used is contribution to profit, which means that the costs and expected benefits of each

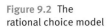

Figure 9.2 The rational choice model

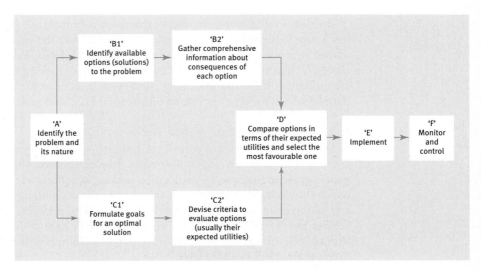

alternative need to be known. Although this sounds simple, gathering the information can be quite complex. To start with, costs occur in the present, whereas benefits might be spread over several years, which adds an element of uncertainty to the decision. Thus criteria such as associated risk and the timing of the payback come into play. Almost inevitably, information of this type consists of estimates and, for this reason, while the method is called 'rational choice', an element of subjectivity tends to be injected into the process, the results of which can be seen in the description of the next step.

Step 'B1': Identifying or generating potential solutions

This step is the essence of the rational choice model. It consists of developing a range of feasible alternative solutions to the problem and usually there are several alternative ways of achieving the desired goal. While it can be relatively easy (but time-consuming) to do this for a bounded problem, it is clearly a much more difficult step for one that is unbounded, because there is often a lack of clarity about what the problem is.

Step 'B2': Information gathering

Here the decision maker gathers precise, detailed information about the outcomes of each alternative solution, for example, investment costs, expected returns and so on.

Step D: Compare options and select one

In a truly rational decision, if all of the options are compared, the one that ranks highest in terms of expected utility should be chosen. Suppose, for example, that three alternatives 1, 2 and 3 have been identified, the costs and benefits of which are as follows:

	Costs	Benefits (profits per annum)
1.	£15,000	£5,000 for 5 years
2.	£20,000	£6,000 for 6 years
3.	£30,000	£8,000 for 8 years

Because of inflation and the interest that is foregone from risk-free investments, money has a time value and so it is commonplace to discount the value of future cash flows to their equivalent in net present values, after which a decision is taken. Although techniques such as this appear to add a greater degree of rationality, the assigned values are estimates. Thus they inevitably contain an element of subjectivity, which reflects the preferences for safety or risk on the part of the decision makers (Weber *et al.* 1992).

Steps 'E' and 'F': Implementation and monitoring

Strictly speaking, these are part of the broader issue of problem solving and so they are only described here for completeness. Implementation speaks for itself, and the more significant issue so far as decision making is concerned is step 'F', monitoring, which should be designed to evaluate whether the decision has had the desired effect and has no unanticipated consequences. If necessary, remedial action is then taken to achieve the desired outcomes. However, even in the light of evidence that a problem has not been solved there are times when people simply press on regardless and a return to this matter will be made later.

Criticisms of the Rational Choice Model

There are three main streams of criticism of the idea of rational choice, all of which are concerned with its underlying assumptions. These are:

* In terms of uncertainty, while the model assumes that decision makers have complete information about the consequences of alternatives, this is rarely the case and the use of hunches and intuition is probably far more prevalent than people would care to admit (Fagley and Miller 1987).

* The model assumes that decision makers have fixed and consistent preferences, whereas they are probably far more pragmatic; their preferences are seldom set in tablets of stone, but in many cases evolve gradually in the light of experience (Singh 1986).

* There is an assumption that decision makers have unlimited resources at their disposal and an unlimited capacity to process information, which can be far too optimistic a picture in many organisations (Simon 1978).

The second and third points are probably the most damning. In terms of preferences there are times when people are not completely sure of what they want until they know what is available and, in the meantime, the only options considered are those that are currently politically and socially acceptable. In terms of information processing capacities and resources, decisions sometimes have to be taken quickly, and so the long, drawn-out process of the rational choice model would be unworkable or inappropriate (Perlow *et al.* 2002). Indeed, the one resource that is frequently not available to a decision maker is time. Thus, March (1982) suggests that being a rational decision maker can come down to taking short-cuts, and aiming for a decision that is 'good enough' rather than optimal. This optimises the use of time, which is sometimes the most precious resource of all. For these reasons, the conditions in which rational choice methods can be used are probably the exception rather than the rule.

In addition there is a more recent stream of criticism that points out that, even when the right conditions exist, the use of rational choice methods can be extremely unlikely for cultural reasons. This is a matter that will be explored in more detail later, when considering contextual factors, and here it is sufficient to note that there are strong arguments that every step in the rational choice model can be handled in a different way according to the cultural context in which decisions are made (Adler 1997).

In summary, although the rational choice model is often portrayed as the most logical and appropriate way to make decisions, few people would seriously argue that it represents an accurate picture of what always occurs in practice. Simon (1978), who was awarded a Nobel Prize for his research on decision making, notes that the assumptions underpinning the idea of perfect rationality are far from being an account of the processes that people use in everyday situations. As an alternative, he proposes a descriptive model, which identifies processes actually used by decision makers, and this is considered next.

Bounded Rationality

The rational choice model tends to portray decision making in stark terms. Either the decision maker behaves rationally by adopting an optimising approach, or accepts a sub-optimal solution, in which case the person is deemed to have behaved irrationally. However, as Simon (1957) points out, there are several types of rationality:

- objective rationality, which in decision making means that the person seeks to maximise given values in a given situation
- *post hoc* rationality, in which a decision is made quickly, and is legitimised after the event by developing an argument that it was rational in the prevailing circumstances
- subjective rationality, where an attempt is made to maximise the outcomes within the constraints of limited information.

The rational choice model only deals with the first of these and *post hoc* rationality will be dealt with later in the chapter, when considering what can happen after a decision is made and it fails. Therefore it is important to examine the matter of subjective rationality, which is dealt with in Simon's (1957) model of *bounded rationality*.

The basic premise underpinning Simon's ideas is that, in most circumstances, decision makers are subject to a huge variety of constraints that limit their capabilities to make decisions in the way envisaged by the rational choice model. For example, they have a limited capacity to process information (Jones 1995) and are often confronted with unbounded problems that are inherently so complex and full of uncertainty, that they have only the vaguest idea of what information needs to be collected. In addition, there is often a shortage of information, a lack of knowledge concerning how critical the decision is and, above all, pressing time constraints. In these circumstances, which are often triggered by signs of a shortfall in some aspect of organisational performance, decision makers have a strong imperative to simply 'do something'. This is often because they have a much wider range of matters to which they must attend, and this precludes an exhaustive consideration of all the possible alternative actions; often in order to make the best use of time. As such, they tend to reduce the information processing demands involved in the rational choice model, and find a solution that largely relies on past experience. Any search for remedies tends to be very limited and local, and this makes use of decision heuristics, which will be considered presently. All this, however, introduces potential biases into decisions, the net result of which is that decision makers are not really able to *optimise*, and instead, have to *satisfice*. They do not seek a perfect or best solution, but one that is satisfactory or 'good enough' in the circumstances (Bowen and Qui 1992). To put matters another way, decision makers tend to accept a solution that makes the problem 'go away'. Thus, in searching for solutions, they will usually accept the first alternative that is good enough, without any comparison of alternatives. These ideas are reflected in the model shown in Figure 9.3.

In step 1, there is a recognition that decision makers are usually too busy to go looking for problems to solve and that unless one appears, their attention falls on a host of other matters to which they must attend (step 1a). If, however, a significant problem comes to light, a local search for a solution is made, which involves the use of heuristics (step 2). If a solution is located that makes the problem go away (step 3), it is implemented (step 3a) and this prompts a return to step 1, where monitoring to verify that the problem no longer exists is undertaken. Should the solution fail to resolve the problem, the decision maker then has two alternatives: to keep repeating the cycle

---

Bounded rationality: the recognition that a person's ability to take a position of perfect rationality in decision making is constrained by limited time, limited information, or a limited capacity to process information

Optimise: to seek a solution or decision option that maximises expected utility

Satisfice: to seek a solution or decision option that is 'good enough' rather than perfect

Figure 9.3 The bounded rationality model of decision making

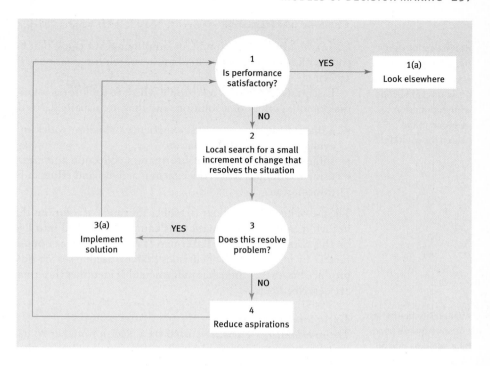

until a satisfactory solution is found, or to reduce his or her aspirations, for example by choosing a solution that is good enough and which produces results that the person can 'live with'.

In this model the first and last steps illustrate an interesting facet of organisational life: the 'if it ain't broke, don't fix it' point of view. In most organisations, where things function without apparent problems, there is virtually no search for alternative or better ways of doing things. This means that *slack* (unexploited opportunities, undiscovered economies and under-utilised resources) tends to accumulate. It is only when performance falls below the standards set by goals that there is an imperative for a search for alternatives. When one is found, it results in slack being taken up.

However, step 4 draws attention to the idea that when a decision maker conducts a search for an alternative, he or she sometimes becomes aware that there are limits to what can be achieved and, if reserves of slack have been used up, it is more than likely that the person will reduce the goals to match what is actually achieved. For instance, the easiest and quickest way to reduce the defect level is to lower the standards of inspection.

Simon's bounded rationality model is generally accepted as far more realistic than the rather abstract concept of rational choice, but it is important to recognise that the difference between the two models is one of degree. While they are both theories that make use of the concept of rationality, the rational choice model assumes that objective rationality is possible, whereas Simon recognises that rationality is usually subject to severe constraints. Thus, the main difference between the two models is in terms of how much attention is allocated to a particular problem.

Slack: unexploited opportunities or undiscovered economies such as surplus resources

The Use of Heuristics

Heuristics are rules-of-thumb, or simplifying strategies, that help a decision maker to cope with information overload in the search for solutions (Tversky and Kahneman 1974).

Essentially, heuristics tell people where to look for a solution or something about the potential utility of a solution, and they are usually derived from three sources:

- a (mental) summary of past experience, which provides an easy way of evaluating the current situation
- subjective rules that guide information collection and interpretation
- using techniques that reduce mental activity and effort in processing information.

The use of heuristics is likely to reduce the range of solutions that are examined, which in turn means that systematic bias can be introduced into decisions. Some evidence on this matter is given by Bazerman (1994), who takes bounded rationality one step further by identifying the heuristics that are used in search procedures and how these produce biases that influence judgement. He identifies three major heuristics and these are described below.

The availability heuristic

The *availability heuristic* is used by a decision maker to assess the probability of the outcome of a decision, which is done by recollecting the outcomes of a similar decision in the past. The problem here is that for most people the past events that are most accessible in the memory are usually those that are vivid and easily recalled because they evoke an emotional reaction. For example, if a decision maker has used a particular solution to a problem in the past and it backfired, causing some embarrassment, the person would probably avoid taking a similar step in the present, even though it could be appropriate.

The representativeness heuristic

The *representativeness heuristic* is used by a decision maker to judge the likelihood of the outcome of a current option by using a stereotyped similarity to something in the past. In the case of decision making, for example, it might well be assumed that the successful solution to every decline in sales is to increase advertising.

The anchoring or judgement heuristic

With the *anchoring or judgement heuristic* the decision maker makes a judgement by starting at an initial position which is then adjusted to reach the solution that is eventually chosen. Usually the initial position is chosen on the basis of historical precedent, or by the way the problem is presented. If, for example, the decision maker has used a similar option in the past, which resulted in unanticipated consequences, he or she would probably avoid the same option again. However, if the problem is an urgent one, and something needs to be done quickly, he or she might reason that given certain precautions the same thing will not happen this time.

Although Bazerman's explanations are complex, his work tells us a great deal about how decision makers conduct localised searches for solutions under conditions of bounded rationality. Moreover, there is an emerging body of research evidence to show that the heuristics he identifies are widely used (Allinson *et al.* 1992).

The Garbage Can Model

This model (Cohen *et al.* 1972) was also derived because the rational choice model is unable to explain how many decisions are made in practice. However, unlike the models presented so far, it avoids the assumption that decision making follows an orderly sequence of steps and instead argues that some decisions are taken in a haphazard, random fashion.

Essentially, Cohen *et al.* argue that the decision making context in many organisations is so complex that it becomes impossible to specify the steps used in a decision process. Rather, problems, their solutions, the opportunity to take decisions and decision makers co-exist in a turbulent state of flux. This being the case there is no neat, orderly set of decision steps, but a disordered collection of circumstances, that consists of:

- problems looking for a solution
- solutions looking for issues to arise to which they can become the solution
- decision makers looking for decisions to make
- opportunities for making a decision that are looking for a problem about which to make a decision.

At first all this might seem contradictory, but matters can be more easily explained with the aid of the so-called garbage can model shown in Figure 9.4.

Event Streams

Figure 9.4 portrays the idea that problems, solutions to problems, participants and participants' choice opportunities are all independent entities that flow into the organisational decision situation as streams of events. This is metaphorically regarded as a garbage can in which these things get dumped until, by chance, they become connected and then interact. For this reason, problems can exist independently of solutions and the existence of a particular problem does not mean that a solution will be found.

Problems

In this model problems are a shortfall of some sort in organisational performance.

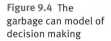

Figure 9.4 The garbage can model of decision making

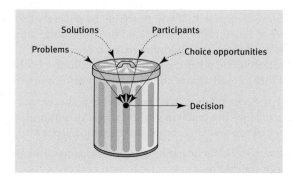

Solutions

These are the answers to problems and, because ideas constantly flow through an organisation and can remain unused until a problem arises, they sometimes exist before a problem is identified. Therefore, solutions are not always identifiable courses of action that are put into effect, although they often consist of available, but as yet unused, ideas about how to handle a particular problem if it arises. For this reason problems often go unrecognised until people are confronted with a solution. To give an example from everyday life, you might not recognise that you have run out of some essential household item, such as toilet paper, until you go shopping for food on Saturday and a shelf full of toilet paper reminds you.

Participants

These are the organisational members concerned with making decisions, all of whom bring different priorities, attitudes, values and prior experiences to the decision making situation. Some of them will have solutions to problems of which they have not yet been made aware, and others will be aware of problems to which their prior backgrounds contain no clue of a solution.

Choice opportunities

While these occur frequently in organisations, this happens in an irregular and unpredictable way (Cohen *et al.* 1972). There are the occasions when a decision *can* be made, but there is no guarantee that this will happen. For instance, some opportunities occur regularly in terms of regular meetings, but others are unique because a crisis might well prompt a special meeting.

The Interaction of Streams of Events

The four independent streams of events interact in a highly random fashion in most organisations and so the elements are all mixed together in the organisation's decision environment (garbage can). This means that decisions are only taken as and when the appropriate elements of each stream connect with each other. Since these connections also occur randomly, luck or timing sometimes influence whether a decision is taken. Decisions therefore tend to be made when a situation comprises a certain combination of circumstances. For example:

- when a problem exists that is sufficiently important to warrant the attention of those concerned, otherwise it will probably be pushed into the background
- when a potential solution is known and brought to the attention of someone who has the authority and energy to make a decision
- most important of all, when a problem and a solution both surface in sequential order, and this state of affairs coincides with a choice opportunity.

There is fairly strong evidence that the model is an accurate but complex picture of the way that decisions are made in organisations (Levitt and Nass 1984). Moreover, it has a number of far-reaching implications, which are that:

- some decisions will only be made when the streams coincide and this introduces an element of randomness into the decision process

- because some decision makers are guided by political motives and have their own personal agendas to pursue (see Chapter 14), the timing of connections between the four streams of events is open to manipulation, which can delay the making of decisions

- the whole process of decision making is likely to be extremely volume sensitive because if people are extremely busy, they are likely to absent themselves from events that constitute choice opportunities

- flowing directly from the previous point, as the number of problems in an organisation rises, people can find that the time they have available to attend meetings declines, and so the opportunities to make decisions that could solve problems tends to decrease

- this means that important and novel problems are more likely to be solved than those which are mundane and routine, particularly if they are problems experienced by power holders, who can create choice opportunities, perhaps by calling special problem solving meetings.

REPLAY

- Decision models can be divided into two main groups: normative and descriptive.
- Normative models (e.g. the model of rational choice) give prescriptions for what decision makers should do and strongly endorse the aim of 'rational' procedures to achieve an 'optimal' solution.
- Descriptive models explain how decisions are made in practice.
- The (descriptive) model of 'bounded rationality' explains how decisions are made under conditions where only a limited degree of rationality can be applied, because of pressures on time and other resources.
- The 'garbage can' model describes how decisions are made in conditions of greater uncertainty, i.e. unbounded problems.

POST-DECISION BEHAVIOUR

Escalation of commitment to a failing course of action: a decision maker's tendency to persist with a failing course of action, in the face of clear evidence that the decision taken is inappropriate

Both rational choice and bounded rationality models contain implementation and monitoring stages which occur after a decision is taken. Hopefully, most decisions will resolve problems, but in the face of evidence that this has not happened it is reasonable to suggest that a decision maker would seek another solution. In some situations, however, a decision maker can become so enamoured of the chosen course of action that he or she disregards signals that the decision was an inappropriate one. There are many examples of this and one that hit the headlines a few years ago was the decision to build the Millennium Dome. This phenomenon has been labelled '*escalation of commitment to a failing course of action*' (Staw 1980) and the question of why and how it happens has been addressed by Staw and Ross (1989), who identify four primary reasons for escalation: psychological factors, social factors, project factors and organisational factors.

Psychological Factors

If a decision goes wrong, the threat to self image and ego can be significant and one result of this is that a decision maker can ignore the negative signs of failure and 'press on regardless'. In addition, he or she can interpret incoming information in a biased way, for example by underplaying the risk of complete failure and emphasising the necessity of recovering the costs of implementing the decision.

Social Factors

Because people are naturally reluctant to advertise the fact that they have made a poor decision, it can be extremely difficult for a decision maker to reverse a decision that he or she strongly advocated. This is particularly the case if other people rallied around the decision maker to give public support, which can become a silent pressure on the decision maker to stay with the decision, otherwise he or she 'lets the team down'.

Project Factors

Because most projects have a delayed return and benefits do not appear for some time, project factors usually have the greatest impact on escalation. In this situation there is an almost inbuilt tendency to regard any sign that the decision was incorrect as temporary, or something that can be remedied with a little more expenditure (Garland 1990). For these reasons there is little sense of urgency to seek an alternative course of action.

Organisational Factors

In many organisations, once a decision has been taken, there is a sense of relief that the matter is now in the past, and this can be particularly strong when the search for a solution has been an extensive one. In addition, there can be vested interests at stake in a particular solution, and this sets up political pressures to stay with the course of action.

 TIME OUT

Carefully reflect on your past and try to identify a decision that you made that went wrong, but was one where you still tried to see things through, despite evidence that the decision was inappropriate. If this has never happened to you (be honest with yourself) try to complete the exercise for someone that you know well. How do you account for your commitment to the failing course of action?

Reducing Escalation Tendencies

Staw and Ross (1987) suggest a number of measures that can be put in place to reduce tendencies towards escalation. These receive support from empirical work (Simonson and Staw 1992) and are:

- set minimum targets for performance and insist that the decision maker compares performance with the target

- ensure that the people who make the initial decision and those who evaluate its success are different
- try to ensure that decision makers do not become too ego-involved with a project
- provide more feedback about project completion and costs
- reduce the risks or penalties of failure
- try to ensure that decision makers are aware of the consequences of persistence.

 OB IN ACTION: Improving decision making with videoconferencing

On a cold crisp morning at Cisco Systems' European headquarters near Heathrow Airport, Rob Horn, an internal consultant at Cisco, is using a videoconferencing link to talk to a colleague in another part of the building. The link is one that has been developed by a Norwegian-based videoconferencing specialist, Tandberg, and, in Mr Horn's estimate, Tandberg has saved Cisco's European operations some $4.5 in the last 18 months. This comes mostly from reduced travel costs across Cisco's European, Middle East and African region since the system was introduced, and executives can now see and talk to each other without needing to travel, which has freed-up a lot of people's time, and reduced the stress and costs that travel can cause, he says.

The system links Cisco offices to each other – and to customer sites – using both ISDN and Internet Protocol networks, and Cisco also uses the system to record meetings for people who cannot attend. One attraction is the system's relative portability and another is that it does not need to be hard-wired into dedicated connection points, but can plug into Ethernet or ISDN connections and quickly integrated into the corporate network.

However, cost savings are only part of the story because videoconferencing can help to streamline decision making and allow busy employees to join meetings to which they would not have wanted to travel. Moreover, it is often very useful to be able to extend a meeting to people who would not have been able to attend in person. An unquantifiable – but real benefit – is that videoconferencing allows participants to gauge each other's feelings better than on 'voice only' calls, because it gives sight of non-verbal aspects of communication such as posture and facial expressions.

Videoconferencing is often sold as a cost-reduction tool, but the intangible benefits frequently outweigh the financial ones. Cisco's travel cost savings – while no doubt real – are more the exception than the rule says Neil Rickard, a research director at IT consultancy Gartner. Indeed, Mr Rickard notes that he tends to tell his clients not to hang their hats on cost savings that might never happen, but instead concentrate how systems like this can make the decision making process more effective and more rapid.

Source:

Hayward, D (2003) *Financial Times*, 14 February

FACTORS AFFECTING DECISION MAKING

So far the chapter has treated the decision making process in a rather abstract way, as something that can be separated from everything else in an organisation. However, this is not how things take place in the real world and it is important to recognise that the nature of decision making is affected by the surrounding context and, in return, the resulting decisions have an effect on this context. With this in mind, it is now time to bring together some of the matters covered in the chapter and add some detail, to give a more comprehensive picture of the factors that can shape the nature of the decision process. To structure the discussion Figure 9.5 portrays three major groups of influential factors and these are considered in what follows.

Individual Factors

Individual differences can have a profound influence on how people approach the matter of making decisions and, in particular, four differences can be significant.

Personality Variables

These can have an impact on a person's preferred behaviour in a particular decision context. For instance, highly manipulative people can view the decision situation as an opportunity to manipulate others for their own personal gain. Thus they might have a tendency to keep decisions to themselves, or withhold vital information to maintain control over other people. Depending on their status in an organisation, authoritarian people can behave in one of two ways. Many authoritarians have a low tolerance to ambiguity and endorse the idea of a highly ordered environment, which can prompt them to rely on precedents and rules to guide decision making. If people of this type

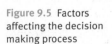

Figure 9.5 Factors affecting the decision making process

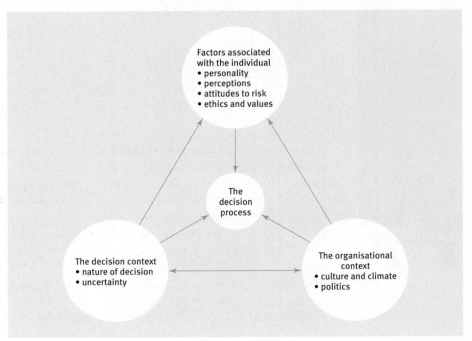

occupy positions of high status, they may also view decision making as something that should not be shared with subordinates but as a prerogative of their rank.

Perceptions

Perceptions can strongly influence the way that people view a problem and so they are likely to interact with personality variables to shape preferred decision strategies (MacCrimmon 1974). For instance, if a person's prior experience has been confined to a restricted range of situations involving only bounded problems, he or she will probably have a tendency to see most new problems as similarly bounded. Depending on the person's occupational history, he or she can develop a bias towards seeing all problems in a particular way and to seek solutions accordingly (Beck and Kieser 2003).

Attitudes towards Risk

People vary in their acceptance of risk (Bass 1983) and, in general terms, individuals can be placed along a continuum, the extremes of which are 'risk-takers' and 'risk-averters'. According to where they are located on this continuum, people tend to display characteristic patterns of behaviour in decision making (MacCrimmon and Wehrung 1986) and the behaviours associated with the extremes are summarised in Table 9.2. Notwithstanding this, recent evidence suggests that people's tolerance of risk can change over time. For instance, repeated exposure to risky situations can lead to progressively lower perceptions of the riskiness of a situation and an increase in the tolerance to risk (Brown 2005).

Ethics and Values

As noted in Chapter 2, ethical behaviour is not solely determined by individual predispositions, but is usually the result of an interaction between individual factors and contextual variables. Since concern about ethics injects a degree of uncertainty into a decision, and for most people uncertainty can be uncomfortable, this can have a huge impact on the decisions that are taken. At one extreme, people can try to shield their core values by either not making a decision or behaving with excessive ethical zeal. At the other extreme, they can try to shut out their values by rationalising that anything goes so long as they 'put the good of the organisation before their own feelings'.

Table 9.2
Characteristics of risk averters and risk takers (adapted from MacCrimmon and Wehrung 1986)

Characteristics of the decision	Risk averters tend to look for:	Acceptable to risk takers:
Conditions of possible loss	A low maximum loss, with low probability of loss	Higher maximum loss, with higher probability of loss
The context in which decision is taken	A familiar environment, a high provision of information and higher degree of control over decision implementation	Higher degree of unfamiliarity with environment, less information, higher uncertainty and less control over the decision and its implementation
Decision style	Shared responsibility, consensus contingency planning, easy exit when risk arises	Sole responsibility, tolerance to conflict, less contingency planning, risk

The Decision Context

The Nature of the Decision

This has been covered earlier in the chapter when discussing bounded and unbounded problems and a glance at Table 9.1 shows that it is much easier to grasp the nature of a bounded problem than one that is unbounded. Providing there are sufficient resources and time is not pressing, something akin to the rational choice method can be used for some bounded problems; for example, a decision about where to locate a new factory might be made in this way. This, however, does not mean that all the assumptions of rational choice decision making, such as complete information about alternatives, apply. Rather, it is far more likely that with the importance of the decision and the considerable expenditure that is involved, people will feel far more comfortable with acting in a way that looks as though it is completely rational. These situations are comparatively rare in organisations and the vast majority of decisions made at middle levels, where there is an imperative to respond quickly to a shortfall in performance or 'to be seen to be doing something' about a problem, will be made using a 'bounded rationality' method. Finally, at both middle and upper levels in an organisation the garbage can mode of decision making can come into play. This is particularly the case where unbounded problems are encountered and, although decision makers are likely to have preferences for certain courses of action, in unbounded problems preferences are seldom set in tablets of stone. The sheer ambiguity of this type of problem sometimes means that preferences only emerge in the light of experience, and in some cases it is not a matter of identifying the best way to achieve goals but of deciding what the goals should be.

Uncertainty

The degree of uncertainty surrounding the outcomes of a decision can shape how the decision is made. In most organisations the degree of risk involved is regarded as a reflection of the potential success of a particular decision option, whereas uncertainty is a characteristic of the problem itself; for example, the clarity of the problem, incomplete information, or whether the alternative courses of action are clear. If these circumstances exist, it makes the problem an unbounded one and work by Lipshitz and Strauss (1997) indicates that decision makers tend to treat unbounded problems as bounded; for example, by trying to reduce uncertainty by collecting additional information, relying on experts, making assumptions, or even by suppressing information about the degree of uncertainty.

The Organisational Context

Organisational Politics

This facet of organisational life can strongly shape the nature of decision making. The topic of organisational politics will be explored in depth in Chapter 14, where it is explained that certain types of decision situation provide unrivalled opportunities for organisational politicians to manoeuvre to pursue their own personal goals (Mintzberg 1985). This means that decision making can become a matter of 'game playing' and when this happens the whole process can be shaped and re-shaped as power bases are built up and alliances made.

Organisational Culture and Climate

The culture of an organisation can have a profound influence on the way that a decision is handled by its members, and an abbreviated definition of culture is 'the way we do things around there' (Deal and Kennedy 1982). In certain organisations the culture is highly risk aversive, and in some of them decision making is regarded as a matter for shared responsibility, while in others it is strictly the responsibility of individuals (Ouchi 1981). Climate which is a shorter-term phenomenon, also has an impact on decision making. In some organisations, for example, behaviour is strongly governed by formal rules and regulations, which results in a strong tendency to make decisions according to past precedents and, wherever possible, rules are formulated to remove the necessity for decisions to be taken.

Cross-cultural Effects on Decision Making Styles

Just as individual organisations can differ in their cultures, the national culture of different countries can result in people conducting themselves differently in the decision making situation. For example, in the rational choice model given earlier, the decision making process is divided-up into a set of steps, each of which consists of certain specified activities. Work conducted by Adler (1997) draws attention to the idea that some of these steps are likely to be perceived differently in certain cultures, and for this reason they attract distinctive, culturally induced variations in the way that they are handled. These ideas are summarised in Table 9.3, which shows that in each step there are

Table 9.3 Culturally induced variations in the way that decisions are made (adapted from Adler 1997)

Steps in decision making process	Extremes of culturally induced variations in step		
1. Recognition of problem	In Great Britain and the USA there is a tendency to see problems as situations requiring solutions that will involve changing the *status quo*	←→	In Indonesia and Thailand there is a tendency to adopt a more fatalistic view, in which some problems have to be lived with
2. Search for information	In cultures where people seek to avoid uncertainty, decisions are normally deemed to require 'facts' that allow a 'one best solution' to be identified	←→	In cultures where there is a higher tolerance to uncertainty, information is sought to open up a range of possible alternative solutions
3. Developing alternative solutions	In the USA there is an assumption that because people are easily able to adapt and change, solutions requiring radical change are acceptable	←→	In Great Britain there is an assumption that because people find it hard to change, alternatives should preferably involve small, incremental changes
4. Choosing between alternatives	In individualistic and masculine cultures such as Great Britain and the USA, decisions tend to be made quickly and only by those people who have decision making authority	←→	In more collectivist cultures such as Japan and Germany, decisions tend to be made in a careful, deliberate way, and preferably by all those who have to implement the decision
5. Implementation	In Great Britain and the USA this is managed in a top-down way, by individuals with authority	←→	In Japan there is a shared responsibility for implementation, that involves a high degree of participation

predictable variations, because the culture induces people to approach the matter of making decisions in distinctly different ways.

OVERVIEW AND CONCLUSIONS

Decisions come in all shapes and sizes and, in organisations, they are all taken in an attempt to resolve a problem, real or anticipated. However, decision making and problem solving are not the same thing, and the decision process is more correctly viewed as part of the wider process of problem solving. In this respect, a distinction can be made between two main classes of problem: bounded and unbounded. Each type has its own characteristics and the decision making methods appropriate for one type are not necessarily appropriate for the other.

In many organisations decisions are the prerogative of managers, most of whom prefer to think of themselves as taking decisions in a rational way. However, the evidence suggests that this is not always the way that decisions are made and a number of decision making models have been evolved to explain the process. These fall into two broad types: normative and descriptive. Normative models, the best known of which is the rational choice model, give a highly prescriptive recipe for how decisions 'should' be made. Problematically, the assumptions that underpin the model mean that very grave reservations exist about whether it can be used in its pure form.

Descriptive models, which are usually based on substantial research evidence, seek to explain how decisions are made in practice and, since they recognise the limitations of the normative models, they tend to give a far more realistic picture of decision making.

When decisions are made and implemented, they sometimes turn out to be inappropriate. In these circumstances decision makers do not always recognise their mistakes and instead doggedly stick to the initial decision and become embroiled in 'escalation of commitment to a failing course of action'. Finally, it is worth remembering that decision makers are individuals, with all that this means in terms of personal idiosyncrasies. It is rare to find two decisions that are identical and the way that decisions are made can vary considerably and be influenced by three important groups of factors: those associated with the individual decision maker, the nature of the decision itself, and the organisational context in which the decision is made.

REPLAY

- The phenomenon of 'escalation of commitment to a failing course of action' explains why, when a decision has been implemented and found to be wanting, the decision maker does not abandon the chosen course of action, but persists with implementation of the original decision.
- There are three major groups of factors that shape the nature of the individual decision making process: individual factors, decision context factors and factors associated with the organisational context.

FURTHER READINGS

Bazerman, MN (1994) *Judgement in Managerial Decision Making*, 3rd edn, New York: Wiley. A very comprehensive and penetrating exploration of the heuristics used by managers, as identified in the research of Kahneman and Tversky.

Beach, LR (1997) *The Psychology of Decision Making*, London: Sage. The book gives a comprehensive introduction from a psychological perspective of the way the individuals make decisions in organisations. It also gives a useful description of how contextual factors in organisations shape the decision process and decisions that are made.

Brown, LS (2005) Relationships between risk-taking behaviour and risk perceptions, *British Journal of Psychology* 96(2): 155–164 An illuminating empirical paper giving some evidence that increased exposure to risky situations increases a person's tolerance to risk.

Cook, S and H Slack (1991) *Making Management Decisions*, 2nd edn, London: Prentice Hall. A useful book that is now regarded as a standard text on the subject of organisational decision making.

Hammond, JS, RL Keeney and H Raiffa (2006) The hidden traps in decision making, *Harvard Business Review* May: 114–126. An interesting paper that deals with the use of heuristics in (bounded rationality) decision making. These are described by the authors as 'hidden traps' that often lower the quality of decisions, and some advice is given on how tho avoid falling into these traps.

Harrison, EF (1994) *The Managerial Decision-making Proc*ess, 5th edn, Chicago, IL: Haughton Mifflin. This book has a focus on middle and top management levels to explain organisational decision making.

Kahneman, D and A Tversky (eds) (2000) *Choices, Values and Frames*, Cambridge. Cambridge University Press. A book of readings, which gives an account of some of the more recent research evidence on decision making and, in particular, that concerning biases and the use of heuristics.

Schick, F (1997) *Making Choices: A Recasting of Decision Theory*, Cambridge: Cambridge University Press. A penetrating and scholarly analysis of decision theory, but written in a very readable and non-mathematical way.

Shapira, Z (1997) *Organisational Decision Making*, Cambridge: Cambridge University Press. A book that brings together contributions from scholars who approach decision making from a cognitive perspective, together with those who study organisational aspects.

Case Study 9.1: Project Taurus

Background

In the 1990s Project Taurus was commissioned by the then Council of the London Stock Exchange, a body which subsequently became its board of directors. Taurus was an advanced information technology initiative that sought to catapult the Stock Exchange into the information age. Its cost was originally estimated at £50 million and it was scheduled to be up and running within one and one-half years. The project was subsequently cancelled in 1993, by which time it was still not completed and had cost the Stock Exchange over £80 million. In addition, it has been (conservatively) estimated that the financial sector of the City of London had incurred costs of over £400 million in preparing for its introduction.

Aims of Project Taurus

The prime aim of the Taurus system was to streamline procedures and methods for the settlement of transactions involved in buying and selling shares along lines recommended by an international group of investment bankers; the 'Group of Thirty'. Until then these activities were dominated by paper-driven methods and the intention was to produce a virtually instantaneous registration of share transactions. This would considerably reduce the risk of failure and lack of security associated with prior methods, in which there could often be a delay of months between a transaction and the settlement of an account.

British securities are bought by a wide range of customers ranging from large institutional investors such as insurance companies and merchant banks at one extreme, to small private investors at the other, and normally shares can only be bought and sold through stockbrokers and other authorised institutions. All of these parties had different requirements for the proposed Taurus system and initial discussions about its design specification, which took place for several years before it was commissioned by the Stock Exchange were characterised by infighting, as each constituency fought to have its interests dominate those of others. This produced a near crisis situation, which was only resolved when the Bank of England stepped-in at the end of 1988 to insist that Taurus must be able to operate without compromising any of these different interests.

Development of Taurus

The Bank of England's edict resulted in an immensely complicated design specification and, even when this was produced, different interest groups continually insisted on changes to meet their own requirements. This gave an inbuilt tendency from the outset for complexity to increase even further. As noted earlier, the original plan called for Taurus to be operative within 18 months (approximately mid 1991), but with each constituency manoeuvring to get the design changed, the specification became more and more complex. For this reason, the official decision makers (the directors of the Stock Exchange) quickly lost touch with the reality of the situation and tended to underestimate the problems involved in trying to develop a system that would be 'all things to all people'. To oversee the project the board set up a structure of two powerful sub-groups: the technical group charged with solving technical problems, and a monitoring group (effectively a sub-committee of the board of directors) whose task was to oversee matters such as budgets and compliance with user requirements.

The Stock Exchange had insufficient resources to design and develop new software for Taurus and in the light of the short time scale, the technical group argued for the purchase of a software package that would be tailored to meet the needs of Taurus; a suggestion that was accepted. After a survey of available options, three main packages were identified. Using criteria such as relative capital outlay, ease and cost of modification and versatility, these were closely compared as alternative solutions to the problem and eventually a software package called Visa was chosen, and a budget of £4 million was allocated to tailor it to the needs of Taurus. Importantly, the method used to evaluate and choose software had significant implications on subsequent developments. It cloaked the choice in an aura of scientific impartiality, and resulted in the technical team being the best informed about the workings of the intended system, both of which placed the technical team in effective control of most future decisions. Thus rather than having a veto over technical decisions that might result in Taurus failing to achieve its objectives, the monitoring group was relegated to the role of choosing between any shortfalls in performance that came to light.

While all this was in progress different user constituencies continued to manoeuvre for alterations to the design specification and so the requirements for software capabilities continued to change. There is a limit on the number of major modifications that can be made to a programme, beyond which its basic architecture virtually rules out further changes. Thus the decision to buy-in software and modify it, subsequently turned out to be an inappropriate one and by the time the project was eventually cancelled, software development costs had risen to approximately £14 million.

Since the technical team was always trying to cope with changing requirements, in January 1991 things were so far behind that the Taurus launch date was put back by six months. In order to try to solve the myriad problems with which it was confronted, from then on the technical team had to work extremely long hours, which exceeded 80 hours in most weeks. At this point the monitoring team tried to exert its authority and started to demand more information from the technical team. However, as new requirements for the Taurus system emerged, more and more design problems surfaced and at times it seemed as though the project had taken on a life of its own. At the end of 1991 the board of the Stock Exchange held a meeting at which the introduction of the Taurus system was postponed until 1993 and, in an attempt to resolve all the outstanding problems, the development budget was doubled. By now the originally envisaged time scale for introducing Taurus had doubled, as had its budget, and there was a furious emphasis on trying to solve technical problems, without ever asking why so many problems existed.

By October 1992 there was still no definite date for the introduction of Taurus, and a further review was commissioned by the chief executive of the Stock Exchange. In its report the review panel argued that it could be another two to three years before the system came on stream, by which time it could well be outdated and incapable of accommodating ongoing changes in the nature of the securities industry. At this point therefore, Project Taurus was officially cancelled.

Questions

1. At what point in the events recounted above were 'rational choice' methods used to make decisions?

2. How successful were rational choice methods in reaching an appropriate solution to the identified problem?

3. Are there signs that 'bounded rationality' came to dominate decision making at certain times?

4. What do you feel prompted the use of 'bounded rationality' methods?

5. To what extent do you feel that the phenomenon of 'commitment to a failing course of action' is reflected in the events described and if so, why do you feel that this happened?

Reference: This case study gives only a very abridged version of events and fuller details can be found in Drummond (1996)

REVIEW AND DISCUSSION QUESTIONS

1. Describe the differences between bounded and unbounded problems. Explain what could happen in an organisation if what was thought to be a bounded problem turned out to be one that is unbounded. Give examples of when this could occur.

2. Describe the types of problem in which it would be possible to make successful use of the rational choice method of decision making, giving examples to illustrate your answer.

3. Consider each stage of the rational choice model of decision making and identify what 'irrational' things could happen in each one that could call into question a decision that is made. Give examples to illustrate your points.

4. At which levels in an organisation – supervisory, middle, top – are the following modes of decision making likely to be most prevalent: rational choice, bounded rationality, garbage can?

5. Describe the circumstances in which escalation of commitment to a failing course of action could occur, the factors responsible for it occurring, and what could be done to prevent escalation in organisations.

Chapter 10

Workplace Stress and Work–Life Balance

LEARNING OUTCOMES

After studying this chapter you should be able to:

- define stress, explain its importance and describe the stages of the General Adaptive Syndrome

- define workplace stress, how it arises and, in outline, describe a model of the important variables in workplace stress

- describe the four main groups of stressors that can impinge on people in the work situation: contextual, organisational, social and individual

- describe the four outcomes at which stress can manifest itself: physiological, psychological, cognitive and behavioural

- describe the six important groups of moderators of stress: individual characteristics, lifestyle, social support, appraisal of stressors, life events and biographic and occupational factors

- describe approaches to the management of stress at individual and organisational levels

INTRODUCTION

A degree of work-related stress has probably always existed in organisations but, in the last three decades, there has been a considerable acceleration in the pace of life, together with a radical change in the nature of many organisations. In the light of these changes it is not surprising to find that work-related stress is commonplace and most people experience it at some time. For this reason, it is important to draw attention to the inclusion of the expression 'work–life balance' in the chapter title. As will be seen presently, workplace stress has been on the increase for several years. To a large extent this is because the pace of life in many organisations is so frenzied and unremitting that many employees have genuine difficulties in separating their life at work from their lives outside and it is their inability to do so that makes them so prone to stress-related problems. The reasons for this are complex, but for an example see the OB in Action Box below.

Stress itself is a poorly understood phenomenon, and our knowledge of how to cope with it is still less than perfect. Therefore, the chapter starts by defining stress and tracing its increasing importance to organisations and this is followed by an examination of stress as a psycho-physiological process. The remainder of the chapter focuses more explicitly on stress at work. To structure the discussion, a model of the stress process is presented. The first feature of this model is the factors that can give rise to stress, which is followed by a description of the four major effects that stress can have on a person. Since stress is a highly individualised reaction to workplace conditions, the next matter to be considered is the factors that can moderate how a person reacts to a particular set of stressors. Managing workplace stress is discussed next and the chapter closes with a section that reviews and integrates its contents.

 OB IN ACTION: Is stress really a sign of success?

We keep going for the medal, postponing living until we get there, but there is always another objective or promotion to aim for. For Felimy Greene, 38, work at an international corporate bank used to be like climbing a mountain. No matter how many peaks he reached, there was always another one just a little bit higher waiting to be climbed.

Greene generally worked more than 60 hours a week, rarely taking a lunch break or his full leave. He was not alone and had friends and peers who work just as long. 'I think it is because of the modern consumer-driven lifestyle, we are always aiming for the medal of achievement,' he says, adding that 'being stressed and overwhelmed by your workload is something we interpret as a sign of having an important job'. In other words, to be stressed means you're somebody. Eventually, Greene decided enough was enough and gave up his job but overwork remains a way of life for many people in Britain. Julie Hamilton, managing director of Mavrix Connect, which helps business executives lead healthier lives, says many of her clients are working so hard that they put their lives on hold. 'They leave home early and get

back late, which can affect families and relationships.' 'Weight problems, lack of healthy eating and exercise, and sleeping problems are also common', she says. It is not only detrimental to their health. 'An unhealthy executive will have impaired judgement and make bad decisions.'

For Greene the situation was finally brought into perspective by the sudden death of a colleague. It shocked him out of his busy work lifestyle and he knew then that he couldn't postpone living a normal life any longer. It was at this point that he took advice and, through a series of psychometric tests, realised that he wasn't actually enjoying the hierarchical nature of the company he worked for. Decisions were always being taken upstairs and there was little sense of ownership of his work. He quickly left for a smaller firm but along the way took two months out to go sailing and learn yoga.

Source:

Little, W (2006) *Financial Times*, 26 August

STRESS: BASIC CONSIDERATIONS

Stress: an adaptive response to external stimuli that place excessive physical or psychological demands on a person

Stress is as old as mankind itself and, in one way or another, all animals are susceptible to it. While there are many ways of defining stress, the definition adopted for this chapter, is:

> an adaptive response, mediated by individual differences and/or psychological processes, that is a consequence of any external action, situation or event that places excessive physical and/or psychological demands on a person.
>
> (Ivancevich and Matteson 1993, p 244)

The idea underpinning this definition is very simple. When humans are subject to an external pressure, there are two alternative reactions: to try to withstand the impact of the pressure (fight) or move away from it (flight). Stress usually arises when an attempt is made to withstand the pressure, and a number of important points, should be noted:

- Stress is a reaction to an external force or demand and while anything physically or mentally demanding or burdensome can create stressful conditions, this does not necessarily mean that it occurs.

- For this to happen the situation must have sufficient impact on the person to attract his or her attention, perhaps because it evokes feelings of disappointment, annoyance, anger or hostility, or simply because the individual feels that the situation should not exist.

- More importantly, the pressure needs to be experienced as something of such magnitude that the person finds it difficult to cope with.

Stressors: external factors that impinge on a person and potentially result in stress

- While stress can be debilitating, it is an adaptive response to the *stressors*, and not simply a state of anxiety or nervous tension; both of these can result from stress, but they are purely emotional or psychological reactions, whereas stress often has physical effects as well.

- When subject to stressors, the amount of stress experienced is a highly individual matter and, as Lazarus (1966) points out, there are no objective criteria that can be used to define whether a situation will be stressful.

- Individuals vary considerably in the way that they experience stressors, and no two people are likely to experience the same stressor in the same way.

- People also vary considerably in terms of their capabilities to cope with different stressors and the only person who can accurately define whether and to what extent a situation is stressful is the person on the receiving end.

To some extent everyone encounters stressors and, in some degree, stress inevitably follows or, as Selye (1974) puts it, 'a complete absence of stress is death'. Although it is almost universally thought of as something bad, stress has a potentially positive aspect, and many people find a mild degree of pressure stimulating and they often report that it seems to make them more alert, attentive and clear-thinking so that they function better (Cavanaugh *et al.* 2000). Therefore, it seems likely that each person has an optimum level of stress and this idea is portrayed in Figure 10.1.

The Importance of Stress

Stress is now acknowledged to be a very widespread phenomenon. For example, survey evidence (Natvaney 1996) suggests that over 50 per cent of European employees experience some degree of occupational stress, and in America the collective cost of stress from sickness absence, premature retirement and lost productive value has been estimated at $150 billion (Cooper 2005). In Great Britain, direct and indirect costs, which include NHS treatment for stress related illness, have been estimated at 5–10 per cent of the Gross National Product (GNP) each year. Indeed, a survey conducted by the Chartered Institute of Personnel and Development (CIPD) in 2004 identified it as the leading cause of long-term sickness absence and one British organisation is reported as having estimated that 40 per cent of its annual absence could be attributed to stress, the cost of which was estimated as in the order of £5 million (Evans 1995).

Figure 10.1 The relationship between performance and level of stress

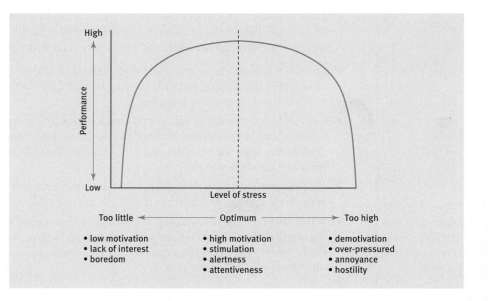

While these figures illustrate the importance of stress in economic terms, there is another reason why it has become significant to organisations. A number of landmark personal injury cases for stress have been brought against employers in the last few years and these have resulted in high levels of compensation for employees. Indeed, the Appeal Court has recently ruled that the criteria for psychiatric injury are essentially the same as for physical injury. Thus an employer has a duty to prevent foreseeable injury and is liable if it fails to take reasonable steps to do so (Aikin 2005). Perhaps more significantly, The Health and Safety Executive (HSE) has now launched the final version of its new management standards that are designed to help employers and employees avoid stress at work (see OB in Action Box following). Although these do not have the status of statute law, they clearly set-out the standards that employers are expected to meet (see Gyngell and Patmore 2006).

Unlike many topics in Organisational Behaviour, stress has implications that directly translate into costs, or loss of reputation for organisations. In addition, there are more humane reasons for being concerned about occupational stress. Stress-related illnesses, for example coronary disease, psychoses, alcohol dependence and tension-related disorders, are all on the increase (Arnold *et al.* 1998) and the personal costs for those affected can be enormous.

 OB IN ACTION: HSE management standards

HSE management standards are aimed at workplace stressors that affect the majority of employees in an organisation and establish a blueprint for the characteristics of an organisation in which stress is managed effectively. They cover six key areas of work design which, if not properly managed, are associated with stress at work. Importantly, whether or not the standards are being met is established in conjunction with employees (using the firm's records or a survey instrument developed by HSE) and an organisation achieving the standards will have systems in place locally, to respond to any individual concerns. The six key areas are:

Demands: employees indicate that they are able to cope with the demands of their jobs.

Control: employees indicate that they are able to have a say about the way they do their work.

Support: employees indicate that they receive adequate information and support from their colleagues and superiors.

Relationships: employees indicate that they are not subjected to unacceptable behaviours (e.g. bullying) at work.

Role: employees say they understand their role and responsibilities.

Change: employees indicate that the organisation engages them frequently when undergoing an organisational change.

Source:

http://www.hse.gov.uk/stress

Stress as a Psycho-physiological Process

In everyday language, stress normally indicates that a person has a distressed state of mind, possibly accompanied by physical symptoms, and that this makes it hard for the individual to function normally. While there is nothing inherently wrong with this conception, it glosses over the complexity of what occurs and infers that stress only results from unpleasant circumstances, whereas pleasant stimuli can also result in stress. The description is also rather one-sided. Its main focus is on a person's performance, which implies that the matter is relatively unimportant if the individual can cope or adapt to the stressors. Finally, the description implies that there is a one-way direction of causality, in which stressors give rise to stress, which in turn affect performance, whereas high performance can often be a stressor in its own right and in the long run it can result in severe stress. For these reasons, it is necessary to explore the processes at work that result in someone experiencing stress.

In the late 1950s a substantial body of work was undertaken by Professor Hans Selye (Selye 1976) who set out to determine whether exposure to unpleasant or noxious environmental conditions resulted in stimulus-specific responses, or in a generalised response to all stimuli. This resulted in the discovery of what Selye called the *General Adaptive Syndrome* (GAS), which provides a physiological explanation of the way in which a state of stress arises. The GAS describes a three-stage defence reaction to a stressor that:

General Adaptive Syndrome: a three-stage physiological process that takes place when an organism is subject to a stressor

- is *general* because the reaction occurs to all stressors and affects several different parts of an organism
- is *adaptive* because it involves stimulation of defence mechanisms which help the body adjust to, or deal with, the stressor
- is a *syndrome* because all three stages occur together, or in very close succession (see Figure 10.2).

Stage 1: Alarm

In this first stage, the person becomes aware of being subject to the effects of a stressor, which can be any environmental stimulus that has a disruptive effect on the individual; for example, something that physically attacks the body such as a virus, or even another person who threatens bodily harm. It could also be a set of conditions, such as overwork, that disrupts psychological well-being. There is an initial reaction to this, in which the body tries to meet the challenge, and this sets up a non-specific response via the body's endocrine system. This commences with activity in the pituitary gland, which sends a chemical messenger (the hormone ACTH) to the adrenal glands, which in turn triggers increased activity in the autonomic nervous system. The autonomic nervous system is divided into two parts: sympathetic and parasympathetic. The presence of the stressor induces dominance by the sympathetic system, which triggers a host of physical changes, such as increases in the heart rate and blood pressure. This prepares the body for action, but does not initiate activity, so at this stage the body is in a state of temporary retreat, which involves a minor loss of efficiency until it has rallied its reserves. If the influence of the stressor continues, this then leads to the next stage.

Stage 2: Resistance

Here the person starts to fight the effects of the stressor. The adrenal glands secrete their own hormones into the bloodstream (adrenaline and non-adrenaline) and this

Figure 10.2 Selye's general adaptive syndrome

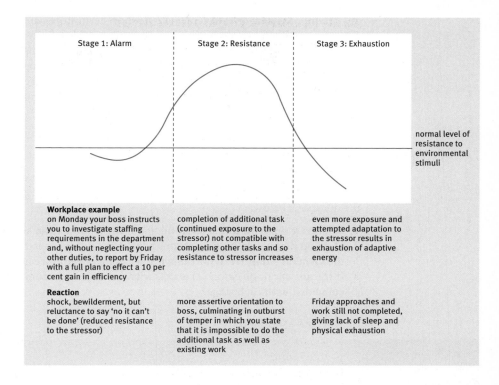

Stage 1: Alarm	Stage 2: Resistance	Stage 3: Exhaustion

normal level of resistance to environmental stimuli

Workplace example

on Monday your boss instructs you to investigate staffing requirements in the department and, without neglecting your other duties, to report by Friday with a full plan to effect a 10 per cent gain in efficiency	completion of additional task (continued exposure to the stressor) not compatible with completing other tasks and so resistance to stressor increases	even more exposure and attempted adaptation to the stressor results in exhaustion of adaptive energy

Reaction

shock, bewilderment, but reluctance to say 'no it can't be done' (reduced resistance to the stressor)	more assertive orientation to boss, culminating in outburst of temper in which you state that it is impossible to do the additional task as well as existing work	Friday approaches and work still not completed, giving lack of sleep and physical exhaustion

triggers action in several organs. The liver releases sugar, the heart beats faster and adrenaline reaches the brain, which stimulates an increase in the level of activity. All this enables the body to isolate the effects of the stressor in order to minimise damage to the organism as a whole. Thus there is a degree of adaptation to the stressor. However, since the body has a finite capacity to adapt, resistance cannot continue indefinitely and if the body is subject to an environmental stressor of sufficient strength for sufficient time, its reservoir of adaptive energy becomes depleted. The problem is that the endocrine system, in which the adrenal glands are strongly involved, gives the body an ability to resist other agents, such as germs and microbes, which are also threatening. When the system is overloaded it cannot cope with everything, which explains why stress is so often accompanied by physical illness. If there is prolonged exposure to the stressors, the depletion of adaptive energy makes it almost inevitable that the third stage of the process will be entered.

Stage 3: Exhaustion

On entering this stage, all reserves of easily available adaptive energy are nearly exhausted and, in order to try to replenish its short-term store, the body shuts itself off from the stressful stimuli. Before long all resistance to the stressor(s) has virtually disappeared and the immune system is seriously affected (Keilcot-Glaser and Glaser 1987). In addition, there are usually attendant psychological effects, such as mood changes, emotional problems and feelings of helplessness, and these can be accompanied by significant behavioural changes, for example, a clenching of hands, fidgeting, finger tremors and weak legs. Unfortunately, because the long-term energy store also has finite reserves, any attempt to draw on it to replenish the short-term store tends to be a debt that can never be repaid and so a stressor can cause irreversible harm.

Although all this paints a somewhat dismal picture, it must be remembered that stress is essentially an adaptive process, at least in the physiological sense. Unpleasant as it may be, the final stage should be viewed as what it is – the body protecting itself from even greater harm by shutting itself off from further exposure to the stressor(s).

TIME OUT

Many students report that they find examinations result in a degree of stress. If you feel this way, carefully consider the last time that you took an examination and answer the questions below.

1. What is it that you found stressful about the examination situation?
2. Did you find yourself going through the three stages set out in the description of the General Adaptive Syndrome, that is, alarm, resistance and exhaustion?
3. If the answer to question (2) is yes, what actions or outcomes on your part coincided with each stage?

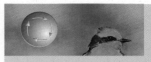

REPLAY

- Stress is an adaptive response to external factors that put physical and/or psychological demands on a person.
- It is possible that each person has an optimum level of stress; that is, a slight amount of stress could help him or her to function more effectively, whereas higher levels are detrimental to performance.
- Stress has important economic, humanistic and legal implications for organisations.
- The way in which an organism reacts to external forces that can result in stress can be explained in general terms of conformity to the General Adaptive Syndrome.

Workplace Stress

Workplace stress: stress that arises from an interaction between people and their jobs

So far stress has been considered in a very general way. However, this book is concerned with matters within organisations, and it is necessary to sharpen the focus onto *workplace stress*. However, there are dangers in compartmentalising human behaviour in this way. While a great deal of stress has its origins in organisations, there are also sources beyond the organisation and because people seldom leave the outside world behind them when they come to work, the effects of stressors outside have a habit of spilling over into the work situation and, in the same way, work-related stress can prompt stress outside work. Thus the effects of stress inside and outside work can be cumulative. With this in mind, and to distinguish the topic from stress in a more general sense, workplace stress is defined here as:

conditions arising from the interaction of people and their jobs, which are characterised by changes within people that force them to deviate from their normal functioning. (Beehr and Newman 1978, p 666)

A WORKING MODEL

Figure 10.3 presents a general working model that will be used to structure the discussion in the remainder of this chapter. It portrays workplace stress as a process having three main stages:

- Stressors, which are shown on the left, are conditions that have the potential to result in a person experiencing a situation as stressful.
- The middle stage, experienced stress, is a reflection of the individual's reaction to the potential stressors.
- Experienced stress then results in a set of outcomes, which are shown on the right of Figure 10.3.

The degree of stress experienced and the ways in which a person reacts to it can be influenced by a number of other factors, and these are shown lower down as the moderator variables.

Before exploring the model it is important to note that, since stress is such an individual matter, there can be no hard-and-fast rules about what happens. The effects of everything shown on the model are relative rather than absolute, and this is particularly true of the potential stressors. What one person experiences as stressful, other people often regard as normal and the effects of potential stressors can be considerably amplified or reduced by cultural factors.

Figure 10.3 A working model of stressors, outcomes and moderators

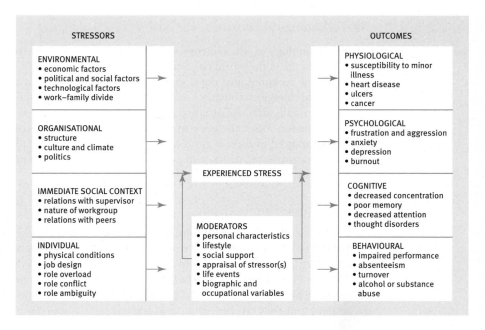

STRESSORS

For convenience, stressors are brought together into four major groups, according to the level at which the potential source of stress originates, and these will be described in turn.

Environmental Stressors

Environmental stressors: forces external to the organisation that can be potential sources of stress for individuals

Environmental stressors consist of forces that can become worrying or potentially disturbing to individuals and they are located in the environment of an organisation.

Economic Factors

In Western society, work is a central feature of our lives and anything that threatens the stability or certainty of future employment can become a stressor. Rising unemployment figures, news of decreased national competitiveness and rising interest rates are all potential threats to a person's economic security, news of which evokes feelings of uncertainty and helplessness.

Political and Social Factors

A new government can have different priorities from its predecessor and so political changes always bring a degree of uncertainty. While some of the changes associated with a new government are likely to appear as economic factors, uncertainty can also be brought about simply because there has been a change in political ideology.

In addition, certain social factors can also induce feelings of insecurity. An element of racial discrimination is still widespread in society and this undoubtedly creates a degree of apprehension for ethnic minorities.

Technological Factors

If a technology exists, someone will find a use for it and the tremendous rate of technical change in the world has a significant impact on people's lifestyles. Keeping pace with new technological developments can be a problem for almost everybody, and technical change establishes a requirement for individuals to adapt, all of which makes for potentially stressful situations. Information technologies, which speed up information transfer, make the pace of life faster and the volume of information that can be transmitted in these ways tends to put people at risk of information overload. In addition, increased traffic and population density in urban areas makes travelling a more frustrating experience.

The Work–Family Divide

Paradoxically, although the family can be one of the most significant sources of support to help people cope with stress (Fryer and Payne 1986), an increased pace of life can often result in tensions and divided loyalties between work and family responsibilities. There seems little doubt that the wave of downsizing and delayering that swept through firms in the 1980s and 1990s resulted in most people having to work harder and for longer hours. Indeed downsizing has rightly been described as 'a constellation of stressor events' (Shaw and Barret-Power 1997). In a downsized organisation it often becomes the norm for people to have to take work home, which makes it much harder for them achieve a satisfactory work–life balance. This problem can be particularly acute in so-called 'dual career families', which seem to be very prone to home–work conflicts (Lewis and Cooper 1987), and there is some evidence that one stressed-out partner can quickly transmit his or her stress to the other (Jones and Fletcher 1993).

 OB IN ACTION: Farewell to work–life balance?

According to the latest British Social Attitudes survey, the elusive goal of work–life balance is proving harder than ever to achieve for families in Britain, often because of increasing working hours for women, and rising workplace stress.

The survey finds that full- and part-time employees of both sexes are finding it increasingly difficult to achieve a balance between life and work, particularly in combining their job with family responsibilities. More than eight out of ten of them would like to spend more time with their family, a figure that is up from under 75 per cent in 1989. Indeed, although working hours have fallen slightly for men, an increase in the hours worked by women means that, overall, the hours worked in two-earner households have risen. At the same time, the pressures of work appear to be increasing, with both men and women expected to work harder.

According to the survey, only 8 per cent of full-time employees say they never or hardly ever find their work stressful, which is half the level reported in 1989. Even among women working part time, just a quarter say they experience little or no stress, which is down from more than a third in 1989. A majority of men and women say the demands of their job interfere at least sometimes with family life.

Rosemary Compton, co-author of the research, said that government moves to increase opportunities for flexible working are unlikely, on their own, to improve work–life balance, if work itself was becoming more stressful. She noted that there needs to be more focus on reducing stress and pressure at work, rather than simply promoting flexibility, and also noted that increasing levels of staffing, as well as reducing hours of work for men and women, could both contribute to the reduction of stress at work. However, she admitted that policies such as this could face opposition on the grounds that they threatened profitability, potentially leading to some difficult choices in future.

The research finds that professional and managerial employees are more likely to find work stressful than people in routine and manual jobs, because people in this type of work are not only likely to work longer hours themselves, but also more likely to live in a household where both partners are working. The study also shows that although women are now at least as committed to employment as men are, if not more so, they still retain the leading responsibility for childcare and work in the home.

Source:

Double whammy of hours and stress rules out more time with the family, *Guardian*, 24 February, 2007 p 9

Organisational
stressors:
characteristics of the
whole organisation
that can be potential
sources of stress for
individuals

Organisational Stressors

Organisational Structure

Structure can have a considerable effect on emotions and feelings. In structures that are too rigid, people can feel that there are few opportunities for growth and personal development, whereas very loose, ill-defined structures can give rise to feelings of role ambiguity and anxiety. Thus, either of these extremes can be stressful to some people. Of equal importance is the effect of structural changes that have become common-place in the last decade. When faced with tight market conditions, downsizing has become an almost automatic reaction in many organisations, and this has left many employees with jobs that are more physically demanding and the feeling that life is now less secure. So pronounced are these effects that one author describes the situation as 'working with pain' (Berggren 1993) and others actually describe the new conditions as 'management by stress' (Parker and Slaughter 1988). As such, demoralisation and anxiety are common in organisational workforces that have been through this experience (Green 2001; Kets de Vries and Balazs 1997). So intense are these pressures that people find it hard to 'shut off' from the sources of stress, even by the simple step of having a good night's sleep (Carpenter 2006; Doward 2005).

Culture and Climate

As will be seen in Chapter 20, one definition of culture is 'the way we do things around here' (Deal and Kennedy 1982). If a highly pressurised work environment is part of the culture, there can be heavy work demands on employees which creates highly stressful conditions (Schaunbroeck and Ganster 1993). Conversely, there is empirical support for the idea that cultures and climates that incorporate a strong element of participative management reduce the stressfulness of conditions (Ivancevich *et al.* 1990).

Organisational Politics

People in organisations are often in interdependent relationships, where they have to rely on each others' efforts. However, if cooperation from others cannot be obtained, this can bring an element of resentment and frustration to the person concerned. In addition, if it is found that these people are going one step further and manoeuvring behind the scenes for their own ends, the effects can be even more devastating. For example, in a survey of 2,500 managers by Kiev and Kohn (1979), respondents rated a poor political climate as one of the most frequent sources of stress.

Immediate social
stressors: features of
a person's immediate
(social) work context
that can be stressful

Immediate Social Stressors

The social aspects of work are as important for most people as the opportunity to earn money. Thus, certain immediate social conditions can result in stress and three in particular can be important: relations with one's immediate superior; the nature of a workgroup; and interpersonal relations with group members.

Relations with Immediate Superior

It is all too easy for the behaviour of an inconsiderate or thoughtless supervisor or manager to create stressful conditions for an employee. A study by Fox *et al.* (1993) shows that a number of behaviours can be particularly stress-provoking. These are:

- inconsistent instructions
- failure to provide physical and emotional support
- lack of concern for employees' well-being
- lack of adequate direction
- too strong an emphasis on productivity
- focusing only on isolated incidents of sub-standard performance
- ignoring good performance.

Nature of a Workgroup

Being a member of a group is an important feature of work for most people, and later in this chapter it will be seen that a person's workgroup can be an important source of social support to resist the effects of stressors.

In current conditions temporary groups and teams tend to be used a great deal. Thus individuals sometimes find that they have to move in and out of new groups, and each time this happens people have to adjust to the personal idiosyncrasies of a new set of people and find a role within the group. A newly formed group is full of unresolved ambiguities and if it is not given enough time to work through the necessary processes of formation (see Chapter 11) these ambiguities can turn into conflicts that persist for some time, all of which create a highly stressful set of conditions.

Interpersonal Relations with Group Members

To some extent this flows from the point above. It has long been recognised that good personal relationships between group members can be a central factor in individual well-being (Argyris 1964) and the major stressors in this respect can be:

- conflictual relations with other group members
- a lack of interpersonal trust
- unsympathetic co-workers.

Individual stressors: features of a person's job that can give rise to stress

Individual Stressors

Certain features of an individual's role can be stressful and five in particular can be highly significant: physical conditions; job design; role overload; role complexity/conflict; and role ambiguity.

Physical Conditions

The effects of physical conditions on individual well-being are covered in some detail in Chapter 7, where it is noted that the physical conditions in which work takes place can have a significant impact upon individual productivity. Many of these have an impact because they are potential stressors and Shostak (1980) notes five that have this effect:

- temperature extremes
- bright or harsh lighting
- too little illumination
- a dusty or dirty atmosphere
- loud noise.

Job Design

A number of features of an individual's job can have the potential to induce stress. Machine-based, repetitive work gives a person low task control or personal responsibility, whereas a job with a high degree of autonomy has the opposite effect and acts as a buffer to the effects of other stressors (Makin *et al.* 1996). Moreover, repetitive work often under-utilises a person's skills, and can result in a degree of anxiety, depression and boredom, all of which can lead to stress (Reeves 2003).

Long working hours or intensified working conditions can be highly stressful (Green 2001; Sparks *et al.* 1997) and shift work disrupts bodily rhythms, levels of blood sugar and mental efficiency. A shift worker's body clock is permanently in disarray and there can be a lack of alertness at work and, because the person attends work while friends and family are asleep and vice versa, there can also be a sense of social isolation, all of which can give rise to a potential for stress and stress-related diseases (Monk and Tepas 1985).

Working with a computer screen for prolonged periods can result in 'repetitive strain injury' from adopting the same posture for long periods and become a significant source of stress (Mackay and Cox 1984).

Role Overload

Most people have some idea of what constitutes a reasonable level of work, and from time to time almost everybody has to exceed this by working long hours or to extremely tight deadlines, to cope with an emergency. If it is temporary, people can usually cope with a *quantitative* overload of this type and some individuals actually like working under pressure in this way. However, if the situation persists it can become highly stressful.

Qualitative overload, in which the requirements of the job are beyond the skills of its incumbent, is a more difficult situation, even in the short term. This occurs for most newcomers, and it is usually accepted that they will underperform until they 'find their feet'. However, the situation can also occur for people who have been re-deployed in an organisational restructuring, and because they are already familiar faces in the firm, there is sometimes no tolerance to their inexperience in a certain task.

Variety overload can occur when someone has a very wide range of different tasks to perform, which demands a constant shift in attention and concentration. Since downsizing and delayering are often quickly followed by empowerment initiatives, in which employees have to take on some of the tasks hitherto performed by supervisors and managers (Claydon and Doyle 1996), these circumstances can result in all forms of overload.

Role Complexity/Conflict

This occurs when two or more different roles held by the same person have competing demands. Thus, complying with one set of demands makes it difficult or impossible to meet demands of the other set(s). It has long been recognised that role conflicts of this type result in a highly stressful situation and Kahn *et al.* (1964) note that these circumstances are associated with:

- high levels of interpersonal tension
- decreased job satisfaction
- poor interpersonal relations

- decreased confidence in the organisation
- decreased commitment to the organisation.

Moreover, this state of affairs is not confined to conflict between roles within an organisation; there can also be significant effects if competing pressures exist between work and family roles.

Role Ambiguity

This occurs when someone is uncertain about:

- what he or she should accomplish in a job
- the expectations of other people
- what needs to be accomplished to meet his or her expectations.

Ambiguities of this type can be uncomfortable and highly stressful and, although some degree of role ambiguity is probably inevitable in today's fluid, downsized organisations, individuals vary considerably in their capacity to live with the situation. Thus individual differences have a strong bearing on the degree of stress experienced. In general, however, the following can all result from role ambiguity and they can all be precursors of stress (French and Caplan 1973):

- low job satisfaction
- low self-confidence
- low self-esteem
- a sense of futility
- low motivation
- depression.

TIME OUT

As for the previous Time Out exercise, carefully reflect on the last time you took examinations, but this time answer the following questions:

1. Were there any stressors emanating from the external environment of your university or college that you felt were impinging on you?
2. What organisational stressors do you feel were present?
3. What stressors emanating from your immediate social context at your university or college do you feel were impinging on you?
4. What individual stressors do you feel were present?

REPLAY

- Workplace stress results from the interaction of people and their jobs and, in particular, from changes that force them to deviate from their normal functioning.
- There are four main groups of stressors (forces that impinge on people and result in stress): contextual, organisational, those in a person's immediate social context and individual factors.

THE OUTCOMES OF STRESS

Stress can manifest itself in many ways, but these can be divided into four main categories as suggested by Beehr (1995). From the perspective of an organisation, the most significant outcomes are those that affect performance, which are included here in the behavioural and cognitive categories. However, it is important to remember that overt behaviour is just the final, most visible symptom and, if behavioural symptoms are evident, it is virtually certain that there will also be psychological and cognitive outcomes. In the long run, physiological problems will also probably appear. Historically, the majority of research on stress has explored its link with physical illness and work on psychological and cognitive outcomes is a more recent development. Thus, in what follows, although the four outcome categories are discussed separately, it is vital to remember that they are all interconnected.

Physiological Outcomes

Physiological outcomes: the effects of stress on a person's bodily health

There is a substantial body of evidence to support the idea that stress has serious effects on physical health (O'Leary 1990), an early indication of which is given in the work of Holmes and Rahe (1967), which will be covered when describing the moderators of stress. The reason why stress has these effects was described earlier when covering the General Adaptive Syndrome. The endocrine system enables the body to resist agents such as germs and microbes, and plays a part in providing the adaptive energy to cope with novelty, uncertainty and conflict; the very conditions associated with stressors. If its reserves are limited and it has to try to provide the energy to cope with stressors, it simply has less energy to resist microbes.

It is also known that high levels of stress are accompanied by an increase in the level of cholesterol in the bloodstream and with increased blood pressure. Since these phenomena are associated with heart disease, there are good reasons for suggesting that stress is a major contributory factor, and there are even arguments to suggest a link between some forms of cancer and stress (Bammer and Newberry 1982).

Psychological Outcomes

Psychological outcomes: the effects of stress on a person's mental health

Frustration and Aggression

As explained in Chapter 7, frustration can occur when goal achievement is blocked. Since goal blocking is an endemic feature of organisational life and many of the stressors described earlier can give rise to frustrating experiences. Where these are fairly limited in duration all will probably be well, but if the experience is prolonged, or the limits of tolerance are exceeded, frustration becomes a driving emotional condition that can all too easily degenerate into aggression. Thus it is not surprising to find that high levels of stress are associated with aggressive actions such as interpersonal hostility, or even sabotage (Chen and Spector 1992).

Anxiety

Anxiety occurs when someone believes that he or she has no effective way of dealing with disturbing circumstances that might occur, while fear is a reaction to danger that is already perceived to exist. Many of the stressors identified earlier are associated with ambiguity and uncertainty about the future, and this is almost bound to prompt a degree of anxiety. Where anxieties are slight or moderate, however, this tends to keep people alert and ready for action, but, where anxiety becomes severe, it can all too easily result in non-adaptive, escapist behaviours, including aggression.

Depression

Because it can take so many different forms, depression can be very hard to define. Nevertheless, Flach (1974) gives some of the symptoms of chronic depression as:

- disturbed sleep
- loss of appetite
- lowered sex drive
- indecision
- fatigue
- poor concentration
- avoidance of social contact
- inability to find pleasure in almost anything
- feelings of being trapped and helpless.

At times most of us become mildly depressed and because this makes us slow down and build up our reserves of energy, it has a useful function and most people seem to pull themselves out of mild depression. However, there are others who find depression harder to shake off and they sink deeper into self-defeating patterns of behaviour. The great paradox is that depressed people tend to feel that they have no control over events, but at the same time blame themselves for feeling depressed (Abramson and Sackheim 1977).

Clearly many of the stressors described above have the capability to induce mild depression and, if several of them are present in combination and for a sufficient time, matters could become serious. Moreover, since depression is a condition that can lead to even more serious problems with mental health, it is sometimes one that needs psychiatric attention.

Burnout

Burnout: a chronic outcome of stress characterised by a general feeling of complete exhaustion, depersonalisation, disinterest and lack of personal accomplishment

Burnout can be defined as 'a general feeling of exhaustion that develops when an individual experiences too much pressure and too few sources of satisfaction' (Moss 1981). While it is more commonplace than depression, it is almost exclusively associated with work-related stressors and some of its associated symptoms are:

- emotional exhaustion
- physical exhaustion
- disturbed sleep
- absence of any positive feelings about work
- feelings of hopelessness and futility
- a cynical perspective about almost everything associated with work.

There is general agreement that the key component of burnout is emotional exhaustion (Gaines and Jermier 1983). When this occurs the person becomes callous towards, or withdrawn from, colleagues and clients, and then develops a sense of a lack of personal accomplishment about work. It seems to be far more prevalent in people whose jobs include a large component of interaction with other people who have their own problems; for example, the police, teachers, nurses and other caring professions (Evans and Fischer 1993).

Jobs such as these often attract people with high ideals and the nature of their work places strong emotional demands on them, but if these demands cannot be met, they develop burnout through frustration. For this reason burnout can seldom be associated with a specific stressor that appears at a set point in time. Rather, it is an outcome that appears and then gets progressively worse. This idea is cogently expressed in a review of the literature by Cordes and Dougherty (1993), from which the model shown in Figure 10.4 has been synthesised.

Cognitive Outcomes

Cognitive outcomes: the effects of stress on thought processes

The word cognitive refers to thought processes and the main cognitive problems associated with stress are:

- lowered concentration
- impaired memory

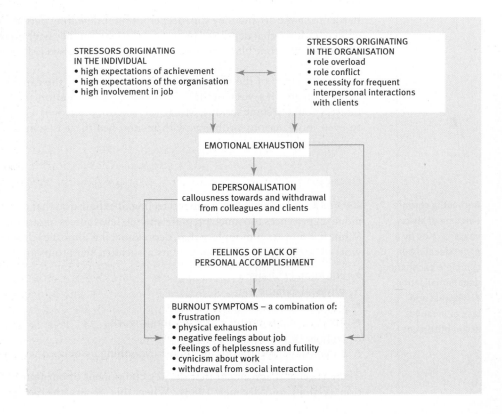

Figure 10.4 The development of burnout (adapted from Cordes and Dougherty 1993)

- lowered attention
- distorted perceptions
- (in extreme cases) thought disorders.

However, these are symptoms and, because the relationship between stress and thought is so complex, it can be hard to pinpoint a definite effect because highly circular processes are likely to be at work; for instance, a person's thoughts about a stressor can give rise to an emotional reaction that becomes an additional source of stress. However, while we know that certain cognitive processes are affected by stress, we do not really know why. What is known is that, when stress occurs, hormones that affect brain functioning are released, and in mild cases this increases brain activity and sharpens thinking, alertness and concentration. Problematically, when this stress-induced arousal reaches a certain level, more primitive reactions occur. The person becomes less sensitive to his or her surroundings, the intake of information and its interpretation can be impaired, and this results in hasty action and mistakes.

Behavioural outcomes: the effects of stress on overt behaviour

Behavioural Outcomes

Work Performance

Because there are moderating variables that can mitigate some of the effects of stressors, it is hard to identify the direct effects of stress on job performance. There are people who argue that it can only have a negative effect, while others adopt the view that a moderate degree of stress probably improves performance. Nevertheless, if the stress is too severe, performance is inevitably undermined and Cohen (1980) draws three significant conclusions:

- In most cases, stressors have no immediate effects on behaviour because, in the short term, the majority of people adapt in order to maintain performance.
- The adaptive process has its penalties and, while these take time to have an effect, reduced tolerance to frustration and less efficient working eventually start to appear.
- Importantly, the whole process takes less time in the presence of multiple stressors and so it seems safe to conclude that a decrease in performance is a function of the aggregate number of stressors, and the time for which they are experienced.

Other Behavioural Outcomes (Absenteeism, Turnover, Substance Abuse)

A whole host of other behavioural outcomes have been linked to stress. There is evidence of a relationship between stress levels and absenteeism and staff turnover (Steers and Rhodes 1978), although some employers are skeptical about whether absenteeism is necessarily stress related (see OB in Action Box on page 292). Other outcomes that have attracted increasing interest are alcohol and drug abuse but, because of the secretive nature of both practices, it is difficult to find hard evidence that they are related to stress. Nevertheless, it is more than possible that people seek solace in alcohol and drugs as a result of stress, even if this only shows up as unauthorised absence the following day.

 OB IN ACTION: Employer attitudes towards stress

Many employers think that workers are using the excuse of 'stress' to take days off to which they are not entitled, according to a recently published survey. The revelation has added a twist to the issue of stress at work, which health chiefs say is emerging as a serious problem for employers. Although the survey provoked protest from the largest private-sector trade union, it elicited evasiveness and embarrassment from business organisations, who refused to endorse employers' widespread suspicions.

Nevertheless, 51 per cent of human resource professionals believe that over half the days that employers lose to stress are not 'genuine', and 40 per cent of private-sector businesses said they did not want to raise the profile of stress, in case this encouraged increased reporting of it. Roger Lyons, joint general secretary of the Amicus trade union, complained that employers were 'utterly wrong' to believe that many workers were taking sick days for dubious reasons. 'Modern living and modern working places huge stress on families', said Mr Lyons, and 'failure to recognise this is part of the problem.' However, while Ben Willmott, of the Chartered Institute of Personnel and Development, conceded that 'we will always have a few employees who will use stress as the excuse to take the odd day off', stress is a real problem, although some managers, under pressure themselves, perhaps do not have a lot of sympathy for a stressed employee.

The Federation of Small Businesses warned that employers were 'increasingly aware of vexatious claims, and are concerned about an area which is vaguely defined at the moment'. Elizabeth Gyngell, head of 'better working environment' at the Health and Safety Executive – which has led the campaign to increase awareness of stress – said if companies tackled the causes of stress they would be 'in a stronger position to tackle the people they might think are skiving'.

Source:

Turner, D (2003) Stress used as 'excuse to skive', *Financial Times* 21 October

 TIME OUT

Returning to the subject of examinations used for the previous Time Out exercise, now answer the questions below about the outcomes of stress that might have been present.

1. Were there any physical symptoms and, if so, what were they?
2. Were there any psychological symptoms and, if so, what were they?
3. Were there any cognitive symptoms and, if so, what were they?
4. Were there any behavioural symptoms and, if so, what were they?

- There are four main outcomes of stress, and while these can sometimes appear in isolation, it is common for them all to appear together.
- Physiological outcomes have effects on the person's health.
- Psychological outcomes include frustration, aggression, anxiety, depression or burnout.
- Cognitive outcomes affect thought processes.
- Behavioural outcomes are manifested as changes in the individual's work performance, possible absenteeism and/or staff turnover.

THE MODERATORS OF STRESS

Research has revealed a number of factors that can moderate the effects of stressors, in one or both of two ways:

- by influencing the amount of stress that a person experiences
- by influencing the person's reactions to the experience of stress, which has an impact on the outcomes he or she exhibits.

Although the effects of the moderators are well documented, our knowledge of the mental processes through which these effects are produced is still far from perfect. In what follows they will all be considered separately, but it is important to point out that there are connections between some of them and several can act in combination.

Personal Characteristics

Self-efficacy: a person's belief in his or her ability to act in a certain way

Self-efficacy

This, which is a characteristic of personality, can be defined as an individual's perception of his or her ability to act in a certain way, which in this case would mean remaining in control of the work situation (Bandura 1982). In terms of stress, this probably comes down to the person's belief in his or her ability to withstand or adjust to change.

It is also likely to be an important determinant of a predisposition to succumb to stress, and a case study by Fox *et al.* (1993) indicates that people who are high in self-efficacy maintain a relatively low blood pressure when exposed to stressors. It is perhaps for this reason that participative decision making, which can give people a feeling of having some element of control over matters, can reduce the stress-inducing potential of work (Jackson 1983). The reverse of feeling 'in control' is what Seligman (1975) dubs a state of 'learned helplessness', which predisposes people to give up easily and accept that they will be stressed.

Hardiness: a psychological characteristic that helps a person withstand the effects of stressors

Hardiness

This is a global predisposition that was first identified by Jackson (1983), who noticed that under stress some people tend to go to pieces much more readily than others. In an investigation of managers subject to stressful conditions, those who experienced lower rates of stress-related illnesses were classified as having what the researchers (Kobasa *et al*. 1982) called 'a hardiness disposition', which was associated with three distinct characteristics:

- **commitment:** they were highly involved in their work
- **challenge:** they felt that change rather than stability was normal
- **control:** they felt able to influence the outcome of events.

From these results Kobasa and her colleagues reasoned that these characteristics help people to resist stress by erecting a buffer between themselves and workplace stressors.

Negative affectivity (NA): a tendency to focus strongly on the negative aspects of work and life

Negative Affectivity (NA)

This is a tendency to focus on the negative aspects of work and life, and it is a characteristic that seems to predispose people to be more affected by stress (George 1990). Those high in a negative affectivity tend to become easily angered, afraid or depressed about events in their lives, and this could well shape their appraisals of workplace stressors. Indeed, there is fairly strong empirical support for the idea that, when exposed to the same stressors, individuals high in NA tend to experience higher levels of stress than those low in this characteristic (Schaunbroeck *et al*. 1992).

Lifestyle (Type A and Type B Behaviours)

Following a lengthy and exhaustive programme of research into cardiovascular (heart) disease, the scientific world was shaken by the findings of two researchers who uncovered the risks of what they identified as Type 'A' behaviour (Friedman and Rosenman 1974). Prior to this, it had been assumed that the main risk factors in heart disease were diet, high blood pressure and a genetic predisposition. However, the researchers uncovered another factor, which consists of a set of behavioural traits that dominate the lives of those most at risk. These are Type 'A' people, who display the following characteristics:

- To achieve maximum efficiency and output they strive to do a multitude of things at the same time.
- They are aggressively competitive, ambitious and forceful.
- They are impatient, and so tend to do everything at a frenzied pace and consider any delay a chronic waste of precious time.
- They are highly combative with people, events and objects.
- They have a tendency to speak in a rushed explosive way and are impatient with others who speak slowly and often try to finish other people's sentences.

In contrast, Type 'B' people, while still having drive and ambition, have a much steadier pace of doing things.

Research has amply demonstrated the inherently stressful nature of Type 'A' behaviour (Jex *et al*. 2002). Instead of condemning the pace of organisational life, these people may well have a tendency to use the circumstances as an unrivalled opportunity to behave according to their preferred pattern, which places a huge amount of stress on themselves and those around them.

Social Support

Social support:
emotional support
received through
interaction with
other people

While receiving and giving *social support* is usually advocated as a way of helping to combat stress, it also has a role in resisting stress and can be a powerful moderator of the effects of stressors. Social support is derived from the give-and-take relationships that are built up with other people, particularly those who give support at an emotional level and Williams and House (1985) argue that this helps combat the effects of stressors in three important ways:

- by creating a setting in which needs for affection, approval, security and social interaction are met
- by reducing the likelihood that poor interpersonal relations will become a source of stress, which makes the work environment a much more pleasant place
- perhaps most importantly, by acting as a buffer between an individual and stressors; that is, stressors can sometimes be brought into perspective by discussing them with other people.

(Cognitive) Appraisal of Stressors

Cognitive appraisal: a
person's perception
of a stressor, e.g.
whether it is harmful,
threatening or
challenging

Different people often evaluate the same stressor in different ways, and this has a significant impact on whether it is perceived as threatening, harmful, challenging or, alternatively, benign. In addition, it has some bearing on the strategies that a person might use to cope with stress. For instance, Dewe (1991) points out that if a person judges that a particular situation is likely to require resources that he or she does not possess, this poses a threat to the individual's personal well-being and stress can be experienced. According to Dewe, this appraisal takes place in two stages:

- *Primary appraisal*, which involves thoughts or feelings or emotions about a stressor, for example whether it is felt to be harmful, threatening or challenging.
- *Secondary appraisal*, where more detailed consideration of the stressor's characteristics takes place.

Clearly, both of these stages can have an impact on how the stressor is experienced but, according to Dewe, in terms of coping with the stressor, primary appraisal is by far the most important; a point to which a return will be made when considering stress management.

Life Events

Stress is a reaction to the need to adapt when people undergo significant changes, either at work or outside. This idea was examined for a wide variety of life events that were mainly non-occupational in nature by Holmes and Rahe (1967), and it led to the development of a test instrument called the Social Readjustment Scale. This places potential stress values on a number of life events that require people to make adjustments, and is reproduced in outline in Table 10.1.

The assumption underpinning the scale is that because the life events shown in Table 10.1 are all changes that require people to adapt, they are potential stressors, and this can predispose the person to illness. The usual way of applying the scale is to identify the events that a person has encountered in a 12-month period, and then to total the scale values of these events which are shown in the right-hand column. According to Holmes and Rahe, this can be used to predict the likelihood of illness in the following year. For a score of up to 150, people are said to be at no great risk; if the total is between 150 and 300, there is a 50 per cent probability of serious illness; if the total is above 300, the probability of illness rises to at least 75 per cent.

Depending on how it is viewed, the scale can be regarded as a warning list of potential stressors, or as a list of extra-organisational stressors that can exacerbate the effects of those in the workplace. It is in the second way that it is used here, and a high score on the scale means that there is a high potential for stress in outside events, which in turn makes it more likely that the person may succumb to workplace stressors.

Note that while a number of the events listed in Table 10.1 are what most of us would regard as pleasant events, they still require a person to undergo change and, in Holmes and Rathe's terms, they are potential stressors. This contradicts the popular view that stress is totally associated with aversive conditions and gives rise to one of the most frequently voiced criticisms of the scale – the assertion that aversive and pleasant events are equally important as stressors. Nevertheless, follow-up work using the scale indicates that the relationship between life events and subsequent health problems, although relatively modest, is robust (Perkins 1982). Thus the work has sufficient predictive validity to have encouraged other workers to develop new and improved scales. The most important inference that can be drawn from the work concerns the cumulative effect of multiple stressors. Stress outside work almost certainly lowers the ability to resist stress at work and, as a corollary, stress at work spills over into a person's private life.

Table 10.1 The Social Readjustment Scale (adapted from Holmes and Rahe 1967)

Life event	Scale value	Life event	Scale value
Death of spouse	100	Son or daughter leaving home	29
Divorce	73	Trouble with in-laws	29
Marital separation	65	Outstanding personal achievement	28
Prison sentence	63	Wife begins or stops work	26
Death of close family member	63	Begin or end school	26
Major personal injury or illness	53	Change in living conditions	25
Marriage	50	Revision of personal habits	24
Dismissal from employment	47	Trouble with boss	23
Marital reconciliation	45	Change in work hours or conditions	20
Retirement	45	Change in residence	20
Major change in health of family member	44	Change in schools	20
Pregnancy	40	Change in recreation	19
Sex difficulties	39	Change in church activities	19
Gaining new family member	39	Change in social activities	18
Business readjustment	39	Very small mortgage or loan	17
Change in financial state	38	Change in sleeping habits	16
Death of close friend	37	Change in number of family gatherings	15
Career change	36	Change in eating habits	15
Change in number of arguments with spouse	35	Vacation	13
Having a large mortgage	31	Christmas	12
Foreclosure of mortgage or loan	30	Minor violations of the law	11
Changed responsibilities at work	29		

Biographic and Occupational Factors

In addition to the factors covered above, there is evidence that a number of biographical and occupational factors is associated with stress. Where biographics are concerned, the sex of an individual is likely to be a moderator. All other things being equal, women seem to experience greater psychological effects of stress, while men suffer far more from physical outcomes (Geller and Hobfall 1994).

Certain occupational factors also seem to be influential. Dentists seem to be particularly prone to stress because of time and scheduling demands and negative patient perceptions (Cooper *et al.* 1988), while civil servants are particularly prone to the effects of role ambiguity (Erera-Weatherley 1996). In a study of burnout, Evans and Fischer (1993) draw attention to the idea that different occupations suffer most from different outcomes. The caring professions exhibit the symptom of de-personalisation very strongly, whereas technical occupations, such as computer hardware and software designers, are more aware of the feeling of lack of personal accomplishment that results in burnout.

TIME OUT

In the previous Time Out exercises you have noted some of the features of the stress that you felt you experienced during the time that you last took examinations. Now answer the questions below:

1. How would you classify the amount of stress that you feel you experienced: mild, medium or high?
2. Were there any moderators present that helped you either resist the effects of the stressors, cope with the stress, or made it harder for you to resist or cope? If so, try to classify the moderators into:

   (your own) personal characteristics
   (your own) lifestyle
   social support from others
   your appraisal of the stressors.

REPLAY

- There are a number of factors that can moderate an individual's reaction to workplace stressors. These are:

  personal characteristics such as personality
  lifestyle
  availability of social support
  how the person appraises the stressors
  other life events
  biographic and occupational factors.

STRESS MANAGEMNT

The expression stress management is misleading, if only because it implies that the level of stress in an organisation can be varied at will. In addition, a great deal of so-called stress management is simply concerned with enabling people to 'learn to live with high levels of stress'. Nevertheless, it is a widely used expression and, to maintain continuity with other literature, it will be used here.

A number of ways can be used to deal with stress in organisations and, in order to structure the discussion, the approaches are distinguished by locating them along the two dimensions shown in Figure 10.5.

The horizontal dimension categorises approaches according to the *level of stress management*, that is, the level in the organisation at which the matter is addressed – at the level of the individual, or the organisational level. The vertical dimension reflects the timing of the approach; for example, whether it is a *reactive approach* that aims to equip people to cope with conditions that are stressful, or a *proactive approach* that is concerned with removing or minimising stressors, so that stress is no longer experienced.

Note, however, that Figure 10.5 merely portrays four theoretical categories. In practice these are not mutually exclusive and reactive approaches at either level are usually concerned with coping. Since it is far easier and less disruptive for an organisation to try to change the individual rather than itself (Cooper and Cartwright 1994), even organisational-level initiatives are largely confined to helping people to function under higher levels of stress. Thus it is convenient to commence the discussion at the individual level.

Individual Level Stress Management

Because stress is an individually experienced phenomenon, there is a sense in which all stress management approaches have some focus on the individual, because he or

Level of stress management: whether dealing with stressors is focused at the level of the individual or the level of the organisation

Reactive approach: attempts to help people better cope with the effects of stress after it has occurred

Proactive approach: attempts to remove or lessen the influence of stressors before stress occurs

Figure 10.5 A typology of stress management approaches

	LEVEL OF (STRESS MANAGEMENT) FOCUS	
	Individual	Organisation
Reactive	**Aim:** to equip specific individuals to cope with, or recover from, the effects of stressful conditions after stress has occurred **Example:** stress management techniques	**Aim:** to equip (on request) any individual in the organisation to be able to cope with, or recover from, the effects of stressful conditions as and when encountered **Example:** Employee Assistance Programmes
Proactive	**Aim:** individuals take action to resist the effects of stressors, or remove stressors from their working environments **Example:** negotiate change to working environment or quit	**Aim:** redesign of the working environment to reduce or eradicate stressors **Example:** structural, operational and role redesign

TIMING OF STRATEGY

she is the only person who knows whether a particular technique for combating stress works. Nevertheless, recent research indicates that there can be strong differences between employees and managers as to where the onus lies for diagnosing stress. Managers are likely to feel that having an 'open door' policy, which allows employees free access to complain about being stressed is all that is necessary, whereas employees are likely to feel that managers owe employees a duty of care and, therefore, should behave more proactively and seek-out stress sufferers (Pryce *et al.* 2006).

So far as coping with stress is concerned, Beehr (1995) notes that there are two ways in which an individual can try to cope. By using either:

- an emotion-focused strategy, in which the person reacts to the situation by attempting to remove or lower its emotional effects without actually trying to do anything about the situation itself
- a problem-focused strategy, which attempts to tackle the root cause of stress.

If, for example, a person finds that lack of personal autonomy or the nature of the work is stressful, one emotion-based strategy can be to reconcile him or herself to living with the situation. However, Oakland and Ostell (1996) suggest that a range of other mental and physical behaviours also fall into this category, for example fantasising, wishful thinking, substance abuse, or turning to religion or mysticism. Conversely a problem-focused strategy can be to try to negotiate more interesting work with more responsibility.

A more explicit set of alternatives is given by Terry (1994), who distinguishes between three strategies:

- The *control strategy*, which broadly corresponds to a problem-focused attempt to take charge of matters by anticipating a continuation of the situation and acting in a way that tries to solve the problem.
- The *escape strategy*, which is roughly equivalent to an emotion-focused approach that involves using thought processes and behaviour that involve accepting the situation in a passive way.
- The *symptom-management strategy*, which consists of using methods that alleviate the effects of the stressors.

To some extent, the strategy a person adopts will depend on prior experiences of its usefulness in similar situations. For this reason cognitive appraisal of the situation, which was mentioned earlier when considering the moderators of stress, is all important. The way this process works is portrayed in Figure 10.6, which is based on the ideas of Lazarus and Folkman (1984).

While there is quite strong evidence that individual appraisal of a stressful situation correlates strongly with the choice of coping strategy (Lowe and Bennett 2003), it is not clear, which of the three coping strategies is the most effective in different situations (Dewe 1992). Since the vast majority of techniques used fall firmly into the symptom-management category, the remainder of the discussion will be focused on these. They are summarised in Table 10.2 and described in what follows.

Relaxation Techniques

One of the greatest problems for the person suffering from stress is that he or she finds it hard to relax. Thus anything that can help in this respect is likely to be beneficial.

Control strategy: a problem-focused attempt to tackle the root cause of stress by changing the nature of the situation, to remove or reduce the impact of stressors

Escape strategy: an emotion-focused attempt to lower the impact of stressors, but without trying to change the nature of the situation

Symptom-management strategy: an attempt to live with, but mitigate, the effects of stressors

Figure 10.6 Cognitive appraisal and the coping process (adapted from Lazarus and Folkman 1984)

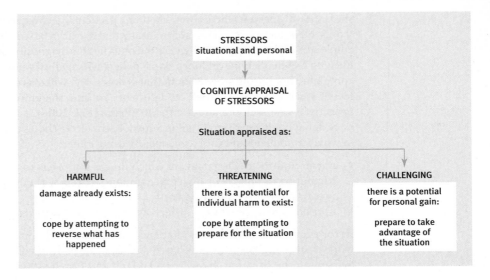

Table 10.2 Some personal stress management techniques

Technique	Examples
Relaxation training	Breathing exercises, muscle relaxation
Physical exercise	Jogging, walking, workout in fitness centre
Biofeedback	Take pulse rate, check own breathing rate
Assertiveness training	Learn to reappraise stressful situations and address root causes of problems
Behavioural self-control	Learning how to manage one's own time better, learning how to recognise potentially stressful situations and making plans to cope with them
Seek social support	Discussing stressful situations with colleagues, peers and friends
Professional help	Psychotherapy, counselling, etc.

For instance, the person could force him or herself to take a holiday (or even be ordered to do so). In addition, there are a number of easily taught relaxation techniques that can be used, for example breathing exercises and muscle relaxation.

Physical Exercise

Regular physical exercise not only improves blood circulation, lowers blood pressure, muscle tension and cholesterol levels, it also has more subtle effects. The feeling of general well-being it creates can help combat some of the symptoms of stress and, when people are physically tired, they tend to sleep more soundly, which provides periods of intense relaxation and enables them to marshal reserves of energy.

Biofeedback

This is a technique of learning to monitor one's own bodily functioning, sometimes with the help of instruments. In biofeedback people are also taught elementary ways of controlling certain body functions, such as heart rate, muscle tension and blood pressure, all of which can help alleviate some of the symptoms of stress.

Assertiveness Training

Assertiveness should not be confused with aggression. The assertive person is more likely to stand his or her ground and refuse to be trampled on, whereas aggression is often an attempt to trample on someone else. Helping someone to be more assertive is perhaps the one technique that can encourage people to adopt a more problem-focused approach to stress, and there is some evidence that initiatives of this type may be highly beneficial in the long term (Bunce and West 1996). For example, assertive people are more likely to reappraise a stressful situation and try to address its root cause rather than its symptoms.

Behavioural Self-control

The aim here is usually to get people to analyse and take control of their own actions, in this case to identify ways in which their behaviour gives rise to stress. One technique is for people to learn how to manage their time more effectively and prioritise work tasks. Another is for people to learn to recognise situations that put them under stress and make plans for handling them so that the situations are less stressful.

Social Support

Social support has been mentioned earlier, when describing the moderators of stress. Here, people are usually advised to build up networks of colleagues, co-workers and friends, from whom they can receive a sympathetic ear and give the same service in return. While the link between receiving social support and the reduction of stress is complicated, there is fairly strong empirical evidence that it has beneficial effects (Schonfeld 1990) and these are greater when support comes from inside the organisation, rather than from outside (Lim 1996), perhaps because the recipient feels that these people can more readily appreciate the problems.

Professional Help

If all else fails, because the level of stress has gone beyond the point where the person can bring about an improvement alone, he or she might need guidance from a clinical expert. This can involve some sort of psychotherapy and, while this might seem to be a drastic step, it must be remembered that in its severest form stress can be so debilitating that people may be incapable of working out what to do to alleviate their symptoms. In situations such as this it can be near impossible for even the most devoted friends or family members to give useful help, and these well-intentioned interventions may actually do harm. Where expert help is needed, a wide variety of techniques, such as behavioural therapies, insight-orientated approaches or even hypnotherapy, may be required. Firth-Cozens and Hardy (1992), who conducted research into the effects of clinical treatment of stress sufferers, report in highly positive terms on the outcomes of these therapies. However, a note of caution is also sounded. While anxiety tends to be lowered and people come to view their job more positively, they are no more tolerant of the organisation for allowing the stressful conditions to exist in the first place.

All of the individual techniques given above have some utility in appropriate circumstances, and the evidence suggests that they can provide a degree of help in coping with workplace stress (Ivancevich *et al.* 1990). Nevertheless, it should be noted that these methods only deal with the symptoms of stress, rather than addressing the stressors that give rise to the malady. Thus they tend to sweep the real problem under the carpet.

Organisational Level Stress Management

Just as a distinction can be made at the individual level between reactive and proactive approaches, the same is true at the organisational level. To date, it is fair to say that the vast majority of organisational initiatives have been distinctly reactive. They deal with stress in individuals as and when it occurs, effectively deflect responsibility away from the organisation to place it on the shoulders of individuals, which allows stressful conditions to remain (Dewe and O'Driscoll 2002). To some extent, this is tantamount to shutting the stable door after the horse has bolted – what Berridge *et al.* (1997) call the 'band aid' or inoculation approach. Thus, where they exist, organisational initiatives tend to have a highly reactive element, and the currently fashionable step is to introduce Employee Assistance Programmes (EAPs). These can be defined as:

> a programmable intervention at the workplace, usually at the level of the individual employee, using behavioural science knowledge and methods for recognition of certain work and non-work related problems (notably alcoholism, drug abuse and mental health) which adversely affect job performance, with the objective of enabling the individual to return to making his or her full work contribution and to attaining full functioning in personal life.   (Cooper and White 1995, p 121)

From the late 1980s onwards, these programmes have increasingly been run by specialist consultancy firms, with the result that the provision of EAP services has become something of a growth industry. However, they are expensive to put in place, and it is probable that a small firm, where the potential for stress could be higher because of the hectic pace of activity, would find an EAP beyond its resources.

A wide variety of techniques and methods can be deployed in EAPs and, to a large extent, there is a very strong emphasis on the individual methods described above. Cooper and White (1995) note that there are a number of focal issues that need to be addressed in a programme of this type, and these are summarised in Table 10.3.

Table 10.3 tells us that the reason for introducing an EAP is almost always reactive, usually because stress has become noticeable in a large number of employees. However, once installed, there is no reason why an EAP cannot be used to take remedial action at a very early stage with employees who are only just starting to experience stress.

Evidence about the success of stress management training of this type is very mixed (Cooper and Sadri 1991). Although these initiatives are well meaning, there are a number of problems. First, they have an in-built tendency to put the burden of doing something

Table 10.3 Focal Issues for EAPs (adapted from Cooper and White 1995)

Issue	Reason for focus on issue
Decrease in job performance	Can be used to identify individuals suffering from stress
Consultative assistance	Provides help for managers who are responsible for achieving goals, and identifies where manager's performance and that of subordinates is critical to achieving goals
Constructive confrontation	To get affected employees to recognise that they are experiencing stress and thus provide the motivation to become involved in EAP activities
Individual micro-level linkages	Develop planned, systematic programmes that help employees to identify how EAP can provide assistance and clarify their individual responsibilities
Macro-level (organisational) linkages	Clarify the organisation's responsibilities (towards employees) and identify how EAP can best be used by the employer
Organisational culture	The existence and use of EAP needs to be incorporated into the organisation's culture
Improved job performance	The criterion of success for the EAP is whether its use results in a sustained improvement in the performance of affected employees

about stress on the shoulders of the individual. Second, they usually only provide training and facilities that can be used by individuals to try to avoid becoming stressed, or to cope with an attack of stress. Finally, they are probably underpinned by an assumption that organisations are, and will continue to be, more stressful places. Thus they tend to focus on ways of enabling employees to function in ever more stressful environments.

Turning now to less reactive steps, there is no shortage of advocates of a more proactive organisational approach and, for example, this is the line taken by the Institute of Personnel and Development (IPD 1998). Creating a stress-free workplace is not a simple task, if only because the rapid rate of change makes it difficult to forecast whether future conditions will be stressful. Nevertheless, one of the more encouraging signs about EAPs is that some employers are reported to be looking beyond the need simply to treat stress after it has occurred, and have started to address the issue of making the organisation a less stressful place.

To this end, Elkin and Rosch (1990) list a wide range of steps that can be used by organisations as part of a stress reduction strategy, the efficacy of which is well supported by the literature on Organisational Behaviour. Examples of these are:

- redesigning tasks
- redesigning work environments
- using more flexible work schedules
- using more participative management styles
- involving employees in drawing up career development plans
- involving employees in establishing their work goals
- providing social support and feedback
- building cohesive teams
- establishing fair employment and rewards practices.

Figure 10.7 A five-step problem solving approach to dealing with workplace stress (adapted from Cooper and Cartwright 1994)

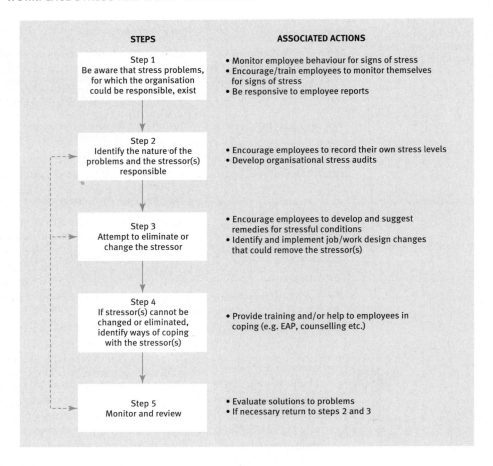

STEPS	ASSOCIATED ACTIONS
Step 1 Be aware that stress problems, for which the organisation could be responsible, exist	• Monitor employee behaviour for signs of stress • Encourage/train employees to monitor themselves for signs of stress • Be responsive to employee reports
Step 2 Identify the nature of the problems and the stressor(s) responsible	• Encourage employees to record their own stress levels • Develop organisational stress audits
Step 3 Attempt to eliminate or change the stressor	• Encourage employees to develop and suggest remedies for stressful conditions • Identify and implement job/work design changes that could remove the stressor(s)
Step 4 If stressor(s) cannot be changed or eliminated, identify ways of coping with the stressor(s)	• Provide training and/or help to employees in coping (e.g. EAP, counselling etc.)
Step 5 Monitor and review	• Evaluate solutions to problems • If necessary return to steps 2 and 3

A more comprehensive strategy, which potentially involves both organisational level and individual level measures, is suggested in a five-step, problem solving approach given by Cooper and Cartwright (1994), which is shown in outline in Figure 10.7.

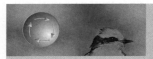

REPLAY

- Approaches to stress management can be categorised along two dimensions: the level (individual or organisational) at which stress management occurs; and whether the approach is proactive (attempts to remove stressors) or reactive (concerned with coping with stress once it has occurred).

- Individual level methods are dominated by reactive strategies.

- Organisational level approaches, for example Employee Assistance Programmes (EAPs), are also dominated by reactive methods that mainly employ individual techniques, but there are signs that some organisations have an interest in more proactive methods.

OVERVIEW AND CONCLUSIONS

Stress is a word used with increasing frequency in organisations and it is doubtful whether the phenomenon can ever be completely eradicated. It is a psycho-physiological defence mechanism through which a person tries to adapt to burdensome external pressures and, where this is not possible, he or she shuts off from the stressors to avoid greater harm. This process is known as the General Adaptive Syndrome, and it has three stages: alarm, resistance and exhaustion.

Workplace stress arises from an interaction between people and their work milieu. Stressors emanate from four main sources: contextual stressors, which are located in the environments of organisations; organisational stressors, which emanate from within the organisation as a whole; stressors in the individual's immediate work context; and, finally, stressors associated with the individual's role. Because conditions outside the workplace can either exacerbate the effects of workplace stressors or ameliorate them, there is a two-way interaction between stressors within and beyond the organisation.

Just as there are several sources of stress, the outcomes of stress can show themselves in many ways: physiologically, in terms of lowered resistance to disease and infection; psychologically, as frustration, aggression, anxiety and depression; cognitively, when thought processes become impaired; and, behaviourally, in terms of changes in a person's patterns of behaviour.

Stress is an individually experienced phenomenon and it is unlikely that two people will react to the same set of stressors in exactly the same way, because a number of factors can moderate the impact of stressors, and these can also influence the way that a person tries (or fails) to cope with a stressful situation. There are six important groups of moderators: personal characteristics such as personality; the person's lifestyle and whether this predisposes an individual to stress; the extent and nature of social support available to the individual; the individual's cognitive appraisal of stressors; other life events to which the person is subject; and a number of biographical and occupational variables.

As noted above, stress can never be completely eradicated and there are arguments that a low level of stress is beneficial to humans and improves their functioning. Nevertheless, it is important to recognise that severe stress can be highly debilitating and, for this reason, individuals and organisations need to explore ways of reducing the potential for stressful conditions to arise, and to find ways of helping people to cope with stress. In general terms there are two levels at which these matters can be addressed. At the individual level, people can either equip themselves with a number of coping techniques that enable them to withstand the effects of stressful conditions, or they can attempt to change the characteristics of the situation in which they find themselves. However, since organisations are ultimately responsible for the existence of most workplace stressors, they should shoulder some responsibility for developing solutions, perhaps with initiatives that make the work milieu a less stressful place. This approach is comparatively rare and, for the most part, organisations confine themselves to providing assistance for those who already show signs of stress. Thus most organisations have a regrettable tendency to expect employees to deal with the stress that may have been brought about by the organisation.

CASE STUDY 10.1: Stress management at Bradford and Bingley

Bradford and Bingley, a major financial services company, began looking at the link between line managers and stress in early 2005, when a member of staff complained to the local authority about the firm's management of stress. Although an investigation by an environmental heath officer failed to result in formal action, it highlighted improvements that the company could make in terms of its policy and practice for stress management.

Initial analysis using absence data, annual staff survey results and focus groups established that Bradford and Bingley's stress issues centred around change management and the demands placed on staff. In response, the company devised a stress management plan that defined responsibilities for everybody in the organisation. It also launched a training programme for all 600 line managers to teach them how to carry out local risk assessments and execute control measures.

A large part of the education initiative consisted of getting managers to realise that in many cases they were already implementing good stress control measures, they just didn't realise it, says John Hamilton, head of group health and safety. Citing the daily 'huddles' – five-minute get-togethers held by many teams across the business – he adds that this is an absolutely fantastic stress management control measure: it helps people to balance their workloads, pick up on issues and award praise, and allows everybody to have their say in an informal way.

Managers soon became engaged in the training when they realised that stress management simply amounted to good business practice, and that quarterly appraisals, making sure the business was properly resourced, that staff were trained, and that bullying wasn't tolerated, could all have positive effects. The training didn't change the way they used these control methods, but it changed the emphasis they put on them, says Hamilton. He and the rest of the health and safety team also worked closely with their HR colleagues, because many of the policies and initiatives that supported stress management were linked to HR processes such as performance reviews, grievance processes, and issues such as bullying and harassment, equality and diversity. They also had to overcome some initial hesitancy from middle management about the potential cost and relevance of this issue to their jobs. Feedback from the interviews with managers helped in this respect, prompting them to focus on case studies in the training sessions.

The training itself seems to have gone down well, with 83 per cent of managers giving it a positive response. A recent health and safety audit also showed that the quality of the risk assessments being produced by managers was now high. However, there is still a long way to go, says Hamilton. This is not a T-shirt and mouse-mat exercise; you are talking about massive cultural change in a business, and you don't do that with just six months of training.

Source: Clarke, E (2006) Pressure soars, *People Management*, 31 August, pp 31–32

Questions

1. Using Figure 10.5, classify the approach to the stress management initiative adopted by Bradford and Bingley.

2. What do you feel prompted the firm to adopt this particular approach?

3. Many of the steps undertaken in the programme were focused on line managers, for example all 600 of them were re-trained. Why do you feel that it was decided to focus on these people?

4. Critically examine some of the other things on which the group health and safety head comments favourably; for example the daily 'huddles' – do you feel that his praise is justified?

5. Compare the case material with the OB in Action Box given earlier in the chapter, which describes the HSE Stress Management Standards. Can you identify anything that Bradford and Bingley might have overlooked, or which might also need attention?

FURTHER READING

Beehr, TA (1995) *Psychological Stress in the Workplace*, London: Routledge. A very readable account of the causes, consequences and handling of workplace stress.

Cartwright, S and CL Cooper (1996) *Managing Workplace Stress*, London: Sage. The book gives penetrating insights into stressful workplace events and happenings, and explores attempts to alleviate their impact.

Benson, H (2005) Are you working too hard?, *Harvard Business Review*, November: 53–58. A novel article that explains the author's ideas about stress management techniques, which he calls the 'Breakout Principle'.

Cooper, CL (1996) *Handbook of Stress, Medicine and Health*, Boca Raton, FL: CRC Press. A book that highlights a great deal of the research that links stress with ill health.

Cooper, CL and MJ Davidson (1991) *The Stress Survivors*, London: Grafton Publishing. Although the main focus of the book is on coping with stress, it also deals with many other features of stress at work.

Cooper, CL and R Payne (1988) *Causes, Coping and Consequences of Stress at Work*, Chichester: Wiley. A comprehensive book, the title of which reflects its contents.

Daniels, K, R Hartley and CJ Travers (2006) Beliefs about stressors' impact: evidence from two experience-sampling studies, *Human Relations* 59(9): 1261–1285. An interesting and useful paper that reports an empirical study of cognitive appraisal of stressors; specifically, the predicted beliefs about the relationship between the anticipated occurance of a stressor and the effect that this is likely to have on work performance.

Fontana, D (1990) *Managing Stress*, New York: Routledge. A useful overview of stress and stress management from an American perspective.

Lepine, JA, NP Podsakoff and ME Lepine (2005) A meta-analytic test of the challenge stressor – hindrance stressor framework: an explanation for inconsistent relationships among stressors and performance, *Academy of Management Journal* 48(5): 764–775. The paper reports the results of an interesting and innovative research study to explore the effects of 'good stress' and 'bad stress'. Using a conceptual framework that purposely frames the research questions in the light of motivation theory, the authors show that there is some support for the idea that it is probably only hindrance stressors that have debilitating outcomes, whereas challenging stressors do not.

Robinson, O and A Griffiths (2005) Coping with the stress of transformational change in a government department, *Journal of Applied Behavioural Science* 41(2): 204–221. A useful paper that reports the results of an empirical study that attempts to identify: (i) why employees experience change as a stressful event; (ii) how they attempt to cope with changes.

Roney, A and CL Cooper (1997) *Professionals on Workplace Stress*, Chichester: Wiley. This book illustrates the problems of workplace stress that are encountered by a number of professionals, such as medical doctors, human resource managers, academics and lawyers.

REVIEW AND DISCUSSION QUESTIONS

1. It is sometimes asserted that a certain level of stress is necessary to induce high work motivation and performance. Identify the implications of this assertion and the problems associated with putting it into practice.

2. What developments in the last decade have tended to increase stress in organisations and are there any that have tended to decrease it? In the next decade, what developments can you foresee as being likely to increase or decrease levels of workplace stress?

3. Which causes of stress are the easiest to identify and which are the hardest to deal with?

4. Explain why different individuals in the same situation can experience different levels of workplace stress.

5. Review the model of burnout given in the chapter and describe the circumstances leading to burnout. Explain why individuals and organisations should be concerned about burnout and what can be done to try to ensure that it does not occur.

Integrating Individual Characteristics and Processes

Individual differences that can be used to distinguish between people in terms of their psychological characteristics were brought together in the previous integrative section of the book, which appeared immediately after Chapter 5. These can be likened to the basic building blocks of individual psychology, which manifest themselves as the individual processes covered in the previous five chapters; that is, *memory and learning*; *motivation* (which also has implications for the design of jobs); *decision making*; and *workplace stress*. The task of this integrative section is to trace some of the links between individual characteristics and the ensuing processes. Clearly, since the number of such links is potentially endless, space precludes an extensive coverage and only the most prominent ones will be dealt with here. To do this a broadly similar method will be used as for the previous integrative section. That is, the individual characteristics will be taken one by one, and some of the links with processes covered in this section of the book will be explored. Note, however, that some of these links are recursive in nature. Just as an individual characteristics can give rise to effects in an individual processes, in some cases a process can have an impact on characteristics.

LINKS BETWEEN PERSONALITY AND INDIVIDUAL PROCESSES

All personality theories have clear implications for individual motivation. For instance, Freud's (1940) theory of development tells us that whichever of the three components of personality (id, ego, superego) becomes dominant has a huge impact on a person's needs and wants, and thus the behaviour directed at satisfying them. In addition, research that maps the typical patterns of behaviour of people in either Eysenck's (1947) or Jung's (1971) personality types gives strong clues about what is likely to motivate people of each type, and also some indication of their likely decision making styles.

Another link, but this time more directly between personality and decision making, can be seen in Spector's (1982) work on 'locus of control'. To give an example, those with an internal locus like to feel in control of events and, perhaps because of this, they are more likely to be decisive people (De Brabender and Boone 1990; Gist 1987). This, together with Eysenck's results, clearly has direct implications for the organisational roles for which people of certain personality types are temperamentally most suited and, to some extent, these conditions are those that are most likely to motivate them. Internals, for example, work better where clear goals are set and incentives are available for good performance (Kren 1992).

There are also likely to be links in the reverse direction. According to Freud, personality is largely the result of subconsciously held memories. Thus the process of learning is likely to have significant effects on this important individual characteristicl.

LINKS BETWEEN INTELLIGENCE AND INDIVIDUAL PROCESSES

As was noted, the way that intelligence is normally measured can mean that it reflects stored experiences as much as anything else, and this is precisely one of the major criticisms of intelligence testing. Moreover, what has been learned and held in the memory creates expectancies that some objects, phenomena or social situations are more likely to exist than others, and this probably has a huge impact on the object recognition stage in perception.

LINKS BETWEEN PERCEPTION AND INDIVIDUAL PROCESSES

As was explained in Chapter 4, if a person has an unsatisfied need, this has a bearing on the environmental features likely to attract his or her attention. Therefore, an individual's motivational state may well have an influence on the person's perceptions.

LINKS BETWEEN ATTITUDES/EMOTIONS AND INDIVIDUAL PROCESSES

Because attitudes are dynamic in nature and are subject to a degree of change in the light of experience, in one sense an attitude can be regarded as either a characteristic or a process. Strictly speaking, however, it is the change of an attitude that is a process, which makes it more convenient to regard an attitude as a characteristic. What this means, however, is that the connection between attitudes and processes is likely to be recursive.

Attitudes are predispositions to behave in certain ways towards certain objects, and this is likely to have a fairly clear influence on motivation. For example, the cluster of related attitudes known as job satisfaction has been shown to be associated with both labour turnover (Tett and Meyer 1993) and absenteeism (Steel and Rentsch 1995). Moreover, direct experience of an object or phenomenon also has a tremendous impact on a person's evaluation and subsequent behaviour towards it (Fishbein and Ajzen 1975). Thus, there is also likely to be a strong connection between memory and attitudes.

To summarise, there are clear indications of links between different characteristics, and between characteristics and processes at the individual level. Therefore the initial model given in Figure I1, at the end of the first integrative section, can be expanded to the one given in Figure I2.

Figure I2 Interactions between individual characteristics and processes

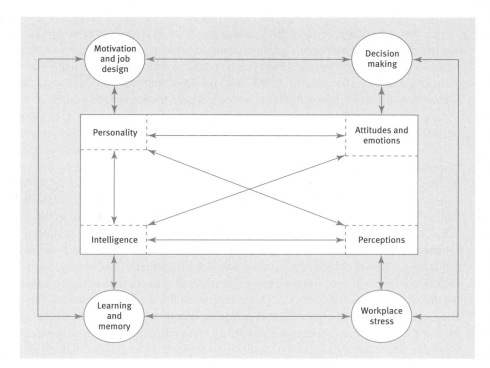

Integrative Case Study No. 2: Developments at David Orton plc

Note To familiarise yourself with the background scenario to this case you are recommended to re-read Case Study No. 1 in this series, which deals with events at Costwise in the period between early 2004 and mid-2005. This episode of the case reports events in its merger partner (David Orton plc) across the same time period, and subsequent cases will focus on events affecting both partners after this later date.

By mid-2005 it was becoming clear to Orton's senior managers that the takeover of Costwise had given rise to a number of irritating problems, one of which had its roots in the firm's prior history. In the past, the Orton group had largely grown organically and its enlargement was financed from retained profits. Thus growth, which involved opening new larger stores, essentially involved applying its tried and trusted strategy to do 'more of the same'. This had the strength of allowing the company to enlarge its geographic spread beyond the north of England and the Midlands, but at the same time leaving its strategic approach towards retailing unchanged. It was unashamedly proud of its northern roots, Thus its strategy consisted of delivering an efficient, cost-effective service that was predominantly focused on groceries and home wares (with fewer electronics, clothing and furnishings) at lower retail prices than its competitors. In the recent past it had focused on doing this from larger stores, where a higher than average turnover per square foot of floor-space could be obtained.

▶

However, when Orton acquired the Costwise group, which in terms of turnover was more than twice the size of Orton, it found itself with a portfolio of sites that varied considerably in size and product range, and with a variety of different approaches to retailing. While this enabled it to acquire a presence in other areas of the UK, notably the home counties, the south-west and Scotland, this was its first incursion into a takeover situation, which gave rise for a need to integrate the more diverse Costwise stores.

One of the first problems to appear was that the Orton group eventually had to pay more than originally intended for Costwise. Here it will be recalled from Case Study No.1 in this series that the Orton bid for Costwise opened up a bidding war from other competitors, and also a warning from the Competition Commission (CC) that it might well insist on Orton divesting itself of a number of stores (subsequently the number it was required to dispose of was slightly more than 50). Although the CC subsequently banned other competitors from bidding for Costwise while this was being sorted out, by then the damage had been done, and Costwise's shares were being quoted at a significantly higher price by the stock market; so high, in fact, that Costwise had to withdraw from its acceptance of Orton's offer, which in the original bid was set-out in terms of a deal that only involved an exchange of Orton's shares for those of Costwise. Here it should be noted that Coswise's withdrawal was virtually inevitable, and in no way indicated a cooling of enthusiasm for the merger. It was simply a step that had to be taken to provide a period of grace in which the market could re-value Costwise's shares, thus providing a more realistic valuation that that would allow its shareholders to obtain the appropriate value of their holdings. Nevertheless, it resulted in the value of Coswise's shares rising, which had to be taken into account in any new offer by Orton, and this inevitably meant that the cost of the takeover was somewhat higher than originally planned.

In preparation for the merger, Orton had become deeply engaged in an exercise to re-brand itself with the public. This involved considerable expenditure on advertising, and a complete refurbishment and facelift of all of its portfolio of property. When details of the takeover were finalised in mid-2005 (including details of the 50 stores to be divested in accordance with ruling of the CC), Costwise stores were added to this programme and by late 2006 the Costwise fascia disappeared from large stores in Great Britain. This left Orton with approximately 370 stores bearing its own name. Since then, however, the group has continued to sell or close stores that were not covered by the original CC ruling. These are stores that it felt did not fit with its new image and in total 254 stores were scheduled for sell-off in this way by late 2006; mainly smaller, 'compact' stores, which to be sold to competitors.

Problematically, since the re-branding/refurbishment exercise started, Orton has struggled to hold onto its turnover. To some extent this was because its stores were being remodelled or refurbished at the rate of three or four per week, and by early 2006 the group had issued no less than five profits warnings; although by later in the year it released figures that suggested that it had finally turned the corner. The warning was also made necessary by the divesting of stores to conform with the CC ruling, the effect of which was to reduce its turnover by £1 billion, with £80m less in profits. Set against this, however, it is due to obtain income from the sale of parts of its property portfolio. Nevertheless, Orton finds itself in a position where it desperately needs to boost turnover, and this has become critical to the success of the merger. One factor that seems likely to have had a significant effect on this is the reaction of ex-Costwise customers in the new converted stores.

As noted above, Orton unashamedly has a gritty, north of England self-image, and prides itself on giving value for money to its customers. Costwise, however, has a somewhat more upmarket image. For example, market research shows that Costwise attracts customers in the ABC1 social groups, while Orton sells mainly to lower social groupings. Indeed, in the eyes of typical Costwise customers, Orton's product range has too strong a focus on 'bangers and mash and meat pies'. Thus there has been some confusion among ex-Costwise customers, many of whom seemed to be deserting the stores in droves when they are re-branded as Orton. In addition, there have been strong criticisms from customers about the internal layout of the converted stores; for instance, that they are too cramped and congested, that the aisles are too narrow, that they can't locate what they want to purchase, and that it all seems to reflect a policy of 'pile it high and sell it cheap'. It is not known whether this trend will continue – or for how long – but it is not helped by the statement of the somewhat charismatic and forthright chairman of Orton that he puts these criticisms down to southern snobbery, and that as far as he is concerned 'he does not know [or particularly care] what a middle class shopper is'.

Be this as it may, but there seems to be a possibility that it is less associated with the type of customer who now shops at converted (from Costwise to Orton) stores, than the different approaches to people management traditionally used in Costwise and Orton. In Costwise, store managers at a local level had the authority to plan their own local strategies; for example, to stock certain items, vary prices according to local competitive pressures and even recruit additional staff. This gave a strong element of decentralised control, which recognised the needs of different localities. With Orton, however, all these things were strictly controlled from the centre. There was a high degree of uniformity across all stores, who sold the same range of products at the same prices, regardless of location. This strategy had worked very well in the past, but was probably less well suited to the diverse locations of former Costwise stores. While product policy has now been loosened slightly, pricing is still controlled from the centre at Ortons and store managers have nothing like the flexibility enjoyed by Costwise managers.

Questions

1. List what you feel to be the main problems confronting the senior managers of David Orton plc at this point in time.

2. Are these problems primarily associated with Staff Motivation; Learning; Decision Making; Job Design; or Workplace Stress?

3. To what extent do you feel that the existence of problems such as these is attributable to the top management of the Orton group, or is it attributable to employees?

4. What do you feel that Orton's management team could do now to address these problems?

5. What do you feel that Orton's management team could do now to address these problems?

As indicated by the diagram, this section of the book consists of five chapters, all of which deal with group level processes. Important as they are, the individual characteristics and processes covered in the previous two sections of the book do not completely explain human behaviour in organisations because, for the most part, people work in groups and teams. A group exerts a powerful influence on the behaviour of its members, and it is also true that the individual members of a group play a part in deciding what the nature of this influence will be. For this reason there are strong connections between individual and group level matters in an organisation and these are considered in the integrative section that follows Chapter 15.

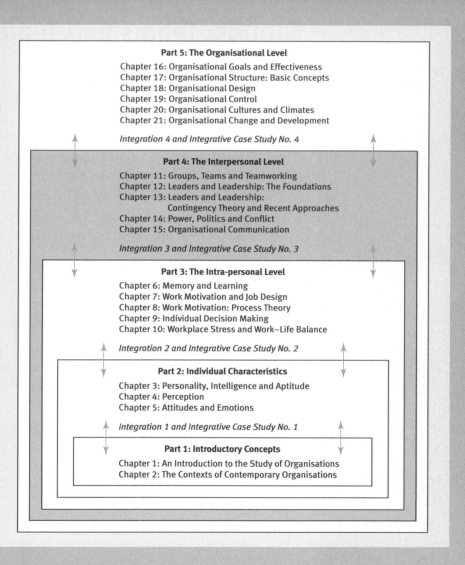

Part 5: The Organisational Level

Chapter 16: Organisational Goals and Effectiveness
Chapter 17: Organisational Structure: Basic Concepts
Chapter 18: Organisational Design
Chapter 19: Organisational Control
Chapter 20: Organisational Cultures and Climates
Chapter 21: Organisational Change and Development

Integration 4 and Integrative Case Study No. 4

Part 4: The Interpersonal Level

Chapter 11: Groups, Teams and Teamworking
Chapter 12: Leaders and Leadership: The Foundations
Chapter 13: Leaders and Leadership:
              Contingency Theory and Recent Approaches
Chapter 14: Power, Politics and Conflict
Chapter 15: Organisational Communication

Integration 3 and Integrative Case Study No. 3

Part 3: The Intra-personal Level

Chapter 6: Memory and Learning
Chapter 7: Work Motivation and Job Design
Chapter 8: Work Motivation: Process Theory
Chapter 9: Individual Decision Making
Chapter 10: Workplace Stress and Work–Life Balance

Integration 2 and Integrative Case Study No. 2

Part 2: Individual Characteristics

Chapter 3: Personality, Intelligence and Aptitude
Chapter 4: Perception
Chapter 5: Attitudes and Emotions

Integration 1 and Integrative Case Study No. 1

Part 1: Introductory Concepts

Chapter 1: An Introduction to the Study of Organisations
Chapter 2: The Contexts of Contemporary Organisations

Chapter 11

Groups, Teams and Teamworking

LEARNING OUTCOMES

After studying this chapter you should be able to:

- define the term group, explain why groups are important in organisations, and distinguish between formal and informal groups and the functions they perform

- explain why groups are able to influence certain aspects of the behaviour of their members and describe the stages of group development

- explain the significance of group role structure, group norms and group cohesiveness

- discuss decision making in groups and explain what is meant by group effectiveness

- identify important factors that influence the relationships between groups and the factors that should be taken into consideration in managing them

- describe group-based job designs that attempt to utilise the positive features of group functioning

INTRODUCTION

In organisations people are usually located in groups, and groups exercise a powerful influence on a person's behaviour, and, in return, a group's behaviour is affected by its individual members. Thus some knowledge of groups and how they function is vital to understanding the behaviour of people in organisations.

This chapter provides the reader with some of this knowledge. It commences by defining groups and then describes different types of group that are found in organisations. The importance of group membership to individuals is then considered, which is followed by an explanation of the influence that groups exert on the behaviour of their members. The next topic to be explored is the internal processes of groups, which embraces the process of group formation, the structures and nature of a group and group decision making. The matter of group effectiveness is then considered, and this is followed by a consideration of relationships between groups.

In appropriate circumstances some of the effects that groups have on their members can be highly beneficial to an organisation. Therefore the next section of the chapter describes group-based job designs and the chapter concludes with an overview section.

A DEFINITION OF GROUPS

Familiar as it is, the word group does not have a universally accepted meaning, but, after Schein (1980), a group is defined in psychological terms as any number of people who:

- interact with each other
- are psychologically aware of each other
- perceive themselves to be a group
- purposefully interact towards the achievement of particular goals or aims.

Note that this description would exclude a collection of people who just happen to be together at the same time and place; for instance, in a queue at a supermarket checkout. Also note that the people must all interact with and be aware of each other. Thus, in practical terms, there is an upper limit on group size. For instance, it is very unlikely that everyone in a large department would interact, and neither is it likely that they would be psychologically aware of each other. Thus the number usually has to be small enough to permit people to interact in a face-to-face way. Moreover, if they interact in pursuit of a common goal, group members are likely to have some sense of shared identity. However, this does not necessarily mean that a group's goals are necessarily the same as the objectives of the organisation. A return to this final point will be made later, but for the present it is more important to consider the different types of group that are normally found in organisations.

TYPES OF GROUP

Formal Groups

Formal groups: groups brought into existence by the structure of an organisation

An organisation's structure breaks down its overall task into a number of sub-tasks and makes provision for these activities to be coordinated and controlled, which brings *formal groups* into existence. The people who make-up these groups are usually allocated to them with very little choice in the matter and one way of making sense of the variety of formal groups that can exist is to classify them according to their relative degrees of permanence.

Permanent formal groups arise from the relatively fixed structure of an organisation, often by bringing together people who perform similar activities under a single manager, for which the term *command groups* is sometimes used. In most organisations, structure also establishes clear connections between groups, and one interesting theory views an organisation as an elaborate set of overlapping groups (Likert 1961), in which the supervisor or manager of a group is also a subordinate member of a group at the next level upwards, who should act as a linking-pin to facilitate coordination and control. This is illustrated in Figure 11.1.

Command groups: permanent groups of people, all under a single manager, who perform like activities

These days many organisations have a strong emphasis on flexible structures, which has resulted in a widespread use of temporary formal groups. For instance, *task groups* might be formed temporarily to tackle a specific problem or special project, and be dispersed as soon as the task is completed. While this can be a very useful device to deal with a one-off issue, its usefulness crucially depends on how quickly the people transform themselves into a well-functioning group: a matter that will be considered in some depth later.

Task groups: temporary formal groups formed for a specific short-term purpose

A term that is also encountered frequently in the literature on organisations is that of '*teams*'. Indeed, these days, the virtues of teams and teamworking are extolled very widely (Katzenbach and Smith 1993). Teams can be permanent or temporary and a 'team' would conform to the definition of a group given above. The way the term is used in the organisational literature, however, makes it easier to think of a team as a distinctive class of group that is highly task orientated (Adair 1986). Thus teams are essentially formal groups that are very good at achieving the goals and objectives set for them by the organisation.

Teams: strongly task-orientated formal groups

Informal Groups

Whether they are permanent or temporary, formal groups have two things in common:

- they exist because someone at a high level has decided that they are necessary to achieve specific aims and objectives
- people are conscripted into membership.

However, in most organisations there is usually an informal structure that parallels the formal one, and this is made up of informal groups that exist for different purposes. While people primarily work for organisations to earn a living, they also have social

Figure 11.1
Overlapping structure of groups and linking pins (adapted from Likert 1961)

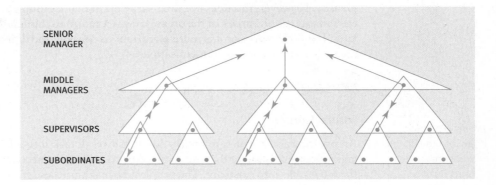

needs and informal groups often play a crucial part in satisfying these social needs. Because membership of an informal group is voluntary, and only happens if existing group members consent to a new person being admitted, an informal group can often exert a far more powerful influence on a person's behaviour than a formal one. These groups often exist because a formal group fails to satisfy people's psychological needs (Argyris 1964) and sometimes informal groups can take on a life of their own. While this can prompt the manager of a formal group to feel that he or she lacks control, the disruptive potential of an informal group is almost certainly exaggerated, and whether or not it has negative effects can often depend on whether the manager of a formal group recognises it has come into existence (Hussein 1989). Depending on how we look at it, the group illustrated in the following OB in Action Box could be either an informal group or a formal one: what do you think?

 OB IN ACTION: Benefits of a different kind

John Nash is a jobless 30-year-old ex-bale operator. With no work experience other than heavy manual labour, no academic background and two newly slipped disks that prevent him ever lifting anything heavy again, he could be a prime candidate for long-term unemployment. Nash, however, has joined the Cotswold Canal Trust (CCT), a canal restoration volunteer workgroup. He learns skills such as hedge-laying and stone walling, as well as general tool work. He much prefers working outside to sitting around at home, gets an extra £10 a week benefits, and it's very likely that his new skills will land him an outdoors job that he enjoys. 'They should do this for a lot more unemployed people,' he says.

The CCT's scheme embraces two linked canals: the Stroudwater Navigation and the Thames & Severn. And the current phase consists of restoring seven miles of the most dilapidated section, which will cost £25m. In the end, the CCT hopes to rebuild 36 miles of canal, opening new routes from the Midlands and the west to London, at a cost of £100m. The journey by inland waterways from Stroud to the capital currently takes two weeks, whereas after restoration it will take five days.

But the canal was forced into extinction by the development of faster and cheaper transport methods, so what's the point in spending so much money to revive an outmoded dinosaur? The most obvious advantage of the scheme currently is the joy and benefits it brings to its amateur work-group. Supervised by Keith Lloyd, a retired Ministry of Defence project manager, every Monday and Wednesday around ten people meet to work on the canal. The group is comprised of retired people and the long-term unemployed, such as John Nash. The retired canal-hands are by no means dodderers desperately seeking a social life. They know what they're doing. Brian Ward-Ellison, 72, gives regular talks on local transport history. Roger Wells, 55, took voluntary retirement after 30 years as a nuclear engineer.

Source:

Watson, A (2004) *Financial Times*, 4 December

THE MEANING AND FUNCTIONS OF GROUPS

Without realising it, group membership has a strong psychological impact on most people and, from an organisation's standpoint, there are certain advantages in bringing people together into groups, six of which are listed by Schein (1980):

- working on complex tasks that are not easily undertaken by an individual
- as a means of stimulating creativity and generating new ideas
- to act as a liaison/coordination mechanism which integrates different parts of an organisation
- for problem solving purposes, where multiple viewpoints are important
- to implement decisions; that is, so that a common objective or goal can be set for a number of people
- as socialising devices, so that a common message, especially with respect to an organisation's culture, can be communicated and reinforced.

These, however, are the advantages to the organisation and Schein also gives a number of less formal but extremely important functions that groups perform for their members. They:

- fulfil social needs for friendship and interaction
- allow people to develop, test and confirm their sense of identity and self-worth
- allow people to establish and test beliefs, reality, experience and meanings
- reduce feelings of insecurity, anxiety and powerlessness
- allow people to achieve mutually agreed informal aims and objectives.

Although these two sets of functions might look like separate lists, they strongly complement each other. While people usually have no choice about the formal group to which they are allocated, the group can also fulfil some of the informal functions. For example, working with others on a complex task usually requires people to share their definitions and meanings, which helps them to test reality, reduce anxiety and confirm a sense of identity. Sharing ideas with other people also allows individuals to know what is going on in the organisation. To some extent it results in people absorbing a group's culture and, providing this does not conflict with the culture of the organisation, there can be highly beneficial outcomes. For instance, commitment to the aims of a local constituency (the group) can bring about a degree of commitment to the organisation as a whole. In addition, the opportunity to engage in meaningful interactions with other people can be a source of stimulation that allows people to tolerate the nature of tedious, repetitive and boring work.

TIME OUT

Identify at least two groups of which you are a member. One should be a formal group, for example people you work with on a regular basis either in your employment or at college. The other should be a more informal group that only exists because its members decide to associate with each other. Now look carefully at the two lists of functions of groups given above and answer the following questions.

1. To what extent does the formal group facilitate the formal functions being achieved?

2. To what extent does the formal group fulfil some of the informal functions?
3. Although the informal group probably has no explicit formal functions, are there any that it seems to have adopted?
4. To what extent does the informal group provide for meeting the informal functions of its members?

GROUP INFLUENCES ON INDIVIDUAL BEHAVIOUR

A group can have many influences on its members, perhaps the most significant of which is that individuals stifle some of their own preferences in favour of the group's code of behaviour.

The evidence about individual conformity is unequivocal and some of this will be described presently. What is not quite so clear is why people conform. One way of making sense of this phenomenon is to adopt a social exchange theory perspective (Blau 1964) and start at a simplified level by considering the group of two people (dyad) shown in Figure 11.2.

Social exchange theory acknowledges that the basic motivation to enter into a relationship with someone else is the expectation of obtaining rewards of some sort. However, to obtain rewards, both people have to provide something for the other one. Thus, as well as getting benefits, they both incur costs and, to ensure that they continue to receive benefits, each person has to continue to meet the costs. This tells us why groups are able to exert control over the behaviour of their members.

Group norms: the rules of behaviour adopted by the members of a group

While individuals derive several practical and psychological benefits from group membership, to continue to receive benefits, each one has to be trusted by the others to incur his or her costs. One of the most visible ways that a person can demonstrate trustworthiness is to abide by *group norms*; that is, the rules that the group has evolved to regulate how individuals will behave towards each other. This makes everybody's behaviour more predictable, which in turn makes it easier for people to trust each other. Thus, one reason (perhaps the main reason) why a group is able to exert an influence over the behaviour of an individual is the unvoiced implication that the benefits of membership will be withdrawn unless he or she observes the norms.

Because any group has a vested interest in trying to ensure that the conduct of a new member is predictable, these principles are equally applicable to a larger group. Indeed, evidence shows quite clearly that groups that have developed a distinctly anti-social climate quickly induce new members to behave in the same way, and the longer a person remains within the group, the greater is the tendency for the person to adopt these patterns of behaviour (Robinson and O'Leary-Kelly 1998).

Figure 11.2 The basic social exchange process

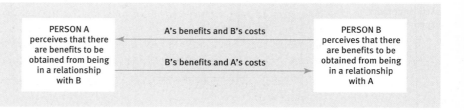

| PERSON A perceives that there are benefits to be obtained from being in a relationship with B | A's benefits and B's costs ← | PERSON B perceives that there are benefits to be obtained from being in a relationship with A |
| | B's benefits and A's costs → | |

Different groups tend to evolve their own, unique ways of getting new members to conform and some of these will be described later in the chapter. For the present it is more important to examine the rather surprising degrees of conformity that groups can obtain and to do this three classic, and by now venerable, research studies will be described.

The Asch Experiments

In the Asch (1951) studies, groups of six people (the members of which were apparently selected at random) were shown a line drawing similar to the one illustrated in Figure 11.3. Individuals were asked to state which of the other vertical lines most closely matched the length of the reference line 'A'. Unbeknown to the one true subject in the group, the other five members were confederates of the experimenter and all had been instructed to respond unanimously with a judgement that was incorrect.

Thus, the true subject either had to agree with the rest of the group or contradict them. Even when subjects were initially hesitant about giving an incorrect answer, over one-third eventually agreed in public with the group's judgement, and only where a supporting 'ally' was planted in the group was resistance continued. This illustrates the capability of a group to obtain conformity, even where conforming means making a public statement that a person knows to be untrue. In these experiments the participants were comparative strangers, which only adds weight to the conformity effect. In a close-knit group that had existed for some time, the pressures to conform would probably be even greater.

Sherif's Experiment

This work (Sherif 1936) demonstrates that a group can bring about conformity, even to the extent of shaping individual perceptions. Subjects were placed in a darkened room and asked to track a small spot of light projected onto a screen, and to report its direction of movement as either upwards, downwards, or diagonally to the right or the left. This is a difficult task because 'autokinetic effects' tend to result in perceptual distortions, in which the light appears to move when it is really stationary. Thus there were often wide initial differences in what individuals reported. Where group members were allowed to exchange information before making the judgement, they all tended to report the same direction of travel. When the size of a group was increased, the tendency to conform became much stronger, probably because a non-conformist finds it much harder to resist if his or her opinions conflict with many people rather than just a few.

Figure 11.3 Line drawing used in Asch conformity experiments

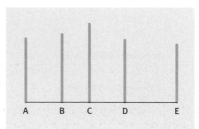

The Milgram Studies

In the first phase of Milgram's (1965) study volunteers were asked to take part in what was described as 'an experiment to investigate the effects of punishment on learning'. They were asked to sit at a table and to converse through a microphone with an unseen individual in another room. On the table there was a control dial, and subjects were informed that this enabled them to regulate the voltage of an electric shock, which would be given to the unseen person. Using the microphone, the subject read out a printed passage of text to the other person, who then had to repeat the passage. If a wrong answer was given, the subject was instructed by the experimenter to administer an electric shock, the purpose of which was said to be 'to assist learning'. For each successive wrong answer the subject was required to increase the voltage, which was clearly labelled on the control panel as varying between 'light shock' and 'danger: extreme intensity'.

Subjects were unaware that the person in the other room did not actually receive an electric shock, but was a 'stooge' who had merely been instructed to give clear, audible signs of receiving a shock. Nevertheless, so far as the subjects were concerned, the other person received a shock which caused a great deal of distress and pain. Screams were clearly heard, and occasionally there was a period of complete silence, from which subjects inferred that the person had collapsed. Many subjects baulked at the task, particularly when there were pleas to terminate the experiment. Nevertheless, the experimenter pressed them to keep increasing the voltage, if necessary, up to the maximum and, despite their reluctance, most subjects did exactly as ordered. This phase of the studies clearly demonstrates that most people have strong tendencies to obey the instructions of an authority figure.

For a further series of experiments, there was a slight change in procedure. During the first phase subjects had been kept apart so that they could not communicate, but in the second phase they were allowed to socialise over a coffee break. Most of them had an initial reluctance to discuss what had taken place, but the longer they were allowed to mix the more likely it was that the truth would come out. The net effect was that they became more willing to defy the authority of the experimenter and many refused to continue with the experiment. Thus Milgram's results demonstrate that conformity can extend to resisting authority and this can have important implications for organisations.

When a person conforms to a group's behavioural expectations, he or she is given the stamp of legitimacy by the group. Almost all formal groups are placed under an appointed authority figure, who is granted a degree of power by the organisation, but if a group does not legitimise this person's actions, extremely potent forces are unleashed which can result in resistance to authority.

TIME OUT

Reflect on an informal group of which you are a member. This could be a group at your place of work or at college.

1. Try to identify any rules of behaviour that the group seems to have evolved; that is, ways of behaving that it expects everybody in the group to observe.

2. What evidence have you that these norms exist? For example, what happens if somebody breaks one of these rules?
3. How do members of the group go about ensuring that someone who breaks one of these rules, either inadvertently or consciously, conforms in the future?

REPLAY

*   A group is a number of people who interact, are aware of each other, perceive themselves to be a group, and purposefully interact to achieve goals or aims.
*   The existence of formal groups is sanctioned by the organisation, whereas informal groups primarily exist to serve the needs of their members.
*   Formal groups serve two main sets of functions: those concerned with achieving organisational ends, and those concerned with serving the social and psychological needs of their members.
*   Irrespective of an individual's personal characteristics or inclinations, groups are able to enforce a degree of conformity in their members to the behavioural norms of the group.

GROUP FORMATION AND DEVELOPMENT

The Stages of Development

It takes time for strangers to fuse together into a mature, cohesive group, and one way to describe this transformation is to document the different stages through which a group passes. Although several 'stage' models of this type have been proposed, the best known is Tuckman's (1965) integrative model, which suggests that groups normally pass through a number of identifiable stages before they function effectively. However, it should be remembered that these stages seldom occur in a single meeting, and it can take weeks or even months before the final one is reached.

Forming: the first stage of group development, in which it is essentially a collection of individuals

Stage 1: Forming

When people first come together they are little more than a collection of individuals, who at best recognise that they have come together to achieve something, but as yet have no clear consensus about what it is, or how it will be done. As such there is little focus on completing the task and people will probably devote their time to getting to know each other, perhaps by making tentative bids for the roles or positions they want to occupy, or trying to create a personal impression. Nevertheless, they will probably recognise that they have to achieve something, and towards the end of this stage will tentatively explore the job that has to be done, and how it will be undertaken. To reach this point, however, the social interaction and testing outlined above needs to have taken place.

Storming: the second stage of group development, which is characterised by interpersonal conflict

Stage 2: Storming

In this stage people become more aware of each other and are willing to bring their views into the open. This sometimes occurs forcefully, as individuals make bids for territory and position in the group, and as these personal agendas and goals surface, a degree of interpersonal hostility and conflict can emerge as people compete to get their ideas adopted. This is often a highly uncomfortable stage for everybody concerned. Sometimes the bonds and alliances made in the first stage are broken, and new ones are formed. However, although it seldom seems so at the time, this stage has a highly positive function. Before convergence can take place, it is usually necessary for polarised views to come out into the open and, unless this happens, differences can remain beneath the surface as unresolved problems. This stage is vital if the group is eventually to fuse into one that can effectively accomplish its task and, if it is not skilfully handled, the group can fragment into cliques or cabals that carry on the battle afterwards. However, if the group successfully comes through this stage, it is ready to pass on to the next one, which is often much more comfortable and rewarding for those involved.

Stage 3: Norming

Norming: the third stage of group development, in which ground rules for a group's way of functioning begin to emerge

In this stage conflict and hostility subside and there is a sharper focus on the task in hand. The group starts to hammer out what it must accomplish and the methods it will use. As well as having a stronger focus on the task, the nature of the interaction between members also changes. Signs of cooperation and sensitivity to others start to appear and the rules for social interaction are established. Although these are not set down in a formal way, they become the code of conduct that regulates group activities and makes future behaviour more predictable. This all helps to reduce future ambiguities and gives the group a firmer foundation that makes it ready to pass into the next stage.

Stage 4: Performing

Performing: the final stage of group development, in which the group becomes capable of effective functioning

Structures and procedures are now in place and the group is ready to get on with the job in hand. If it has successfully passed through the previous three stages, and resolved the problems and issues inherent in each one, the task aspects and the social aspects of the group complement each other. Members are not only mutually supportive and flexible, but have also learned to trust each other and the group is better equipped to perform its role effectively.

Adjourning: the group is disbanded

In a later development, Tuckman and Jensen (1977) identify a further stage: *adjourning*. This refers to the disbanding of the group, perhaps because people move on or because its task has been completed. Almost by definition, teamworking is only possible for groups that have successfully reached the fourth stage, which means that they are relatively cohesive. Because people tend to reflect nostalgically on their positive feelings about the group's achievements and other group members, adjournment is said to be full of sadness and anxiety, and this can be particularly relevant in today's conditions where the use of temporary groups and teams is commonplace.

The idea of a sequence of stages such as those in Tuckman's model is widely accepted, and while most new groups probably go through a similar process, there are exceptions. In some circumstances it is possible that all four stages occur together. For example, if the task in hand is so pressing that something needs to be done immediately, the group may have to pitch in and resolve task problems and its own process together. Similarly, there may be circumstances which make it unnecessary for the group to pass through the stages. An example is an airline cockpit crew. These people can sometimes be complete strangers who have never worked together before, but because they customarily come together with clear definitions of their respective roles and responsibilities, they form into a small, highly effective group in less than ten minutes (Ginnett 1990).

Tuckman's scheme gives a useful set of guidelines for anyone who is charged with starting up a new group and guiding its development. It also reveals why some groups fail to cohere and become effective. This is often because one of the first three stages has not been successfully completed, which leaves unresolved issues or emotional baggage lurking beneath the surface. Thus it is important to allow sufficient time for each stage, and the person in charge of the group needs the patience to allow the process to run at its own pace. It is also useful if a group leader can recognise when a stage has been successfully concluded, so that matters can progress to the next one and, where managers find themselves allocated to temporary, *ad hoc* groups or working parties, this can be particularly important. Because it stands in the way of resolving important social issues, too early a focus on the group's task to the exclusion of everything else is, therefore, to be avoided.

Before moving on it should also be pointed out that Tuckman's scheme is almost completely concerned with the internal dynamics at work in a group. However, these are not the only matters that can give rise to difficulties in development. To this end, in his model of work group behaviour, Homans (1950) stresses that the nature of the context within which a group operates can also play a prominent part in shaping its characteristics; for example, such things as:

- the group's task
- the technology it uses
- the personal background of its members
- management styles in the organisation.

These can all be very important factors, particularly in teamworking, which currently receives a great deal of emphasis in organisations. Nevertheless, it is probably fair to suggest that one of the things that is required for teamworking to work well, is that teams should desirably have passed through the four stages of development. In addition, the nature of the work given to teams should also be conducive to them working with the organisation, rather than against it. While these conditions are present in some organisations, they do not exist everywhere. Moreover, getting the best from teams also requires an ongoing understanding of the ways in which mature groups function, and this is explored in what follows. However, a computer technology that is said to be able to speed-up group development processes for temporary groups is described in the OB in Action Box opposite.

REPLAY

- Most groups pass through a number of sequential stages before emerging as an effective unit.
- These processes all take place within a context within which a group exists and this also has a powerful influence on the characteristics of the group that emerges.

OB IN ACTION: Swarming

Swarming, a technique pioneered by the USA army, is emerging as a peer-to-peer (P2P) networking technique to help civilian organisations reduce the time needed to react to new business opportunities. It was devised to enable small forces to coordinate with each other directly, rather than through a central command post, which cut the time needed to plan military operations from ten hours to just ten minutes, by allowing networks in the field to talk to each other and make snap decisions.

In swarming, employees use P2P collaboration tools to pull-together an *ad hoc* team of people from anywhere in an organisation – or even outside it – to work on a specific task. When problems arise, a team can add new members with the additional skills required, and the team's composition evolves until the project is successfully completed. To large companies the potential prize is worth billions of dollars. The breakthrough technology (P2P) links individuals around the world into a unit with a common focus very quickly, whereas alternative collaboration systems, which are based on centralised servers, are unsuitable because they relatively inflexible and require too much time-consuming administration before new members can be added.

For example, when account managers at Hewlett Packard Services (HP) receive requests for proposals from potential customers, they invite technical architects, product specialists and other experts from all over the world into a swarm in a matter of minutes. This uses a P2P collaboration platform called Groove, which cuts the time needed to generate a response by up to 60 per cent. In addition, Lowe & Partners Worldwide, an international advertising agency, uses swarming to generate creative ideas for new business proposals, by bringing together appropriate staff from offices around the world. Clearly security is important and, while P2P technology allows traffic to pass through corporate firewalls, it uses 192 bit encryption which can't be turned off and is approved by the USA government. Thus the system could be used with a Wi-Fi connection in an internet café and still be highly secure. While several armies worldwide have adopted swarming, corporate adoption of P2P technology has been slow. But as it becomes more common it seems likely that it will be used with increasing frequency as a business tactic.

Source:

Rubens, P (2003) Army tactics are the business, *Financial Times*, 26 November

GROUP CHARACTERISTICS

A group that successfully emerges from its process of development is said to have 'matured'. However, even mature groups that perform similar functions often have unique characteristics that distinguish one from another, the three most important and noticeable of which are structure, norms and cohesiveness.

Group Structure

For a group to accomplish something, individual activities have to be linked and coordinated in some way. Since individuals differ in their capabilities and inclinations, some division of labour is usually necessary and this results in a group structure. There are many ways of describing these structural arrangements, but here three different aspects of structure will be explained: role structure, status structure and communication structure.

Role Structure

Role: a set of expectations and obligations to act in a specific way in certain contexts

Role theory uses a dramaturgical analogy to explain human behaviour and *role* is defined here as:

> a set of expectations and obligations to act in specific ways in certain contexts.

Role has much the same connotations in a group situation as it has in a dramatic setting: it permits people to know roughly how others will behave, and to play their own parts in what happens. To use a dramatic analogy, imagine yourself playing Juliet and speaking 'Oh Romeo, Romeo! Wherefore art thou Romeo?', only to find that the reply you get is from *Macbeth*: 'Double, double, toil and trouble.' Ridiculous as it is, the analogy makes two important points:

- Unless a person knows the requirements of a role, the part cannot be played properly: for example, it is Juliet's role to stand on the balcony and summon Romeo.
- The whole performance breaks down unless other role occupants play their allotted roles; Juliet's words require an appropriate response from Romeo, not the three witches in *Macbeth*.

Thus, in playing roles, people are involved in 'trading performances' (Goffman 1971).

The allocation of group roles usually occurs during the processes of formation and the role a person comes to occupy can be influenced by a number of factors, generally a combination of:

- **Functional factors**   the tasks that will need to be performed in the group; the relative status that people bring with them into membership; influence or authority compared to other people; and position in the necessary communication network of the group.
- **Personal factors**   the personality, attitudes, skills and abilities of the people.

In formal groups job descriptions usually lay down certain aspects of a role. However, these only specify 'what' should be done, not 'how' it should be done, and because a role is a set of expectations and obligations to act in a specific way, the *how* is as important as the *what*.

People are seldom completely free to choose their own roles and, to explain this, consider a formal group of 12 people working under a manager in a design office. The office is sub-divided into three sections and each section leader is in charge of a group of four subordinates. Imagine that you are one of these section leaders and that as part of the job you have to interact with a fairly large number of people:

- those in the design office
- people in other departments
- people outside the firm, for instance customers and suppliers.

Figure 11.4 The role set of the section leader

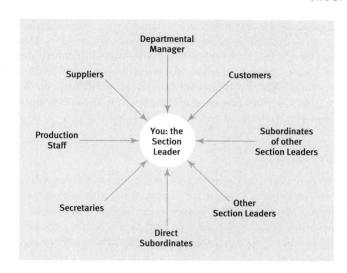

Role senders: individuals who have behavioural expectations of a role occupant

Role set: the total of all role senders for a given role

Role expectations: the role occupant's expectations about what the role entails

Altercasting: the process of tacit negotiation between a role occupant and senders about behaviour which is acceptable to both

Expected role problems: a clash between role sender and role occupant about the content of their respective roles

Perceived role problems: a misinterpretation by a role occupant of a role sender's expectations

Enacted role problems: inappropriate role behaviour

Role ambiguity: the role occupant is unsure of the requirements of his or her role

All of these people will have some expectations about what you will do and how you will do it. They are the *role senders*, who make up your total *role set*. An example of a role set is shown in Figure 11.4.

Unlike an actor on a stage, you have no formal script to tell you how to behave, so how do you find out what the role is? Initially you will probably have your own opinions and your behaviour will reflect this, and your behaviour sends a signal to members of the role set about your *role expectations*. However, there will almost certainly be clues from other people about what is appropriate, for example that the office manager should be shown a certain amount of deference, that other section leaders should be treated as equals and that subordinates will need to be able to approach you for advice and help. Over time, each role occupant constructs a sort of 'working agreement' about the general form of the relationship with all of these role senders. McCall and Simmons (1966) call this *altercasting*: a process in which people cast themselves and others in roles which are then tacitly negotiated and firmed up by imputation and improvisation.

Sometimes, however, things can go disastrously wrong. There can be *expected role problems*, in which there is a clash between role sender and role occupant about what is an appropriate relationship. In other cases there can be *perceived role problems* because sender and role occupant misinterpret each other's signals, and this results in *enacted role problems* of inappropriate role behaviours.

Agreeing on roles can sometimes be a long, drawn-out process and in the early stages of group development poorly conveyed and misinterpreted messages are quite common. This explains why the storming and norming stages need sufficient time to run their course. Even when these matters are resolved, if a group's task or function changes, or new people enter the group, the system of roles can be thrown into disarray and a number of other problems can arise. One of these is *role ambiguity*, which occurs when a person is unsure of the requirements of a role (Katz and Kahn 1978), often because there is a lack of clarity about what is expected in terms of tasks to be performed or how to go about performing them.

Role conflict: a clash between the different sets of role expectations

Another problem is *role conflict*, which covers any situation where there is a clash between the multiple expectations of different role senders. Here a role occupant who tries to meet one set of expectations will find it difficult to meet the expectations of others. Because people usually find it stressful to perform an unclear role, and this leads to very low levels of job satisfaction and job performance. Thus, role conflict of any type can have serious consequences for both organisations and individuals (Fisher and Gitelson 1983).

Status Structure

While there is no foolproof way of predicting what roles will emerge, a feature that is almost inevitable is a hierarchy of authority, with a leader or head at the top. If the group is a formal one, this person is normally appointed by someone higher in the organisation, which gives the role occupant a degree of formal authority over other group members. Note that there are crucial differences between 'heads' and 'leaders', not the least of which is the consent of subordinates to be led. Thus, putting someone in charge of a group does not ensure that he or she will occupy a role of leadership. For this reason, it is not unusual to find that more than one leadership role emerges in a group:

Task leader: the person who occupies the role concerned with ensuring that a group completes its task

- a *task leader* (or *specialist*), who ensures that the group completes its task (Bales 1950)
- a *socio-emotive* or *group maintenance leader*, who ensures that group members have their social needs catered for.

Socio-emotive or group maintenance leader: the person who ensures that group members have their social needs catered for

From then on, and according to the group's needs, other roles, which are seldom formally appointed, start to emerge. Three of the most noticeable and necessary roles are:

- *guardians*, who perform the role of shielding the group against external pressures
- *scouts*, who maintain contact with the group's environment and import vital information
- *ambassadors*, who represent the group across its boundaries and often negotiate with other groups.

Guardians: group members who shield the group from external pressure

Communication Structure

Scouts: group members who maintain contact with their environment and import information

Another important aspect of structure is its internal communication channels. Bavelas (1950) identifies five prominent patterns of communication found in groups, and these are shown in Figure 11.5.

An investigation by Leavitt (1951) reveals that each of these has certain advantages and disadvantages:

Ambassadors: group members who represent a group with other groups

- Since the 'y' and 'wheel' patterns have a focal point through which messages pass, the person in this role tends to emerge as the group's leader.
- Since a single person receives and distributes all information, the 'wheel' and 'y' patterns are also the fastest means of communication and give rise to fewer distorted messages.
- If a group's task is highly complex and requires a great deal of interaction between all members, the 'circle' and 'all-channel' structures, which involve

Figure 11.5 Group
communication
structures (adapted
from Bavelas 1950)

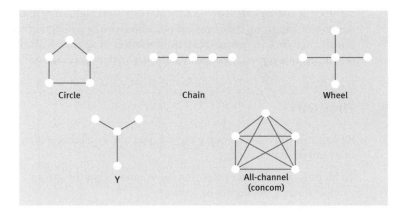

everybody, can be the most effective and often result in the highest degree of
member satisfaction.
- The 'chain' is usually the slowest structure of all and is prone to chinese-whisper
effects that distort messages.

Group Norms

These provide group members with a code of conduct to guide their actions in terms
of behaviour that is important to the group. The four most important functions they
serve are identified by Feldman (1984) as:

- making life more predictable, because people know what behaviour is expected
of them, so that time is not wasted in continual re-negotiation of roles and the
group can function smoothly
- an expression of the central attitudes, values and beliefs of a group, which
projects the group's self-image beyond its boundaries, and signals something
about its nature to those outside
- facilitating group survival, for example by ensuring that the majority subscribe
to the idea that, if a member's behaviour threatens the group's integrity, he or
she should be brought into line. For instance, a common norm for many groups
is that internal dissent can be tolerated to some extent, but woe betide the group
member who criticises the group beyond its boundaries (Hornsey *et al.* 2005)
- avoiding embarrassing problems and issues that can disrupt the group's smooth
functioning.

In general, however, norms will exist with regard to two aspects of group life:

- Norms about ends, which specify what the group should achieve and give it
some degree of consensus about what constitutes success or failure.
- Norms about means, which signal behaviour that is considered acceptable in
achieving the ends.

Although task performance is important, there are usually limits to which a group
will go to achieve success and so both types of norm are necessary. For instance, while

member flexibility can improve task performance, if this means that people can be made redundant, the group will probably place limits on its willingness to be flexible. Therefore, norms can work in favour of an organisation or against it, and it is unwise to assume that a group's norms necessarily coincide with organisational rules and procedures.

TIME OUT

Reflect carefully on a group of which you are a member, either at your place of work or at university or college.

1. Identify any distinct roles that have emerged in the group, for example are there guardians, gatekeepers or scouts?
2. What is your own role in the group?
3. Does role ambiguity or role conflict ever arise for you and, if so, what type of ambiguity or conflict occurs?
4. Does the group have one leader or more than one?
5. What sort of communication structure does the group have?
6. Are there any distinct norms of behaviour for group members? Are these norms about ends or norms about means?

Group cohesiveness: the attractiveness of a group to its members and their desire to retain membership

Group Cohesiveness

The cohesiveness of a group is something that is often immediately obvious and it can be defined as:

> **the attractiveness of the group to its members, together with their motivation to remain as part of the group and resist leaving it.** (Piper *et al.* 1983, p 3)

Because cohesiveness tends to have very strong effects on performance, it is a characteristic that has received a great deal of attention and it is strongly influenced by three sets of factors: those associated with the group itself; those associated with its immediate environment; and those associated with the organisation.

Group factors: characteristics of the group and its members that affect its degree of cohesiveness

Group Factors

* **Member similarity**: people who are alike in their objectives, attitudes and values, will probably derive satisfaction from being in each other's company, whereas a heterogeneous membership makes it more likely that people will split into potentially competitive factions and sub-groups.
* **Past success**: gives people a sense of being part of a winning team, whereas a past record of failure lowers morale and reduces the desire to be associated with a group.
* **Frequency of interaction**: this means that there are many opportunities to identify common interests and shared perceptions.
* **Member turnover**: frequent changes in membership result in a smaller proportion of people who have been socialised into accepting the group's culture and norms.

- **Size:** also reduces cohesion, because in very large groups people can come to regard other members as unfamiliar or anonymous, from which it is but a short step to the formation of sub-groups and factions.
- **Membership criteria:** are also influential. Where it is hard to become a member of a particular group, people can feel that they are part of something exclusive, which in turn prompts them to search for other points they have in common.
- Where **dominance by focal group figures** occurs, it lowers the opportunity for people to share in group decisions, which not only reduces the sense of commitment and ownership of decisions but also the need for members to interact.

Environmental factors: characteristics of a group's environment that influence its degree of cohesiveness

Environmental Factors

- **Group isolation** makes a group physically or geographically remote from other groups. Thus its members can come to think of the group as 'something different'. While this promotes cohesiveness, it can also have negative effects, which will be described when discussing relations between groups.
- **Perceived external threats** promote cohesiveness, because people tend to put internal differences aside to deal with the 'threat'.
- **Favourable self-evaluations** can have much the same effect as past successes. Members tend to feel there is something prestigious about belonging to the group and this prompts individuals to look for similarities with other members.
- **Rewards** also have an effect on cohesion. Where the members of a group are rewarded collectively for its performance, this increases the desirability of group success and members look for ways of cooperating to achieve this.

Organisational factors: organisational features that influence a group's cohesiveness

Organisational Factors

These were briefly identified earlier, when discussing the Homans model.

TIME OUT

In the previous Time Out exercise you identified a group to which you belong and examined its roles and structure. Now reflect further on this group and answer the following questions.

1. Would you consider the group to be a cohesive one in terms of the definition of group cohesiveness given earlier?
2. What evidence have you used to come to this conclusion about the group's cohesiveness?
3. What are the outcomes of this cohesiveness: for example, is it simply that the people like being together in a group, or is it a highly productive group in terms of completing its tasks?
4. From your point of view, can you identify any drawbacks to the cohesiveness of the group?

The Outcomes of Group Cohesiveness

A cohesive group tends to have a stable structure of roles, which brings predictability into its members' lives and increases their willingness to conform to its norms. Whether this is judged to be a satisfactory state of affairs, however, depends on the circumstances surrounding the group and who makes the judgement. In broad terms, group cohesiveness has a number of advantages to an organisation:

- Cohesive groups are much better at meeting their objectives (Keller 1986).
- Members have a higher degree of job satisfaction than those in non-cohesive groups, which shows up in the energy that they devote to achieving group goals (Shaw 1981).
- Morale is likely to be higher and, because people will have worked through and resolved most interpersonal problems, members tend to have fewer work-related anxieties (Seashore 1954).
- There will usually be a lower degree of problem behaviour, such as absenteeism and quitting (Hodgetts 1991).

Other things being equal, therefore, cohesive groups will achieve their goals with fewer resources and a lower expenditure of energy, mainly because energy and resources are directed at the task in hand and not absorbed by internal squabbles. Nevertheless, a very high degree of cohesiveness can have its problems and whether the organisation benefits depends on several factors:

- Productivity, as the organisation would want it, is only likely when the goals that a group has for itself are the same as those of the organisation (Keller 1986). Thus, unless organisational productivity is a group norm, its potential contribution to the organisation will be limited.
- A manager can try to persuade a group to adopt productivity as a behaviourial norm, but if the group is cohesive there is the risk of a backlash, particularly where a group feels that its existing norms are the appropriate ones, in which case the manager's attempts to influence the group will be resisted (Buller and Bell 1986).
- In a cohesive group the *status quo* is comfortable and satisfying, which results in an extremely potent set of forces to resist change.
- Cohesive groups have a higher potential to generate inter-group conflict because a cohesive group is likely to view itself as unique (Dion 1973), which in extreme cases can all too easily result in a perceptual bias against outsiders.
- In certain circumstances, cohesiveness can result in strongly impaired decision making processes.

The last point is a special problem with cohesive groups and since it warrants separate consideration it is dealt with next.

Group Decision Making

At some time most groups need to make a decision and a matter that has received some research attention is whether a decision made by a group is likely to be better than one reached by an individual. While the evidence on this matter is complex and beyond the scope of this chapter, there are three general conclusions that have been drawn:

- First, because there is a levelling effect in groups, working together usually results in a better decision than one that would be produced by the average individual in the group; but not, however, as good a result as that which would be produced by the best individual working alone (Miner 1984).
- Second, groups are more likely than individuals to produce accurate, workable decisions (Michaelsen *et al.* 1989).
- Third, while group decision making has the advantage of involving everybody, it usually takes more time than when an individual works alone. Thus the advantages are only realised where time is available, or implementation requires a decision that everybody accepts (Bottger and Yetton 1988).

All this suggests that there are enough advantages for group decision making to be preferred. However, this conclusion only holds good where sufficient time is available to allow the slower (group) process to work, and only then if nothing stands in the way of the process being an effective one. Because there is some evidence that cohesive groups are particularly prone to an impaired decision making process, the second proviso is a very important one, and two problems can arise, which will be described separately.

Group Polarisation (Risky Shift)

Risky shift: the tendency of groups to make riskier decisions than their members would as individuals

This phenomenon was first identified by Stoner (1961) and has been well documented in a number of subsequent experimental studies (Clark 1971). It describes the tendency of some groups to opt for polarised and much riskier decision alternatives than individuals, the usual explanations for which are:

- **Diffusion of responsibility**. A group decision is less likely to be attributed to a single individual and so blame for one that goes wrong is taken away from any single person and shared by everybody.
- **Valuing risk**. Taking risks is sometimes associated with being macho, dynamic and adventurous; therefore riskier alternatives have some degree of social prestige.
- **Familiarisation**. As the risk is discussed and people in the group become more accustomed to it, it starts to look less risky.
- **Prominence/leadership effects**. The people most likely to speak out in group decision making meetings are often those who have most influence in the group and their suggestions are sometimes adopted without full consideration.

There is much debate about which of these explanations is the most valid and also about the circumstances in which each is most likely to apply (Clark 1971; Schein 1980). Nevertheless, there is a consensus that 'risky shift' is more likely in cohesive groups because they exert strong pressures on individuals to conform, which enables people to abandon their cautious positions and move towards those that involve greater risk.

Groupthink

Groupthink: impaired decision making by a group because the desire for unanimity overrides examining the consequences of a decision

Another process that can stand in the way of effective group decision making is particularly significant for a highly cohesive group that has a strong record of past success. This phenomenon has been dubbed *groupthink* and is defined as:

> a mode of thinking in which people engage when they are deeply involved in a cohesive group, in which strivings for unanimity override motivations to realistically appraise alternative courses of action.
>
> (Janis 1972, p 9)

Janis's research led him to examine famous and controversial political decisions, some of which turned out to be disastrous and highly inappropriate in the circumstances. From this, Janis and his colleagues concluded that in each case the process was characterised by the group just 'drifting along', which gave rise to a sense of false consensus, with nobody questioning suggestions made at an early stage. In his view, the signs of groupthink are unmistakable, and he identifies eight main symptoms:

- An **illusion of invulnerability**, in which almost or all group members overemphasised the group's strengths and played down its weaknesses. This induces a bias towards feeling that its decisions are inevitably correct, taking risks and ignoring danger signals, which should have resulted in the assumption being questioned.
- **Assumptions of morality**, where the group believed that its own aims and means were morally superior and unquestionable. This in turn results in any decision made going unquestioned.
- **Realisations**, in which prior decisions, or emerging information that would necessitate the group looking again at its decision, or its underlying assumptions are swept under the carpet as irrelevancies.
- **Stereotyping**, where its views of competing or opposing groups are distorted and simplified, which results in other groups being perceived as weak, evil, corrupt and unprincipled, and enables the group to disregard any opposition from outside.
- **Self-censorship**, in which members suppress any doubts, disagreements or misgivings to maintain cohesiveness and mutual support.
- **Illusions of unanimity**, which occur because individuals censor any misgivings that they may have, and nobody wants to be the odd one out who challenges what is perceived to be the unanimity of others.
- **Mindguarding**, where some group members take it upon themselves to keep negative views or bad news from reaching others and, in particular, any decision leaders in the group.
- **Direct pressure**, in which anyone who injects a note of questioning or caution is quickly pressured to get in line with the rest of the group.

There are several potential consequences of these symptoms:

- The group tends to curtail discussion and considers only a very limited range of alternatives.
- The search for any information that can be relevant in examining the potential consequences of its decision is limited.
- Since outsiders are not given the same credibility as group members, it fails to import expert opinion when it is needed.
- It does not develop contingency plans.
- Information which can indicate that the decision needs to be reappraised tends to be ignored.

The net result is a failure on the part of the group to audit its own decisions and their potential outcomes. Moreover, dissent and self-criticism, which are sometimes very necessary, are suppressed. Thus Janis argues that groupthink arises from a group's natural tendency to maintain a favourable self-image and notes certain conditions in which it is most likely to arise, for example:

- where a group is highly cohesive
- where it has a strong record of past success
- where it is insulated from the outside world
- where it has high prestige with outsiders
- where there is a strong or powerful leader who promotes his or her own preconceived solutions.

REPLAY

- Mature groups usually evolve a distinctive set of roles, internal communication structures and evolve their own norms, which become a code of behaviour that their members are expected to observe.
- The cohesiveness of a group is influenced by a number of factors particular to the group and its members, together with factors emanating in its environment.
- While cohesive groups are usually more productive than those that are not, there are potential problems inherent in highly cohesive groups, the most significant of which is the possibility of impaired decision making processes.

GROUP EFFECTIVENESS

As will be seen in Chapter 16, one way to evaluate the effectiveness of an organisation is against the criterion of whether it achieves its goals. For a group the equivalent of this is whether it accomplishes its task(s). With a group, however, task accomplishment acutely depends on member satisfaction and, with this in mind, it is normal to evaluate group effectiveness against two criteria:

- **task criteria**, for example, high quantity and quality of work output, speed in completing work, economy in the use of resources
- **member satisfaction criteria**, consisting of cohesiveness, member satisfaction with the group, wanting to be part of it and to remain a member.

These criteria make it clear that an effective group is one in which both task and socio-emotive needs are met and there seems little doubt that this occurs because individual members occupy highly compatible roles. Recent approaches, which deal with the matter of developing effective management teams, often use this idea as a starting point. The best known of these is Belbin's (1993) scheme, which identifies nine key roles that are present in an effective group. Belbin and his co-workers point out that effective and creative groups or teams seldom consist of people who are all of the same type, but require a balanced mix of individual characteristics, so that the positive attributes of each person complement those of the others. The nine types of person needed, together with their main characteristics, are given in Table 11.1.

For the most part, independent empirical studies show strong support for Belbin's assertion that teams which are well-balanced in terms of different member roles are the most effective (Senior 1997b). However, although there is some debate about whether the number of distinctly different roles is as high as nine (Fisher *et al*. 1998), and for smaller groups it might be necessary for some people to occupy more than one role.

Table 11.1 Outline of Belbin's team role types (adapted from Belbin 1993)

Team role type	Personal characteristics	Strengths	Potential weaknesses	Contributions to team task
Implementor (IMP)	Disciplined Tough minded Reliable Tolerant	Conscientious Self-controlled Outward looking Practical	Conservative Lacks flexibility	Often performs tasks that others do not want. Systematic and efficient planning to transform plans into practical actions
Coordinator (CO)	Calm Self-confident Trusting Outgoing Dominant	Impartial Self-disciplined Enthusiastic Positive thinker	Average ability Average intellect	Organises team operations and resources to meet its objectives. Good at evaluating and handling people and maximising team members' potential
Shaper (SH)	Highly strung Outgoing	Dynamic Achievement-orientated	Argumentative Impatient Provocative	Establishes objectives and priorities. Often has an arousing, challenging and motivating effect on others, but at times can be disruptive
Plant (PL)	Introverted Individualist Serious minded	High intellect Knowledgeable Unorthodox Creative thinker	Aloof Impractical Loner Lacks attention to detail	The ideas person who brings innovation and creativity to goals and activities
Resource Investigator (RI)	Low anxiety Sociable Extrovert Enquiring	Versatile Innovative Communicative Strong social skills	Can easily become bored	Good at creating useful contacts outside the team. Gathers useful resources and manages interactions across team boundary
Monitor-Evaluator (ME)	Sober Unemotional Detached Hard-headed	High intellect Discreet Objective	Uninspiring	Helps team analyse and evaluate objectively and prevents impulsive decisions being made
Team Worker (TW)	Gregarious Sensitive Sociable	Team player Responsive to others	Indecisive in crisis	The builder of team relationships and team spirit. Helps reduce levels of interpersonal conflict
Completer-Finisher (CF)	Conscientious Anxiety prone	Perseverance Perfectionist Attention to detail	A worrier	High contribution of effort and strong attention to detail. Good at planning and carrying through. Helps ensure team progresses the activities necessary to achieve goals and deadlines
Specialist (SP)	Single minded Self-starter	Dedicated	Dwells on technicalities	Provides knowledge and skills in rare supply. Only contributes on a narrow front

In addition, there are also some criticisms of the methodology Belbin used to derive his conclusions. Nevertheless, the scheme has intriguing implications for organisations in current conditions. For example, Conger (1993) argues that in today's delayered and downsized organisations, empowered employees tend to be highly interdependent, which puts a strong emphasis on working in groups, much of which occurs in temporary task groups and project teams. For this reason it can be vital to assemble teams that function effectively from the start. If some of the characteristics of potential team members are known before the team assembles (for example, their preferred team roles) this enhances the prospects of assembling a team which knits together very quickly. To this end, Belbin and his colleagues have developed a questionnaire – the Belbin Self-perception Inventory – which enables people to identify their preferred team roles. While there are questions about the reliability of this instrument (Furnham *et al.* 1993), with care it can be used to slot appropriate people into a team.

RELATIONS BETWEEN GROUPS: INTERGROUP CONFLICT

Since groups are not usually independent entities, the effectiveness of an organisation as a whole can often depend on smooth relationships between them. Nevertheless, each group tends to be judged by how well it performs, and this can sometimes put cooperation with other groups at risk. Therefore, some degree of conflict or competition between groups may well be inevitable.

In addition, a cohesive group has its own norms and values, which means that it can put its own goals before those of the organisation or another group. Thus, cooperation between groups cannot be taken for granted. Moreover, since an organisation's structural design often creates interdependencies between formal groups, the goals and activities of one can impinge upon those of another, and from this it is but a short step to a highly competitive situation, which can turn into outright hostility.

From an organisational viewpoint, intergroup conflict is clearly counter-productive. It tends to result in winners and losers, and the after-effects can sometimes be as disruptive as the conflict itself. For instance, winning groups can become extremely complacent and develop feelings of superiority and invulnerability that make them susceptible to groupthink. Losers can become tense and demoralised, which makes them all too anxious to pick up the cudgels again.

The structure of an organisation is often fertile ground in which intergroup conflict can flourish because it establishes different groups and gives them separate identities. Thus each group can come to see itself as 'different' from others. Over time, there can be a tendency for people to view their own group as the 'in group' (the one about which everything is correct) and other groups as 'out groups' (those that are nowhere near as correct), simply because they are different. Indeed, some scholars believe that when permanent groups with different identities are established, some degree of polarisation is bound to occur (Campbell 1965).

In addition, structure sometimes places groups in competition and, as a result, perceptions of the other group can become distorted, with each one perceiving the other as a distinct threat, or even a potential 'enemy'. This has a number of predictable consequences. To prop up their own morale and sense of 'rightness', members tend to overevaluate their own group, its members tend to develop an increased liking for each other, and the pressure to conform to group norms gets even stronger. Further confirmation of its goodness is also obtained by denigrating the other group, which is now firmly cast in the role of 'the enemy'. The other group then has little alternative but to respond in a like way, and there is a great deal of evidence to suggest that the 'in group' and 'out group' phenomenon can arise even where there is no conflict.

Underlying all this may be extremely potent forces at an individual psychological level. Allport (1954b) notes that telling a person that he or she is better than somebody else is the easiest idea to sell in this world. Thus, when an individual devalues another person, he or she gets an immediate boost to self-esteem. Group membership gives people an opportunity to play this game on a larger scale and enhance their self-esteem in three very powerful and mutually supporting ways:

- It gives a positive value to those things which distinguish the 'in group' from the 'out group'.
- As individuals, this enables them to consider themselves as different from and superior to other individuals.
- They receive signals from other people in the 'in group' that their judgement is sound.

TIME OUT

Reflect further on the group you examined in the previous Time Out exercise and answer the following questions.

1. To what extent do you consider the group an effective one in terms of the two sets of criteria given above; that is, the task criterion and the member satisfaction criterion?
2. Do you feel one set of criteria is considered more important by the group? Are both considered equally important? Or does their relative importance vary from time to time?
3. Now consider Belbin's list of nine team roles (Table 11.1). Which one do you fit most closely, and can you identify other members of the group who fit some of the other roles?
4. Does the group have any tendencies to compete or come into conflict with other groups, and what circumstances are likely to give rise to this state of affairs?

REPLAY

- From an organisational perspective, an effective group is one that achieves its goals, but this is only one criterion of effectiveness; the other is whether a group satisfies the needs of its members and, unless this criterion is met, it is doubtful if the first will be achieved.
- Effective groups are likely to consist of people with different patterns of skills and abilities so that the attributes of one group member complement those of the others.
- While conflict between groups is not inevitable, there are a number of structural features in most organisations that are likely to result in groups competing with each other, and this can all too easily become outright conflict.

GROUPS AND JOB DESIGN

As noted in Chapter 7, job design can have a huge impact on the motivational state of people. For the most part, traditional approaches to job design focus exclusively on individuals, but in the last three decades there has been an increasing awareness of the need to take account of some of the positive influences that groups can have on their members. Thus, at the present time, the most popular methods of trying to bring about improvements in motivation and performance are pitched firmly at the level of the workgroup (Alford 1994).

While initiatives of this type have a wide variety of names, for example semi-autonomous work groups, high performance work systems and, more recently, team-working, all of them are group-based job designs that aim to bring about a level of performance that is superior to that achieved with previous, individual designs. Although his description refers explicitly to high performance work teams, Vaill (1982) nicely captures what is intended to result. That is, a workgroup which:

- has excellent performance in terms of known external standards
- exceeds expectations by performing at a higher level than that which is assumed to be its potential best
- strives to makes constant improvements by performing excellently in comparison to its prior level of performance
- is judged by informed observers as having substantially better performance than other comparable groups
- is efficient because it achieves its level of performance with fewer resources than are normally assumed to be necessary
- is seen as an exemplar and a source of ideas and inspiration
- is seen to achieve the ideals of the culture within which it is located.

Socio-technical Systems

Group-based work designs owe much to the pioneering work of Trist *et al.* (1963) which resulted in what is now known as the *socio-technical systems* approach to work design. In outline terms the approach holds that:

Socio-technical systems: an approach to work design in which the people and the technical systems (and the relationship between them) are accorded equal importance

- two major organisational systems interact at the point at which work is undertaken: the technical system, which includes the task to be completed, the machinery and tools used, maintenance, location, etc.; and the social system, which includes the social and psychological needs of the people involved

- it is never possible to completely satisfy the needs of one system without failing to satisfy the needs of the other

- an effective design sub-optimises to some extent by aiming to satisfy (so far as this is possible) the most important demands of both systems.

In practice this usually means that individual jobs are deliberately clustered into groups in which people are interdependent (Cherns 1987). In addition, the group that results is often allowed a great deal of autonomy in the way that it addresses the task in hand (Cummings 1978).

Semi-autonomous Work Groups

Semi-autonomous work groups: self-managed teams that have a high degree of responsibility for their own work activities

Semi-autonomous work groups, or as they are sometimes called self-managed work teams, are an important development in job design that emerged as a natural outcome of the socio-technical systems approach. The best-known example of the use of this design started in the mid-1970s in Volvo, the Swedish car manufacturer. Hitherto, Volvo had produced cars using assembly line methods, which are widely used in vehicle manufacture throughout the world, and, in common with other mass production industries, it had experienced the usual problems associated with extreme job simplification, for example low employee motivation, poor quality, etc. On opening a new plant at Kalmar in 1974, Volvo introduced radically different work methods. Instead of a moving conveyor with workers completing very small, simple tasks, cellular manufacturing techniques were employed. The total number of tasks of the whole conveyor line was distributed between a number of work cells, each of which consisted of a team of between 15 and 20 workers. Teams were given complete responsibility for completing an entire job, for example the car's electrical system, its upholstery and trim, or the transmission and brakes. Within each cell, workers normally divided themselves into a number of smaller teams and, instead of a continuous conveyor, the vehicles were mounted on computer-controlled carriers that moved the car from cell to cell.

Cells were responsible for their own scheduling, planning and work allocation within the group and, in new plants opened later at Torslanda, Tuve and Uddevalla, group responsibilities were extended to include a measure of decision making responsibility for hiring and training new workers and holiday scheduling. Thus the essential features of the work design were:

- Goals (output and quality) were set for each group of workers (the cell) but the group itself decided the most appropriate way to achieve them.
- Groups had a large measure of choice and discretion over allocation of jobs, planning and control of the work.
- A group policed its own activities with little or no external supervision; indeed, although supervisors still existed, they tended to become advisers to groups rather than overseers.
- Any evaluation of the group was based on its performance as a whole, with evaluation of individuals being done within the group, by the group.
- To some extent, the group became responsible for ensuring that it had the necessary spread of skills and abilities to complete its tasks.

Although some tensions were evident in supervisors and managers, who felt somewhat uncomfortable and threatened by the greater autonomy of workers, most reports of the Volvo experience emerged in highly positive terms, for example enhanced job satisfaction, productivity and quality (Bailey 1983). Thus, semi-autonomous work groups appeared to be a resounding success story and a number of American firms were prompted to try the method, notably General Foods at its manufacturing plant at Topeka in Kansas. Because it gave significant improvements in quality, productivity, job satisfaction, cost reductions and a lowered incidence of problem behaviours such as absenteeism, this initiative has also been widely cited as a success (Walton 1977). However, a subsequent review and analysis by Whitsett and Yorks (1983) calls some of these findings into question and points out that sufficient tensions arose in the Topeka initiative to merit a strong degree of caution about the use of the method.

Nevertheless, studies of other semi-autonomous work groups have also found that people tend to have higher levels of job satisfaction and organisational commitment than those whose jobs are designed to more traditional criteria (Cordery *et al.* 1991). Thus it would not be surprising if these methods also give enhanced productivity. Perhaps more importantly, organisational conditions that have become widespread across the last two decades might well make something akin to semi-autonomous groups inevitable. For instance, Peters (1985) argues that this work design is entirely consistent with the increased emphasis on flatter organisational structures, quality, multi-skilling and flexibility that are required in an age of globalised competition. For this reason it is to the current version of this group-based design that the discussion turns next.

Teamworking

Teamworking: the current name for use of semi-autonomous work groups

Teamworking is by no means a new idea and in many respects it only amounts to a new and currently fashionable title for the use of semi-autonomous work groups. What is different, however, is that whereas semi-autonomous group designs were used in a small number of organisations, teamworking seems to have caught the imagination of managers, and it is now impossible to open a management journal without finding an article that extols its virtues.

Across the last two decades many firms have downsized and delayered. While this was originally a response to economic conditions, these steps now tend to be seen as an essential prerequisite for survival in the fast-moving, globalised marketplace. This, it is argued, requires that organisations take a number of steps, such as: removing surplus manpower; using much flatter hierarchies in order to make decisions faster; using multi-skilled, highly adaptable workforces that have a strong customer orientation; and developing the ability to change quickly and smoothly with minimal disruption.

To a large extent these characteristics are more likely to be obtained if responsibility for day-to-day operational problem solving and innovation is devolved to the lowest possible level (Colenso 1997). However, a lot more is required than simply telling people that from now on they will be 'teamworking'. In theory, teamworking requires that a large measure of responsibility for the day-to-day running of an organisation is devolved to an empowered workforce that is able to cope with a more dynamic set of conditions. Moreover, the decisions and actions of one team can have a strong impact on the performance of other teams, and this occurs in a situation where there are fewer managers to coordinate their activities. For this reason it can be argued that teams need to have a more strategic orientation to performance, and this often runs counter to the prior work experiences of team members, many of whom simply required to focus on working hard (Parker *et al.* 1997). Therefore, a great deal of preparatory work is needed to introduce teamworking and Holbeche (1997) sets out a number of cardinal rules for doing so:

- **Communication,** employees need to be kept well informed of what is required, why it is required, why change is necessary and of the new culture, values and beliefs of the organisation.

- **Leadership,** a lean organisation often needs to rely on temporary teams, which not only requires training and support for people, but also for leadership to be fostered in team leaders so that they carry people with them, without having to rely on formal authority.

- **Careers,** the organisation needs to establish a career framework in which people can develop their skills and enhance their employability.

- **Development,** the lean organisation is only likely to grow and retain skilled, flexible people if it invests heavily in development, which not only means training, but also creating an environment in which people continually learn.

- **Reward and recognition,** an appropriate reward system that recognises performance of the team and its individual members needs to be established.

Research conducted for the Institute of Personnel and Development (see Kinnie and Purcell 1998) bears out many of Holbeche's assertions. For example, that how team-working is introduced has a tremendous impact on how well teams perform. Thus, a teamworking initiative requires a great deal of prior thought and planning before its introduction, otherwise it may well result in the opposite of what it is intended to achieve.

So far, the evidence on whether teamworking achieves the outcomes that managers desire (usually productivity and lowered costs) is very mixed. There have been a number of reported success stories (Banker *et al*. 1996; Macduffie 1995) and one such initiative appears as a case study at the end of this chapter. Conversely, there are many other examples that report the abject failure of teamworking initiatives (Cully *et al*. 1999; Wilkinson 1998; Gallie *et al*. 1998). Indeed, in some cases so-called teamworking has been used to drag employees into a method of working where jobs were no more interesting, enriched or empowered – merely harder and more exhausting (Danford 1998; Delbridge *et al*. 2000).

The problem is that although there are a high proportion of managers who lay claim to having adopted teamworking (perhaps because it gives the appearance of being a firm that is on the cutting edge of modern developments), in practice, the number who have actually done so is far less. For example, in Germany, where there was a similar glut of firms who reported to be engaged in introducing teamwork in the late 1990s, less than 3 per cent of them actually persevered with the initiative (Minssen 2005). Teamworking, it should be noted, requires senior managers to abandon control by hierarchy and treat workers as mature experts in their own right who are coordinated by team-leaders, rather than remaining as the passive recipients of orders. Problematically, even in Germany, which in other respects has highly democratic systems of control, managers are still firmly wedded to hierarchical control methods.

Much the same can be said of what goes on in Great Britain, where there has been a great deal of 'talking-up' teamworking, with very little teamworking in practice. For instance, an extensive survey by Hales (2005) set-out to determine whether the role of first-line managers (formerly the supervisors and foremen of the 'pre-teamworking' age) has changed. Specifically, Hales sought to discover whether there has been a significant trend for supervisors to become 'team-leaders' who coordinate the activities of teams and perform more managerial tasks, because team members are now part of a workforce that now largely manages its own activities. On this matter Hales reports that for the most part supervisors are still heavily involved in the direct supervision of workers. Why? Because this is what most senior managers want them to do with their time. Indeed, he concluded that, by and large, so-called self-managed teams are not trusted by senior managers to manage their own activities.

OVERVIEW AND CONCLUSIONS

Groups are fundamental to the structure of society and have a prominent place in work organisations. Formal groups are established by the structure of an organisation, but if groups are only viewed in terms of what the organisation wants them to achieve, their role in serving a number of important social purposes tends to be ignored.

Groups often become like societies in miniature. To make life more predictable they evolve a structure of complementary roles and a set of rules (norms) to regulate the behaviour of their members and, if necessary, pressure to conform is brought to bear on people who step out of line. Self-regulation of this type is a characteristic of mature groups, but to reach this degree of maturity fairly clear role structures and behavioural norms must have emerged. For this to occur, it is usually necessary for a group to go through a number of characteristic stages of development. What emerges, however, is not simply a function of the personality and attitudes of the individuals involved; a host of important features of the work context also play a part in shaping its characteristics and subsequent behaviour.

Cohesion is an important feature of some groups and in one that is cohesive, people identify strongly with the group and its aims. Although a cohesive group is often more effective in achieving its aims, the aims do not necessarily correspond with those of the organisation. Cohesion can also have implications for the effectiveness of group processes, notably how it reaches its decisions. Too much cohesion can also give rise to the 'in group' and 'out group' phenomenon, in which a group can all too easily come into conflict with others in the organisation. For these reasons the role structure of a group can be crucial. Effective groups and teams – those that meet task requirements as well as socio-emotive needs – usually need an appropriate mixture of different roles.

Largely for economic reasons, current fashions in work design often seek to cash-in on the positive outcomes of working in groups, usually under the generic banner of 'teamworking'.

FURTHER READING

Ackroyd S and P Thompson (1999) *Organisational Misbehaviour*, London: Sage. An amusing but nevertheless serious academic study of groups, and how they often misbehave to pursue their own ends.

Adair, J (1986) *Effective Team Building*, London: Pan. A very easy-to-read book, the contents of which are based on its author's extensive research.

Belbin, RM (1993) *Team Roles at Work*, Oxford: Butterworth Heinemann. A comprehensive description of the team roles concept and its application in organisations.

Brown, R (2000) *Group Processes*, Oxford: Blackwell. A recent and thorough review and assessment of research and theoretical developments on group processes.

Ericksen, J and L Dyer (2004) Right from the start: exploring the effects of early team events on subsequent project team development and performance, *Administrative Science Quarterly* 49(2): 438–471. Reports an empirical study of high performing and low performing temporary project teams and their characteristics.

Guzzo RA and W Dickson (1998) Teams in organisations: recent research on performance and effectiveness, *Annual Review of Psychology* 49: 307–338. A review of recent research on groups and teams. Rather technical in places but full of useful information.

Hayes, N (1997) *Successful Team Management*, London: Thomson. A useful book that covers research and theory on groups/teams, and which also makes practical suggestions for improving their performance.

Hogg, MA and GM Vaughan (1998) *Social Psychology*, Hemel Hempstead: Prentice Hall. An introductory textbook containing an excellent chapter on basic group processes.

Marchington, M (2000) Teamwork and employee involvement: terminology, evaluation and context. In S Proctor and F Mueller (eds) *Teamworking*, Basingstoke: Macmillan. A useful commentary on teamworking, which includes a number of criteria that need to be satisfied if teamworking is to work well.

Proctor, S and F Mueller (eds) (2000) *Teamworking*, London: Macmillan. A book of readings with contributions by several prominent authors, that brings together many different perspectives which reflect current views on teamworking.

Sinclair, A (1992) The tyranny of a team ideology, *Organisation Studies* 13(4): 611–626. The paper presents a damming indictment of managerial obsession its latest panacea: teamworking.

Spector, P (1995) *Industrial and Organisational Psychology: Research and Practice*, Chichester: Wiley. A wide-ranging book that contains easy-to-read chapters on groups.

West, M (1994) *Effective Teamwork*, Leicester: BPS Books. A practical guide to teams and teamworking, albeit one with a 'how to do it' flavour.

West, M, D Tjosvold and K Smith (2004) *Teamworking: International Perspectives*, London: Wiley. A useful commentary on the do's and don'ts of teamworking in an international context.

Whelan, SA (1999) *Creating Effective Work Teams*, London: Sage. Another 'how to do it' book that makes practical recommendations for building high performance teams.

Womack, JP, DT Jones and D Roos (1990) *The Machine that Changed the World: The Triumph of Lean Production*, New York: Macmillan. By now a classic that in a rather 'over-the-top' way enthuses about Japanese lean production methods, which have now been widely adopted in the West. The book has been heavily criticised in academic circles as being rampantly managerialist.

CASE STUDY 11.1: Self-managed teams at Vesuvius

Vesuvius is located in Ayrshire in Scotland and is part of the Cookson group, a large diversified conglomerate with plants located in 21 countries, that that makes specialist ceramics and other components for the steel industry.

Realising the competitive nature of life as part of a multinational conglomerate, Vesuvius wanted to be seen as a high performer in the group. Thus, in the early 1990s, it reviewed its operational policies and procedures and, in particular, those concerning the use of human resources. In the mid-1990s it embarked on a change programme built around the business excellence model derived by the European Foundation for Quality Management (EPQM). This involved building a culture in which production staff were to be grouped into self-managing teams, who would take full responsibility for improving performance in all the tasks they undertake. The chosen vehicle for this initiative was the adoption of 'teamworking' and to facilitate this there was a radical break with the past, in which many barriers needed to be overcome. For example:

- across a three year period the diverse wage rates for different production activities were replaced with a simplified single wage structure that effectively resulted in a salaried workforce
- multi-skilling was introduced to give labour-flexibility across all jobs and production workers were re-trained to enable them to do all jobs within their respective teams
- teams took responsibility for all the tasks they undertook, from materials used, problem solving and quantity and quality of output
- two-way communication meetings between management and workers were instituted and although this gave rise to initial apprehensions on the part of trade unions, these eventually subsided when it was made clear that there would be no job losses
- foremen, who had hitherto performed a first-line supervisory role, were initially apprehensive about job security and also needed to be re-trained to become 'facilitators' rather than overseers.

While these changes all took time to implement, the management of Vesuvius is well pleased with the outcomes. For example, enthusiasm, job satisfaction and satisfaction with health and safety, as measured by employee opinion surveys, has increased significantly. Financial turnover has also increased by nearly 50 per cent over a five year period, market share has grown, the number of customer complaints has decreased and costs have been lowered. Indeed, so convinced is the management of Vesuvius that these outcomes are the result of the introduction of teamworking, that it has been extended to all other functions and departments in the company.

Source: Adapted from Arkin, A (1999a) Peak practice, *People Management*, 11 November: pp 57–59

Questions

1. After reading the above case material, to what extent do you feel that the decision to adopt teamworking at Vesuvius was an appropriate one?

2. What do you feel was the main factor that prompted the managers at Vesuvius to pursue this initiative?

▶

3. What of the outcomes of the initiative; in your view, have the outcomes been worthwhile in view of the considerable disruption and expenditure that was likely to have been incurred?

4. From whose perspective, the company and its managers, or the employees who had to adopt the changes, have you answered questions 1, 2 and 3?

5. Now answer the questions again, but this time answering them from the perspective of the party you ignored the first time through.

REVIEW AND DISCUSSION QUESTIONS

1. Explain the criteria that need to be satisfied in order for a number of people to be considered to be a group.

2. Explain the difference between the two types of group commonly found in organisations, and what distinguishes a 'team' from other types of group.

3. Explain why groups are able to exert such a powerful influence over the behaviour of their individual members and describe some of the aspects of individual behaviour that can be influenced by a group.

4. Describe the four stages of the group formation process and explain what occurs in each one.

5. Explain what is meant by group cohesiveness, the three sets of factors that influence a group's degree of cohesion and whether cohesiveness is a good or a bad thing.

6. Describe two phenomena that can affect the quality of a group's decision making, and why and in what ways the phenomena have these effects.

Chapter 12

Leaders and Leadership:
The Foundations

LEARNING OUTCOMES

After studying this chapter you should be able to:

- define leadership and distinguish between leadership and management

- distinguish between descriptive and functional approaches to the subject

- describe trait theories of leadership, their general assumptions, and their strengths and weaknesses

- describe style theories of leadership, their general assumptions and their strengths and weaknesses

INTRODUCTION

In Chapter 11, which explored the nature of groups, it was noted that a mature group has a structured system of roles, one of which is its leader. This chapter and the one that follows both deal with the topic of leadership, a concept that has long fascinated the organisational sciences. Because there are many different theories of leadership, to avoid overwhelming the reader with more information than can be digested in a single sitting, the topic is covered in two chapters. This one deals with traditional ideas, while Chapter 13 covers more recent approaches.

The chapter starts from basic principles by defining leadership and this is followed by a section that distinguishes between two very different approaches to the study of leadership: the descriptive approach and the functional approach. The next matter to be examined is whether, and to what extent, the words 'leader' and 'manager' mean the same thing, which is followed by a brief examination of the significance of leadership to organisations. The chapter then goes on to explore two of the earliest ideas in the area, and these are discussed in the sequence in which they emerged. The first to be considered is trait theory, which deals with the attributes and personal qualities that leaders are assumed to possess. This is followed by an explanation and description of style theory and its derivatives, which focuses on the behaviour that is associated with effective leadership. Finally, as a prelude to Chapter 13, traditional and contingency approaches to leadership theory are compared.

THE NATURE OF LEADERSHIP

There are many definitions of leadership, but one that is frequently quoted is:

> **the process whereby one individual influences other group members towards the attainment of defined group, or organisational goals.** (Barron and Greenberg 1990)

Unfortunately, this tells us very little. For example it says nothing about how the influence process occurs which would, for example, cover situations where coercion is used; something that is beyond what most people associate with leadership. The main problem, however, is that it infers that leadership is a one-way process, in which followers passively respond to what a leader does, or what a leader is, which tends to oversimplify the processes at work. Another, but unrelated problem, which confuses matters even more is that the word leadership has two commonly accepted meanings: first, to describe a process, in which influence is used to direct and coordinate the activities of a group towards its objectives; and, second, to express the idea that a group of people perceive that their leader has certain attributes or characteristics that enable him or her to exert influence over them (Jago 1982). Taken together, a number of important implications arise from these two meanings:

* Since a leader's influence is non-coercive, followers must consent to be influenced with a view to achieving something.
* Although this can simply mean that the group completes its tasks, it is possible that it might want something else as well; in Chapter 11, for example, it was explained that group members invariably have socio-emotive needs in addition to task needs and, if they consent to be influenced by someone, it can be because they anticipate that the person will bring about satisfaction of both sets of needs.

- Finally, since followers may well believe (but do not know for certain) that these outcomes will be achieved, leadership tends to be conferred on someone that followers perceive they can trust to make the desired outcomes more likely.

With these points in mind, a working definition of leadership used for this and the following chapter is:

a process in which leader and followers interact in a way that enables the leader to influence the actions of the followers in a non-coercive way, towards the achievement of certain aims or objectives.

TWO APPROACHES TO THE STUDY OF LEADERSHIP

Descriptive approach to leadership: theories that describe leadership in terms of either what a person is or his or her distinctive style of behaviour

All theories of leadership adopt one or other of two approaches. The *descriptive approach to leadership* focuses on whether a leader is a special type of person and/or whether there is a most appropriate style of behaviour for a leader to adopt. For the most part this approach has dominated theory and research into leadership and the majority of theories covered in this chapter, and the one that follows, fall into this category. However, while theories of this type have much to say that is important in understanding leadership, they fail to address a very important point, which, phrased as a question, is: 'What functions does a person have to perform vis-à-vis a group in order to be considered by them as their leader?' This matter is addressed by the *functional approach to leadership* and, since theories of this type have important implications for whether leadership and management are the same thing, it is appropriate to examine this approach in greater depth.

Functional approach to leadership: theories that explain leadership in terms of the functions performed by the leader with respect to the followers

The Functional Approach to Leadership

As noted above, theories of this type address the question of what functions a person needs to perform in order to be considered as a leader by others. A number of different ways has been used to try to answer this question. For example, Scott and Podsakoff (1982) approach the question from an operant conditioning perspective (see Chapter 6). Starting from Bowers and Seashore's (1966) argument that leadership is 'behaviour that results in a difference in the behaviour of others', they reasoned that since leaders get psychological rewards when they successfully get followers to do something, follower behaviour prompts leaders to behave in a certain way to obtain this reward. This gives a unique perspective on the leader–follower relationship by introducing the idea of *reciprocal causality*.

Reciprocal causality: the idea that followers affect leader behaviour as well as the leader influencing followers

Most traditional models of leader behaviour simply assume that leaders affect the behaviour of followers, which treats followers as passive recipients of influence. However, this oversimplifies matters by failing to acknowledge that while the behaviour of a leader can have effects on followers, it is equally true that there are effects in the opposite direction (Green 1975). For this reason a potentially fruitful way to view leadership is from the perspective of social exchange theory. Perhaps the simplest way to express this idea is that leaders are able to be leaders if they provide something that followers want and, in return, followers provide something that the leader wants. Two models which adopt this perspective will be described in what follows, and while neither of them is explicitly framed in social exchange terms, both are capable of being interpreted in this way.

Action-centred Leadership

The action-centred theory of leadership is based on extensive research by John Adair (1984), which has subsequently been developed into a highly successful method of leadership training by the Industrial Society. Adair points out that effective leadership consists of meeting three sets of interrelated needs, which give rise to three functions that a leader must perform:

- **The task-related function**, meeting the needs of the group to complete its task by helping members to clarify the task and its nature, and enabling them to overcome barriers to completion.
- **The team-related function**, meeting the group's need to hold together as a cohesive unit.
- **The individually orientated function**, ensuring that the diverse but important individual needs of group members are met.

In terms of group performance, the theory explicitly recognises that these three areas affect each other. For instance, a leader who focuses too much on the task can find that individual needs are not met, and this in turn can demoralise certain individuals to the extent that the group becomes fragmented. This is demonstrated symbolically by Adair in his overlapping circles model, shown in Figure 12.1.

In practical terms, balancing these three functions requires that the leader must have three vital skills:

- An awareness of the group's processes, which requires knowing the characteristics of people in the group and displaying some sensitivity to the finer nuances of behaviour, in order to be able to diagnose how the group interacts, and take remedial action to resolve any difficulties.

- An ability to be able to spot which of the three functional areas needs attention.

- The interpersonal skills that are necessary to bring about changes to achieve the right balance between the three functions.

Figure 12.1
Interaction of task, team maintenance and individual needs (Adair 1979)

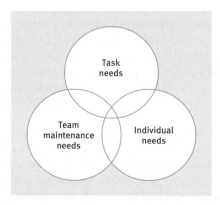

From this it follows that being effective as a leader is not just a matter of choosing a specific style of behaviour, but arriving at an appropriate balance between the three functions. What is crucially important is that one of these three functions requires the leader to serve the interests of the group as a whole. Indeed, Grint (2005) argues that it is followers who (silently) teach the leader how to lead. Or to put matters another way, followers create leaders by making (tacit) demands to be treated in a particular way (Nicholson 2005). This means that leadership is a social function and essentially a process of facilitating social exchange (Barker 2001). In most circumstances the leader will be held accountable by people inside and outside the group for whether it accomplishes its task. Thus if he or she serves the interests of the group as a whole, and in return the team completes the task, leader and followers exchange performances that are important to each other.

The Vertical Dyad Linkage (VDL) Model

Most conventional leadership models have the same fundamental weakness. They assume that a leader uses the same behaviourial style with all group members (Danserau *et al.* 1975). However, unless people are identical in all respects (and this is very unlikely), a leader would usually take account of peoples' idiosyncrasies. Thus, Danserau and his colleagues believe that it is more realistic to view leader–member relations dyadically (in pairs), in which a group consists of a set of vertical dyadic linkages, with the leader as one person in a particular dyad and another group member as the other one. Strictly speaking, this means that there will be as many dyadic relationships as there are subordinates but, to simplify matters, Danserau and his colleagues deal only with two distinct sub-groups of subordinates, each of which has a different relationship with the leader.

In-group members: those on whom the leader relies to go beyond the minimum level of performance required

In-group members are those who, in the leader's eyes, can be relied upon to go beyond the minimum level of effort and initiative required to undertake the group's task. These people are often self-starters who obtain satisfaction from added responsibility, and the leader tends to form a more open relationship with them, in which they are taken into his or her confidence and allowed a fair amount of latitude in how they do things. Since this is often the relationship that people of this type wish to have with the leader, they respond by giving more than the minimum.

Out-group members: people who give only a basic level of performance

Out-group members are people who the leader recognises as not wanting to go beyond performing at a basic level. Therefore, so long as they do what is necessary, they are not usually pressed to do more, and this gives another distinct type of relationship. These people are usually more distant from the leader, who simply uses the power of his or her position (rather than person-orientated behaviour) to obtain the required task performance. As such, expressed in terms of social exchange, there are clearly two different types of relationship at work. In-group members obtain different benefits from those people in the out-group and incur different costs in doing so. In return, the manager obtains different benefits from each sub-group and incurs different costs to reap these benefits.

There is a fairly strong body of evidence to show that leader–member relations in groups are often structured like this (Dunegan *et al.* 1992). Moreover, research indicates that appropriate patterns of leader–member exchange have positive effects in terms of member satisfaction, group effectiveness and productivity (Wayne *et al.* 1997), all of which has strong implications for how leadership effectiveness is conceptualised.

It is all too common to find that effectiveness is viewed purely in terms of productivity or task completion, with a consequent neglect of the ways in which these outcomes are obtained. By focusing on leader–follower relations, Danserau and his colleagues provide one explanation for some of the processes that may be at work; for example, an effective leader may be someone who is able to perform two vital functions vis-à-vis subordinates:

- an ability to identify those subordinates who have needs to perform in-group roles and those who would prefer to be in the out-group
- to follow this up with different but equally appropriate behaviours towards the two sub–groups, so that each makes its respective contribution to the group task.

Moreover, detailed research work continues to this day to flesh-out finer nuances of the leader–member relationship (see, for example, Sparrowe and Linden 2005; Erdogan *et al.* 2006).

The great strength of functional theories such as these is that leadership is treated as a negotiated role, concerned with meeting the needs of both followers and leader. This avoids the trap of dealing only with situations where a leader is endowed with formal organisational authority, and for this reason it is now time to consider the important question of whether there is a difference between being a manager and being a leader.

LEADERSHIP AND MANAGEMENT

The words 'leader' and 'leadership' carry a great deal of prestige in modern society and, since there is a tendency to use the words interchangeably, some managers probably believe that the positions they occupy confer the mantle of leadership upon them. Thus it is important to examine whether leadership and management are synonymous; are they, for example, just different words that express the same idea?

One way to address this question is to examine the widely acknowledged functions of management. These are usually taken to be some combination of planning, organising, directing and controlling the use of resources at his or her disposal, and when someone is appointed as a manager he or she is normally granted a degree of formal authority over subordinates, which in turn gives some capability to influence their actions. All this really means, however, is that power has been conferred from above and, in technical terms, the person occupies a position of *headship*, which means that a manager can be defined as:

Headship: the formal authority over subordinates granted as part of a manager's position

> A person formally appointed to a role in the organisational hierarchy, associated with which is the formal authority (within prescribed limits) to direct the actions of subordinates. Among other things the role is concerned with some combination of planning, organising, directing and controlling the activities of human resources towards the achievement of set organisational objectives.

Most people intuitively feel that there is more to leadership than simply wielding formal, delegated authority, and the following can be noted:

- From the earlier discussion of the functional approach, leadership is a two-way process, in which both leader and followers get some of their needs satisfied.

- A person does not become a leader simply because he or she wants to take on the role, but because other people confer on him or her the authority to influence their behaviour, which essentially means that leadership is conferred from below, not from above, as in headship.

- Would-be leaders will probably have their own ideas about how the role should be performed, for instance how much influence they are entitled to exert over followers, and followers will have expectations about how the leader should behave, including the amount of influence the leader should have over their behaviour.

- Whether they are prepared to concede the amount of influence that a leader wants will probably depend on whether this is felt to be an acceptable price to pay for satisfaction of their needs.

- From this it follows that the leader–follower relationship is a potentially fragile state of affairs, because, if conditions change, the needs of both leader and followers can change. Thus it is possible that the group will come to see the leader as an inappropriate person for the new situation and, if this happens, pressure can be brought to bear on the leader to change his or her behaviour, and if these moves are not successful, attempts can sometimes be made to replace the leader with someone else.

For these reasons, a leader can be defined as:

> Someone who occupies a role which involves conforming to a set of behavourial norms and expectations emanating from followers, in return for which they confer on the leader a degree of power that (within prescribed limits) allows the leader to influence their actions.

Where does all this leave the manager in terms of being a leader? Because a manager has some formal authority to influence subordinate behaviour, he or she clearly has a flying start in coming to occupy a role of leadership. However, just because the authority is there, it does not mean that subordinates will willingly assent to its use. They may simply comply with instructions, and this is far from being a situation where leadership is at work. Therefore, although managers can be leaders as well as heads, this is not an inevitable state of affairs and, even though it is widely assumed that leadership can be taught to anybody (see OB in Action box below for an example), it is probably far more realistic to regard management and leadership as two complementary activities (Kotter 1990), each one having its own unique functions.

 OB IN ACTION: Leadership training at Barclays

When Barclay's University, the training unit of the UK-based high street banking group, was looking for a way to encourage junior team leaders to adopt more of a leadership role, it turned to Epic, the quoted e-learning consultancy. It needed a programme to provide an integrated and consistent leadership proposition for up to 5,000 potential users (from junior team leaders, who may have responsibility for two to three people, up to heads of strategic business units). Senior management

▶

wanted these people to take a more active leadership role, explains Donald Clark, Epic's chief executive. In partnership with Barclay's University, Epic developed a training programme dubbed 'Take the lead . . .'. This is a leadership training programme built around a blended approach, integrating offline and online training resources and delivery systems. Mr Clark explains: 'A key component of this blend is the "take the lead" website, which forms a single gateway for leader development within Barclays.' The content is specifically designed to engage students by focusing on leadership issues and role models, drawn not only from within the financial organisation, but also from contemporary society and popular culture – examining Sven-Goran Eriksson's leadership style, for instance, or the dynamics of team building within the 'Big Brother' house on television. The site is also the jumping-off point for a series of e-learning modules, theories, just-in-time performance support tools and online reference materials. 'Take the lead in style' is the first module to be released and other recently introduced modules include take the lead courses in performance, change, teamworking, innovation, communication, time, life and the business world. Other elements of the blended training programme include Barclay's University learning 'nudges' – short pieces of 'just-in-time' learning also developed by Epic – supporting links and suggested reading, diagnostic tools, face-to-face workshops and support through telephone tutoring.

Source:

Taylor, P (2003) Barclay's University: taking the lead in staff training, *Financial Times* 23 June

THE SIGNIFICANCE OF LEADERSHIP TO ORGANISATIONS

Leadership is an attribute that is highly prized in most organisations and, as a result, it is an extensively studied and debated topic in Organisational Behaviour (Meindl *et al.* 1987). There is a widely held belief that leadership is one of the factors (if not the most important factor) which determines whether a group or organisation will be successful (Drucker 1984). However, as noted above, managers are usually granted a degree of power to influence subordinate behaviour and so it can be asked: what makes leadership so important? Here the answer is comparatively straightforward and can be found in the distinction between headship and leadership made earlier.

The naked use of power is a somewhat blunt tool for obtaining compliant subordinate behaviour when compared to leadership, because in a leader–follower situation followers willingly consent to coming under another person's control and, in so doing, they become the authors of their own subordination. Indeed, because the whole situation is partly 'their idea', they are more likely to be committed to performing well. Therefore, to the extent that a manager or supervisor is able to be a leader as well as a head, it is more likely that the human effort will be deployed in exactly the way the organisation wishes and this gives us one reason why leadership is considered important in organisations; because it is likely to be a cheaper, less obtrusive and a more effective means of control than simply directing people's efforts and monitoring compliance.

There is, however, another reason why it is considered important, and this is probably more connected with the symbolic significance of the word than anything else. The word 'leader' has an almost heroic ring which conjures up an image of someone who brings order, success and triumph to a situation of potential failure or defeat; a saviour figure, without whom a group might flounder in its own lack of direction or, as one author describes matters, the CEO as an all-action Superhero (Reeves 2003). This is an image firmly imprinted in our minds in the West, where our literature and childhood stories are replete with hero figures such as King Arthur, Robin Hood or Beowulf. We are also taught that society is (or should be) a meritocracy, in which the most able people rise to positions of authority. Therefore, the concepts of leader and leadership may well have considerable appeal to managers because this is how they like to think of themselves – as those who exercise authority because all those around them acknowledge their fitness to command.

TIME OUT

Think carefully about your own experience of being a member of a group, either at your place of work, in your social life, or at college or university. Think of a situation where the group chose its own head, either by formally electing the person or in a less formal way, for example the captain of a football or hockey team is sometimes chosen this way. Now identify a situation where someone was chosen to be in charge by people outside the group, for example in a work situation.

1. Which of the two people had the most real authority with those beneath them?
2. Try to identify examples of how one person had more real authority than the other, for example which one of them could give instructions that would most readily be followed?
3. What conclusions do you draw from this exercise about the importance of leadership as opposed to headship for organisations?

REPLAY

- Leadership is a process in which leaders and followers interact in a way that enables the leader to influence followers' actions in a non-coercive way.
- Leadership theories fall into one or other of two main approaches: descriptive or functional.
- Because they derive their authority from above, managers are not necessarily leaders, but occupy positions of headship; whereas in leadership authority is conferred from below by followers who willingly consent to a chosen leader influencing their behaviour.
- In organisations, leadership is important because employees are likely to work in a more committed way for someone they look upon as a leader than for someone who simply occupies a position of headship, to whom they may just give compliance.

LEADERSHIP THEORIES AND MODELS

Theorising and research into leadership have a long pedigree in the social and organisational sciences. Over the years a number of theoretical strands have emerged, each representing a different perspective on the subject. This sometimes leads to confusion about what the different perspectives have to offer and one way to make sense of this is to classify the different approaches on the two-dimensional matrix shown in Figure 12.2.

The horizontal dimension shown across the top of the matrix reflects the extent to which a theory results in a universal or situation-specific view of leadership. Universal theories, which are the main focus of this chapter, claim to be applicable in all situations and normally reflect the assumption that there is a 'one best way' to lead. Conversely, situation-specific theories, which are covered in Chapter 13, draw attention to the idea that different forms of leadership can be more appropriate in certain circumstances. The vertical dimension reflects the extent to which a theory focuses on the leader as a person, or on the leader's behaviour. Person-centred theories deal with the leader's personal characteristics, which are usually treated as relatively fixed, while behavioural approaches focus on leader behaviour and are concerned with the way that different patterns of behaviour can affect leadership.

As in most fields of study, the theories appeared in a sequence because scholars perceived shortcomings in a prior approach. To enable the reader to appreciate how ideas in the area have developed, the theories will be described in the order in which they appeared. Many of the theories originate in the USA and focus exclusively on leadership in organisational settings. While none actually states that being a leader and being a manager are the same thing, they all focus on the management role and treat this person as someone who occupies a position of leadership: a perspective that is commonplace in most American leadership theories.

Figure 12.2 A typology of leadership theories

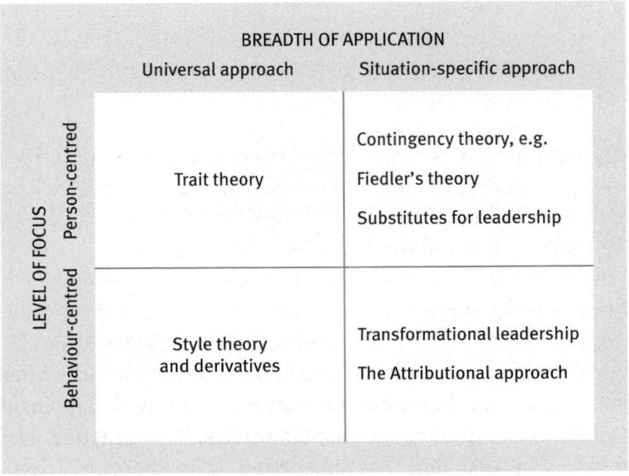

	BREADTH OF APPLICATION	
	Universal approach	Situation-specific approach
Person-centred	Trait theory	Contingency theory, e.g. Fiedler's theory / Substitutes for leadership
Behaviour-centred	Style theory and derivatives	Transformational leadership / The Attributional approach

LEVEL OF FOCUS

TIME OUT

Reflect carefully on the person you identified in the previous exercise as the leader of a group to which you belong or have belonged in the past. Now identify the characteristics of the person which, in your view, resulted in him or her being chosen by the group as its leader.

1. Was this because the person had a distinctive character or personality that others looked up to?
2. Was this because the person had particular skills and/or abilities that the group found useful?
3. Was there something else about the person which was instrumental in him or her coming to occupy a position of leadership?
4. Bring all the information in questions 1–3 together and in one or two sentences say why you feel this person became the leader.

TRAIT THEORY

Trait theory: the assumption that certain people have inherent characteristics which enable them to be leaders

This consists of a very broad set of ideas, which has its origins in work that pre-dates the development of leadership theories. The basic tenet of *trait theory* is that leaders have personality characteristics that are either inherited or developed early in life which result in them emerging as leaders in most situations. While this view first appeared around the turn of the twentieth century, it is a remarkably persistent idea and even today it is not uncommon to hear people speak of the 'born leader' or the 'natural leader'.

The three basic assumptions inherent in all theories of this type are:

- In order to be an effective leader, an individual must have certain personal characteristics (traits).
- Traits are stable and transferable across situations so that a person who leads effectively in one situation is equally likely to be effective elsewhere.
- Traits are clearly identifiable and measurable, which means that the leadership ability of a person can be predicted.

Work in this area was largely focused on attempts to identify the required traits, usually by cataloguing those people who are widely acknowledged to be good leaders; for example, great generals such as Julius Caesar, or statesmen such as George Washington and Abraham Lincoln. Like so much else in psychological research, the initial findings looked promising, but the end results turned out to be less than satisfactory. Literally dozens of seemingly important traits were identified, so many that it is impossible to find any that are common to all those people who could be identified as effective leaders. In what was perhaps the most penetrating review of the area, Stogdill (1948) pointed out that most research points to five key traits that differentiate leaders from followers: intelligence, dominance, self-confidence, high levels of energy and task-related knowledge. However, while acknowledging that these are important, he also noted that traits are very poor predictors of who emerges as a leader; for example, some traits are also commonplace among followers. For this reason there is a number of strong criticisms of the trait approach, which are summarised below.

- Because the list of influential traits is virtually endless, there is no real agreement about those which are the most important, and some that are said to be the most important are not even characteristics of all successful leaders.

- Even if it were possible to establish consensus about the most important traits, defining a successful leader often turns out to be a matter of subjective judgement. To identify traits associated with effective leadership it is first necessary to define leader effectiveness in very precise terms. However, trait theories simply assume that someone who is prominent or successful must be a good leader, which is a highly circular argument that effectively says 'here is a great leader, the great leader has these traits, therefore the leader is a leader because of these traits'.

- Since success or prominence can be due to many factors other than leadership, for example inherited wealth or the old-boy network, the trait approach is clearly a wildly inaccurate assumption.

- Strictly speaking, traits are personality variables whereas many of the characteristics identified as traits can more accurately be described as patterns of behaviour and a person's behaviour is partly a function of a specific situation.

Despite the above weaknesses, it would be unwise to dismiss trait theory completely. A review of the literature (Kirkpatrick and Locke 1991) suggests that effective leaders are different from other people and even Stogdill, who initially dismissed trait theory, eventually revised his stance and cautioned against the assumption that leadership is totally situational and devoid of any personal effects (Stogdill 1974). The current thinking is that, while there are probably no universal leadership traits, there are some traits that are likely to be crucially important in a selected range of situations (Judge *et al.* 2002; Taggar *et al.* 1999). In addition, Kenny and Zaccaro (1983) note that there are people who seem to gravitate to leadership positions in whatever they do, probably because they have a strong ability to predict what a situation requires and to modify their own approach accordingly. This is not the same as saying that they have important traits that guarantee their emergence as leaders, but it may indicate that they have two important characteristics:

- the ability accurately to sense the requirements of a situation
- a repertoire of behaviours that gives a capacity to adapt to the situation.

Arguments such as these have recently given the trait approach a new lease of life in a much more sophisticated form, which suggests that certain traits have an impact on the way that someone is perceived and experienced by other people. If these traits induce other people to perceive the individual as someone who has leadership ability, then it is far more likely that he or she will be accorded the status of leader (Lord *et al.* 1986). Therefore, if the person can recognise what has happened, he or she will be well placed to manipulate the situation to ensure occupancy of a position of leadership (Smircich and Morgan 1982). Chapter 13 will return to this idea, but for the present it is more important to explore the next major development in leadership thinking.

STYLE THEORIES

Trait theory failed to predict the success of people in leadership positions. Nevertheless, traits are generally assumed to lead to characteristic patterns of behaviour, and so the next development focused on a somewhat simpler question: what patterns of behaviour are most closely associated with leadership success? Work within this approach was heavily influenced by human relations theory and an early piece of research which acted as the trigger to almost everything that followed was a study of 20 eleven-year-old boys who met under adult leaders in a hobby club to undertake such activities as model building (Lewin *et al.* 1939). Lewin and his colleagues were able to place the behaviourial styles of leaders into one or other of three categories, each of which had identifiable effects on followers.

Autocratic leaders made all the major decisions and exerted a high degree of control over the children. Thus, while followers were very clear about what to do, they were less sure why it needed to be done and were often unwilling to accept any responsibility when things went wrong. They also tended to have a low level of morale and some hostility towards each other and the leader.

Democratic leaders involved followers in decisions and delegated much more responsibility to the group. This was said to lead to higher-quality decisions, a much stronger team spirit, commitment to implementing decisions and satisfaction among followers.

Laissez-faire leaders had a strong tendency to abdicate from the leader role. Although they did not make decisions for followers, or exercise control, this was not because of a conscious desire to delegate or stimulate participation, but simply because they had little desire to provide leadership. Thus, unless followers were competent and self-motivated, they opted out of trying to complete tasks and looked for their satisfactions in the social side of group life. This was by far the least effective style in terms of getting tasks completed.

The researchers came down heavily in favour of the democratic style, which probably reflected the dominant social values of the day. Nevertheless, the work gave a strong impetus for a shift in focus away from the trait approach, and this resulted in research of a more penetrating nature.

The milestone development in style theory came from a pair of independent studies conducted by two highly prestigious American universities: the **Ohio State Leadership Studies** and the **Michigan Leadership Studies**. Both studies focused on the behaviour of people in actual work settings and started from an explicit definition of two criteria of leadership effectiveness: task completion and follower satisfaction. The researchers examined the effects of different leader styles on subordinates' perceptions of these outcomes and, since the conclusions and assumptions are slightly different, it is convenient to describe each study in turn.

The Ohio State Leadership Studies

These took place in the late 1940s and resulted in what is now known as the *two-factor theory of leadership* (Flieshman 1953). Prior to the main body of work, questionnaires were developed to measure subordinate perceptions of leader behaviour and leaders' self-perceptions of their own behavioural styles. Using these questionnaires, data were collected and two primary dimensions of leader behaviour were isolated:

Autocratic leaders: those who strongly control subordinates and make all major decisions

Democratic leaders: those who involve followers in decisions

Laissez-faire leaders: those who abdicate from the leadership role

Two-factor theory of leadership: that there are two independent dimensions to leader behaviour, that is, initiating structure and consideration

- **Initiating structure**, behaviour concerned with achieving the group's formal task. Supervisors and managers scoring high on this dimension were firmly focused on completing the task and tended to tightly structure the work of subordinates.
- **Consideration**, behaviour focused on interpersonal relations within the group, for example trying to develop mutual trust between themselves and subordinates, or showing some concern for their feelings and involving them in decisions.

The researchers drew the conclusion that these two dimensions of behaviour were unconnected. Thus a supervisor might only pay attention to one of them and, even where there was a focus on both, the score on one was independent of the score on the other. This gave four basic leadership styles:

1. High consideration and high initiating structure.
2. High consideration and low initiating structure.
3. Low consideration and high initiating structure.
4. Low consideration and low initiating structure.

Leader effectiveness was defined in terms of two group outcomes – task completion and member satisfaction – and an important finding was that the two dimensions of leader behaviour had different implications for these outcomes. Supervisors high on initiating structure were highly productive in terms of task completion but, because their focus was solely on output, grievance rates and turnover were also high. Conversely, highly considerate supervisors were found to have groups with very high morale and member satisfaction but low productivity. Thus the conclusion was drawn that both dimensions are important for leader effectiveness. Unfortunately, however, a number of later theorists over-generalised from this conclusion, by assuming that the ideal leader is someone who is high on both consideration and initiating structure. In practical terms, however, it can be extremely difficult, if not impossible, for a single person to have this dual orientation. Indeed, in many groups, these two aspects of leadership are often provided by different people.

The Michigan Leadership Studies

In terms of methodology and findings this work has strong similarities with the Ohio Studies (Likert 1961). Almost identical criteria of effectiveness were derived, supervisors and subordinates were also used as data sources, and two contrasting dimensions of leadership behaviour were identified. However, unlike the Ohio Studies where the dimensions were deemed to be independent aspects of behaviour, the Michigan researchers drew a different conclusion: that the two dimensions were different styles of behaviour that lay at the extremes of a continuum, stretching from production-centred leadership at one end, to employee-centred leadership at the other. In the production-centred style the supervisor's primary focus was on task performance, so any interactions with subordinates were confined to briefing them on the job in hand and supervising their work. With the employee-centred style, although the supervisor still focused on productivity, this was achieved by developing a satisfied, cohesive work group.

Clearly there are strong similarities between the Ohio and Michigan studies, bothof which identify similar dimensions of leader behaviour and draw similar conclusions about which of these is the most desirable. Thus the ideas have found widespread application

Figure 12.3 The
leadership grid
(*Source*: Blake and
McCanse 1991)

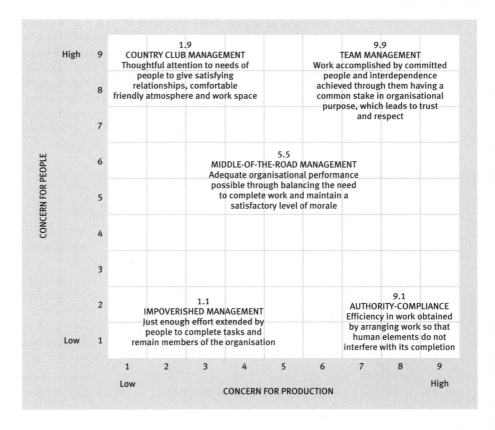

Managerial grid: an
application of style
theories of leadership
used for training
and development
purposes

in leadership training for supervisors and managers, perhaps the best-known example
of which is the Blake and Mouton (1964) *managerial grid* (Figure 12.3).

The grid is really intended to be used as a diagnostic tool in the first stage of a more
extensive programme of organisational development (see Chapter 21), which starts with
managers exploring their own leadership styles. As can be seen, the terms 'concern for
people' and 'concern for production' replace the expressions used in the Ohio and Michigan
studies, and scores on the two dimensions can be anywhere between 1 and 9. Blake and
Mouton suggest that a 9:9 style (high concern for both people and production) is the
ideal. For this reason, although the grid has been widely used for a number of years –
long enough, in fact, for the method to have been updated and revised (Blake and McCanse
1991) – the ideas have been strongly criticised. The assumption that the 9:9 style is universally superior has never been convincingly demonstrated (Bernardin and Alvares 1976)
and, since this is also a criticism of all style theories, it is relevant to conclude this
section by evaluating their contribution to leadership theory.

Although style theories moved thinking about leadership out of the cul-de-sac of
trait theory, they still give a universalist view of leadership, which assumes a 'one best
style' for all occasions; for example, the alleged superiority of the 9:9 style on the Blake
and Mouton grid, and even today it is still common to find universal prescriptions for
what makes a good (or poor) leader (see OB in Action Box on page 364). Although
they show that behavioural styles influence the supervisor–subordinate relationship,
and that this in turn has an impact on the output of a group, the theories also quietly

ignore something of potential importance. This is that the circumstances surrounding the relationship can also have an impact on a supervisor's style (Tracy 1987). For instance, even when it is not a supervisor's natural style, there can be compelling reasons why he or she behaves in a production-centred way, which could well be because the supervisor's boss emphasises output above everything else. Style theory can also be criticised for the way it assumes that the supervisor or manager is a leader of some sort, and that subordinates are followers. This is a very one-sided view that underestimates the subtleties and complexities of leadership. Thus, style theories probably have more to say about differences in manager behaviour (headship) than about leadership.

OB in ACTION: Seven failings of really useless leaders

What really useless leaders do	How they do it	How to avoid the same trap
1. Kill enthusiasm	Micromanagement, coercion, disrespect	Try better delegation and informal feedback, plus better, easier appraisal
2. Kill emotion	Aggression, lack of emotional intelligence, lack of empathy, no work-life balance	Publish a personal work-life balance manifesto; develop greater empathy; encourage assertiveness
3. Kill explanation	Partial, inconsistent communication	Make communication consistent, clear and two-way
4. Kill engagement	Individual objectives dictated by managers; limited team goals	Allow teams to set their own goals; encourage participation in decision-making
5. Kill reward	Rewarding the wrong things and offering the wrong sort of rewards (e.g. money for someone not motivated by money)	Give the right rewards to the right people at the right time; establish team rewards; give managers greater flexibility in rewarding staff
6. Kill culture	Ignoring the differences in cultures during mergers and acquisitions; punish risk-taking while trying to foster a culture of innovation	Offer training for managers on influencing culture; allow managers to evolve their own personal mistakes policy
7. Kill trust	Unfair recruitment or reward decisions	Offer training for managers on procedural justice and fairness; help managers to develop trust in others

Source:

Sonsino, S (2007) It's the fault that counts, *People Management*, 11 January: pp 37–38

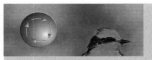

REPLAY

- Style theories were an important breakthrough in leadership theory beyond trait ideas.
- They draw attention to the idea that the way a leader behaves has an important impact on the effectiveness of a group.
- Nevertheless, style theories still have significant weaknesses, the most important of which are that leaders and managers tend to be regarded as the same thing and that there is assumed to be a single style of leader behaviour suitable for all circumstances.

UNIVERSAL VERSUS CONTINGENCY THEORIES

When it was realised that there is probably no such thing as a 'one best style' of leadership, there was a change in focus of research in an attempt to identify key situational variables that can make one style more appropriate than others. This is a contingency approach, which is underpinned by an assumption that effective leadership requires a person to use a style of behaviour that matches the conditions in which leadership is exercised. The precursor to this way of thinking emerged when style theories were still very much in vogue and appeared as a theoretical model developed by Tannenbaum and Schmidt (1958), the basics of which are shown in Figure 12.4.

Tannenbaum and Schmidt's ideas were influenced by the basic distinction between job-centred (boss-centred) and employee-centred (follower-centred) behaviour, which are shown at the extremes of the continuum. Between these extremes a variety of styles is shown, each of which corresponds to a different pattern of interaction between subordinates and manager. The appropriateness of these styles is said by Tannenbaum

Figure 12.4
Continuum of leadership styles (adapted from Tannenbaum and Schmidt 1958)

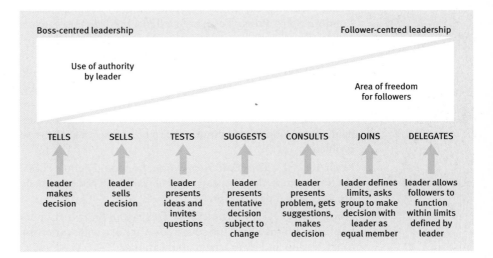

and Schmidt to depend on a number of factors, for example the manager's value system, personal wants, his or her confidence in employees and the willingness of subordinates to accept responsibility. Since the authors did not develop their ideas beyond this point, no indication is given of which style is the most appropriate according to the factors at work. Nevertheless, by pointing out that there are several factors that can influence the appropriateness of different styles, it paved the way for work by others, some of which is covered in Chapter 13.

TIME OUT

Using the group and its leader that you identified in the earlier Time Out exercise, use the Tannenbaum and Schmidt model to answer the questions below.

1. Where would you place the leader's style on the Tannenbaum and Schmidt continuum?
2. How personally acceptable to you was/is the leader's style?
3. Why is it that you find the style either acceptable or unacceptable?
4. How acceptable do you feel the leader's style is to other group members?
5. Can you identify any reasons why they find the style acceptable or unacceptable?

FURTHER READING

Bass, BM and RM Stogdill (1990) *Bass and Stogdill's Handbook of Leadership: Theory, Research and Managerial Applications*, New York: Free Press. What is certainly the most comprehensive text yet written on leadership theories and their application.

Bryman, A (1996) Leadership in organisations. In SR Clegg, C Hardy and WR Nord (eds), *Handbook of Organisation Studies*, London: Sage. An easy to read critical review of leadership theory and research, which, among other things, contains an excellent exploration of the links between leadership and organisational culture.

Diehl, C and M Dennelly (2001) *How Did They Manage? Leadership Secrets of History*, London: Spiro Press. To a large extent, the title is self-explanatory. Using what is essentially a trait theory approach, it has a strong 'how-to-do-it' flavour and purports to convey the essence of effective leadership by examining great leaders from history.

Grint, K (2005) *Leadership: Limits and Possibilities*, Basingstoke: Palgrave, Macmillan. An ambitious but nevertheless succinct text that highlights the limits of our understanding of leadership. In particular it addresses the matter of the limited impact that so-called leaders have on organisations; something that flies in the face of the widely held assumption that obtaining the right leader is a sure-fire solution to all of a firm's problems.

Koch, R (2002) *The 80/20 Revolution*, London: Nicholas Brealey. In essence the book is a testament to the persuasiveness of trait theory ideas, which according to its author are as timely today as ever.

Northouse, PG (1997) *Leadership: Theory and Practice*, London: Sage. A very readable book. It contains a brief but sound coverage of a wide variety of theoretical approaches to leadership and its practical applications.

Wren, T, D Hicks and T Price (eds) (2004) *The International Library of Leadership*, Cheltenham: Edward Elgar. A collection of three volumes of readings, which survey the development of leadership theory: (i) Traditional Classics on Leadership; (ii) Modern Classics on Leadership; (iii) New Perspectives on Leadership.

Wright, P (1995) *Managerial Leadership*, London: Thomson. A very practical approach to leadership, which is mainly be of interest to the manager (actual or would be).

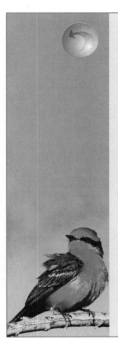

REVIEW AND DISCUSSION QUESTIONS

1. Using the concepts of 'headship' and 'leadership', explain whether and to what extent the words 'leader' and 'manager' are just expressions that have the same meaning.

2. Why is it that most organisations give formal authority to managers to direct and control the activities of their subordinates, but at the same time stress the importance of leadership skills in managers?

3. Explain the underlying assumptions of trait theories of leadership and the extent to which these theories have a practical utility for modern organisations.

4. Explain the fundamental way in which style theories of leadership differ from trait ideas and the extent to which this results in a more realistic perspective on leadership.

5. Describe a development of style theory that has found widespread use as a vehicle for expressing leadership style and whether the fundamental assumptions of this model make it one that has practical utility for organisations.

Chapter 13

Leaders and Leadership:
Contingency Theory and Recent Approaches

LEARNING OUTCOMES

After studying this chapter you should be able to:

- distinguish between the contingency approach to leadership and traditional theories

- describe Fiedler's LPC contingency theory and the Substitutes for Leadership model

- discuss recent approaches to leadership theory, including the difference between transactional and transformational leadership and the attributional approach

- appreciate the potential effects of national cultures on the appropriateness of different leadership styles

INTRODUCTION

This chapter follows on from Chapter 12. It starts with an exploration of 'contingency theory', a major group of leadership theories that deal with the circumstances that are likely to make one leadership style more appropriate than another. It then examines some of the more recent developments in ideas about leadership. Since many theories covered in this chapter acknowledge the importance of the context in which leadership is exercised, it gives a brief consideration of the implications of national cultures for the appropriateness of different leadership styles. Finally, the different approaches in this and the previous chapter are compared and contrasted, and general conclusions are drawn.

CONTINGENCY THEORIES OF LEADERSHIP

The realisation that there is probably no such thing as a 'one best style' of leadership appropriate in all circumstances prompted a new direction in leadership research. Although this continued to use the concept of leadership style, instead of attempting to identify a single style that would be appropriate everywhere, its aim was to pinpoint variables that make one style more appropriate than others in certain specific circumstances. As such, a contingency perspective was adopted, which was underpinned by the assumption that effective leadership requires a leader to adopt a style of behaviour that matches the conditions in which leadership is to be exercised.

Fiedler's Contingency Theory

This was the first true contingency theory of leadership. It first appeared some 30 years ago (Fiedler 1967) and is sometimes referred to as the LPC (least preferred coworker) model. In Fiedler's view, the most appropriate style of leader behaviour is that which results in high task performance by a group, which is said to be the outcome of two important factors: the preferred behavioural style of the leader and the contextual circumstances in which the group operates. The way that these variables interact is shown in Figure 13.1.

Figure 13.1
Interaction of variables in Fiedler's contingency theory

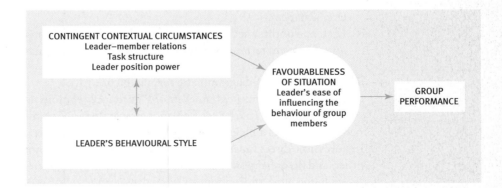

The three key contextual variables that affect the appropriateness of a particular style are said to be:

- **Leader–member relations:** which broadly corresponds to the quality of the relationship between leader and followers. If these are good, leader and followers have confidence, liking, trust and respect for each other, which gives a situation that is favourable to the leader in terms of making it relatively easy for him or her to influence subordinate behaviour.
- **Task structure:** the nature of the group's task. If this is clear, unambiguous and routine (a high task structure) the leader will find it comparatively unnecessary to guide, direct and supervise the group's work, which also works in his or her favour.
- **Leader position power:** the formal organisational authority vested in the supervisor's role. If position power is high, the supervisor has the authority to assign tasks directly to subordinates and to reward and punish them for good or bad performance. Again, this is a situation which is favourable to the leader.

Least preferred co-worker (LPC): the subordinate that a supervisor was least able to work with successfully on a prior occasion

A supervisor's preferred leadership style is normally assessed by using a psychological scale that taps his or her orientations towards his or her *least preferred co-worker (LPC)*. This is the subordinate that the supervisor was least able to work with successfully in the past. The supervisor is asked to rate this person (together with other subordinates) on 18 bipolar scales, which are shown in Table 13.1. Responses to all scales are added up and an average obtained, which gives the LPC score for the supervisor. The idea here is that a supervisor with positive orientation towards a subordinate who is liked least (high LPC score) will be someone who is sensitive to other people and gets satisfaction from interacting with them at work, which indicates a 'relationship-orientated' supervisor. Conversely, low LPC supervisors (those with negative orientations towards their least preferred colleague) are basically 'task-orientated', and their work satisfactions are mainly obtained from successfully achieving output goals.

An extensive programme of research by Fiedler and his colleagues resulted in two general conclusions:

- That the favourableness of a situation (how easy it is for a leader to influence the behaviour of followers) is strongly affected by certain combinations of external circumstances.
- Each one of these sets of circumstances has a leadership style that is most appropriate in terms of obtaining effective group performance.

This is illustrated in diagrammatic form in Figure 13.2.

In the column on the extreme left of Figure 13.2 relations are good, the task structure is high and so is the leader's position power. In terms of influencing subordinate's behaviour, this is a highly favourable situation for the leader, because the task itself requires little direct supervision; the leader and subordinates are tolerant towards each other; and his or her power position allows rewards to be given for good performance. As such, the most appropriate style involves a primary focus on the task.

Table 13.1 Dimensions of the LPC scale

	8	7	6	5	4	3	2	1	
Friendly									Unfriendly
Supportive									Hostile
Pleasant									Unpleasant
Tense									Relaxed
Rejecting									Accepting
Distant									Close
Boring									Interesting
Cold									Warm
Quarrelsome									Harmonious
Gloomy									Cheerful
Open									Guarded
Considerate									Inconsiderate
Backbiting									Loyal
Untrustworthy									Trustworthy
Insincere									Sincere
Agreeable									Disagreeable
Kind									Unkind
Nasty									Nice

Figure 13.2 Fiedler's contingency theory – circumstances and leadership styles

CONTEXTUAL CIRCUMSTANCES								
Leader–member Relations	Good	Good	Good	Good	Bad	Bad	Bad	Bad
Task Structure	High	High	Low	Low	High	High	Low	Low
Leader Position Power	Strong	Weak	Strong	Weak	Strong	Weak	Strong	Weak
FAVOURABLENESS OF SITUATION	HIGH				MEDIUM		LOW	
MOST APPROPRIATE BEHAVIOURAL STYLE	Low LPC Task-orientated				High LPC Relationship-orientated		Low LPC Task-orientated	

At the opposite (right-hand) extreme, relations are relatively poor: the supervisor has little position power and, importantly, the task is more ambiguous. This ambiguity requires that the leader becomes more involved in directing subordinates, but this has to be done without the benefit of being able to use rewards or punishments as inducements. Therefore, to spur people on to give maximum effort, the most appropriate style is also one which is strongly focused on the task.

In the fourth column from the left there is a also a degree of task ambiguity and, once again, this requires that the supervisor gives more direction. However, while position power is weak, and rewards and punishments cannot be used, relations are good, which means that subordinates would not resent a high degree of supervisor involvement, and may even welcome it. Thus the most appropriate style for effective group performance is that of helpful, relationship-orientated behaviour.

Fiedler states that since a leader's style (as measured by LPC score) is a function of his or her personality, it is relatively fixed and unchanging. Therefore, if it does not fit the circumstances, there are two alternatives: either the leader can be removed and a new one appointed, or the circumstances must be changed. In Fiedler's view, the latter is by far the most appropriate step and (to use his own words) he advocates 're-engineering the job to fit the manager' (Fiedler 1965). This might sound a difficult, or even impossible task. However, in more recent work (Fiedler and Garcia 1987) give a range of actions that can be used to bring about changes in the three contextual variables. These form the basis of a scheme for developing managers in leadership, the 'leader match' programme, which has a somewhat unusual approach to leadership training. In most cases, training of this type attempts to change a person's style of behaviour, but in Feidler's method the aim is to teach the manager ways of changing the situation. An outline of his suggested ways of doing this is given in Table 13.2.

Although Fiedler's model is a huge advance on style theories, there are criticisms. Studies to test the validity of the theory have yielded mixed evidence about its accuracy (Graen *et al.* 1971). There are also arguments that variables other than the three suggested by Fiedler could influence leader effectiveness (Peters *et al.* 1985). Moreover, there are criticisms of using LPC scores to evaluate a leader's normal behaviour; mainly because, while LPC probably gives an indication of a person's attitudes or even personality, these are often poor guides to actual behaviour. It should also be noted that Fiedler's sole criterion for evaluating supervisor effectiveness is task performance, which neglects the equally important factor of follower satisfaction. Perhaps most damming of all, it has been argued that Fiedler's model can take in virtually any set of research findings and show that they support his ideas, which ultimately means that it can be little more than a self-fulfilling prophecy.

For all these criticisms, Fiedler's work was a significant contribution to leadership theory and, in recognising that contextual circumstances can have a strong impact on the appropriateness of a leader's behaviour, the theory broke the strait-jacket of a 'one best style' approach. Perhaps more importantly, his work prompted an ongoing search for other potentially influential variables, and so subsequent developments owe a great deal to his ideas.

Table 13.2 Leader actions to change the state of contingency variables

Contingency variable		
Leader–member relations	**To improve leader–member relations**: • spend more time with group members on an informal basis • ask for specific people to be allocated to the group • offer help or direction to difficult group members • transfer particular people in or out of the group • raise feelings of satisfaction by obtaining positive outcomes for group members	
Task structure	**To increase task structure**: • obtain structured and straightforward tasks for the group, together with detailed criteria for completion • break down the jobs and tasks into more tightly structured parts	**To lower task structure**: • obtain novel and unstructured problems or tasks to be solved by the group and/or • involve subordinates in working jointly with leader to solve problems
Leader position power	**To enhance position power**: • exercise in full those powers granted by the organisation to reinforce the appearance of being in charge • become the sole channel for information coming into the group	**To decrease position power**: • share decisions with group members • allow more autonomy to group members

Source: Fiedler and Garcia 1987, pp 49–93.

Substitutes for Leadership

If a group is to perform well, almost all leadership theories take it for granted that a leader is necessary. However, there are many examples of people performing well without supervision, for instance highly skilled professionals such as barristers or doctors. An analysis that addresses the matter of leaderless groups is provided by Kerr and Jermier (1978) who point out that there are a number of circumstances in which leadership can be relatively unimportant. These fall into two classes:

Leadership substitutes: situational factors that enable subordinates to function well without leader guidance

Leadership neutralisers: workplace factors that remove the capability of a leader to influence subordinate behaviour

• where there are *leadership substitutes*: situational factors that give subordinates the necessary guidance and/or provide them with some degree of work satisfaction and thus enable them to perform well
• where there are *leadership neutralisers*: where something is absent from the work milieu, that would normally make leadership important and its absence removes the capability of a leader to influence the behaviour of subordinates.

Kerr and Jermier argue that substitutes and neutralisers emanate from three possible sources:

• the characteristics of the followers
• the characteristics of the task
• the characteristics of the organisation.

Table 13.3 Substitutes for leadership

Characteristics	Neutralises relationship-orientated leadership	Neutralises task-orientated leadership
Of the subordinate		
Ability, experience, training, knowledge	No	Yes
Need for independence	Yes	Yes
Professional orientation	Yes	Yes
Indifference towards organisational rewards	Yes	Yes
Of the task		
Unambiguous and routine	No	Yes
No variation in method	No	Yes
Provides its own feedback on accomplishment	No	Yes
Intrinsically satisfying	Yes	No
Of the organisation		
Formalisation (explicit objectives, plans and job specifications)	No	Yes
Inflexibility (fixed rules and procedures)	No	Yes
Active advisory staff roles with clear areas of responsibility	No	Yes
Close-knit, cohesive work groups	Yes	Yes
Organisational rewards that are not within the leader's control	Yes	Yes
Physical distance between superior and subordinates	Yes	Yes

Source: Kerr and Jermier 1978, p 378.

However, some of these do not completely remove the need for either or both aspects of leadership. Some, for example, only reduce the need for task-orientated aspects, others make relationship-orientated behaviour unimportant, and some negate both. These effects are shown in Table 13.3.

There are three ways to look at the Kerr and Jermier theory. First, it can be viewed simply as a theory of non-leadership. Second, it can be regarded as another set of contingency factors and, finally, as the ultimate in contingency theory. Whichever perspective is adopted, it should be noted that there is fairly strong empirical support for the idea that a leader is redundant in certain situations (Howell *et al*. 1990). As such, the ideas of Kerr and Jermier are very important, particularly in today's conditions where a number of popular initiatives such as downsizing and empowerment place a very strong emphasis on employees working without direct supervision.

TIME OUT

Think carefully about the classes you attend at university or college as part of your programme of studies. While your lecturers cannot really be considered to be leaders, or even heads, they are still responsible for achieving what could loosely be described as a task-related output; that is, a class that successfully passes the course or module. However, achieving this is something that relies on student endeavours as well. Examine Table 13.3 and try to answer the questions below.

1. To what extent does achieving the task-related output rely on leadership substitutes or leadership neutralisers?
2. Do these reduce the need for relationship-orientated behaviour, or task-orientated behaviour?
3. Do these substitutes or neutralisers exist because of characteristics of the students, of the task or of the organisation?

AN OVERVIEW OF CONTINGENCY THEORIES

Like style theories, contingency models all focus on leader behaviour and leader styles are invariably categorised as somewhere between relationship-orientated and task-orientated. What is different about these ideas is that the situation itself is deemed to make one style more appropriate than another, and no style is appropriate for all situations. Beyond this, the various contingency theories differ in two important respects: first, the situational factors that are taken to be the most important; and, second, whether the leaders are assumed to be able to vary their style to meet the needs of the situation. These similarities and differences are summarised in Table 13.4.

Perhaps the most important point to note from Table 13.4 is that while neither of the theories are identical in terms of the contingencies covered, one of them assumes that leaders can change their behavioural style at will. In this respect, Fiedler's theory is unique because he believes that style is relatively permanent and reflects deep-rooted psychological characteristics.

Table 13.4 Summary comparison of contingency theories

	Fiedler's contingency theory	Kerr and Jermier substitutes for leadership
How leader styles are classified	Task- or relationship-orientated	Task- or relationship-orientated
Assumptions about leader's style	Fixed and cannot be varied	None
Implications of assumptions about style	Choose the leader to fit the situation	Leadership not necessary in certain circumstances
Major aspect of leadership addressed by theory	Which style is most appropriate to the circumstances	None
Contingency variables assumed to influence appropriate style	Nature of task, leader position power, leader–subordinate relations	Subordinates, task and organisation
Measures of leader effectiveness	Task completion	Task completion, subordinate satisfaction

Since the theories deal with slightly different combinations of circumstances, they are complementary rather than contradictory. Once again, however, it is necessary to draw attention to a common feature that places limits on the application of the models. In every case a leader is regarded as someone who has been selected by people higher up in an organisation to be 'in charge', and this fails to distinguish between 'headship' and 'leadership'. To apply the word 'leader' to situations such as these is misleading because, if all else fails, the person can resort to the use of formal authority to influence the actions of subordinates. Subordinates are likely to be aware that this 'reserve' basis of authority exists and, although they might well comply with instructions (perhaps grudgingly), this can be far from a situation where they give their willingly consent to be led, which casts doubt on whether the theories describe leadership, rather than variations in styles of 'headship'.

REPLAY

- Unlike style theories, which assume that there is a single leadership style suitable for all situations, contingency theories assume that the situation itself makes a certain style more appropriate than others.
- There are a number of theories of this type and they tend to deal with different sets of circumstances that make particular styles of leader behaviour more or less appropriate.
- Because none of the theories deal with all possible circumstances that can influence the appropriateness of a leader's style, they should be regarded as complementary rather than in opposition.

RECENT PERSPECTIVES ON LEADERSHIP

As noted earlier, it is commonly assumed that a leader exerts influence on the behaviour of followers and most of the theories covered so far are built on this assumption. However, the theories are silent about how the processes of influence work and, unless we understand how people are able to exert influence without using power or coercion, leadership remains an abstract 'black box'. To some extent the functional approach discussed in Chapter 12 gives some hint about the processes at work and, in addition, more recent theories purposely address this issue. Most of them adopt what has come to be known as the *influence perspective*, which argues that leaders influence the perceptions and attitudes of followers by setting them a personal example. Compared with other theoretical approaches, this is still in its infancy, and tends to focus strongly on the personal behaviour and characteristics of leaders, which makes it remarkably similar to older trait ideas, albeit in a more sophisticated form.

Influence perspective: an approach to leadership theory which explicitly addresses the issue of 'how' leaders influence follower behaviour

Transactional versus Transformational (Charismatic) Leadership

Transactional leadership: the leadership style that is said to be the most appropriate to stable conditions

The expressions transactional and transformational leadership, were originally coined by Burns (1978), who contrasted successful leadership in stable situations with that in changing circumstances. These ideas were later amplified by Bass (1985), who contrasts two types of leadership: transactional and transformational (see OB in Action Box below). In *transactional leadership* the relationship between leader and subordinates is akin to the normal management role in stable-state conditions, where the crucial skills required by the leader are the ability to diagnose subordinate needs and adopt an appropriate style of managing the relationship.

Transformational leadership: the approach to leadership which is said to be most appropriate in times of significant organisational change

However, where organisational change is required, perhaps because the environment is subject to rapid fluctuation, a leader's task is somewhat different from just keeping things ticking over. Here Bass believes that another pattern of leader behaviour, *transformational leadership*, is called for. This requires the leader to have a vision of what needs to be done to cope with the situation, the ability to communicate this vision to followers and the capability to energise or inspire them to change their current way of doing things. Bass then sets out what he believes to be the four key characteristics of the transformational leader: charisma, vision, intellectual stimulation of followers and an ability to take their emotional needs into account.

 OB IN ACTION: Transformational leadership

What is it?

Some leaders see their relationships at work as a series of one-off deals. These transactional leaders are fixated on immediate results but, for transformational leaders, every decision is interrelated, part of a continuously developing story. They see the bigger picture, are more ambitious about long-term goals and do not hesitate to share their vision with other people. Their eyes are on the hills. This approach seeks to offer a narrative or vision, to instil a sense of purpose and direction. It coaches staff rather than telling them what to do, winning hearts and minds instead of controlling them.

Where did it come from?

Pulitzer prizewinner James MacGregor Burns introduced the concept in his book *Leadership* published in 1978. For him, it characterised the great leaders of history. The idea gradually became more fashionable and fits in with other trendy ideas such as chaos theory, the notion that an organisation is a complex adaptive system that resists linear instruction or change. Incrementalism is out. Transformational leadership may also reinforce the myth-making that surrounds the stock market hero CEOs, who leave the little details to little people, while engineering dramatic commercial success.

Where is it going?

The jails could soon be full of transformational leaders whose integrity and accounting practices let them down. Down-to-earth, practical execution – transactional leadership – is making a comeback. So, if you want to be a transformational leader, don't broadcast the fact: expectations will be raised, and dramatic results will be required. Leaders who promise more than they can deliver soon find themselves out of a job; a transformation you could do without.

Management Fad Quotient (out of 10)

Seven, with the potential to go higher.

Source:

Management Today, November 2003

Charisma

The idea that someone with charisma is endowed with a natural authority is an old one; Max Weber (1947), for example, viewed charisma as one of the three primary bases of authority. This idea re-emerged in the late 1970s as part of the theory of charismatic leadership and has more recently been incorporated into views on the necessary attributes of transformational leaders. However, while most people would acknowledge that charisma can exist, it is much harder to be precise about what makes someone charismatic. Nevertheless, attempts have been made do this, and the main attributes identified are expertise, articulateness, perceived trustworthiness, and perception and sensitivity to surrounding circumstances (Conger and Kanugo 1987). Unfortunately, these attribute names are plagued with the same problem that bedevilled the attribute lists in trait theory: what do the words mean? Having any one of these attributes is more a question of perception than objective reality, and what can be seen as articulate by one person can be seen by someone else as garrulous.

Vision

This is also extremely difficult to define. For instance, how much vision is required and vision about what? The word is well used by management gurus such as Wesley and Mintzberg (1989), but all too often it is used in a very loose and imprecise way. However, Selznick gives a precise description:

> sensitivity to changes in an organisation's environment, together with an accurate perception of the direction in which the organisation must move if it is to take advantage of environmental changes.
> (Selznick 1984)

Although this looks fine at first sight, it still leaves a feeling of unease. It implies, for example, that those with vision are unique and are able to foretell the future.

Intellectual Stimulation

This attribute is said to reflect an ability to energise followers, usually by showing them that problems can be viewed in an alternative way and convincing them that the leader's way of solving the problems is a sound, rational path to follow. Once again this poses problems of definition. Moreover, it comes uncomfortably close to Hermalin's (1998) somewhat cynical definition of leadership as 'a mechanism by which leaders convince followers that they are not misleading them'.

Consideration and Sensitivity to Followers

This means that transformational leaders pay close attention to followers and their differences. Since this is a pattern of behaviour, rather than a vaguely defined attribute, it is less controversial than the others. In some respects it is very similar to *emotional intelligence* (see Chapter 3) and has been shown to be a distinctive characteristic of transformational leaders (Rubin *et al.* 2005). Usually a person of this type will be good at spotting where a skill or ability needs to be imported into a group and at selecting the appropriate person to meet this need. He or she will often spend a great deal of time with group members, and perhaps devote time and energy to such activities as coaching and mentoring to develop their talents. In return, group members are likely to obtain satisfaction of their higher order psychological needs, such as achievement and recognition (Kotter 1990).

To summarise, although the contrast between transactional and transformational leadership is a useful one, it almost inevitably results in a feeling that leadership theory has come full circle. So far, it adds little to the body of knowledge and only tells us what most people already know: that the prevailing circumstances surrounding a group dictate what type of leader is required. The main problem is that most of the attributes of the transformational leader are extremely difficult to define, let alone identify. By far the most problematic of these is charisma and, while advocates of the theory usually acknowledge that charisma on its own is not enough to make someone a transformational leader (Bass 1985), it still tends to be viewed as a vital prerequisite, and is often described in terms that verge on 'hero worship' (see Kets de Vries 1998a). This is not to deny that there is such a thing as charisma, or that charismatic people are able to influence others. However, protagonists of these ideas somehow manage to convey the impression that transformational leadership is greatly superior to the transactional style and, in their enthusiasm to glorify the transformational type, the transactional style almost inevitably gets denigrated. For instance, a recent 15-month study of job advertisements for senior management positions indicates that the attributes associated with transformational leadership had virtually become 'must haves' for the organisations concerned (Hartog *et al.* 2007). Perhaps, more importantly, there could well be drawbacks in the assumed superiority of these people. For example, Maccoby

(2000) argues that many charismatic leaders are likely to be narcissists, who have an overpowering self-image, that leads them to believe that whatever they suggest is right. Moreover, they often lack empathy and are more than willing to impose their visions on dissenters. This, it can be noted, is the typical behaviour of fanatics and despots (Tourish and Pinnington 2002), which can all too easily lead to what has become known as 'the Hitler problem' in leadership (see Kets de Vries 2006). In all probability transactional and transformational types are complementary rather than mutually exclusive, and both are needed in organisations.

Notwithstanding these points, theories of transformational leadership have attracted a great deal of attention and the idea of charisma is extremely popular in management circles, perhaps because the word has a certain cachet that gives it an almost heroic ring. It implies that the person with charisma is both exceptional and exemplary, and the idea might well be popular because being charismatic is how many managers like to think of themselves.

The Attributional Approach

Attribution theory, which was introduced in Chapter 4, holds that humans are seldom content to take the behaviour of another person at face value: they also try to attribute a cause to a person's actions. This idea can be applied to leadership by asking whether the effects that a person has on a situation are a result of his or her leadership abilities.

Most leadership theories unswervingly accept that outcomes such as performance or employee satisfaction are the result of a leader's actions, and this is particularly true of ideas about transformational leaders, where it would be near heresy to even question that leadership is a crucial determinant of an organisation's success. Importantly, however, attribution theory alerts us to the possibility that attributing success to a leader in this way could be little more than an act of faith.

People in organisations have just as much need to explain events and happenings as those elsewhere. Since the words 'leader' and 'leadership' are endowed with almost mystic connotations, 'the effect of the leader' is a highly convenient factor that can be used to attribute a reason for success or failure (Meindl *et al.* 1987). As such, so-called leadership might well be little more than the results of image building or myth making, and Pfeffer (1977) developed a cogent argument to support this proposition by giving three reasons why leaders are unlikely to have the effects on organisational performance that are usually attributed to them. First, if success or failure arises because an organisation has changed its way of doing things, the change is very unlikely to have been prompted by a change in leadership behaviour. People are usually selected for positions of authority in organisations because they 'fit in' and have certain acceptable attributes and styles of behaviour. Thus they have every encouragement to stick to these behaviourial patterns. Second, and flowing from the first point, even if a person with a different style should gain admittance to an organisation, the individual is usually socialised very rapidly into conforming to accepted patterns of behaviour. Finally, the success or failure of an organisation is often largely determined by contextual factors, over which even very senior managers have no control.

Pfeffer's arguments are very powerful and are quite strongly supported by empirical evidence. For example, Reich (1985) analysed the performance of a number of organisations, in which success had been attributed to the dynamic leadership of a person in control. In almost every case success turned out to be more directly attributable to economic boom conditions than anything else. In more general terms, the way that success almost inevitably gets attributed to the leader of a group was demonstrated by a tightly controlled experiment by Staw (1975). Groups were placed in a competitive situation, in which their success in a task was beyond each group's control and completely in the hands of the experimenters. Irrespective of whether a group had actually succeeded in the task, when groups were told they had succeeded, group members almost always attributed success to the effects of the leader.

Flowing from evidence such as this, it is possible to identify three important implications of tendencies to attribute success or failure to leaders. The first and most obvious of these concerns the assumption that a leader has a direct effect on subordinate behaviour, and that this necessarily produces desired outcomes. This can be a completely false assumption and, while leaders undoubtedly have some effect on followers, the effect might not be a direct one. That is, the leader might have an effect on some other factor, and this in turn influences the behaviour and emotions of subordinates, for example by bringing about a change in the contextual circumstances in which they operate, which makes it much easier for them to succeed in their task.

Second, it is possible that simply calling someone a leader unleashes very powerful forces. People seem to be most at ease in situations where they belong to a group that has a head, and if that person is called 'the leader', it allows the person to take on the mantle of leadership, which from then on becomes a self-fulfilling prophecy.

The third point, which follows from the second, has very direct implications for the rather romanticised and hyped-up ideas about the charismatic nature of so-called transformational leaders. These people may just have an intuitive grasp of how to act in a way that makes them appear as a leader to others. In addition, they could be sensitive to situations where people feel more comfortable if there is a leader and have a good intuitive grasp of what potential followers believe the characteristics of a leader to be, together with the ability to convey the impression that they have these characteristics. Put this way, leadership may turn out to be simply a matter of impression management, in which potential followers are encouraged to put themselves in a subordinate role and to cast the would-be leader as occupying a position of authority. There is a growing body of evidence that effects such as these actually take place (Weierter 1997) and while this paints a somewhat less romantic picture of leadership than the one that is normally encountered, we should note that impression management is an activity in which almost everybody engages to some extent – some more successfully than others. It is also a technique that can be taught. Witness the long-lasting success of Dale Carnegie's book, *How to Win Friends and Influence People*, which for the last 50 years has been one of the consistent bestsellers in management literature. Even a cursory examination of Carnegie's book shows that some of its interactive principles are remarkably similar to the behaviour that is said to characterise transformational leaders.

- A comparatively recent development hinges on the distinction between transactional and transformational leadership, in which the former is portrayed as more appropriate to stable circumstances while the latter is needed for change situations.
- Another recent development is the attributional approach, in which people are attributed with leadership characteristics as a way of explaining the past success of a group.

LEADERSHIP IN A CROSS-CULTURAL CONTEXT

Wider Social Cultures

Culture is defined here as the customary patterns of behaviour and thinking that are shared by most people in a society (Jaques 1952). Thus, those who have absorbed a particular culture share deep-seated and taken-for-granted assumptions that exercise a subtle and powerful influence over their actions. While we can all think of ways in which people in other countries seem to have cultural norms different from our own, it is misleading to speak of national cultures because cultures do not confirm neatly to national boundaries and, for this reason, the expression 'wider social culture' is used here.

Dimensions of Cultural Difference

Importantly, individuals in an organisation will expect to be able to conform to the wider social norms that they have absorbed. Indeed, if they come to occupy a role in an organisation where values and beliefs are different from their own, they can have great difficulty in adjusting (Feldman and Thompson 1992). For this reason, the culture of an organisation normally replicates many of the characteristics of the wider social culture in which it is located (Nelson and Gopalan 2003). Thus cross-cultural differences and how they can influence patterns of behaviour in organisations, have now become important areas of study in OB and OA (Alder and Bartholomew 1992). Nevertheless, while there is a long pedigree of trying to identify the way in which national cultures can affect the behaviour of people in organisations, until the late 1970s the majority of work simply consisted of comparisons between two countries. Since then, however, attempts have been made to conduct wide-ranging international comparisons, the foremost example of which is the work of Geert Hofstede (1980).

Hofstede: The Hermes Study

Hofstede's original study was based on two surveys of employees in a large multinational corporation (IBM) that had branches in over 100 different countries. In total, over 116,000 completed questionnaires were obtained from subsidiaries in 40 countries and, to allow strict comparisons to be made, Hofstede used only sales and service staff, all of whom were nationals of the country in which the subsidiary was based. Samples in each country were matched as closely as possible in terms of age and gender composition, and so the most significant difference between the samples was in terms of the nationality of the people. Therefore, any differences in attitudes and values could be mainly attributed to cultural rather than demographic or organisational factors.

Hofstede identified four basic dimensions along which the differences between national cultures could be expressed but, before describing them, the reader should be aware that in later work (Hofstede 1991) a fifth dimension (time orientation) is added, which is said to be based on Confucian values. While this looks appealing, several scholars, such as Newman and Nollen (1996) argue that it is the least relevant and most difficult to understand of all the dimensions, and in a penetrating exploration of the theoretical roots of the dimension, Fang (1998) points out that it is a gross distortion of Confucian philosophy. Therefore, in the interests of simplicity, Hofstede's original scheme is used here. This uses only four dimensions: power–distance; uncertainty avoidance, individualism–collectivism and masculinity–femininity, and these are considered next.

The Hofstede Dimensions

The Power–Distance Dimension

This portrays the extent to which a culture encourages superiors to exercise power and for subordinates to accept that this is a legitimate way for superiors to behave. In a high power–distance culture, power inequalities between people are accepted and this is how the boss is expected to behave, but, where power–distance is low, superiors and subordinates treat each other more as equals, this is accompanied by a tendency to minimise social inequalities.

The Uncertainty Avoidance Dimension

Here the dimension reflects the cultural acceptance of risk taking. In a culture characterised by strong uncertainty avoidance, people tend to feel threatened, uncomfortable, anxious and stressed by ambiguous situations, and prefer highly stable conditions where there are clear rules of behaviour. Conversely, where uncertainty avoidance values are weak, the ambiguities of life are more readily accepted, rules are not sacrosanct and can be abandoned with ease.

The Individualism–Collectivism Dimension

This dimension reflects the extent to which people derive their sense of identity from being individuals rather than as part of a group. In an individualistic culture, a person's identity is derived from his or her sense of uniqueness, and individual initiative and achievement are highly prized. Thus, a person's loyalty is primarily to him or herself, and privacy of thought and life are strongly respected. In contrast, collectivist cultures are characterised by much tighter social frameworks and the aim of most people is to be a good group member.

The Masculinity–Femininity Dimension

This dimension can perhaps most easily be described as the extent to which being 'macho' is what counts. In masculine cultures, performance, wealth, material possessions and driving ambition epitomise what is seen to be good. Conversely, the so-called feminine cultures are characterised by a far stronger concern for the quality of life. People rather than possessions are considered important and a high value is placed on service to others.

Classifying Cultures with the Dimensions

Using the dimensions described above, Hofstede classified the 40 countries examined according to their scores on each one. From this he derived a set of eight 'cultural groups', each of which consists of countries that have similar cultural characteristics that differ strongly from those in other groups. The names given to the groups are somewhat arbitrary and these were chosen on the basis of prominent countries located in each one. The clusters are shown in Figure 13.3.

Figure 13.3
Hofstede's country clusters and their characteristics

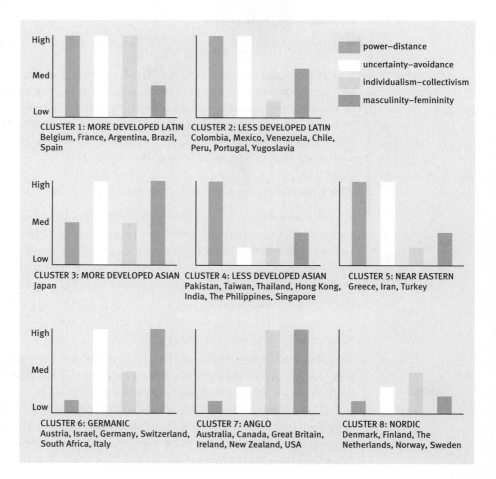

As can be seen, the groupings fit well with the historical and linguistic development of the countries, which gives a plausible feeling to the clusters. Note, however, that the values should not be taken to mean that everybody in a particular nation has the same cultural characteristics, and the scales only portray what can be described as the commonly encountered core values of the culture. A feature that stands out clearly from the results is that there are clear and systematic differences in work-related attitudes in the different cultural groups. Therefore, Hofstede argues that since the cultural values in each one are likely to give rise to different conceptions of what are the appropriate ways to behave, we should not expect leadership styles, management practices and organisational processes to be the same everywhere.

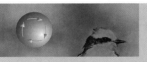

REPLAY

- The culture of an organisation needs to be compatible with the wider social culture within which the firm operates.

- Wider social cultures give rise to distinctive patterns of attitudes, values, beliefs and behaviours on the part of people who have absorbed these cultures.

- Hofstede's scheme distinguishes between national cultures by classifying them along four dimensions (the power–distance dimension, the uncertainty avoidance dimension, the individualism–collectivism dimension, the masculinity–femininity dimension) and, using this scheme, different countries can be located in one of eight clusters according to the characteristics of their cultures.

- Each cluster has its own cultural characteristics that have implications for the way in which people think and behave.

Management Style (Leadership)

As noted earlier, most so-called theories of leadership are simply explanations of why certain styles of management behaviour are more appropriate in some circumstances than in others and, for this reason, the expression 'management style' is used here. The manager–subordinate relationship does not exist in a vacuum and normal patterns of behaviour in an organisation are often a function of what is considered appropriate in its wider social culture. For instance, Hofstede (1991) points out that only in the USA is the manager regarded as a cultural hero, whereas in Germany people expect their immediate superior (the person who assigns them tasks and evaluates their efforts) to be a person of proven technical competence in a particular field (a qualified engineer or its equivalent in other occupations). Perhaps the most straightforward way to illustrate that different management styles are needed in different cultural contexts is to apply the work of Hofstede (1980), who argues that different cultures

Figure 13.4 Locations of France, Japan, the UK and the USA on Hofstede's four dimensions of culture

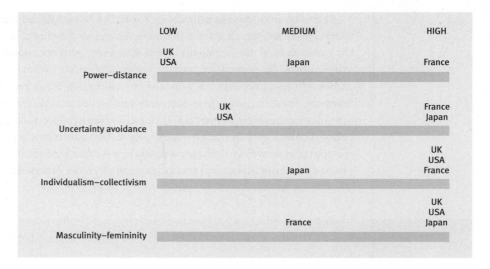

have different work-related values which, in turn, produce implicit mental models of what is considered to be an appropriate way for a manager to behave. To illustrate the point, four of the countries studied by Hofstede – France, the UK, the USA and Japan – will be contrasted. Their positions on Hofstede's four dimensions are shown in Figure 13.4.

In the United Kingdom and USA scores on the power–distance dimension are low, which means that most employees would find autocratic, distant management styles unwelcome. In addition, uncertainty avoidance scores are medium to low. Thus, people are fairly comfortable with ambiguity and are willing to take some responsibility for their own actions. These cultures also prize individuality and achievement, and have high scores on the masculinity–femininity dimension. If all these features are brought together, it is fairly easy to see why employees in the UK and USA strongly prefer participative managers who involve their subordinates in decision making.

In France, however, power–distance is high and hierarchical structures, in which people lower down are not expected to shoulder responsibility, are accepted. Thus, employees are strongly encouraged to pass decision making upwards, which also suits the strong uncertainty avoidance characteristic of the culture. Individualism is also high and there is a medium level of masculinity. Therefore, managers are unlikely to delegate and, in any event, subordinates probably expect to be told what to do and would not adapt easily to the self-monitoring that goes hand in hand with autonomy. Thus, less participative styles are likely to fit well with the culture.

In Japan power–distance and individualism are only of medium strength, but uncertainty avoidance and masculinity are both high. Being part of a team is fundamental to the Japanese way of life and it verges on bad manners to stand out too much as an individual. Therefore, people avoid uncertainty by submerging their identities in a group, which militates strongly in favour of a shared ownership of decisions. This means that subordinates expect to shoulder some responsibility for solving the group's problems and in return, managers tend to be less concerned with the decision itself than with whether it can be implemented without problems. Indeed, an ideal decision is one where everybody is fully committed to its implementation. Usually this means that everyone has been involved in reaching the decision and so participative leadership styles fit best with the cultural characteristics.

Even a brief contrast such as this shows that culture can have a strong impact on whether employees are likely to feel comfortable with certain management styles. Perhaps the most important point to note is that the UK and USA have cultures in which the participative style is important but so is employee autonomy. Therefore, participation needs to take a form in which the manager shares decision making with subordinates, but also gives them some independence in action. In Japan, however, participation tends to be interpreted in a different way. It is generally taken to mean that manager and subordinates share decision making and also act collectively as a group to implement the decisions – a difference that is highly important. A style that is viewed as participative in the Western sense may well be interpreted altogether differently elsewhere.

OVERVIEW AND CONCLUSIONS

In its comparatively short history leadership theory has come a long way. While the topic now contains a rich diversity of different approaches, this can give rise to some problems. The word leadership can be is used in different ways by different theorists and this makes it difficult to be sure what the word means. The trait approach, which is the simplest and oldest of all leadership theories, conspicuously failed to isolate characteristics that are common to all effective leaders, and turned out to be a sterile line of enquiry.

The next development, style theory, sought to identify the way in which effective leaders behave, 'effectiveness' usually being defined by the twin criteria of goal attainment and follower satisfaction. This approach resulted in many different theories and the two dimensions of leader behaviour – concern for task and concern for people – are still very much alive in the leadership vocabulary.

The next stream of theoretical development, contingency theory, also accepts that the most valid way to describe leadership style is along the two dimensions of concern for task and concern for people. However, rather than specifying a 'one best' universal style, these theories try to identify which of the two dimensions should receive the most emphasis according to the circumstances in which leadership takes place. While this escapes the trap of assuming that there is a best way to lead, it gives rise to the problem of identifying the important factors that should influence style. A number of different contingency theories have emerged and these deal with different contingent circumstances but, as yet, there is no single contingency model that incorporates them all. One of the most interesting developments in this area is the 'substitutes for leadership' approach, which identifies certain circumstances in which leadership may well be redundant and unnecessary. Another promising but as yet comparatively underdeveloped approach is the idea that culture, either national or organisational, could be an important contingency variable.

In recent approaches to theorising there is a sense in which ideas about leadership have come full circle. This is particularly noticeable in the distinction between transactional and transformational leadership, where the emphasis on vaguely defined characteristics such as charisma, vision and empathy are regarded as vital attributes of the transformational leader, which is something of a return to earlier trait ideas.

With such a rich diversity of ideas it can be difficult to draw generalised conclusions about leadership, but six major points are worth noting.

1. Almost every book that discusses leadership stresses the point that leadership and management are not necessarily the same thing, but having made the point, it is then ignored. Indeed, there is currently a deplorable tendency to equate the word leader with positions at the very top of an organisation, which creates the myth of the Chief Executive as a 'superhero'. Even where this is not the case, most leadership theories focus exclusively on the supervisory or management role, and it is not uncommon to find that the words 'leader' and 'manager' are used interchangeably, as are the words 'follower' and 'subordinate'. This tends to ignore the point that supervisors and managers invariably have a degree of position power that, in the final analysis, can be used to influence or control subordinate behaviour. Thus, much of what is called leadership theory actually deals with headship and, at best, only gives guidance on how headship can most effectively be exercised.

2. The distinction between headship and leadership is an important one, which concerns the source of authority in the role. In headship authority is conferred from above and headship exists because a manager is given the right to command the actions of subordinates, whereas leadership occurs where followers confer authority on someone (upwards) to command their actions. Because most theories deal with headship, they sidestep the important issue of how and why some people come to be seen as leaders and have this power conferred upon them. Nevertheless there are theories which address this issue by treating leadership as a two-way process, for instance the vertical dyadic linkage model, action-centred leadership theory and, to some extent, the attributional approach.

3. As it has developed, leadership theory has become increasingly complex and so, while recent theories are regarded as more valid in academic circles, they have probably lost a degree of utility to managers. This probably accounts for the continued popularity of simpler, universal models and has a strong parallel with motivation theory, an area that has also become more rigorous and complex but now tends to be beyond the comprehension of many managers (see Chapters 7 and 8).

4. The leadership theories described in this chapter are all products of Western thought, and for this reason they usually extol the virtues of the participative or democratic styles of behaviour. While this behaviour fits well with the cultural values of the USA and UK, it should be noted that other countries have cultures that can make this style of behaviour somewhat less appropriate.

5. It is important to stress that leadership is not a discrete activity in organisations, nor is it a discrete topic in Organisational Behaviour. It therefore has strong connections with other topics in this book; for example, motivation is also concerned with influencing people's behaviour and, to the extent that someone is able to provide stimulating and motivating conditions for others, they are more likely to be seen as a leader. Similarly, whatever style of behaviour a leader adopts, he or she will need to be able to communicate ideas to others and so communication skills can be a vital part of being a leader.

6. Although leadership and headship are different in terms of the source of authority, in practice both processes involve the use of power. Power is a complex topic in its own right and is important enough to deserve the next chapter to itself.

FURTHER READING

Adair, J (1998) *The Inspirational Leader*, London: Kogan Page. A useful book that is partly a reflection of the author's action-centred approach, with a strong emphasis on the need for leaders to connect strongly with those that they lead.

Adair, J (2004) *Effective Leadership Development*, London: CIPD Publishing. Another well written and easy-to-read text that gives a faithful explanation of the author's theory of action-centred leadership principles.

Bass, BM and RM Stogdill (1990) *Bass and Stogdill's Handbook of Leadership: Theory, Research and Managerial Applications*, New York: Free Press. Almost certainly the most comprehensive text yet written on leadership theories and their application.

Bryman, A (1992) *Charisma and Leadership in Organisations*, London: Sage. The book gives an extensive and constructively critical analysis of current approaches to leadership.

Felfe, J and B Schyns (2006) Personality and the perceptions of transformational leadership: the impact of extraversion, neuroticism, personal need for structure and occupational self-efficacy, *Journal of Applied Social Psychology* 36(3): 708–739. Reports the results of a research study to trace some of the personality characteristics of transformational leaders.

Hickman, GR (ed.) (1998) *Leading Organisations: Perspectives for a New Era*, Thousand Oaks, CA: Sage. A book of readings that has a strong American bias and is lacking in critical perspectives. However, it is comprehensive and up to date.

Lim, BC and RE Ployhart (2004) Transformational leadership: relation to the five-factor model and team performance in typical and maximum contexts, *Journal of Applied Psychology* 89(4): 610–621. Another research study identifying the effects of the personality characteristics of transformational leaders.

Northouse, PG (1997) *Leadership: Theory and Practice*, London: Sage. A very readable book giving a brief but sound coverage of a wide variety of theoretical approaches to leadership and its practical application.

Parry R (2003) *Enterprise – the Leadership Role*, London: Profile Press. While containing lots of useful advice the book is very much an anthem to the CEO as the 'all action superhero' school of thought. That is, it equates management (particularly top management) and leadership as being the same thing.

Piccolo, RF and JA Colquitt (2006) Transformational leadership and job behaviour: the mediating role of core job characteristics, *Academy of Management Journal* 49(2): 327–340. Reports the results of an interesting study of transformational leaders and the effects that they are said to have on subordinate behaviour.

White, RP, P Hodgson and S Crainer (1996) *The Future of Leadership: A White Water Revolution*, London: Pitman. Rather a prescriptive text, but interesting because it speculates about the nature of leadership in the future.

Wright, P (1995) *Managerial Leadership*, London: Thomson. A very practical approach to leadership that will mainly be of interest to the manager (actual or would be).

CASE STUDY 13.1: Leadership Training at British Petroleum

Front-line managers, are often the unsung heroes of any large organisation. Yet without their effort and commitment, business performance often suffers. Until recently, British Petroleum (BP) had no comprehensive development programme for the people who ran its retail outlets, supervised teams at oil-refineries and chemical plants, or managed operations on drilling platforms, all of whom had different job titles in different parts of the corporation: for example, team leaders, supervisors or front-line managers. However, after a series of mergers and acquisitions, BP had become the world's third largest oil company and its new chief executive, John Browne, decided to set-up a team of senior executives to re-think the organisation's approach to learning and development.

The upheaval involved in creating a single entity out of British Petroleum, Amoco, Arco and several smaller firms had taken its toll of the workforce and employee surveys showed that front-line managers were especially dissatisfied, with many of them complaining about their supervisors, or the absence of clear career paths. These people work in every continent and constitute roughly 10 per cent of BP's 100,000-strong global workforce, and it was clear that they had long felt disconnected from the rest of the organisation. As one of them put it: 'there are no signs that the company wants to hear from people like me'. 'We may not be aiming to rise to the top, but we have leadership ability and ambition – and we feel ignored.' In retrospect, remarks like this were hardy surprising. For the most part, their training consisted of short *ad hoc* courses, designed and delivered locally and with little or no follow-up. Thus, although 70–80 per cent of all BP employees reported to these managers, they often found it difficult to see how their individual decisions contributed to the performance of the corporation as a whole. Neither was it clear how the skills and experience that a manger had gained in one part of the world could be transferred to another.

The eight senior executives on Browne's learning and development team recognised that this state of affairs was not sustainable, and were given the go-ahead to develop an ambitious training programme for a cohort that came to be known as 'first-level leaders' (a title chosen to emphasise their importance to BP). This was to be one of several initiatives intended to improve the quality of leadership throughout the organisation, and a project team working under Dominic Emery, a senior BP executive, was charged with undertaking this task. At its inaugural meeting the team started by identifying three potential constraints.

- It was recognised that that while some companies ran training programmes in a way that enabled entire teams to attend two or three sessions over the course of a year, this wasn't a practical option for BP. It had too many first-level leaders in too many different locations for that. Thus it needed a programme design that would enable some people to go to one session, and others to two or more.
- Since many of the first-level leaders worked on offshore oil rigs, or in other remote locations that had no internet access, BP could not rely on using web-based courses.
- It was envisaged that the 'owner' of the leadership programme would be BP itself, with local business units and regions using different elements of it as they saw fit, and paying for courses and materials out of their own learning and development budgets. However, it was recognised that this would be a break with past practice of the local design and delivery of courses, which might cause some resentment among learning and development professionals in BP's regional offices.

As a starting point for an overall design, Dominic Emery noted that employee surveys revealed that a diverse range of topics needed to be covered, which suggested that the programme should consist of a number of separate modules, which should, as a minimum consist of:

1. a module covering the basics of supervisory management
2. a slightly longer module explaining BPs overall business strategy
3. a longer and more intensive module on leadership skills
4. a peer coaching session in which new first-level leaders would be paired with more experienced colleagues.

Source: Priestland, A and R Hanig (2006) Fuelling the fire, *People Management*, 23 February: pp 41–42

Task
Assume that you have been co-opted onto Dominic Emery's project team; answer the questions below.

1. What do you feel prompted BP to choose the generic job title of 'first-level leaders' for the people to be trained; do you see any potential advantages and disadvantages in doing this?
2. Identify the potential advantages and drawbacks of BP itself (rather than its subsidiaries) being the 'owner' of the leadership programme.
3. What are your views on the tentative design of the programme suggested by Dominic Emery; for example, does it cover the most appropriate topics? Is it comprehensive enough, or is it too comprehensive?
4. Do you feel that the programme element covering leadership skills should attempt to draw on theoretical material on leadership? If your answer is yes, what theories of leadership should be included?
5. What other information do you feel that the project team might need before embarking on more detailed programme design activities?

REVIEW AND DISCUSSION QUESTIONS

1. Explain the underlying assumptions of the contingency approach to leadership and comment on Fiedler's theory in terms of its practical utility to organisations.

2. Explain Kerr and Jermier's argument that there are circumstances in which leadership can be relatively unimportant.

3. Explain the difference between 'transactional' and 'transformational' leadership and assess the practical utility of the transformational concept for devising programmes of leadership training.

4. Evaluate the assertion that 'most so-called theories of leadership tell us very little about the nature of "leadership"'.

Chapter 14

Power, Politics and Conflict

LEARNING OUTCOMES

After studying this chapter you should be able to:

- define power, describe the interpersonal and contextual bases of power in organisations, and explain some of the ways in which power is used

- define organisational politics, describe the factors that give rise to behaviour of this type and describe the tactics of its use

- define organisational conflict, distinguish conflict from competition and explain traditional and current perspectives on conflict in organisations

- describe the factors that give rise to conflict in organisations and explain the stages of a conflict episode

- explain what is meant by functional and dysfunctional conflict and describe methods that can be used to resolve or stimulate conflict in organisations

INTRODUCTION

This chapter covers what are, to many people, three of the most uncomfortable aspects of organisational life: power, politics and conflict. While the first of these is an attribute or characteristic of a person or group, and the other two are processes, it is important to realise that they are all closely related.

The first to be considered is power, and this section of the chapter starts with a definition, and explains the sources (bases) from which individuals and groups derive their power. Discussion then turns to the use of power and the most frequently used power tactics.

The next section deals with organisational politics. It defines the phenomenon and describes the organisational circumstances which tend to give rise to political activity. The pervasive nature of political activity is then considered, together with the ethics of this type of behaviour, and the section closes with a description of some of the political tactics used in organisations.

The final topic is that of organisational conflict. A definition is given and conflict is distinguished from competition. Traditional and contemporary perspectives on conflict are examined and, following this, the nature of organisational conflict is examined, together with an explanation of the factors that give rise to conflictual behaviour. Although it can exist beneath the surface for some time, conflict only tends to become visible when a conflict episode occurs. A model of a typical episode is given, followed by an explanation of methods of conflict management. The chapter closes with a conclusion and overview that highlights the interconnected nature of power, politics and conflict and some of the more significant implications for people in organisations.

POWER

Until fairly recently there was considerable debate about whether the use of power in organisations is widespread and, because there is a potential imbalance of power in all social relationships, any attempt to describe human behaviour in organisations would be incomplete without a consideration of power. Since power is an extremely complex topic, this chapter only gives an introduction to the subject. Historically, there have been numerous definitions of power, many of which imply that it is essentially an individual attribute but, since this chapter also deals with power as something that can be wielded collectively, it is defined here as:

> **the capacity of an individual or group to modify the conduct of other individuals or groups in a manner which they desire and without having to modify their own conduct in a manner which they do not desire.** (Tawney 1931, p 229)

A number of important implications flow from this definition and the reader is asked to keep them firmly in mind throughout the chapter. These are:

- that power does not exist in isolation, but is a characteristic of a relationship between two or more individuals or groups
- for power to exist there must at least be a possibility that it can be exercised, otherwise it is only latent power

- power is situational; a person or group seldom has the same amount of power in all circumstances and, sometimes, it is the situation itself that confers power on someone who is otherwise relatively powerless
- few people have no power whatsoever; some might only have a small degree of power in a limited range of circumstances, and others have not yet mobilised their power so that it remains latent
- in using power, what often matters most is not the absolute amount that a person or group has, but the relative amount compared to the other party.

Power is a very abstract concept and different people use the word in different ways. For instance, although some texts use the words 'power' and 'authority' interchangeably, strictly speaking they are not the same thing. Authority is a special type of power that exists when a specific position or role is endowed with the right to make decisions or command the actions of other people. It is not a property or characteristic of a person, but is delegated from above (Weber 1947) and comes with the job, often outlives the individual's occupancy of a role, and its use is usually regarded as legitimate by those over whom it is exercised (Katz and Kahn 1978). However, since it confers the rights to make decisions only about certain matters, authority is bounded and if someone exceeds these rights, it can sometimes be challenged. It is, of course, the most visible type of power in organisations.

Some writers also distinguish between power and influence, by stating that power involves a stronger element of force or coercion, while influence is more persuasive in nature. This, however, poses a huge conceptual problem. All forms of power, including coercion, are used to influence the behaviour of other people, and so it makes little sense to distinguish between influence and power (Mintzberg 1983).

TIME OUT

1. Think of someone, whom you either know well or come into contact with regularly, whom you perceive to be a person who has power over other people, perhaps even over yourself. Try to identify why it is the person has this power over others; that is, where does his or her power come from?

2. Now consider yourself and your own situation. Do you have power over other people in any way (if you examine matters deeply you may be surprised to find that you have)? Where does your power over these other people come from, that is, what gives you this power?

THE ORIGINS (SOURCES OR BASES) OF POWER

In order to understand more about power and its use the first step is to identify why some individuals or groups have more power than others. Power often comes from several sources at the same time, some of which are located within an individual or group, some arise from the nature of an organisation and others may be more a reflection of specific context or situations. These all tend to have a cumulative effect and so they are all brought together in the comprehensive model shown in Figure 14.1.

Figure 14.1
Interpersonal and contextual bases of power

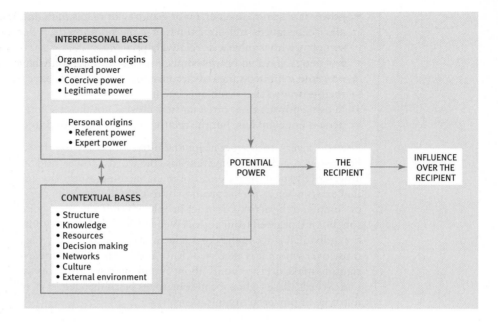

The Interpersonal Bases of Power

At this level, power is exercised personally by one individual over others. Several different schemes have been suggested to categorise the sources of power of this type, the best known of which is probably French and Raven's (1959) 'five bases of power'. The original scheme simply describes these bases, but since some are derived from the power holder's position, while others are more a function of personal characteristics, they are split into two groups.

Organisational Origins

Reward Power

Providing that they value the rewards, someone who controls the distribution of rewards to other people has a degree of power over them. The more formally structured an organisation the more likely it is that this type of power will be limited by rules, for instance supervisors might only be able to make recommendations about increased rewards for subordinates, but the actual decision is the prerogative of a higher-level manager. To some extent the use of *reward power* is also influenced by informal 'custom and practice' arrangements. Although a supervisor can have the official right to award paid overtime, it may be the normal practice to share it out between subordinates, and woe betide the supervisor who ignores this custom.

Reward power: the capability to confer rewards on others

Coercive Power

Coercive power is the opposite of reward power. It reflects a person's capability to compel someone else to behave in a particular way, usually because a sanction can be

Coercive power: the capability to compel others to behave in a certain way

imposed or a reward withheld in the event of non-compliance. Usually this is also a matter of delegated authority, and in most organisations the use of coercive power tends to be very strictly controlled. For instance, while supervisors commonly deal with all minor rule transgressions, the sanctions that they are allowed to impose are usually strictly limited and more severe sanctions are normally the prerogatives of higher levels of management.

Legitimate Power

Legitimate power: the authority to command the actions of other people that goes with a particular role

Legitimate power exists where someone occupies an organisational role that carries the authority to make decisions or command the actions of others. Once again, the more formal and elaborate the structure of an organisation the more likely it is that boundaries will be placed on a person's legitimate power. For instance, while supervisors can instruct subordinates to undertake certain activities it is often the case that these can only be from within a strictly specified range. Subordinates also play a role in the exercise of legitimate power. For example, a supervisor might have the power to allocate a number of duties to subordinates, some of which are considered to be more unpleasant than others. Where it is the custom for everyone to take their turn at doing the dirty jobs, and the supervisor shields certain people from this work, he or she can easily find that the others take steps to demonstrate that power is being used unwisely, perhaps by refusing to cooperate over other matters.

Personal Origins

These are associated with the personal characteristics of a power holder. Unlike the three bases discussed above, which can be removed or reduced by a person's superior, whether or not personal bases remain intact is largely in the hands of the power holder.

Referent Power

Referent power: the capability to influence others that comes from having attributes or characteristics that make someone a source of reference or role model for other people

Someone with strong personal attributes that make the person a source of reference or a role model to others is said to have *referent power*. Usually this means that other people who come into close contact with the individual recognise these attributes, so power of this type is not necessarily associated with position in the organisational hierarchy. One of the more tangible signs that someone has this type of power is that others imitate his or her characteristics, which can result in the person being perceived as a leader. However, as will be recalled from Chapter 13, leadership tends to be situational, and someone who is seen as the most appropriate person to lead in one set of circumstances may not be viewed in this way when the circumstances change. Thus referent power can sometimes be highly transient.

Expert Power

Expert power: the ability to influence others that exists because a person is seen to possess a particular expertise

In all organisations there are people who occupy specialist positions and, in situations where their expertise is required, this gives them a degree of power. Because pockets of expertise often reside low down in an organisation, this type of power is not necessarily associated with rank. Indeed, people higher up can sometimes be strongly dependent on those below, which means that *expert power* can be deployed upwards.

Contextual Bases of Power

Lukes (1974) draws attention to an important distinction between *power over* (others) and the *power to* achieve something. The 'power to' is often derived from the contextual circumstances that surround an individual or group, and these sources tend to complement and reinforce interpersonal bases. At least seven contextual sources can be identified and these are explained below.

Organisational Structure

An individual's formal authority in an organisation is primarily determined by its structural design, which establishes certain patterns of communication and the authority to make certain decisions (Pfeffer 1981). Therefore, structure largely determines the extent of a person's reward, coercive and legitimate power, and an organisation chart is little more than a map of power and authority.

Knowledge and Information

There is a great deal of truth in the adage that 'information is power'. Information is required for most decisions, and if someone controls its flow he or she has power over other groups to whom the information is vital. People in a position to do so often acquire this power base by becoming 'information gatekeepers'. An example of this is given in Pettigrew's (1973) study of a large retail firm that was one of the first in Great Britain to computerise its operations. Pettigrew describes how a single individual managed to manoeuvre himself into a position where he controlled the flow of information from the computer manufacturers who were able to supply a new machine. In this way, although the directors of the firm formally made the choice of which one to purchase, he was able to shape their decision in a way that was highly beneficial to himself.

Resources

Access to appropriate resources often gives an organisational sub-unit the ability to achieve its goals. However, in most organisations, resources are often rationed or shared out between sub-units, which makes subordinate units dependent on higher-level managers, and helps ensure their compliance. Therefore, access to a plentiful supply of resources not only gives a degree of independence from the power of those above, but also gives a better likelihood of achieving goals.

One of the most subtle uses of resource power occurs when one sub-unit becomes a vital resource for most other sub-units. In his description of the relationship between production and maintenance departments in a French tobacco factory, Crozier (1964) gives a penetrating insight into this situation. Since the key to the profitability of the factory lay in a smooth and uninterrupted flow of production, production departments had a great deal of formal power. However, real power was in the hands of maintenance workers, because they determined whether production machinery was kept in continuous operation. Thus, to achieve output goals, production departments were acutely dependent on the goodwill of maintenance.

Using Crozier's ideas, Hickson *et al.* (1971) developed a theory of sub-unit power based upon the concept of *strategic contingencies*. This was subsequently verified by

Strategic contingencies: events or activities that are crucial in achieving organisational goals

Hinings *et al.* (1974), who examined power relations in seven manufacturing firms in the USA and Canada. In each firm, four departments (engineering, marketing, production and accounting) were examined to assess their power along the following dimensions:

- **Substitutability:** whether the service provided by a department could be obtained elsewhere.
- **Work flow pervasiveness:** whether the flow of work in a department affected work flow in one of the others.
- **Uncertainty:** ambiguity about the future.
- **Work flow immediacy:** the extent to which the work flow of a department had a rapid and noticeable effect on the output of the whole organisation.

Departments were then ranked in terms of overall power, according to the number of dimensions on which they had achieved high scores. If a department had a high score on just one of the power dimensions, it was found to have a low degree of power relative to the others. From this, Hinings and his co-workers concluded that relative power lay in the ability to cope with the three key contingency factors shown in Figure 14.2.

Decision Making

The ability to affect how decisions are made considerably enhances power, and sometimes it is possible to do this without actually taking part in the decision making process. For instance, a team that is charged with studying a range of options for marketing

Figure 14.2 A strategic contingency model of sub-unit power (adapted from Hickson *et al.* 1971; Hinings *et al.* 1974)

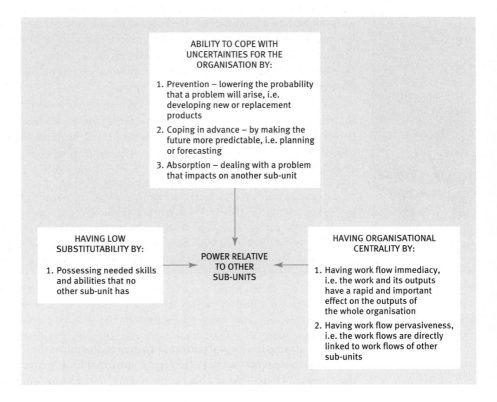

ABILITY TO COPE WITH UNCERTAINTIES FOR THE ORGANISATION BY:

1. Prevention – lowering the probability that a problem will arise, i.e. developing new or replacement products
2. Coping in advance – by making the future more predictable, i.e. planning or forecasting
3. Absorption – dealing with a problem that impacts on another sub-unit

HAVING LOW SUBSTITUTABILITY BY:

1. Possessing needed skills and abilities that no other sub-unit has

POWER RELATIVE TO OTHER SUB-UNITS

HAVING ORGANISATIONAL CENTRALITY BY:

1. Having work flow immediacy, i.e. the work and its outputs have a rapid and important effect on the outputs of the whole organisation
2. Having work flow pervasiveness, i.e. the work flows are directly linked to work flows of other sub-units

a new product may examine a very limited range of options, which leaves decision makers little to do but rubber-stamp the option that makes the team more influential in the future. Indeed, since some decisions are made sequentially in organisations, the individual or group that makes its decisions early can limit the range of options open to those who make their decisions later on.

 OB IN ACTION: 'The club' still reigns supreme

There is a fairly extensive raft of legislation that tries to ensure equality of opportunity and, in addition, many organisations have policies that proclaim their commitment to this aim, all of which gives an impression that organisations are meritocracies. Nevertheless, being 'one of the chaps', or 'networking' as current jargon politely calls it, still seems to have tremendous advantages for those admitted to 'the club'. For instance, there are certain occupations, such as the law, where the 'old boy' discrimination network is highly effective in creating a barrier for those entering the profession. In addition, the system of taking 'informal soundings' from existing members of the judiciary before a new judge is appointed only serves to confirm the idea that the judiciary is a rather exclusive club. To some extent the same can be said in medicine; in recent cases of incompetence and/or malpractice, it seems likely that members of the club 'closed ranks' with the result that even though well-documented complaints from patients existed, matters remained concealed for many years. 'The club' is just as commonplace and is an equally potent force in many large business organisations. For instance, a recent survey revealed that even younger senior executives rated 'knowing the right people' as one of the most important factors influencing career progression.

A new twist, however, is that while there seems to be some tendency to unseat the old elite, it is almost inevitably replaced by a new one. While the criteria of membership may not be the same, for example hard drinking, competitiveness and brashness replace the old school tie and an Oxbridge education, the end result is the same. The old adage of 'it's not what you know, but who you know' still operates as before, and members of the club are given preference over those who are not.

Source:

Palmer, C (2000) A job old boy? The school ties that still bind, *The Observer*, 11 June, p 18

Networks

Structure establishes formal patterns of interaction and, as the OB in Action Box above indicates, those who interact often create informal links that are useful for enhancing their power. These links enable people to stay 'in the know' and trade favours so that power can be exercised in the future. Pfeffer and Salanick (1978) argue that these networks are often more influential than formal mechanisms because people are liable to increase their power by forming coalitions, or power blocs, that enable them to draw on each other's power when necessary.

Organisational Culture

Culture can often be a silent and highly unobtrusive source of power. It reflects implicit understandings and assumptions about the way that certain matters should be dealt with, and these become embedded in codes of behaviour that often confer a great deal of power on certain individuals and groups. These norms are often so taken for granted that they become what Lukes (1974) has called the third dimension of power. They determine whose viewpoint dominates, whether an issue can be brought out into the open or is regarded as non-discussable, and they often result in an acceptance of power holding by one group as the natural order of things.

The External Environment

Because a firm has little control over its environment, it is usually regarded as something that reduces organisational power. However, as will be seen in Chapter 18, most firms try to buffer their technical cores from the effects of environment so that they can operate under stable conditions (Thompson 1967). Where environmental effects are particularly crucial, organisations often have sub-units to deal with segments of the environment that are subject to a high degree of change. Because these sub-units shield others in the organisation from the effects of change, they can come to occupy positions of great power, an example of which was given earlier when describing the work of Hinings *et al.* (1974).

THE BASIS OF POWER

To close this description of the bases of power and link it to the next section, a number of important points can be made. First, the distinction between interpersonal and contextual bases of power is an artificial one. In practice, the bases are strongly connected and some of the contextual sources, for example structure, culture, knowledge and resources, reinforce the coercive, reward and legitimate powers of individuals. Similarly, some of the interpersonal bases, notably expert and referent power, enable people to manipulate circumstances to acquire contextual power.

Second, the bases of power are additive, which is why interpersonal and contextual bases converge in Figure 14.1. Thus, someone who can draw on all the interpersonal bases has much more power than someone who can draw on only one, and individuals or groups that have access to both contextual and interpersonal bases will usually be much more powerful than those who can only draw on one source.

Third, as can be seen from Figure 14.1, the bases only give someone 'potential power'. In some situations, power has to be used to demonstrate that it exists so that it can be used to exert influence in the future.

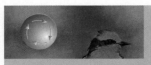

- The three main bases of interpersonal power that emanate from the organisation are reward power, coercive power and referent power.
- Two additional bases of interpersonal power that emanate from within the power holder are referent power and expert power.
- A number of other bases of power can be derived from the context within which power is exercised.
- The bases of power are additive, so that normally an individual or group that can draw on several bases is more powerful than an individual or group that relies on just one base.

MISCONCEPTIONS ABOUT THE USE OF POWER

There are many misconceptions about the use of power, but two of the most common ones concern its assumed direction of flow and its assumed visibility, and these will be addressed in turn.

The Direction of Power Flows

The use of power in organisations is often assumed to be synonymous with formal authority, which gives the impression that power is always exercised downwards, through the hierarchy. However, some of the interpersonal bases of power result in conditions where it can just as easily be exercised upwards. For example, expert power sometimes makes a manager dependent on subordinates, whose cooperation can be vital. This is particularly the case at the current time, when the workforce in many organisations has been cut back to the bare minimum and many managers are dependent on the active cooperation of employees. Whereas compliance can be enforced, this is not the case with cooperation, which needs to be given willingly, and it is this need for cooperation that enables employees to exert power upwards.

Hidden Power

The second misconception is that power is always a visible attribute, whereas hidden power is often the most potent form. For example, people who keep their power hidden can often be one step ahead of the opposition and act before an opponent becomes aware. A simple explanation will perhaps demonstrate the point. People of high status can use their position power to control the agendas of committees where certain issues are discussed and, because most of us have some awareness of this practice, it is only a semi-hidden use of power. However, other people, notably those with expert or referent power, sometimes have access to these individuals, which enables them to exert a degree of hidden influence that prevents some of these items ever being discussed.

Power Tactics

There are many ways of using power. Some were briefly mentioned when describing the bases of power and others in contrasting the use of invisible and visible power. Here the discussion will mainly focus on power tactics that are used at individual and intra-group levels, where people, including managers and supervisors, use power in their immediate surroundings. To do this, some of the research evidence will be described, and these results will be used to draw conclusions at the end of this section.

The Kipnis Study

Kipnis *et al.* (1984) give a comprehensive picture of the tactics that are used by supervisors and managers to influence each other and their subordinates. Seven main tactics were identified and these are shown in Table 14.1, together with the behaviour associated with each one.

The range of tactics identified by Kipnis and his co-workers is quite extensive and tactics were found to be used upwards, downwards and laterally. Some, however, are clearly more usable in one direction than another. For example, trying to use coercion

Table 14.1 Power tactics (after Kipnis *et al.* 1984)

Tactic	How the tactic operates	Typical associated behaviours
Assertiveness	Direct use of authority	• Issue direct instruction to comply • Set deadline dates for completion • Emphasise importance of compliance • Remind other person(s) of obligation to comply
Friendliness or integration	Induce favourable disposition in other person(s) to comply	• Praise prior to requesting compliance • Exaggerate importance of compliance • Act humbly to obtain cooperation and wait until other person is in receptive mood before making request
Rationality	Use the force of logical argument	• Present information in a way that makes non-compliance seem illogical • Develop well-argued case to show that other person is highly competent if he or she complies • Explain exactly what is required
Sanctions	Compel compliance – the argument of force	• Use or threaten to use the coercive power of organisational rewards and punishments, e.g. future performance appraisal, salary increases, privileges
Higher authority	Obtain support and backing from above	• Support obtained and shown to be obtained before requesting others to comply
Bargaining	Obtain support from other power holders	• Exchange favours to obtain compliance • Call in debts for giving favours on prior occasions
Coalitions	Enlist the support of other people	• Build up alliances with others (subordinates and co-workers) • Network to identify where favours can be done for others and asked in return

Figure 14.3 Preferred power tactics for using upwards or downwards influence (adapted from Kipnis *et al.* 1984)

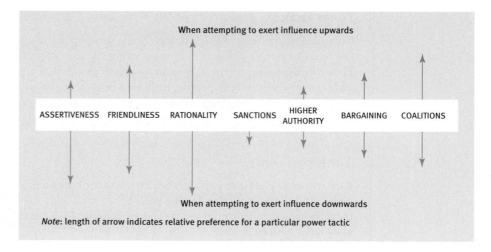

upwards is likely to provoke unresistable coercion in return. Thus, the order of popularity of a particular tactic tends to vary according to the direction in which it is used, which is shown in Figure 14.3.

AN OVERVIEW OF POWER AND ITS USE

When brought together with other points made in the chapter the results of Kipnis *et al.* (1984) allow general conclusions to be drawn about power and its use.

- To some extent, successfully using a particular base of power depends on the type of person on whom it is used. For instance, aggressive or assertive managers, who are perhaps most likely to use sanctions or face-to-face confrontations to extract obedience, are often those who get the least compliance from their subordinates. Thus, the power tactic used must be appropriate to the circumstances.

- Power is used within a context, and all contexts have their own rules about how power should be exercised. For instance, in most cases an attempt to use coercion upwards would be a breach of the rules. Moreover, power bases can also be very fragile and have their own limitations in certain contexts. For example, managers who are legitimate experts in certain areas can seriously undermine perceptions of their expertise if they try to create an illusion that they are experts on everything. Similarly, people who have genuine referent power because they are seen by others to have high ethics and ideals can lose all credibility in a momentary lapse in which they use less reputable tactics.

- There are sometimes occupational or professional biases for or against the use of certain power bases. Technical experts and professionals (for example, engineers, scientists, lawyers or accountants) are probably more amenable to the tactics of rationality and friendliness from an expert in another field than they would be to other types of power. Thus it is unwise to rely too much on one power base and a variety of sources may be needed as the circumstances dictate.

- The effectiveness of certain power bases and tactics can depend on the circumstances of the moment. In a crisis situation, legitimate or expert power and, in some circumstances, coercion can often be considered appropriate. For instance, if your house was burning down and the fire brigade arrived, would you be happy to see the chief firefighter get the others in a circle and painstakingly persuade them what to do with a long-winded process of rational argument? However, the same power tactics can be highly ineffective in non-crisis circumstances, even if they are used by the same people.

- The sources of power do not appear overnight. While people acquire legitimate power and the reward and coercive bases that go with it when they are promoted to a position of authority, to be sustained, even these bases have to be nurtured.

- Because the effect of different bases of power is additive, it is sensible to cultivate as many interpersonal and contextual bases as possible. To do this often means that a versatile range of tactics for acquiring, maintaining and using power has to be developed, and this is the next topic in the chapter.

REPLAY

- Although power is most visible when it is used downwards, it can also be exercised upwards and laterally.
- Power is not always used in a visible way and often invisible power is the most potent form.
- A wide range of tactics of power use can be identified, some of which are more commonly used in different directions and in specific contextual circumstances.

ORGANISATIONAL POLITICS

To quote what is by now is the most widely accepted definition, organisational politics:

> involves those activities taken within organisations to acquire, develop and use power and other resources to obtain one's preferred outcome in a situation where there is uncertainty or descensus about choices. (Pfeffer 1981, p 7)

To many people this smacks of unsavoury manipulation, chicanery and devious under-hand behaviour. Nevertheless, it gives rise to three implications:

- Although political behaviour is clearly related to the concept of power, conceptually, politics and power are two different things.
- Politics tend to occur in situations of uncertainty, where an individual or group can use the situation to their own advantage.
- The definition refers to descensus about choices, which means that if there is disagreement about whose preferences should dominate, the political process can be activated to resolve the issue.

It should also be recognised that because matters dealt with by top managers are usually more uncertain and ambiguous than those dealt with by people lower down, political behaviour is more prevalent at these levels. Indeed, Gandz and Murray (1980) comment that, while most managers declare behaviour of this type to be unfair, bad and unhealthy, they also feel that being a good politician is a prerequisite for advancement to high levels.

In addition, it is worth noting that much of the political behaviour used to pursue the interests of individuals or groups, is at the expense of the organisation as a whole (Madison *et al.* 1980).

FACTORS GIVING RISE TO POLITICAL BEHAVIOUR

Organisational Factors

While certain personality characteristics can play a part in prompting political activity, these characteristics only identify the more willing users of politics, which says nothing about situations that provide an opportunity to bring political tactics into play. These, however, are well documented in the works of Miles (1980) and Robbins (1998), and are covered in what follows.

Ambiguous Goals

In some organisations, goals are stated in highly ambiguous terms. While goals such as 'increase the market share', or 'enter new markets' are commonplace, they fail to specify exactly what should be achieved. This vagueness can be used to justify almost any course of action (even something that can be use for purely personal gain) simply by saying that it will help achieve the goal.

Scarce Resources

Few people get everything that they desire when resources are distributed in an organisation, especially when cutbacks are in progress. This creates a situation of winners and losers and the losers can engage in all sorts of tactics to try to acquire resources simply by presenting misleading information or exaggerating budgets.

Technology and Environment

Changes in the technology used by an organisation increase the uncertainty of organisational life. This often gives a tremendous opportunity to engage in manoeuvres that are designed to enlarge or preserve the power bases of individuals and groups.

Non-programmed Decisions

Where a decision is required on how to deal with a completely novel situation there are seldom any precedents to guide decision making. This gives huge scope for individuals to manoeuvre to get their definition of the situation adopted. If this is successful, it virtually guarantees that the person will be regarded as knowledgeable, which brings expert power.

Organisational Change

Since any situation involving change contains a degree of uncertainty, the circumstances are ripe for someone to redefine the situation and how it should be handled to his or her own advantage. In addition, uncertainty and ambiguity have been shown to result in heightened perceptions that political activity is commonplace in others (Ferris *et al.* 1994), which in turn prompts the perceivers to engage in political actions themselves.

Role Ambiguity

If someone occupies a role in which the required behaviour is unclear or ambiguous, the person has a golden opportunity to redefine the role in way that best suits him or herself.

Unclear Criteria for Evaluating Performance

Those who appraise the performance of others often rely on very subjective evaluation criteria. Sometimes only a single measure of performance is used, and there are long intervals between the time that performance occurs and the point at which it is evaluated. In the interim period the appraisee clearly has a great deal of scope to redefine his or her role in a more advantageous way.

Organisational Culture and Structure

The more that a culture contains values that encourage people to view situations in win–lose terms the greater is the incentive never to be a loser. Thus, any type of behaviour that facilitates winning can come to be considered as justifiable. In addition, where a structure centralises decision making in the hands of a small number of people, others can feel starved of information and influence, which prompts them to engage in politicking.

Low Trust

Where people do not trust each other their tendency to use covert manoeuvrings in their dealings is greater. This is particularly the case when they perceive that others regularly engage in politicking, because in this situation they can come to believe that they have no alternative to behaving the same way themselves (Valle and Perrewe 2000).

TIME OUT

Imagine that you are an official of the student union at your university or college. Also imagine that the government announces that in the interests of saving money, as from the start of the next academic year, it will reduce its subsidy to each university by an amount equivalent to last year's expenditure on the student union. Most student unions run a number of services for students, and there are a large number of societies and activities that are subsidised in this way.

1. Would this situation be likely to result in an increase in the use of political tactics within the student union?
2. Of the factors discussed above, which ones in particular are likely to prompt increased political activity within the union?
3. What form do you feel this political activity would take?

THE PERVASIVENESS OF ORGANISATIONAL POLITICS

Although many people condemn organisational politics, there is little doubt that it is extremely widespread. For instance, a survey of 428 managers by Gandz and Murray (1980) revealed that, while 55 per cent felt that behaviour of this type was unfair and unhealthy, over 75 per cent believed that successful executives need to be good politicians. Moreover, work by Lenway and Rehbein (1991) affirms this picture and indicates that most managers see political behaviour as an undesirable but inevitable part of organisational life. As such, the conclusion that can be drawn is that politicking is highly prevalent and to a large extent this is connected with the circumstances outlined above, which are very common in most organisations. Indeed, Mintzberg (1985) argues that the incentives to use political behaviour are so strong that it can never be completely eradicated. However, this still leaves unanswered the important question about whether political activity has a positive or negative effect on an organisation.

Political Behaviour: Positive or Negative Functions?

Political behaviour probably has both positive and negative organisational functions. For example, in his earlier work, Pfeffer (1981), while not actually condemning political behaviour, is far from endorsing its use. In more recent work, however, he argues that it is often the only way to overcome the inertia that is commonplace in hierarchically structured organisations, and may well be the only way to make things happen (Pfeffer 1992). Thus, like power, politics is *Janus-faced* and, depending on how it is used, it can be a force for good or a force for evil. The twin faces of politics have been cogently analysed by Mintzberg (1985), who draws a similar conclusion: it is not political behaviour itself that is dysfunctional but how politics are used and the ends to which they are directed. A summary of Mintzberg's ideas is given in Table 14.2.

Janus-faced: having two (good and evil) aspects

POLITICAL TACTICS

Having considered organisational politics at a theoretical level it is now time to examine some of the more practical considerations. Although a wide range of political behaviour is possible, Schein (1977) notes that what is used tends to depend on three factors:

● Goals – what a person hopes to achieve.
● Personal characteristics – some people are more comfortable with using certain tactics than others.
● The situation – which places limits on the behaviour that can be used, for example some behaviour is easier to defend and so it can be used in a visible way, while other tactics have to be concealed.

Table 14.2 Positive and negative functions of organisational politics (adapted from Mintzberg 1985)

Positive functions		Negative functions	
Organisational flexibility	The use of politics can correct the slowness of more formal methods of influence and add flexibility to these methods	Inequality, discrimination and unfairness	Political activity tends to result in 'in-groups' and 'out-groups', in which the interests of minority groups, who have little formal influence, can be ignored
Meritocracy	Political usage acts to ensure that the fittest and strongest in organisations are brought into positions of influence and leadership	Distorted decision making	Political activity tends to be used by individuals and groups to promote only their own interests, which means that decision criteria can be narrow and parochial
Promotion of multiple perspectives	Politics can help ensure that all sides of an issue are aired and debated, while more conventional forms of influence can result in only one side being heard	Ignores interests of stakeholders	Because some individuals or groups are able to exercise the real power within an organisation other stakeholders simply have their interests ignored
Facilitates change	Politics can be used to promote changes that are otherwise blocked by normal systems of influence	Inefficiency and time wasting	Political behaviour, which often involves extensive lobbying, alliance building and subversion of the formal influence processes, uses up inordinate amounts of energy that could be put to better use
Decision implementation	Political activity can help ensure that decisions get implemented	Unequal power and the results of decisions	Power corrupts and once tasted is an addictive drug. Thus, the use of political behaviour develops a taste for power, which can all too easily gyrate in only one direction. Power difference in organisations should desirably be minimised rather than allowed to become greater

Several authors have attempted to catalogue political tactics, an exacting task because it is very difficult to observe politics at work. Nevertheless, using the writings of Pfeffer (1981) and Mintzberg (1983), a list of tactics can be brought together and these are described in what follows. Since the purpose of these tactics is to acquire or maintain power, it should be noted that some of them have a connection with the bases of power described earlier in the chapter.

Control of Information

Where certain information is crucial the smaller the number of people having access to it, the greater the influence of those who have the total picture. Thus, an extremely potent political tactic is to become the sole conduit for certain information.

Dominate Information Flows

Where it is not possible to be the sole source of information, people who are able to become 'gatekeepers' who control access to it acquire a great deal of power. For instance, they can divulge only certain parts of the information, so that only they have the complete picture.

Use of Outside Experts

Outside experts such as consultants have an air of impartiality and neutrality, and the people who sponsor their entry into an organisation are often able to frame the consultants' terms of reference in a way that enables only one set of conclusions to be drawn. In this way it is possible to obtain the support of an outside expert for proposals that might otherwise attract internal opposition.

Control of Agendas

Rather than get into an argument when alternative proposals are debated, it can be more effective to control the agenda and limit the number of proposals that appear. For instance, under the guise of saving the valuable time of the main committee, a sub-committee can be set up to vet the alternatives. Where control over the whole agenda cannot be exercised, choosing the order in which items appear can be nearly as useful. This way it is sometimes possible to arrange for opponents to be absent, or at least ensure that supporters are in the majority.

Image Building

If people are seen as experts on a particular matter, or have the backing of people in power, their judgement is less likely to be questioned. Thus a useful tactic is to create an image that conveys this impression.

Coalition Building

There is a saying that 'It's not what you know, it's who you know.' Thus a viable tactic is to build up a network of alliances, perhaps by doing favours for others, so that support can be called on in return when it is needed.

Control of Decision Parameters

Astute politicians often ensure that the outcome of a decision most benefits themselves by establishing the criteria against which the acceptability of a solution to a problem is evaluated. Suppose, for example, that a manager favours a particular location for a new warehouse. If he or she is able to persuade the decision making body that certain criteria (such as location, ease of access, room for eventual expansion, etc.) are the ones to use, information can be presented in a way that makes the manager's preferred option the automatic choice.

Game Playing

In one sense, game playing can be regarded as just another political tactic. However, Mintzberg (1983) views all tactics as 'games that are played within a political arena'

Figure 14.4 The political arena (adapted from Mintzberg 1983)

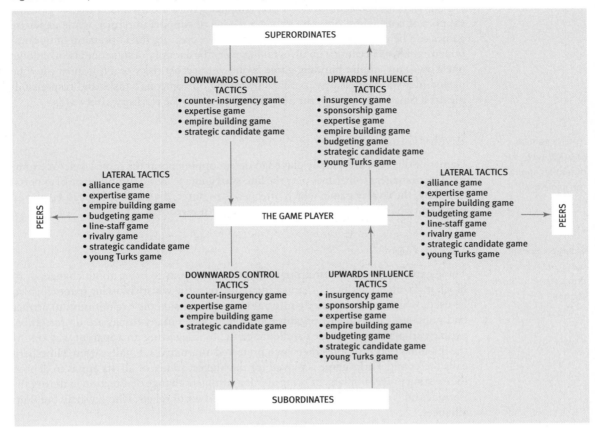

and this perspective has the advantage of illustrating that tactics can be used in several directions depending upon those one is trying to influence. This is portrayed in Figure 14.4.

Authority Games

Authority games:
political tactics to resist authority from above or counter resistance to authority from below

These are used either to resist authority from above or counter resistance to authority from below. The former are what Mintzberg calls **insurgency games**, which range from outright mutiny to mild resistance or, to avoid taking action, the use of delayed messages. These tactics can be used by individuals, groups or even a whole workforce, if it has been collectively organised. As the name implies, **counter-insurgency games** are played by people in authority to retain or regain compliance; often by making threats or introducing a stricter regime of control.

Power Base Games

Power base games:
political tactics to build or maintain a power base

Tactics of this type can be used in all directions to build or maintain bases of power. The **sponsorship game** is used to obtain resources, backing or prestige by convincing a senior, powerful figure of one's loyalty. A **budgeting game** simply involves making exaggerated bids to acquire resources. **Alliance games** are used laterally, to gain the support of colleagues, often by giving a pledge of support in return, while **expertise games** can be played in any direction and involve creating the impression of unquestioned expertise. Because it involves taking away the territory of someone else to enlarge one's own, the **empire building game** is one of the most risky of all. It must often be played in a very covert way, perhaps by taking on someone's tasks and responsibilities at a time of crisis, with the aim of holding on to the territory afterwards.

Rivalry games: political tactics to defeat an opponent at the same level

Rivalry Games

Games of this type are usually played to defeat opponents at the same level, for example, line managers sometimes play the **line-staff game** to avoid the influence of experts. Similarly, the **rivalry game**, which often leads to bitter, divisive battles, can be played between two individuals or groups competing for territory.

Change games: political tactics to bring about or block change

Change Games

These games come to the forefront when someone wants to bring about change, or to block it. To alter unethical organisational practices the **whistleblowing game** can also be used, which involves quietly informing people outside the organisation to attract bad publicity. At a time of organisational flux, when many things are up for grabs, people can play the **strategic candidate game**, by suggesting an apparent way out of the dilemma that promotes their own preferred alternatives. Finally, what Mintzberg calls the **young Turks game** is played for the highest stakes of all. Its aim is to depose the existing power holders, or bring about a complete change of direction in the organisation, and is usually played by a very dedicated set of rebels, who covertly build up alliances.

 OB IN ACTION: Environmental groups – political tactics

The battle over so-called 'ghost ships' has turned the spotlight on the politics and tactics of the environmental movement. However, lobbyists, led by Friends of the Earth, have come under attack for scaremongering and exaggerating the scale of the problem. Peter Mandelson, Hartlepool's MP and a former cabinet minister, has complained of a 'ferocious propaganda battle'. The group's detractors accuse it of successfully hyping the issue – with its potent mix of fear, symbolic imagery and anti-American sentiment – as part of its battle for members, money and media attention. They say there is a history of 'green' lobbyists distorting evidence, while choosing emotive but relatively unimportant issues for their campaigns. Long-established campaign groups, such as FoE (Friends of the Earth) and Greenpeace, try to avoid making factual errors, realising that they reinforce the public's suspicion that pressure groups are often cavalier with facts. Nevertheless pressure groups are often accused of choosing emotive, irrational issues on which to campaign. Shell was forced

to give up its attempt to sink the Brent Spar platform in the North Sea despite having convinced many scientists that deep sea disposal was the most environmentally sound solution.

Professor Ulrich Steger of IMD, the Lausanne-based business school, argues that one reason why FoE chose to campaign on the ghost ships was its collective memory of a series of incidents in the mid to late 1990s when the UK accepted hazardous waste from other European countries, creating fears that it was being used as a waste dump. He notes that the largest campaigning groups have, in effect, divided the agenda between them, rarely speaking on the same issues. They also tackle issues in different ways: at one extreme are groups bent upon confrontation with businesses, while at the other are those striking alliances with businesses. Professor Steger says companies are often taken off guard when attacked by a pressure group and, with the exception of a few battle-hardened companies, such as those in the oil or tobacco industries, most businesses are ill-prepared for an onslaught of this type. The costs can be devastating, as Monsanto discovered in its battle against UK non-governmental organisations over genetically modified food. Even in less extreme cases, a tarnished reputation can cost customers and staff dearly, says Professor Steger. 'You only realise what your reputation is worth when you have lost it.'

Source:

Holder, V (2003) Campaigning to win war of words, *Financial Times*, 13 November

POLITICAL BEHAVIOUR: AN OVERVIEW

Clearly the range of political tactics is almost limitless. Some, however, are inherently more risky than others; for instance, violating the chain of command, losing personal control, or saying no to the ultimate power holder. Because they are visible, other tactics tend to be viewed as deviant and are difficult to defend; for example, divide and rule – excluding rivals from a decision making forum and settling old scores. For this reason milder tactics, such as controlling information, image building and deflecting attention from oneself when something goes wrong, tend to be the ones that are most favoured (Madison *et al.* 1980).

REPLAY

- Political tactics are used to acquire, develop or maintain power and other resources or to bring about personally desired outcomes, and they are widely used in organisations.
- A number of personal and organisational factors are likely to give rise to political behaviour.
- A wide range of political tactics can be identified, and a useful way to view them is as games that people play to pursue desired outcomes.

TIME OUT

Using the scenario given in the previous Time Out exercise, which concerns the mythical situation where student union funding is withdrawn, answer the questions below.

1. Which political tactics do you feel would be most likely to come into play? Develop an example for each one that you feel would be used.
2. Which people do you feel would be most likely to use these tactics?
3. What do you feel that these people have to gain by the use of political tactics?
4. Is it possible that these ends could be pursued in some other way?

ORGANISATIONAL CONFLICT

The word 'conflict', which is often used in an imprecise way, is defined here as:

> the behaviour of an individual or group that purposely sets out to block or inhibit another group (or individual) from achieving its goals.

Note that conflict involves one party purposely standing in the way of another achieving its goals, which distinguishes it from competition, a word with which it is sometimes used interchangeably. As Schmidt and Kochan (1972) point out, in a competitive situation, although the parties can have incompatible goals, people can usually pursue their aims without impeding each other, but, in conflict, it is impossible for one party to achieve its aims without doing so.

Perhaps the easiest way to appreciate this distinction is to examine sports activities. Although these are often called competitive, many are inherently conflictual. For instance, in football, cricket and squash, each party sets out to prevent the other from achieving its aim, but in sports such as gymnastics or mountaineering, each person or group tries to do its very best, with no attempt to thwart the other's goal attainment. There are many parallels to this in organisations. For example, individual salespeople might all try to be the top one but, as long as they stick to their own geographical territories they do not block each other, they simply compete. However, if some start poaching customers from other territories, goal-blocking activity has started and conflict is likely to ensue. This illustrates a point that is often overlooked: the dividing line between competition and conflict is sometimes very blurred. In many organisations competition is encouraged because it is assumed that it improves performance, but sometimes things go too far and conflict is triggered.

CONFLICT: TRADITIONAL AND CONTEMPORARY VIEWS

Because it is seen as something harmful and unpleasant, conflict is often viewed with distaste, usually because people have very traditional views on the matter (Pinkley 1990). However, there is an alternative viewpoint, which holds that conflict is a normal state of affairs and, in controlled amounts, can even be beneficial (Edwards 1986). Thus it is important to examine these alternative philosophies.

The Unitarist Perspective

Unitarist perspective: a management frame of reference in which an organisation is seen as one large family, all on the same side and pulling in the same direction, and in which conflict is seen as deviant behaviour

This is very much the traditional view. It sees harmony and cooperation as the natural state of human affairs, from which it follows that conflict is at best an undesirable interruption to smooth-flowing normality, and at worst has negative or destructive effects. In organisations this results in an assumption that everyone is really on the same side, united behind one leader and in pursuit of the same goals, but that they sometimes fail to recognise this, either because of faulty communication, poor leadership, or simply because they have been led astray by wilful troublemakers. While there are cooperative elements in most organisations, this perspective grossly oversimplifies matters, and fails to acknowledge that there could be in-built differences of interests that make conflict a perfectly normal occurrence. Nevertheless it is a remarkably resilient view: Drucker (1984), for example, writes about organisations as places where everyone works (or should work) towards a common goal. Moreover, it has long been recognised that a unitarist ideology is very strong in British managers (Poole *et al.* 2005), who often make appeals for all employees to pull together in a team spirit. Indeed, the team idea is almost certainly popular with managers simply because it is a unitarist concept; that is, an appeal to pull together as a team is a way of discrediting anyone who questions the manager's wisdom.

The Pluralist Perspective

Pluralist perspective: a management frame of reference in which an organisation is seen as a collection of different groups, all with their own legitimate aims to pursue, and so a degree of conflict is a normal state of affairs

Although this perspective acknowledges that cooperation and harmony can exist in organisations, neither is viewed as a natural state of affairs. Rather, an organisation is regarded as a collection of groups which can have some goals in common, but others that are different and potentially opposed. Thus, conflict is seen as perfectly natural and pluralists advance the idea that specific channels for handling conflict should be set up so that it can occur in a relatively ordered way that does not disrupt the whole organisation. At a theoretical level this viewpoint is widely accepted as more realistic than the unitarist perspective but, because it tends to side-step the issue of wider social factors as a source of conflict, it has its critics.

The Radical Perspective

Radical perspective: organisational conflicts reflect conflict in wider society between capital and labour

The basic tenet of this view is derived from the Marxist idea that organisational conflict reflects inherent conflicts in society as a whole; that is, between the interests of those who own an enterprise and those who simply work in it. Although it takes a somewhat broader set of social forces into account, it views all organisational conflict as part of the struggle between capital and labour. Indeed, managers are seen as merely the agents of the owners, which assumes that all conflict is vertical, and fails to recognise that managers can have interests that are different from those of owners, subordinates, or even other managers. As will be seen, not all organisational conflict takes place vertically, and much occurs between people at the same level.

The Interactionist Perspective

Interactionist perspective (conflict): organisational conflict is seen as neither bad or good but simply inevitable

Current views on conflict correspond to what is often called the *interactionist perspective*, which in many respects is a more refined version of pluralism. Conflict is seen

Figure 14.5
Relationship between
levels of conflict and
organisational
performance

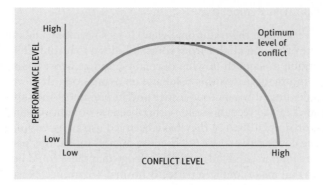

as neither inherently bad nor good, just inevitable. It recognises that too much conflict will hamper an organisation's welfare and absorb a great deal of energy that could be devoted to doing other things. However, it also accepts that, where no conflict exists, ideas are never challenged and this stilts any impetus to change things for the better. Thus an important difference between this and pluralism is the idea of an optimum level of conflict (see Figure 14.5).

There are two important implications of this idea. First, a great deal of conflict is concerned with challenging the *status quo*, which can have a positive outcome in dealing with complacency and lack of innovation. This idea has a strong intuitive appeal and, from what we know of organisations, is highly plausible. However, the main problem lies in identifying an optimal level of conflict, something that is often conveniently sidestepped by theorists in the area. The second implication is more practical and indicates that, rather than suppressing conflict, it is more important to learn how to manage it effectively. Since this is the view that currently holds sway, a return will be made to the important topic of conflict management later in the chapter.

TIME OUT

Carefully reflect on the organisation in which you work. If you are not in employment, consider your own university or college. Which perspective on conflict – the unitarist, pluralist, radical or interactionist – seems to you to most accurately reflect the nature of the organisation? Try to address this by answering the questions below.

1. Do people in the organisation express the view that everyone is on the same side and pulling in the same direction?
2. If your answer to question 1 is no, what are the different groups, what aims do they have in common and what aims do they have which could come into conflict?
3. Does any conflict in the organisation reflect divisions within wider society?
4. Is there an optimal level of conflict for the organisation, and how would you characterise the state of affairs when this exists?

THE NATURE OF ORGANISATIONAL CONFLICT

Two general points need to be made about the nature of conflict in organisations:

- that the roots of a conflict can go very deep, so deep that the people involved do not even realise what prompts their disagreement
- while conflict is extremely widespread, it is rare to find that people engage in continuous hostilities; rather, these occur spasmodically, and while they are in progress people stop doing other things to pursue the conflict.

In practice it is often hard to divorce the roots of a conflict from how it is pursued, but since both are important in their own right they will be explored separately.

The Causal Factors in Conflict

Figure 14.6 gives a simplified model of a large number of factors that can prompt organisational conflict. For convenience, they have been broken down into four main groups.

Organisational Structure and Design Factors

The two most visible features of an organisation's structure are **horizontal differentiation** and **vertical differentiation**. The first divides an organisation into specialised activities and, although this gives the advantage of efficiency, it has a number of potential drawbacks. The more separate the activities the more each one is likely to develop its own particular viewpoint and have a tendency to pursue their own goals at the expense of others, which can all too quickly lead to conflict.

Figure 14.6
Causal factors in organisational conflict

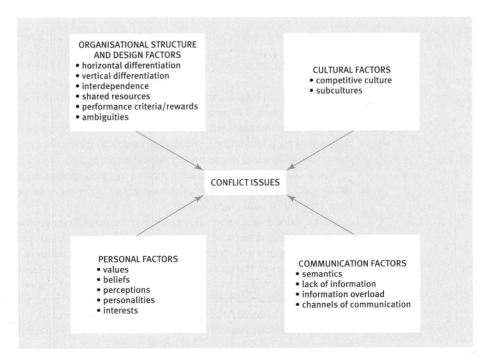

Vertical differentiation has a somewhat different effect. It establishes a hierarchy of authority. In theory this is used to coordinate the activities of different departments, thus avoiding horizontal conflicts. However, it can give rise to conflict in another way. Differences in authority result in decisions that affect people below and, while limits are normally placed on a person's authority, when someone is perceived to have exceeded his or her legitimate powers, those down below sometimes challenge the decision. A fairly obvious example of this is industrial relations conflict.

Departmental or **functional interdependence** is another feature of structure that can give rise to conflict. To achieve successful outcomes it is often necessary for two or more functions to coordinate their activities. This can mean that the performance of each one depends on the performance of the other(s), and to some extent they have to run their activities partly for the benefit of the other party. In this situation there is always a temptation for one function to put its own goals first.

Interdepartmental dependence and **shared resources** can have similar effects to interdependence. When resources are limited or rationed, departments do not always get all that they need, and if they are required to share resources, severe conflicts can occur about whether the distribution of resources is fair.

Performance criteria and **rewards** can magnify these problems. Like resources, rewards are usually rationed and one unit can be rewarded at the expense of another, which can lead to very bitter conflicts.

Ambiguities reduce the clarity about who is responsible for performing a certain activity and increase the likelihood that people will conveniently perceive that it is someone else's job. Ambiguities of this type are often the result of a badly thought-out structure and can lead to *post hoc* recriminations and conflicts when a job does not get done.

Personal Factors

Values are the positive and negative feelings that people have about the world, and, because they shape whole patterns of behaviour and outlook, they give rise to differences about the underlying purpose of an organisation. Thus they can be potent sources of conflict.

Differences in **beliefs** sometimes result in conflicts about the means to an end, rather than the end itself. For instance, there can be strongly contrasting beliefs about what the expression 'organisational effectiveness' means. Some people hold that it simply means making a large profit, while others stress that effectiveness involves being responsible to a much wider constituency of stakeholders.

We do not see reality, but infer it from our **perceptions** and, since people's perceptions vary, this sometimes results in genuine differences of opinion about what has been implied or said (see Chapter 4).

As explained in Chapter 3, people have unique **personalities**, and these can result in them finding it hard to get on together – the so-called 'personality clash'. While people are usually able to get over these conflicts, the incident sometimes affects their willingness to see things from the other party's point of view, which not only gives rise to further conflict but makes the conflict harder to resolve.

People also have different **interests** in terms of what they want from work. To some, prestige and status are the most important rewards, while to others it is autonomy, job satisfaction and remuneration. These days many organisations are in an almost constant state of change, which upsets traditional patterns of reward and, since it is natural that people should want to hold on to what they already have, conflicts can arise when they try to do so.

Cultural Factors

An organisation's culture gives its members a guide to how they should conduct themselves. Problematilcally, different parts of an organisation often have their own subcultures and, where these result in an issue being viewed in different ways, sub-cultures can give rise to conflicts.

Another way in which culture can establish a predisposition towards conflict is in those organisations where the culture emphasises competition. If top managers believe that it is good for sub-units to compete, they often establish structures and processes that encourage such behaviour, and matters can quickly get out of hand and turn into conflict.

Communication Factors

As will be seen in the next chapter, misunderstandings can all too easily arise in communication. There can be **semantic problems,** in which people attribute different meanings to the same information and **lack of information** creates ambiguity, which provides an opportunity for the use of political tactics that can eventually lead to conflict. Too much information leads to **information overload** and in this situation people tend to take in only that which is important to them. The use of **inappropriate channels** of communication can also give rise to conflict. Finally, it is important to recognise that even perfect communication will not ensure an absence of conflict. Differences in interests are inevitable in organisations and, in some cases, good communication only serves to highlight them (Pondy 1967).

CONFLICT EPISODES

One of the things that probably encourages the view that conflict is abnormal is that organisations tend to be characterised by long periods of apparent calm, interrupted by outbreaks of visible conflict, sometimes known as conflict 'episodes'. This does not mean, however, that prior to an episode there was no conflict. Indeed, conflict may well have been in progress in a less visible way for some time before an episode occurs. Thus the main value of the concept of a conflict episode is to highlight the idea that conflict often follows a predictable pattern of stages. Figure 14.7 shows a simplified version of a more complex model derived by Kelly and Nicholson (1980), which deals with industrial relations conflicts. This has been adapted to embrace a wider range of organisational situations and by reading the model from left to right, a chain of conditions and events can be traced.

Pre-episode Factors

All conflicts involve an **issue** and, as is explained in the above, a large number of factors can be **sources of issues.** However, the presence of an issue does not guarantee that a conflict episode will occur – merely that a set of circumstances exists in which

Figure 14.7 A simplified model of conflict causation and process (adapted from Kelly and Nicholson 1980)

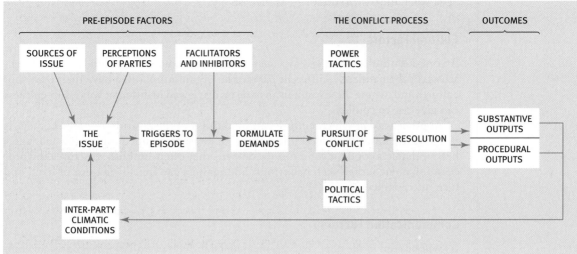

one party might block the goal attainment of another. For instance, at an individual level two people in the same department might see themselves as the logical choice for a promotion vacancy.

The **perceptions** that the parties have of each other can also strongly influence what happens. In the example above, if either person has started to perceive the other as a potential threat, he or she is likely to become more willing to put up a fight.

Inter-party climatic conditions consist of a cluster of attitudes and frames of reference that influence the way the parties view each other. In the case of the two individuals, although both wish to get the job they may also be good friends, which establishes a climate where neither one desires to harm the other. Conversely, they may be relative strangers, which gives a climate more conducive to conflict.

None of these factors on its own is enough to give rise to open conflict. A **trigger** of some sort is required and this is usually something that brings it home to one or both of the parties that goal blocking is likely to occur. In the case of the two individuals, this might happen if the promotion vacancy is advertised internally. However, even this does not ensure open conflict will occur.

In most situations a number of **facilitators** and/or **inhibitors** to conflict exist. Facilitators are push factors that make conflict more likely and inhibitors have the reverse effect. One such factor is the behavioural predispositions of the parties. Are they, for example, people who have a distaste of overt conflict? Another factor is a past record of success in conflict episodes. People who have engaged in conflict before and have emerged as the winner can often be more willing to use the same tactics again. In the case of the two individuals, one of them might get a 'buzz' out of conflict and might have used it in the past to get his or her own way.

All these pre-episode factors are at work together, and the final step before conflict actually occurs is usually that the parties will **formulate their demands**. One or both of them will become much clearer about what he or she wishes to achieve, and acutely aware that aims could be blocked by the other party. This is usually accompanied by some indication to the other party that an impasse has been reached and that, if the matter is not resolved, the next phase could be entered. In the individual conflict above, one of the people might insult the other in some way.

The Conflict Process

When entering this phase both parties tend to have a clear aim of emerging as the winner, and many different tactics can be used to try to achieve this goal. In general terms these can be categorised as either **power tactics**, where the aim is to force the other party into compliance, or **political tactics**, which are used to undermine the opponent's power or acquire sufficient power to enable power tactics to be used. Since previous sections of this chapter have dealt with the topics of power and politics, the ground will not be covered here. However, it is worth noting that many people have characteristic ways of handling conflict situations and this will be discussed in a later section of the chapter.

Most conflicts are capable of being **resolved** in one way or another. How this is done depends on handling styles and some of the factors leading up to the conflict, for instance the importance of the issue to the parties, their perceptions of each other, the inter-party climate and whether there are facilitators or inhibitors to continuing the conflict. It is also important to note that how the conflict is resolved has a huge impact on the phase which is considered next.

Outcomes

In general terms, there are two types of output from most conflicts: substantive outputs and procedural outputs. Also note that in Figure 14.7 a feedback loop runs from the outputs of the conflict process to inter-party climatic conditions at the left-hand side. This reflects the idea that the terms on which the matter is resolved can have a huge impact on what happens in the future.

Substantive outcomes are the terms of settlement that result in the parties abandoning the conflict. In the example of the two individuals in conflict over promotion, this could be a decision to promote one and not the other, or even to award the promotion to an outsider. Although this resolves the matter for the immediate future, it is important to recognise that substantive outcomes can have a strong impact on the other type of output.

Procedural outcomes are in part a result of the substantive terms of settlement but, since they can also be affected by how the conflict has been handled, they can have longer-term climatic effects. If the settlement has produced a clear winner and loser, the result can often be disastrous. In the euphoria of victory, winners can become very complacent and, in certain cases, assume an air of moral superiority, while losers can become tense and demoralised. More importantly, the situation can result in the inter-party climate becoming much worse. Nobody likes losing, and so losers sometimes try to save face and recover their morale by convincing themselves that the other party has only won the battle, not the war. From this it is but a short step to them actively looking for opportunities to engage in combat again and for this reason conflict management and resolution are all-important.

CONFLICT MANAGEMENT

Current ideas imply that the level of conflict in an organisation needs to be carefully managed – if there is too much, conflict needs to be reduced, and if there is too little, the level may need to be increased in a controlled way. In practical terms this means that a decision has to be made about whether to stimulate conflict or to resolve any conflicts that exist. Since the conditions under which conflict will need to be resolved are probably more prevalent in organisations, and this has a strong connection with previous sections of the chapter, only the matter of conflict resolution will be covered here and discussion of conflict stimulation will be deferred until later in the chapter.

Assertiveness: a person's desire to satisfy only his or her concerns in a conflict situation

Cooperation: the willingness to look for a solution to a conflict that satisfies the other party's concerns

Conflict Resolution

One of the things that can make conflicts hard to resolve is the way that the parties behave towards each other. This is sometimes quite relentless and the key to a resolution is often found in a fuller understanding of their styles of behaviour. A useful analytical framework for doing this is given by Thomas (1976), who categorises conflict handling along two dimensions:

- *assertiveness*: a person's desire to satisfy only his or her own concerns
- *cooperation*: the willingness to satisfy the other party's concerns.

These can be used to identify the five distinct styles (shown in Figure 14.8).

Figure 14.8
Alternative approaches to handling conflict (adapted from Thomas 1976)

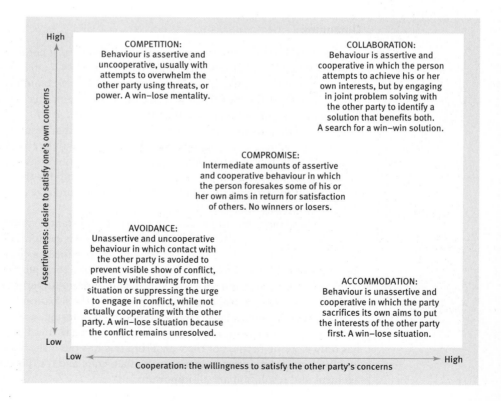

High

Assertiveness: desire to satisfy one's own concerns

Low

COMPETITION:
Behaviour is assertive and uncooperative, usually with attempts to overwhelm the other party using threats, or power. A win–lose mentality.

COLLABORATION:
Behaviour is assertive and cooperative in which the person attempts to achieve his or her own interests, but by engaging in joint problem solving with the other party to identify a solution that benefits both. A search for a win–win solution.

COMPROMISE:
Intermediate amounts of assertive and cooperative behaviour in which the person foresakes some of his or her own aims in return for satisfaction of others. No winners or losers.

AVOIDANCE:
Unassertive and uncooperative behaviour in which contact with the other party is avoided to prevent visible show of conflict, either by withdrawing from the situation or suppressing the urge to engage in conflict, while not actually cooperating with the other party. A win–lose situation because the conflict remains unresolved.

ACCOMMODATION:
Behaviour is unassertive and cooperative in which the party sacrifices its own aims to put the interests of the other party first. A win–lose situation.

Low ← Cooperation: the willingness to satisfy the other party's concerns → High

While it is probably true that the collaborative style is the most preferable, 'it takes two to tango'. Thus, for a conflict to be resolved collaboratively, both parties need to approach the matter in this way. If either or both has already become locked into a win–lose approach, it can take a considerable time before a search for collaboration even starts. Moreover, some conflicts (for example those about pay) are essentially win–lose in nature and others need to be resolved very quickly, perhaps because they have become highly disruptive to everyone else in the vicinity. Here it often falls to a higher-level manager to resolve the situation as a mediator and in a later paper (Thomas 1977) gives guidelines for selecting the style that is most appropriate to the circumstances. Indeed, he suggests that these can also be used by the protagonists to adjust their own styles. However, this is a controversial point. From what we know of personality differences, people may well have a predisposition to approach episodes in a relatively fixed way and it will often be necessary for a third party to intervene. In this situation, the guidelines for selecting what style to use are given in the OB in Action Box following.

 OB IN ACTION: Selecting conflict resolution approaches

Use competition when:
- quick, decisive action is necessary
- the future popularity of the decision is unimportant
- the matter is essential to organisational success
- one or both of the parties would take advantage of the other's less competitive behaviour.

Use avoidance when:
- the issue is trivial
- when someone else can resolve the conflict more effectively
- neither party has a chance of satisfying its concerns
- disruption cannot be allowed to continue
- people need time to cool down
- more information is needed to bring about a resolution
- there are hidden agendas and the apparent issue could mask something more fundamental.

Use compromise when:
- the parties' goals are important but not worth the disruption that could arise from using more assertive approaches
- the parties have equal power and stalemate is likely
- temporary settlements are needed
- time is short
- when collaboration or competition is unsuccessful (as a backup).

Use accommodation when:
- one party is patently in the wrong
- the issue is much more vital to one party than the other
- a trade-off for an issue that comes later needs to be established
- it is necessary to find a way for one party to retreat with dignity
- a party needs to be able to learn from its mistakes
- when future harmony and stability are particularly important.

Use collaboration when:
- time is relatively plentiful
- it is vital that both parties learn from the experience
- gaining commitment of both parties to implementation is vital
- it is necessary to work through feelings that might give rise to future conflicts
- it is necessary to gain insights from parties that have very different perspectives.

Someone who has to intervene to try to get the parties to adopt an appropriate style can use a number of strategies. For example, one way to induce collaboration is to set a **superordinate goal** that can only be achieved if both parties collaborate. Another tactic, but this time one that can be used to reduce tendencies to compete, is to **expand resources,** which attacks the root of the conflict by allowing both parties to have what they want; unfortunately, however, this is seldom possible. Finally, if all else fails, it may be necessary to **impose a solution.** However, this has to be done with great care. While it often works in the short term, if the solution suits neither party, there is always a danger that the apparent resolution has been achieved at the price of both parties uniting against the arbiter, who is now seen as a common enemy.

Conflict Stimulation

As noted earlier, the current view is that in certain circumstances there can be benefits in stimulating a degree of conflict within an organisation (Van de Vliert and De Dreu 1994). In situations such as this, the matter needs to be handled in a very careful and controlled way so that matters do not go too far and result in something that is highly dysfunctional. A great deal seems to depend on the type of conflict that exists, and here it can be useful to distinguish between *relational conflict* (conflict in interpersonal relations) and *task-related conflict* (conflict within a group about how it should complete its task). Recent research evidence suggests that people find relational conflict highly stressful, which can prompt them to perceive that others in a group are engaged in playing politics (Darr and Johns 2004). As such, it often evokes strong emotional responses that lower productive effort and employee satisfaction. Conversely, mild task-focused conflict tends to result in a more rigorous examination of the way things are done, which can lead to innovation, productivity and satisfaction (Jehn 1997). With this in mind, methods that can be used to stimulate conflict are described in what follows in an ascending order of risk that unwanted behaviour could be provoked.

Relational conflict: conflict in interpersonal relations

Task-related conflict: conflict within a group about how it should complete its task

Stimulating Competition

This is probably the least risky strategy of all, and many organisations have measures of this type in place. A fairly common one is the use of incentives, such as awards and bonuses for outstanding performance.

Communication

Because it tends to mark the point where political tactics can come into play, this is a more risky way of stimulating conflict and, if not used with great care, can result in emotional conflicts. One tactic that can be deployed is to carefully use information to create ambiguity, or even an element of apprehension or fear. One way of doing this is the judicious use of rumors; for example, that a major reorganisation is being considered. Although this can sometimes stimulate ideas and create competition among sub-units, it can also have the undesirable result of prompting a 'rush to the door', in which the organisation loses the very people it most needs to retain.

Altering Organisational Structure

This is another measure that contains pronounced risks. While structure can be used to make conflict less likely, it can also be a major source of conflict in its own right. A carefully selected structure can give a healthy degree of competition between sub-units and encourage innovation and improved performance but, like other things, matters can go too far: it is all too easy to pit units against each other in a way that produces something akin to outright war.

Bringing in Outside Individuals

This is often the most risky strategy of all. It is usually underpinned by the belief that if someone with different background values and attitudes is imported, he or she will be a source of inspiration to current employees and jerk them out of their complacency. However, it can also go sadly astray and result in a high degree of relational conflict because the people come to see the newcomer as a threat, and they all unite against this person.

REPLAY

- Organisational conflict can be an emotive subject and there are four main perspectives on its inevitability and legitimacy: unitarist, pluralist, radical and interactionist.
- The sources of conflict can usually be located in one or more groups of factors: organisational, personal, communication and cultural.
- Conflict can lie beneath the surface for some time before becoming visible as a conflict episode, which usually takes the form of a sequence of identifiable stages.
- Since some degree of conflict is probably inevitable, it can be vital to resolve conflicts in an appropriate way.

OVERVIEW AND CONCLUSIONS

To many people, power, politics and conflict are three of the least pleasant aspects of organisational life. There is a saying that 'power corrupts', which perhaps explains why those who seek power are viewed with suspicion and, because politics is mostly concerned with the pursuit and maintenance of power, the word probably has an even stronger effect. Conflict also gives rise to feelings of unease, not only because it can be disruptive, but because many of us are brought up to believe that harmony and cooperation are part of the natural order of things. Nevertheless, power, politics and conflict are all part of organisational life, and people have derived pleasure from wielding power since time immemorial.

Since all organisations are hierarchically structured, it is possible that organisational life appeals to some people because it gives them the opportunity to pursue and use power. Political activity is often a way of doing this and so, where power exists, politics is never far behind. Since it can also be used to wrest power and territory away from someone else it has a strong potential to generate conflict.

What, then, are the implications of power, politics and conflict in an organisation? There are four that are highly significant. To start with, it is important to shed our preconceptions about whether these features of organisational life are inherently right or wrong. Rather than condemn any of them, or work for their eradication, it is more practical to accept that they are inevitable.

Second, it is worth remembering that there are many bases of power, not all of which are immediately obvious. Thus it can sometimes come as a surprise when we realise how much power other people have. Because of the formal authority vested in their positions, managers often think that they are the only people who have power, and it can come as an unpleasant shock when they discover how much dependence they have on those below them.

Third, using politics is a tricky business. It is never without risk and the problem is, that if one person refrains from playing politics, he or she can never be entirely sure that others will behave similarly. However, two wrongs do not make a right. Therefore, when faced with a choice about whether to use political tactics it is important to think matters through carefully and examine whether political behaviour is defensible, not only to oneself, but also in the eyes of others.

Finally, in contemporary organisations some degree of conflict is probably unavoidable, and it is unlikely that anybody will escape becoming embroiled at some stage. For this reason it is important to avoid taking matters too personally. Thus, provided conflict occurs for constructive purposes and takes place in an orderly way, it probably does no harm and, in the long run, it may well do a considerable amount of good. However, a note of caution is necessary here. Conflict can be extremely stimulating in its own right and, like the people who fought duels in the eighteenth century, an increase in appetite can grow from what it feeds on.

FURTHER READING

Ackroyd, S and P Thompson (1999) *Organisational Misbehaviour*, London: Sage. The authors adopt a radical prspective on conflict and use it to examine employee resistance and conflict.

Clegg, SR (1989). *Frameworks of Power*, London: Sage. A text that is full of useful insights and which has become a classic in the area.

De Dreu, C and E Van de Vliert (eds) (1997) *Using Conflict in Organisations*, London: Sage. A book of readings which contains a wide variety of perspectives on the functional and dysfunctional aspects of organisational conflict, and how it can be used constructively.

Fox, A (1973) Industrial relations: a social critique of pluralist ideology. In J Child (ed.) *Man and Organisation*, New York: Halstead. The author was the first person to distinguish between unitarist, pluralist and radical perspectives on conflict. Despite its age, a very readable analysis that is full of useful insights.

Hardy, C (ed.) (1995) *Power and Politics in Organisations*, Aldershot: Dartmouth Publishing. A book of readings, which gives a diverse range of views on power and political activity in organisations.

Lee, R and P Lawrence (1985) *Organisational Behaviour: Politics at Work*, London: Hutchinson. A useful text, which gives a political perspective on many topics in Organisational Behaviour.

Mintzberg, H (1983) *Power in and Around Organisations*, Englewood Cliffs, NJ: Prentice Hall. An easy-to-read book that makes a major contribution to thinking about power in organisations.

Pfeffer, J (1981) *Power in Organizations*, Marshfield, MA: Pitman. One of the most authoritative books yet written on the use of power and the ways that political tactics are used to acquire and maintain it. A classic text in the field.

Pfeffer, J (1992) *Managing with Power: Politics and Influence in Organisations*, Boston, MA: Harvard Business School Press. An immensely practical guide to using power and politics in organisations.

CASE STUDY 14.1: A company at war with itself

Speak to executives, investors and other German businessmen and one thing is clear about Volkswagen – it is not a normal company. One supervisory board member describes running it as like trying to ride a chariot with four or five horses, each of which pulls in a different direction, and another influential director says: 'VW is an awful advertisement for Germany and the structure of German companies, but it is a one-off'. 'I've known many companies but I've never known one like this with all the politics that are involved.' The problem is one that Bernd Pischetsrieder, who was forced to resign in November 2006 knows only too well. VW and, in particular, its supervisory board have several poles of interest, most of which are competing against each other at any given time.

Anyone who wants to know what VW is thinking needs to talk to at least five different groups: Porsche and Lower Saxony, the two biggest shareholders; Ferdinand Piëch, the still dominant chairman who is a controlling shareholder at Porsche; IG Metall, the powerful engineering union that controls half of the supervisory board; and, last but not least, VW's management. Politics between each of the groups plays a huge role, and it is extremely difficult to avoid offending at least one of the parties with any decision.

▶

Supervisory board members say Mr Pischetsrieder fell foul of the nefarious arrangement when he walked into an ambush led by Mr Piëch which was supported by the unions and Porsche. Lower Saxony, alone among the members of the board's top praesidium committee, tried to resist, before Mr Pischetsrieder eventually threw in the towel. Directors say this is not the first time that Mr Piëch, who was chief executive from 1993 to 2002, has ganged up with IG Metall to thwart Mr Pischetsrieder. For example, a year ago they imposed Horst Neumann, a former IG Metall official, as personnel director against the wishes of Mr Pischetsrieder, Lower Saxony and other members of the board including the chairmen of Siemens and ThyssenKrupp. It shows just how difficult it is to run this company because Piëch just won't leave it alone, one director says. It also shows how co-determination [the system under which workers sit on company's boards] can be totally misused. It is now a company at the beck and call of Piëch and IG Metall.

Henning Gebhardt, head of German equities at the country's biggest fund manager, DWS, says: 'It's very important the supervisory board, big shareholders and management act in union; otherwise, you won't solve the problems at the company. It is another sign that politics is very important in this company, and that is very difficult to manage.'

A chairman of a Dax-30 blue-chip company says it is the classic sign of the 'unholy alliance of the losers' that can take place under co-determination. This takes place when a desperate manager does nothing to offend his workers, who in turn prop him up. VW directors suggest that this is exactly what Mr Piëch has done here – adding examples that include Jürgen Schrempp, former head of carmaker Daimler Chrysler, and Michael Frenzel, current head of tourism and shipping group, Tui. Indeed, one VW director admits that it shows the problem with co-determination. But this drinking with the devil does not exist anywhere else. VW has gone further than almost any other German company in this respect. Under Mr Piëch's reign as CEO, the 'VW system' was set up in which unions played such an active role in decision making that it became known as co-management.

Many reformers at VW, including Mr Pischetsrieder, hoped a sex and bribery scandal last year would lead to an end of the system, but Mr Piëch's backing of Mr Neumann as personnel director was widely seen as thwarting that ambition. Some directors at VW and investors are now worried about the fate of Wolfgang Bernhard, the head of the VW brand and the instigator of the carmaker's recent restructuring. Bernhard is the driving force behind VW's recent progress, says one. Together with Pischetsrieder he has put VW on the right path. But what does Piëch want to do with Bernhard? The unions certainly don't like him. The departure of Mr Bernhard would be a big blow for investors who have put their faith in him to turn around the underperforming VW brand. His confidants say he has no interest in the political machinations at the company, only in making good cars at the right price. But they also say he has a poor relationship with Martin Winterkorn, the head of Audi and chief executive-designate at VW, and this is another peculiarity of the carmaker. Although VW and Audi are two brands owned by the same group, they are more often than not at loggerheads. Maybe Mr Winterkorn can change that, but as one senior VW executive says: 'there are some days here where it feels like everybody is fighting a war against you.'

Source: Milne, R (2006) VW – a company that's at war with itself, *Financial Times*, 9 November

Task

Read the above case study material, then working in groups of four or five students answer the questions below.

1. What in your view are the roots of the conflict at Volkswagen; do they lie in structures, cultural factors, personal factors or communication?

2. To what extent do you feel that this conflict has been in progress for some time?

3. Which of the four philosophies of conflict given in Chapter 14 gives the most realistic explanation of the conflict at work in Volkswagen: the unitarist perspective; the pluralist perspective; the radical perspective; or the interactionist perspective?

4. In your view is the conflict dysfunctional, or does it have positive aspects (justify your answer with examples)?

5. What do you feel would be a realistic way of removing any dysfunctional aspects of this conflict, while retaining any positive aspects that exist?

REVIEW AND DISCUSSION QUESTIONS

1. Identify the main interpersonal and contextual bases of power in organisations and describe how and in what circumstances these sources of power can complement each other.

2. Distinguish between the tactics identified by Kipnis *et al.* (1984) that are used more frequently in a downward direction and those that tend to be used upwards. Explain why these differences are likely to exist.

3. Organisational decisions are often said to be political. What are the advantages and disadvantages of reaching decisions in this way?

4. Identify the characteristics of unitarist, pluralist, radical and interactionist perspectives on organisational conflict and explain how each one can influence how conflict is handled in an organisation.

5. Describe the three main stages in a conflict episode and the important factors and processes in each one.

Chapter 15

Organisational Communication

LEARNING OUTCOMES

After studying this chapter you should be able to:

- define effective communication and understand its importance for organisations

- using the communication model, explain the communication process and describe the barriers to effective communication

- explain the main directions of information flow in organisations and distinguish between formal and informal communication

- describe the strengths and weaknesses of the two traditional methods of communication used in organisation: verbal (face-to-face) methods and written communication

INTRODUCTION

This chapter, which deals with communication in organisations, adopts a 'back to basics' approach to the topic. It starts by defining communication and then highlights its crucial importance to organisations.

Although communication is often viewed as a straightforward matter, it is a complex process in which many things can go wrong. Therefore, the next section of the chapter presents a model of communication that illustrates its complexity and this is applied in the following section, to consider the barriers to effective communication. The remainder of the chapter focuses more explicitly on communication in organisations, first by considering the main flows of information, and then by exploring in detail two important ways of communicating: by face-to-face methods and written communication. The chapter closes with a section that integrates and overviews its contents.

THE IMPORTANCE OF COMMUNICATION

Communication: a process in which information and its meaning is conveyed from a sender to receiver(s)

'*Communication*' is a widely used (and in some ways misused) word. It has been defined in many different ways, perhaps the simplest of which is 'the process of transmitting information from one person to another' (Weick and Browning 1986, p 244). This, however, is overly simplistic. Taken at face value it covers situations where information is transmitted, but is only understood by the sender and more penetrating definitions usually point out that 'meaning' (rather that just 'information') must be conveyed, and some go much further by stating that communication must involve an exchange of information. Desirable as it may be for other reasons, this feedback is not necessarily part of the communication process and, with this in mind, communication is defined here as:

> a process in which information and its meaning is conveyed by a sender to receiver(s).

An elementary, but important implication can be drawn from this definition, and the reader is asked to keep it in mind for the remainder of the chapter. This is that whatever the message conveys, and, whatever means are used to convey it, the sender and the receiver must have consensus about its meaning, otherwise communication has not taken place, merely the transmission of information.

Effective communication: the extent to which the sender and receiver of a message both attribute it with the same meaning

It is virtually impossible to identify an aspect of organisational functioning that is not affected by communication and serious problems can arise if communication is not effective. In accordance with the definition above, *effective communication* is defined here as:

> the extent to which the sender and receiver of a message both attribute it with the same meaning.

In general terms, there are three aspects of organisational functioning in which effective communication can be particularly crucial, each of which will be considered in turn.

Coordination

Organisational structure establishes different functions and departments that make their own contributions to an organisation's overall task. Unless they inform each other about what is required, coordination of activities is pretty well impossible.

Control

Achievement of goals cannot be left to chance and so it is normal to set up a method of control that monitors goal achievement. Clearly, therefore, control activities are acutely dependent on a flow of accurate information (see Chapter 19).

Human Factors

Inadequate or ineffective communication probably has its most visible effects in terms of the impact on employees. If employees do not know what is required of them, or how they are affected by changes, the effects on morale, motivation and the psychological contract can be disastrous (Guest and Conway 2002). In some organisations, employees do not get to hear about matters that impact on their working lives until they are overtaken by events. As a result, they impute sinister motives for being kept in the dark and if the situation persists for any length of time, those who are starved of information become only too ready to listen to rumours, which quickly become accepted as 'the truth'. With this in mind the next section of the chapter explores the communication process in some depth to uncover what is necessary for it to be effective.

 REPLAY

- Communication can be defined as a process for conveying information and its meaning between people.
- The effectiveness of the communication process can be evaluated in terms of the extent to which the sender and receiver both attribute the same meaning to a message.
- The effectiveness of communication in an organisation can have a strong impact on its performance and, in particular, on its ability to coordinate and control its component parts and to make effective use of its human resources.

THE COMMUNICATION MODEL

Most of us tend to take communication for granted and when we find that communication is not effective, we blame the other person. The problem is that the process is much more complex than it appears at first sight and to appreciate this, it is useful to start by exploring it from a theoretical standpoint.

The approach that dominates thinking and research in the area is the 'information processing' perspective, and a model derived from the works of Berlo (1960) and earlier workers is given in Figure 15.1. Despite its age, this model has stood the test of time and it is still the most widely used conceptualisation of the process.

Figure 15.1 The communication model

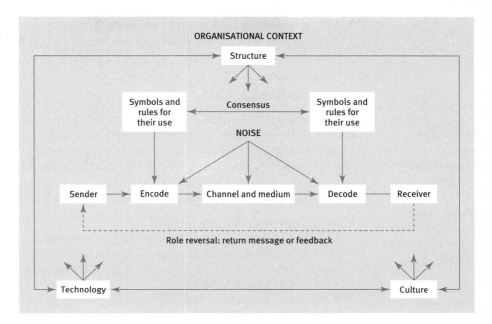

Before exploring the model, however, it is necessary to make three important points:

- The model is not intended to be a faithful representation of communication in practice, but a specification for the components that should be present and the functions that they should perform.

- Strictly speaking the three elements (structure, technology and culture) shown as part of the organisational context are not part of the process itself and were not included in earlier information processing models. However, since they can have a huge impact on communication in organisations, they have been included for completeness.

- As shown in Figure 15.1, the process portrays a one-way flow of information from sender to receiver. In practice, many messages evoke a response in which the receiver becomes the sender of a new message and the sender becomes the new receiver. This is reflected in the model by the dotted line labelled 'role reversal: return message or feedback'.

Source of message: the person from whom a message originates

Components of the Model

The Source of the Message (Sender)

All messages originate in the brain of the sender, for whom they have a meaning.

Encoding: a process in which a message is transformed into a set of symbols that can be conveyed by a channel

Symbols and Encoding

To be transmitted messages have to be encoded from thoughts into a set of symbols, for example, words (spoken or written) or diagrams. The essentials for this are:

- a set of symbols that are in common use by both sender and receiver
- a high degree of consensus about the rules for using the symbols so that they convey common meanings.

The Channel and Medium

Channels of communication: the carriers of the message

The same message can usually be transmitted in more than one way, but the two basic *channels of communication* are verbal and written. Within these channels there are a number of different *media* that can be used, and these have different capacities to carry information. This idea is reflected in what Lengel and Daft (1988) refer to as *information richness*, which can be defined as 'the potential information-carrying capacity of the medium', which is a reflection of four factors:

Media: specific ways of conveying a message along a channel

- whether multiple channels are used
- whether the channel and medium permit rapid feedback to the message sender
- the type of communication – personal (person-to-person) communication that occurs in the here and now, or impersonal communication that is not addressed to anyone in particular
- the language sources used, together with the variety of information cues available for establishing meaning.

Information richness: the potential information-carrying capacity of a communication medium

These ideas are summarised in Table 15.1 and the work of Lengel and Daft permits a number of generalisations to be made about selecting an appropriate channel and medium in order to achieve effectiveness in communication:

- Spoken channels are best for some messages and written ones for others, and for some messages a mixture of both is more appropriate.
- Certain messages can be notoriously difficult to encode in written form, notably sincerity, integrity and trustworthiness, which are all much more difficult to detect on paper than they are in the face-to-face situation.

Table 15.1 The information richness of selected communication media (adapted from Lengel and Daft 1988)

Medium	Channel(s)	Potential for feedback	Type of communication	Sources of language (symbols)	Information richness
Face to face	Verbal and visual	Immediate	Personal	Words, intonation, gestures, eye contact	Very high
Telephone	Verbal	Fast	Personal	Words, intonation, phraseology	High
Personal written: memos, letters and e-mail	Written	Slow	Personal	Words	Medium
Formal written: bulletins, notices etc.	Written	Very slow	Impersonal	Words	Low
Formal numeric: budgetary reports	Written and encrypted	Very slow	Impersonal	Numerals	Very low

- Certain types of message can seriously overload a channel; it is hard to avoid confusion if an attempt is made to give a purely oral description of something very complex, such as details of new organisational structures or methods of work organisation, which can often be done more effectively with the aid of diagrams.
- Face-to-face communication is usually much richer than the written form because it has a more personal focus and there are many additional clues to help the receiver understand what is said.
- Face-to-face communication also allows instantaneous feedback from the receiver, which in turn allows the sender to check whether the receiver has correctly interpreted the message.

Decoding

Decoding: a process in which the receiver of a message uses the symbols in which it is conveyed to attribute it with a meaning

The receiver must decode the symbols into thoughts in order to be able to understand the message. Thus, if the receiver is to be able to attribute the same meaning to the message as its sender, both parties need to have a high degree of consensus about the meaning of symbols and the rules for their use.

The Receiver

Receiver (of the message): the person to whom a message is directed

Assuming that we are not dealing with a case of eavesdropping, this is the person to whom the message is directed. The person not only has to take in the message using his or her sensory processes, but also process the information mentally to attribute it with a meaning.

Noise

Noise: any extraneous signal that interferes with or masks a message

Noise can be defined as any extraneous signal that interferes with, or masks, the message. Since this is something that acts as a barrier to effective communication, it is more appropriate to consider it later in the chapter, where barriers are dealt with in more detail.

Feedback

Feedback: a process in which sender and receiver exchange roles, so that the receiver responds to a message

In many situations sender and receiver exchange roles, and this is acknowledged in the model by a feedback loop. However, since some communication is purposely designed to be one-way, this does not always take place.

Where it is available, feedback has great value to the sender because it enables the person to gauge the receiver's reaction to the message (Ashford 1986). However, unless sender and receiver intentionally exchange roles, or the receiver reacts in a way that makes the sender pause, this exchange tends not to happen (Windahl *et al.* 1992). Feedback can be of two types. **Direct feedback** occurs if there is an almost instantaneous exchange, as described above. The verbal channel gives far greater opportunity for this to take place, particularly if it is in a face-to-face situation where non-verbal cues such as facial expression and body language can be used. Nevertheless, direct feedback is also possible with written channels, for example where a message evokes or calls for a response. Because this is delayed feedback, however, it is less helpful in adding to the immediate effectiveness of the process.

Indirect feedback occurs when the sender does not obtain an explicit signal from the receiver about whether the message has been attributed with its intended meaning. Thus it tends to be less useful in maintaining the ongoing effectiveness of the process. For example, a receiver might interpret a message in a different way from that desired by the sender and in good faith do exactly the opposite to that which the sender requires. While this is still feedback, the message has already given rise to a problem.

Although very simple, this basic model alerts us to the complexity of communication and some of its inherent problems:

- it is a discontinuous process, containing several breaks
- the sender of a message has to translate his or her thoughts into a message *before* it can be sent and the receiver has to translate the message back into thoughts *before* he or she can attribute it with a meaning
- the channel needs to be capable of conveying the intended meaning and some messages can be notoriously difficult to transmit via certain channels.

Contextual Factors

Like any other aspect of human behaviour, communication can be influenced strongly by contextual factors and that can have a particularly strong impact on effectiveness.

Organisational Structure

As is pointed out in Chapter 17, structure not only reflects a hierarchy of power, it determines the flow of work through an organisation and gives rise to a number of necessary information flows. It not only influences who talks to whom about what, it also tends to shape styles of communication. For example, very tall structures are characterised by a large number of levels in the management hierarchy and associated with centralisation of authority at the top. Where this type of structure exists, top-down, one-way communication methods dominate, and this tends to give communication a very authoritarian flavour (Luthans 1995). In addition, tall structures have more levels through which a message has to pass in travelling downwards, which delays its journey and makes it less likely to reach its destination with the same meaning that the sender intended.

Organisational Culture

Culture gives organisational members strong guidelines about acceptable patterns of behaviour and can influence all manner of organisational practices, including communication. If deference to authority is a characteristic of the culture, this can influence the way that managers communicate with subordinates and also has a bearing on whether people feel free to be the originators of messages, or feel they have to content themselves with being passive recipients. Since information is power (see Chapter 14), if power holding and the exercise of power are high in the organisational value system, this can influence how much information people withhold in the interests of protecting their power bases.

Most large organisations, particularly those with a high degree of specialisation, are likely to have a number of sub-cultures. To some extent, sub-cultures develop their own identities and this can result in them developing their own repertoires of 'buzzwords', which make communication with other parts of the organisation more difficult.

There is usually a high degree of correspondence between the structure of an organisation and its culture. For instance, in a formal bureaucratic structure, anything other than communicating through formal lines of authority is likely to be discouraged. Perhaps more importantly, if the structure is one in which a free flow of information through formal channels is difficult, a compensatory mechanism of relying on informal channels (the grapevine) can spring into existence, a matter that will be considered in more detail later.

Finally, there is an ongoing trend for organisations to become more culturally diverse, and these organisations have their own inbuilt difficulties with communication. People are likely to speak different languages and can also have different norms and values, which sometimes results in a whole host of different meanings being attributed to verbal, non-verbal and written messages (Lewis *et al.* 1995).

Technology

Communication does not depend on technology, but on the people who communicate. Over the last decade, however, there have been significant developments in the technology of communicating, and such things as fax, e-mail, voicemail, intranet and internet are now commonplace. Where it is available, and providing it is used in an appropriate way, technology has a tremendous part to play in effective communication. Note, however, that there is a caveat of 'providing it is used in an appropriate way', and there are different schools of thought on whether the widespread and unrestrained adoption of new information and communication technologies has produced a desirable state of affairs in organisations.

Nevertheless, so widespread is the use of these technologies that they warrant consideration in their own right, and a return to this matter will be made later in the chapter.

TIME OUT

Carefully consider a particular class that you attend at your university or college and use the communication model to identify the following components in the instruction process:

1. Who or what is the source of the message(s)?
2. What is the main channel used to convey the message(s)?
3. What media are used in the channel(s)?
4. Who or what is the receiver?

REPLAY

- The basic components in the communication process are the sender or source of a message (who has to encode his or her thoughts into symbols that can convey the message via the channel), the channel that carries the message and the receiver of the message (who must then decode the symbols into a message that has a meaning).

- Each channel uses one or more media to carry its messages.

- In order for meaning to be conveyed, it is vital that both sender and receiver have a high degree of consensus about the meaning of the symbols used and the rules for their use.

- Noise (extraneous signals that obscure or distort the message) can enter the process via the sender, channel or receiver.

- All communication takes place within a context and factors within the context can have an impact on the way that messages are sent and interpreted on receipt.

BARRIERS TO EFFECTIVE COMMUNICATION

Many things can impair the effectiveness of the communication process. Some are associated with the source of a message, some with the receiver, some are common to both, while others are associated with the channel of communication.

Barriers Associated with the Sender

Message Formulation

While the originator of a message can have a clear idea of the meaning he or she wishes to convey, people differ considerably in their capabilities to express their thoughts. Where skills are undeveloped, there can be considerable barriers to communication.

Perceptions

Our perceptions of other people are not necessarily the truth, but are our own versions of reality. This can sometimes lead to problems in the way that messages are formulated. For instance:

- If a sender perceives that a message is unlikely to be well received, it can be toned down to the extent that its real meaning is obscured.

- A sender can underrate the receiver's capability to cope with a complex message, which can prompt the person to 'talk down' to the recipient, who can then feel that he or she is being patronised, with all the annoyance and resentment that this causes.

- If the sender perceives that the intended recipient is a 'difficult' person to deal with, there can be a tendency to tell the receiver what he or she wants to hear, which can give rise to huge distortions.

Encoding

Even when the sender can clearly express thoughts and has accurate perceptions of the receiver, there can still be problems. Most communication in organisations uses words as symbols and while these can be expressed in written or verbal form, people differ in the meanings they attribute to the same words. A common problem here is the use of jargon, which can be a distinct barrier when people hold different conventions about the meaning of jargon words.

These problems are not confined to words alone. Although diagrams and models can sometimes be a considerable aid in communicating an idea, a diagram or model is just a simplified representation of reality. Thus, while one person can assume that an organisation chart primarily represents the distribution of power in an organisation, someone else can regard it as a way of portraying the degree of specialisation. Errors of this type often result because the sender fails to put him or herself in the position of the receiver and to do this is to tantamount to expecting the receiver to be a mind reader.

In summary, the major barriers associated with the sender are shown in Table 15.2.

Barriers Associated with Media and Channel

Noise

This is the most readily identifiable barrier associated with these components of the model. Noise can be of two types:

- **Physical noise**, which involves an extraneous signal masking or drowning out a message; for example, the din in a factory workshop, or bright sunlight that shines on a screen and makes a projected image almost invisible.
- **Psychological noise** has an impact when something concerned with either the message itself or the setting in which communication takes place interferes with its transmission or attributed meaning.

In face-to-face communication, a significant source of psychological noise can be an unintended clash between what is said and the speaker's non-verbal signals. These have a huge impact on verbal messages and in a face-to-face situation evidence suggests that a only about 7 per cent of the impact of a message comes from the words used; 39 per cent from the way the words are uttered (inflection, tone and content) and 55 per cent from non-verbal cues such as a facial expression, eye contact and body language

Table 15.2 Communication barriers associated with the sender of a message

Type of barrier	Associated problems
Message formulation	Inability to transform thoughts into appropriate symbols for the channel selected
Perceptions	Inaccurate perceptions of receiver's ability to understand the message or reactions to the message
Encoding	Semantics (word meanings), jargon and use of media are unable to convey the complexity of the message

(Mehrabian 1971). More importantly, where a clash between verbal and a non-verbal cues occurs, it is the non-verbal message that is taken to be the factual one (Eckman and Friesen 1975).

The setting in which communication takes place can also be a potential source of psychological noise and if, for example, a manager berates someone in front of other subordinates, the chastised person can sometimes focus more on the reactions of his or her colleagues than on the message itself.

Space proxemics, the use of interpersonal space when communicating with others, can also be a source of noise. Hall (1966) shows that there are four zones of proximity for communicating with others, which, for most Americans, were identified as:

- an intimate zone – from actual contact to about 18 inches
- the personal zone – from 18 inches to 4 feet
- the social zone – from 4 to 12 feet
- and the public zone – over 12 feet.

An individual's intimate and personal zones are private space reserved for very close and intimate encounters. To enter these without invitation can often make the receiver feel so uncomfortable that barriers are erected which interfere with the message.

Finally, the timing of a message can often erect huge perceptual barriers to its reception and accurate interpretation. For instance, announcing a drop in profits can be interpreted in different ways according to when the message appears. If it is said at one time it could be taken by employees to mean that productivity needs to be improved, but if it is said in the middle of wage negotiations, it can be interpreted as an underhand trick by management to pave the way for a meagre offer.

Inappropriateness of Media and/or Channel

Written and oral channels tend to be more appropriate for certain types of message. Because written material gives the recipient the facility to go over the information at his or her own pace, it can be highly effective for lengthy, detailed messages. It also provides a permanent record and so it tends to make the sender more precise about what is said. Moreover, because it can be difficult for a receiver to hold and integrate different parts of a long, complex verbal message in his or her memory, the latter parts of the message can interfere with understanding of what has been said earlier. Written communication can overcome this obstacle.

The verbal channel, however, is much richer than the written form, particularly if it is used in a face-to-face situation where it has a more personal focus and gives the receiver an opportunity to use additional, non-verbal signals that can aid understanding. It is also faster than many written channels, both in transmission and feedback. Perhaps most important of all, feelings and emotions are much more easily communicated in this way, and so where a message is controversial and its sender needs to convey honesty, integrity and trustworthiness as part of the message, it has tremendous advantages.

These days, the facility to use multi-media methods for a message is much greater. Video-conferencing can use both written and verbal channels simultaneously, and even a face-to-face presentation supplemented by visual aids gives this facility. The great advantage of using multiple channels is that these methods are able to make use of

Table 15.3 Communication barriers associated with media or the channel

Type of barrier	Associated problems
Noise: physical	Swamping or covering of message
Noise: psychological	Conflicting symbols (e.g. verbal and non-verbal) result in contradictory message The setting conveys its own (sometimes contradictory or intimidating) message Space proxemics: the invasion of the receiver's personal space
Inappropriate media and/or channel	Meaning of message cannot be fully conveyed by the channel or medium

redundancy – the repetition of the same message in different ways – which vastly increases the likelihood that the message will be received with its meaning intact (Hsia 1977). As such, these methods can be particularly appropriate where complex ideas need to be communicated in an emotionally charged atmosphere, for example, in employment relations.

These potential barriers associated with media and channel of communication are summarised in Table 15.3.

Barriers Associated with the Receiver

Decoding

Perception and selectivity can be huge barriers to the accurate receipt of messages. Recipients can have preconceived ideas about the message they 'expect' to see or hear, which can distort their perceptions and interfere with the sender's intended meaning. A great deal can depend on whether the receiver has faith in the honesty and integrity of the sender, which tends to be influenced by prior experience. If someone has been less than honest on a prior occasion, people can suspect an ulterior motive for the current message and assign a meaning before all of it is received. As such, the receiver attends only to those parts of the message that confirm existing beliefs and the remainder is blocked out.

Information Overload

This is becoming a significant problem in many organisations and to some extent it is associated with the increased use of information technology. When information overload occurs, the receiver is swamped with a surfeit of messages and is unable to cope with them all. The sheer difficulty of trying to assimilate everything forces the person to ration his or her attention (Finholt and Sproull 1990) with the attendant risk of something important being overlooked or messages receiving no attention at all (see the OB in Action Box on page 442).

These potential barriers are summarised in Table 15.4.

Table 15.4 Communication barriers associated with the receiver

Type of barrier	Associated problems
Decoding	Selectivity: attention is paid to only part of message Perceptions and value judgements about sender or meaning of message
Information overload	Receiver has too many messages to which he or she must attend

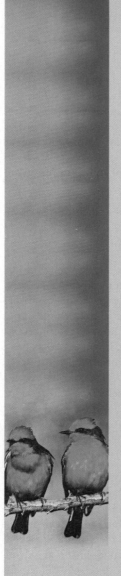

 OB IN ACTION: The hazards of information overload

These days we are often forced to absorb as much information as possible in the shortest time possible; not only in business but increasingly in our private lives. While this can create excitement, it can also result in crippling fear and, according to Edward Hallowell, an American psychiatrist, when this fear is mixed with the daily gush of information, the brain risks overheating and undermining the individual's best efforts.

This 'hot' state of mind resembles a medical condition called attention deficit disorder (ADD) and, in people that suffer from it, the brain has a tendency to run like a racing car that can win races, but is more likely to crash because it has faulty brakes.

These people are often highly talented and creative, but unfortunately in the workplace their performance is frequently inconsistent, veering from brilliance to under achievement. However, in most cases the modern heated-up brain does not have true ADD, which is a genetic disorder that is often aggravated by contextual factors, but rather a contextually induced condition similar to ADD, which Hallowell calls attention deficit trait (ADT). This mimics the symptoms of true ADD, such as heightened distractibility; frequent lapses in memory; and trouble in organising data. Those afflicted are often mavericks, who have trouble taking direction and managing their own time. They have an impulsive decision making style, combined with impatience, irritability and restlessness, and tend to be in a state of constant action, without ever pausing to ponder or reflect on what they do.

These symptoms all become manifest when the brain is asked to process more information than it can handle. Once the frontal and prefrontal lobes of the brain (the parts that handle thinking, decision making and planning) reach full capacity, other parts of the brain devoted to survival and other basic functions begin to take over, and the individual starts to react as if his or her physical survival is threatened. In response to what is happening in the brain, the rest of the body then goes into crisis mode, which further impairs the brain's functioning, and once in this survival mode, they lose the capacity to think clearly. They rush to solve problems when the lower regions of the brain drive them to destroy the perceived threat before it destroys them. For example, at one extreme they might throw tantrums or blame others and at the other extreme go into denial and avoid the problems confronting them.

With sensible precautions, however, ADT is said to be avoidable and a person's underlying abilities can prevail. Nevertheless, the first crucial step in doing this is

for the person concerned to acknowledge that he or she has ADT. This way he or she gives him or herself time to look at the situation and think clearly about how to deal with it. This also helps to dissipate fear, as does discussing things with other people. Other personal steps can be to add structure to one's work practices; breaking-down a large task into a set of smaller tasks; allowing enough time to do a good job; planning one's day instead of just reacting to demands; get enough sleep at night; eat properly.

On the part of the organisation there are also things that can be done to prevent ADT occurring. For example, by matching people's tasks with their skills; having people spending most of their time doing what they are good at, not trying to become good at what they're bad at.

Source:

Hallowell, E (2005) Fast and furious, *People Management*, 16 June, 39–40

A Short Note on Cross-national Influences

Conceptually, the communication problems that can exist in a cross-national situation are the same as those that occur within a single country. That is, for effective communication to occur it is vital that senders and receivers of messages have consensus about the meaning ascribed to symbols that are used to communicate. However, in a cross-national situation where people use different languages, there is clearly a higher risk that the same word will mean different things to different people. Thus the problem of consensus can be particularly problematic, and any of the barriers to effective communication identified above can be considerably magnified. Moreover, even where a common language is used, there can be huge differences in the meanings attributed to non-verbal signals and, as was noted earlier, where there is a clash between the spoken message and the one conveyed non-verbally, it is the latter that tends to be believed.

In Greece for example, shaking one's head up and down means 'no' and wagging it from side to side means 'yes' (Bragganti and Devine 1984) – the opposites to the meanings normally attributed in Great Britain. If everybody freely agreed that these differences exist and made allowances accordingly, there would probably be few problems. Problematically, almost all cultures have a degree of *ethnocentricity* – the 'our culture is right syndrome' – which is probably inevitable because a culture promotes certain values and behaviour above others. A spin-off from this is the phenomenon of stereotyping (see Chapter 4) and in cross-national situations this can result in people being attributed with a whole host of characteristics just because they come from another country (McAndrew *et al.* 2000). This creates strong perceptual barriers in communication in which people develop preconceived notions about the meaning of messages.

Moreover, there is another effect. Schneider and Barsoux (1997) argue that inbuilt cultural preferences for certain structural features in organisations, such as hierarchy, formalisation, or participation, raise expectations about what information should normally be communicated, how it should be communicated and to whom. For instance, French organisations tend to be highly structured, with clear hierarchical distinctions

Ethnocentricity: a frame of reference in which members of a cultural group view their culture as superior to all others

between different levels. Thus the flow of information is very limited and French managers tend to see information as power, which is not something that is shared with those at a lower level. For this reason French employees tend to rely much more on informal communication networks. Conversely, in the Swedish culture, which is much more egalitarian, there is a correspondingly greater willingness to share information with anyone who wants to know (Holden 1999).

As Varey (1999) points out, while the acquisition of linguistic skill is necessary for establishing a cross-cultural dialogue, this on its own may not be enough to convey meaning. Competence in communication also involves the ability to appreciate the differences between our own culture and the culture of those with whom we try to communicate and, because culture gives rise to different world views, which can sometimes erect barriers to effective communication, we also need to be aware of some of the less visible effects of national cultures.

TIME OUT

In the previous Time Out exercise, you considered a class that you attend at your university or college and identified the main components in the communication process. For the same class, now try to identify any barriers to communication. Are there:

noise barriers?
barriers associated with the source of the message?
barriers associated with the media and/or channel?
barriers associated with the receiver?

REPLAY

- The main barriers to effective communication associated with the sender are poor message formulation, perception and encoding difficulties.
- The main barriers associated with the channel and media are physical and psychological noise and inappropriate channel selection.
- The main barriers associated with the receiver of a message are perceptions, decoding difficulties and information overload.
- The effects of barriers can be amplified when people from different countries or cultural backgrounds attempt to communicate.

COMMUNICATION IN ORGANISATIONS

Although many organisations are awash with information, not all of this is intended and some of it might not even be sanctioned by an organisation. For this reason, it is more convenient to distinguish between formal and informal communication and consider these separately.

Figure 15.2 Formal
and semi-formal
information flows in
organisations

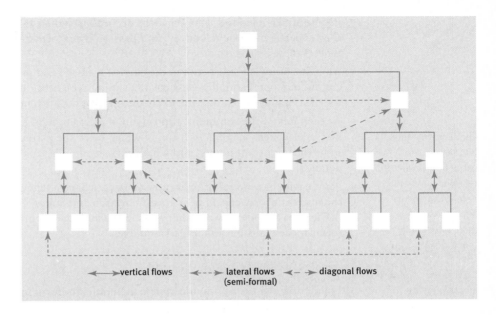

←——→ vertical flows   ←- - -→ lateral flows   ←- - → diagonal flows
(semi-formal)

Formal Communication

Formal communication normally occurs in three directions: vertically (upward and downward); laterally and diagonally (see Figure 15.2).

Vertical (Downward) Communication

This is the dominant form of internal communication and it normally follows the hierarchical lines established by an organisation's structure. A great deal of what is communicated originates at the highest level and while there is evidence that employees who receive the information they need from above usually perform better – either as individuals or groups (O'Reilly 1977). There is also evidence that this state of affairs is not as commonplace as it should be (Callan 1993).

Unfortunately there is often a significant information loss as messages are conveyed downward. This was uncovered over 40 years ago in a classic survey of 100 firms undertaken by Nichols (1962), who convincingly demonstrated that, by the time information has progressed down through five organisational levels, the clarity and understanding of the message had decreased by 80 per cent. One explanation for this state of affairs comes from research by Erez (1992), who shows that as messages travel downwards systematic distortions occur, which are of two main types:

Sharpening of messages: selective attention to only part of a message

Levelling of messages: omission of certain details of a message as it is transmitted onward

- *Sharpening of messages*, in which selective retention on the part of receivers at each level prompts them to exaggerate certain parts of a message.
- *Levelling of messages*, which is the selective omission of other details.

These distortions seldom come about by conscious intent, but occur for a number of predictable psychological reasons:

- People attach meaning to information according to their **expectations** of what they expect a message to convey, and pass-on the information in a form that reflects these expectations.
- An **association** is made between the current message and prior messages that had certain outcomes and, if a message of a similar type heralded certain outcomes in the past, it is assumed that the likely meaning of the current one is the same.
- At each link in the communication chain, a recipient who has to pass on a message engages in *condensation*, in which he or she extracts what are perceived to be the important points, and what gets passed on is typically shorter and less detailed.
- People who have to relay ambiguous messages have a tendency to try to absorb the uncertainty by engaging in *closure* (March and Simon 1958); that is, they fill in the gaps and amplify certain points in the message to turn it into one that seems more plausible and understandable.

Condensation (of messages): the extraction of what the receiver of a message perceives to be its key points and transmitting only these onward

Closure (of messages): the receiver fills in what he or she perceives to be gaps in a message before transmitting it onward

Vertical (Upward) Communication

Although downwards communication is the dominant form, many organisations try to make some provision for information to flow in the opposite direction. For instance, it can often be beneficial for managers to receive open, honest and accurate information for control purposes, and an effective upward flow of communication is said to be a key element in the success of Japanese organisations (Erez 1992). One way for this to occur is through the use of employee opinion surveys, which are discussed in Chapter 5. In addition, in today's fast-moving conditions, where employee commitment and enthusiasm are strongly desired attributes, some knowledge of how people react to top management's decisions can be vital. However, the problem is that many employees can be wary of raising their concerns without invitation and to some extent this can be because they feel that those above them pay little attention to what they say. Thus they develop an attitude of 'why bother'. So, if upwards communication is to occur, it usually needs to be actively encouraged, which requires a distinctly participative approach by management.

Diagonal Communication

Because it cuts across the hierarchy of an organisation and tends to be disliked by many managers, this type of formal communication has traditionally been the least used. Nevertheless, some degree of diagonal flow of information is probably inevitable and Bedeian (1984) notes that most communication of this type occurs between line managers and staff specialists, such as personnel officers and industrial engineers. This is hardly surprising since the primary role of many staff specialists is to gather information and disseminate it throughout the organisation.

Lateral Communication (Networks)

Most of the lateral communication that occurs in organisations happens through networks and, while these are not always part of an organisation's structure, they are sometimes acknowledged to exist. Indeed, some of them, such as cross-functional liaison teams and project groups eventually become a formal part of the structure, and in a matrix structure (see Chapter 17) lateral communication would be the main method of coordinating functional activities. As such, formal networks do not exist in a random way, and a number of distinct network structures are identifiable, for instance 'circle', 'chain', 'wheel', 'Y' and 'all-channel' (Bavelas 1950; Leavitt 1951), which are described in Chapter 10.

Informal Communication

The Grapevine

Grapevine: an
informal channel of
communication

In most organisations, informal communication channels usually exist alongside formal mechanisms. This is often referred to as the *grapevine*, and while its existence is not officially recognised, almost everyone acknowledges that it operates and it is found almost everywhere.

It is a powerful means of communication that does not depend on formal organisational channels and, for the most part, it supplements any formal system that exists. Its prime function is to disseminate information that is of interest to people – usually information that is not available through formal channels. Thus it is an important, if not *the most important*, part of the communication network for any social group in an organisation (Noon and Delbridge 1993). As such, there are a number of reasons why it exists and flourishes, which is normally because:

- there is a lack of information available through formal channels
- people feel insecure, which prompts them to communicate with each other to seek comfort in the face of perceived threats
- there are conflicts between a superior and his or her subordinates, in which the latter feel the need to share information
- people engage in political tactics, in which protagonists circulate negative information about each other
- because there is a need to spread new information quickly.

The last point illustrates a distinctive feature of the grapevine. It is often much faster at carrying a message than formal channels and research evidence tells us that it is somewhere between 75 and 95 per cent as accurate (Watson 1982). Indeed, most employees regard it as a more reliable source of information than that handed out by management (Robbins 1998), mainly because the message gets to almost everybody, even though only about 10 per cent of employees are active message carriers.

For the most part, managers deprecate the very existence of these informal channels, although they sometimes deliberately make use of them when it is convenient. Thus formal methods are often introduced with the aim of eliminating the grapevine, one of which – team briefing – will be described presently. The problem is that informal channels are so useful to employees that it is unlikely that they can ever be completely eliminated. For this reason, it has been argued that managers are foolish to try to do so and, instead, they should take greater pains to ensure that official channels match the informal ones, so that both reinforce the same message (Foy 1983).

Rumour and Informal Communication

Rumour: unverified
information of
uncertain origin

A much criticised feature of the grapevine is its ability to circulate (and sometimes originate) rumours. Although a *rumour* is unverified information of uncertain origin, this does not mean that a rumour is untrue. Mishra (1990) identifies four general types of rumour that commonly occur in organisations, all of which are likely to arise in conditions of ambiguity and uncertainty about the future:

- **pipe dreams/wishful thinking**, which express the wishes or desires of the people who spread the rumour; perhaps with the hope that, if a rumour is started, it will come true
- **bogeys**, which express fears and anxieties, often because there is speculation about the future
- **wedge drivers**, which spread aggressive, damaging and sometimes downright untruthful information about someone, often because political manoeuvring is in progress
- **home-stretchers**, which are items of information that anticipate the future in a prophetic way.

The Effects of the Grapevine

As noted above, the grapevine is often faster and more efficient than many formal means of communication and assertions that it has a detrimental impact on organisational effectiveness are probably grossly exaggerated. For instance, Zaremba (1988) draws attention to a number of its highly beneficial features:

- It can act as a safety valve that enables people to release their frustrations and anger about those in authority.
- Because it gives people a sense of being 'in the know', the grapevine can also give groups and their members higher morale, feelings of security and belonging.
- It can be a reminder to managers that they may need to be more effective in their own communications.
- If taken in the right spirit, it can become a valuable source of feedback to management about how subordinates actually perceive managers and their decisions.

TIME OUT

Reflect carefully on communication at your university or college and try to identify the following:

1. Any formal provisions that are made for the institution to communicate with its students.
2. Any formal provisions that exist for students to be able to communicate upwards to lecturers, more senior academics and the management of the institution.
3. Any formal provisions that exist for students in one school or department to communicate with students in other schools and departments.
4. Any informal communication networks of which you may be aware.

DIFFERENT FORMS OF ORGANISATIONAL COMMUNICATION

The two main channels of communication in organisations are verbal and written. Since each has its own strengths and weaknesses, it is convenient to consider them separately.

Verbal Communication

Verbal methods are widely used in organisations and evidence suggests that over three-quarters of managerial communication occurs in this way (Luthans and Larsen 1986). Because most verbal communication occurs in a face-to-face situation, this will be the main focus of discussion.

Theoretical Considerations: Communication Styles

Many of the problems that influence the effectiveness of face-to-face communication can be traced to perceptual differences on the part of sender and receiver. People interpret the world according to their own backgrounds and prior experiences, and this has a strong impact on how they behave when communicating. One approach to understanding the effect that this has on the process is to use the concept of *interpersonal communication style*, which can broadly be described as the way that people prefer to relate to other people in the communication situation.

In a conversation between two people, it is seldom (if ever) the case that either of them knows everything that the other person knows. This unknown information not only concerns the substantive topic of conversation, but also includes knowledge about personal feelings and potential reactions. For instance, if I talk to someone about food, I may be unaware of the other person's tastes, or whether he or she has some religious or ethical objection to certain foods. Similarly, he or she may not know this about me, and so we can both have a degree of wariness about what we say. Thus communication situations can be classified according to how much each person knows at the outset about three matters:

- substantive knowledge about the topic of communication
- his or her own stance on the matter
- the other person's stance.

For a dyadic (two-person) interaction, this can be classified along two dimensions: the amount of information possessed by self and the amount of information possessed by the other person. The usual way of expressing this is by using what is known as the 'Johari window' (Hall 1973), which can be used to portray the four communication situations shown in Figure 15.3.

In the **blind spot** situation, the receiver has an advantage over the sender because he or she knows more about the substantive issue, his or her own likely reactions to what might be said and the likely feelings and emotional reactions of the sender. Thus the sender is at a disadvantage and communication can be impaired.

The **unknown situation** is one where neither party knows anything about the substantive issue or the other person. Here there is a danger of the blind leading the blind,

Figure 15.3 The Johari
window

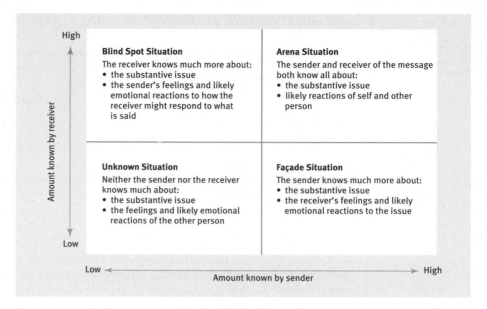

Figure 15.3 The Johari window

and since any meaningful dialogue only occurs by chance, interpersonal communication will be poor.

In the **façade situation**, the sender of the message knows much more than the recipient. Therefore, the receiver may try to convey the impression that he or she understands everything, or, for fear of offending the receiver, the sender can withhold information. Either of these is merely a façade of effective communication in terms of transferring understanding.

The **arena situation** is said to be the one that is most likely to result in effective interpersonal communication because sender and receiver both know all that needs to be known about the issue and each other. However, for this situation to occur, the parties must first gain a clear understanding of each other's feelings, together with the meaning of the information that is to be exchanged.

Three of the situations shown in the Johari window result in communication that is only partially effective. Thus Polsky (1971) points out that effectiveness comes down to a willingness to engage in self-disclosure (revealing ourselves to others) and a willingness to give and receive feedback. People vary considerably in these respects and this gives rise to characteristic patterns of behaviour (interpersonal styles) that impair effectiveness. This is shown in Figure 15.4.

Where the sender of the message has a **self-exposing** style of behaviour, he or she encourages the receiver to focus on the sender, probably by constantly asking for feedback. However, because the person is essentially self-centred, little attention is given to any feedback the receiver provides, and there is little feedback given to the receiver. Thus a 'blind spot' situation is created.

If people in the role of sender have a **self-bargaining** style, they are willing to open up to the receiver and also give a measure of feedback. This, however, is something like a game of 'tit-for-tat'. Because the sender is only willing to engage in these behaviours to the extent that he or she perceives that the receiver does the same, an 'unknown situation' is created.

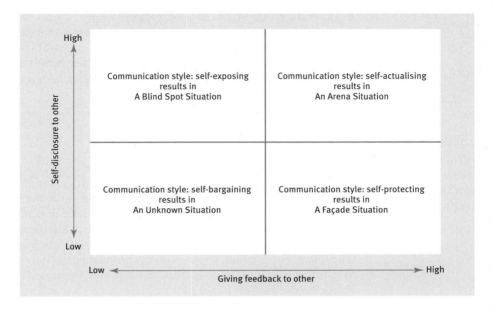

People with a **self-protective** style are unwilling to be open with the receiver about their own feelings and views, but tend to probe the other person's meaning and give a great deal of feedback. In effect, therefore, a 'façade situation' results.

Finally, those who have a **self-actualising** style are willing to provide a great deal of information about themselves, and give and receive feedback, all of which tends to bring about an 'arena situation'.

Polsky suggests that the self-actualising style is universally the best and that something is wrong if it is not used everywhere. While this is far too sweeping an assertion to be plausible, the idea that using a self-actualising style encourages effective communication is a useful one. However, because this depends acutely on a person's ability to adopt a self-disclosing approach and to give feedback, it is worthwhile considering these aspects of behaviour.

TIME OUT

Carefully reflect on a recent face-to-face communication that you experienced with a single individual. This could be a colleague at work, a fellow student, a friend or parent, or a lecturer at your university or college. Try to identify the following:

1. What was the communication style that you used in this encounter: self-denying, self-exposing, self-protective, self-bargaining or self-actualising?
2. Is this your normal style with most people or was there something special about this encounter that prompted you to adopt the style? If so, what?
3. What was the communication style that the other person used in this encounter: self-denying, self-exposing, self-protective, self-bargaining or self-actualising?

4. Do you feel that this is the other person's normal style with most people, or was there something special about this encounter that prompted him or her to adopt the style? If so, what?

5. Having identified the styles that you and the other person used, to what extent do you feel that these made it easier to communicate, or inhibited effective communication in the encounter?

Self-disclosure

Self-disclosure: information that people consciously communicate about themselves to others

This can be defined as information that people consciously communicate about themselves to others, which can happen non-verbally, as well as through the spoken word. To some extent many people do this unconsciously but, because people can be wary of revealing too much, lest the other person take advantage of them, this is different from intentionally disclosing personal details. Moreover, the willingness to self-disclose can be affected by the context and circumstances in which communication takes place. For instance, people who have formal power over others can be reluctant to self-disclose because they see it as part of the job to conceal their personal likes and dislikes in the interests of not putting pressure on their subordinates.

Feedback

Nobody can give accurate feedback unless he or she is fully cognizant with what the other person has said. Thus the key to being able to give (and receive) useful feedback is to understand a message. This means listening, and listening in an active way, which involves a conscious effort to search for the speaker's meaning, suspending judgement until he or she has finished and, if matters are still not clear, asking questions to obtain clarification (Brownell 1986).

Clearly neither self-disclosure nor giving feedback comes easily to everyone, but if Polsky (1971) is correct, effective interpersonal communication is less likely to be achieved unless this happens. One of the things that can stand in the way of this is that in a 'one-to-one' situation, people can feel inhibited about being too open and a method that makes some allowance for this is considered next.

Face-to-Face Communication in Practice

Team briefing: a cascade system of communication starting at the top of an organisation, in which managers at each level brief their direct subordinates about matters relevant to the subordinates

In organisations it is often more convenient to disseminate information in a situation where there is one sender and several receivers and a method of doing this that has been in vogue for several years is *team briefing*. This is essentially a cascade system, which commences at the top, with managers at each level briefing the next level below, and continuing downwards throughout the whole organisation. It is important to note that while briefings include some information about company-wide matters, the main emphasis is on issues specific to the workgroup being briefed. The operational guide to the process produced by the Industrial Society (Middleton 1983) lays down the six cardinal principles on which it is based.

1. **Face-to-face:** although time is left for questions at the end, this is primarily to check that the message has been understood and general discussion is discouraged.

2. **Small briefing teams**: usually not less than four and no more than 15 people.
3. **Leaders**: briefing is by the line manager or supervisor responsible for the team.
4. **Regularity**: it should occur regularly, preferably at fixed intervals of about one month, and briefing itself should last no more than 30 minutes, including questions.
5. **Relevance**: it primarily concentrates on local information that is considered to be most relevant to the team. The 'core brief', which comes from higher levels of management, should occupy no more than one-third of the session.
6. **Monitoring**: leaders need to be trained on how to brief others and it is usually considered important for higher levels of management to monitor the effectiveness of a supervisor's briefings.

As can be seen, although there is a built-in check that those who are briefed understand what is said, team briefing focuses heavily on top-down, one-way communication. The benefits claimed for it are:

- it reinforces the role of line managers and supervisors because, as providers of information, it differentiates them from their subordinates
- by giving work a purpose and relating people to the organisation as a whole, it increases the commitment of subordinates
- it reduces misunderstandings by avoiding the assumption that people know what is going on, and instead explicitly sets out to ensure that all employees receive a common message
- because the early provision of information can assist in people's understanding of why changes are necessary, it helps with the acceptance of change
- because employees receive a common official message, it helps control the grapevine
- it should not be used for consultative or decision-making purposes, but because if people are better informed, this can promote feedback to management via other channels and thus improve the flow of upward communication.

Having noted these points, whether the stated advantages are obtained in practice is a contentious point. While most employees would rather be better informed than kept in the dark, the ideas underpinning team briefing are aimed at reinforcing managerial prerogatives, and it can be expected that in certain circumstances employees may well be suspicious that the information being conveyed is rather one-sided and selective. Indeed, what evidence there is on the outcomes of communication schemes such as these tends to show that the expected benefits of improved employee attitudes are seldom realized (Marchington *et al.* 1989).

Written Communication

Evidence suggests that written channels are still the major method used by organisations for communicating with their employees. For instance, a wide-ranging survey of both large and small organisations undertaken as part of the Workplace Employment Relations Study gives interesting insights into this matter, a summary of which is given in Table 15.5.

As can be seen, written methods are heavily used within organisations, which is hardly surprising because they are relatively cheap and convenient. Moreover, if used well, they can be highly effective in many circumstances; for example, where:

Table 15.5 Frequency of use of different methods of workplace communication (Source: IRS 2006)

Method	Frequency of use for communicating about workplace matters (%)
Bulletins and notice boards	96
Team briefing	86
Newsletters	76
House journals	63
Roadshow meetings	63
E-mail or other electronic	48

- accuracy or precise wording is vital
- a detailed explanation is desirable
- there are a large number of employees dispersed over several locations
- there is a need for employees to have a permanent record.

While this does not mean that the written channel is always the most effective, there are several ways in which it can be used to good effect. Some firms develop *employee handbooks*, which can be particularly useful for new entrants, or as a source of reference for information that is relatively unchanging. Many companies also provide summary annual reports to inform employees about the activities and performance of the enterprise.

As Table 15.5 shows, bulletins and notice boards are probably the most widely used methods and, in the case of the latter, these are sometimes the only form of written communication. The great problem here is that not everybody stops to read notice boards and so it can never be guaranteed that the message has been received. For more regular dissemination of information, many large organisations also produce in-house journals and newsletters, which often contain social as well as organisational items.

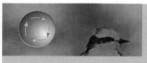

REPLAY

- The main formal flows of information in an organisation are vertical (upward and downwards); lateral through networks; and, more rarely, diagonal.
- Informal communication (the grapevine) also takes place through networks, which are sustained by employees because they serve a useful purpose.
- The main ways of communicating in organisations are interpersonally, using face-to-face methods and different forms of written communication.
- All channels of communication have their own strengths and weaknesses and each one is more suitable for some types of message than others.
- Face-to-face communication is potentially the richest form in information, but taking advantage of this richness requires people to adopt appropriate communication styles.

Electronic Communication

Across the last two decades huge advances have been made in methods of electronic data transmission. Voice messaging facilities now allow desktop computers to act as sophisticated answering machines that can reply to a message and relay it onwards to interested parties. Electronic bulletin boards, which are similar to notice boards but operate through computers, can communicate routine information to large numbers of people, thus reducing paperwork and filing. The internet allows literally millions of people to obtain information on nearly everything, and potentially makes it possible for anyone who has a computer to communicate with others who are also equipped in this way. Finally, the intranet, which is really only an internal form of the internet, allows people inside the organisation to send written messages to each other with tremendous ease. All of these can be of great benefit to organisations, but because in many cases these methods have been the subject of a great deal of 'hype', there are a number of issues that require examination in greater detail and each will be explored separately.

E-commerce

One of the greatest boons of electronic communication seems to be its potential for so-called e-business. By using the internet, organisations can potentially reach customers in markets that they have not yet tapped. It can also bring convenience to customers, who can now order even mundane articles such as the weekly groceries via the internet. However, while services such as this attract a great deal of publicity, so far it is the business-to-business sector in which the most significant level of activity lies. Firms availing themselves of this facility are reputedly able to achieve savings equivalent to 15 per cent of turnover by eliminating paperwork and unnecessary warehouse stocks. In the USA, for example, the three largest car manufacturers – Ford, General Motors and Chrysler – have created a single automotive parts service run via the internet, and other groups of manufacturers in different industries are forming similar alliances. In the light of these developments, traditional companies are said to be finding it increasingly difficult to market their goods and services.

Nevertheless, not everything in e-business is plain sailing. The comparatively low cost of setting up a website to take orders for goods seems to have encouraged a degree of unscrupulous trading practices. Taking orders is easy, but being able to fulfill an order and get the goods to the customer is much more difficult and expensive. A number of firms selling via the internet seems to have forgotten (or conveniently ignored) that warehousing and delivery facilities are required to do this and so this has resulted in a degree of wariness on the part of consumers (Naughton 2000). Finally, the more that individuals and organisations make use of the internet, the more susceptible they become to a complete breakdown because their computer system has been sabotaged by the unwitting importation of a virus (Davidson 2003) (also see the OB in Action Box overleaf).

Electronic Communication within Organisations

Like most things, while there are huge potential benefits in using electronic methods to communicate, the benefits are not always realised, and some of the disadvantages

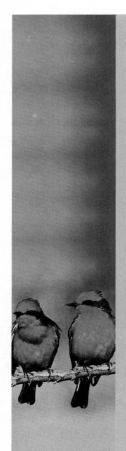

 OB IN ACTION: The hunt for virus writers

In November 2003 Microsoft put $250,000 (£150,000) in bounties on the heads of two computer virus writers, as it stepped up its fight against the tide of malicious code aimed at desktop PCs. The software giant and law enforcement officials in the US also sought to turn public sentiment against virus writers, who are often depicted as underground heroes in technology circles and popular culture. The bounty follows a spate of attacks by viruses and worms, many aimed at weaknesses in the Windows computer operating system. Steve Ballmer, Microsoft's chief executive officer said the company had been humbled. The onslaught also brought an attempt by class action lawyers in the US to hold Microsoft responsible for loses suffered by computer users. However, while software companies are excluded from product liability claims by contract, this has not been tested in the courts.

Microsoft said it would pay rewards of $250,000 for information leading to the arrest and prosecution of the people behind two viruses this year One, known as Blaster or MSBlast, spread through an estimated 1.2m computers. Three people face prosecution in connection with variants of the virus, including an 18-year-old in Minneapolis and a man in Romania. Microsoft said the reward was tied to 'variant A' of the virus, designed to attack the website the company uses to distribute fixes for security flaws. The other reward covers the SoBig virus, designed to turn infected computers into machines that outsiders could use to send spam e-mail.

Source:

Waters, R (2003) Microsoft offers reward to catch virus writers, *Financial Times*, 6 November

are now beginning to show. With voicemail, for example, while it was supposed to be an aid to efficiency and cutting costs, many organisations now consider it to be useless and about half of all new voicemail systems are abandoned within one year (Gwyther 1999). Quite simply, callers do not like being treated as an anonymous entity that can be kept 'on hold' or shunted around from person to person until someone can be found to answer a query. As such there are signs of a significant customer backlash to this service (Caulkin 2005).

Similarly, while e-mail can be a great boon in many circumstances, a number of drawbacks is also starting to appear. Not everyone has the skills to encode their thoughts into the written word, and it seems likely that the ability to communicate in writing has declined considerably in the population over the last 30 years. So serious is this problem that several large companies, for example, Marks and Spencer, Tesco and Unilever, are having to spend significant sums of money in teaching staff how to write simple written communications (Arlidge 2000). In addition, because e-mail permits information to be sent and received with great ease, there is a distinct possibility of information overload and 'spam' (unsolicited messages) (Clegg 2003). This can all too easily lead to messages not being read and, in the case of e-mail, there is a danger that something that was intended to be a means of sending messages cheaply and more effectively has actually become a distinct barrier to communication (Gleick 2003; Naughton 2007). Moreover, there are other, less visible effects. While e-mail is a convenient way of sending messages, it is very impersonal compared to face-to-face methods and it can all too easily become a substitute for face-to-face communication, and this tends to deprive people of one of the things that they value most about work – the social experience.

Finally, more insidious features of e-mail are beginning to appear. There is no such thing as a 'confidential' e-mail, and so it can become a control tool that intrudes into a person's private life and innermost thoughts. Even worse is the recently recognised and growing phenomenon of a *flamemail* (Welch 1997): the use of e-mail to abuse others in the workplace. In essence this is a form of bullying that can all too easily lead to higher levels of stress for individuals.

Flamemail: the use of e-mail to abuse others in the workplace

OVERVIEW AND CONCLUSIONS

As the definition given at the start of the chapter points out, communication is much more than simply transmitting and receiving information. It consists of conveying meaning and, for this reason, the effectiveness of communication can be gauged by the extent to which the sender and the receiver of a message are in agreement about its meaning. From this it follows that, if agreement is absent, communication has not taken place, only the output of information from the source of a message. As such, an abiding theme in the chapter has been to focus on the effectiveness of the process.

Despite its apparently straightforward nature, communication is a complex process. It involves the interaction of many components, all of which need to function in the correct sequence and in an appropriate way for meaning to be conveyed. Two of these, the sender and the receiver, are human and for both of them human sensory and cognitive processes are involved. Since these processes are unique to individuals, people can attribute different meanings to the symbols used to communicate an idea, which means that there is no certainty that a sender will produce a message that it is interpreted in the same way by its recipient. Moreover, because the channel selected for a message may be inappropriate for conveying its meaning, other problems can arise.

Like all human activities, communication occurs within a context, and this can also have an impact on the way that messages are interpreted. Therefore, the effectiveness of communication is not something that can be taken for granted. It is an activity that requires thought before any attempt at communication takes place, and it is almost certainly one in which the amount of mental activity that preceeds the activity is directly proportional to its effectiveness.

In terms of the cues they provide to convey meaning, certain methods of communication are much richer than others. Verbal methods, particularly if they take place in a face-to-face situation, provide a host of non-verbal cues as well as the words that are spoken. This method is also more likely to result in the provision of a degree of feedback to the sender, which can be used to check whether meaning has been conveyed. However, for face-to-face methods to work effectively, the parties need to adopt appropriate interpersonal communication styles by being open to each other and providing feedback.

Many organisations now place emphasis on face-to-face verbal communication with employees. Nevertheless, written channels are still the dominant method used for this purpose and the effectiveness of the process is almost certainly impaired by the oft-quoted decline in effective writing skills. This problem is compounded by the increasing use of methods made available by cheap and reliable electronic technology, for instance e-mail. Because people may have little experience in exercising written communication skills, many of them are ill-equipped to use these methods, and so other problems that impede effectiveness in communication, are starting to appear, for example, information overload.

FURTHER READING

Beck, CE (1999) *Managerial Communication: Bridging Theory and Practice*, London: Prentice Hall. A useful book which, as its title implies, covers organisational communication in theory and practice.

Carysforth, C (1998) *Communication for Work*, Oxford: Butterworth-Heineman. For those who like the 'how to do it' approach, a useful volume that contains many practical tips that can be used to improve personal communication skills.

Hargie, O and D Tourish (eds) (2000) *Handbook of Communication Audits for Organisations*, London: Routledge. A book of readings presenting a number of methodologies to evaluate the effectiveness of communications with a view to making improvements.

Lewis, PS, SN Goodman and PM Fandt (1995*) Management Challenges in the 21st Century*, St Paul, MN: West Publishing. An interesting book, which among other things deals with the implications of communication in organisations that in the future, are likely to be more culturally diverse.

McNeill, D (2000) *The Face*, London: Penguin. A penetrating analysis of the extremely rich variety of signals that we communicate (non-verbally) in our facial expressions.

Pease, A (1997) *Body Language: How to Read Other's Thoughts by Their Gestures*, London: Sheldon Press. An interesting guide to decoding non-verbal communication.

Rosenfeld, P, RA Giacalone and CA Riordan (1995) *Impression Management in Organisations: Theory Measurement and Practice*, London: Routledge. An impressive book that draws widely on the research evidence in the area.

Windahl, S, B Signitzer and TJ Olson (1992) *Using Communication Theory: An Introduction to Planned Communication*, London: Sage. A very useful introduction to communication theory and its application.

CASE STUDY 15.1: Customer loyalty

With frustration verging on despair, marketing gurus and brand managers worldwide bemoan the erosion of customer loyalty. The global power of consumer brands is not what it used to be and marketers resent it. They think their customers are fickle ingrates and in the pungent phrase of Marian Saltzman, an executive trend spotter at WPP, the world's second largest advertising conglomerate, consumers today are 'brand sluts' who are most loyal to instant gratification.

This 'consumer-as-slattern' attitude is a far cry from advertising grand master David Ogilvy's marketing admonition that: the consumer isn't a moron; she's your wife. However, look at a typical block of network advertising in the US and you will see at least a quarter of the prime-time brand advertisements portray their target customers and prospects as idiots and nincompoops. While these are meant to be edgy and humorous, mega-brand fast food, breakfast cereal and telecommunications companies such as McDonald's, Kellogg's and Verizon in effect cast their own consumers as wimps and weasels, while at the same time chief marketing officers complain that brand loyalty is dead.

In reality, the declared demise of brand loyalty is 180 degrees misunderstood and a review of the past decade reveals that customers have not been cavalierly unfaithful to established brands; quite the opposite. Established brands have cheated on and betrayed their most loyal customers, who have been charged more and more for less and less, because firms chase after the youth market or the hot segment *du jour*. Indeed, their so-called innovations frequently add more complexity than value; and their willingness to apologise and compensate for errors or mistakes is nil. Thus the more provocative marketing argument is that it is brand inertia rather than brand loyalty which has kept many customers attached to many companies for so long.

However, consumers are neither sheep nor fools. They can sense when companies are consistently more loyal to investors, employees and regulators than to the people who buy their products and services, and they behave accordingly. Customers are not being disloyal; they are being discriminating and the central marketing question confronting brand leaders therefore is not how can we radically increase customer loyalty, but how can we radically increase our own loyalty to customers?

This distinction is enormous and is analogous to companies who say that they promote a culture of employee loyalty while cutbacks and lay-offs surge during economic slowdowns and mergers. Top management demands loyalty from below while regretfully declining to reciprocate. Yet the moral authority and value of loyalty comes from the courage to hold fast during difficult times. It is the defiant unwillingness of enterprises to be loyal to their best customers that has produced the promiscuous consumer behaviour they deplore and the real sin here is that companies have wilfully confused brand loyalty with customer retention. Just as employees can learn to hide behind a perfunctory loyalty of compliance rather than giving pride or passion, so can consumers. Companies demonstrate loyalty to employees by investing in them, fairly compensating them, tapping their expertise and declining to throw them overboard when times get tough; so why should customers deserve any less?

This is where traditional marketing and brand advertising fail. Often, it is not the brand attribute of flawless service but the real-world performance in rapidly recovering from a mistake that wins customer loyalty and return business. For instance, airline reservationists who waive change fees for inadvertently misbooked flights, or mobile telephone operators who politely and without complaint remove rightly

▶

disputed charges from a bill. These are less acts of customer service than demonstrations of loyalty to customers. Brand value comes not from promises of perfection, but gracefully compensating for acknowledged weakness. At least one global luxury hotel chain and a British Telecom provider have conducted customer research revealing that their most persuasive word of mouth support comes more from individuals who have had an unpleasant problem happily resolved than those who simply enjoyed good or excellent service. The willingness and ability to see a difficult situation through to success despite cost and risk is what defines loyalty. Many companies already know this and invest accordingly. To be fair, financial pressures, increasing transparency and the demands of hydra-headed corporate social responsibility movements make it more difficult than ever for companies to balance customer loyalty with loyalty to customers, but consumers are far quicker to see a brand as a mask that the company hides behind.

This is where new technology creates new opportunities for reciprocal loyalty. Increasingly, cutting-edge companies such as Google and Apple – strong brands in their own right – create online spaces where customers can collaborate and interact around new features and technical problems. Established brands such as Procter and Gamble and the BBC have used digital media to listen to customer ideas and shape new products. Customers know that these organisations have invested millions of dollars, pounds and euros into taking them seriously. In this millennium, brand value comes from investing as much in valued customers as in valuable products and services.

Source: Schrage, M (2007) Customers want loyalty not perfection, *Financial Times, 2 May*. Note: the author is a researcher at the Massachusetts Institute of Technology, where he explores the economics of innovation

Tasks

Working in small groups of up to four students read the above case material, which gives the opinions of an academic about a dilemma confronting many large corporations in America. Then answer the questions below.

1. Assuming that it has occured widely, to what extent do you feel that the erosion of customer loyalty is a serious problem for an organisation?

2. In the author's view, what has brought about this phenomenon? Is it likely to be because:
   - consumers have now developed a taste for novelty?
   - there are mismatches between the views that consumers hold of organisations and their experiences of dealing with these firms in practice?
   - there are barriers to effective communication between firms and their customers that interfere with messages between the two parties?

3. The author comes down strongly on the use of new information and communication technologies to overcome the current problems. To what extent do you feel that these will provide a remedy for firm's dealings with their customers?

4. What else is likely to be necessary to give a long term solution that brings about a change in consumer confidence?

REVIEW AND DISCUSSION QUESTIONS

1. Define communication, state the criterion against which its effectiveness can be evaluated and explain why effective communication is vital to organisations.

2. In outline, describe a model of the communication process and explain the respective roles of the key components in the process.

3. Describe the major barriers to effective communication that are associated with:
- the sender of a message
- the channel and media used to convey the message
- the receiver of a message.

4. Explain the advantages and disadvantages of face-to-face verbal communication and written communication, together with the types of message best suited to each channel.

5. What is the informal communication network in an organisation called? Explain why it exists and critically comment on its effectiveness, speed and accuracy.

Integrating Group Characteristics and Processes and the Links Between Individuals and Groups

Although a group is made up of individuals, what emerges is an entity with its own characteristics, and these have an impact on how the group functions. This is not simply a matter of a one-way cause and effect relationship, but something that arises from complex reciprocal influences, in which characteristics affect processes and in return, new or modified processes have an impact on characteristics. To a large extent this is also true of the links between a group and its individual members, and to explain these matters it is convenient to consider groups first, and then to explain some of the links between groups and their members.

LINKS BETWEEN CHARACTERISTICS AND PROCESSES AT GROUP LEVEL

In terms of a group's patterns of behaviour, one of its most important characteristics its cohesiveness. To a large extent this depends on the group's degree of maturity; that is, whether the group has successfully negotiated its processes of formation (Tuckman 1965), the outcome of which is usually a significant impact on its internal processes. For example, cohesive groups usually devote more energy to their tasks (Shaw 1981), they have higher morale (Seashore 1954) and generally have a lower incidence of problem behaviour such as absenteeism and turnover (Hodgetts 1991).

However, there can also be problems associated with cohesiveness, and one of these can be the impaired decision making that can result from risky shift and groupthink effects, which seem to be far more prevalent in cohesive groups (Janis 1972; Stoner 1961). Since cohesive groups have their own norms and values they also have an in-built potential for conflict with other groups (Ashforth and Mael 1989) and when this happens a cohesive group can come to view another group in a stereotyped way or as an enemy, which has huge implications for the use of political tactics.

In organisations, groups tend to have formally appointed heads, for example managers or supervisors. Whether or not these people also occupy the position of leader is, however, a moot point. Leadership, as opposed to headship, is conferred from below and arises out of tacit negotiation, the result of which is that leader and followers accept complementary roles, and both of them get some of their important needs satisfied (Adair 1984; Danserau *et al.* 1975; Dunegan *et al.* 1992). Thus followers affect the behaviour of the leader just as much as the leader affects follower behaviour (Green 1975), and this has strong implications for processes within groups.

Formally appointed heads of groups usually have certain bases of delegated power (reward, coercive and legitimate) that they can use to try to influence the behaviour of group members (French and Raven 1959). However, this is not necessarily the same thing as exercising leadership, where referent power and expert power can be more important. Thus the style of behaviour adopted by a group's formally appointed head can have a huge impact on the behaviour of a group. In Chapter 13 a number of contingency theories were described, all of which point to the idea that, according to the prevailing circumstances, some styles of behaviour on the part of the head are more appropriate than others.

LINKS BETWEEN INDIVIDUAL AND GROUP LEVELS: CHARACTERISTICS AND PROCESSES

As with many things, there are reciprocal influences between individuals and groups. In a group's early, formative stages, individual characteristics and processes are likely to dominate matters. However, the process of formation (if successful) is one in which individuals give up a certain amount of self-determination in order to accommodate to other group members, but retain enough of themselves to avoid feeling that self-identity is compromised. Thus a fuuly-formed group tends to be able to satisfy those individual needs that can only be satisfied in a social situation, but at the same time allow individuals to occupy roles in which they feel comfortable (Schein 1980). For this reason a well formed group is much more than simply the sum of all of its members' characteristics. The group develops norms of behaviour that become a code of conduct for their members. They also develop systems of roles, each of which has its own expected behaviours. Indeed, groups police the actions of their individual members, and in an extraordinarily successful way they enforce the patterns of behaviour that are expected (Asch 1951), even where this means that individual members have to adjust their perceptions (Sherif 1936) and this can have effects on individuals. For instance, since occupying a role means that the individual has to conform to the behavioural expectations of others, this sometimes means that he or she encounters ambiguities in performing the role. In addition, performing the role can result in role conflicts, which can be stressful to the individual concerned and result in adverse attitudes and impaired performance (Fisher and Gitelson 1983).

One of the roles that emerges is that of leader, which is used here in a generic way, to denote someone who occupies either an appointed headship role, or a person who is acknowledged by followers as someone who provides leadership. As was noted above, followers can affect the behaviour of leaders just as much as leaders affect followers. Nevertheless, the personal characteristics of the person occupying the leader or head role can have an impact on group behaviour. People with a Machiavellian tendency, for example, are inclined to be manipulative with group members and are somewhat more inclined to drag the group into using political tactics in conflicts with other groups (Gemmil and Heiser 1972), as are authoritarians. Strangely enough, where authoritarians are group members rather than heads they tend to be the most slavish followers of orders (Szegedy-Maszak 1989), and this provides another example of how individual personalities can shape the nature of a group.

As noted in Chapter 13, the design of jobs can make leadership of any type superfluous in certain circumstances (Kerr and Jermier 1978) and, where this is the case, trying to exercise either a headship or leadership role may well have adverse effects on individual motivation and attitudes. Moreover, as was also pointed out in Chapter 13, some of the personal characteristics of both leaders and followers, for example their values, personalities and beliefs, can be potent sources of intragroup and intergroup conflict.

In summary, there is an ongoing interaction between individual-level characteristics and processes and those at the group level. Thus, Figure I2 given at the end of Integrative Section 2 of the book, can now be expanded to include group-level interactions as shown in Figure I3.

Figure I3 Interactions between group- and individual-level factors

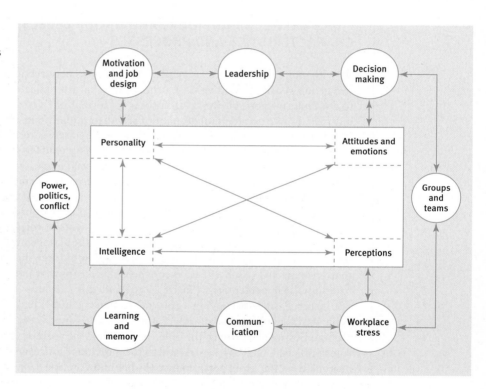

Integrative Case Study No. 3: David Orton plc

Note To refresh your memory about earlier details relevant to this matter, you are recommended to re-read case studies 1 and 2 in this series.

Across the period in which Costwise stores were being integrated into the Orton group, a number of significant changes in management structure took place, some of which had far-reaching effects on the company. The origins of the most prominent change can be traced to difficulties encountered in the early stages of the integration exercise, where it will be remembered that the price Orton had to pay for Costwise had been seriously underestimated. In addition, the pace of upgrading stores had moved far more slowly than had been intended, and price cutting and discounting in an attempt to wooing former Costwise customers into shopping at re-branded Orton stores had also added to costs. Thus the Costwise sites were not turning-out to be anywhere near as profitable as had been hoped and, when taken together, the cumulative effect these things had resulted in Orton having to issue a number of profits warnings. Indeed, in the early stages, the Orton group actually made a loss. For this reason serious doubts were beginning to circulate in the financial press about whether the takeover of Costwise would ever be the success that had been promised, and in some quarters the opinion was being voiced that Orton should perhaps have avoided linking its fortunes to Costwise. For these reasons there was a great deal of personal criticism of the Chairman of the Orton group, who had been the prime mover in the takeover of Costwise, and who, from the start, had always spoken in 'upbeat' terms of the excellent prospects that the merger offered for the company.

As noted in an earlier case episode, Mr Orton was a dynamic and charismatic character, albeit somewhat forthright in his opinions. He was at this time in his mid 70s, and had inherited control of the company in the 1950s on the death of his father. Since then he had been the driving force in building-up the firm to its present size, the final stage of which had been the takeover of Costwise. Although the Orton group was a public limited company, he had virtually run the firm single-handed for more than 40 years, and the only other directors were either family members (his two sons) or long-serving employees. His management style was such that he and he alone made all the major decisions and the firm was run in a way that has been likened to a medieval fiefdom. Thus, when the criticisms surfaced, there were strong attempts to make him the scapegoat for what was then beginning to look like a takeover that might not work out. To cut a long story short, this took the form of a palace coup, led by a small number of very powerful institutional investors, who attempted to force him to stand-down from the chairman's role. While this was narrowly avoided, the institutional investors did manage to engineer a change in his status from executive chairman to non-executive status and, at their insistence (to wrest some of the control out of Mr Orton's hands) a search commenced for a Chief Executive Officer of the company, and eventually Mr Richard Brewer was appointed to this post. Shortly after this, a number of other senior executives were appointed to strengthen the senior management team. These were Dominic Murphy (Director of Marketing) and Brian Guilt (Director of Finance). Some time later it was announced that David Orton would stand down from the chairman's role in early 2008 and, at in what was widely interpreted at the time as a visible sign that the Orton era was due to become corporate history, Mr Edwin Griffin was appointed as Deputy Chairman and Chairman designate. A little later (after the structure of the company had had time settle down) there were also changes lower down in the management hierarchy. Stores were grouped together into six areas of the UK, namely:

Scotland	53 stores	North England	71 stores
Midlands	74 stores	South East	76 stores
South West	53 stores	South Central	61 stores

In addition, and to reflect the wider geographic spread of the group, a number of regional distribution centres were closed and others opened. In addition, the reporting lines for subsidiaries and franchising arrangements (with bakeries, etc.) were reviewed. Finally, the Orton group opened its new, large modern headquarters at Harrogate in Yorkshire and the head office of Costwise was closed and sold-off. In summary, therefore, Orton emerged from these changes with a management structure which, in the words of one of its more prominent instutional investors, is 'one that is now more typical of a modern, well managed company, and has equipped itself well to compete in the new millennium, by shedding its outdated and ageing image'. So far as David Orton is concerned, he appears to be remarkably sanguine about the whole affair. Nevertheless, those who know him well caution that there is bound to be some resentment about what happened and that, although he will be standing down in 2008, in his own eyes he is still too young to be 'put out to grass'.

So far as the continued integration of Costwise stores is concerned, there are recent signs of some recovery of turnover. However, it has been noted that while 2007 started well, a marked downturn appeared in the second half of the year, which the management of the company blamed on rising interest rates, which had cut into customer spending. Moreover, investors were warned that, if anything, trading conditions were likely to worsen due to steep increases in commodity prices. As such, it was stated that the senior management team had noted a need to be increasingly vigilant in the future, with a strict adherance to cost targets. Indeed, there are some signs that a tighter financial regime is starting to take hold in the company. This was a particularly unpleasant surprise to many of the ex-Costwise employees who, from the very start of the merger process, had been aware that they were paid somewhat less than Orton's staff, and had hoped to see their pay levels rise to at least parity.

Problematically, however, the reverse seems to have occurred, and there has been an increased tightening of belts. For instance, staff point to a number of initiatives in which the company seems all too willing to 'level down' in order to harmonise the conditions of staff at Orton and Costwise, but never to 'level up'. Moreover, ex-Costwise staff have noted how quickly they have come to be 'taken for granted' by the management of the company. For instance, in the early days of the integration, management at Costwise seemed to take great pains to keep staff in the picture about everything, but these days report that they are rarely briefed about even major changes. For example, only recently there had been a disquieting rumour that the Orton group had been approached by a private equity fund about yet another takeover. Having recently just come to terms with the takeover by Orton, this provoked near panic reactions in staff, who were aware that Orton owned the property portfolio of their stores outright. This, of course, made the group highly attractive to a private equity fund, because a 'sale and leaseback' arrangement is a frequently used tactic by private equity funds to raise a great deal of cash quickly. Despite the fact that this news was reported widely in the financial press, it was simply denied by management. What was worse, no sooner had this rumour subsided than another one surfaced; this time linking Orton with Woolworth's in a takeover deal.

When referring to themselves, ex-Costwise staff openly express the opinion that they are little more than second-class citizens in the new company, and one example that they feel typifies things is the recent announcement about staffing arrangements for the new group headquarters. Despite the closure and sell-off of the old Costwise heaquarters complex (which was expected), it turned out that the number of original staff who were to be offered jobs at the new Orton HQ was very small. Indeed, of the 1,800 who were to lose their jobs, only 200 were to be transferred to Harrogate.

Another sign in the eyes of ex-Costwise staff that they were not to be 'looked after' was what they interpreted as a rather blatant breach of trust. This matter concerned a decision reached by the management of Costwise in 2004, when, to try to safeguard staff morale and keep them 'on side' in the period leading-up to the official takeover, they undertook to pay retention bonuses to all staff to avoid a 'rush for the door'. Eventually, when the new structure of the company was agreed (included in which was divestment of some sites to conform with the decision of the Competition Commission) Orton decided to close and dispose of three distribution depots. This involved making staff at these depots redundant, which at the best of times is a highly emotive issue. Not only was the consultation process for these redundancies poorly handled, but when the staff concerned received their redundancy payments, these failed to acknowledge retention bonuses.

All in all, therefore, ex-Costwise staff felt that they were being handed a raw deal about virtually everything. They also felt that somehow the major part of the blame for the takeover not working as well as it might have done was being shifted onto their shoulders. For instance, although David Orton was usually bullish about the future prospects for the group, he was seldom reticent about criticising the performance of the Costwise staff, and was on record as saying 'Costwise was an addition that was rapidly getting dusty on the shelf'.

However, it should not be inferred from the above that it is only ex-Costwise staff who feel they have cause for complaint. The new group is much larger and more geographically diverse than the Orton group had been before. It is also more conventionally structured as an impersonal modern company, rather than as a family-run firm. Moreover, the new more formalised strata of board members and senior managers on high salaries (and in some cases incentivised bonus payments) clearly feels that tight cost control is important and, that there is an onus on them to deliver high performance. An example will perhaps illustrate how they perceive matters.

These days virtually all sites of a large retailing organisation are open seven days each week, although not always for the full possible trading hours on every day. Full-time employees are normally contracted to work for something near to 40 hours each week and, in addition, most retail organisations employ considerable numbers of part-time staff, which is an arrangement that suits both management and the staff concerned: management because it keeps paid hours down to the number actually required; and part-time staff because they want to work for less than a full working week. Thus in a large store the manager might have a mixture of anything up to 350 full- and part-time staff to manage, and balancing staff supply with demand can be something of a perennial headache. For example, few people want to work every evening or Sundays. Thus staff have to be 'rostered'. Whereas in the past it had mostly been possible to do this on friendly 'give and take' basis, things have now definitely changed. Staff who query their rostered working hours for a particular week are much more likely to attract a response of 'if you don't like it, you know what you can do' from the manager. In addition, and to control staffing costs, Orton has ceased to pay premium rates for overtime (e.g. time and one-half), although bank holiday working still attracts an overtime premium (but not for part-time workers).

▶

Questions

1. List what you feel to be the main problems confronting the senior managers of David Orton plc at this point in time.

2. Are these problems traceable to issues associated with Groups and Teams; Leadership; Power, Politics and Conflict; Communication?

3. To what extent are any problems you identify associated with more than one, or several of these things working in conjunction?

4. To what extent do you feel that the existence of problems such as these are attributable to the top management of the Orton group, or are they mainly attributable to the actions or perspectives of employees?

5. What do you feel that Orton's management team could do now to address these problems?

The Organisational Level

This section of the book consists of six chapters dealing with matters at the level of the whole organisation. Here the distinction made in some earlier chapters between characteristics and processes is nowhere near as clear-cut as at lower organisational levels.

An overriding theme of this book is that understanding behaviour in organisations requires that account be taken of both macro and micro levels of organisation. Thus, as with all other sections of the book, this one culminates in a section that brings its six chapters together to trace some of the links that bind macro and micro levels together, plus an integrative case study to apply these principles.

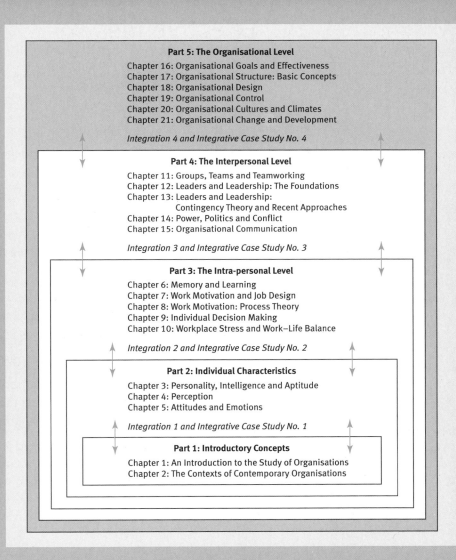

Part 5: The Organisational Level

Chapter 16: Organisational Goals and Effectiveness
Chapter 17: Organisational Structure: Basic Concepts
Chapter 18: Organisational Design
Chapter 19: Organisational Control
Chapter 20: Organisational Cultures and Climates
Chapter 21: Organisational Change and Development

Integration 4 and Integrative Case Study No. 4

Part 4: The Interpersonal Level

Chapter 11: Groups, Teams and Teamworking
Chapter 12: Leaders and Leadership: The Foundations
Chapter 13: Leaders and Leadership:
                Contingency Theory and Recent Approaches
Chapter 14: Power, Politics and Conflict
Chapter 15: Organisational Communication

Integration 3 and Integrative Case Study No. 3

Part 3: The Intra-personal Level

Chapter 6: Memory and Learning
Chapter 7: Work Motivation and Job Design
Chapter 8: Work Motivation: Process Theory
Chapter 9: Individual Decision Making
Chapter 10: Workplace Stress and Work–Life Balance

Integration 2 and Integrative Case Study No. 2

Part 2: Individual Characteristics

Chapter 3: Personality, Intelligence and Aptitude
Chapter 4: Perception
Chapter 5: Attitudes and Emotions

Integration 1 and Integrative Case Study No. 1

Part 1: Introductory Concepts

Chapter 1: An Introduction to the Study of Organisations
Chapter 2: The Contexts of Contemporary Organisations

Chapter 16

Organisational Goals and Effectiveness

LEARNING OUTCOMES

After studying this chapter you should be able to:

- define organisational goals, distinguish between goals and related concepts, describe the five generic types of goal adopted by all organisations and distinguish between the official and operative goals of an organisation.

- state the key results areas for which an organisation needs to formulate goals and explain the concept of the means–ends hierarchy for organisational goals.

- describe the goal-setting process in theory and in practice and the processes of goal adaptation and goal displacement

- explain the significance of organisational effectiveness and distinguish between efficiency and effectiveness.

- describe the three major approaches to evaluating organisational effectiveness (the goal approach, the system resource approach and the multiple constituency approach) and explain their strengths and weaknesses

INTRODUCTION

This chapter deals with two allied topics: organisational goals and organisational effectiveness. The first to be considered is that of organisational goals and the discussion commences with a section that defines goals and distinguishes between the term goal and other related concepts. This is followed by an exploration of the types of goal normally held by organisations, after which an explanation is given of the benefits that accrue to an organisation that has a system of clear and explicit goals. Goal formulation is covered next. This is considered in theory and practice and is followed by a brief exploration of goal adaptation and change.

The section on organisational effectiveness starts with an explanation of why effectiveness is an important attribute for organisations. Effectiveness is distinguished from efficiency and the remainder of the chapter deals with the three main approaches that can be used to evaluate effectiveness, each of which focuses on a different aspect of organisational functioning and has its own perspective on what being an effective organisation means. The chapter closes with a short section that overviews effectiveness and traces connections between this concept and that of organisational goals.

ORGANISATIONAL GOALS

Why Study Organisational Goals?

Chapter 1 of this book draws attention to the idea that organisations do not exist in nature. They are brought into existence by humans to serve a purpose, and without goals to achieve there would be no purpose in their existence. For this reason, if we want to understand the behaviour of an organisation, we cannot hope to do so unless we know something about its goals.

Essential Definitions

A perennial problem when discussing goals is the use of a bewildering array of different terms, for example, goals, objectives, aims, targets, policy and strategy. Since some authors use these interchangeably, it is necessary to start by being explicit about the way that the words are used here.

Goals

Goal: a desired state of affairs, which an organisation attempts to realise

Perhaps the most explicit definition of a *goal* is given by Etzioni (1964), who defines it as:

> **a desired state of affairs which an organisation attempts to realise.**
>
> **(Etzioni 1964, p 6)**

Since this definition is widely endorsed by many authors such as Rouillard (1994), it is adopted here because it captures the three essential characteristics of a goal:

- it is an expectation that a future state will be achieved
- the desired future state is specified in advance
- (by implication) there will be activity directed at achieving the future state.

Objectives

Objective: specific, short-term statement of results that should be achieved

As used here, *objective* describes a specific, short-term statement of results that should be achieved, which means that there are three important differences between goals and objectives:

- objectives specify desired outcomes over a shorter time horizon than goals
- they are normally subordinate to goals and can be thought of as concrete steps necessary to achieve a goal
- for each goal there may well be a number of corresponding objectives.

Mission

Mission: a statement of an organisation's fundamental reason for existence

The *mission* is normally taken to be a somewhat global (and vaguer) statement of an organisation's goals, which expresses the fundamental reason for its existence (Barney and Griffin 1992). Almost inevitably this means that there can be confusion about whether an organisation's mission statement is also a statement of its goals and this point will be clarified presently when discussing types of goal.

Associated Terms

One term that is frequently encountered is the word 'aim'. Strictly speaking, this simply means a purpose or intention. As such, aims can sometimes be nothing more than vague statements of the direction in which an organisation intends to move. However, because the word is frequently used in conjunction with the term 'target', it is more convenient to think of aims and targets as another way of expressing objectives.

The Issue of Strategy and Policy

The words 'goal' and 'objective' are inescapable in the subjects of business policy and corporate strategy. Johnson and Scholes (1999) define strategy as:

> the direction and scope of an organisation over the long term, which achieves advantages for the organisation through its configuration of resources within a changing environment to meet the needs of markets and fulfil stakeholder expectations.
> (Johnson and Scholes 1999, p 10)

Strategy: a plan or design to achieve aims, goals or objectives

Put simply, *strategy* is essentially a plan or design to achieve aims, goals or objectives. *Policies* can be described as guides to action that indicate how the tasks of an organisation might be accomplished, or (after Ansoff 1965) as 'rules to guide future decision making, if and when certain contingencies arise'. The important points to note about strategies and policies are:

Policies: rules to guide future decision making, if and when certain contingencies arise

- Strategies are the chosen ways of achieving the desired end states and their formulation can sometimes occur after goals have been set.
- While goals and strategy are both strongly influenced by an organisation's environment, they also include considerations about things internal to the organisation and involve choices about structure, technology and a host of other matters.
- Policies, on the other hand, are more closely connected with constraints that an organisation tries to observe in attempting to achieve goals and objectives, which means that policy often tends to exist before strategy is formulated and policies can put a limit on the strategies adopted.

Figure 16.1 The relation of goals, objectives, policy and strategy

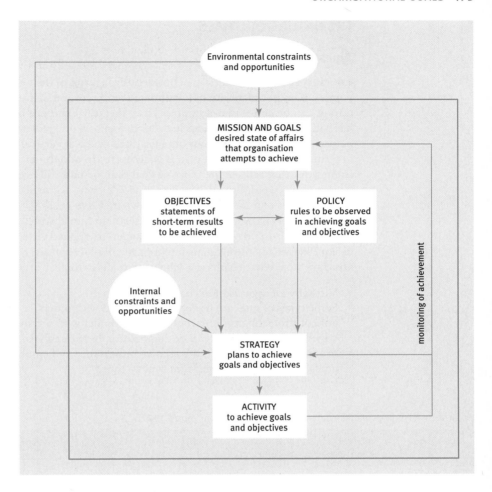

Bringing all the above terms together, matters can be expressed in the simplified form shown in Figure 16.1.

REPLAY

- The words 'goal' and 'objective', together with associated terms such as 'target' and 'mission', can be a source of some confusion.
- Goals are desired future states that an organisation wishes to achieve.
- Objectives are more specific short-term statements concerning results that should be obtained in order to achieve goals.
- There are strong connections between goals, strategy and policy. Strategy is the chosen way of achieving goals and policy is a set of decision guidelines that limit the strategies that can be used.

THE NATURE OF GOALS

Types of Goal

Even very similar firms can vary considerably in terms of their goals. As Perrow (1972) points out, most organisations have limited resources and so it is unlikely that an organisation can be active in everything. Thus, the very existence of a goal implies that it has had to forego certain things in order to focus on others. For this reason the diverse nature of activities in different organisations makes it very difficult to compare them in terms of their goals. To do so it is necessary to adopt a more abstract conceptual framework that reflects the types of goal that virtually all organisations embrace. A scheme of this type is provided by Perrow (1972), who distinguishes between five generic types or levels of goal and these are shown in Table 16.1.

Although Perrow's framework may seem unduly abstract, it has to be because it explicitly aims to provide a typology that can be applied virtually everywhere. While he concedes that slotting goals into a particular level or category can be a somewhat arbitrary step, what results is a scheme that has a number of important implications:

- Virtually all organisations have multiple goals.
- Some types of goal are not easily reconciled with others, for example a derived goal of protecting the environment can conflict with a system goal of profit, which means that there can be competition between goals.
- From the previous point, the relative importance and emphasis placed on certain goals may need to change from time to time.

Table 16.1 A typology of organisational goals (adapted from Perrow 1972)

Type of goal	Referent (whose point of view is recognised by the goal)	Function of goal	Examples
Societal goals	Society in general	Distinguishes what the organisation is *vis-à-vis* its environment	Whether it produces goods or services, whether it generates or maintains the core cultural values of society
Output goals	The public in contact with the organisation	Defines types of output in terms of consumer functions	Whether outputs are consumer goods, business services, healthcare, education, etc.
System goals	The organisation itself	Specifies the state or manner of organisational functioning, irrespective of the goods or services it produces	Relative emphasis on growth, stability or profits modes and functioning such as loose or tight control
Product goals	The goods/services produced	Specifies characteristics of the goods or services produced	Relative emphasis on quality, quantity, variety, styling, uniqueness, innovation
Derived goals	Top management	Specifies what top management chooses to do with the power and resources accumulated in pursuing other goals	Political aims, community service, employee development, environmental protection

- There can also be competing views about the category to which a goal belongs, for instance, is equal opportunities a societal, system or derived goal?

Most organisations have a multitude of different stakeholders and, as Chapter 2 points out, some attention should desirably be directed at catering for the interests of all of them. Since it is virtually impossible to derive a single goal that would do this, formulating organisational goals is typically a political process concerned with reconciling the potential conflicts between the interests of different stakeholders.

TIME OUT

Carefully consider the organisation for which you work (or that part of it in which you are located). If you have no experience of employment, use the university or college at which you are a student. Try to uncover its main goals and classify them into the types shown in Table 16.1.

Official versus Operative Goals

Despite its apparent simplicity, the concept of organisational goals can be one of the most slippery and treacherous concepts employed by those who analyse organisations, because organisations are not always what they seem (or pretend) to be, and this is as true of their goals as other aspects of their behaviour. Perrow (1961) draws attention to this when he distinguishes between two classes of goals: official and operative.

Official goals: ideal states that an organisation would wish to achieve

Espoused theory: the theory of action officially espoused by an organisation

Operative goals: the actual goals pursued by an organisation

Theory in use: the theory of action actually implemented by an organisation

Official goals are the general aims of an organisation expressed in its charter, mission statement, annual reports and other items intended for public consumption. Inevitably these are very broad, general statements of purpose and, while there are examples where these goals are reflected in concrete behaviour, these are all too rare. Thus official goals often reflect what Argyris and Schön (1978) call the organisation's *espoused theory* of action. Indeed, in recent research by Murphy and Davey (2002) there is evidence that many employees tend to regard the values expressed in company mission statements as little more than 'corporate claptrap'. *Operative goals*, however, are the real intentions of an organisation, as revealed by how it actually operates. They reflect what Argyris and Schön call its *theory in use*; that is, the real theory of action, which means that these goals may not correspond with the organisation's professed aims.

An example which can be used to illustrate the difference is that of a prison. Officially, prisons have the aim of rehabilitating criminals and eventually returning them to society as reformed characters. In reality, perhaps because of overcrowding or shortage of appropriate staff and other resources, many prisons are unable to devote sufficient time or effort to rehabilitation and, instead, primarily focus on keeping inmates away from society by holding them in custody.

This is not to say that official goals have no utility. Even where they differ significantly from operative goals they still perform a number of useful functions. For example, they:

- can give an organisation a favourable public image that legitimises its existence and activities

- send a signal to existing and potential employees about what the organisation stands for
- describe something of the organisation's value system and what it would prefer to be.

Nevertheless, there are often significant differences between official and operative goals, which begs the question of how these differences come about. Bedeian and Zammuto (1991) suggest four potential reasons: disagreement about goals; different perceptions of how to achieve official goals; unrealistic official goals; and bargained goals.

Disagreements about goals

There can be considerable differences between people in an organisation about what its goals should be. While these can sometimes be resolved with a compromise goal, people often say nothing, but quietly go about 'doing their own thing'.

Different perceptions of how to achieve official goals

Even when people agree about what the goals should be, they can have very different ideas about how they are best achieved. For example, in a manufacturing organisation, marketing people might argue that a good return for shareholders is best achieved by having a wide product range, whereas production staff argue that a narrow product range with long production runs minimises costs. Again, both functions can quietly go about pursuing what they believe is the most appropriate operative goal.

Unrealistic official goals

Official goals can be unrealistic and to avoid failure people adopt more realistic alternatives. For instance, an organisation that uses timber for its products might have an official goal of protecting the natural environment, which can result in it trying to avoid the use of hardwoods from the fast-depleting tropical rainforests. However, if customer tastes are such that it finds it difficult to sell its products unless this type of wood is used, it might well ignore its official goal.

Bargained goals

As will be seen later, operative goals are typically compromise affairs that result from bargaining between groups or coalitions of organisational stakeholders. As such, operative goals tend to reflect the shifting balance of power between groups and, as Quinn (1977) argues, this often results in organisations purposely setting very vague official goals so that competition between groups is avoided.

In summary, it can be almost impossible to identify an organisation's actual goals from what it says in public pronouncements and its real goals can be identified more accurately from what it does, rather that what it says it does.

The Benefits of Goals

Those at the very top of an organisation usually spend considerable time in formulating, refining and clarifying goals because if an organisation is not clear about *what*

Table 16.2 The benefits obtained from having clear and explicit goals

Benefit obtained	Rationale
Signalling action guidelines	Goals tell employees the future results that are required and where they should focus their efforts
Constraints on action	By signalling what should occur, goals indicate priorities and (by implication) things that should not occur
Sources of legitimacy	Goals justify an organisation's existence and activities to external stakeholders and, providing stakeholders consider the goals legitimate, this helps with the acquisition of necessary resources
Standards of performance	By indicating what should be achieved, standards are set against which future performance can be evaluated, for example how close the organisation has come to achieving the goal
Evaluation and control	The existence of a goal implies that performance should be monitored and allows provision to be made for remedial action to be taken to correct performance deficiencies
Sources of motivation	Fair, but explicit statements of what should be achieved can be a source of challenge to employees, which has a motivational effect
A basis for organising	Clear goals not only indicate what should be achieved, they prompt consideration of factors such as structure, technology and the human resources that are necessary for goal achievement
Facilitation of planning	Clear and explicit goals not only specify what should be achieved, but also time horizons, which enables activities to be coordinated and resources to be available when they are needed

it wishes to achieve, it is difficult to decide *how* it should be achieved, to say nothing of whether the organisation has succeeded in doing so. Thus there are likely to be a number of advantages in having clear and explicit operative goals, and these are summarised in Table 16.2.

REPLAY

- Although goals are always unique to a particular organisation, Perrow's (1972) framework gives a scheme that describes the five generic types of goal adopted by all organisations.

- An important distinction can be drawn between the official and operative goals of an organisation: official goals are broad statements of organisational aims and purpose, whereas operative goals reflect an organisation's actual and more immediate intentions.

- There are often significant differences between official and operative goals, the reasons for which are well understood and documented.

- Although workable goals can be hard to formulate, there are clear benefits for an organisation in having clear, well understood and specific goals.

GOAL FORMULATION

Having discussed goals and their benefits, it is now time to turn to the matter of how goals are selected. Here it is important to stress that, while organisations are goal-directed systems, this does not mean that an organisation itself has goals. As Cyert and March (1963) point out, it is people who have goals, not organisations. Therefore, the so-called goals **of an organisation** are really the goals **for the organisation** and probably those selected by its dominant power holders. This leaves two main issues to be considered: what goals should an organisation have and how they are derived? Each of which will be considered in turn.

The Goals Required

Key results areas: areas of activity vital to an organisation's existence

Most writers in the area, for example Rouillard (1994), assert that an organisation should establish goals for all *key results areas*; that is, the areas or activities vital for its survival and continued existence. These, of course, are likely to be specific for each organisation. Nevertheless, a generic scheme has been proposed by Drucker (1984) and, although this is highly prescriptive and is primarily designed for profit seeking firms, with thought, it is also applicable to public sector and not-for-profit organisations and is shown in Table 16.3.

THE MECHANICS OF GOAL SETTING

Goal setting in theory

In theory there are three main ways in which goals can be set, each of which envisages a different direction for the flow of influence and power in an organisation. These are shown in Figures 16.2(a), 16.2(b) and 16.2(c).

Top-down goal setting: goals for a particular organisational level can be imposed from above

In *top-down goal setting* (Figure 16.2(a)), which is by far the most common method, the goals for any level in an organisation are set by the level immediately above. If necessary, this can be done by imposing the goals, but these days it is widely accepted that the process of goal setting should include a degree of prior consultation. The advantages of this method are said to be:

- it ensures that goals and objectives at a given level support those of the level above
- it usually results in ambitious but achievable goals.

However there are also three pronounced disadvantages:

- those who set the goals for a particular level can be remote from the reality of having to achieve them, which can result in goals being unrealistic and demotivating
- senior managers can be out of touch with the realities of organisational life at lower levels, which means that goals can become outmoded
- because people lower down are not involved in formulating them, goals can come to be seen as the property of top management, which can result in a lack of commitment to achieving them lower down.

Bottom-up goal setting: people set their own goals which are then agreed with their immediate superiors

In *bottom-up goal setting* (Figure 16.2(b)) power flows in the opposite direction. The process starts at the bottom of an organisational hierarchy, with people

Table 16.3 Key areas for organisational goals (adapted from Drucker 1984)

Goal	Purpose	Example: profit-orientated organisation	Example: not-for-profit organisation
Market share	Signals the organisation's intended position *vis-à-vis* competitors	Increase market share from 10 to 15 per cent over five-year time period	A charity: increase the organisation's share of charitable donations by the public from 5 to 8 per cent over three years
Innovation	To stay apace with, or ahead of, competitors	At least 20 per cent of sales revenue to be derived from products less than five years old	Shift the percentage of revenue acquired from public collections, as opposed to long-term covenanted donations from 90 to 70 per cent over five years
Productivity	To promote internal efficiency	Reduce production and distribution costs per unit of output by 5 per cent over the coming year	Local authority: provide specified additional services to ratepayers over the next year at no additional cost
Physical and financial resources	Ensure adequate finance and other resources for the business	A supermarket chain: increase number of retail outlets by 10 per cent over three years	Local authority: increase size of land bank available for building public housing by 200 acres over two years
Profitability	To ensure adequate return to financial stakeholders	Increase earnings per share by 10 per cent each year for the next five years	Local authority: maintain present level of services over the next three years, with no increase in council tax (adjusted for the rate of inflation)
Manager performance and development	Manager quality is assumed by Drucker (1984) to be the most important factor in organisational success	Increase the number of graduate trainees taken on each year; introduce annual performance and development reviews in the coming year	As for profit-orientated organisation
Employee performance	If an organisation develops, its managers, it should also develop other employees	Decrease absenteeism to a level of no more than 3 per cent per annum; reduce accident rate by 30 per cent over the next year	As for profit-orientated organisation
Social responsibility	To ensure that the firm responds appropriately to wider society	Sponsor five university scholarships each year for children of disadvantaged parents	Introduce collection points for recyclable waste materials such as bottles

suggesting their own goals and individuals then have to agree the goals with their immediate superior. According to a number of writers, including Latham and Steele (1983), this has the following advantages:

- goals are more likely to be realistic
- goals are more likely to reflect current conditions and what can be achieved in practice
- because people play a part in setting their own goals, they are more committed to achieving them.

Figure 16.2 (a) Top-down goal setting; (b) bottom-up goal setting; (c) interactive goal setting (arrows indicate the direction of the flow of influence)

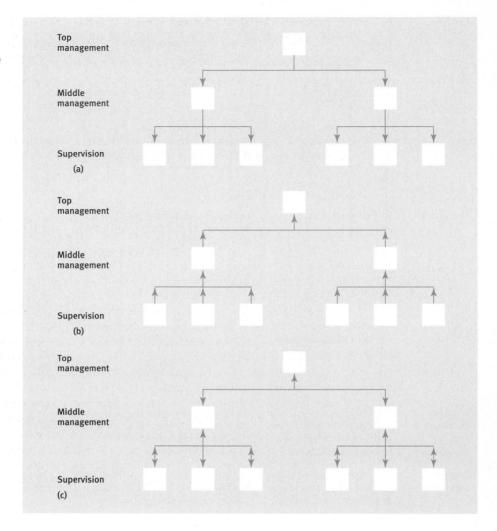

Nevertheless, Lathan and Steele also note the following disadvantages:

- goals tend to be unambitious
- because goals at a particular level are set in isolation, it is only by accident (rather than design) that they support goals at other levels
- the goals that result seldom provide clear direction and purpose for the whole organisation.

Interactive goal setting (Figure 16.2(c)) starts with people at each level stating their views about what the goals should be. However, superiors cannot impose goals on those below, but have to negotiate with subordinates to reach a consensus. This is said to have all the advantages of bottom-up goal setting, but few of its disadvantages. That is:

- goals are realistic and up to date
- people are more committed to achieving the goals

Interactive goal setting: goals are initially set for a particular organisational level by its head, but are then negotiated to a consensus with subordinates at that level

- goals can be coordinated to support each other at a particular level and at different levels.

Nevertheless, there is one disadvantage of this method:

- negotiating to reach a consensus is usually a complicated, time-consuming process.

Several authors, for example Pascale and Athos (1981), recommend the interactive process as the best all-round method, noting that it is a feature of Japanese companies and is associated with the success of these organisations.

Goal Setting in Practice

The work of Cyert and March (1963) points to the idea that goal setting is a political process in which the (sometimes covert) influence of a number of parties is at work. As such the organisational goals that get adopted are often the outcome of covert negotiations between an array of internal and external interest groups, all of whom make competing claims on an organisation. Cyert and March reason that individuals or groups seldom have sufficient power to force an organisation to adopt goals that completely satisfy their interests. Therefore, stakeholders form *coalitions*; that is, temporary alliances of individuals and/or groups who perceive that something that they value can be obtained if they collaborate. The members of these coalitions can come from inside or outside the organisation but the important point is that, while members of a coalition probably have divergent interests, their interests are not actually opposed, which means that they can exert pressure in a collaborative way.

According to Cyert and March, while organisational goals appear to be set by a select group of top managers, they are actually determined by a process of continual bargaining among coalitions. Thus, goals are compromise solutions which reflect the relative power of different stakeholders and stakeholder coalitions at a certain point in time. Here it is important to recognise that bargaining does not necessarily mean that all stakeholder groups sit around a table to thrash out goals, because bargaining can be a much more subtle and covert process than this.

Coalition: an alliance of groups and/or individuals who perceive that something they value can be obtained by collaboration

How Stakeholders Exert Influence

Because different stakeholders have different amounts of potential power to influence an organisation, a range of influence strategies can be expected. A general scheme for mapping the dynamics of influence, which also gives some clues about where coalition formation could be expected to occur, is provided by Frooman (1999), who addresses two basic questions:

- What are the different types of influence strategy available to stakeholders?
- What determines the choice of a particular influence strategy?

Frooman then uses resource dependency theory to answer these questions. The theory will be examined later in the chapter when exploring organisational effectiveness and for the present it is sufficient to note that it hinges on the idea that a firm's need for resources provides an opportunity for other organisations or groups to exert influence on its actions. There are two basic strategies for doing this:

- a **withholding strategy**: where a stakeholder discontinues or rations the supply of a resource to make the firm change its behaviour (or exerts a credible threat to do so)
- a **usage strategy**: where the stakeholder continues to supply the resource but attaches conditions to its supply.

Clearly the withholding strategy is potentially the most potent, but either of the strategies can be exercised in two different ways:

- directly, in which case the stakeholder itself takes the action
- indirectly, where the stakeholder induces someone else, who has a direct relationship with the firm, to exert the influence.

However, much depends on whether, and to what extent, the firm is dependent on the stakeholder, or whether the stakeholder is dependent on the firm. Thus there are four types of influence relationship, which are shown in Figure 16.3 and are discussed in what follows.

The 'Stakeholder Power' Relationship

This is shown in the bottom left-hand quadrant of Figure 16.3 and here it is possible for the stakeholder to exert influence directly by using a withholding strategy. Usually this can only occur if the stakeholder is a monopoly supplier of a certain product and an example is Microsoft, which is the sole owner and producer of the 'Windows' computer operating system that is virtually a 'must have' for any manufacturer of personal computers.

The 'Firm Power' Relationship

This is illustrated in the top right-hand quadrant of Figure 16.3. Here it is the stakeholder who is dependent on the firm. Thus he or she cannot risk exerting direct influence for fear of retaliation, and for the same reason the possibility of using a withholding strategy is very low. Thus the stakeholder's only option is to set conditions on its supply of resources to the firm, and to do so indirectly. For example, if the stakeholder is a supplier to firm A and is also a customer of firm B, which in turn is a monopoly supplier to A, it could seek a coalition with B, who could then exert direct pressure on A.

Figure 16.3
Firm–stakeholder relationships, influence strategies and exertion of influence (adapted from Frooman 1999)

| | | Whether the stakeholder is dependent on the firm | |
		No	Yes
Whether the firm is dependent on the stakeholder	No	**Relationship:** Low interdependence **Influence Strategy:** Withholding **Strategy Exerted:** Indirectly	**Relationship:** Firm power **Influence Strategy:** Usage **Strategy Exerted:** Indirectly
	Yes	**Relationship:** Stakeholder power **Influence Strategy:** Withholding **Strategy Exerted:** Directly	**Relationship:** High interdependence **Influence Strategy:** Usage **Strategy Exerted:** Directly

The 'Low Interdependence' Relationship

This is shown in the top left-hand quadrant of Figure 16.3, where neither the firm nor the stakeholder are dependent on each other. Therefore, the stakeholder would need to seek a coalition arrangement with another stakeholder who could exert influence directly.

The 'High Interdependence' Relationship

This is shown in the bottom right-hand quadrant of Figure 16.3 and, because neither the firm nor the stakeholder can do without each other, it is by far the most interesting situation. The classic example of this relationship is employment relations, where an employer needs the services of employees just as much as employees need the pay from their jobs. Assuming that the stakeholder is employees, who are adamant about obtaining a certain level of wage increase, they would need to induce top management to meet their requirements. To do this it can sometimes be sufficient for employees to demonstrate their willingness to forego the pay for a period of time, for example by holding a ballot on strike action.

Side Payments

Side payments: inducements that are paid for cooperation or collaboration

As can be seen from the examples given above, in some cases the only way that influence can be exercised is through a coalition of stakeholders in which one party gives its support to another(s). This support seldom comes free; it has to be paid in one way or another. Cyert and March (1963) refer to this as making *side payments* and they are commonplace in goal setting. These inducements can take many forms, such as the promise of future cooperation, or foregoing something now in order to receive something in the future. For instance, in return for wages, employees agree to expend effort and, in return for the promise of future dividends, shareholders agree to invest. Therefore, in order to satisfy their goal of obtaining a good rate of return on money invested, shareholders make a side payment (usable finance) to the organisation. In doing this they may well attach conditions about the minimum rate of return expected. It is important to recognise that side payments to one group normally have to be found from contributions made by other groups. For example, when customers place orders, there is an implicit promise to pay for the goods, which allows the firm to borrow money from the bank to pay for employees and other resources to produce the goods. When this finance is acquired, the money then enables the organisation to honour its implied promise to manufacture and deliver the goods to customers. With some validity, Cyert and March argue that an organisation can only survive and prosper if it is able to maintain this reciprocal flow of inducements and contributions and this applies to contributions and inducements from all stakeholders.

Organisational Slack

Organisational slack: the difference between the total resources available to an organisation and those necessary to make side payments to ensure contributions from stakeholders

Under favourable conditions an organisation is sometimes able to accumulate excess resources, over and above those necessary to make current side payments. Cyert and March call this surplus *organisational slack*. Essentially, it is a cushion of excess resources that enables a firm to adjust to unforeseen internal and external pressures. The most obvious form of slack is liquid financial assets or unused fixed assets such as property. The important point about slack is that, if it is available, it allows an organisation to weather temporary storms such as downturns in the market, or to acquire resources in order to make significant changes without interrupting the current pattern of reciprocal flows of inducements and contributions. Where slack exists, it is also much easier to satisfy the competing demands of different groups, because slack enables an organisation to avoid the situation where an increased level of demands by one group can only be met by offering a reduced level of inducements to another one.

In summary, while the above is a very simplified picture of a very complex theory, it illustrates a number of important points about goal setting in organisations:

- Organisational goal formulation is essentially a political process.
- Goals are the outcome of reciprocal relations between groups with diverse interests.
- Any group that accumulates enough power to force other groups to pay attention to its preferences is likely to have an impact on the goals that are adopted.
- Goals are more accurately viewed as complex statements that reflect the multiple (or compromise) requirements of many groups, rather than the prerogatives of one group (top management).
- In organisations that accumulate slack, the goal formulation process and the process of change are likely to be far easier than in organisations with no reserves of slack.

TIME OUT

Carefully reconsider the organisation you identified in the previous Time Out exercise and answer the questions below.

1. Who are the stakeholder groups that could influence the goals of the organisation?
2. What are the side payments that are likely to be made to stakeholders to obtain their support?
3. Does the organisation accumulate slack and to what use is it put?

The Goals and Objectives Hierarchy

Means–ends hierarchy: goals at one level in an organisation are the means of achieving the goals of the level immediately above

Since virtually all organisations have multiple goals, it is important that goals at a particular level in an organisation do not conflict with each other. It is also important there should be no conflict between goals at different levels in an organisation. For this reason goals and objectives are usually set out in a hierarchical way. This is sometimes referred to as the *means–ends hierarchy* and the principle used is that goals for any particular level are the means of achieving the goals of the level immediately above. The exception to this is the organisation's mission, which exists at the very top of the hierarchy and, as can be seen from the example that follows, consists of very broad, all-encompassing goals which are ends in their own right. Goals at other levels can conveniently be classified into one of three types, each of which is associated with a particular level in the organisation: the strategic level, the tactical level and the operational level.

Using the example of a university this will be illustrated shortly, but first it is appropriate to set out the mission statement of the university in full. This is:

> The university's prime objective is to enable students to reach their full potential by equipping them with the knowledge, attitudes and skills they need to meet with confidence the requirements of work and society in the twenty-first century. It will draw its students from those seeking learning opportunities throughout their lives as well as those from suitably qualified school leavers and postgraduates, from both the United Kingdom and overseas.

Like most mission statements, this one consists of goals that are expressed in very general terms that can be interpreted in a number of ways. These are the official goals of the organisation and, although mission statements are commonplace, they can sometimes be misleading documents; note that the one above makes no mention of the financial viability of the institution because at this level a goal of this nature tends to be assumed to exist. Everything that follows is likely to be in more specific terms. Assuming there is no clash between official and operative goals, the goals at each level are shown in outline in Figure 16.4, where it can be noted that because it is important

Figure 16.4 The goals and objective hierarchy for a British university

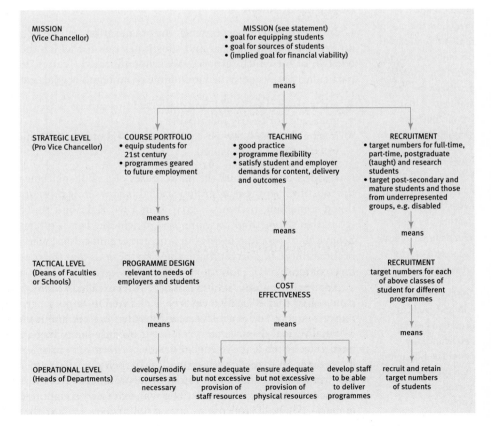

Goal succession: the goal(s) of an organisation is deliberately replaced with another one because the original goal(s) has been achieved or has become seriously outdated

Goal displacement: an organisation or one of its sub-units substitutes a goal for which the organisation was not created, or for which resources were not allocated, for its legitimate goal(s)

Means–ends inversion: the method of doing something becomes a goal in its own right, which displaces the end state (goal) that the method was supposed to achieve

Number magic: the tendency to replace an important and necessary goal with another one that can be measured, simply because it can be measured

Sub-optimisation: sub-unit goals are accorded greater importance (by people in sub-units) than the goals of the organisation as a whole

to goals lower down, for completeness, a goal for financial viability has been inserted at the mission level.

GOAL ADAPTATION AND CHANGE

Adaptation and change of goals tends to occur in a continuous way, sometimes as a response to changes in an organisation's environment and sometimes because there have been (or will be) internal changes. In general terms there are two ways in which this happens: goal succession and goal displacement, both of which will be considered separately.

Goal Succession

Goal succession occurs when the primary goal of an organisation has been achieved (or has become seriously outdated) and it is deliberately replaced with a new one. This can be particularly important when it becomes clear that there has been a shift in the requirements of an important element in an organisation's environment and that staying with the existing goal threatens its very survival.

Goal Displacement

Goal displacement occurs when an organisation or one of its sub-units abandons an existing legitimate goal and substitutes one for which the organisation was not created, or for which resources were not allocated (Etzioni 1964). This is said to be particularly prevalent when intangible or ambiguous goals exist, for instance if:

- goals are incapable of being expressed in a precise way
- goals are not clearly identifiable
- it is hard to operationalise goals in a way that permits achievement (or failure) to be observed and measured.

It is widely accepted that the main causes of goal displacement are threefold. By far the most frequent reason given is called *means–ends inversion*. Here the method of doing something becomes a goal in its own right and this displaces the end state (goal) that the method was supposed to achieve. This is often said to characterise the behaviour of people in highly bureaucratic organisations, where following procedures becomes more important than achieving the ends that the procedures were supposed to accomplish.

The second cause is what Gross (1968) has called *number magic*. When this happens a goal that is easily measured is elevated in importance (or substituted for) an important goal where achievement is harder to ascertain or measure.

Finally, goal displacement can occur because many large, complex organisations have a strong tendency to engage in *sub-optimisation*, in which people have a limited focus that only extends to the boundary of their own department or function. As such, they can sometimes come to regard the goals or objectives of the sub-unit as more important than those of the whole firm. This is an extremely common phenomenon that occurs in many, if not all, large organisations (Mintzberg 1979a), the underlying reasons for which can often be found in an organisation's structural design, a point that will be covered in Chapters 17 and 18.

REPLAY

- Although the phrase 'the organisation's goals' is commonplace, organisations do not have goals, only people do, and so it is more accurate to speak of the 'goals for the organisation'.

- Theoretically goals can be formulated in three ways, each of which reflects a different pattern of the flow of power and authority in an organisation: top-down goal setting in which managers at each level set and, if necessary, impose goals on their immediate subordinates; bottom-up goal setting where subordinates set their own goals and agree them with an immediate superior; interactive goal setting where the manager and the subordinate negotiate to reach a consensus on the goals to be achieved.

- In practice goal setting is a political process that reflects the shifting balance of power between various coalitions of stakeholders, each of whom attempts to ensure that its interests are recognised in the goals adopted for the organisation.

- The goals of an organisation should desirably be capable of being arranged into a means–ends hierarchy, so that the goals or objectives at any level are designed to be the means of achieving the goals of the level immediately above.

- From time to time the goals of an organisation change, either by a process of goal succession, in which new goals are formally selected to replace a prior set, or by goal displacement, which is a more informal process in which goals that are still officially active are displaced by others that are more acceptable to organisational actors.

ORGANISATIONAL EFFECTIVENESS

The Significance of Effectiveness

'Effectiveness' is one of the most frequently used (and misused) words in discussing organisations. There is no universally accepted theory of organisational effectiveness, and neither is there a universally accepted definition and set of criteria that allows the effectiveness of an organisation to be evaluated. Nevertheless, since organisations are brought into existence to achieve some purpose, early theorists such as Barnard (1938) argued that an effective organisation is one that achieves its goals and, as will be seen later, this still remains an influential approach.

However, one problem that besets the use of the word 'effectiveness' is that it can be applied at all levels of an organisation and at each level it is likely to mean something completely different and be influenced by a different set of factors. Important as it is, effectiveness at individual and group levels will largely be ignored in this chapter, because these matters are considered in earlier chapters of the book. As such, the main consideration is effectiveness at an organisational level, the first step being to clarify some of the terms used.

Table 16.4 Effectiveness and efficiency compared using goal achievement as the criterion of effectiveness (adapted from Bedeian and Zammuto 1991)

	Efficiency without effectiveness	**Effectiveness without efficiency**
Goal	1 million units to be produced at a maximum cost of £2 each	
Outcome	750,000 units produced at a cost of £2 each	1 million units produced at a cost of £2.30 each, due to wastage of labour and materials
Effectiveness	Not effective: output goal not achieved	Effective: output goal achieved
Efficiency	Highly efficient	Inefficient

Effectiveness and Efficiency

How 'effectiveness' is defined rather depends on the perspective adopted. For this reason definitions will be considered when the different approaches to evaluating effectiveness are presented. However, a common error that occurs is to use the words 'effectiveness' and 'efficiency' interchangeably, which is incorrect because they refer to two different attributes of an organisation.

Efficiency is a measure of resource usage, usually expressed as a ratio of the inputs used to produce a given level of outputs. Effectiveness is a much more ambiguous concept and it can be defined in a number of ways according to the approach used in evaluating the attribute. At a conceptual level, however, what all these methods have in common is that they judge effectiveness on the basis of whether the organisation as a whole behaves in an appropriate way. Where they differ is in terms of the particular aspect of behaviour that they consider to be the most important. For this reason, Bedeian and Zammuto (1991) crisply distinguish between the two concepts by noting that efficiency is 'doing things right', whereas effectiveness is 'doing the right thing'. It is therefore possible to be efficient without being effective and vice versa (see Table 16.4).

> **Efficiency:** a measure of resource usage, usually expressed as a ratio of inputs used to produce a given level of outputs

APPROACHES TO EFFECTIVENESS

As noted earlier, effectiveness can be defined in several ways, each of which has its own distinctive approach. To avoid dealing with theories that have had very little impact on the topic, only the three most influential approaches will be considered here. These are: the goal approach, the system resource approach and the multiple constituency approach, each of which will be considered separately.

The Goal Approach

The *goal approach* is by far the oldest and best-known approach and mention of it can be found in the work of early theorists such as Barnard (1938). It defines effectiveness as 'the extent to which an organisation achieves its goals', which means that its main focus is on the outputs of an organisation. The approach is underpinned by two major assumptions:

> **Goal approach:** evaluation of organisational effectiveness against the criterion of the extent to which an organisation achieves its goals

- that the goals of an organisation can be clearly established
- that all the necessary resources to achieve the goals are available.

In theory, so long as the evaluation includes multiple goals, both official and operative goals can be considered (Etzioni 1964). However, because official goals are often vague and abstract, a number of writers argue that only operative goals should be used (Strasser *et al*. 1981). The advantages of the approach and the rationale for its use can be simply stated as:

* it is easily understood
* organisations unquestionably have goals and achieving them is what an organisation is supposed to do
* it is the way that most firms evaluate themselves
* it fits well with many other methods of evaluating effectiveness that are used at lower organisational levels, for example management by objectives and budgetary control.

Nevertheless, since it is beset with a host of problems, in academic circles the model has been much criticised because:

* it is immensely difficult to use the approach with an organisation that does not produce tangible outputs, which makes it unsuitable for many not-for-profit organisations
* most organisations have multiple goals and achieving one of them often precludes achieving another; for example, since safety costs money, maximising profits can sometimes be incompatible with providing a safe working environment
* the idea that an organisation has a set of goals, to which all of its members are committed, is highly questionable
* goals are essentially 'ideal' (target) states and since some discrepancy between goals and performance is virtually inevitable, using only goals to evaluate effectiveness is to invite an assumption of failure (Etzioni 1964)
* if goals are set too low and are achieved too easily the organisation can look effective when it is not
* some goals are so inherently ambiguous that achievement can be virtually impossible to ascertain; for example, employee satisfaction or human resource development.

Notwithstanding these criticisms, the goal model is still the most widely used approach to evaluating organisational effectiveness, probably because all organisations set goals of some sort and attempt to determine whether they have been achieved.

The System Resource Approach

The *system resource approach* was first suggested by Georgopoulos and Tannenbaum (1957), largely as a way of overcoming some of the shortcomings of the goal approach. It purposely adopts an open systems view of an organisation, an important feature of which is that it regards an organisation as something that is in continuous interaction with its environment. As was pointed out when discussing goals earlier, an organisation that is able to acquire more inputs than those necessary to produce its outputs accumulates slack, which gives it tremendous advantages. In this approach,

System resource (or resource dependency) approach (to effectiveness): evaluation of organisational effectiveness against the criterion of whether the organisation maximises its bargaining position *vis-à-vis* the environment in order to acquire an optimal level of scarce and valued resources

therefore, effectiveness is evaluated against the criterion of whether an organisation maximises its bargaining position *vis-à-vis* the environment, in order to acquire an optimal level of scarce and necessary resources.

Here it should be noted that the model takes a somewhat broader view of resources than the one that is normally adopted. As well as the conventional resources that most immediately spring to mind (money, raw materials, physical facilities and labour), in appropriate circumstances it would view such things as knowledge, ideas and reputation as scarce and valued resources. In general terms, however, the evaluation of effectiveness is set against criteria that are less precise than for the goal model, four of which are suggested by Cunningham (1978):

- the ability of an organisation to exploit its environment in acquiring scarce and valued resources
- the ability of organisational decision makers to interpret correctly the true properties of the environment; for example, the constraints and opportunities it presents
- whether day-to-day activities run smoothly in the organisation
- whether the organisation responds appropriately to changes in its environment.

Note that the model is focused almost exclusively on input relationships, which means that it is underpinned by an assumption that all will be well if sufficient resources are acquired. As such, little or no attention is focused on what is done with the resources. Nevertheless, the system resource model has the great advantage of being able to deal with situations where achieving output goals can otherwise be hard to evaluate. For instance, in the case of not-for-profit organisations, output goals are often ambiguous or difficult to measure and so it is sometimes hard to evaluate whether they have been achieved. For organisations of this type input goals sometimes have to be used as surrogate measures. Using the example of the university portrayed in Figure 16.4, the vague output goal of providing a good education for the widest number of students tends to be evaluated in terms of the institution's ability to attract sufficient students from a wide range of backgrounds. Here the assumption is made that students will not be attracted to the university unless it achieves its output goal. Nevertheless, while the system resource model directs attention to the organisation's relationship with its environment and this gives an important alternative to the goal model, it has a number of widely recognised limitations, of which the three given below are the most important:

- Although the model emphasises optimal exploitation of resources, no indication is given of what is an optimal state of exploitation, which makes it difficult to evaluate effectiveness. If, for example, a firm draws too heavily on resources from the environment, it can deplete them and jeopardise its own long-term survival. Is this being effective?
- No guidance is given about determining what the scarce and valued resources are, without which effectiveness can hardly be determined.
- Because the approach focuses totally on resource acquisition, it ignores the equally important issue of the uses to which resources are put, which can be crucial to both effectiveness and efficiency.

TIME OUT

Carefully consider the organisation for which you work (or that part of it in which you are located). If you have no experience of employment, use the university or college at which you are a student. Try to identify the scarce and valued resources that it needs to obtain from its environment to operate in a satisfactory way and to safeguard its longer-term survival. Now answer the questions below.

1. What are these resources?
2. How good is the organisation at obtaining the resources you have identified?
3. Are the resources it obtains primarily used to pursue short-term operating efficiency, or longer-term survival?

The Multiple Constituency (Stakeholder) Approach

Clearly the goal and system resource approaches have something to offer and both provide valid, if somewhat restricted, views on effectiveness. The problem is that neither tells a full story, and using either one in isolation has inherent dangers.

The current approach to effectiveness, which first appeared in the late 1970s (Pfeffer and Salancik 1978), has a more comprehensive and integrative view. This is the *multiple constituency (stakeholder) approach.* In common with the system resource model, it addresses the matter of an organisation's relationship with its environment and, like the goal model, it directs attention to the outcomes of an organisation's performance. This is shown in Table 16.5, where the major features of all three approaches are compared.

The basic premise of the approach is surprisingly simple; that all stakeholders who enter into a relationship with an organisation do so in the anticipation that there will be some gain for themselves. Therefore, each group (constituency) of stakeholders has preferences for the way in which an organisation will behave; that is, in terms of satisfying a constituency's particular interests. Thus, each one will have its own criteria against which it judges the effectiveness of an organisation, some examples of which are shown in Table 16.6.

Because an organisation cannot exist, function and prosper without the support of all these groups, the multiple constituency approach defines effectiveness as 'the extent to which the organisation satisfies the interests of its internal and external

Multiple constituency (stakeholder) approach: an evaluation of effectiveness against the criterion of the extent to which an organisation satisfies the interests of its internal and external stakeholders

Table 16.5 Goal, systems resource and multiple constituency approaches compared

Approach to evaluation of effectiveness	Focus of model	Criterion of effectiveness
Goal model	Organisational outputs	Achievement of output goals
System resource model	Ability to acquire scarce and valued resources	Organisational inputs
Multiple constituency (stakeholder) model	Organisational inputs and outputs	Satisfaction of the interests of internal and external stakeholders

Table 16.6 Stakeholder constituencies and their effectiveness criteria

Stakeholder constituency	Stakeholder effectiveness criteria
Shareholders	Dividends, share value
Employees	Pay, working conditions, work satisfaction, security
Customers	Price of goods or services, quality, delivery, after sales service
Suppliers	Prompt payment, creditworthiness, future sales
Government	Tax revenues, observation of laws
Immediate community	Community support
Wider society	Provision of employment opportunities, social responsibility, care for the environment

stakeholders', which in general terms, is widely acknowledged to have a number of advantages over the goal and system resource approaches:

- it gives a much richer picture of effectiveness than other approaches
- it considers factors inside and outside the organisation
- it considers both inputs and outputs to be important criteria of effectiveness
- it acknowledges that effectiveness is a complex, multidimensional phenomenon, for which there is no single measure
- it can, if used appropriately, be applied in a way that reconciles both the goal and system resource views (Tsui 1989)
- it is compatible with goal-setting theory and, in particular, with the political nature of the goal-setting process.

Nevertheless, the approach gives rise to three fundamental problems:

- organisational performance is likely to be viewed by stakeholders in a self-interested way
- almost any aspect of the performance of an organisation is likely to benefit some stakeholders more than others
- since resources in all organisations are likely to be limited, increased satisfaction for one stakeholder group can mean decreased satisfaction for another group.

The burning question therefore tends to be 'whose interests should the organisation attempt to satisfy'? One way out of this dilemma is suggested by Connolly *et al.* (1980), who advocate making the assumption that all stakeholder interests are equally valid. An alternative and more pragmatic stance is suggested by writers who approach the question from a perspective of 'relative stakeholder power'. For example, Pfeffer and Salanick (1978) argue that while every stakeholder constituency has control of resources that are valued by an organisation, at some point in time, certain resources are more important than others. For this reason, being effective comes down to satisfying the interests of the stakeholder group that controls access to the most important resources at that particular time. A third suggestion (Keeley 1984) advocates taking a 'social justice perspective', which has a strong focus on satisfying the needs and expectations of the organisation's most disadvantaged stakeholders.

In summary, therefore, although there is no shortage of suggestions about how to resolve the dilemma, unfortunately there is little consensus about which one is the most appropriate way forward. This inevitably detracts from the practical utility of the multiple constituency approach and, for this reason, it is time to direct attention to a theory that goes some way towards explaining what organisations do in practice.

TIME OUT

In an earlier Time Out exercise in this chapter you identified the stakeholders of an organisation and their potential effect on its goal-setting process. For the same stakeholders, identify the interests that you feel they expect the organisation to satisfy. Now rank the stakeholder groups in terms of what you perceive to be the organisation's order of priority in satisfying their interests. Rank those that you feel are given the highest priority as 1, those who are next in priority 2 and so on.

What conclusions can be drawn from your analysis?

Competing values model: an explanation of how manager values influence the criteria used to evaluate an organisation's effectiveness

The Competing Values Model

This stream of work has its origins in the ideas of Robert Quinn and his co-workers (Quinn 1988; Quinn and Rohrbaugh 1983). It is not so much a theory of organisational effectiveness, but more an account of where managers put their major emphasis in conducting the affairs of an organisation, which, by implication, tells us something about how they evaluate its effectiveness.

Quinn and his colleagues start from the proposition that all judgements about effectiveness are value judgements. For this reason, they argue that if we want to understand what organisational managers believe to be the best indicators of effectiveness, we need to know something of their values. Quinn and his colleagues conducted extensive research from which the conclusion was drawn that managers are virtually forced to choose between value systems that can vary along two dimensions:

- **structure:** whether tight control or flexibility is emphasized in the organisation
- **focus:** whether the manager primarily directs his or her attention to the interior of an organisation or outwards towards its environment.

According to the combination of choices made, a matrix of four main styles can be derived (see Figure 16.5) and the implied criteria of effectiveness that would be used by managers are also given in the figure.

Quinn points out that there is always a certain amount of pressure on managers to try to satisfy everybody. However, managers have their own value systems and these will be reflected in where they choose to put their emphasis, which in turn will influence the criteria that they use to evaluate organisational effectiveness. By implication, this also gives some indication of the stakeholder interests that managers consider to be the most important. For instance, an internal focus combined with a flexible structure implies a strong emphasis on employees as important stakeholders, whereas an internal focus with an emphasis on control through structure places satisfaction of shareholder interests high in the order of priority.

Figure 16.5 The competing values matrix (adapted from Quinn and Rohrbaug 1988)

	FOCUS	
	Internal	External
STRUCTURE — Control	**Values:** primary focus is internal to the organisation and top-down control is preferred **Implied Effectiveness Criteria:** productive efficiency and profit	**Values:** primary focus is external to the organisation and top-down control is preferred **Implied Effectiveness Criteria:** whether organisational goals are achieved
STRUCTURE — Flexible	**Values:** primary focus is internal to the organisation and flexible structure is preferred **Implied Effectiveness Criteria:** employee satisfaction and employee development	**Values:** primary focus is external to the organisation and flexible structure is preferred **Implied Effectiveness Criteria:** competitiveness and the organisation's ability to develop and renew itself

REPLAY

- The words 'effectiveness' and 'efficiency' are sometimes wrongly taken to mean the same thing. However, efficiency is the ratio of inputs to outputs used in a process or activity, whereas effectiveness can be defined in a number of ways, all of which are concerned with whether an organisation as a whole behaves appropriately.

- The goal approach evaluates effectiveness according to the extent that an organisation achieves its goals.

- The system resource approach evaluates effectiveness according to the extent to which an organisation maximises its bargaining power *vis-à-vis* its environment in order to acquire scarce and valued resources.

- The multiple constituency (stakeholder) approach evaluates effectiveness in terms of the extent to which an organisation satisfies the interests of its internal and external stakeholders.

- The competing values model of effectiveness points out that according to their particular value systems, managers direct their attention to certain aspects of organisational functioning, and success in the chosen aspect becomes the criterion against which they evaluate organisational effectiveness.

OVERVIEW AND CONCLUSIONS

Since organisations are brought into existence to serve a purpose, they all have goals of some sort. Although the concept of a goal is clear enough in theory, considering goals in a practical way is sometimes made more confusing by the imprecise and interchangeable use of different terms such as 'goal', 'objective', 'mission' and 'aims'. With respect to the goals of a particular organisation, an important distinction can be made between its official goals and its operative goals. The former are broad general statements of aims and purpose that are designed for public consumption, whereas operative goals reflect the actual intentions of the organisation, which may or may not correspond to is professed aims. Where differences between official and operative goals exist this is usually because a combination of well understood forces are at work.

There are distinct benefits for an organisation in having a system of clear, explicit goals that are arranged hierarchically, so that goals at one level are the means of achieving goals at the level immediately above. Formulating, refining and clarifying goals can be a time-consuming business which, in theory, can be accomplished in one of three ways: top-down, bottom-up or interactively. In practice, however, goal formulation is more likely to be the outcome of political processes which reflect the shifting balance of power between alliances and coalitions of different stakeholders.

'Effectiveness' and 'efficiency' are much used words when discussing organisations and there seems little doubt that they are prized attributes. However, while the words are often used interchangeably, they are not the same thing.

While all approaches to evaluating effectiveness judge an organisation against the criterion of whether its behaviour has been appropriate, there are considerable differences in terms of the behaviour used as the basis of evaluation. The goal model focuses on outputs, the system resource model focuses on inputs and the multiple constituency perspective evaluates effectiveness in terms of whether the interests of internal and external stakeholders are satisfied – essentially a mixture of inputs and outputs. However, different stakeholders are likely to have divergent interests and since most organisations do not have a superfluity of resources, satisfying the interests of one stakeholder group can mean that other groups will not have their interests satisfied. This gives rise to the main difficulty with the model, which is encapsulated in the question of whose interests should take priority? This is illustrated by the competing values model of effectiveness, which clearly shows that managers select their own criteria of effectiveness according to the aspects of organisational functioning that they consider to be the most important, a conclusion that is supported in recent research by Walton and Dawson (2001).

FURTHER READING

Barney, JB and RW Griffin (1992) *The Management of Organisations: Strategy, Structure and Behaviour*, Boston, MA: Houghton Mifflin. The book has an excellent, if rather managerialist chapter on the subject of organisational goals.

Bedeian, A and RF Zammuto (1991) *Organizations: Theory and Design*, Orlando, FL: Dryden. An excellent, comprehensive text that gives a thorough consideration of goals and organisational effectiveness.

Cyert, RM and JC March (1963) *A Behavioural Theory of the Firm*, Englewood Cliffs, NJ: Prentice Hall. A classic text that explores the political processes involved in goal setting. Some readers might find the econometric/mathematic approach heavy going though.

Daft, RL (1996) *Organizational Theory and Design*, 3rd edn, St Paul, MN: West Publishing. Gives a useful, if brief coverage of organisational goals and effectiveness.

Etzioni, A (1964) *Modern Organizations*, London: Prentice Hall. A classic text that gives a detailed consideration of organisational goals.

Rouillard, LA (1994) *Goals and Goal Setting*, London: Kogan Page. A very comprehensive text that gives an extensive, if somewhat managerialist coverage of the problems and issues involved in setting organisational goals.

Simon, NA (1964) On the concept of organisational goals, *Administrative Science Quarterly* 10(1): 1–22. A classic paper, which gives a penetrating exploration of the whole concept of organisational goals.

Walton, EJ and S Dawson (2001) Managers perceptions of the criteria of effectiveness, *Journal of Management Studies* 38(2): 173–199. An interesting paper that supports Quinn's contention that in practice managers choose their own criteria for evaluating the effectiveness of their organisations.

CASE STUDY 16.1(a): Imperial Chemical Industries

Imperial Chemical Industries (ICI) looks likely to be the next British manufacturing icon to fall under foreign control; the Dutch firm Azko Nobel having made a £7bn bid for the company, although ICI boss John McAdam has so far rejected the offer as too low.

Turn the clock back 40 years and no one would have believed that ICI would face being gobbled up by a foreign predator. Worldwide the firm employed 130,000 people and, like British Petroleum, it was viewed as practically an arm of the British state. Today, however, ICI is a shadow of its former self and following three decades of rationalisation its market value has fallen from £11bn to £5bn, and the workforce has shrunk to just 26,000. To some extent the company's demise mirrors the UK's own post-imperial decline as a manufacturing nation. A former industrial bellwether, ICI supplied raw materials to a country in which hundreds of thousands were still employed in ship-building, steel and aluminium production and making cars, and heavy chemicals helped to oil the wheels of industry in Britain and the old Commonwealth. However, the company's top brass remained wedded to imperial values in a post-imperial world. Writing in 1961, ICI chairman Paul Chambers scorned the notion that the company should move into expanding and more profitable sectors. Instead, he said: 'There is a public duty to go on making essential, basic, chemicals even though sales may appear to be less progressive and less profitable. ICI could not, for example, withdraw from the production of industrial explosives without giving the government and the public many years' notice of its intention.'

However, history worked against ICI. Before the Second World War, the world chemicals industry was composed of just three companies: IG Farben of Germany, which dominated Europe; DuPont, which controlled the US; and ICI, which spoke for Britain and the Empire. They set their own prices and never competed in each other's markets, but all that changed after the war, when regional markets began to break down and firms were exposed to the icy winds of international competition. Arguably the sheer size of ICI worked to its disadvantage and a former senior manager commented 'We were too big, trying to do too many things. We were in bulk chemicals, pesticides and biosciences. ICI was more diverse than even its main global rivals and something had to give.' What gave, eventually, were the company's profits. In 1980 ICI reported its first ever loss and cut its dividend, which sent shockwaves around the City. The problem was that the whole business was under pricing pressure, which affected ICI's ability to maintain its competitive edge. 'We would come up with a new product, but it was soon copied by rivals in the Middle East or eastern Europe, who could supply the same thing for less money,' and in the long run, ICI, like many of its competitors, was always on a sticky wicket because there has been a re-shaping of the chemicals industry and production is now shifting to lower cost entries in the Far East and elsewhere.

At ICI, there was a brief renaissance in the mid-1980s when it was the first company to make £1bn profit under Sir John Harvey Jones, who had sold off lower margin businesses such as soda ash (which goes into glass) and industrial explosives, to focus on petrochemicals, polymers, agrochemicals and the fast expanding pharmaceuticals operation. But when the recession came in 1990, chairman Henderson discovered that the company hadn't done enough. Then Lord Hanson struck, buying a stake in 1991 and seeking discussions with the board. ICI conducted a remarkable lobbying campaign, convincing even some ministers in the Major government that a Hanson style break-up of ICI would be against the national interest. In the end, Hanson didn't bid but the cat was out of the bag. A former director says: 'We all knew that if Hanson had broken up the company, he would have made a lot of money. The new mantra was shareholder value, so we began to work on ways to break the company up ourselves.

'ICI brought in rising investment banking star John Mayo from SG Warburg to help with the project. He decided that the firm was in too many product ranges and too many geographies.' He and his team realised that ICI was a chemicals company wrapped in an expanding pharmaceuticals business. That realisation led to the demerger of the pharma arm, renamed Zeneca, which became separately quoted. Zeneca eventually merged with Astra to become one of the FTSE's top 30 companies. However, the chemicals business seemed to lurch from one crises to another and in the mid-1990s, chief executive Charles Miller Smith reshuffled the portfolio again, selling what one analyst described as the 'cyclical, smelly industrial bits', and buying Unilever's higher-margin speciality chemicals. Nevertheless, debt hit £3bn, almost the same as the company's market valuation and it was time for another round of cost-cutting and rationalisation.

Under McAdam, ICI has paid off its borrowings to emerge as a paints company with Dulux as its most famous brand. It also owns National Starch, the US-based adhesives business. Adeney says: 'The ICI story is that its home market disappeared with the demise of British manufacturing industries. Linked to that trend has been stiff global competition and constant pressure from shareholders for ICI to reinvent itself.' In the end, the City viewed ICI as a conglomerate that had overstretched itself and was ripe for unbundling.

It would be wrong, however, to conclude that ICI has been an unmitigated disaster. Zeneca has been successful and so too has ICI's Australian business, now called Orica, the world's number one industrial explosives company. A number of ICI's chemicals operations have been acquired by Ineos, the profitable and privately owned UK multinational, but the fact that parts of the group are still flourishing under new ownership will be little comfort to those who rue the demise of yet another once-great British industrial giant.

Source: Wachman, R (2007) How competition ate away Britain's chemicals giant, *The Observer*, 24 June, pp 4–5

CASE STUDY 16.1(b): Imperial Chemical Industries

After Land Rover and Jaguar, ICI looks likely to be the next British manufacturing icon to fall under foreign control. Unfortunately, its history is full of painful ironies, the most poignant of which is that its eclipse is entirely home-made and the brutal truth is that ICI has imperilled its independence by dutifully complying with the approved nostrums of financial management over the last two decades.

After the second world war, ICI's board decided that the future of chemicals lay in pharmaceuticals and among the clever young scientists it hired was James Black, whose discovery of beta-blockers laid the foundations for ICI's pharmaceuticals division, later re-named Zeneca. It took 20 years for ICI's pharma operations to break even, but patiently growing its stock of resources was what ICI was for, as its mission statement in the late 1980s made clear where the stated aim was to be:

> the world's leading chemical company, serving companies internationally through the innovative and responsible application of chemistry and related science . . . through achievement of this aim, we will enhance the wealth and well being of our shareholders, our employees, our customers and the communities which we serve and in which we operate.

It is possible to identify the exact moment when all that changed. In 1991, Hanson, a company which in many of its methods anticipated today's private equity houses, bought a small stake in ICI which was widely thought to be the precursor of a full bid. It wasn't, but the threat was enough to spur the company to do exactly what the raiders wanted: to break itself up, float off pharma and arm itself with a new, managerially correct mission statement that was more in tune with the age of shareholder value:

> Our objective is to maximise value for our shareholders by focusing on businesses where we have market leadership, a technological edge and a world-competitive cost base.

Instead of growing through its own R&D, ICI now saw its strategy as dealmaking – dumping commodity chemicals and buying its way up the value chain in the shape of fragrances and a sheaf of speciality chemicals acquired from Unilever. So far, so fashionable. But ICI went one better. Again anticipating what is approved practice today, it burdened itself with £4bn of debt to do the Unilever deal. Unfortunately, it failed to sell off the old assets as quickly as it hoped, turning the debt into a millstone that prevented it from doing anything else. Thus earnings and share price declined.

Under the latest regime, ICI is thought to have done quite well, paying down the debt and beginning to grow again. But it has paid dearly for the five-year period when it was paralysed by debt; and you might say that, in the longer term, the Dutch bid is its reward for having faithfully reflected in its strategy the financial orthodoxy of the time, an orthodoxy that it helped create. Moreover, ICI has now crafted itself yet another vision. This one is:

> to become the leader in formulation science, creating complex mixtures that deliver the effects valued by consumers and customers . . . To achieve this leadership goal, and through this create superior returns for shareholders, the group is building a portfolio of businesses that are leaders in their respective industries, bringing together consumer understanding, outstanding knowledge of customer needs and processes, and leading edge technology platforms to provide a distinctive, competitive advantage'.

Source: Caulkin, S (2007) How ICI settled on the wording of its epitaph, *The Observer*, 24 June, p 8

Tasks

Working in small groups of three or four students, read both case studies on Imperial Chemical Industries, which give somewhat different explanations of the potential demise of ICI. Then answer the questions below.

1. How does Wachman (Case 16.1(a)) explain the potential demise of ICI?

2. How does the Caulkin article (Case 16.1(b)) explain the potential demise of ICI?

3. Who, in your view, has the better of the argument?

4. In your view, what could ICI have done in the last two or three decades to avoid putting itself in a position where it became an attractive target for a predatory takeover bid?

REVIEW AND DISCUSSION QUESTIONS

1. Distinguish between official goals and operative goals and explain why the official goals of an organisation can differ from its operative goals.

2. Describe three theoretical ways in which the goals of an organisation can be determined and explain how goals tend to be derived in practice.

3. Define the terms 'coalition', 'side payments' and 'organisational slack', and describe their roles in the goal formulation process.

4. Explain the difference between efficiency and effectiveness and the circumstances in which it is possible for an organisation to be efficient without being effective and effective without being efficient.

5. Contrast the goal approach and system resource approach to evaluating organisational effectiveness in terms of their strengths and weaknesses, and explain why the goal approach tends to be seen by many people as the most appropriate one to use.

6. Describe the multiple-constituency approach to evaluating organisational effectiveness and why this has strong connections with what we know of the ways in which organisational goals tend be derived in practice.

Chapter 17

Organisational Structure:
Basic Concepts

LEARNING OUTCOMES

After studying this chapter you should be able to:

- define organisational structure

- discuss the purpose of structure and identify some of the consequences of structural deficiencies

- describe the structure of an organisation using the dimensions of configuration, centralisation, specialisation, formalisation and standardisation

- describe recent developments in the structural features of organisations

INTRODUCTION

The preceding chapter took an 'outside looking in' perspective in order to examine certain facets of organisations. Although this chapter still focuses on an organisation as a whole, it delves into its interior to consider structure – the way that an organisation's parts are related to each other to make up the whole.

It starts by exploring the meaning of the expression organisational structure and examining its importance in terms of effectiveness and performance. This is followed by an examination of the nuts and bolts of structure, which includes an explanation of the dimensions that are commonly used to categorise and describe the structural features of an organisation. The next section of the chapter explores evolving trends in organisational structure, which is followed by a description of some of the more recent structural initiatives adopted by organisations.

ORGANISATIONAL STRUCTURE

The Meaning of Structure

If someone is asked to describe the structure of a familiar organisation, the person usually sketches some sort of organisational chart, perhaps something like the one shown in Figure 17.1.

Assuming the chart is accurate, it tells us something about structure, but in other ways it is an incomplete description, because all that it portrays is two features: how the organisation is split up horizontally and its hierarchy of authority. Although these are important, there are many other equally important aspects of structure not shown; for instance, it tells us nothing about the flow of work through the organisation, or how orders are transformed into finished products and then delivered to customers. In addition, an organisation chart only gives a very restricted idea of the flow of communication and information in the organisation, which might be crucially necessary for it to achieve something, or to run smoothly.

Figure 17.1 An organisational chart

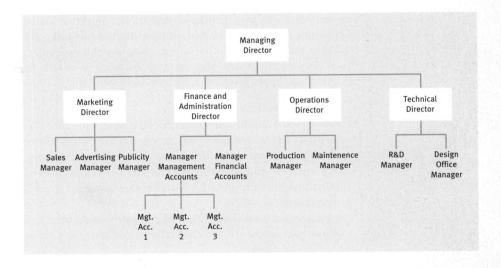

Thus, although organisation charts have their uses, they can be a rather impover-ished way of expressing the complexities of structure. Indeed, structure can be a rather abstract concept, and it is unlikely that anybody has actually seen an organisational structure in totality and, at best, all that can be seen is some evidence that a structure exists (Gibson *et al.* 1994). With this in mind it is as well to define how the expression will be used in this chapter:

> **Organisation structure is taken to be the fundamental and relatively unchanging features of an organisation which are officially sanctioned by those who control it and consist of the way activities and component parts are grouped, controlled and coordinated in order to achieve specific aims and outcomes.**

A number of important points arise from this definition, which the reader should try to keep in mind when reading this chapter and the one that follows:

- Although an organisation's structure is relatively permanent and is intended to facilitate achieving something, this does not mean that it never changes; what has to be achieved can change, or changes in structure might come about because top management alters its views about the most appropriate structural form to achieve certain outcomes.

- The formal structure of an organisation is chosen by its top management and, by inference, this is a matter of considered choice.

- Since structure divides up the organisation into component parts and specifies what roles these will play in achieving specific aims and outcomes for the whole organisation, it also provides for control and coordination of the parts to achieve these goals.

THE IMPORTANCE OF STRUCTURE

To survive, all organisations have to achieve something and this requires completing certain tasks. Structure divides the task of the whole organisation into manageable sub-tasks and allocates them to organisational units that are held responsible for their completion. It also ensures that all the different sub-tasks are coordinated and con-trolled in a way that results in the organisation achieving what it has to achieve. While this is only a very general statement of the purpose of structure, it is clear that, as a minimum, an appropriate structure should ensure that:

- tasks occur in the correct sequence
- activities are monitored so that coordination and control can occur
- decisions can be and are taken at appropriate points to ensure that adjustments which may be necessary to achieve goals and objectives are made
- responsibility and authority for completing certain tasks is assigned to individuals and groups, and also that they accept accountability for task completion
- resources are used effectively and efficiently so that the level of resource utilisation matches the level of activity and resources are only deployed on what needs to be done.

Figure 17.2 Aspects of structure (adapted from Child 1984)

ASPECT	PURPOSE	HOW PURPOSE IS ACHIEVED	ASSOCIATED ACTIVITIES	EXAMPLES
BASIC STRUCTURE	To indicate in a general way what behaviours are expected of the organisation's members	By specifying how the work of the organisation is divided up and assigned to individuals, groups and departments	Specify and define what tasks need to be undertaken Allocate tasks and responsibilities to individuals and specify their decision making freedoms	Organisational chart Job descriptions Membership of boards, committees, working parties, etc.
		By specifying how different tasks will be coordinated	Define how tasks shall be brought together and what formal reporting relationships for task completion shall exist	
OPERATING MECHANISMS	To indicate in greater detail what is expected of individuals	Attempts to ensure that individuals accomplish objectives that contribute to organisational goals and motivate them to do so	Division of main activities into sub-activities and delegation of authority Provide methods of setting objectives and monitoring activities and motivating members of the organisation	Control procedures (e.g. budgets and budgetary control) Operating procedures Staff appraisal Training & development Planning procedures

Basic structure: expresses the general form of structure and what is expected of organisational members

Operating mechanisms: indicates in greater detail what is expected of individuals in a structure

Therefore, structure is concerned not only with what is in place to facilitate achieving goals and objectives, but also with the mechanisms or processes for doing so. For this reason it is helpful to look upon structure as having two aspects: the **what** and the **how**. These are known respectively as *basic structure* and *operating mechanisms* (Child 1984) and, as can be seen in Figure 17.2, together they make provision for two inter-related facets of operations.

An important feature that distinguishes these two aspects of structure is the human element. Basic structure attempts to ensure that the necessary parts of an organisation exist and a parallel can be drawn with the human anatomy. With no stomach or an ineffective digestive tract, the food that fuels the body cannot be converted into energy. Similarly, if an organisation is to survive and achieve its goals it needs an appropriate set of parts. However, basic structure only provides a facility for the organisation to operate effectively and it can never guarantee that this will happen. As Drucker (1984) points out, while an ineffective (basic) structure makes high performance impossible, the best structure in the world will not ensure good performance and so the second aspect of structure is needed. This is much more deeply concerned with the human element and specifies in greater detail how things are to be done.

Whatever it is that organisations do, it is ultimately done by humans. People are not just passive recipients of their experiences – they are affected by their surroundings and, in turn, they react to what they encounter. For instance, the way that their work is organised affects how they relate to their tasks and this influences their attitudes, behaviour, morale and productivity. Therefore, it is important that operating mechanisms specify how things are done in a way that makes the most of human resources.

If a structure is too rigid people can feel that there are very few opportunities for personal growth and self-fulfilment (Argyris 1964) and if it is too loose, or lacks clarity, it can be equally damaging because it tends to give rise to feelings of role ambiguity, anxiety and stress. For this reason, it is worthwhile examining in more detail the potential outcomes of structural deficiencies, which are considered next.

The Consequences of Structural Deficiencies

Structural deficiencies not only stand in the way of goals being achieved, they can also result in a whole host of human problems. Five of these are cogently articulated by Child (1984) and are given in the OB in Action Box that follows.

OB IN ACTION: The consequences of structural deficiencies

Motivation and morale can be adversely affected because in the absence of standardised rules decisions appear to be inconsistent and arbitrary. Narrow spans of control, together with insufficient delegation, can result in people feeling that there is little recognition of their worth or that they have little responsibility or opportunity for achievement. Poorly defined roles can also result in people being unclear about what is expected of them and how their performance is assessed, and unclear priorities or work schedules can mean that people are subjected to competing pressures from different parts of the organisation.

Decision making can be slow and of poor quality where there are no adequate procedures for evaluating the results and learning from similar decisions made in the past. This can also occur where the hierarchy has too many levels or where key decision makers are cut off from each other in separate units. It also tends to be common where there is inadequate provision to coordinate the activities of decision takers, or where they are overloaded because they fail to delegate.

Conflict and lack of coordination can occur if goals have not been structured into a single set of objectives and priorities because people can come under pressure to follow departmental priorities at the expense of product or project goals. Where people are not brought together into teams, or where liaison mechanisms have not been laid down, they can also work out of step with each other. Conflicts between planning and operations can happen when those who are aware of changing contingencies are divorced from those who carry out operations.

Failure to respond innovatively to changing circumstances tends to be commonplace where the structure does not include specialised jobs concerned with forecasting and scanning the environment. It also tends to occur where innovation and planning of change are not mainstream activities that receive the support of top management and adequate resources. In addition, lack of innovation and capability to change is frequently encountered where there is a lack of coordination between

those parts of an organisation that identify changing market needs and those who are responsible for producing technological solutions.

Rising costs can be particularly prevalent in administrative areas where there are tall, extended hierarchies with a high ratio of 'chiefs' to 'indians'. It also tends to occur where there is an excess of procedure and paperwork that distracts attention away from productive work and leads to administrative overstaffing.

Source:

Adapted from Child, J (1984) *Organization: A Guide to Problems and Practice*, London: Harper and Row

TIME OUT

Reflect on the structure of an organisation with which you are familiar. If you have no experience of working for an organisation use your university or college for this exercise. Now answer the questions below.

1. What do you perceive the major goals of the organisation to be?
2. How is the whole organisation split up into major parts and what roles do you think these play in achieving its goals?
3. Can you conceive of ways in which these parts can be or are coordinated and controlled so that they contribute towards the organisation as a whole achieving its goals?
4. Can you identify any of the problems that arise from structural deficiencies in the organisation and what do you feel causes these problems?

REPLAY

- One purpose of structure is to divide up the overall task of an organisation into manageable tasks and allocate responsibility for their completion.
- The second purpose of structure is to provide for coordination and control of those tasks so that the organisation achieves its goals.
- There are two main aspects of structure: basic structure and operating mechanisms.
- Structural deficiencies can result in a number of organisational problems, some of which are not just concerned with goal achievement, but can also affect human motivations and morale.

DIMENSIONS OF STRUCTURE

To describe organisational structures it is useful to be able to highlight important features in a way that allows the similarities or differences of organisations to be compared. One way of doing this is with an organisation chart, but, since this only gives a very crude representation of basic structure, a multidimensional scheme, in which each dimension consists of a specific structural characteristic, is required. Many such schemes exist, all of which have some degree of overlap. Therefore, a compromise scheme which describes the five most prominent structural dimensions (configuration or grouping, centralisation, specialisation, formalisation and standardisation) is used here. Although these are all described separately, it is important to recognise that some are strongly connected.

Dimension 1: Configuration or Grouping

To achieve its aims and objectives, an organisation has to accomplish an overall task, and to do this usually requires that many different activities are undertaken. A sound structure will allocate these activities to groups of people and/or individuals according to a basic criterion or organising principle and also establish a coherent link between the activities to provide a basis for their coordination and control. This is referred to as the organisation's structural *configuration* and can be described in terms of two features: **horizontal differentiation**, which is concerned with the **division of labour** and is sometimes referred to as the basis of departmentalisation; and **vertical differentiation**, which is more concerned with integration and coordination of the parts.

Configuration: the basic arrangements for differentiation and integration in a structure

Horizontal Differentiation

Horizontal differentiation: the division of an organisation's overall task into different activities according to a set, organising principle

Horizontal differentiation can take a number of forms; theoretically each one is underpinned by a different organising principle that is intended to cope with a particular set of circumstances. **Functional grouping** is by far the most common basis and is shown in Figure 17.3(a). This groups activities together according to the major functional specialisms of the organisation and is widely used in both manufacturing and service organisations. Its major advantages are:

- all the experts in a particular field are brought together, which encourages efficient use of resources and discourages duplication
- because specialists understand each other, coordination within these groups is made easier
- the structure is easily understood by those involved.

Figure 17.3(a)
Functional grouping

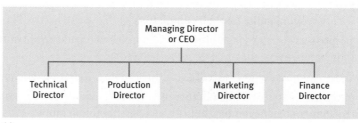

(a)

Figure 17.3(b)
Process grouping

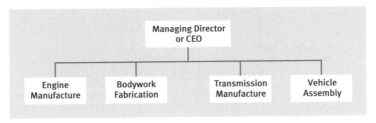

(b)

Nevertheless, there are some potential drawbacks:

- very parochial viewpoints can arise
- functional goals can be pursued at the expense of those of the whole organisation, which can result in sub-optimal performance.

A variant of this is **process grouping**, in which work activities are more specifically grouped according to a narrower range of specialist skills. It is most often found in manufacturing when a functionally grouped firm gets very large and complex. Figure 17.3(b) illustrates the principle at work for a car manufacturer. To a large extent the advantages and disadvantages are the same as for functional grouping, but because the degree of specialist differentiation is greater, these can be somewhat amplified.

Product or **service grouping** is shown in Figure 17.3(c) and is most often found where an organisation has a number of distinct product lines, which happens when a firm diversifies, or when it is taken over or merged. Usually each product or service group is managed separately and this has a number of advantages:

- Everything connected with a particular product line is brought together, making coordination and specialisation easier.
- Each product line is identifiable as a cost or profit centre which facilitates financial control.
- Rather than coordinating day-to-day activities, top management can spend its time focusing on longer-term strategic issues.

Like all structural forms, however, it also has disadvantages:

- People can become too focused on their own product or service and lose sight of advances made in other product groups.
- Because all divisions want to control everything that affects their own product area, some overresourcing and duplication of effort can be almost inevitable.

Figure 17.3(c) Product
or service grouping

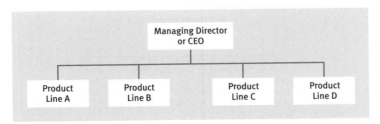

(c)

Figure 17.3(d) Market or customer grouping

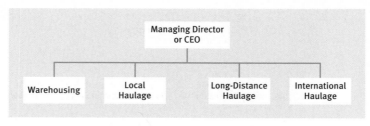

(d)

Market or **customer grouping** brings together all the jobs or activities that serve the specialist needs of particular groups of customers. However, it is more commonly used where the same basic product or service is provided for distinct groups of customers, albeit with slightly different needs. Figure 17.3(d) gives an example which illustrates how a road transport company might have different units to deal with long-haul, local and international goods transport. The main advantage is that:

- specialist activities and/or resources can be used to fine tune the product or service to the needs of different types of customer.

Its potential disadvantages are:

- there is a possibility of duplication of effort
- specialists in one customer area can be unaware of innovations in other areas.

Geographic grouping is shown in Figure 17.3(e) and is really a form of market grouping that is used where localised populations need to be served, for example bakeries. The advantages are:

- reduction in transport costs
- an ability to cater for different local tastes
- for international operations units can adapt to different legal, political and economic constraints.

Its potential disadvantages are:

- coordination and control of the whole organisation is made much more difficult
- there is some danger that regional loyalties will take precedence over those of the whole organisation.

Figure 17.3(e) Geographic grouping

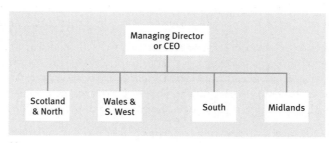

(e)

Figure 17.3(f) Matrix grouping

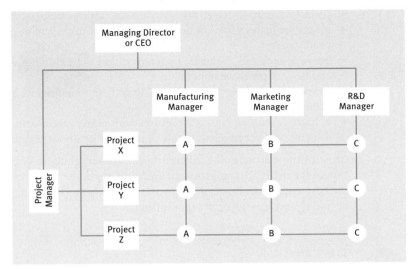

(f)

A **matrix grouping** attempts to gain the advantages of both functional and product grouping but minimise the potential drawbacks of each one. The basic principle is to superimpose a horizontal, product-based structure on to a conventional functional arrangement, and this is shown in Figure 17.3(f).

The aim is to provide the different products or projects with the specialised functional expertise they require, but without incurring the duplication of resources that is often found in a conventional product-grouped organisation. In Figure 17.3(f), for example, there are three project managers who oversee projects X, Y and Z respectively. Each project manager needs the services of one-third of a manufacturing engineer, a marketing specialist and a designer. By locating the specialists A, B and C respectively in manufacturing, marketing and design departments the firm has the same range of expertise as in a conventional functional structure, and these people are the subordinates of functional managers. However, each person from each function divides up his or her time equally between the three projects, and for the time spent working on each one acts as a subordinate of its project manager.

This structure originated in the American aerospace industry, in which highly complex products are designed, developed and brought into production with their own dedicated teams, and where obtaining the most efficient use of resources is a constant problem. The matrix organisation is said to be the most appropriate structure for these circumstances (Davis and Lawrence 1977). Its potential advantages are:

- improved coordination of diverse activities which does not rely on cooperation between separate functional heads but is undertaken by the product manager
- the multiple perspectives of different functions are brought to bear on problems and this tends to give fast and highly innovative solutions
- efficient utilisation of scarce resources and improved lateral communications.

A structure like this can be a confusing place to work, and commentators such as Davis and Lawrence (1977) have highlighted a number of potential problems:

- people never have fewer than two bosses, which can give rise to dual loyalty issues
- power struggles often occur about use of resources and decision making prerogatives
- because decisions are made by teams rather than individuals, decision making can be very time-consuming
- cooperation between specialists with different viewpoints is not always easy to achieve
- in highly complex matrix structures with many specialisms it can sometimes be difficult to determine who really has authority about certain aspects of a task.

Most of these structural configurations have one thing in common: with the exception of the matrix organisation all are 'pure' types that represent different ideas about the best way to handle the division of labour. In practice, however, it is quite common to find mixed structures in organisations.

TIME OUT

In the Time Out exercise before this one you were asked to identify the basic structure of an organisation with which you are familiar. What is the configuration principle used by this organisation?

Vertical differentiation: the establishment of a hierarchy of authority in the organisation

Scalar chain: a direct line of authority from the top to the bottom of an organisation

Span of control: the number of subordinates reporting to someone

Vertical Differentiation

While horizontal differentiation divides up the overall task into sub-tasks, to accomplish the overall task requires that these sub-tasks be integrated and coordinated. By far the most common way to do this is through a hierarchy of authority, in which those higher up the organisation bear a greater degree of responsibility for outcomes. This gives the characteristic pyramid shape of organisation charts, and produces a *scalar chain*, the direct line of responsibility from top to bottom. In practical terms this is bound up with another feature, the average *span of control*, which refers to the number of subordinates reporting to each level in the hierarchy. Where the average span of control is wide, it is normally the case that there are fewer levels in the hierarchy,

Figure 17.4(a) Flat organisation

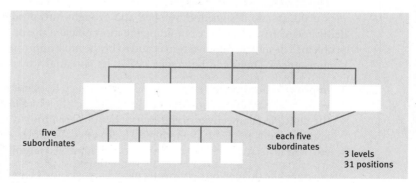

(a)

Figure 17.4(b) Tall organisation

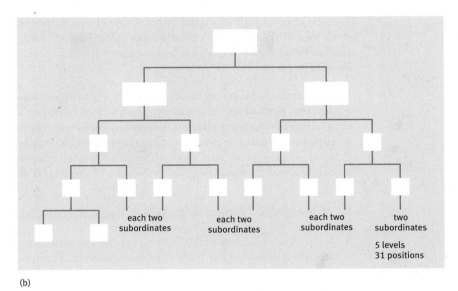

each two subordinates

each two subordinates

each two subordinates

two subordinates

5 levels
31 positions

(b)

Flat organisation: a relatively small number of levels in the management hierarchy

which gives the *flat organisation* configuration shown in Figure 17.4(a). Conversely, narrow spans of control usually result in a large number of levels and give the so-called *tall organisation* shown in Figure 17.4(b).

Classical management theory, which is discussed at the beginning of Chapter 18, assumed an ideal span of control that is equally applicable in all circumstances, and narrow spans were assumed to be better because supervising a relatively small number of people means that each one receives more of the supervisor's attention. However, a wide span of control results in more autonomy for subordinates, which later research associated with increased job satisfaction and employee performance (Ivancevich and Donnelly 1975). The current trend is for so-called **delayered** designs, which gives very wide spans of control lower down, often accompanied by the use of **empowerment** techniques. Because these are assumed to result in employees having more satisfying and interesting jobs, they are often portrayed in glowing terms (Pickard 1993). However, it is likely that the main reason for their use is the desire to cut costs and to increase effort by employees, rather than to make a concerted attempt to improve the quality of their working lives. A return will be made to these recent initiatives towards the end of the chapter.

Tall organisation: a relatively large number of different levels in the management hierarchy

Centralisation: the locus of decision making in an organisation

Dimension 2: Centralisation

Centralisation expresses the locus of decision making in an organisation, thus reflecting patterns of responsibility and authority in a structure. Put simply, *responsibility* places an obligation on someone to achieve something. The other side of the coin is that a degree of *authority*, which is the legitimate power to take decisions, should be delegated as well, so that a person can meet his or her delegated responsibilities.

Responsibility: the obligation to achieve something

In **centralised** structures decision making tends to be retained in the hands of a small number of people at the top of the organisation, while in those that are **decentralised**,

Authority: the legitimate power to make decisions in a given area of activity

decision making authority is delegated. As will be explained later, certain basic structures lend themselves to decentralisation more than others, so there is a strong connection between this dimension and configuration. The arguments for centralisation are said to be:

- those at the top can coordinate the whole organisation more effectively
- different parts of an organisation are prevented from duplicating resources, which results in more efficient resource utilisation and economies of scale
- common policies are easier to adopt throughout the organisation because sub-units are prevented from 'doing their own thing' and becoming too independent
- decision making tends to be faster because of the smaller number of people involved.

On the other hand, there are a number of arguments in favour of decentralisation:

- the organisation is more flexible and special circumstances can be taken into account if decisions are made at a point closer to operational levels
- control is distributed more evenly which develops people lower down
- it frees top management to devote its attention to longer-run strategic issues
- by engendering a feeling of participation it can contribute positively to the development of an organisation's culture
- effectiveness, efficiency and cost control are improved if the levels at which decisions are taken are made at cost or profit centres.

There is, however, very little hard evidence to support either point of view and the degree of decentralisation probably reflects top management philosophies (or possibly even what is currently fashionable) more than anything else. Although decentralisation has been very much in vogue for some time, there are still many influential writers who continue to praise a relatively high degree of centralisation (e.g. Jaques 1990). What is more interesting is that while managers and management gurus have strongly preached the virtues of decentralisation for the last two decades, recent evidence suggests that a growing number of organisations is now moving in the opposite direction, although 're-centralisation' is a word that most of them seem fearful of using (Arkin 1999b).

Dimension 3: Specialisation ✓

Specialisation: the degree of division of labour and patterns of work organisation at lower organisational levels

Specialisation, which expresses the division of labour and general patterns of work organisation at lower levels, has some relationship to configuration. However, it is much more strongly focused on the micro elements of structure and reflects management philosophies about whether it is advantageous to have narrow, specialised jobs rather than those that are broad and multiskilled. In theory, a high degree of specialisation has the following advantages:

- Economic efficiency: a narrow, specialised task only requires a small range of skills, which makes it easier for a person to pick up speed and, because the person does not have to regularly interrupt one operation to do another, the job can be simplified and operators can be trained quickly so that people are easily replaced.

- Because a specialised structure is easily understood, people tend to feel comfortable with it, particularly if the degree of specialisation reflects past ways of doing things and the way a firm has evolved.

Set against these advantages, there are also some potential drawbacks:

- Boredom, tedium, lack of interest and a shortage of intrinsic satisfactions often occurs and, as a result, absenteeism, labour turnover and (in some cases) antagonisms between the workforce and management can arise.
- Specialisation can sometimes result in duplication of effort, overmanning and rigid job demarcation; for example, even where they are capable of doing so, craftsmen will often refuse to handle the smallest task which is regarded as part of the job of another trade.

In a competitive world where economic efficiency is vital, it is seldom possible to abandon job specialisation altogether. However, its potential for demotivating employees is well recognised and, while there are strong economic advantages, potential disadvantages can negate some of the economic gains. Attempts to mitigate some of the demotivating effects of high specialisation are sometimes made by using techniques such as job rotation, enlargement, enrichment and empowerment, which are discussed in more detail in Chapter 7. Once established, any pattern of specialisation can also be very difficult to change and is often only possible if specialisation is 'bought out' with increased pay rates (Ingram 1991).

Dimension 4: Formalisation

Formalisation: the number of formal rules and procedures governing organisational activities

Formalisation reflects the extent to which formal rules and procedures govern activities in an organisation and, in particular, whether the nature of work is prescribed in rules that specify what shall be done and, often, how it will be done. Rules and procedures can be implicit as well as explicit, and can be used either to prescribe what should be done or to proscribe what is forbidden. Explicit rules are usually set down in writing, for example in job descriptions, policy documents and standard operating procedures. However, these cannot cover all the day-to-day adjustments that are necessary to adapt to changing conditions. Thus implicit or informal rules are often constructed in an *ad hoc* way (Brief and Downey 1983) but, unless they are eventually formalised, these tend not to become part of an organisation's formal structural arrangements.

To some extent, increased formalisation is a function of organisational size. Once an organisation grows beyond a certain point it becomes almost impossible to rely on the personal and informal interactions that are commonly used to control and coordinate activities in a small firm. As an organisation gets larger it also tends to employ more specialists, the number of levels in the hierarchy increases and top management may need to divorce itself from day-to-day activities to concentrate on strategic issues. Thus procedures and rules become the main way of controlling activities and introducing a degree of predictability into the organisation.

Dimension 5: Standardisation

Standardisation: the extent to which formal rules and procedures are applied in all circumstances

In practice, although *standardisation* has a strong practical connection with formalisation, in theory it is a different dimension of structure. Formalisation simply reflects the number of rules and procedures, whereas standardisation expresses whether they are applied in all circumstances. For instance, in a firm with low standardisation there may be a large number of rules and procedures, but some are only applied in certain parts of the organisation. Conversely, a highly standardised organisation can have comparatively few rules, but apply them strictly throughout.

Like formalisation, standardisation is essentially a method of coordinating activities and Mintzberg (1979) distinguishes between three forms that it can take:

- **Standardisation of work process**, where coordination is achieved by designing the flow of work to link different activities together as, for example, on an assembly line, where one operation leads naturally to the next.

- **Standardisation of work output**, where task elements are coordinated by relating them all to an end result, for example in stock levels, where the aim is to avoid the high costs of large inventories but also to avoid a 'no stock' situation.

- **Standardisation of worker skills**, which tends to be used only where the other two forms of standardisation cannot be applied and specifies what knowledge and skills are needed for a particular task; for example, although nurses in a hospital are responsible for day-to-day patient welfare, the diagnosis and prescription of a patient's treatment is strictly in the hands of medical doctors.

Mintzberg also points out that the size and complexity of an organisation normally governs how strongly standardisation and formalisation go together. In small firms, where employees adjust to each other using informal communication methods, standardisation is seldom needed to achieve coordination and control; but as firms get larger it becomes more difficult to rely on these methods and so supervisors coordinate the activities of people. In very large organisations the scale and wider scope of activities are much more complex and so standardised procedures are used to reduce the coordination burden on supervisors.

The Relationship between Dimensions of Structure

For the purposes of this discussion it is convenient to simplify matters by viewing configuration and specialisation as dimensions that are primarily concerned with differentiation, while centralisation, formalisation and standardisation are those that integrate the parts.

All structures are a compromise between the competing demands of different pressures. For instance, although specialisation gives efficiency and economy, it can result in people losing sight of the goals for the whole organisation. Therefore, where it is used, specialisation gives rise to the need to integrate and coordinate the tasks of sub-units using a combination of formalising activities through rules and procedures, standardising the activities that take place and centralising the authority to take decisions. However, this can give rise to another problem. The more these integrating methods are used, the more the organisation lacks flexibility and, to some extent, personal initiative is stifled as well. This makes it clear that there are no easy answers in the matter of structural design. However, it is possible to draw two general conclusions about what tends to happen in practice:

- Where a functional configuration with a high degree of specialisation is used there seems to be a strong tendency for formalisation, centralisation and standardisation to be adopted together as coordinating mechanisms (Grinyear and Yasai-Ardekani 1980).

- As organisations grow, some delegation of authority to specialists becomes virtually inevitable and this brings about a decrease in centralisation that is counteracted to some extent by strong tendencies to increase formalisation and standardisation (Pugh and Hickson 1976).

However, there are limits to the extent that these two conclusions can be applied in a general way. Above a certain size, firms tend to have much more diverse product lines, and this makes it much harder to use a pure functional grouping. Thus product-based, market-based and geographic configurations become more common. With these configurations it is often necessary to decentralise authority to divisions and, within a division, the structural form that is used tends to depend on the nature of its markets or the technology. Thus, beyond a certain point it is probably necessary to view a division as a separate organisation (Mintzberg 1979b).

REPLAY

- The most significant dimensions of structure are: *configuration*, which describes the basic pattern of differentiation and integration; *centralisation*, which reflects the extent to which decision making is centralised; *specialisation*, which reflects the extent of lower-level division of labour and patterns of work organisation; *formalisation*, which indicates the number of formal rules and procedures governing organisation activities; and *standardisation*, which indicates the extent to which rules and procedures are applied in all circumstances.

- The dimensions are not independent and there tend to be characteristic patterns of combinations of those described.

RECENT DEVELOPMENTS IN ORGANISATIONAL STRUCTURE

The dimensions described so far can be found in virtually all organisations and, as explained above, to some extent the positioning along different dimensions of structure go hand-in-hand. Nevertheless, for many years there has been a tendency for organisations to adopt more flexible structures and a number of the more recent developments will be described presently. To put these in context it can be useful to examine a scheme given by Morgan (1989), which portrays what he considers to be an almost inevitable move from the rigid structures of the past to the highly flexible structures that are now beginning to emerge. This is given in outline in Table 17.1.

As can be seen, what prompts the evolution of increasingly more flexible forms of structure is the nature of an organisation's environment. The more this becomes variable and diffuse, the more the organisation needs to remove the rigidities from its structure in order to speed up its responses to environmental demands. All of the first three types are variant on the classical bureaucratic structure that will be described in more detail in Chapter 18. Organisations of this type are still very common because

Table 17.1 The changing nature of organisational form (adapted from Morgan 1989)

Organisational type	Environment	Characteristics
1. Rigidly organised bureaucracy	Highly stable	Similar to classical Weberian bureaucracy (see Chapter 18). Under strict control of head of organisation. Functional configuration, with high degree of centralisation, specialisation, formalisation and standardisation. Integration by hierarchical authority
2. Bureaucracy run by a senior executive team	Slightly more variable with some novel problems arising	Similar to type 1
3. Bureaucracy with cross-departmental teams and task forces	More variable with novel problems arising even more frequently	Similar to type 1 but with a greater degree of integration and coordination at operational level by permanent cross-departmental teams. Bigger problems are referred upwards to be resolved by senior managers
4. Matrix organisation	Diverse and diffuse with higher rate of change, giving rise to an even greater number of unique problems	A product-based structure is superimposed on a conventional functional structure to give a matrix in which equal emphasis is given to traditional functions and to different business or product areas. Dual focus allows operating teams to combine functional skills with an orientation to particular problems in their respective product areas
5. Project-based organisation	Similar to type 4 but more volatile	Nominally a functional structure may exist but it only plays a supporting (servicing) role to project teams (usually based on product areas) who run the core activities of the organisation. Frequent exchange of ideas and information between teams
6. Loosely coupled network organisation	Similar to type 5 but even more volatile	The organisation becomes a loosely coupled network of small (usually product-based) teams who are semi-autonomous mini firms that operate under a common identity. Teams handle strategy and operations in their respective product areas, but virtually all operational work is sub-contracted to outside the organisation

as they grow (and some of them are very large indeed) they tend to acquire a capability to exert a degree of influence over their environments, which is a force for stability. However, not all organisations are this big and powerful and, for those that are not, some degree of progression to types 4 and 5 are said to be necessary. Type 6, however, is still comparatively rare and a move from type 5 to type 6 is a step of quantum proportions. Thus a return to this type will be made at the end of the chapter, and in the meantime it is sufficient to note that many organisations prefer to adopt minor incremental adjustments to structure, and some that have emerged across the last two decades are described presently.

Many of these changes appeared in response to recessionary conditions, more volatile markets and a perceived need to cut back on the number of people employed – often as 'off-the-shelf' solutions or prescriptions to obtain increased efficiency and profits. They tend to have an intuitive appeal to managers, and fashionable names that trip easily off the tongue have now become part of the acceptable vocabulary of 'management speak'. While the names differ, virtually all of them involve reducing the size and altering the shape of an organisation (at least below the level of the board room). In addition, they all have remarkably similar prescriptions for the desirable characteristics of a structural design, asserting that in today's conditions a sound structure should provide for:

- a closer relationship with customers
- a rapid response to environmental changes
- where necessary, the use of advanced technologies
- the effective and efficient use of human resources.

Before describing these techniques, it is worth examining the origins of the ideas and arguments that underpin them.

Customer Relations and Adaptability

Flexible specialisation: the argument that organisational survival now depends on gaining the economic advantages of specialisation, but being flexible at the same time

The argument that structure must allow for a closer relationship with customers and a rapid response to their needs and wants first appeared in the early 1980s and can be traced to Piore and Sabel's (1984) *flexible specialisation* thesis. This argues that most large firms have hitherto been based on a Fordist production paradigm, in which the aim was to cater for a large market for standardised goods. This virtually dictates the use of mass production techniques, with a high degree of task specialisation in order to obtain the economies of scale that enable a firm to compete on the basis of price. Piore and Sabel argue that a radical change in customers' tastes has resulted in the disappearance of mass markets for standardised goods. Thus firms are faced with fragmented markets, composed of discerning customers who have diverse tastes and requirements, which means that survival depends upon the ability to cater for a high degree of change and customisation of outputs. This does not mean that customers are automatically willing to pay the price of custom-made goods. Rather, that the dominant theme has changed from 'everything the same' to 'variations on a standard product', and to be successful firms have to find ways of being specialist and flexible at the same time.

Whether flexible specialisation is just a catchy phrase or represents a new order in manufacturing is a contentious issue. Nevertheless there are signs that firms are willing to cater to more diverse consumer tastes.

Advanced Technology

There is much stronger evidence about the widespread adoption of new technologies and, in terms of structure, two particular developments are worth noting. The first is **computer-integrated manufacture,** in which different operations are controlled and coordinated electronically. This enables inputs of raw materials and components, various operations and the output of finished goods to be synchronised. In addition, machines are often computer controlled and sometimes robotically operated, so that when a machine is switched from one operation to another it does not have to be reset by hand. Instead, resetting instructions are fed into the computer that controls the machine, which saves considerable time and adds flexibility to the production system. Before the availability of this technology, large economies of scale were only obtainable using mass production techniques, in which machines were dedicated to specialist operations. While this works if there is a mass market for the same product, where product life cycles are shorter and a more varied range of products is required, the technique is inherently inflexible and restrictive (Buitendam 1987). Thus, computer-integrated manufacture gives the flexibility of multipurpose machinery together with unit costs that are nearly as low as in mass production.

Another development is **advanced information technologies**, which are deployed in data networks that greatly increase efficiency and streamline coordination and control. Perhaps the easiest way to illustrate the point is with the example of 'Electronic Point of Sale' (EPOS) technology, now widespread in large supermarket chains. When an item passes through the checkout an electronic scanning device reads the bar code, and records the item and its sale price. Because the cashier does not have to punch the price into a cash register this clearly saves time. If the information is also sent to the stock room, shelves in the sales area can be replenished as necessary. Moreover, if the same data are supplied to the central warehouse of a supermarket chain, it can be used to decide what should be included in the next delivery to a particular store.

Human Resources

Productivity through people has been a much emphasised theme since the mid-1980s, and the idea has been strongly linked with arguments about the performance of so-called 'excellent' companies (Peters and Waterman 1982). Moreover, the drive for cost savings, coupled with a desire to cultivate customer loyalty, has introduced an emphasis on 'quality' of output as much as quantity. Thus new production methods and their associated technologies often go hand in hand with methods such as **total quality management** and **just in time**. However, because there are fewer routine or specialised jobs, and the different activities are often coordinated by the machinery or its associated control software, other demands are placed on employees. The pace of work can be faster and workers are often required to maintain the machinery and solve minor problems. These features not only require new skills, such as judgement and literacy, but also increased levels of willingness, flexibility and commitment (Walton 1985). Thus, most of the new structural initiatives emphasise methods such as teamworking, empowerment and employee involvement.

In what follows, while the suggestions for redesign will be described in the approximate order in which they appeared. It should be noted that this is only approximate, because there is a considerable degree of overlap in their introduction and some of the older ones are only just being introduced into some organisations.

The Flexible (Core–periphery) Firm

Functional flexibility: an organisation's capability to vary what is done and how it is done

Numeric flexibility: an organisation's capability to vary its number of employees and, in so doing, its level of activity

Across the last two decades the environments of many organisations have become increasingly volatile and this has resulted in two significant problems. The first is the problem of changing products and production methods to cater for changes in customer tastes and to take advantage of new technologies. The second is to be able to respond rapidly to changes (either upwards or downwards) in the level of demand for products. To address these two problems, the organisation needs to be flexible in two different ways. Rapid adjustment of products and processes requires *functional flexibility*; that is, being flexible in what is done. Coping with changes in the level of output, however, requires *numeric flexibility*, usually in the number of people employed. A structural remedy for both of these problems is suggested in what has become known as the 'flexible firm or core–periphery' model (Atkinson and Meager 1986), which is shown in Figure 17.5.

Figure 17.5 The
flexible firm

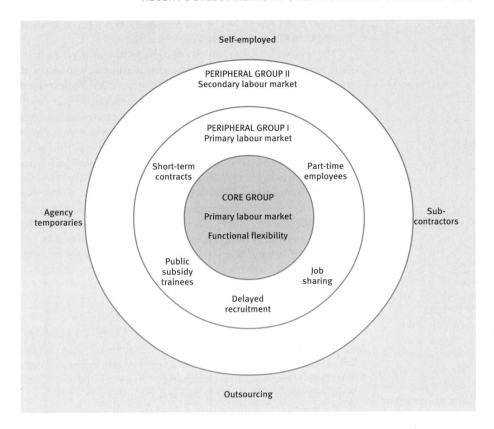

The flexible firm concept is most applicable to large manufacturing organisations, and the key idea is that the firm becomes much more responsive to changes in its product markets if the workforce is structured into two main groups. The first consists of a relatively small but permanent core workforce of highly competent, multi-skilled workers, which is obtained from the primary (internal) labour market and is shown at the centre of the model. To ensure that this core group has the skills to deliver the needed flexibility, the firm has a vested interest in providing training and retraining as necessary and, because the skills of the workforce are akin to an investment, the organisation seeks to retain this group of employees with an attractive package of rewards.

To obtain numerical flexibility so that the organisation can adjust its levels of output, the firm has up to three peripheral sub-groups of workers. The first consists of employees with skills that are important to the firm but which are general skills that are relatively easy to import at short notice. These are normally permanent employees but are people who tend to exit and re-enter the labour market – for example, typists and word-processor operators – and gives a fairly high level of natural turnover that can be used to adjust numbers. This sub-group also consists of employees such as part-time workers, whose hours can quickly be adjusted upwards if need be, and people on government-sponsored training schemes who are employed by the firm in an even less permanent way. The second sub-group of peripheral workers is drawn from secondary (external) labour markets as and when necessary, and these people are shown in the next circle outwards. Finally, beyond the outer circle are workers who are never employed by the firm itself, but who enter it from time to time to give an additional degree of numerical flexibility.

The model is essentially a conceptual one and was never designed to present a picture of what is taking place in a wholesale way. Neither does it offer a universal prescription for success. Rather, it is simply a theoretical framework that explains steps taken by some firms to achieve higher degrees of labour flexibility. Having said this, since flexibility has become something of a watchword in organisations, the model is an important one. For some years flexibility in the use of human resources has been widely seen as an essential ingredient of an organisation's ability to weather market conditions and the flexible use of labour is seen by many managers as one of the key characteristics that explains the success of Japanese companies.

So far as adoption of this structural form is concerned, there is a small amount of historic case study research that supports the real-world utility of the core-periphery model (Kallenberg 2001). Nevertheless, the evidence suggests that, until recently, a full core–periphery design is rare and confined to about 10 per cent of organisations, with most firms tending to use only selected elements from the core-periphery menu (Hakin 1990).

Downsizing, Rightsizing and Delayering

These measures are not really structural designs so much as strategies for reducing the head count. All are predictable extensions of the trend that started in the 1980s, when vast numbers of employees at the lowest organisational levels were declared redundant in response to a tightening of market conditions, and those remaining were required to work differently and much harder.

Kozlowski *et al.* (1993) define *downsizing and rightsizing* as a choice made to reduce the workforce, which is intended to improve organisational performance. They distinguish between two main approaches to this matter:

- **Proactive:** a planned approach which is part of a business strategy to re-orientate the organisation to its environment and which usually involves reductions in targeted business areas.
- **Reactive:** an approach in which the organisation makes a 'knee-jerk' reaction to conditions in its environment, usually aimed at cost-cutting using across-the-board reductions in headcount.

Most evidence (see Kinnie *et al.* 1998) strongly suggests that the majority of downsizing initiatives adopt the second of these approaches and that far from making an organisation more successful, performance often declines severely (Morris *et al.* 1999). Although the reasons for this are very complicated, Evans *et al.* (1996) draw two general conclusions about why reactive downsizing fails to deliver its expected benefits:

- Because headcount reductions tend to occur across the board, removing organisational fat only occurs by accident and, quite frequently, the very people who will be needed to ensure future organisational success disappear as well.
- There is a huge impact on the survivors, many of whom become demoralised, dispirited, insecure, demotivated and highly stressed to the extent that they are unable to deliver the commitment and performance required to rescue the organisation.

Delayering: a reduction of the number of levels in an organisation's hierarchy, usually by removing one or more levels of supervision and/or middle management

Downsizing and rightsizing: a reduction in the size of an organisation or the scale of its activities, theoretically to attain the appropriate size for its volume of sales

 OB IN ACTION: Some perils of structural change

The primary purpose behind restructuring is to find an organisational structure that will help the company meet its goals. Commonly, the existing structure is seen as too rigid or too complex, with too many divisions, departments and layers of management. In such cases, restructuring tries to simplify the organisation and make it more responsive by reducing the number of divisions and cutting out layers of management.

However, other, less laudable reasons for restructuring exist. Fad-prone managers are often attracted to new forms such as matrix organisations or network organisations, believing these to be more efficient, regardless of whether they actually fit the organisation's purpose. Sometimes methods of restructuring are carried to extremes. Business process re-engineering, a perfectly sound set of techniques when used to understand and design process flows, was overused and misapplied to the point where even its founding gurus, Michael Hammer and Thomas Davenport, began to criticise their creation. Finally, companies that are in financial trouble sometimes use restructuring in the hope that the stock market will take this as a positive sign and this rarely works.

Restructuring often means removing elements of the structure that have built up gradually, but no longer serve any useful purpose. Like removing growths from a living organism, restructuring can be painful, invasive and have many unfortunate side effects. It is not often appreciated how closely a company's structure and its culture are tied together. Changing structure means changing personal relationships and responsibilities; and very often it also means downsizing and unless these changes are carefully handled, they can lead to resistance. Edwin Artzt, former chief executive of Procter and Gamble, once noted that 'the hardest thing for a company is to change its thinking and failure to do this accounts for many restructuring failures'. Moreover, successful restructuring takes time, planning and resources, without which there is a high risk of failure and when this happens, the temptation is often to undertake another restructuring programme to cure the problems caused by the failure of the first one.

Source:

Witzel, M (2004) Be principled for a change, *Financial Times*, 23 August

Empowerment

So far as delayering is concerned, the introduction of new information technologies has resulted in organisations dispensing with the services of whole layers of supervision and middle management. In theory this means that hierarchies are flatter, day-to-day decision making is devolved to the operational level, and lateral rather than

Empowerment: giving people the authority to make decisions in their own area of operations without the approval of someone above

vertical communication is much more common. Almost inevitably this has been accompanied by some of the human resource measures outlined above and a buzzword in organisations where this has happened is '*empowerment*'. The aim is usually to mobilise the skills, energies and commitment of employees to enhance operational effectiveness and efficiency, and its use is underpinned by an assumption that if certain aspects of control and responsibility are devolved from senior levels to lower down, this confers benefits on everybody. For example, employees supposedly have greater satisfaction because they have more interesting and responsible jobs. In return managers get a more efficient, effective and flexible workforce.

This, however, is empowerment in theory. In reality there would seem to be a great deal of ambiguity about what managers mean when they speak of an 'empowered' workforce (Cunningham *et al.* 1996). In addition, a number of rigorous empirical studies has shown that many empowerment initiatives fail to deliver their expected advantages and that employees can end up less committed than before (see, for example, Cunningham and Hyman 1999).

Business Process Re-engineering

Business process re-engineering: a fundamental re-think and, if necessary, radical redesign of business processes, with the aim of making dramatic improvements to critical aspects of performance, such as cost, quality, service and speed

In theoretical terms *business process re-engineering* can be most easily conceptualised as the 'scrap it and start again' approach to organisational structure. Its originators (Davenport 1992; Hammer and Champey 1993) argue that the aim is to force an organisation to think itself through from first principles. This starts with attempting to discover what it is that customers really want, followed by a strategy and design to cater for customer needs. The fundamental principle that is supposed to guide these considerations is 'do only that which is necessary'. Thus, nothing, be it organisational processes, existing procedures and rules, or structural form, is immune from consideration. The aim is to ruthlessly dispense with anything that is not vital to obtain cost savings. In theory, although it is not usually envisaged by the advocates of re-engineering, this can just as easily result in an organisation deciding to do something extra, and so there are no clear-cut structural implications. However, there are a number practical lessons that can be learned.

Since the publication of Davenport's and Hammer and Champey's books a wave of re-engineering mania seems to have swept the USA and, to a lesser extent, Great Britain. When the books first appeared, the management perception of the business and economic environment seems to have prompted a belief that re-engineering had only one aim: cost cutting. Thus many such initiatives quickly became nothing more than an exercise in downsizing and/or delayering. Indeed, it seems that most re-engineering has been so badly applied that one of its originators has criticised what tends to occur as 'a fad that forgets that there are people in organisations' (Mumford and Hendricks 1996). Moreover, as at least two penetrating analyses reveal (see Blair *et al.* 1998; Grey and Mitev 1995) there are huge contradictions in business process re-engineering. To deliver the advantages it promises, re-engineering is heavily dependent on engendering high levels of employee commitment, but since it has become so strongly associated with headcount reductions and redundancy, this is analogous to asking turkeys to vote for Christmas, and has the same predictable consequences.

THE DIGITAL AGE AND THE VIRTUAL ORGANISATION

The expression 'digital (or information) age' is now widely used to convey the idea of a society in which information and communication technologies (ICTs) will result in a new wave of economic development. Predictions on this matter first came to prominence in the 1980s in the writings of a number of self-styled prophets of the new age such as Drucker (1988) and an example of this is given earlier in the last item in Table 17.1. These arguments have a strong element of *technological determinism*, in which the new ICTs are seen as an irresistible driving force for change, the key to which is said to be the so-called 'information superhighway' (internet), which will create boundless opportunities for the revitalisation of industry.

To some extent, the efficacy of the new ICTs has probably been 'talked up' as an off-the-shelf solution to reverse the decline of Western economies. Moreover, it is widely argued by these 'gurus' that failure to modernise in this way is a sure recipe for further deterioration (Birchall and Lyons 1995). For this reason, governments everywhere have exhorted organisations to become involved before it is too late (Bangemann 1994).

Off-the-shelf recipes for success seem to have an irresistible appeal to managers. One of the things that makes this one so acceptable is the argument that the new technology will inevitably result in a radically different form of organisation, and this is considered next.

New Organisational Forms

The new organisations that are said to result from embracing ICTs are known by a number of names, for example 'networked organisations' (Miles and Snow 1986) or the 'virtual organisation' (Davidow and Malone 1992). In some cases, ICTs are merely seen as the enabler of this type of organisation, while others argue that the technology forces an organisation to adopt new ways of working. Nevertheless, it is argued that, in the information age, economic advantage accrues to organisations that turn information into usable knowledge, rather than those that turn physical inputs into outputs. In essence the resulting organisational form would be an extremely loose network of relatively high-status knowledge workers. Unlike conventional firms, these organisations do not exist in a physical sense but only in cyberspace, as what have been described as 'organisationless organisations' (Nohria and Berkley 1994), which have fluid boundaries that expand or contract as required, and with capital and other inputs assembled as they are needed for a particular endeavour. By those who advocate these arrangements these organisations are said to deliver the ultimate in economic efficiency and flexibility. Their main characteristics would be:

- lean, flat and stripped down to the bare necessities
- an absence of hierarchy
- support functions, such as accounting and personnel, are outsourced, as are manufacturing and delivery
- most tasks are accomplished by project teams which vary in size according to the task in hand
- the organisation does not need to exist at any particular location but is an *ad hoc* assembly of skills required for a particular project
- people are connected by ICTs and work collaboratively.

Technological determinism: the belief that technological advances drive changes, e.g. to organisational structures

The advantages of these arrangements are said to be:

- a strong competitive advantage because knowledge can be exploited almost immediately
- the organisation is in continuous interaction with its environment, from which it learns almost instantaneously, with very rapid reaction to environmental changes
- economy in the use of resources
- people work in an empowered, autonomous and therefore enthusiastic and committed way.

Teleworker: someone who works at a place other than the one where the results of the work are needed, by using information and communication technology

Virtual organisations are assumed to be staffed by some form of *teleworkers*; that is, people who work at a place other than the one where the results of the work are needed, using ICTs (Bertin and Denbigh 1996). Some advocates of the virtual organisation, such as Negroponte (1995), argue that many of these people will be portfolio workers who work for a whole range of organisations on a freelance basis. Since it is argued that routine work will largely disappear in the information age (EC 1996), it is also assumed that people who work in virtual organisations will be technical, managerial or professional staff who can be trusted to work enthusiastically without supervision (Handy 1995), and these enterprises are portrayed as exciting, stimulating places in which to work. All this sounds a near perfect situation for both organisations and those who work in them. For this reason it is important to examine the evidence on virtual organisations.

The Virtual Organisation

The technology enabling the creation of virtual organisations already exists. The internet has been up and running for a number of years, and software that enables people to work collaboratively in teams also exists (Nunamaker 1997). However, while other developments, such as video-telephony, that might also facilitate the virtual organisation have been developed, commercially they are only partially successful (Kraut and Fish 1997).

So far as the existence of virtual organisations is concerned, the most significant thing is that, except for a small number of isolated cases, they do not actually exist (Furnham 2000). The notable exceptions are sportswear manufacturers Reebok, Nike and Puma, in the field of computing Dell Computers and Gateway, and in furniture retailing IKEA (Stanworth 1998). These are all high-profile organisations, which only serves to fuel the unfounded assumption that a mass transformation to the virtual organisational form is in progress. Nevertheless, there are a fairly large number of companies who call themselves virtual organisations, probably because the expression has a catchy, up-to-the-minute ring that appeals to managers who wish to convey the impression that their organisations are at the cutting edge of innovation. Thus there seems to be a tendency for any firm with a flat structure and an emphasis on teamworking to identify itself as a virtual organisation. However, most of these firms are merely traditional organisations that have restructured themselves with downsizing and delayering initiatives, and, where it is used, teamworking is not necessarily of the empowered and autonomous variety because workers are still controlled through traditional hierarchical arrangements (Stanworth 1998). Thus, while ICT is probably widely used in these firms, this is mostly to speed up communication or perform traditional co-ordination and control activities in a more economical way (Nathan *et al.* 2003).

Accounting for the Lack of Virtual Organisations

One reason for the dearth of organisations of this type may be that the arguments for their existence are based upon a false premise; that is, that the very existence of the technology results in the formation of virtual organisations. Moreover, because the evidence that structures are not solely determined by technology is so overwhelming (Child 1997), this idea must be discarded in favour of the idea that a host of social rather than purely technical considerations prompt management's choice of technologies (Clear and Dickson 2005; Haddon and Brynin 2005; Martin 2005).

In addition, Symon (2000) gives a penetrating analysis of the supposed link between ICTs and the predicted organisational form, which reveals other reasons why the virtual organisation is unlikely to exist. She argues that there are five major assumptions that underpin the existence of this link, all of which are contradicted to some extent by the prior research evidence and this is explained in what follows.

Assumption 1: That All the Required Information can be Transmitted Electronically

While this is theoretically possible, it is also likely that too much information would be made available, so that information overload occurs. Here Symon points out that several studies, such as the work of Finholt and Sproull (1990), show that people develop strategies to cope with overload, the most favoured of which is simply to ignore many of the messages. More important perhaps is the point that media such as e-mail are devoid of many of the social cues that support interpersonal relations; for example, non-verbal signals such as eye contact and facial expression that convey meaning and intention are all absent (Garton and Wellman 1995). Since interactions between geographically dispersed strangers who make up project teams would be acutely dependent on quickly establishing meaning and intent, one of the main advantages of this type of organisation – rapid decision making – would be lost. For these reasons, Symon argues that there are grave doubts about whether ICTs can transmit all the required information.

Assumption 2: That Most Employees are Willing Users of Electronic Forms of Communication

Here Symon points out that people usually act in accordance with previous group norms about the appropriate way of communicating certain types of message (Zack and McKenney 1995). If these norms dictate face-to-face methods for certain messages, people will find ways of using this method and ignore electronic methods.

Assumption 3: That an Increase in Electronic Communication Links Will Overcome Barriers to Communication and Participation

A participative, collaborative and non-hierarchical work environment is said to be essential to reap the full advantages of the virtual organisation. However, as Symon points out, ICTs in themselves do not create these conditions (Ciborra and Patriotta 1996). While the anonymity afforded by electronic messaging can lead to increased openness, participation and democracy are much more dependent on prior organisational contexts and cultures (Zack and McKenney 1995). Thus, if the organisation is already riddled with notions of status and hierarchy, introducing electronic methods is unlikely to remove the effects of these features.

Assumption 4: That Electronic Networking Enables More Autonomous and Flexible Working

In order to encourage workers to give of their best in terms of knowledge and creativity, autonomy and flexibility are said to be essential features of the virtual organisation. While ICTs may help by providing communication links, so far as employees are concerned there can be distinct drawbacks about flexibility. It usually results in people becoming more dispensable and job losses, particularly among lower-status clerical workers, are commonplace (Boddy and Gunson 1995). Moreover, a combination of teleworking and globalisation has raised the spectre of jobs being exported to developing countries where labour costs are lower (Webster 1996). It is no coincidence, for example, that India has been the preferred location for call centres for a number of years, because of lower labour costs. For this reason there is also a possibility of insecurity for higher-status workers.

Employees are usually well aware of these matters and so it is by no means certain that they willingly accept autonomy or give flexibility, no matter how much is provided in the way of electronic communications technology. As if this were not enough, Symon also points out that teleworking is not necessarily a liberating experience. For instance, call centres demonstrate how little autonomy and flexibility can be allowed to people who work in this way and so there are grave doubts about whether ICTs always result in more autonomous and flexible working conditions.

Assumption 5: That Work Using Communication Technologies Supports Achievement of Management Goals

According to Symon, while the use of ICTs can lead to much more efficiency and effectiveness in the way people work, a number of studies have shown that there are also counter-tendencies. For instance, e-mail can result in time wasting on social chatter and it can also be used for politicking or even to support personal aims that are counter to those of the organisation (Romm and Pilskin 1998). Thus it is far from certain that ICTs always result in an easier achievement of management's aims.

Overall, therefore, Symon's analysis provides a number of convincing reasons that explain the rarity of virtual organisations. At present there is no widespread transformation from prior organisational forms, and ICTs have merely been introduced in a piecemeal way to support management's traditional methods of controlling the workforce (Murray and Willmott 1997).

Teleworking

While teleworking can be used in many other contexts than the virtual organisation, it is envisaged that teleworkers will staff organisations of this type, and so it is relevant to examine trends in work of this nature. An extensive examination is provided by Stanworth (1998), who notes that while there has been some growth in tele-working in Great Britain, and that this is forecast to continue, there are several types of teleworker and the forecasts are different for each one.

Employed Teleworkers

There are a significant number of these workers in Great Britain (Brewster *et al.* 1993), which is associated with the growth of the call centre industry and the increased number of remote offices set up by banks to deal with clerical work formerly undertaken in high street branches (Cressey and Scott 1992). This is usually routine, semi-skilled work, often undertaken by part-time employees, and the volume is expected to grow in the future.

Self-employed Teleworkers

Although there has been a small amount of research to examine these working arrange-ments, it tends to have been undertaken for specific occupations such as publishing or language translation. This makes it is impossible to extrapolate the results to the whole working population and no future trends can be determined. However, little future expansion is envisaged.

Home-based Teleworkers

Here there are three discernable sub-groups. Those based at home for part of the week are usually high status, regular employees, who periodically work at home, sometimes because an employee's services can only be retained if he or she can achieve a better balance between work and home life. With the exception of possible crisis periods, such as a complete breakdown of transport services, a major growth in this area is not expected.

People who are home-based for all of their working time are usually women doing low-skilled clerical work for low pay, and are similar in employment status to 'out-workers' that were once commonplace in some manufacturing industries. They often have unpredictable workloads and work unsocial hours. However, in terms of the economic advantages that accrue to organisations from using them, a modest increase in numbers can be expected.

Finally, freelance teleworkers are usually reluctant recruits to this type of work. They are rarely people who are attracted to the idea of self-employment as is predicted by the virtual organisation model. Rather, they tend to be former full-time employees made redundant by a downsizing or other cost-cutting initiative, to whom the job has now been outsourced as a self-employed person.

As can be seen, most forecast growth in teleworking is likely to be in low skill occu-pations. Thus the vision of a new generation of highly skilled technical and profes-sional teleworkers who staff virtual organisations is probably no more that a figment of the imaginations of those who prophesied the rise of this type of enterprise. When taken together with Symon's arguments, this means that, while the virtual organisa-tion may be the direction in which things move in the future, any movement is likely to be at a very slow pace.

OVERVIEW AND CONCLUSIONS

This chapter has been strongly focused on explaining the elementary principles of structure; for example, defining what structure is, its importance, how it can be portrayed in an accurate way and describing some of the recent trends in structural design. To do this it has been necessary to adopt a very descriptive approach and this has its drawbacks. It can, for example, convey the impression that structure is a relatively straightforward topic and that the subject extends no further than simply being able to describe a structure. In reality there is much more to structure than this, but like many things in Organisational Behaviour and Organisational Analysis, it is necessary to understand the basics before trying to master more advanced concepts. While the dimensions of structure described in this chapter will be found in virtually every organisation, no attempt has been made to explain why different organisations adopt different patterns of structure. This is covered in the following chapter, which deals with the matter of organisational design; that is, on the main factors that impinge on an organisation and limit its choice of where it should position itself along each of the five dimensions of structure.

FURTHER READING

Atkinson J and N Meager (1986) *Changing Work Practices: How Companies Achieve Flexibiity to Meet New Needs*, London: National Economic Development Office. A comprehensive but easy-to-read explanation of the 'flexible firm' concept.

Bedeian, AG and RF Zammuto (1991) *Organizations: Theory and Design*, Orlando, FL: Dryden. A readable and thorough exploration of organisation theory and organisational design.

Blair, H, SG Taylor and K Randle (1998) A pernicious panacea – a critical appraisal of business re-engineering, *New Technology, Work and Employment* 13(2): 116–128. A penetrating analysis of the pitfalls of re-engineering.

Child, J (1984) *Organization: A Guide to Problems and Practice*, 2nd edn, London: Harper and Row. Perhaps the most thorough and penetrating consideration of structure yet written, but one that is very easy to read and understand.

Hammer, M and J Champey (1993) *Re-engineering the Corporation: A Manifesto for Business Transformation*, New York: Brearley. A highly influential book, widely read by managers because it gives a detailed recipe for the practice of re-engineering.

Mintzberg, H (1979) *The Structuring of Organisations*, New York: Prentice Hall. A classic of its type, which gives an easy-to-read account of how organisations are structured.

Piore, MJ and CF Sabel (1984) *The Second Industrial Divide: Possibilities for Prosperity*, New York: Basic Books. By now, a classic book. It explains its authors' 'flexible specialisation' thesis, to which can be traced many of the current trends in organisational structuring.

CASE STUDY 17.1: Heathrow Airport

In June 2007, the flood of letters complaining about overcrowding, etc. at Heathrow Airport rivalled Santa's postbag in the days before Christmas. Tony Douglas, the airport's managing director, apologised, but his apology demonstrated regret rather than willingness to take responsibility. And yet there is some right on Mr Douglas's side: the primary fault lies not with the British Airports Authority (BAA) but with a structure that has been flawed from its inception.

The natural sphere of the commercial sector is something in which there is a direct connection between the revenues of the business and its effectiveness in meeting customer needs. That connection is real for airlines (as long as travellers have a choice) but there is no similar relationship between cash and performance in other areas such as water supply, rail networks, schools or hospitals, broadcasting; or indeed, in managing Heathrow airport. For BAA, the activities that generate customer satisfaction – providing seats, enough security guards, clean toilets and travelators that work – are costs, not a source of revenue. Profits are derived from landing charges, parking fees, or even selling Burberry scarves and smoked salmon sandwiches. Thus only a basic knowledge of economics is needed to explain why there are longer queues at the X-ray machines than for the scarves and the salmon.

More competition would help, but Gatwick has limited capacity and Stansted is a longer journey from Heathrow than many short-haul flights. Nevertheless, the idea is still current that the scope for commercialisation can be extended by having a central regulator set standards of service or writing customer service contracts. The Civil Aviation Authority, BAA's regulator, has tried this, although in a feeble manner. A handful of service indicators are backed by financial penalties (which are miniscule in the light of the airport's revenues). Also note that Railtrack was subject to a similar regime, which continued until its failures were so evident that its licence to operate was withdrawn. The obligations on water companies and broadcasters are more demanding and the contracts for most private finance initiative contracts immensely detailed.

However, this process does not work well. Specifications for the London Underground public/private partnerships will be the subject of continuous dispute and negotiation throughout the life of the projects. The experiment of trying to achieve centrally prescribed objectives by imposing targets and penalties has already been tried, on an extensive scale. This was in the Soviet Union between 1917 and 1989 and the experiment did not work. If targets are not detailed and the penalties are modest – as at Heathrow – they have little effect on behaviour, but if the targets are detailed and the penalties large, they distort behaviour – as with hospital waiting lists. Moreover, if the targets are very detailed, the people setting them then become the managers of businesses about which they know very little. The mistake is a failure to recognise that a different approach is needed to activities that cannot be commercial, but need to be distanced from day-to-day political control. There was too much haste in following up on successful early privatisations, in a perhaps justified belief that almost any organisational structure would be better than the British conception of nationalised industry. Thus the activities for which a different model is required now veer from crisis to crisis. The crisis at Heathrow is infuriating its passengers; and before that it was Channel 4 broadcasting ripping off its viewers on premium-rate phone lines. Before that the problem was Railtrack, and before that Yorkshire Water. These activities are not and never will be normal businesses, which is why privatising Channel 4 would be a mistake and the acquisition of BAA by Ferrovial was

▶

inappropriate. The solution is a differentiated financing and governance structure for these hybrid corporations: a structure that emphasises that their prime accountability is to customers not shareholders.

Source: Kay, J (2007) Heathrow's problems result from a flawed concept, *Financial Times*, 25 June

Task

Working in small groups of three or four students, read the above case material, together with the OB in Action Box at the start of the chapter. Then answer the questions below.

1. The author of the case material argues that the problems facing Heathrow Airport can largely be traced to its inappropriate control structure; what are these problems and in what ways are they likely to be associated with BAA's organisational structure?

2. The author also argues that the same or similar problems beset many other public sector organisations; identify some of these problems and show how they can be traced to organisational structures?

3. To what extent could you envisage that these problems give rise to the sorts of problematic outcomes identified by Child (1984) in the OB in Action Box earlier in the chapter?

4. Assuming that the author is correct in saying that 'corporations of this type require structures that emphasise that their prime accountability is to customers rather than sharehoders', what steps could be taken to reflect this in their structural designs?

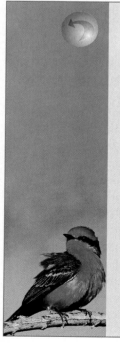

REVIEW AND DISCUSSION QUESTIONS

1. Define the term organisational structure and describe the five primary purposes fulfilled by an appropriate structure.

2. What characteristics of an organisation are described by the structural dimension of configuration (grouping) and describe six common configurations that can be used by organisations?

3. In what ways are the structural dimensions of configuration, centralisation, specialisation, formalisation and standardisation connected?

4. In what ways can measures such as downsizing, rightsizing and delayering be said to be structural responses to the four principles that recent thinking suggests should be reflected in a sound structural design?

5. In what ways does business process re-engineering represent a new theory of structure?

6. Explain what is meant by the expression 'virtual organisation' and the likelihood that this form of organisation is likely to be dominant in the future?

Chapter 18

Organisational Design

LEARNING OUTCOMES

After studying this chapter you should be able to:

- contrast classical and contingency approaches to organisational design

- understand the ways in which the characteristics of an organisation's environment influence the appropriateness of its structural design

- understand the ways in which its size influences the appropriateness of an organisation's structural design

- understand the ways in which technology influences the appropriateness of an organisation's structural design

- understand the ways in which the culture of an organisation and the culture of its top management group influence its structural design

- describe different types of cross-national organisations, distinguish between them in terms of their strategic foci and how this influences the structural form typically found in each type

INTRODUCTION

While the previous chapter was largely confined to explaining dimensions that can be used to describe organisational structures, this one has a rather different aim: to give the reader an understanding of important factors that restrict an organisation's choice of its structural design. It commences by contrasting two perspectives on organisational design. The first is derived from classical organisation theory and gives universal principles that are said to be applicable in all organisations. The second is what is now known as the 'contingency approach'. This rejects the idea of a set of universally applicable design principles and reflects the argument that the most appropriate design for an organisation is the one that best suits its circumstances in terms of the presence of certain contingency factors. The most important of these are usually taken to be its environmental circumstances, size and technology. Each of these is considered in turn, together with some of the research evidence that indicates that each factor has a significant effect on structural design. The chapter then examines the idea that organisational culture is also an important contingency factor and this is followed by a description of the theory of strategic choice, which gives insights into how, in practice, top managers make decisions about structural design.

These days many large organisations seek to expand beyond the traditional boundaries of their country of origin and do so by adopting strategies that have strong implications for their structural designs. This is examined by distinguishing between different types of cross-national organisations and how their expansion strategies affect their structures. The chapter closes with an overview section that reviews matters covered in this and the previous chapter.

ORGANISATIONAL DESIGN: CLASSICAL VERSUS CONTINGENCY APPROACHES

The Classical Approach

Max Weber and Bureaucracy

Weber's (1948) contribution to organisation theory is one of the most misunderstood and misquoted pieces of work to find its way into textbooks on Organisational Behaviour. His description of the bureaucratic organisation is part of a much more extensive examination of power and authority in society as a whole, in which he distinguishes between three basic forms of authority: *charismatic*, *traditional* and *rational–legal*, and it is the latter in which his study of bureaucracy is grounded.

Above all, Weber was a social scientist who observed and documented the world of his day. In the nineteenth century, scientific rationality was considered to be the essential vehicle of social progress and the bureaucratic form of organisation, which is based on highly rational principles, was seen as having a number of characteristics that made it the most suitable for emerging institutions. Through patient observation, Weber documented the characteristics of the 'ideal type' bureaucracy, the most significant of which are given below:

- **Specialisation**: in the bureaucracy each office has a clearly defined sphere of influence or set of tasks.

Charismatic authority: that acquired when a person becomes the focus of a particular set of ideals and principles, e.g. Christ

Traditional authority: that which rests on the established sanctity of a traditional position, e.g. a king

Rational–legal authority: that which rests on the assumption that rational rules should guide the conduct of society and hence people in high office should command the actions of those below

- **Hierarchy:** there is a clear chain of command from the top to the bottom of the organisation and a lower office is under the control and supervision of the one above.
- **Rules:** clearly defined rational rules prescribe the functions of an office and these provide uniformity, coordination of effort, continuity and stability.
- **Impersonality:** the conduct of officials is dominated by cool professionalism. Those with whom an official deals, whether they be above, below or from inside or outside the organisation, are treated equitably.
- **Appointment:** officials are appointed on the basis of technical competence rather than family connection or favouritism.
- **Progression:** upwards movement through the bureaucracy is based on merit and/or seniority so that it offers a career for life.
- **Exclusivity:** holding an office is the individual's sole or primary occupation.
- **Segregation:** official activity (and resources) are regarded as distinct from those outside the organisation.
- **Accurate written records:** these are regarded as the lifeblood of the organisation. They ensure impartial treatment of office holders and clients, and give rules, procedures and information to guide future conduct.

The bureaucratic model has been severely criticised and the word 'bureaucracy' is often used in a derogatory way to refer to all that is bad. Crozier (1964), for example, criticises bureaucratic theory as an unreal account of how people behave in organisations, and is particularly scathing about the idea that impersonal, conflict-free behaviour characterises the bureaucracy. Other writers are equally critical and some point out that Weber was incorrect in assuming that rules always promote uniformity, order and rationality. A case in point is Gouldner's (1954) classic study of an American gypsum company, which clearly demonstrated that workers and managers quietly went about bending and ignoring rules as part of a pattern of indulging each other. In addition, Selznick (1966) points out that a surfeit of rules results in disadvantages, such as **goal displacement**, in which slavishly obeying a rule becomes a goal in itself. Finally, there are a number of influential writers who draw attention to the potentially adverse effects of the bureaucracy on its members. Merton (1957) writes of the narrow and restricted experience it provides, which ill equips people to operate elsewhere and results in the trained incapacity of the bureaucrat. Perhaps the severest critic in these terms is Argyris (1964), who considers that high degrees of specialisation, rule-regulated behaviour, impersonality and emphasis on hierarchical decision making restricts their psychological growth and results in feelings of frustration, which stifles creativity and innovation.

Although some of these criticisms are probably valid, Weber's work is seriously misinterpreted by many writers. His description of the main characteristics of bureaucracy is an 'ideal type', which does not mean 'highly recommended', but is simply a situation where all the characteristics exist together at the same time. Thus, Weber's model is essentially a **descriptive tool**, and he acknowledges that relatively few organisations conform to it in every respect. Nevertheless, his work is frequently misquoted in many American textbooks as 'Weber's ideal bureaucracy', where he is also unfairly criticised for offering a prescriptive design that has a number of inescapable drawbacks. In reality, Weber merely argued that a bureaucracy was superior in a technical sense to other systems of authority prevalent in his time and far from advocating bureaucracy, in many respects he was highly sceptical about its effects. For instance, he notes that rationality can stifle the scope for individuality, and so office holders tend to become specialists without spirit, trapped in the bureaucratic iron cage of bondage (Weber 1948). Moreover, for all that they criticise bureaucracy, many of the so-called management gurus of today, such as Peters (1987), give universal prescriptions that are just as unworkable, and more recent thinking points out that the rules and routines that characterise bureaucratic organisations can be a source of flexibility and adaptability (Feldman and Rafaeli 2002; Feldman and Pentland 2003). Indeed, a recent meta-analysis of a large number of prior studies by Walton (2005) revealed just how resilient and permanent bureaucratic structure is over time. Thus for all that current ideas criticize the bureaucracy, in reality comparatively few organisations opt for newer structural designs.

Adhocracy: a loose, very flexible and constantly evolving set of structural features that dispenses with traditional hierarchies, job titles and rules

For example, many of the currently fashionable initiatives such as 'delayering' or 're-engineering' always seem to leave the top two layers in an organisation untouched, and what remains is still a bureaucratic hierarchy, albeit a flatter one. The opposite of the bureaucratic hierarchy is the so-called *adhocracy*, or networked organisation, which has been advocated by a number of writers such as Morgan (1989). This would consist of a loose, very flexible and constantly evolving set of structural features that dispense with traditional hierarchies, job titles and rules. However, power holding is usually very high in the management value system and, because bureaucratic structures centre power in the hands of a small number of top managers, it seems unlikely that they will ever be fully eclipsed by anything else. In any event, more recent work argues that it is not bureaucracy as a set of organising principles that results in the dysfunctional effects. Rather, it is misapplication of the principles that has these effects, which occur because of highly inappropriate organisational designs (Adler and Borys 1996).

Classical Organisation Theory

This is not so much a unified theory as a set of remarkably similar ideas put forward by a diverse group of writers, who set out what they believed to be the guiding principles for designing an appropriate structure. Although these ideas differ in detail, they are remarkably similar in terms of basic approach and, for the most part, they are based on the work experience or personal opinions of their authors. Collectively, the approach is usually referred to as the 'classical management school', which stresses that productive efficiency is most easily obtained by:

* adherence to the bureaucratic organisational form
* narrow spans of control
* tightly prescribed roles
* clear and explicit formal procedures
* a high degree of task specialisation
* a clear and explicit hierarchical system of management.

Perhaps the best-known example which typifies the approach is Henri Fayol's (1916) 14 principles, which are described in outline in the OB in Action Box oposite.

 OB IN ACTION: Fayol's 14 principles of organisational design

- **Division of work:** the object of an organisation is to produce more and better work for the same effort, which means there are advantages to be derived from specialisation of labour.

- **Authority and responsibility:** these must be matched and, in particular, managers should have the right to give orders and expect obedience, which goes hand in hand with the responsibility to reward people for good performance and to punish them if it is not forthcoming.

- **Discipline:** this is essential for the efficient running of the organisation; it is a sign that employees respect the organisation and so it is management's duty to decide on and apply appropriate sanctions where discipline is not forthcoming.

- **Unity of command:** an employee should receive orders from one and only one superior.

- **Unity of direction:** this supports unity of command and dictates that there should only be one plan for activities that are designed to achieve an objective.

- **Subordination of interests:** the well-being of the organisation should come before that of groups and individuals.

- **Remuneration:** this should be fair and satisfy both employer and employee; it should encourage keenness and performance but avoid overpayment.

- **Centralisation of authority:** this is necessary and will always be present to some extent.

- **A scalar chain:** there should be a direct line of authority from the top to the bottom of the organisation.

- **Order:** both material and social order should exist; the former avoids loss and the latter ensures that everyone knows his or her place.

- **Equity:** the desire for equality of treatment should guide the vertical division of authority in the scalar chain.

- **Stability of tenure:** this should be encouraged, particularly in managerial personnel.

- **Initiative:** this should be fostered, the best vehicle for which is said to be the unity of command principle.

- **Esprit de corps:** the team spirit should be promoted because this builds loyalty to the organisation.

Guidelines such as these give a highly prescriptive recipe for organisational design, which has been much criticised. For example, it takes no account of interactions between people and, because it underestimates their mental capacities, it has a very naive view of the way they think. In addition, it understates the potential for conflict in organisations (March and Simon 1958). Indeed, so prescriptive and mechanical is the approach that it has been called a description of 'organisations without people' (Bennis 1959). Nevertheless, it gives a clear and unambiguous set of guidelines that are easy to understand and apply. Thus it is remarkably resilient in management circles and, dressed up in different words, it is still common to find the ideas espoused in current management textbooks. In academic circles, however, the strongest criticism centres on the idea that there is a valid set of principles which is applicable everywhere. Current thinking on organisational design purposely avoids this assumption, and it is this approach which is considered next.

REPLAY

- The classical approach to organisational design establishes principles of structure that are said to be universally applicable in all organisations.
- Modern approaches take a contingency perspective which holds that the most appropriate structural design for an organisation is the one that best suits its particular circumstances.

The Contingency Approach

The great problem with classical management theory is that it ignores the possibility that there are influential factors that make some structures more appropriate than others. In the late 1950s a number of theorists began to seriously question the 'one size fits all' assumptions of the classical approach, and took as their guiding principle the simple but elegant idea that the most appropriate structure for an organisation is the one that best suits its particular circumstances. Although the term was not coined until some time later, this subsequently came to be known as *contingency theory*.

Contingency theory: that the most appropriate structure for an organisation is the one that matches its particular circumstances

CONTINGENCY FACTORS IN ORGANISATIONAL DESIGN

The three variables that have received most research attention in organisational design are an **organisation's environment**, **organisational size** and **organisational technology**, and these will be considered shortly. However, more recent thinking on the subject, for example the strategic choice model, reveals that the **preferences and values of top management** can also have a huge impact on what structures are selected. Since it can be argued that these are a powerful contingency factor they will also be considered. The following discussion starts at the outside of the organisation and works inwards.

Environment

An organisation's environment often contains elements over which it has no direct control, but which can strongly influence its performance. Thus, organisations have little choice but to adapt to their environments, and this has been a concern of organisation theory for a number of years.

Burns and Stalker: Mechanistic and Organic Structures

Burns and Stalker (1994) set out to explore whether differences in the technological and market elements of environment affected the structure and management processes in firms. They investigated 20 manufacturing firms in depth and classified environments between 'stable and predictable' and 'unstable and unpredictable'. Because the organisations studied were drawn from several different industries, they identified diverse structural arrangements, but also found that firms could be grouped into one of two main types, with management practices and structures that Burns and Stalker considered to be logical responses to environmental conditions. Neither type is inherently right or wrong. Rather, the firm's environment is a contingency factor that prompts a structural response. The two contrasting forms, the names used by Burns and Stalker to identify them, and the general structural and management style which characterises each one are given in what follows.

The Mechanistic Organisation

Mechanistic organisation: roughly corresponds to a more bureaucratic firm and is best suited to stable environmental conditions

The *mechanistic organisation* has a more rigid structure, is typically found where the environment is stable and predictable and is an appropriate response to these conditions. Its characteristics are:

- tasks facing the concern as a whole are broken down into **specialised, functionally differentiated** duties and individual tasks are **pursued in an abstract way,** that is more or less distinct from the concern as a whole
- the **precise definition** of rights, obligations and technical methods is attached to roles, and these are **translated** into the responsibilities of a functional position so that there is a **hierarchic structure** of control, authority and communication, in which performance requirements for each level in the hierarchy are reconciled by **immediate superiors**
- the hierarchic structure is reinforced by locating **knowledge** of the whole organisation exclusively at the top of the hierarchy, with greater importance and prestige being attached to **internal** and **local** knowledge, experience and skill rather than that which is general to the whole organisation, which gives a tendency for interactions between members of the concern to be **vertical,** that is between superior and subordinate
- a tendency for operations and working behaviour to be **governed by superiors** with **insistence on loyalty** to the concern and obedience to superiors as a condition of membership.

The Organic Organisation

Organic organisation: an organisation that has more fluid structural arrangements, and is better suited to variable and dynamic environments

The *organic organisation* has a much more fluid set of arrangements and is an appropriate response to an environment that is turbulent and which requires new and innovative responses to changing conditions. Its characteristics are:

- special knowledge and experience is valued for its **contributive nature** to the common task of the concern and the **nature of individual tasks** is seen to be set by the total situation faced by the organisation
- a **continual redefinition** of individual tasks through interaction with others, with little **shedding of individual responsibility** upwards, downwards or sideways

- the **spread of commitment** to the concern beyond any technical definition, and a **network structure** of control, authority and communication that has a **lateral** rather than a vertical direction of communication through the organisation

- omniscience is not imputed to the head of the concern and **knowledge** may be located anywhere in the network, with this location becoming the centre of authority

- communication consists of **information** and **advice** rather than instructions and decisions, with **commitment** to the concern's tasks and to the 'technological ethos' of material progress and expansion being more highly valued than loyalty

- importance and prestige are attached to those **affiliations** and **expertise** that are valid in the industrial and technical and commercial milieux external to the firm.

Although mechanistic and organic types are quite different they are only the extremes of a continuum and, in some firms, a mixture of both types could be expected. Nevertheless, the broad structural characteristics that are likely to be associated with each of the two types follow fairly naturally from the descriptions given above.

Mechanistic organisations are likely to have tall structures, a high degree of specialisation, centralisation of authority and standardised rules and procedures. Employees are likely to be 'procedure-orientated' and most interactions and communications, including resolution of conflict, will take place through the chain of command. Conversely, organic organisations will have much flatter structures and lower degrees of specialisation, centralisation of authority and standardisation. People are likely to be much more 'goal-orientated' and there will be more lateral interaction between them. Management will tend to give advice rather than orders, and prestige and status will come from expertise rather than position.

When first published, the Burns and Stalker results were something of a milestone. They not only demonstrated a clear link between environment and structure but also showed that the successful use of different structures requires people in the organisation to have appropriate patterns of values and attitudes. This means that structural arrangements need to be matched by appropriate organisational cultures, and a return to this point will be made later in the chapter.

Lawrence and Lorsch

The work of Lawrence and Lorsch (1969) is regarded as the classic study linking the effects of environment to structure. The authors set out to identify the most appropriate structural characteristics for dealing with different environmental conditions and addressed four important issues of whether:

- the different demands placed on organisations by their environments relate to their structural designs;

- organisations with stable environments make greater use of centralised patterns of authority to achieve coordination and control, and, if so, whether this is because fewer integrating decisions are required, or because decisions can be made more effectively by a small number of people at a high level

- organisations in different environments have the same degrees of specialisation of functions

- firms in different environments have greater degrees of functional specialisation, giving rise to differences in the extent to which organisational functions are coordinated, or use different ways of integrating functional activities.

To address these issues, the authors coined three terms which have subsequently become an important part of the vocabulary used in organisational design. **Differentiation,** which, as used by Lawrence and Lorsch, goes beyond the normal meaning of specialised functional activities. They point out that different organisational functions usually deal with distinct segments of the environment, which can mean that people in different functions develop unique perspectives and emotional orientations. For instance, marketing people can be far more focused on the pressures exerted by customers; this can give them a very different perspective from production people, who tend to be more sensitive to the views of trade unions and suppliers. Therefore, the Lawrence and Lorsch view of differentiation took cognisance of whether some functions:

- focused more on their own goals and objectives, rather than those of the whole organisation
- had longer time horizons because of differences in the time taken for the results of their decisions to become apparent with respect to that part of the environment with which they dealt
- were managed differently in terms of being task-orientated or person-orientated
- tended to be more bureaucratically managed than others.

Integration reflects the ways in which functional activities are coordinated and controlled to achieve the goals for the organisation. Lawrence and Lorsch acknowledged that different functions are likely to have different orientations, but they avoided the assumption that integration is just a matter of minimising differences to produce a common outlook. Rather, their aim was to determine whether ways had been found to allow the differences in orientation to exist, while getting the functions to focus on achieving organisational goals. Thus attention was directed on two alternative methods of coordination: 'vertical coordination' using rules and procedures through the hierarchy to control functional behaviour; and 'horizontal coordination', using lateral processes designed to encourage functions to make mutual adjustment to each other.

Environment was not conceptualised as 'everything out there' but as three specific sub-environments, normally dealt with by three major specialist functions in firms:

- The **market sub-environment:** dealt with by the marketing function.
- The **technical–economic sub-environment:** dealt with by the production function.
- The **scientific sub-environment:** dealt with by research and development.

They reasoned that each sub-environment can differ in a number of important ways:

- its rate of change
- the certainty about prevailing conditions at any particular time
- the time-span of feedback before the results of a decision with respect to the environment become known.

These differences were reasoned to result in the three functions having to deal with different degrees of ambiguity or uncertainty, which can result in them evolving their own functional sub-structures and processes. This gives rise to three testable predictions about the functions, that:

1. **Production** would have a short time horizon focused on the demands of the here and now, such as meeting quality and output targets. It would operate in a fairly stable internal environment of known methods and rely mostly on rules and procedures.

2. **Research and development** would operate on a much longer time horizon and deal with an unstable, moving situation concerned with innovation. As such it would have a fluid, organic type of structure.

3. **Marketing** would tend to lie somewhere between these two extremes.

Several studies were conducted, but the one giving the most definitive findings was a comparative study of firms in three different industries, chosen on the basis of their environmental characteristics.

- The *plastics industry* had a very dynamic, highly uncertain environment characterised by rapid changes in customer requirements and a high rate of scientific and technological development.
- The *containers (canning) industry* had a stable, certain environment with predictable customer requirements and an established, unchanging technology.
- The *consumer foods industry* had an intermediate environment and a moderate rate of change in customer requirements and technology.

In each industry high-performance firms (high profits and many new product innovations) were compared with low performers and two general sets of findings and associated conclusions emerged:

- The more uncertain the environment the greater the degree of differentiation within firms; that is, plastics (high), consumer foods (medium), containers (low), giving the conclusion that the more dynamic and uncertain the environment the more that specialist sub-units are needed, each dealing with the dynamics of its own sub-environment.
- Within each industry, the more successful firms were those that also had the highest degrees of integration, giving the conclusion that success (in the terms measured) is associated with mechanisms that are concerned with ensuring that all sub-units contribute towards achieving a common goal.

However, the most interesting finding is related to the methods of integration used. Successful firms all had high degrees of integration, but the mechanisms used in each industry were quite different and depended on the amount of differentiation needed. Firms in the canning industry, which had a very stable environment, had the lowest degrees of differentiation and tended to integrate activities by using rules, procedures and centralised decision making. In consumer foods, where the environment was intermediate in uncertainty, these integrating devices were also used but, in addition, lateral integrating mechanisms, such as cross-functional task groups or special coordinating roles, were sometimes found. The plastics industry, with the most dynamic and uncertain environment of all, invariably had permanent, lateral integrating mechanisms; for instance, cross-functional coordinating teams at several levels and sometimes permanent departments whose role was to integrate functional activities.

Figure 18.1 Causal
chain implied by
Lawrence and Lorsch

The work of Lawrence and Lorsch occupies a prominent position in organisation theory and, because its major focus is on the link between strategy, structure and performance, its findings are widely accepted and well respected in academic circles. To some extent it can be viewed as an extension of the ideas of Burns and Stalker. However, Burns and Stalker treat an organisation as an undifferentiated whole that is either organic or mechanistic, whereas the Lawrence and Lorsch dimensions of differentiation and integration go to the very heart of organisational design and enable matters to be considered in a more sophisticated way. For instance, they acknowledge that mechanistic and organic structures can exist side by side in different parts of an organisation.

Nevertheless there are criticisms of the theory, the most important of which is that it treats organisations as passive recipients of environmental influence and postulates a one-way chain of causality, such as that shown in Figure 18.1.

In Figure 18.1, environment is shown as the independent variable and performance as the dependent variable, which means that structure is a mediating factor that must be adjusted to ensure excellent performance. This neglects the important idea that, rather than slavishly responding to environmental changes with disruptive structural reorganisations, most organisations try to exert some influence on their environments.

Organisational Size

Size is normally taken to refer to the number of employees in an organisation and a simple example of its effects can be given by considering a small corner shop which develops over time into a large successful business. Initially the owner will also be the manager and do everything – selling, buying, ordering and keeping the accounts. If the business is successful, it may well expand, perhaps by acquiring additional outlets and eventually by having a large store in the city centre. Later on it might even become a national chain. In the first stage of expansion the owner will require managers in each outlet and, to take advantage of bulk-buying discounts, he or she might make purchasing and accounting separate activities, with warehousing and publicity added shortly afterwards. Eventually, if the firm becomes a national chain, it might be decided to group stores into geographical areas, each with its own manager.

Even from a simple story such as this, a general principle emerges which has been shown to be applicable, even with multinational corporations (Malnight 2001). As organisations grow their structures become much more elaborate, internal activities become more specialised and the structure becomes more vertically and horizontally differentiated, which in general terms has two opposing consequences. First, clear economic advantages accrue from specialisation and formalisation, and there is extremely strong evidence that larger firms that adopt these principles outperform those that are more loosely structured (Child 1984). However, this can result in people finding the organisation a less satisfying place in which to work; job satisfaction can be lower and different forms of conflict and protest behaviour can sometimes increase with size.

TIME OUT

Carefully consider your own university or college. Like most other higher education institutions it has probably grown significantly across the last ten or 15 years. Make enquiries to determine what its structure was about 15 years ago and compare this with its structure now, then answer the questions below.

1. In what ways has the structure become more elaborate and complex?
2. Have the problems of coordination and control of the different parts become more difficult?
3. How has the institution tried to resolve the issues?

Technology

Technology is often thought of in terms of machines and hardware, but in the words of Rousseau (1979), it can be more simply described as the application of knowledge to perform work, which has the advantage of embracing both what is done and how it is done. To some extent, technology is dictated by the tasks that must be performed and, once selected, it often completely determines the order in which tasks are undertaken. Thus there can clearly be a relationship between technology and structure, which can be examined at a number of levels. In this section the perspectives of two influential theorists will be examined.

Thompson and Organisational Interdependencies

Thompson (1967) deals with the technology of a whole organisation and distinguishes between the three basic technologies portrayed in Figure 18.2. Each one is associated with a particular flow of work, which results in the interdependence of an organisation's parts in a characteristic way. It is also related to the amount of discretion in making decisions in its operation. This all gives rise to differences in the degree of complexity inherent in coordinating the activities of the interdependent parts, together with characteristic remedies to shield the organisation's operating core from the uncertainties of the environment.

Figure 18.2
Thompson's technological types and associated interdependencies: (a) the mediating technology (pooled interdependence); (b) the long-linked technology (sequential interdependence); (c) the intensive technology (reciprocal interdependence)

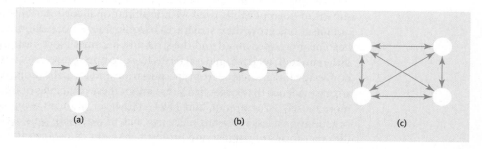

(a)   (b)   (c)

Mediating technology: the parts of an organisation are linked through its centre

Pooled interdependence: organisational sub-units safeguard each other by contributing discretely to the whole, which safeguards them all

Long-linked technology: all activities have to be performed in a set sequence

Sequential interdependence: each stage is interdependent with the one before and the one after

Intensive technology: all parts contribute together to perform the task

Reciprocal interdependence: the parts are dependent on each other to perform their respective tasks

In the *mediating technology* the parts of an organisation are linked together through its centre. Each renders its own contribution to the whole and in return receives support from the centre. This is a situation of *pooled interdependence*. There is little direct interaction between sub-units, but they are interdependent in the sense that unless each one makes a contribution to the whole, others are placed in jeopardy. Examples of organisations using mediating technologies are banks, building societies, retail chains and insurance companies. Providing each sub-unit follows procedures and makes the same contribution in the same way, this technology is the least complex in terms of coordination, which is done by **centralising authority** and by **formalising** and **standardising operations**.

The *long-linked technology* is exemplified by the mass production line, where task A must be performed before B, B before C and so on. This is *sequential interdependence* and, because everything else has to be adjusted if one of the operations in the chain does not perform as required, it is rather more difficult to coordinate. An organisation using this technology tends to devote a great deal of time and effort to planning and scheduling to coordinate activities. Dealing with environmental fluctuations is also more of a problem, and this is typically addressed by vertical integration, either backwards or forwards. For example, a car manufacturer could integrate backwards by acquiring a component supplier, or forwards by owning car dealerships.

In terms of coordination, the *intensive technology* is the most complex of all. Each sub-unit is in an interdependent relationship with all the others, which results in *reciprocal interdependence*. Organisations of this type, for example hospitals or travel agents, offer a custom operation where the tasks undertaken, the skills used, the mix of techniques deployed and the order in which they occur are determined by feedback from the client or customer. Sub-units need to be highly responsive to one another and there can be an ongoing need for mutual adjustment. Because it is always hard to predict what is required in advance, coping with environmental uncertainty is extremely difficult, and sometimes this can only be done by acquiring surplus resources that are held in reserve, just in case they are needed.

Thompson points out that the effectiveness of an organisation's 'technical core' (the operational units that transform inputs into outputs) depends on it being able to get on with its tasks in a smooth, uninterrupted way. This requires shielding the core from environmental fluctuations, which is done by incorporating appropriate sub-units into the structure to deal with the problematic parts of the environment. For example, the core of the mediating technology is particularly vulnerable to fluctuations on the output side, and so stability is sought by having a very active marketing function. The long-linked technology is vulnerable to fluctuations on both input and output sides, and so it devotes a great deal of effort to forecasting demand and usually has specialist departments that plan activities and ensure continuity of supplies. In the intensive technology, fluctuations on the input side are the greatest problem, and the only way the core can be shielded is to have a surplus of resources. However, it is not just a matter of the different technologies having different structures. The progression from mediating, through long-linked to intensive technology results in an exponential increase in the difficulties associated with coordination, which in turn gives a corresponding increase in structural complexity. This is because if sequential interdependence exists, there is also a degree of pooled interdependence. Similarly, the existence of reciprocal interdependence means that sequential and pooled interdependence are present as well.

Thompson's ideas stand up well to empirical examination, for example Mahoney and Frost (1974) tested the relative importance of the different coordinating mechanisms in firms conforming to the technological types and the results obtained strongly support Thompson's predictions.

TIME OUT

Review the Thompson scheme of classifying organisational technologies and carefully examine the structure of the organisation in which you work or study.

1. Which of the three technologies do you feel is used by the organisation or institution?
2. Identify the component parts that are interdependent in some way and show what type of interdependence exists between them.
3. What would you identify as the organisation's technical core?
4. In what activities does the organisation or institution engage to shield its technical core from environmental uncertainties?

The Woodward Studies: Technology, Structure and Performance

The original aim of Woodward's (1965) work was to determine whether an association exists between business success and the structural prescriptions given by classical organisation theory. Data were collected from over 100 manufacturing firms, all of which were larger than 100 employees. Business success was measured in the usual financial terms and, in addition, data were collected on a number of structural variables, such as the number of levels in the management hierarchy, span of control and what is now referred to as administrative intensity (the ratio of managers and supervisors to direct production workers). Firms were classified in terms of performance as below average, average and above average. Initially, no consistent relationship was identified between structural variables and performance, but subsequent re-analysis revealed that if technology was held constant, there was a connection between structure and performance. To explain this it is necessary to describe Woodward's scheme for classifying manufacturing technology. This used three broad technology types and represents what Woodward and her colleagues called a scale of increasing *technical complexity*, in which coordination and control become more difficult as the scale is ascended. The types are:

Technical complexity: a measure of the ease of coordination and control of a manufacturing technology

- **Low technical complexity: unit and small batch production,** for example unique products made to a customer's specification, prototypes and small batches made to customer order.

- **Medium technical complexity: large batch and mass production,** which involves large batches made using multipurpose machinery, or on assembly lines equipped with purpose-designed machinery.

- **High technical complexity: process production,** for instance production of chemicals liquids and gases under continuous flow (24 hours per day, seven days per week) conditions.

This classification needs to be interpreted with some caution because, although it classifies process technology as the most technically complex, unit and small batch production is also full of unpredictability and it is equally valid to argue that this is the most difficult to coordinate and control. Nevertheless, Woodward found that in each technology type the most successful firms had structures that were the average of all firms in the type; that is, the most successful unit and small batch production firms were those where supervisors had the average span of control, etc. for firms using this technology. Moreover, when the structural characteristics of the successful firms were plotted against the type of production technology used, distinct relationships were revealed, some of which are shown in Figure 18.3.

The important conclusion that Woodward draws is that different production technologies require their own structural arrangements, and replication studies provide strong support for this idea (Collins and Hull 1986). Nevertheless there are criticisms of her findings, one of which is noted above and concerns the way that technical complexity is evaluated. In addition, the work is exclusively focused on manufacturing industry and since there are no direct equivalents of the technological types in service industries, it is hard to generalise the findings beyond manufacturing. Another important point is not really a criticism of Woodward, but of the way that her results are sometimes taken too much at face value and it is rather simplistically inferred that technology alone determines structure. As firms grow or acquire more stable markets the volume of work they undertake can result in a move from small batch methods into mass production. Thus there is an increase in size (or at least in scale) of the organisation, as well as a change in production technology, and structural changes are almost certainly the result of both variables being at work together.

Culture as a Contingency Variable

Organisational culture is considered in greater detail in Chapter 20 and for the purposes of this discussion it will be defined as:

> the basic values, ideologies and assumptions which guide and fashion individual and business behaviour. (Wilson and Rosenfeld 1990, p 229)

Although organisational design is mainly concerned with structure, we need to recognise that there are strong connections between culture and structure and this gives rise to two important issues. First, a culture prompts people to behave in characteristic

Figure 18.3
Woodward studies – selected relationships between structure and technology type

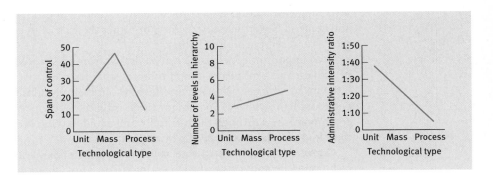

ways and, since structure also has this effect, the behaviour required by a culture needs to be compatible with the behaviour required by its structure. Second, the values of the top management group in an organisation can have a huge impact on its decisions. Since values are a central part of culture, the culture of top management can influence decisions about structure. In practice, this gives rise to two issues, which, for convenience, will be called the **limiting factor on design** and the **limiting factor on top management decisions**.

Issue 1: Culture as a Limiting Factor on Design

Until comparatively recently, technology was thought to have the major determining effect on structure. However, there is an alternative argument: that culture and structure are so interconnected that they both go hand in hand. A simple way to illustrate this is to use the basic four-part classification scheme for cultures set out by Harrison (1972), which is given below.

The **role culture** typifies the bureaucracy or mechanistic organisation in which the duties, responsibilities and the authority attached to roles are tightly specified, with activities controlled and coordinated by senior managers. In organisations of this type, power resides in a person's position and the activities of individuals are regulated by rules and procedures.

The **task culture** roughly corresponds to the organic organisational form and is the complete opposite. There are few rules and procedures, and getting things done tends to be far more important than how things are done. Status comes from expertise and adaptability in achieving results and this is facilitated by giving individuals a considerable degree of autonomy.

The **power culture** is also lacking in formal rules but tends to be one in which a powerful individual or small group is the source of all authority. This elite controls and coordinates everything and often changes the rules as it goes along. The essential qualities required of those employees who are not part of the power structure are personal loyalty to power holders, working extremely hard and doing what they are told without question. Again this promotes a set of values and sentiments that enable people to work and survive within this structure.

The **person culture** is seldom found outside small voluntary groups and is only described for completeness. This type of organisation exists to serve its members and is often brought into existence by those who staff it. To some extent it allows its members to collectively pursue aims that would not be possible as individuals, and is often no more than a loose alliance of people who share some common facilities. Other than behaving with mutual respect to each other, there will probably be no coordination and control. Nevertheless, structure, or rather the lack of it, goes hand in hand with the cultural sentiments and values.

Two important conclusions can be drawn from this typology. In each case, a set of values and sentiments that promotes characteristic patterns of behaviour is interwoven with a set of structural features. In the role culture, for example, people perform their own roles and do not trespass on the territory of others. They channel communications through the hierarchy and avoid making decisions that are beyond their formally designated level of authority.

Conversely, in the task culture, roles are extremely flexible and people are expected to be versatile and act on their own initiative. Thus, these structural arrangements can effectively become a mental programme that indicates the reality of 'how the organisation should operate', which suggests that an organisation's culture should be an important consideration in the design of its structure.

Issue 2: Culture as a Limiting Factor on Management Decisions

In organisational design the dictum that 'structure follows strategy' (Chandler 1962) is often accepted without question, but, from what has been said earlier, decisions about the structural design of an organisation are not this straightforward. They usually require a balance to be struck between the sometimes competing demands of size, technology and environment. Since an inappropriate design is likely to jeopardise achievement of business strategies, a more sophisticated view of the strategy formulation process is needed. This is provided by the model of strategic choice (Child 1997), which reflects the idea that when constructing strategies top managers can purposely incorporate measures that leave existing structures and processes relatively unaltered. Child argues that top managers are like other people: they have their own foibles, preferences and personalised performance criteria. As such, they do not always pursue high profitability and growth, but sometimes sacrificed these in favour of an organisational structure with which they feel comfortable, because it reflects their philosophies about control and coordination. Thus top management's values and culture, both of which are neglected in the conventional contingency approach, can be important contingency variables in their own right.

There is a considerable body of evidence to show that the personal preferences of top managers, particularly those about methods of monitoring performance, can have a strong influence on decisions about structure (Hinings *et al.* 1996) and this alone makes the strategic choice model an important one. In addition, there is a body of knowledge that suggests that the prior experience, preferences and ideologies and values (cultures) of key decision makers actually influence the way that they perceive the environment (Finkelstein and Hambrick 1996; Winter 2003). For instance, Weick (1979) observes that managers 'perceive' environments, rather than actually see the totality of what is there – they tend to focus their attention on only specific parts of the whole environment and other parts are excluded from consideration. Weick calls this the *enacted environment*, and it is this to which top managers respond in terms of structural arrangements. To illustrate how organisations define and modify their environments, by selecting strategies that have an impact on structural design, these ideas have been developed further by Miles and Snow (1978) who examined the extent to which enacted environments produce predictable patterns in structural design. They give three distinct patterns of strategy–structure linkage used by successful organisations.

Enacted environment: management's mental construction of what the environment is, which arises from its selective perceptions of environment

Defender strategies involve having a relatively restricted field of activity in terms of product lines and markets served. The firm's aim is to have a secure, stable niche in the market and it tries to protect this by offering outputs of a higher quality or lower price than competitors. An organisation of this type is not usually an innovator in terms of products or services, but concentrates on internal efficiencies so that it can focus its efforts on doing a job well in a limited field, and this has distinct structural implications. Internal efficiency is typically obtained by a high degree of specialisation and centralisation of authority and a reliance on rules and procedures for coordination and control.

The **prospector strategy** aims to obtain market advantage by being the first organisation with a new product or service. To do this it usually has to serve a very broad environment, watch closely for changes and respond to them very quickly, which also has structural implications. Responding quickly to opportunities that arise usually requires decentralised decision making, together with lateral communication. Thus project and product teams are often used for coordination and control.

The **analyser strategy** falls between the above two types. Here the aim is to have a stable but limited product line and this is used to finance fairly quick moves into carefully selected new developments. This strategy seldom involves the organisation being the first into a developing area. Rather, it monitors what other firms do and can often enter a market in its early stages of development with a product or service that is more cost-efficient. This tends to produce a mixed structural form. Those parts of the organisation operating in the stable part of the environment will have structures similar to the defender, and those dealing with the emerging part will tend to have market-based, fluid structural characteristics.

Miles and Snow also identify a fourth strategy type: **the reactor**. Because this tends to result in inconsistent strategy–structure arrangements, often because an inappropriate structure is used to pursue a particular strategy, firms are seldom successful and the type is not considered further here.

The Miles and Snow strategic choice perspective has received a great deal of support and currently receives much attention in organisation theory. Since empirical studies are highly supportive of the original work (Boschken 1990), a number of important conclusions may be drawn:

● Managers seldom react to all of the environmental factors that can affect an organisation, but tend to focus on specific parts and thus 'enact' an environment.
● Different organisations operating in the same environment can perceive it in different ways, which results in diverse strategies for dealing with the same environment.
● Because strategies not only involve choices about the markets that are served, but also the ways of serving markets, this results in different structural designs.
● Once a strategy and structural design are put in place it is likely to result in what Miles (1982) has called a **strategic disposition**, which establishes a 'mind set' about what is seen to be an appropriate strategy for the organisation.

This final conclusion is tremendously important. Put another way, it means that the structural choices that have been made earlier can inhibit the adoption of alternative strategies, and even affect views on whether future strategies are viable (Hinings *et al.* 1996).

An Integration of Contingency Factors

Depending on the particular factor on which a contingency theory is focused, it gives valuable insights into the way that the factor influences structure. However, most theories usually focus on a single contingency factor, and this conveys the impression that this factor has the major influence on an organisation's structural characteristics. The exception here is the strategic choice model, which is much more behavioural in its approach. It incorporates the idea that managers who exercise choice can try to influence organisational environments, or even serve them selectively, which gives them greater a degree of freedom about structural options.

However, the strategic choice perspective does not contradict conventional contingency theories. Indeed, by introducing values and ideologies of senior decision

Figure 18.4 Structure and strategic choice

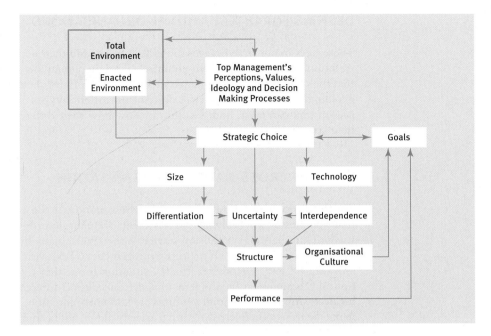

makers as another contingency factor, it gives a theory that is complementary rather than contradictory. Nevertheless, it results in a somewhat more complex view of the determinants of structure, and, in order to bring all these influences together, Figure 18.4 reflects the inferences about that can be drawn from all the contingency theories covered in this chapter.

REPLAY

- The classical approach to organisational design establishes principles of structure that are said to be universally applicable in all organisations.

- More recent approaches take a contingency perspective, which holds that the most appropriate structural design for an organisation is one that best suits its particular circumstances.

- Contingency theorists have attempted to identify how structural design needs to vary to accommodate particular organisational circumstances, and the three factors that have received most attention are organisation size, the technology an organisation uses and an organisation's environment.

- In addition, because an organisation's culture needs to match its structure, there are grounds for arguing that culture is also an important contingency variable.

- The cultural values of top management are also likely to exert an influence on the structural designs chosen for an organisation.

DESIGNS FOR INTERNATIONAL ORGANISATIONS

These days many large organisations seek to expand their activities well beyond the traditional boundaries of their countries of origin. Doing this, however, often means that the strategies they adopt have strong implications for their structural designs. To explain this it is first necessary to describe the different types of cross-national organisation that can exist, and, second, to show how their different strategic foci affect their structural arrangements.

TYPES OF CROSS-NATIONAL ORGANISATION

The difference between an organisation whose markets are in a single country and one that operates on a worldwide basis is a leap of quantum proportions. When the first wave of international expansion started in the 1960s, many firms attempted to do so through international joint venture arrangements (IJVs) with foreign partners (Park and Ungson 1997). However, the IJV situation is one that is fraught with coordination and communication problems arising from cultural differences, so many IJVs were unsuccessful. Although joint ventures are still fairly common, many firms now try to make the transition to cross-national activity alone, but becoming a globalised organisation is seldom accomplished in a single step, as is graphically illustrated by Barney and Griffin (1992), who describe the transitional stages in the following way:

Stage 1: From national to international, in which domestic organisations that derive their revenues within a single country seek to become international organisations, still based in the country of origin, but with additional operations elsewhere.

Stage 2: From international to multinational, where some of the firms go on to become even more dispersed, with subsidiaries and facilities spread across the globe, for example the Ford Motor Company.

Stage 3: From multinational to globalised, which is a much more recent phenomenon and consists of a tendency to transcend national borders. The firm not only operates on a global scale, but thinks of itself as one that is no longer primarily located in its country of origin.

These intermediate stages give rise to different types of cross-national organisation, each of which has its own strategic focus. This enables organisations to be located along a continuum, the extremes of which are the large domestic organisation and the global or transnational organisation. Drawing on the work of Bartlett and Ghoshal (1991) and others, the differences between these types of organisation are summarised in Table 18.1. However, caution needs to be exercised in drawing conclusions from this table. It simply reflects the idea that there are five different types of organisation, and it should not be inferred that a progression from left to right indicates superiority. Indeed, whether an organisation can move from one extreme to the other is greatly dependent on the markets for its products. For example, Beamish *et al.* (1991) provide convincing reasons why some product markets push an organisation into serving only local markets, whereas for others the nature of the product market means that failure to compete on a worldwide basis can be commercial suicide.

Table 18.1 Major strategic characteristics of different types of cross-national organisation (adapted from Bartlett and Ghoshal 1991)

	Domestic organisation	International organisation	Multinational organisation	Global organisation	Transnational organisation
Markets served	Home market in country of origin	Home and overseas	Home and overseas	Worldwide	Worldwide
Strategic assumptions	There is one best way of serving the market	There are several best ways to satisfy different markets	There is a single least cost way to satisfy different markets	There are many good ways to satisfy different markets, all of which can be used simultaneously	As global organisation
Strategic focus and competitive strategy	On home markets alone	Transfer of knowledge and technology from country of origin to produce at home and abroad	Products or services developed and made to suit different markets at home and abroad	Develop standardised products that can be produced for a wide variety of markets, but customise to meet specific requirements of each market	Develop skills, products and technology in all units and transfer to wherever needed
Responsibility for strategy formulation	Headquarters in country of origin	Centralised at headquarters in country of origin	Decentralised to overseas subsidiaries	Shared between all divisions around the world	Shared between all divisions
Structure and control	Functional with divisions	Functional with an international division; hierarchical control exercised from the country of origin	Several different lines of business, decentralised semi-autonomous overseas divisions	Independent overseas divisions whose activities are coordinated by headquarters	Interdependent units operating nationally and worldwide
Degree of adaptation to host countries	None necessary	High in legal terms, but managers usually from home country	High degree of social and cultural diversity	High: very diverse culturally and socially	As global organisation

Domestic Organisations

Domestic organisations: mainly trade within the borders of their country of origin

Although *domestic organisations* can be very large, for the most part they do not trade outside their country of origin, although they might well engage in a level of export activity. Their dominant focus is on home markets and they try to find a strategy that captures the largest possible market share. If large, they are often multi-product companies and so they can use any of the structural designs described in Chapter 17; for example, functional or divisional designs. These organisations are usually controlled from the centre.

International Organisation

International organisation: one that is primarily located and managed in its country of origin, but also either export to or produce identical or similar goods and services in overseas subsidiaries

This represents the first stage beyond being primarily a domestic organisation. These companies tend to have some overseas operations, the scope of which can vary considerably, but even in its most advanced form, the organisation simply attempts to expand its markets overseas, using the same or very similar products as those sold at home. To do this it exports its technology and knowledge to one or more host countries, with operating subsidiaries to handle production and marketing. This arrangement is fairly commonplace in manufacturing industries that produce standardised products that are very similar the world over, for example car tyres and chemicals. Overseas divisions are usually responsible to, and controlled by the organisational headquarters in the country of origin.

Multinational Organisation

Multinational organisation: one that is primarily located and managed from the country of its origin, but produces goods or services in relatively autonomous overseas subsidiaries to meet the needs of local markets

Here the aim is to expand even further, but doing so requires servicing more diverse markets. Because new products can be required to satisfy different overseas markets, overseas subsidiaries often need a higher degree of operating autonomy, for example to be able to design, develop and market their own products. Examples of this type of organisation can be found in industries that produce branded goods that have some degree of similarity worldwide but also need to be varied to meet the requirements of particular overseas markets, for example food and clothing (Beamish *et al.* 1991).

Global Organisation

Global organisation: one that is not tied to a single nation, but operates wordwide as an independent set of subsidiaries coordinated by a headquarters

This type of organisation aims to produce standardised products that can be easily adapted to suit the requirements of a wide range of different markets. The product can be designed or developed anywhere so long as it is adaptable to other markets. In this type of organisation strategy is a shared responsibility of all divisions and although control is centralised in the hands of corporate headquarters, this is less concerned with detailed regulation of the activities of subsidiaries than with getting them to work with each other. Thus the organisation has a strong emphasis on the interdependence of its parts in order to be able to service worldwide markets.

Transnational Organisation

Transnational organisation: one that operates simultaneously as an international, multinational and global organisation

In terms of strategy, these organisations are by far the most complex and sophisticated type. They try to incorporate the productive efficiency found in the globalised organisation with the ability to the transfer technology and know-how found in international organisations. Where necessary, they also try to be highly responsive to localised markets in the same way as a multinational (Harzing and Russeveldt 1995). If anything, therefore, the degree of interdependence between subsidiaries is even higher than in the globalised organisations.

Each of these different types of organisation has its own characteristic way of operating and this can be seen in the penultimate row of Table 18.1, which indicates that structures tend to be very different. Thus the next step is to examine structure and organisational design in the different types.

TIME OUT

Carefully examine the different types of cross-national organisation, the details of which are described above and summarised in Table 18.1. Imagine that you are just about to leave university or college, having completed your degree, and have been offered four different positions as a management trainee: one in a large domestic organisation, one in an international organisation, one in a multinational and one in a global organisation. Assuming that all four jobs have the very similar remuneration conditions:

1. Which would you accept?
2. Why would you choose this job in preference to the others?

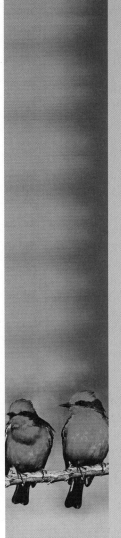

 OB IN ACTION: Beyond the transnational organisation

Sumantra Ghoshal first came to prominence through his work with Christopher Bartlett in the late 1980s. This set out the concept of the 'transnational' corporation and suggested that a new model of international business strategy and organisation was emerging. They argued that old-style multinational and global corporations were increasingly being forced to change by the simultaneous demands of global efficiency and local responsiveness, and that rather than choosing between globalisation and localisation, they are forced to adopt both strategies at the same time. The result, they said, was the emergence of the 'transnational' corporation, which had the characteristics of both big and small companies, and could operate globally and locally. Rather than centralised, hierarchical structures, transnational companies operated as networks, with increasingly specialised units worldwide, which are integrated into a seamless whole that works in harmony. At the heart of all this was a mindset that requires managers to work across boundaries, pulling far-flung teams and resources together to achieve strategic goals.

Their most recent book, *The Individualised Corporation*, takes a more far-reaching look at the changes in business. They argue that a revolution is in progress, which is being led by pioneering companies, such as ABB and General Electric, who no longer force employees to conform to a rigid conception of what an employee should be and do, but reconfigure the organisation itself, to fit around the talents and abilities of its employees: the 'individualised' corporation of the title. By doing this these organisations are said to be able to release 'entrepreneurial hostages', thus allowing individuals the room to be creative and add value to the business. In these firms, Ghoshal argues, purpose is more important than strategy or systems, and the aim is to infuse every member of the organisation with a sense of common purpose, which becomes the key to organisational change. Indeed, the most successful big corporations today are those that have realised the importance of purpose and made this, rather than preconceived ideas about organisation or strategy, their central focus.

Source:

Witzel, M (2003) Champion of the individual, *Financial times*, 7 August

Structure: A Brief Review

In theory, if not always in practice, structure follows strategy. Structure is intended to facilitate achieving organisational goals and the two main features intended to serve this purpose are:

- differentiation, which divides the organisation into component parts and specifies what role each will play in achieving specific aims and outcomes for the organisation
- integration, which provides for these parts to be controlled and coordinated so that their activities mesh together to achieve organisational goals.

As organisations grow, they tend to develop more elaborate and complex structures. In most cases the degree of specialisation increases with size, authority becomes more centralised, and procedures and practices become more formalised. Indeed, if allowance is made for such factors as size and industry type, these general tendencies hold good for many countries in the world (Hickson and McMillan 1981). However, this does not mean that organisations are the same everywhere, because, as the final row in Table 18.1 indicates, it is often necessary for cross-national organisations to adapt themselves to social and cultural factors in their overseas subsidiaries.

Structural Designs for Cross-national Operations

The functional, divisional and matrix designs given in Chapter 17 meet the needs of most domestic organisations, but, even so, mixed designs are quite common. Many years ago Stinchcombe (1965) pointed out that new organisational designs only tend to appear when two conditions arise together:

- where existing designs cannot adequately cope with a new situation; and
- when social and technical conditions make it possible to adopt a new design.

To a large extent these conditions came together when each of the different cross-national designs emerged. The designs for international and multinational organisations evolved some time ago, and the latest one to emerge is that which is often used by global organisations. To make it easier to understand the differences, the designs that can be used for domestic, international and multinational companies will be described first.

Domestic Organisations

Strictly speaking these are not cross-national organisations, but the first step towards international activity is often exporting products made in the home country. At this stage organisations use what Porter (1986) calls an '*international trade strategy*', in which an international division is grafted on to an existing functional or product structure. This allows company headquarters in the country of origin to exercise tight control and coordination and a typical structure is shown in simplified form in Figure 18.5.

International and Multinational Organisations

A simplified example of the structure used by these types of organisation is shown in Figure 18.6. Both international and multinational organisations can be regarded as

International trade strategy and structure: one that is primarily geared to serving a wider set of markets by exporting goods or services from the home country

Figure 18.5
Structural design for
international trade

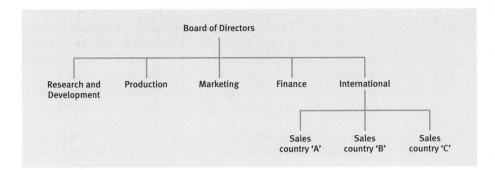

Figure 18.6 Country-
focused structural
design

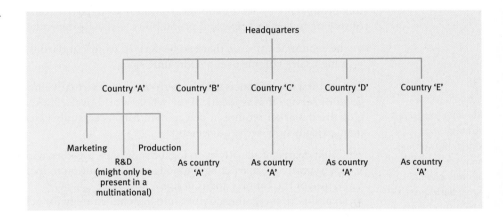

Country-focused
strategy and
structure: primarily
geared to serving a
wider set of markets
by producing goods
or services in
overseas subsidiaries
for sale in local
markets

federations of divisionalised operating units, which service different national or regional markets. In general terms both tend to use what can be described as a '*country-focused strategy*' (Porter 1986). However, as Table 18.1 illustrates, they differ in one important respect. In the international organisation, overseas subsidiaries produce the same or slightly modified products and services as they do for home markets. Therefore, activity in subsidiaries bears a strong resemblance to what occurs in the country of origin, which means that authority tends to be centralised at headquarters and subsidiaries are strongly controlled. Subsidiaries in multinationals tend to develop and manufacture different products and services that are specifically targeted at markets in host countries, and the products or services required for one country or region can be very different from those required elsewhere. Thus subsidiaries need a much higher degree of autonomy and there is less direct control by headquarters.

To some extent there is a natural tendency for an organisation to export the structure it uses in its country of origin, particularly its control and coordination mechanisms (Harzing and Sorge 2003). The ability to do this, however, tends to be limited because competing in international markets often depends on knowing the rules of the game, which can sometimes be very different from those learned in the organisation's past. Learning these rules quickly can be vital for organisations that are behind others in entering international operations, a case in point being West German firms which, until comparatively recently, restricted themselves to export-orientated, international trade strategies. When organisations in West Germany eventually entered the field of international operations, in an attempt to make up for lost time they tended to acquire what are sometimes referred to as 'vanguard subsidiaries' (Ferner and Varul 2000) many of which were based in Great Britain, and were already heavily involved in international operations. Know-how and skills were then absorbed into the German parent.

Globalised Organisations

A globalised market for a product or service creates huge expansion opportunities for organisations but, because companies all over the world can enter the same market, the stakes are high for all of them. In an attempt to outbid each other in markets, the rate of development and improvement of products tends to be very fast, which means that product life-cycles are shorter. For this reason the research and development costs of staying in business rise, and profitability is acutely dependent on achieving:

- the economies of scale that can be derived from standardised products
- a high sales volume over a short time span.

Except for a few products such as petroleum, it is virtually impossible to think of any good or service that is identical the whole world over. Thus, taking advantage of a globalised market requires a design than can successfully cater for two separate but diametrically opposed requirements:

- a high degree of sensitivity to local conditions, together with the flexibility to adapt products, marketing methods and distribution to local markets, which is a feature of the country-focus design
- an ability to integrate activities into a global strategy for achieving economic efficiency in all countries where the organisation operates.

To reconcile these requirements, companies tend to adopt what Bedeian and Zammuto (1991) call a '*globally integrated strategy and structure*', a simplified example of which is shown in Figure 18.7.

The design gives a highly interdependent network of geographically dispersed divisions, whose activities are coordinated through headquarters. Interdependence comes from divisions in each country having a degree of specialisation, which reduces

Globally integrated strategy and structure: a diffuse network of highly interdependent subsidiaries, each of which specialises in some degree, but none of which has the capability to operate as a totally independent and autonomous business unit

Figure 18.7 The globally integrated structural design

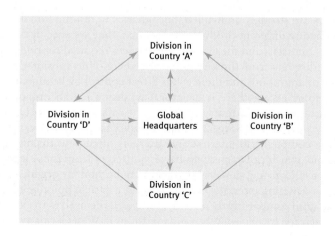

duplication of effort and gives economies of scale. For example, in Figure 18.7 the division in country 'A' may handle research and development, the division in country 'B' production of components, while 'C' and 'D' may handle final assembly, with all divisions undertaking the marketing and distribution of finished goods. As an alternative, as well as marketing and distribution in their own host countries, divisions in countries 'A', 'B', 'C' and 'D' may also produce a distinct part of an overall product line that is exported to the others. The net result is that none of the divisions has the complete capability of a single autonomous organisation and they are all dependent on each other for products, resources, technology, information and exporting opportunities.

In the globalised design, top managers at headquarters have the vital task of coordinating strategic objectives, policies for the whole organisation, activities of divisions and the flow of information. Divisional managers tend to be responsible for adjusting their respective divisions to the overall global strategy, ensuring that headquarters get to know about opportunities in their own areas and servicing their local markets (Bartlett 1986). Note, however, that headquarters and divisions share in devising the global strategy, whereas in the international organisation the strategy of overseas divisions is imposed by headquarters, and in a multinational there are different strategies for each country. Probably the most outstanding example of a globalised organisation is Coca-Cola. Some of its products are sold worldwide, while others that cater for local tastes are sold only in certain countries or geographical areas. To avoid cultural clashes in advertising, products are also marketed in slightly different ways in different parts of the world. Moreover, products are distributed via different channels in different places, according to local customs. For example, in some countries through supermarkets in large bottles, while in others nearly everything is sold ready-chilled in cans (Herbert 1988).

Transnational Organisations

As noted in Table 18.1, these organisations have some of the characteristics of all other types of cross-national organisation. Therefore, structure depends to a great extent on the mix of products and services that each organisation provides and it is impossible to identify any general trends in structural design. Some will be remarkably similar to globalised organisations, while others will be more like multinationals.

TIME OUT

Carefully consider the structural characteristics of the international, multinational and globalised organisation, paying particular attention to how each of these types of organisation controls and coordinates the activities of its overseas subsidiaries.

Now consider the jobs of production manager, design and development manager and marketing manager in each of these types of organisation and try to identify what you think would be the likely characteristics of each of these jobs in terms of: degree of autonomy in the job; freedom to innovate; and career prospects within the organisation as a whole.

REPLAY

- The move from being a purely domestic organisation to one that operates worldwide is a leap of quantum proportions which usually takes place in a number of stages and this results in four different types of cross-national organisation: international, multinational, globalised and transnational.
- Each type has a different strategic focus and different ways of pursuing its strategic aims.
- One of the major tools for pursuing these aims is organisational structure and so international, multinational and globalised organisations tend to have different structural designs.

OVERVIEW AND CONCLUSIONS

Organisational structure can have a significant influence on effectiveness and efficiency. Its basic purpose is twofold: to divide up organisational activities and allocate them to sub-units, and to provide mechanisms for coordination and control of these activities so that the organisation as a whole achieves its aims. The most common way of portraying structure is the organisational chart, which tends to mask the true complexity of matters, but an oversimplified view can be avoided if a multidimensional perspective is adopted. However, since the dimensions are related, they should not be treated as discrete features.

Early ideas on structural design, for example those of the classical management theorists, attempted to identify universal principles that would give a structural design suitable for all organisations. These ideas reflected the belief that high degrees of specialisation, centralisation of authority and the formal specification of activities are all necessary in organisations.

In the last four decades new ideas have emerged that reject universal principles and take a contingency approach, in which the most appropriate structural design for an organisation is the one that best copes with its particular circumstances. Contingency theory has extensively considered the effects of organisational size, the technology used by an organisation, and the demands of its environment. In the light of more recent work, it can also be argued that organisational culture is a factor of some importance.

Most theories in organisational design tend to accept that structure is, or should be, an outcome that flows logically from the goals and strategy of a firm. However, the theory of strategic choice points out that matters are not quite this simple. Because managers are likely to be more at ease with some structural arrangements than with others, the values and ideologies of top management are also influential factors in the choice of a structural design; as is the prevailing culture of the whole organisation. Thus structure does not always flow logically and inevitably from a set of organisational goals and strategies. Strategies and goals can sometimes be subject to a degree of revision in order to accommodate structural arrangements that are more comfortable to managers and employees.

For some time now the market contexts with which organisations have had to cope have changed considerably and many firms now seek to engage in a degree of cross-national activity. This has resulted in different types of international organisation, who differ in terms of their strategic focus. Since structure is concerned with achieving the goals and objectives of a firm, these differences in strategic focus tend to result in corresponding differences in organisational design.

FURTHER READING

Bedeian, AG and RF Zammuto (1991) *Organizations: Theory and Design*, Orlando, FL: Dryden. A thorough but readable exploration of organisation theory and organisational design.

Burns, T and GM Stalker (1994) *The Management of Innovation*, Oxford: Oxford University Press. This is a re-print of the original (1961) book, which is by now a classic in organisation theory.

Child, J (1984) *Organisation: A Guide to Problems and Practice*, 2nd edn, London: Harper and Row. Perhaps the most thorough and penetrating consideration of structure yet written, but one that is very easy to read and understand.

Child, J (1997) Strategic choice in the analysis of action, structure, organisations and environments: retrospect and prospect, *Organisational Studies* 18(1): 43–76. The paper re-states its author's theory of strategic choice and reviews the evidence on this matter.

Donaldson, L (2001) *The Contingency Theory of Organisations*, Thousand Oaks, CA: Sage. The book gives a thorough and comprehensive coverage of contingency theory.

DuGuy, P (2000) *In Praise of Bureacracy*, London: Routledge. In the light of the very bad press that bureaucratic organisations have received across the last four decades, this is a timely book. It explores many of the positive aspects of bureaucracy as well as giving a penetrating counter-argument to its many criticisms.

Hinings, CR, L Thibault, J Slack and LM Kikulis (1996) Values and organisational structure, *Human Relations* 49(7): 885–916. An interesting paper that provides support for the idea of a strong connection between organisational structure and culture.

Lawrence, PR and JW Lorsch (1969) *Organisationa and Environment: Managing Differentiation and Integration*, Homewood IL: Irwin Dorsey. Despite its age, the book is still a classic in the literature on organisational design.

Smith, V (1997) New forms of work organisation, *Annual Review of Sociology*, Vol. 23: 315–339, Palo Alto, CA: Annual Reviews Inc. A useful review of recent thinking on organisatonal design.

CASE STUDY 18.1: Organisational design at British Petroleum

The half-year results presented by Tony Hayward, the new chief executive of British Petroleum (BP) reveal that it is a company that still has many strengths. It has good assets in places such as Angola and Azerbaijan, and with the resolution of the dispute over the Kovykta gas field in eastern Siberia, it appears to have stabilised its position in Russia. In addition, the potentially significant exploration deal signed with Libya has raised hopes about its future. Nevertheless, even with his talk emhasising a future focus on 'safe and reliable operations', Mr Hayward is widely acknowledged to be facing a daunting challenge in his bid to turn the company around and in the view of some analysts, he will need to overturn the entire structure and culture of the company.

The roots of today's BP go back to former chairman and chief executive Sir Robert Horton's 'Project 1990' restructuring plan, which had a strong emphasis on cutting back the corporate centre and giving more autonomy to individual business units. Later in Lord Browne's era, BP was characterised by a combination of strict financial controls imposed from the centre, and a high degree of managerial independence in operational terms. For example, business unit leaders (BULs) were put in charge of an operation such as an oil field or group of fields, with staff numbers ranging from a few hundred to a few thousand. They were set demanding financial objectives and then told to get on with it. As one former executive put it: 'The business unit leader was pretty much a medieval lord, as far as the running of his fiefdom was concerned.'

This contrasted sharply with **ExxonMobil**, the acknowledged global leader in the industry for safety and engineering excellence. This is organised on functional lines, so that the global exploration operation is a single division, which helps to spread best practice and new technology rapidly around the company. Rex Tillerson, the chairman, said recently: 'Wherever you travel in the ExxonMobil world, you will hear consistent strategies and approaches, consistent expectations of high standards for safety and operational performance.' Moreover, senior management also takes a hands-on approach.

BP's much less centralised approach to operational decision-making has many strengths: it encourages entrepreneurialism and initiative; it smoothed the rapid integration of the companies that BP acquired between 1998 and 2001, and it helped drive down costs to deliver outstanding financial performance. Nevertheless, it also has its weaknesses. BP was very well configured for the low oil price environment: it could outsource and slash costs very effectively, but getting resources into the right projects is a different challenge altogether and the main challenge now is to get projects executed and completed on time and on budget. Decentralised operations have also inhibited BP's ability to share best practice around the group, which can be vital when investing in challenging and high-value projects, such as the notoriously troubled Thunder Horse platform in the Gulf of Mexico. They also hinder the board in knowing exactly what is occuring on the ground. Indeed, there is a sense that the centre doesn't want to hear bad news, reports a former executive. Moreover, the incentives for the BULs to conceal problems, and the lack of effective ways for top management to check what it is being told, have been blamed for slip-ups such as BP's embarrassing failure to hit its production targets in 2002. In the worst case, top management's lack of detailed operational knowledge has also led to lapses in safety. For example, an internal BP probe into the 2005 Texas City explosion found that John Manzoni, the then-head of refining and marketing, who left BP in May, should have carried out a much deeper probe into the true state of the refinery after clear warning signals from previous accidents. However, attempts at BP to pool the knowledge of its staff worldwide have had a mixed record.

While Mr Hayward, who is an avowed admirer of the standards set by Exxon, does not want to replicate its centralised structure, he does want to strengthen BP's global functions, which could help BP curb its costs. In the past few years, when the emphasis has been on expansion rather than contraction in the industry, cost inflation has been rampant and BP's structure has failed to control costs effectively. Moreover, allowing so much operational independence to the business units has encouraged them to develop their own activities, often chasing up blind alleys or duplicating initiatives. Taking on BP's barons will not be easy, however. Trying to strengthen global functions without adopting Exxon-style centralisation risks foundering, the way that earlier efforts have failed and creating additional costs. The outcome is likely to be decisive in determining whether Mr Hayward's tenure is seen as a success or failure.

Source: Crooks, E (2007) Hayward set his first BP challenge, *Financial Times*, 23 July

Tasks

Working in small groups of three or four students, read the above case material, then answer the questions below.

1. While BP is clearly an international organisation, at present, which of the different categories of cross-national organisation does it fall into?

2. If BP makes the changes that are advocated in the case material, what type of cross-national organisation will it become?

3. What changes will it have to make to do this?

4. In your view, will the advantages of doing this outweigh any disadvantages?

REVIEW AND DISCUSSION QUESTIONS

1. State nine prominent characteristics of Weber's 'ideal type' bureaucracy and explain what each one describes.

2. Define what is meant by a contingency approach to organisational design and explain how this differs from classical organisation theory.

3. Distinguish between mechanistic and organic organisations, and the type of environmental circumstances to which each is most suited.

4. State the four research questions addressed by Lawrence and Lorsch (1969) in their studies of the relationship between environment and structure, and describe the three prominent conclusions that emerged from their work.

5. Name the three types of technology that Thompson (1967) uses to distinguish between organisations and explain the distinguishing features of these technologies.

6. What is the major conclusion of Woodward's study of the effects of technology on structure in manufacturing organisations?

7. Describe the way in which the culture of an organisation can place limits on its freedom to adopt a new structural design and the ways in which the culture of the top management group in an organisation can be a limiting factor on decisions about a structural design.

8. Name five different types of cross-national organisation and describe the structural designs associated with each type.

Chapter 19

Organisational Control

LEARNING OUTCOMES

After studying this chapter you should be able to:

- define control and distinguish between three alternative perspectives on control in organisations

- distinguish between open-loop (feedforward) and closed-loop (feedback) control and use the control model to diagnose potential weaknesses in different management control systems

- in outline, describe the main features of seven traditional methods of behavioural control used by organisations and compare these with recent developments in management control regimes

- explain why employees sometimes resist control

- evaluate whether recent developments in management control regimes are likely to result in the demise of employee resistance

INTRODUCTION

To ensure that goals and objectives are achieved, it is necessary to coordinate an organisation's activities and this makes control an important process in any organisation. However, because this involves controlling the behaviour of people, which smacks of coercion, manipulation or even exploitation, control can be a controversial activity. To cover these issues the chapter starts by defining control and tracing its purpose in organisations. This is followed by an exploration of three contrasting perspectives on control, after which the control model, a device for analysing control systems, is presented.

The remainder of the chapter focuses on behavioural control; first by describing some of the traditional ways of controlling human behaviour in organisations and, second, by explaining recent developments in managerial control regimes. Resistance to control is then explored and the chapter closes with a short overview section.

THE PURPOSE OF ORGANISATIONAL CONTROL

There are many definitions of control, but this chapter purposely opens with a broad one, which is:

> the regulation of organisational activities so that some targeted element of performance remains within acceptable limits.   (Barney and Griffin 1992, p 329)

As was noted in Chapter 1, organisations are brought into existence to achieve something and this involves structuring human activity in an enterprise. The primary purpose of control is to coordinate different organisational activities in order to achieve the goals for the whole organisation. For this reason, control is normally applied at all organisational levels: the organisation as a whole has to be controlled in order to ensure that it adopts an appropriate stance *vis-à-vis* its environment and, at lower levels, control is applied to synchronise the activities of groups and individuals to ensure that they play their respective parts in achieving goals. This means that control is not a 'one-off' activity, but an ongoing process that:

- monitors what is achieved
- compares what is achieved with what should be achieved
- takes remedial action (where necessary) to ensure that discrepancies are corrected.

Thus goals and objectives are crucial elements in the control process and, as is pointed out in Chapter 16, goals are normally arranged as a means–ends hierarchy, in which the goals at one level in the hierarchy are the means of achieving the goals at the level immediately above. Therefore, from a purely management perspective it is desirable that a control mechanism should exist for every goal that is set. For this reason, a great deal of effort is normally devoted to controlling organisational and employee activities. Indeed, it is not so much a matter of whether these control activities are necessary, but whether human beings would be capable of coping mentally with a situation in which there was blissful ignorance of whether their plans and goals were successful in achieving the intended outcomes.

TIME OUT

Think carefully about an organisation in which you are, or have been, employed. If you have no experience of paid employment, either full-time or part-time, use the department of the university or college at which you study for this exercise and answer the questions below.

1. What do you feel are the goals or objectives for the department in which you work?
2. Can you identify any controls that attempt to ensure that the activities of the people in the department are coordinated in order to achieve the departmental goals?
3. What goals or objectives are set for these people and how is it determined whether they have achieved their objectives?
4. If everyone in the department achieved his or her objectives, would this result in the goals for the department as a whole being achieved?

REPLAY

- Control systems do not exist in a vacuum, but are intended to make it more likely that formal goals are achieved.
- Any activity that is important enough to warrant a goal being set should normally have its own associated control mechanism.
- Since goals are arranged hierarchically, with those at one level being the means of achieving the goals for the level above, higher level goals are only achieved where operational goals are also achieved.

ALTERNATIVE VIEWS ON CONTROL IN ORGANISATIONS

While few people would question the idea that complex organisations need to be managed and coordinated, this can give a false impression that control is a harmless, neutral activity. Control can exist for a number of reasons, and it can be exercised for a wide variety of motives and in an equally wide variety of ways. There are a number of different schools of thought on the use of control in organisations, but for the sake of simplicity, discussion will be confined to three contrasting perspectives: the

Table 19.1 Three perspectives on control

	Managerialist perspective	Open systems perspective	Political perspective
Underlying assumptions	Control of resources (including human resources) is a legitimate management activity. Therefore, managers have the right to exercise control over the behaviour of subordinates	Control mediates processes that transform inputs into outputs; for instance, budgetary control attempts to regulate financial resources used in the transformation process and performance appraisal to achieve the most appropriate use of human resources While control itself is neutral, it can have adverse consequences for humans	Control is synonymous with the exploitation of human resources
Major concerns of the perspective	Identification of methods that can best be used by managers to exercise control	Modelling control systems for design, analysis and fault-finding purposes	Understanding the internal dynamics of control, e.g. how control is exercised and whether it gives rise to resistance or attempted counter-control

managerialist perspective; the *open systems perspective*; and the *political perspective*. These are shown in Table 19.1.

The Managerialist Perspective on Control

This represents a view that controlling others is a legitimate management activity – the so-called 'right to manage'. Its origins can be traced to the writings of classical management theorists and, in particular, Henri Fayol (1916), who defined the five major functions of management as: planning, organising, command, coordination and control. Since it goes to the very heart of achieving objectives, many managers would argue that control is the most important of these.

While it is not surprising that most managers feel this way, the view is also reflected in a number of academic texts, such as Barney and Griffin (1992) who write about control as something akin to a management right. Mullins (2002) goes even further by suggesting that when an employee asks his or her manager 'how well am I doing?' the person is asking to be controlled, which comes close to portraying the control activity as a piece of managerial social work. Many managers, it can be noted, argue that what differentiates them from other employees is that they are allocated resources and are made responsible for their efficient and effective utilisation. From this it is but a short step to laying claim to a right to command employee actions.

The Open Systems Perspective

This perspective neither condemns nor endorses control. Instead, it takes the view that because of the size and complexity of organisations, control is inevitable and, that this can have a number of benefits, such as:

- improved economic efficiency and the best use of scarce resources
- predictability, stability, order and reliability

- people know what they have to do, which avoids the ambiguity, that many people find distressing.

Notwithstanding these advantages the perspective also acknowledges that what makes control such a controversial matter is its application to people as well as machines. Thus it can be applied inappropriately or for suspect reasons, which can have a number of dysfunctional effects:

- coercion, manipulation or exploitation
- people lose their individuality and innovation can be stifled
- people have little or no say in matters that affect them and can become dependent on being controlled.

These matters will be further amplified presently in discussing the control model.

The Political Perspective

This perspective has become highly influential over the last two decades and a number of authors, such as Willmott (1977), have argued that control in organisations often goes well beyond the search for economic efficiency. Indeed, he notes that much management action has a strong focus on domination and exploitation, which is made relatively easy because managers control the distribution of rewards, which allows them to obtain compliant behaviour that facilitates the strong manipulating and exploiting the weak. For this reason, the political perspective on control has a strong focus on *social control*, in which compliance, conformity and obedience are achieved through processes that occur between groups and individuals. For instance, it has been observed that managers' activities tend to be more concerned with controlling employees than coordinating their efforts and this results in ever-increasing inequalities in the distribution of rewards, and an inbuilt tendency for workers to resist control. Thus the main focus of this perspective is the attempted subordination of labour and employee attempts at counter-control.

Social control: achieving compliance, conformity or obedience through interpersonal or intergroup processes

The roots of this approach can be traced to Marx's (1894/1974) analysis of the capitalist mode of production; something that has subsequently become known as the labour process. There is, of course, a lot more to Marx's work than the examination of industry, and it is a theory that encompasses the whole structuring of society. Nevertheless, Marx notes that under capitalism, the relationship between employer and employee is essentially based on inequality and exploitation. For example, only part of the surplus value created in transforming raw materials into saleable goods is returned to the worker in the form of wages; the rest is retained by the employer.

From the early 1970s onwards, there was a rekindling of interest in the use of Marxist principles to analyse aspects of the employment relationship, which was prompted by a rediscovery of Marx's ideas by Braverman (1974), who argued that in the twentieth century work has been consciously de-skilled by employers by the use of scientific management techniques to lower costs. However, there is an ongoing debate about how widely Braverman's analysis can be applied, and whether Taylorist forms of control have been as absolute as Braverman suggested. Nevertheless, labour process theory has resulted in a very rich stream of work that seeks to explain the process of managerial control and the attendant conflicts that occur at work.

REPLAY

- Organisational control systems do not exist in a vacuum, but are intended to make it likely that formal goals are achieved.
- The managerialist perspective on control views it as something that managers exercise by right.
- The open systems perspective views control as something that is necessary in organisations, but which can have a number of adverse consequences.
- The political perspective focuses on the internal dynamics of the control of people in organisations and assumes that control can lead to exploitation, which in turn leads to resistance to control.

THE CYBERNETIC MODEL OF CONTROL

Cybernetics: the theoretical study of control processes in electrical, mechanical and biological systems

Control model: a symbolic representation of the components necessary for a system of control, how they relate to each other and their functions

As noted, what makes control such a controversial matter in organisations is its application to humans. To understand the processes involved, it can be useful to approach the matter in a detached way, leaving ethical considerations temporarily on one side. For this reason a concept will be borrowed from *cybernetics*: the theoretical study of control processes in electrical, mechanical and biological systems. While cybernetics can be highly mathematical, one of its basic tools – the *control model* – gives a symbolic representation, of the components necessary for a system of control, their functions and how they relate to each other. This model has two main uses: as a checklist for designing control systems and as a diagnostic tool to pinpoint faults if a control system is not functioning correctly. It will be used for both of these purposes at various points in the remainder of the chapter. First, however, it is necessary to explain the model.

Control: the Basic Requirements

The starting point of the control model is that a process or activity exists which needs to be controlled. This is shown in its simplest form in Figure 19.1 and, while the process has inputs and outputs, without exception it is the outputs that employers seek to control. The first requirement for control is to know something about the relationship between the inputs and the outputs. For instance, in an organisational process that produces goods or services, it is necessary to know:

- that the required quantity of labour with the appropriate skills is available
- that tools, machines, raw materials, etc. are all present.

Figure 19.1 The process or activity to be controlled

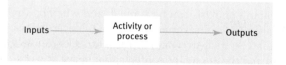

Figure 19.2 Open-loop (feedforward) control

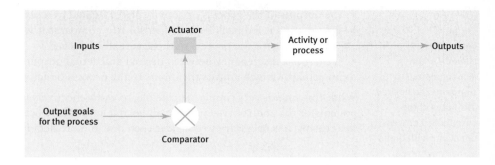

Figure 19.3 Closed-loop (feedback) control

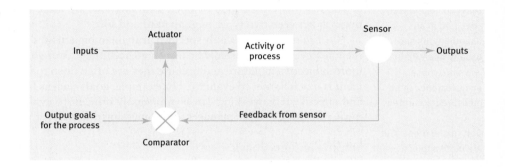

From here onwards it is necessary to select between two basic control options: open-loop (feedforward) control and closed-loop (feedback) control. These are shown in Figures 19.2 and 19.3 respectively.

As can be seen, the only difference between the two options is that in closed-loop control there is a sensor on the output side of the process, together with a feedback loop to a comparator, the functions of which will be considered presently.

Open-loop Control

Open-loop (feedforward) control: a method in which the inputs to a process or activity are carefully determined, but with no monitoring of outputs

In *open-loop control* it is normally assumed that the workings of the process or activity are so perfectly understood that the required outputs will be obtained so long as the required inputs are fed into the process. There are plenty of examples in everyday life where open-loop methods are encountered. For instance, in convenience foods, such as cake mixes and TV dinners, the ingredients all come pre-packaged and if the instructions are closely followed with respect to mixing, cooking times, temperatures, etc. a usable finished product is obtained. In many organisational activities, particularly those with human inputs, the workings of the process are not precisely known so it is not considered safe to rely on open-loop control.

Closed-loop Control

Closed-loop (feedback) control: a method in which the outputs of a process or activity are monitored and, if necessary, inputs are adjusted to achieve the desired outputs

With *closed-loop control* the assumptions about complete understanding of the workings of the process are not made, and the basic sequence of activities is:

- the outputs of the process or activity are evaluated by a sensor
- information is fed back from the sensor to a comparator which compares the output goals for the process to those actually achieved
- if there is a discrepancy between desired and actual outputs, information is fed to an actuator which adjusts the inputs to the process or activity accordingly.

While this sounds very simple in principle, to work effectively it requires that the components of the control system must all be able to perform certain functions and, for this reason, it is necessary to consider each one in more detail.

Comparator: something (or someone) that compares the desired attributes of the outputs of a process or activity with those actually achieved

Goals and Comparator

A first requirement is to be able to specify the output goals for the process, and this is true whether closed-loop or open-loop methods are used. Here it is useful to distinguish between two types of goal: hard and soft.

Hard goals can be precisely specified in an unambiguous and quantifiable way. Thus their achievement can usually be measured accurately. *Soft goals*, however, are much more subjective in nature and because they are often open to interpretation, achievement is much harder to evaluate. For example, goals such as high workgroup morale and effective teamworking can be immensely difficult to evaluate, because they can mean one thing for one manager and something different for another.

Hard goals: those that can be precisely specified in an unambiguous and usually quantifiable way and whose achievement can be measured accurately

Soft goals: those that are more subjective and qualitative in nature, open to interpretation and whose achievement is much harder to evaluate

Sensors and Feedback

Sensors must be able to evaluate the desired attributes of the outputs of the process. For instance, if the workgroup used as an example so far has a quality goal of say a maximum reject rate of 3 per cent, the sensor will need to collect two pieces of information: the number of items produced and the number of rejects. A problem that can occur here is the speed at which information is fed back to the comparator. Because continuous monitoring is prohibitively expensive, most work activity is monitored by *sampling*. And so there can be time lags in taking appropriate remedial action.

Another difficulty that can plague sensing is the effect of monitoring outputs. Machines do not have feelings and monitoring does not affect the process or the activity, but where humans are involved monitoring can have a huge impact on the way an activity is performed. For example, if people resent being observed, they can usually find ways of distorting the situation, which means that monitoring becomes counter-productive.

Sensor: something (or someone) that monitors the attributes of the output of a process or activity

Sampling: the characteristics of the total output of a process or activity is estimated by examining only a proportion of the output

The Actuator

Since many processes or activities have multiple inputs, separate *actuators* are required to regulate the supply of each one. Indeed, separate actuators are often needed to regulate different attributes of an input. For instance, in the case of the workgroup described above, the actuator that adjusts the quantity of labour (number of people or hours worked) would need to be very different from the one that adjusts the skills of the workforce.

While it is usually fairly easy to determine whether an acutator works properly in a mechanical system, this is not always the case with humans. For instance, if jobs are designed by using scientific management principals, payment is usually made contingent on effort, which assumes that the main (if not only) thing that motivates people

Actuators: things that adjust the inputs to a process or activity

Normative inputs:
human values,
attitudes, beliefs
and motivations

is money. Since we know that people also require a degree of intrinsic motivation, this is a half-truth, and it is now widely acknowledged that a host of *normative inputs*, such as values, attitudes, beliefs and motivations, are important inputs to any process that involves human effort. These all come from within the person and although managers might like to think that they can directly control them, this is nothing more than wishful thinking.

The Control Model: An Evaluation

As was pointed out earlier, the control model has two main uses: as a device to design control systems and as a tool to diagnose problems with existing systems of control. While it can be a powerful instrument for either purpose, it is important to recognise that a number of criticisms of the model have been voiced, the most important of which are:

- It treats control as an engineering exercise, in which the properties of everything are unvarying and well known, whereas some of the greatest difficulties arise in the use of highly variable human factors.
- Because it focuses exclusively on achieving goals that have already been decided, it takes these for granted, which ignores the possibility that the goals themselves could be inappropriate.
- It regards goals and goal setting as unproblematic, whereas in Chapter 16 it is pointed out that goals are often compromises rather than statements of unassailable logic.
- It tends to assume that links between cause and effect are perfectly understood, and in many cases this not a safe assumption.
- It tends to assume that all the resources for a process or activity are readily available in sufficient quantities and qualities.

Although these criticisms are perfectly valid, it should be remembered that the model is simply an analytical tool and so everything depends on how it is used. If suitable allowances are made for these points, it is too valuable a model to discard and, for this reason, it will be used at various points throughout the chapter to illustrate some of the problems that arise in control systems.

TIME OUT

Reflect carefully on the study activities that you undertake as a student at the university or college that you attend. Focus on a particular module or subject that you study and answer the questions below.

1. What standards of performance are set for you and who sets these standards?
2. What are the inputs to the process in which you learn the subject material?
3. Assuming that an important output of the learning process is that you understand (and can apply) the subject material, is this output monitored in any way and, if so, how is this done?
4. Is there any provision to compare this output (learning) with the standard of performance you identified in question 1? If so, who or what makes this comparison?

5. If a discrepancy was identified between your actual output and the targeted output you identified in question 1, what provision is there to adjust the inputs to the learning process? Who or what makes this adjustment?
6. Map your answers to questions 1–5 on an appropriate control model. In your view is the learning process controlled by open-loop or closed-loop methods?
7. In your view how effective is this control?

REPLAY

- The control model, which originated in the field of cybernetics, gives a symbolic representation of the components in a system of control, their functions and how they relate to each other.
- Open-loop (feedforward) control assumes that the workings of the process or activity to be controlled are perfectly understood and that the required outputs are obtained by using inputs of the required quantities and qualities.
- Closed-loop (feedback) control contains a stage in which the outputs of a process or activity are monitored in order to detect discrepancies between actual and desired outputs so that remedial action can be taken if necessary.
- Either model can be used as a tool to design control systems or diagnose faults in those that exist.

BEHAVIOURAL CONTROL

Power and Control

Manager-directed control: managers specify exactly how and what should be done and closely monitor employee behaviour

Bureaucratic control: the use of tight job specifications and standard operating procedures to specify employee behaviour, which become the accepted ways of doing things to which employees conform

Control cannot be divorced from the use of power, if only because managers and supervisors usually have a degree of authority in organisations and for this reason they are likely to assume that they have the right to control the behaviour of others. This can have a strong impact on the relationship between an organisation and its employees. And as Stewart (1991) points out, one of the dilemmas created by the desire to be 'in control' is that managers feel a need to obtain two different patterns of employee behaviour that are difficult to reconcile. On one hand they want order and predictability in employees, which implies the need to tightly specify employee behaviour. On the other hand, they also want employees to be flexible, innovative and to show initiative, which implies giving them a high degree of discretion. Paradoxically, these twin requirements are so different that an emphasis on one can lead to a near absence of the other. Thus exerting control over employee behaviour involves a trade-off between order and flexibility and Stewart illustrates this by contrasting three control strategies which can be placed along the continuum shown in Figure 19.4.

Manager-directed control has a strong emphasis on the predictability of employee behaviour, and in control model terms, this corresponds to a strict application of closed-loop control techniques. At the middle position on the continuum is *bureaucratic control*, in which limits are placed on employee discretion by clearly defining an

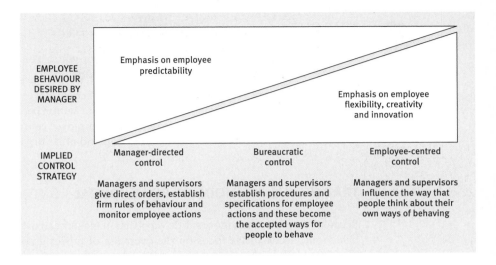

Figure 19.4
Management control strategies (adapted from Stewart 1991)

employee's role with a tight job specification and by using standard operating procedures to specify *how* things should be done. While there would still be some monitoring of employees, this would probably consist of a somewhat looser application of closed-loop methods.

Employee-centred control has a strong emphasis on obtaining a high degree of flexibility, creativity and innovation in employees. In theory this means that they exercise a high degree of self-control and the task of management is to get employees to control themselves in a way that delivers the behaviour that managers want. Since this reduces the need for monitoring, control is much nearer to open-loop methods.

A move from left to right on this continuum represents what Friedman (1977) calls a shift from 'direct control' to 'responsible autonomy', which uses what Walton (1985) calls a commitment strategy. Note, however, that all three options are equally control-orientated. Indeed, over 40 years ago Tannenbaum (1962) argued that by using participation to create an impression of shared decision making, managers can lower employee resentment at being controlled and retain the better part of control to themselves. Thus management control strategies always involve the use of power and it is not so much a question of whether power is used, but how it is used.

Employee-centred control: a 'hearts and minds' strategy that involves influencing the way that employees think about themselves and what they do so that they willingly subscribe to management's aims

REPLAY

- Behavioural control is mainly exercised by supervisors and managers who are granted a degree of formal authority by an organisation to direct the activities of subordinates: thus control cannot be divorced from the use of power.

- Supervisors and managers have control strategies, which relate to their use of formal authority, and one way to classify these control strategies is along a continuum, the extremes of which are manager-directed control and employee-centred control.

TIME OUT

Carefully reflect on the organisation/institution for which you work or study, either full-time or part-time, and answer the question below.

All organisations require their members (whether employees or volunteers) to comply with rules that constrain their behaviour within certain limits. What type of control (manger directed, bureaucratic or employee centred) is used by the organisation to obtain compliance from you and other organisational members?

TRADITIONAL METHODS OF BEHAVIOURAL CONTROL

Portfolio approach to control: the use of different strategies for controlling human behaviour according to which one is seen to be most applicable at the time

Because there are other, more subtle ways that managers can use to influence employee behaviour, an exclusive focus on the overt use of power gives a misleading picture of control. Child (1984) argues that managers are adaptive in their use of control techniques, with many of them employing a *portfolio approach*, in which different control methods are applied to different groups of employees (or at different times) according to what managers hope to achieve. Thus a number of the most commonly used methods will be described, and a return will be made to how they are related at the end of this section.

Input Control: Recruitment, Selection and Socialisation

Although at first sight these activities do not look like a control mechanism, organisations usually try to employ people who can be relied on to behave as required; those who are seen to 'fit in'. In order to make decisions about this, management has a wide range of techniques at its disposal to attract, recruit and select employees. At the selection stage, which relies heavily on open-loop control, the process enables a line to be drawn between those allowed to become organisational members and those who are not, and a recent study by Callaghan and Thompson (2002) illustrates the length to which some employers go to achieve these aims.

Once admitted to an organisation, further closed-loop methods come into play in which people are subjected to a variety of pressures from peers and superiors to conform to established ways of doing things. In essence, this process of *socialisation* is a method of behavioural control in which attempts are made to ensure that those recruited are susceptible to other methods of control. While managers seem to have great faith in their abilities to select appropriate entrants to an organisation, there is strong evidence that the selection process is not very effective in predicting future employee performance. For this reason, it is often socialisation that plays a far bigger part in the process of control.

TIME OUT

Using the same organisation as in the previous Time Out exercise, try to remember the time when you were selected to enter the organisation and answer the questions below.

1. In what ways do you feel that the selection process was a conscious attempt by the organisation to exercise control over the quality of human resource inputs to organisational processes and activities? What evidence do you use to support this idea?

2. To what extent do you feel that any induction process you received when first joining the organisation (including interaction with your peers and immediate superior) was concerned with exercising control over your future behaviour in the organisation? What evidence do you use to support this idea?

Rewards and Punishments

There are many ways in which rewards and punishments are used to try to bring employee behaviour under control. Although it is widely assumed by managers that *all* employees will expend effort in return for rewards, to rely completely on this happening of its own accord would mean relying on open-loop control. Thus some degree of direct control over their efforts has traditionally been regarded as normal. One way of doing this is to link rewards to effort by using incentive payments, and managers seem to have a sublime belief that incentive payments place them (the managers) firmly in control of the effort that people put into their work. Thus, reward power (see Chapter 14) is used to obtain their compliance. With salaried workers, however, it is near impossible to do this because incentives are usually vague and indeterminate; for example, they consist of such things as merit payments, fringe benefits, security or the prospects of promotion. Moreover, most salary earners look upon themselves as distinctly different from those who earn wages, and it is often assumed that higher-level salaried workers have a degree of moral involvement with the organisation.

To some extent punishment – the reverse of reward – is also used to obtain compliance (see Chapter 14). However, trade unions and the law often put limits on management's freedom of action in this matter.

Appraisal, Training and Development

Just as selection can be likened to a filter that admits only some of those who apply to join an organisation, appraisal, training and development are processes that can be used to reinforce the desired characteristics of those who are admitted. In most appraisal schemes, superiors evaluate their subordinates and decisions about whether some form of training or development will be provided are usually made by the immediate superior. Thus the processes are strongly linked and both provide opportunities to control the behaviour of employees.

Since an explicit link between performance and rewards is usually made in appraisal, the process can become little more than a very crude form of psychological conditioning, in which employees learn to shape their behaviour into something that is personally acceptable to their superiors (Salaman 1978).

Direct Control

Employee monitoring by supervisors and managers is the oldest method of behavioural control, and to some extent everybody is subject to it. Nevertheless, the ways in which this occurs can vary considerably, as can the intensity with which control is applied.

For instance, mild control might consist of giving instructions on what should be done, with periodic checks to see that the instructions are observed. At the other extreme, very explicit instructions can be given about what is to be done and how it must be done, with almost continuous surveillance of the subordinate's actions and results.

Because other systems of control are now beginning to appear it is often assumed that these have replaced direct control. However, detailed research in organisations that have adopted modern control methods has clearly revealed that supervisors still have important control functions – either to make the newer methods work, or to exercise control where the newer methods fail to work as intended (Mulholland 2002). Thus the redundancy of direct control is almost certainly exaggerated (Thompson and Ackroyd 1995).

Technology and Job Design

Technology generally denotes the means by which tasks are accomplished. This is usually a management choice, and it can have a huge effect on the ability to exercise control. For example, work on a mass production assembly line is machine-paced, so that it is the speed at which the line moves that dictates how much employee effort is required. The same is also true of newer workplaces such as call centres, where technology dictates the pace of employee–customer interactions (Bain and Taylor 2000).

Another way in which management can attempt to control the efficiency and effectiveness of employees is to design jobs with an eye to their motivational content. How to get the most willing work performance from subordinates has long been a concern of management, and across the years there have been a whole string of theories about what motivates employees, all of which imply that human behaviour can be made more controllable (see Chapters 7 and 8).

Control through Structure

Organisational structure and design, which are covered respectively in Chapters 17 and 18, result in some degree of specialisation of activities, together with a hierarchy of authority. A characteristic way of achieving control is through this hierarchy; for example, by specifying roles and rules that lay down the activities undertaken by role occupants. These details are often included in job descriptions, works rules and operational procedures, and are incorporated into the contract of employment, which gives a large measure of control over employee behaviour.

These features also shape behaviour in other subtler ways. Differences in authority not only map out the formal power of managers to reward some behaviour and punish that which is prohibited, differences in power also have psychological effects. They establish embedded rules of conduct that are taken for granted and which legitimise management power so that those lower down cooperate in their own subjugation. Thus, for many people, pursuing management's will comes to be seen as organisational common sense (Weick 2001).

Output Control

Output control: results to be achieved are specified in terms of outputs, a degree of discretion is permitted in how they are achieved, and outputs are subsequently monitored

As noted earlier, bureaucratic control focuses on two main aspects of a process or activity: *what* is done and *how* things are done. A variant of this approach, which introduces an element of open-loop methods is *output control*, which consists of:

- specifying the desired results (outputs) that should be obtained, perhaps by setting targets and time scales
- holding the person concerned responsible for achieving these ends, but also granting a degree of discretion about how this is done
- reviewing achievement at a later date.

This cycle is fundamental to most schemes of performance appraisal and it is widely used at middle management levels in systems of budgetary control, in which managers are set output and resource usage targets. For managers and other employees who have responsibilities that are not so easily translated into financial results, a similar way of using output control is the use of a scheme of Management by Objectives (MBO). In theory this consists of a number of steps, which are shown in outline in Figure 19.5.

Because it is concerned with achieving goals, monitoring feedback and, if necessary, some regulation of inputs, in control model terms MBO conforms to closed-loop principles and the following advantages are usually claimed for it:

- Since the subordinate is involved in selecting targets and defining his or her own job, the person is said to be more highly motivated to perform well.
- The joint setting of targets also means that the superior gains a better understanding of the subordinate's problems and is able to assess what changes are needed to remove impediments to objectives being achieved.

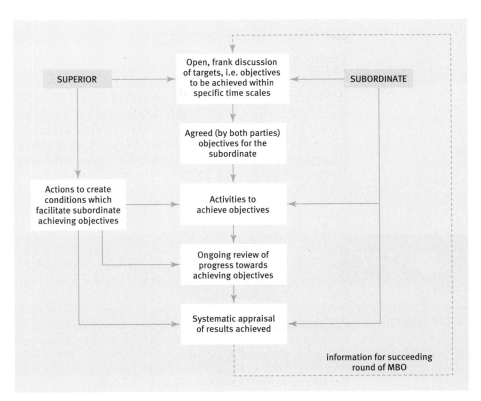

Figure 19.5 An outline of the management by objectives process

- Information from the goal-setting and review stages can be valuable in identifying training needs, education and personal development programmes.
- Information from the MBO process can provide a thorough and systematic method of deciding whether individuals are ready for promotion.
- The criteria (performance achievements) are applied to everybody, which in the case of promotion decisions demonstrates that decisions are fair.

Notwithstanding these points, it is important to stress that what is shown in Figure 19.5 is MBO in theory, and in practice things can be somewhat different because:

- power is unequally distributed in all organisational hierarchies and this results in an ever-present danger that goals are imposed, rather than agreed
- unless jobs can be redesigned before using MBO so that a subordinate becomes responsible for a complete unit of output, the running of which is completely under his or her control, it is hard to see how meaningful goals can be derived and it can even result in resistance to the control (Covaleski *et al.* 1998)
- goals preferably need to be set in quantitative terms and for some jobs, the most important outputs are qualitative.

For these reasons, it should not be taken for granted that MBO works effectively as a control mechanism in all situations and for all employees. Nevertheless, in one form or another, MBO is widely used and, in the guise of performance appraisal, it is applied at almost all organisational levels.

Control by Culture

A culture is a system of shared beliefs and values, which tells people about the behaviour that is accepted as normal by other people in a particular context. Since managers first discovered the topic in the 1980s, their interest has largely been focused on its potential use as a mechanism of control. For this reason, attempts to change cultures have become an essential element in recent developments in control regimes. These will be described presently and, in the meantime, traditional methods of behavioural control are summarised in Table 19.2.

REPLAY

- Traditional methods of behavioural control rely on a combination of: input control (recruitment, selection and socialisation); rewards and punishments; appraisal, training and development; direct control (personal supervision); technology and job design; control through structure; output control; and cultural control.

Table 19.2 Comparison of traditional methods of behavioural control

Method	Aims	Control model components and type of control	Most frequently used in conjunction with
Recruitment, selection and socialisation	To control the quality of human resource inputs	Actuator in open or closed-loop control	All other methods
Appraisal, training and development	To set goals for individuals, monitor performance and identify what is necessary to maintain/improve performance	Goals, monitoring, comparator and actuator in closed-loop control	All other methods
Direct control	To provide instruction and clarity about task performance and obtain compliant behaviour	Goals, monitoring comparator and actuator in closed-loop control	All other methods
Technology and job design	To place constraints on employee behaviour by regulating what is done, how it is done and how much is done	The actuator, monitor and comparator in closed-loop control	Rewards, punishments and structure
Rewards and punishment	Provide inducements to behave as required and disincentives to unwanted behaviour	The actuator, monitor and comparator in closed-loop control	Appraisal, training and development
Structure (bureaucratic control)	Establish rules and procedures to limit discretion and make behaviour more consistent and predictable	The actuator, monitor and comparator in closed-loop control	Appraisal, training and development, and sometimes as substitute for direct control
Output control	To set goals for individuals, monitor performance, and adjust targets	Goals, monitoring and actuator in closed-loop control	Appraisal, training and development, technology, job design and structure

 OB IN ACTION: Is Big Brother watching you?

The recent report of the Information Commissioner (IC) points out that we live in a surveillance society. It catalogues in detail the technologies and processes by which we are all logged, profiled and digitised daily, both at work and at play. For instance: credit, loyalty and swipe cards; mobile phones; congestion charges; work log-ins and activity monitors; and interactions with public- and private-sector call centres, not to mention the ubiquitous use of CCTV cameras. A striking measure of the burgeoning of surveillance is the growth of the industry that provides it: for example, in the three years to 2006 the top 100 US surveillance companies had doubled in value to $400bn.

Nevertheless, individual surveillance uses are hard to track and regulate, and one problem is that technology runs ahead of the ability to foresee its implications.

▶

Another is the phenomenon of 'function creep', in which a mechanism set up for one purpose, such as a travel card, is then used for another, such as tracking movement. Thus increasingly complex networks of information-sharing across the private and public sectors make it almost impossible for people to assert their right to know the information held about them. Indeed, although insulated from the office by mobiles and laptops, some remote teleworkers now find they are more controlled and monitored than before. For reasons such as these, the use of data for racial and postcode profiling and credit checks is probably just the beginning. Indeed, when you contact some call centres you are categorised by level of spending and served accordingly. However, not all surveillance is bad – accurate records can protect the innocent as well as identify the wrongdoers – and some of it, as the IC notes, is an inescapable part of modern life. Nevertheless, although the technology itself is neutral, the use made of it can be anything but. Thus the report warns that it can be naïve and dangerous to sleepwalk into a world where gathering, processing and sorting personal data is no longer just an overlay, like CCTV cameras, but a part of life's basic infrastucture, which occurs without a debate or an understanding of what it means.

Part of the inherent danger is mistakes rather than conspiracy, and at a basic level so much of the information gathered is simply wrong. One study found that 22 per cent of a sample of entries into a police computer contained errors, even when double-checked. Names were misspelled and addresses wrongly coded, and the impact of such errors is compounded by sharing data sources. Even worse, they are not remedied by the enthusiastic addition of more technology. Indeed, as the IC report points out, as well as locking us into the technology, this often makes the original problem still harder to unravel.

Ultimately, surveillance is a substitute for trust. At work or as cititzens, some people break trust, so surveillance is necessary. The dilemma is that by fostering suspicion and making people feel mistrusted, it increases the chances that they act in ways that seem to justify even more surveillance.

Source:

Caulkin, S (2007b) Watch it, or surveillance will take over our lives, *The Observer* 19 August

RECENT DEVELOPMENTS IN BEHAVIOURAL CONTROL

Over 20 years ago Edwards (1979), in reviewing the historic sequence of changes in control methods, predicted that some form of post-bureaucratic control was likely to emerge. He also forecast that this would most likely be based on more sophisticated monitoring techniques, utilising advanced information technology (see the OB in Action Box above for a current commentary on this trend). Even before then, however, managers had long desired self-disciplined employees, who do what managers want in a willing, productive and conscientious way, without the need for their efforts to be directly supervised. Electronic surveillance now offers the tantalising prospect of being able to obtain greater managerial control over employee effort. It also increases the possibility of introducing open-loop control methods, which are infinitely cheaper and more flexible than closed-loop methods, the net result of which is a potentially 'self-correcting' work system. However, as was noted earlier, open-loop control can only be used where two conditions are satisfied: first, where there is perfect knowledge of cause–effect relationships in the process to be controlled; and, second, where inputs to the process are accurately regulated. With work systems, in practice, this would mean that:

- it is known for certain that all the required inputs are fed into the work system in the correct quantities
- the qualitative characteristics of these inputs are exactly known
- there is certain knowledge of the effects that these different inputs have on each other.

With physical inputs these things are not usually problematic, but humans are highly variable. They have feelings, emotions and minds of their own, and react to situations in very different and unpredictable ways. Therefore, open-loop methods can only be used if control can be exercised over what employees 'think', so that they think in the way that managers want them to think, and this is a lot easier said than done.

Because thoughts are invisible, we have no idea of what people think until the results of their thoughts appear as visible actions. Nevertheless, this does not stop managers yearning for self-regulating work systems and so the current trend is to try to get as near as possible to open-loop conditions. To do this, some organisations are beginning to make use of control techniques that were relatively unknown in a prior era. Although there is one school of thought which argues that this is a radical break with the past, the perspective adopted here is that recent systems of control use additional techniques that have been superimposed on older methods, to give new and more intense control regimes (Casey 1999). As yet no definitive model that describes these regimes has yet emerged, but Gabriel (1999) points out that they have some or all of the following features:

- The use of symbolic manipulation of meanings in a concerted attempt by managers to change employee cultures so that workers internalise the importance of service, quality, excellence, teamwork and loyalty.

- Changes to structures and, in particular, the use of flatter hierarchies, flexible working practices, continuous benchmarking and performance measurement.

- Changes in manufacturing techniques to introduce lean production, total quality management (TQM) and just-in-time (JIT) methods.

- Changed methods of surveillance, including widespread use of electronic cameras, performance monitoring technologies, electronic tagging and methods that enable identification of individuals who are the source of operational problems.

An important thing about these features is that they are mutually reinforcing. This is shown in Figure 19.6 and the ways in which they combine is explained in what follows.

Figure 19.6 Current developments in behavioural control: the key elements

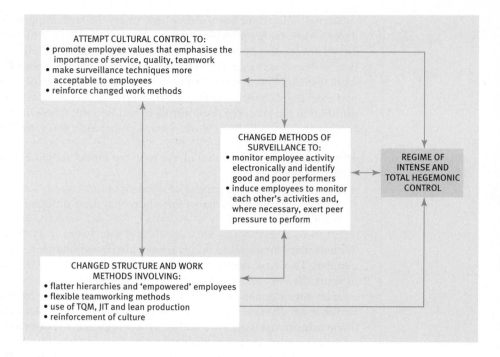

Cultural Control

While rudimentary attempts to manipulate organisational cultures have been attempted since the 1980s, the cultural element in the new systems of control has more specific ends in mind. These are:

- to make the new surveillance practices that are described presently the norm and more acceptable to employees
- to lead to greater effort on the part of employees
- to reduce levels of dissent or discontent, including any form of resistance or protest via trade unions (Casey 1999; Purcell 1993).

The objective is to win over employees in supporting organisational goals, and to induce them to embrace a highly personalised relationship with the organisation, in which the individual's self-identity is largely derived from organisational membership (Jermier *et al.* 1994). The whole approach aims for an image of the firm as one big happy family, to which the employee has (or should have) a strong emotional and psychological attachment. One in which the employee comes to accept that unswerving loyalty, intense effort and unquestioning obedience must be given to remain part of the family. In short, a system of totalised control, in which any allegiances to other bodies, such as unions or occupational or professional bodies, is abandoned.

Cultural change is not easily accomplished and the ways of trying to do this are outlined later in Chapter 19. It is important to stress again that the aim of cultural control is to control hearts and minds and, as Sewell (1998) notes, this is greatly facilitated by replacing earlier forms of bureaucratic control with *hegemonic control* (Rosen and Baroundi 1992). Bureaucratic control is really a rudimentary form of hegemonic

Hegemonic control: control exercised by an elite body whose power is accepted as supreme control, which extracts compliance in a very unobtrusive way, by using apparently neutral rules that employees perceive to be legitimate. However, true hegemonic control is much more personal, and it exists when people come to believe that a source of authority is near infallible. Thus, managers set-out to induce employees to adopt a set of values that leads them to believe that managers and workers are both on the same side, and pulling in the same direction towards the same common goals. If successful, this would result in managers coming to be seen as leaders, whose instructions also represent the interests of the workforce. The net result of this is would be that there would no longer be a need for a set of behavioural rules, because employees can deduce rules to fit any situation by simply asking themselves 'What is it that the manager wants?'

Structure and Work Methods

For a number of reasons that are largely economic, TQM, JIT and lean production often feature strongly in current work systems. However, reaping the full advantages of these methods is acutely dependent on people working cooperatively. Consequently, they are usually accompanied by structural and work organisation changes, notably the introduction of teamworking and empowerment.

In popular management books, teamworking tends to be presented as a humanistic act that frees workers from the drudgery of job designs based on scientific management principles (Katzenbach and Smith 1993). In theory, this results in employees who are more committed, highly motivated and trustworthy because they have feelings of self-control, personal responsibility and autonomy (Tjosvold 1991). However, teamworking often conceals the restrictions of scientific management behind a rhetoric of emancipation and enhances managerial control (Sinclair 1992). Moreover, because empowerment tends to be introduced after a workforce has been cut to the bare minimum, it is less of an opportunity for self-development than an imperative or obligation for people to continually to improve their performance in order to hold onto their jobs (Claydon and Doyle 1996). Therefore, what at first sight looks like a relaxation of control, is, at a psychological level, the reverse. Nevertheless, if people can be persuaded that they have really been empowered, and accept this idea within the culture outlined earlier, the result is likely to be highly significant. Employees will deliver the targets set by managers by making the decisions management want them to make, and will believe that they have made the decisions of their own free will: thus a high degree of behavioural control is achieved in a near-invisible way (Willmott 1993).

Monitoring (Surveillance)

Direct monitoring of employees is very expensive and contradicts the rhetoric of empowerment. Nevertheless, managers have a tendency to feel that they are not 'in control' unless employee behaviour is monitored in some way (Felstead *et al.* 2003) and this poses the problem identified by Sewell (1998): 'How do you achieve control without appearing to control?' One answer to this lies in the way that new surveillance technologies have been introduced.

Poster (1990) argues that technology has enabled highly sophisticated surveillance methods to emerge that are so unobtrusive that they tend to go unnoticed. Moreover, the facility for electronic monitoring of employee activities is advancing by leaps and bounds, and management's interest in remaining 'in control' is so strong that some of the latest advances are highly dubious in ethical terms. For instance, there is the reported case of a lecturer in cybernetics at Reading University who was approached by an American company to design a microchip that could be implanted under the skin of employees, to track their movements throughout the working day (Welch 1999).

Sewell (1998) points out that many of the emerging work systems that make use of teamworking by employees contain two principal forms of surveillance:

Vertical surveillance: a person's actions are monitored by someone above him or her in the organisational hierarchy

Horizontal surveillance: a person's actions are monitored by someone at the same level, who is part of the same workgroup

- *vertical surveillance*, by people above the employee in the hierarchy using electronic monitoring of individual performance
- *horizontal surveillance*, by other people in a workgroup, who observe each other and exert peer pressure on individuals to perform.

Horizontal surveillance is the most significant feature of the new control methods. Instead of monitoring the outputs of a work system, some monitoring is shifted to within the system itself, by having people observe the efforts of their colleagues (Barker 1993) This is relatively cheap and, by introducing closed-loop methods at all stages within a work system, the system as a whole is brought much nearer to being controlled by open-loop methods.

A number of authors has commented on the effects that this has on people who work under these conditions. Far from being the emancipated, empowered and self-actualising experience that is claimed for it, teamworking often turns out to be a highly stressful system, that sets worker against worker (Parker and Slaughter 1988; Taylor *et al*. 2003). The whole process is made possible by attempting to manipulate cultures to promote the values and attitudes of the organisation as though these are somehow the natural order of things. In reality, however, workers are induced to police each other's actions, and are ultimately subject to an immensely tighter control regime.

RESISTANCE TO CONTROL

One of the things we can note about traditional methods of control is that many of them have been in use for some time. Although this does not mean that control is welcome, or that resistance to control is absent, it suggests that many employees have either acclimatised themselves to control regimes, or have been able to shape management control into a form that they can 'live with'. Therefore, it is appropriate to start by re-examining what are said to be the underlying reasons for resistance.

As noted earlier, the *political perspective* on control argues that some degree of resistance is endemic, because workers are likely to resist control in order to avoid being exploited by managers. While there is some evidence for these effects, it is rather overstating the case to suggest that *all* resistance is for economic reasons. For example, a number of scholars have shown that resistance can have distinctly emotional roots, such as fear of change (Dent and Goldberg 1999; George and Jones 2001). In addition, because the opportunity to exercise valued skills is often central to a person's concept of self, and tight control can remove this opportunity, protection of self-identity is also a powerful motive for resistance (Thomas and Davies 2005; O'Doherty and Willmott 2001). Moreover, since changed patterns of control can upset social relationships such as the structure of a workgroup (Bain and Taylor 2000), it is also possible that people resist control as a way of protecting themselves from the effects of impending social changes. Finally, people who have a modicum of power and/or prestige can feel threatened by controls that might transfer this power into other hands (Mulholland 2004).

These, it can be noted, are all circumstances in which control could easily result in adverse emotional reactions. Thus the political approach, which conflates resistance to control with other forms of industrial action and workplace conflict, can present a somewhat oversimplified explanation, which is limited in its capacity to encompass all the other reasons why resistance can occur.

Turning now to newer control regimes, there is no shortage of evidence to suggest that resistance continues to exist. However, as noted earlier, the cultural component in recent developments in control is purposely designed to remove employee resistance. While one school of thought argues that managers have been highly successful in doing this (see Casey 1999), there are also arguments that when managers introduce new methods of control, employees find new avenues of resistance that remain hidden from managers. The middle view, which for the time being appears to be the most pragmatic, is that while it is too soon to tell whether resistance has withered away, and there is a body of evidence to show that it has taken on new forms (Thompson and Ackroyd 1995).

For example, Collinson (1994) points out that workplace resistance can manifest itself in two ways:

Resistance through persistence: an aggressive or assertive and overt way of resisting control

- *Resistance through persistence*, in which employees go on the offensive.
- *Resistance through distance*, which is a defensive form in which people create their own physical and emotional space to opt out psychologically.

Resistance through distance: a defensive way of resisting control by psychologically opting out

For the present, it seems to be true that the first of these is largely absent. Nevertheless, a number of authors point out that in place of the overt resistance of earlier times, employees seem to have found ways of undermining the new control regimes that are equally as subtle as management's new ways of trying to exercise control. For example, Townsend (2005) shows that by seemingly adopting new surveillance methods, call centre employees were able to turn them to their own advantage, and exert a degree of counter-control over management. Moreover, Bolton (2004) describes an interesting example of the ways in which NHS nurses were able to selectively re-interpret what managers stated they wanted, in order to deliver something that was much more in line with their own professional ethos.

In addition, to these examples there are an increasing number of studies that seem to indicate that, far from being naive in their appreciation of what managers hope to achieve by using these new control regimes, employees are only too well aware of managerial intentions. Indeed, there is plenty of evidence to show that workers will, where necessary, find innovative and new ways of subverting managements' control methods (see Bain and Taylor 2000; Geary and Dobbins 2001; Knights and McCabe 2000; Timmons 2003). In particular, Jermier *et al.* (1994) identify the following as employee actions that can have this effect:

- sabotage, pilfering and whistleblowing
- bloody mindedness (being obstructive), legal retaliation and output restriction
- developing counter-cultures, rumour mongering and refusal to accept autonomy and discretion.

With the exception of the first line, it can be noted that none of these are overt acts of defiance that would justify dismissal, and those in the remaining two lines are what used to be called 'dumb insolence'. As many managers have found out to their cost, there is seldom a foolproof way of handling this.

What then are the implications of the above? There would seem to be three that are particularly noteworthy. First, it seems highly unlikely that resistance is completely dead. Rather it has probably taken on a host of new forms to deal with new contingencies.

Second, explaining why resistance still flourishes can often be found in the nature of the new control regimes. These days, managers seem to be aware that unless they attempt to take control of organisational culture, which has accurately been identified as 'the last frontier of control' (Ray 1986), they have no chance whatsoever of exerting control over all the other aspects of organisational life. This, however, is a formidable task, and it would be an act of gross naivety for them to believe that employees are so gullible that they cannot spot that there is an attempt to try and take over their hearts and minds.

Finally, one of the few things that we can be sure of in this world is that a dislike of being under another person's control is a near universal human attribute. Thus, people are likely to resent any attempt to manipulate their psyches. Therefore, new control regimes are virtually an invitation to resist the control that they seek to exercise.

REPLAY

- Current developments in control attempt to use a higher degree of open-loop control of work systems by deploying mutually reinforcing techniques that result in more intense control regimes.
- One technique that is deployed is to attempt to change the culture of the workforce so that employees have values that result in them behaving as management desires.
- Another technique is to change structures and work methods so that employees work in teams which are empowered and held responsible for achieving results.
- Another technique is the surveillance of employee behaviour by electronic methods and further surveillance by group members who exert peer pressure on individuals to behave in ways desired by managers.
- These steps tend to result in more stressful working environments and there are suggestions that employees resist these controls in covert ways.

OVERVIEW AND CONCLUSIONS

If large complex organisations are to achieve their goals and objectives, it is necessary to coordinate activities, which means that control of some sort is vital. Humans react to attempts to bring their behaviour under control and have their own interpretations about why this control is applied. Thus, even though control is often portrayed as a neutral activity, those who are controlled do not necessarily interpret matters in this way.

The control activity can be viewed from a number of different perspectives. Managers tend to believe that controlling the activities of others is a prerogative that comes with the job, while political theorists point out that control cannot be divorced from the use of power and is often used for exploitative purposes. Between these two extremes lies the open systems perspective, which views control as necessary, but also acknowledges that it can have unforeseen consequences and is capable of being used for exploitation. Many of the control activities in organisations attempt to regulate human behaviour and since control is normally exercised by supervisors and managers, it cannot sensibly be divorced from the use of power.

A wide range of traditional methods have been developed to try to bring human behaviour under control in organisations. However, people often have emotional reactions to attempted control and there are arguments that a degree of resistance is commonplace.

In addition, recent developments, which use a number of mutually reinforcing elements to obtain the ultimate degree of behavioural control – control of hearts and minds – have now become more widely used. While it is sometimes argued that newer methods are likely to bring an end to resistance to control, it should be noted that their use results in more intensive control regimes. Therefore, it is not surprising that some scholars argue that these can result in new forms of resistance, that might ultimately turn out to be extremely difficult, if not impossible, to handle.

FURTHER READING

Berry, AJ, J Broadbent and D Otley (1995) *Management Control: Themes, Issues and Practices*, London: Macmillan. A wide-ranging book written from what is basically a managerialist perspective, but which nevertheless gives good coverage of the topic.

Collinson, DL (1994) Strategies of resistance: power knowledge and subjectivity in the Workplace. In JM Jermier, D Knights and WR Mond (eds), *Resistance and Power in Organisations*, London: Routledge. A penetrating chapter which deals with employee resistance to control in organisations.

Etzioni, A (1975) *A Comparative Analysis of Complex Organisations: On Power, Involvement and their Correlates*, New York: Free Press. A revision by the author of his earlier (1964) text, in which he further develops the idea that an organisation's relationship with its employees is strongly influenced by the way power is used and the way that this engenders characteristic patterns of attachment by organisational members. A useful basic text that explains the underpinnings of control and resistance.

Johnson, P and J Gill (1993) *Management Control and Organisational Behaviour*, London: Sage. The book has a focus on organisational structure, culture and power. It uses these to explore the use of formal control systems and behavioural control.

Mitchell, D (1979) *Control without Bureaucracy*, London: McGraw-Hill. A useful text on industrial organisation that takes a humanistic stance on the matter of control.

Purcell, J and R Smith (eds) (1979) *The Control of Work*, London: Macmillan. A penetrating analysis of control from an industrial relations perspective.

Rosen, M and J Baroundi (1992) Computer based technology and the emergence of new forms of control. In A Sturdy, D Knights and H Willmott (eds), *Skill and Consent: Contemprary Studies in the Labour Process*, London: Routledge. A penetrating chapter that fully explores emerging systems of behavioural control.

Thompson, P and D McHugh (1995) *Work Organisation: A Critical Introduction*, 2nd edn, London: Macmillan. A book which has an excellent chapter on power and control.

CASE STUDY 19.1: The Royal Borough of Kensington and Chelsea – control of homeworking

Since 2000, the Royal Borough of Kensington and Chelsea has made a conscious effort to encourage and support homeworking. The biggest area of success has been in the revenues division, which includes council tax and benefits, where there are now 19 employees working from home full-time. In other parts of the council a handful of people work at home full-time, but a much greater number work at home for part of the week. Employees who make a transition to homeworking usually start with one day each week and then move to two days, three days and so on. It allows the council to see whether it's working for them, and people have actually come back and said two days is all that I can do, because I need the contact in the office.

David Tidey, head of information systems, has been leading an internal group responsible for drawing together guidelines on homeworking for the council. He says individuals and their managers need to consider a number of issues before deciding if homeworking is appropriate. On the part of managers it needs to be recognised that homeworking requires them to abandon command and control attitudes, and adopt more empowered forms of management. Above all, it requires them to 'trust' employees to work effectively if they are 'out of sight'.

Employees need to think carefully about homeworking and recognise that it brings a blurring between work and home life.

'You also have to ask yourself whether people are responsible enough to make the best of homeworking and what effect it might have on the rest of the team,' he explains. 'Then there are housekeeping issues, such as accommodation at home and childcare. We want to make sure people don't use it as an excuse to deal with childcare problems.' Health and safety also needs attention. In the revenues division, individual risk assessments have been carried out for all those who work from home. But Tidey admits such an approach will not be viable as the trend towards homeworking spreads. 'Our people live all over the country, so it's not going to be possible to go to everyone's house,' he explains. So, in the future, a full risk assessment will be carried out in the office for each employee and then, as long as they have no previous history of a problem such as repetitive strain injury, the office set-up will be replicated in their home. Staff will also be sent on a half-day training course about working safely at home, which will cover issues such as electrical safety, setting up the workstation and taking breaks.

While there has been reluctance on the part of some managers to allow people to work from home, Tidey says that on the whole feedback has been positive. 'Team leaders say that staff tend to be off sick less if they work from home; there are also fewer problems with travel delays,' he says. Productivity among homeworkers has also increased by an average of about 10 per cent. While flexibility is the obvious benefit for staff. In the long term Tidey envisages there will be an impact on the amount of office space the council needs, which will allow for greater efficiency and reduced overheads. 'We're in the early stages at the moment,' he says, 'but in the council tax department we have reduced space, and in IT we've got a number of people who are hot-desking.'

Source: Edwards, C (2005) Remote Control, *People Management*, 16 June, pp 31–32

Questions

1. In terms of its ease of controlling employee behaviour, compare and contrast homeworking with traditional methods of behavioural control.

2. What particular features of homeworking can you identify from the case material that are likely to make it appeal to:
   (a) Managers of the local authority
   (b) Employees of the local authority

3. Are there any potential disadvantages of which managers of the local authority need to be aware?

4. Are there any potential disadvantages of which employees of the local authority need to be aware?

5. The case material notes that employees who have been approved for homeworking arrangements will be equipped with a set-up in their homes that replicates (as close as possible) the set-up in their traditional work location. Why do you feel that the local authority intends to take this step?

REVIEW AND DISCUSSION QUESTIONS

1. Define what is meant by the word 'control' in an organisational context. What are the purposes of control in an organisation?

2. Compare and contrast the managerialist, open systems and political perspectives on control in organisations.

3. Explain the difference between open-loop and closed-loop control. What are the respective functions of the following components in closed-loop control: actuator, sensor, feedback path and comparator?

4. Explain the connection between power and organisational control. Why is it impossible to divorce power from control in an organisational context?

5. Describe seven methods that have traditionally been used to try to bring human behaviour under control in organisations. Which of these methods are most frequently used in combination?

6. Describe recent developments in behavioural control in organisations and explain why the use of these is likely to result in more intense control regimes.

Chapter 20

Organisational Cultures and Climates

LEARNING OUTCOMES

After studying this chapter you should be able to:

- define and understand the nature of organisational culture, its historical roots, how it is maintained and replicated, and how it affects the behaviour of organisational members

- describe a traditional (Peters and Waterman) perspective on organisational culture and contrast this with the more recent (Goffe and Jones) contingency framework

- describe the methodology and techniques that can be deployed in culture change initiatives

- define the nature of organisational climate, describe its antecedents and consequences and its affect on the behaviour of organisational members

- compare and contrast the concepts of organisational culture and organisational climate

INTRODUCTION

Although the visible characteristics of an organisation can reveal much about how it operates, this tells us little of how people experience organisational life. Nevertheless, if we ask them what it is like to work for a particular firm, they often reply in terms of their feelings or emotions; for example by saying that it is very dynamic, or perhaps that it is chaotic. These people would be telling us is something about their perceptions of the atmosphere in the firm, which is one of the less tangible facets of organisational life and is encompassed by the two concepts covered in this chapter: culture and climate.

The first to be considered is culture, a topic that came to the fore in the early 1980s, largely as a result of the appearance of a number of books and articles linking organisational culture with commercial success. Since culture is rather intangible and difficult to define, the discussion commences with a definition, which is followed by an exploration of its nature and the assumed link with commercial success. This is followed by an outline of some of the more influential theories and perspectives on culture and, since these mostly imply that some cultures are more beneficial than others, the topics of culture management and cultural change are examined. To round off the discussion, a brief consideration of the effects of national cultures on organisations is given.

The second topic of the chapter is that of organisational climate. This is a more mature and well-developed concept, which deals with dynamic and changeable organisational features. Climate is defined and distinguished from culture and is then explored in greater depth by examining the nature, origins and outcomes of organisational climates. The chapter concludes by comparing and contrasting the concepts of culture and climate, together with an examination of the organisational implications of both.

ORGANISATIONAL CULTURE

The word culture has been used by many different people to explain a variety of phenomena, and because each one tends to adopt a slightly different perspective, there is no universally accepted definition. As such, the most appropriate way forward is to define how the word will be used in this chapter, which is:

> a pattern of basic assumptions – invented, discovered or developed by a given group as it learns to cope with its problems of external adaption and internal integration – that has worked well enough to be considered valuable and, therefore, to be taught to new members as the correct way to perceive, think and feel in relation to those problems.
> (Schein 1992, p 9)

Culture has been, and still is studied by several different disciplines, all of which have their own distinct approach. The main disciplines include **anthropology**, which can be defined as the study of human cultures and how they influence the structure and functioning of a society. **Sociology** adopts a somewhat different perspective, linking particular sets of values and beliefs to patterns of social action. **Social psychology** explains the internal dynamics of a social situation, focusing especially on how culture produces observable patterns of behaviour and the ways in which people communicate their expectations to each other. For example, the work of Martin and Power (1983) shows that stories and anecdotes are powerful vehicles for communicating the cultural values of an organisation.

THE NATURE OF ORGANISATIONAL CULTURE

The details of an organisation's culture are carried in people's minds, and even though they may not be aware of doing so, they use this information to interpret what surrounds them, and to react to it. If these meanings are shared by all or most of the people in an organisation, it can be said to have a culture, but the details from which the meanings are constructed can exist at different levels of visibility – some are directly observable while others are near invisible. In this respect Schein (1990) conceptualises culture as a 'layered' phenomenon which has three interrelated levels of meaning: *basic assumptions*; *values and beliefs*; and *artifacts and creations*, which is shown diagrammatically in Figure 20.1.

Figure 20.1
Schein's layered conceptualisation of culture

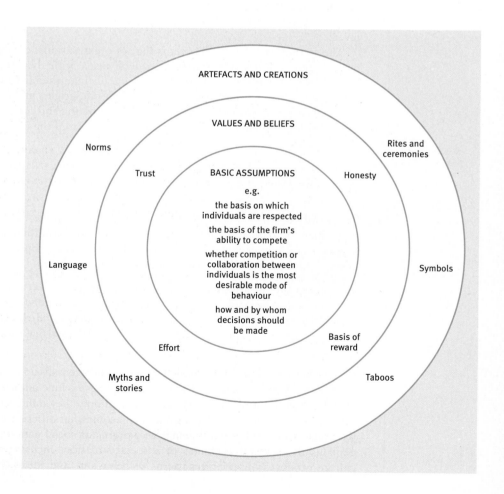

Basic Assumptions

These lie in the innermost core of a culture. In Schein's view they are fundamental and so taken for granted that most people in a cultural unit subscribe to them but not in a conscious way. However, if we dig deep enough, it is not difficult to identify these basic assumptions. For instance, they are quite different in the major political parties in Great Britain. The Labour Party has an assumption that society is or should be a collective body, in which individuals should display a high degree of social responsibility towards each other. Conversely, Conservatives believe that the individual is paramount and their prime responsibility is their own welfare, an idea succinctly expressed in Margaret Thatcher's famous (or infamous, according to one's views) statement 'there is no such thing as society – only individuals'. Business organisations also tend to differ in the basic assumptions contained in their cultures: for example, about whether people deserve respect because of the positions they hold, or because of their skills and abilities; what lies at the root of the firm's ability to compete; or whether competition between individuals is a good thing or should be suppressed.

Values and Beliefs

Values and beliefs exist at the next level of visibility. They consist of consciously held reasons or justifications for people behaving as they do (Sathe 1985) and, are moral or ethical codes that guide behaviour by putting the assumptions into practice. To use the example of British political parties again, values can be seen in their policy guidelines for programmes of legislation. Since Conservatives have a basic assumption about the primacy of the individual, they often express values that dictate how this should be reflected in legislation, for example cutting taxes and encouraging individuals to use the money to make provision for their own health insurance and retirement. Conversely, the Labour Party's basic assumption about collective responsibility strongly advocates the funding of state schemes of social security. Once again there are parallel ways in which values serve as guidelines for action in organisations, such as whether the customers' interests should come first, and whether conflict should be suppressed or is best brought out into the open where it can be handled and resolved.

Artifacts and Creations

These are the most visible manifestations of a culture. They include everything from the physical layout of a building to the way people dress, the way they talk to each other and, often, the things they talk about. Although some of these features are very subtle and it can be dangerous to view them in isolation, they often give vital clues about the underlying values and beliefs (an example of one that is potentially important is given in the OB in Action Box on page 594). It is therefore useful to distinguish between some of these different signs.

Norms

Norms are a code of behaviour brought into being by the underlying assumptions and values, and are perpetuated when people observe the norms. If people only reach high positions by working a 60-hour week, this sets up an expectation that these hours are

 OB IN ACTION: The coffee break – an important cultural ritual

Product obsolescence is a familiar phenomenon in workplaces all over the world and 'filter' coffee making machines are rapidy being phased-out and replaced by individualised 'pod' coffee makers. However, as has been pointed out by a number of commentators, the communal coffee-maker encourages people to drink coffee together; it. is a place to have a quick chat with colleagues, catch up on news and gossip, and generally oil the wheels of the organisation. However, current trends force more and more people to make the solitary walk to a machine that does nothing more than provide them with just one cup of coffee and gone is the idea of the [coffee] pot designed for a group; and gone with it are many of the corresponding opportunities for social interaction. As a result, American workers are increasingly rejecting the in-house option altogether.

But why should managers be bothered by any of this? Who cares where staff get their coffee, so long as it helps keep them awake and they are back at their desks working again before too long? Simply because it has to do with workplace culture.

Who your people drink coffee with, and where, is important. You may not think you need to promote the rise of 'café society' internally, but a coffee culture could be beneficial – for collaboration, networking, and cross-fertilisation. As such, the coffee break and its attendant social interaction could be one of the most important rituals or artifacts that exists in many firms.

Source:

Stern, S (2007) Wake up and smell the coffee on your corporate culture, *Financial Times*, 26 March

a criterion for promotion, which permeates downwards and becomes accepted as the normal behaviour for ambitious people.

Language

The language people use can be a valuable indication of culture. For example, how managers talk to subordinates and vice versa can reveal much about the status values at work, and the use of jargon and current 'buzzwords' are often used to signal who is accepted and who is not.

Symbols

Status symbols communicate social position and pecking order in the hierarchy, and their grandness gives a good indication about how much importance is attached to hierarchy as an organising principle.

Rites and Ceremonies

Formal and informal ceremonies abound in most organisations, and these often have important meanings for those involved. Retirement or farewell parties can be used to signal the idea of a happy family or a caring organisation. The ritual of taking a newcomer around and introducing the person to new colleagues is often a way of speeding up the integration process.

Myths and Stories

These are often a way of communicating core values and assumptions to people. Anecdotes are useful for this purpose because they often have an element of drama and are interesting to hear. Myths are stories that are partly fictional and are of questionable accuracy (Ott 1989), but nevertheless convey a central message in a more dramatic form and increase its salience.

Taboos

These signal what should not be done and an example is the story about the junior employee who addressed a director by his first name. This can be used to provide a humorous illustration for a newcomer that respect for someone higher up is a fundamental part of the culture.

Although it has been convenient to describe all these signs separately, it is important to recognise that they complement each other and are often used in combination as reminders of what the culture is and what is expected. For instance, basic assumptions are often expressed in values and, in turn, artifacts, creations and visible behaviour are practical ways of expressing the values.

TIME OUT

Carefully reflect on the organisation in which you work, either full-time or part-time. If you have no experience of being an employee use another organisation of which you are, or have been, a member. Using Schein's layered concept of culture, and starting with the most visible level, try to answer the questions below.

1. What artifacts and creations are there? For example, are there any identifiable norms of behaviour, particular language mannerisms that are encouraged, symbols, rites and ceremonies, myths, stories or taboos?
2. What basic values are indicated by the things you identified in question 1?
3. What are the basic assumptions underpinning the values you identified in question 2?

CHARACTERISTICS OF CULTURES

Pervasiveness or Homogeneity

In some respects the very expression organisational culture is misleading. It conveys the impression that everyone in a particular firm perceives things in the same way. For

Integrationist
perspective on
culture: culture is an
organisation-wide
phenomenon which
consists of shared
values to which all
or most employees
subscribe

Fragmentationist
perspective on
culture: organisations
are so full of
ambiguities and
inconsistencies that
frames of reference
are individual and
constantly changing
so culture is
inherently unstable

Differentiationist
perspective on
culture: organisations
are made up of
different groups
with their own
sub-cultures

this reason Martin (1992) distinguishes between three distinct perspectives. The *integrationist perspective* (which is the way matters have been discussed so far) views culture as an organisation-wide phenomenon. This is the view that probably appeals most to managers, because it holds out the prospect of using culture as a control mechanism to deliver superior organisational performance. At the other extreme, Martin identifies what she calls the *fragmentationist perspective*, in which organisations are so full of ambiguities and inconsistencies that they cannot be said to have a single culture. Rather, people respond in an *ad hoc* way to constantly changing conditions. Martin also identifies a middle-ground position, which she calls the *differentiationist perspective*. This acknowledges the possibility that within an organisation's overall culture there are variations in which different groups of people have slightly different cultures.

An interesting insight on Martin's ideas is given by Harris and Ogbonna (1998), who show that all three perspectives commonly exist side by side in different parts of the same organisation. Perhaps because they like to view the organisation as one big family, top managers tend to adopt an integrationist view, whereas middle managers, who are more sharply focused on their own functional roles or specialisms, have differentiationist perspectives. At the very bottom of an organisation, where people often have to keep their heads down and focus on their immediate tasks with no sight of a bigger picture, shopfloor workers are prone to take a fragmentationist view.

The evidence for the existence of sub-cultures in anything other than very small firms is overwhelming, and the larger the firm the more likely it is that distinct sub-cultures will emerge. For example, in a study of a large Danish insurance company, Hofstede (1998) identified three highly distinctive sub-cultures (production, administrative and professional) that embraced virtually everyone in the organisation. In the light of this and other evidence, the currently prevailing view is that the differentiationist perspective offers the most realistic view of culture in organisations. Moreover, it can be argued that the advantages accruing from having different subcultures outweigh any disadvantages. Sub-cultures give different perspectives, which makes the 'groupthink' phenomenon described in Chapter 11 less likely. In addition, since sub-cultures are associated with the professional expertise and specialist perspectives of different groups, the resulting differences are of great organisational value. For instance, in a marketing department that deals with a very uncertain environment, a dynamic, thrusting sub-culture of risk-taking can be just what is needed. However, to ensure that matters do not get out of hand, it is probably desirable to counterbalance this with the cautious, risk-averting sub-culture that is often found among accountants. After all, this is why specialists are employed – do we really expect accountants to have the same values as marketeers?

Strength of Culture

A recurring theme in popular texts is that strong cultures are associated with superior organisational performance (Deal and Kennedy 1982; Peters and Waterman 1982). Luthans (1995) argues that cultural strength is a function of two factors:

- **Sharedness,** which corresponds to what has been described above as homogeneity and expresses the extent to which all organisational members have the same core values.
- **Intensity,** which corresponds to the degree of commitment of all the people in the organisation to these values.

Taken together these imply that the strength of a culture needs to be assessed in a multidimensional way, which is probably a very sound point. However, Luthans' ideas about the factors that influence these dimensions are open to severe criticism. He states that both are a function of the way that an organisation rewards its members. This implies that culture is totally under management's control and is easily manipulated by the judicious use of rewards and punishments, which grossly overestimates the extent to which deeply held values and beliefs can be controlled by external stimuli. Moreover, Luthans somewhat uncritically accepts that a high degree of sharedness is desirable and, as was pointed out earlier, there are inherent dangers in having an organisational culture that is too homogeneous. The most controversial point, however, is the way that he accepts that a strong culture leads to organisational success. This point will be addressed in detail later, but for the present two brief points can be made. First, a strong culture may only be a predictor of good performance in the short run and, second, it is only safe to assume that a strong culture is an aid to success if it is also an appropriate one, that is, one that is suitable for coping with the conditions faced by an organisation.

Cultural Evolution and Replication

Although it is important to be able to describe an organisation's culture, two questions of equal significance are: how did the culture come to exist?; and what forces are at work to enable it to persist in this state? Both of these will be considered separately.

Cultural Evolution

Schein (1983) argues that the history of an organisation inevitably has a huge impact on its culture and that some cultural elements can be traced back to the values and ideologies of a firm's founder. Those who bring organisations into existence often have a strong entrepreneurial disposition. They can be highly dynamic people who communicate their vision to others and, in the early days of a firm, they tend to attract and recruit a core of like-minded people. What emerges is a key group that has shared assumptions and values and as the firm grows, these people become role models for new entrants.

Cultural patterns such as these can last a long time and may well persist for generations. For instance, certain British firms founded in the nineteenth century were set up by prominent Quaker industrialists who, because of their religious convictions, felt a sense of obligation and duty to their employees and attempted to mitigate many of the harsh industrial conditions of the day by devoting considerable financial resources and effort into improving the lot of the workforce. In these organisations welfare schemes, medical attention and, in one famous case, the building of a whole village that took employees out of the slum conditions of the industrial revolution were put in place and, to some extent, this tradition of welfare paternalism carries on today.

An imprint of the founder is still often encountered in firms, but what remains, however, is seldom identical to the culture that existed in the early years. As firms grow they face new challenges and cope with these by adopting new structural forms and methods (Beekun and Glick 2001). Clearly this is likely to be a slow and continuous process, which is concerned with two generic problems: that of **ensuring survival and external adaptation;** and that of **ensuring internal integration.** These in turn give rise to more specific problems and what emerges from this ongoing process is that the core

Table 20.1 External and internal problems which, when resolved, partially determine organisational culture (adapted from Schein 1983)

Problem orientation	Potential problem
External problems to be resolved: those concerning adaption and survival	1. Developing consensus on the primary task, core mission and latent functions of the group, i.e. strategy 2. Consensus on goals, with goals being a reflection of core mission 3. Developing consensus on the means to be used to achieve goals, e.g. division of labour, organisation structure, reward systems, etc. 4. Developing consensus on the criteria to measure how well the group is performing against its goals and targets, e.g. information and control systems 5. Developing consensus on remedial strategies that may be needed when the group is not achieving its goals
Internal problems to be resolved: those concerning internal integration	6. Common language and conceptual categories need to be derived so that group members can communicate with each other, without which group functioning is impossible 7. Consensus on group boundaries and criteria for inclusion and exclusion needed in order that one of the most important areas of culture (consensus on who is or is not part of the group and what criteria determine membership) are clear 8. Consensus on criteria for the allocation of power and status are needed so that the organisation's pecking order, its rules for obtaining and retaining power, are understood in order that members can manage their own feelings of aggression 9. Consensus on criteria for intimacy, friendship and love so that rules for the way that peers relate to each other and relationships between the sexes are handled, and the degrees of openness and intimacy that will be used in working on organisational tasks are clearly understood 10. Consensus on criteria for the allocation of rewards and punishments so that people in the group know what behaviours are lauded and what are deprecated, what rewards are available, what behaviours are punished by withdrawing rewards, up to and including exclusion from the group 11. Consensus on ideology and religion because, like societies, groups must have ways of giving meaning to 'unexplainable' events so that people are able to respond to them without feeling anxious in the face of the 'unexplainable'

elements of culture (its basic assumptions and values) re-emerge in slightly modified form. Once adopted, these are held at a subconscious level and are so taken for granted that they are taught to new entrants to the organisation as the appropriate way to view things (see Table 20.1).

Cultural Replication

In the short run, cultures are maintained and replicated by the socialisation processes shown in Figure 20.2.

To a large extent, when new organisational members are selected, those who are allowed to enter are the ones who are perceived to fit in with what is already there. In cultural terms new entrants are seldom a perfect match and, almost immediately, another set of processes come into play, which are concerned with inducing these people to adopt the required feelings and behaviour.

- As an immediate measure, those who are already members and have absorbed the organisation's culture pass on their knowledge so that newcomers 'learn the ropes'. Most newcomers view this in a positive way and inducting a new starter

Figure 20.2
Organisational
socialisation

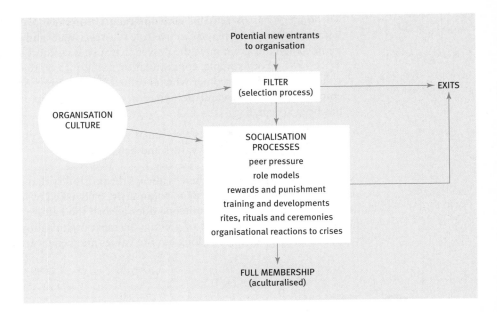

does a great deal to help the person settle in and come to know what is expected
(Reichers 1987).

- Most new entrants are also likely to experience a certain amount of **peer
  pressure**. This can take the form of enquiries about how things were done at the
  previous place of employment which, if necessary, is followed-up with pointed
  comments about how the new situation differs.

- Where cultures are very strong and existing members know that the newcomer
  will find things very different, a new recruit can purposely be put through mildly
  humiliating experiences. For instance, the person might be given particularly
  onerous jobs to do, which tends to have the effect of making people question
  their own prior assumptions, and makes them more open to accepting new
  norms and values (Pascale 1985).

- It is also common for a new entrant to pick up **role models** early on. For
  example, newcomers tend to be placed under the wing of a senior, trusted person
  and it is natural for the newcomer to see this person as someone who fits in well.

- As the newcomer becomes more familiar with the surroundings, he or she also
  picks up clues about the **criteria for rewards and punishments**. Rewards provide
  clear indications of the criteria that are used to evaluate performance and, by
  absorbing this knowledge, the routes to promotion, higher status and prestige
  can be learned. Conversely, punishment is an indication of behaviour that is
  viewed as deviating from what is acceptable.

- Newcomers may well be put through **training and development experiences**
  which, on the face of it, are only designed to teach skills. However, some of these
  processes also act as a powerful means of transmitting culture. For instance,
  many organisations use a formal induction course that often contains a strong
  element of company history, and messages about core values and beliefs.

- The longer a person remains with an organisation the more he or she is likely to witness and come to play an active role in **rites, rituals and ceremonies**. Rites are planned activities that have the power to transmit cultural norms (Beyer and Trice 1987). For example, congratulation gatherings on the promotion of a colleague tell the newcomer what is valued in the culture. Social gatherings emphasise integration and an invitation to attend is often a sign that someone has been accepted.

- **Critical incidents and crises** also signal what culture expects, for instance an 'all hands to the pumps' set of values and behaviours.

Notwithstanding the above, there is always the possibility that someone cannot adapt to the new culture and either exits voluntarily, or is asked to leave. It is also important to recognise that when someone does absorb the culture it does not mean that he or she becomes some sort of a clone. In most organisations there is a degree of tolerance to individuality, so long as core values and beliefs are not violated.

TIME OUT

In an earlier Time Out exercise you examined the culture of an organisation in which you work or, alternatively, the student body at your university or college. Take your analysis one stage further and answer the questions below.

1. How homogeneous is the culture? For example, does everybody seem to be part of the same culture, or are there different groups of people that have their own sub-culture? If so, how different are the sub-cultures?
2. How strong is the culture (and, if they exist, sub-cultures)?

The Effects of Culture on Organisational Performance

Although it is known that culture has a strong effect on people's behaviour, management's interest is less likely to be prompted by curiosity about why this happens, than in its possible bottom-line effects on the commercial or financial performance of an organisation. To a large extent this interest was kindled by the writings of popular authors such as Peters and Waterman (1982) who view culture as a key component in the performance of successful companies. These ideas resulted in an increased awareness among managers of the potential effects of culture but, as is often the case (because these writings conveyed the impression that there is a 'one best culture'), a more dangerous turn of events was set in motion.

Unfortunately, managers have a tendency to look for 'off the shelf' solutions to organisational problems. Therefore, when the cultural characteristics of successful companies were set out in these books in a catchy, marketable and easily grasped way, there was an understandable tendency for some managers to believe that, at last, social science had come up with something of immense practical use – a sure-fire recipe for success.

However, other than in the writings of these popular authors, there is little evidence of a strong association between culture and organisational performance, and none whatsoever for a set of cultural characteristics that are likely to be appropriate in all circumstances. Indeed, when the firms held up as shining examples in the popular works were examined a few years later, no coherent link between culture and performance could be established (Hitt and Ireland 1987). Indeed, several of the firms were in serious financial difficulties (Carroll 1983).

There could be sound reasons why this happens and Miller (1994) notes that, after a period of outstanding success, certain patterns of behaviour can appear in firms, all of which have an adverse impact on future success. For example, a firm can exhibit **inertia**, in which it clings to a past recipe for success, which may no longer be viable. Alternatively it becomes guilty of **immoderation**, in which very bold gambles are made, perhaps because previous success gives a feeling of invulnerability. In addition, the firm exhibits **inattention**, which is similar to a form of institutional 'groupthink', where top managers only pay attention to a very restricted range of environmental signals. Finally, firms show **insularity**, in which there is a failure to adapt to environment, even where the signs that this is necessary are readily available.

It is similarly important to recognise that the idea of a 'one best culture' is over simplistic and is misleading enough to be potentially dangerous. To this end Kilmann *et al.* (1985) reason that there are three features of a culture that could affect performance. These are:

Cultural direction: the extent to which an organisation's culture helps it achieve its goals

Cultural pervasiveness: the homogeneity of an organisation's culture

Cultural strength: the influence of a culture on the behaviour of organisational members

- *Cultural direction*, which broadly corresponds to the extent that a culture actually helps an organisation achieve its goals.
- *Cultural pervasiveness*, which denotes the extent to which an organisational culture is homogeneous. To some extent sub-cultures are probably inevitable, and this has some potential benefits. However, if the sub-cultures are very different and this leads to intergroup conflicts, people can spend more time in internecine warfare than anything else.
- *Cultural strength*, which expresses the influence that a culture has on the behaviour of people. A culture that is positive and strong will clearly have the most beneficial impact, while one that is strong and negative is likely to have adverse consequences. Because it takes time to socialise people into an organisation, one factor that can rapidly dilute cultural strength is staff turnover. Unfortunately, many firms have a regrettable tendency to shed staff when the organisation hits a bad patch and to hire fresh employees when an upturn arrives. Thus they can deprive themselves of the strong culture that they need to take advantage of an upturn, to say nothing of the demoralising after-effects that redundancies have on the culture of those who remain.

In summary, therefore, there are three main conclusions that can be drawn from the above. First, it is all too easy to treat culture as an essential 'must have' to achieve success, whereas if there is a link between culture and success, it could well be a rather tenuous one, and there could be many other factors that produce superior performance. Second, as Killman *et al.* (1985) point out, to have an affect on performance a culture needs to be appropriate to what the organisation seeks to achieve. Finally, Miller's (1994) analysis alerts us to the idea of certain 'perils' of prior success. Thus the characteristics of the culture need to be keyed to future performance, rather than those associated with the past.

- Culture is one of the less tangible features of an organisation and is carried in the minds of organisational members.

- It can be thought of as a layered phenomenon with largely invisible basic assumptions at its core, values that arise out of the basic assumptions as the next level outwards, and visible artifacts and creations that express the culture on the surface.

- Different perspectives exist on whether organisational culture is pervasive throughout a whole organisation or whether sub-cultures exist, but strong cultures, (provided that they are appropriate to an organisation's circumstances) are usually acknowledged to be beneficial in terms of organisational performance.

- The roots of a culture can often be located in an organisation's history, but culture is usually sustained and replicated by socialisation of new organisational members, together with a measure of re-socialisation of people as culture adjusts to changing circumstances.

PERSPECTIVES ON CULTURE

Key variable (application) school: culture is viewed as an organisational property (something an organisation has) that can be changed at will

Smircich (1983) distinguishes five different streams of research that link the concepts of culture and organisation. Although these all have their own underlying assumptions, she also points out that they can be divided into two strongly contrasting schools of thought. The first is what will be called here the *key variable or application school*. This makes use of open systems ideas and views an organisation as something that has to acquire appropriate characteristics to remain in balance with its environment. Viewed this way, culture is a property in the same way that structure and size are properties that enable an organisation to cope with environmental demands; that is, culture is something an organisation '*has*'. A key assumption of this school is that culture is a crucial ingredient of organisational success. It allows the firm to marshal the commitment of its members to achieving the firm's goals and so it is similar to Martin's (1992) integrationist perspective. Since this offers the prospect of using culture to influence organisational performance, it is the perspective that has the strongest appeal to managers and has given rise to a considerable volume of work in the area, the vast majority of which has attempted to identify cultures that promote success, and how to obtain these cultural characteristics (Kanter 1995). In non-academic circles this is by far the most influential school and it spawned a growth industry for organisational development practitioners who have long sought to manipulate cultures to serve the interests of management (see Chapter 21).

Root metaphor school: culture is assumed to reflect the essence of what an organisation '*is*'

The second approach is what Smircich calls the culture as the *root metaphor school*. This views culture as something that an organisation '*is*', which is less concerned with trying to link culture with organisational performance than with trying to understand how cultures are experienced by organisational members, and how this affects the way they behave. While research in this area has great appeal to academics, it finds far less favour with managers, probably because the accounts are difficult to understand and are far too deep and complex for their tastes. Therefore, the better-known perspectives are firmly located in the application school, two of which will be described in what follows. Before giving these descriptions, however, it is important to point out that the first of them appeared nearly 20 years ago, in what could be described as the views of the 'founding fathers' of the cultural movement. In academic circles these are widely acknowledged to be incomplete, if not downright simplistic. Nevertheless, many managers still cling tenaciously to them and it is necessary for the reader to have some appreciation of their origins.

Peters and Waterman: The Characteristics of 'Excellent' Companies

The management interest in organisational culture was greatly stimulated by the publication of Peters and Waterman's (1982) best-seller, *In Search of Excellence*. The two authors, who were management consultants, set out to document management practices that they felt accounted for the superior performance of a number of highly successful American companies (see OB in Action Box on page 604). One of their major conclusions was that these organisations all had similar cultures, the eight most prominent characteristics of which are summarised in Table 20.2.

Bias for Action

Peters and Waterman noted that successful firms have a strong bias for action and outperformed firms where this is absent; for example, managers are expected to make decisions, even in the absence of full information.

Table 20.2 Peters and Waterman – the attributes of excellent companies

Attributes or characteristics	Example
Bias for action	Decisions get made, even in the absence of complete information
Staying close to the customer	The customer is regarded as the source of most of the valuable information the company needs to guide its actions
Autonomy and entrepreneurship	The company is often divided into smaller, more manageable business units to foster innovation and initiative
Productivity through people	People should be treated with dignity and respect and be given opportunities
Hands-on management	Senior managers maintain close contact with operational levels, often by 'walking the floor'
Sticking to the knitting	The company refrains from entering areas of business outside its competence and expertise
Simple form: lean staff	Flat structures with few levels of management and relatively small numbers of headquarters personnel
Simultaneous loose–tight organisation	Tightly knit in terms of common values held by people and at the same time loosely organised in terms of absence of rules and regulations

OB IN ACTION: Corporate culture and the 'excellence' movement

Image is increasingly important to all organisations, which is why companies employ a veritable army of public relations officers, corporate identity consultants, and reputation managers to improve their public perception. Top executives spend vast amounts of time carefully refining their corporate statements and inducting new employees into their corporate culture. Yet a great deal of executives' pre-occupation with corporate culture can be traced to the historical influence of elite management consulting firms, which was itself a product of consultants' attempts to establish the professional credibility of their field long before the concept of corporate culture was commonly understood.

For example, consultants in McKinsey & Company have long been careful not to refer to themselves as a business and, instead, call themselves a professional practice. Indeed, McKinsey's training emphasises professional language, professional metaphors, and professional comportment in the firm's socialisation of recruits. This deliberate development and self-conscious codification of McKinsey's professional practice lay behind the concept of 'corporate culture'. This was something that fascinated management theorists during the 1980s and 1990s, and was popularised by Tom Peters and Bob Waterman (both McKinsey consultants) in their best-selling book, *In Search of Excellence*. Importantly the concept of corporate culture emerged from their analysis of McKinsey's past successes and through a gradual process of calculated image building, the success of consulting firms ultimately became the model for their corporate clients.

Today, management consultancies still use metaphorical language to reinforce their image, yet what is most notable is how the rhetorical language of consulting has become less descriptive of the individual consultancies and more evocative of their clients' inner desires. Instead of offering their clients corporate counsel or greater efficiency, firms such as Accenture and Booz Allen now promise to turn their clients into aggressive winners, and there seems to be no shortage of clients who embrace their siren statements.

For the management consultancies themselves, however, two questions remain to be answered. First, whether their professional image and vague formulations of positive management buzzwords are going to continue to be enough? Second, when will the so-called profession of management consulting finally go beyond rhetoric and accept full responsibility for its many implicit promises?

Source:

McKenna, C (2006) In the business of consulting: image is everything, *The Observer*, 20 November

Note: Christopher McKenna, who teaches corporate strategy at the Said Business School, University of Oxford, is the author of *The World's Newest Profession: Management Consulting in the Twentieth Century* (Cambridge University Press, 2006).

Staying Close to the Customer

The authors argue that firms where the customer is valued above all else outperform firms without this frame of reference. Where this viewpoint is held, the customer is seen as a source of information about the quality of current products and a source of ideas about products for the future. Thus meeting and, where necessary, pandering to customers' needs is argued to be an action that leads inevitably to superior performance.

Autonomy and Entrepreneurship

Peters and Waterman argue that while successful firms are often very large, they actively fight tendencies towards bureaucracy and lack of innovation. This is accomplished by dividing the firm into small, manageable units which are encouraged to be independent and creative within their respective areas.

Productivity through People

The authors note that successful firms have a genuine recognition that their most important assets are people at all levels, and this gets translated into committed action.

Hands-on Management

In many large companies, senior managers tend to lose touch with the fundamentals of the firm, but Peters and Waterman note that successful firms purposely try to counter this tendency by encouraging the view that the best way to manage is to stay in contact with what goes on by 'walking the floor' rather than exercising control from behind closed doors.

Stick to the Knitting

Another value that is said to characterise excellent firms is a reluctance to become involved in business outside their spheres of expertise. There is a strong emphasis on relying on the firm's core competencies and doing well what it does best.

Simple Form, Lean Staff

Unlike many organisations where managers measure their status, prestige and importance by the number of their subordinates, Peters and Waterman noted that successful firms have fewer layers of administrative staff, and a relatively small group of headquarters personnel. In what the authors call 'excellent' companies, a person's importance is measured by his or her impact on the organisation's performance rather than the size of his or her empire.

Simultaneously Loose and Tight Organisation

The final attribute identified by Peters and Waterman looks like a contradiction at first sight – how can something be loosely and tightly organised at the same time? What is meant by a loose and tight organisation is connected to the core values. In one sense they are tightly organised because everyone understands and believes in the firm's values, and these provide the glue that holds the firm together. However, in a physical sense they have fewer staff and fewer rules and regulations, which means they are loosely organised. Peters and Waterman argue that the loose physical structure is only possible because of the strong common value system. Thus the tight structure of common cultural values facilitates the loose control structure which is said to encourage innovation and risk taking.

Comments on the Peters and Waterman Contribution

Peters and Waterman's work has attracted strong criticism for its lack of rigour in terms of research methodology, and it has been forcefully argued that the link between cultures, excellence and performance is tenuous and highly fragile. Some of the so-called excellent companies subsequently encountered huge performance difficulties and, in addition, there are severe criticisms of some of the cultural characteristics used by Peters and Waterman. For instance Silver (1987) is particularly scathing about the reality of the 'people orientation' in some of the firms, and in a descriptive parody entitled 'McFactory' cites McDonald's as an example of one of the companies identified as 'excellent'. He notes that McFactory relies heavily on cheap, minimum-wage, non-unionised labour, which is usually made up of teenage workers in part-time employment. Thus behind the façade of what is portrayed as a stimulating work environment, there is a reality of dull monotony, where the emphasis is on deskilling the work by using the principle of scientific management so that the last ounce of effort can be extracted from employees (Silver 1987).

Notwithstanding these criticisms, the Peters and Waterman research played an important part in stimulating interest in organisational culture and this was accompanied by other work in the same style, which for interest is given in the further readings at the end of this chapter. However, things have moved on since then and it is to more recent developments that attention must now be directed.

A Recent Perspective: The Goffee and Jones Contingency Framework

The Peters and Waterman (1982) perspective was firmly part of what is now known as the 'excellence movement', which holds that culture is a key ingredient in the commercial success of an organisation. Because the authors list cultural characteristics that are said to lead to this outcome, it is easy to see why the ideas have an instant appeal to managers. The problem is, however, that this perspective and others like it imply a 'one best culture' suitable for all organisations. This is a rather simplistic idea and, although culture almost certainly has a part to play in organisational performance, it is only likely to have this effect if it helps in coping with the circumstances that confront an organisation. Since different organisations face different circumstances, the most useful approach to the culture–performance relationship is likely to be a contingency perspective, a matter that is addressed in a more recent development by Goffee and Jones (1998), who start with an assumption there is no such thing as a 'right' or 'best' culture for all organisations. Rather, the most appropriate culture for an organisation is the one that best helps it cope with the exigencies of its own business environment.

Goffee and Jones commence their analysis by giving a framework for classifying the characteristics of different organisational cultures. To do this they return to a stream of sociological work by Durkheim (1966), from which they extract two basic dimensions that reflect the way that humans relate to each other: sociability and solidarity.

Sociability

Sociability: the degree of friendliness in the relationships between people

Sociability expresses the degree of friendliness between members of a community or group and where sociability is high, people help each other because they want to, with no thought of favours in return. This dimension of the relationship between people is essentially based on feelings and emotions and where it exists, people tend to value the relationship for its own sake. While those immersed in a relationship of this type sometimes take it for granted, it is usually recognised by a newcomer to an organisation as something special. For instance, if one person has a reason to celebrate they all celebrate; if someone has a reason to feel low, everyone tends to rally around; when people go into hospital they are visited by colleagues, and the people often socialise away from work.

The advantages to an organisation of a high degree of sociability in its culture are said to be:

- high morale, because most people working in these conditions find work a pleasure and work is viewed as fun
- it fosters teamwork, creativity, openness and sharing of ideas, and, because they genuinely want to help each other rather than simply look good, people are likely to go beyond their formal job requirements
- it promotes innovation and uninhibited cross-fertilisation of ideas
- people seldom have a mentality of being there for the shortest possible time, but work until the job is done.

Nevertheless, high sociability can have its downside because:

- strong friendships can mean that poor performance is tolerated and people can be reluctant to disagree with or criticise friends
- in extreme cases it can degenerate into cliques, cabals, in-groups and out-groups which results in behind-the-scenes politicking
- it can be an unpleasant situation for people who value their own personal space and privacy of thought.

Solidarity

Solidarity: the degree of collectiveness in the relationship between people

This dimension is not so much a reflection of people's feelings and emotions, but their thoughts. It expresses the degree of collectiveness (as opposed to individuality) in the relationship between people. Where solidarity is high, people have a sense of common purpose because they have shared goals, tasks or mutual interests. Thus, even if people do not particularly like or admire their colleagues, they tend to make common cause and work together like a well-oiled machine. Its advantages are said to be:

- a ruthless commitment to getting done what (by consensus) needs to get done
- many people find it stimulating to work towards and achieve mutually agreed goals and the behaviour of other people is a constant reminder of the behaviours that are considered acceptable
- people are usually very clear about the rewards for good behaviour.

Again, however, solidarity can have its dark side:

- cultures that are high in solidarity can be ruthless in suppressing dissenters, even when they are also innovators
- too strong a focus on group goals can oppress or hurt individuals.

Using high and low values for sociability and solidarity, the two dimensions can be brought together to give a matrix of four cultural types, which Goffee and Jones call the 'Double "S" Cube' (Figure 20.3). Notice that there is a third dimension (depth) to the matrix. This reflects the idea that sociability and solidarity can have positive and negative aspects, the latter being expressed in the far (shaded) end of the cube. The four cultural types and the environmental circumstances for which they are said to be most appropriate are described in what follows.

Communal culture: one that is high in sociability and solidarity

The Communal Culture

While this is most frequently found in thrusting, successful, small to medium-sized organisations, it is occasionally found in larger firms that have taken great care to retain a culture of this type since their early, formative years. Examples cited by the authors are Hewlett-Packard and the pharmaceutical company Johnson and Johnson. Strong sociability results in people working in a highly collaborative, flexible and mutually supportive way, and their high solidarity unites them in a common sense of purpose. Thus there is a strong ethos of people being protective of the organisation and what it stands for, or as Goffee and Jones put it, 'the competition tends to be seen as an enemy that needs to be defeated' (1998, p 29). Since maintaining a communal culture

Figure 20.3 'The Double "S" Cube'

Source: Goffe, R and Jones, G (1998) *The Character of a Corporation*, copyright © by Rob Goffee and Gareth Jones. Reprinted by permission of HarperCollins Publishers Ltd and HarperCollins, Inc.

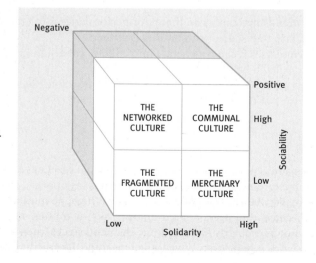

in a large organisation is difficult, a great deal of emphasis is placed on careful selection of new entrants, with only those who are perceived to 'fit in' being admitted. In addition, extensive and somewhat intensive induction programmes are used to inculcate the core values of the organisation and appraisal is not only against performance targets, but adherence to the desired organisational ethos.

The Networked Culture

Networked culture: one that is high in sociability and low in solidarity

This culture, which is high in sociability but low in solidarity, is said to be most appropriate for large organisations that face highly competitive environments. Typically, the critical success factor in these industries is a free and open flow of information across functional, geographic, or even national boundaries and examples cited by the authors are Unilever, Heineken and the international electrical giant Philips. The culture is often found in large, highly successful companies, which perhaps had communal cultures at an earlier stage of development. Because it is hard to retain the right balance of sociability and solidarity to sustain a communal culture, there is a natural transformation to the networked type of organisation. Even so, there is often a strong legacy of sociability and people expect to be friendly with their colleagues.

The Mercenary Culture

Mercenary culture: one that is low on sociability and high on solidarity

Organisations of this type are low on sociability but high on solidarity, and this culture is said to be most beneficial in a fast-changing business environment where competitive pressures are extremely high. In these circumstances, success and even survival can depend on establishing priorities, goals and strategies to beat off the competition, and an ability to move quickly, decisively and cohesively can be all important. Because solidarity is high the culture tends to promote an 'all hands to the pumps' mentality, but this is unencumbered by a compulsion to maintain friendly relations with everybody, which allows the relentless pursuit of effectiveness and efficiency to become the norm. Organisations of this type tend to be highly goal-orientated and goals are usually ambitious and specific – not just improve market share, but improve market share by 10 per cent each year. Here the examples identified by the authors are the confectionery giant Mars, PepsiCo and the financial conglomerate Citicorp. These organisations can be extremely demanding of their employees and the lack of sociability might mean that people only cooperate with each other when they can see a clear personal benefit in doing so. While people are probably well rewarded, the organisation can be merciless and intolerant of those who do not achieve, and so people tend not to remain with the organisation for too long.

The Fragmented Culture

Fragmented culture: one that is low on both sociability and solidarity

This culture is low on sociability and solidarity. It applies to companies in which interdependence between the different activities is low and the critical success factor is having employees who are the star individuals in a particular field. In these circumstances sociability or solidarity are unlikely to have strong effects on performance, and organisations of this type tend to be relatively small in terms of staffing levels, for instance law firms, consultancies or merchant banks. However, this culture is sometimes found in much larger organisations that sub-contract or outsource most of their activities, for example the clothing manufacturer Benetton, or franchised operations such as fast-food chains.

An Appraisal of the Goffee and Jones Framework

The Goffee and Jones framework is an important advance in the study of organisational cultures. Because it is a true contingency theory, it does much to enhance the utility of the culture concept and, since it fits well with other work in the area, it is not a 're-invention of the wheel' but a genuine advance in the body of knowledge. This can perhaps be best illustrated by drawing attention to a number of important implications that arise from the work.

- Although the authors state that an organisation's dominant culture can usually be categorised as one of the four types described above, they also point out that sub-cultures are almost certain to exist in most organisations. Thus they avoid the pitfall of treating culture as an undifferentiated whole, and this is in line with other important work in the area.

- The authors point out that no culture is likely to last forever. Indeed, they put forward the idea that there seems to be a natural life-cycle with three of the four cultural types, which is connected to the changes that inevitably take place as an organisation grows and develops. Companies often start out with communal cultures, which fits well with Schein's (1983) ideas about the effect that the founder of an organisation has on its culture. As it grows, it meets new challenges and for this reason there is probably a natural progression to the networked type in many organisations. Later on, however, complacency can set in and the organisation can come under siege by its competitors. Thus, emergency measures may be needed, which prompts a move to the mercenary culture.

- Goffee and Jones explicitly point out that none of the cultures is inherently good or bad in itself. Sociability and solidarity can both result in human behaviour that is dysfunctional for an organisation in certain circumstances. Thus it is the blend of these two dimensions at a certain point in time that is important. For this reason, the cultural types are more (or less) appropriate at coping with the different environmental exigencies that can be encountered by organisations.

- Although Goffee and Jones do not specifically address the matter of difference in national cultures, they draw attention to the idea that these can have an impact on the cultural type with which an organisation is likely to feel most at ease. For example, in contrasting Procter and Gamble and Unilever, which are direct competitors facing almost identical competitive pressures, they note that the former has long had characteristics typical of the mercenary culture, whereas Unilever has only recently made moves in this direction. The important difference here is that Procter and Gamble is an American organisation, while Unilever is Anglo-Dutch. American organisations are much more likely to be at home with the centralisation of authority, a high task focus, ruthless internal competition and the 'all shoulders to the wheel' ethos of the mercenary culture. European organisations, however, have a much stronger focus on relationships and decentralised authority, both of which characterise the networked culture.

- Finally, although the authors deal with the matter of changing organisational cultures, they avoid the trap of understating the problems involved. Thus, while they view change as possible, which puts them firmly in what has been called earlier the 'application' school, they do not suggest, as do so many others in this school, that culture can be manipulated in an easy way. Indeed, they are at great pains to point out that cultural change is often prompted by a crisis, which itself brings about a degree of modification to culture.

TIME OUT

Before reading the next section, re-examine the culture you explored in the two previous Time Out exercises and answer the questions below.

1. Is the culture an appropriate one from the point of view of:
   (a) the employees (or students)?
   (b) the organisation or institution?
2. If your answer to questions 1(a) and 1(b) is yes, how can this culture be maintained?
3. If your answer to questions 1(a) or 1(b) is no, what changes in culture do you feel the organisation would like to see?
4. How can these changes be brought about?

CULTURE CHANGE AND CULTURE MANAGEMENT

Culture change: modification of an existing culture

Culture management: maintaining or making slight modifications to fine-tune an existing culture

If it is accepted that culture has an important influence on the success of an organisation, managers clearly have a vested interest in being able to influence culture. This can be done in one of two ways: by modifying the existing culture through *culture change*, or using *culture management* to retain one that is felt to be appropriate. However, to regard either of these as a practical possibility it is necessary to assume that culture is something that can be changed at will. This idea still provokes heated debate, and nowhere is it more apparent than in the suggestion that all employees throughout an organisation can be induced to embrace a market-orientated culture; a very fashionable 'must have' in many organisations (Greenley and Foxall 1996). The assumption is that a culture of this type will result in superior organisational performance (Selnes *et al*. 1996). While this may just be a bid for increased power on the part of marketeers in organisations, it can be noted that inculcating a stronger customer focus in employees is also a fundamental part of the new control strategies described in Chapter 19. However, in an extremely penetrating analysis of these ideas, Harris and Ogbonna (1999) conclude that what is proposed is so conceptually and practically flawed that it is doomed to failure because it:

- rests on an integrationist perspective, which assumes that an organisation's culture is common to all its members, whereas the more realistic differentiationist view acknowledges the inevitability of sub-cultures
- assumes that top managers can impose a culture on the rest of an organisation at will, but this is only possible in certain, rarely encountered circumstances

- flies in the face of a substantial body of evidence that cultures perpetuate themselves until such time as culture holders decide that change is desirable.

Many theorists argue that because culture is so deep-rooted, it is highly resistant to manipulation. For example, Ogbonna (1993) points out that while some behaviourial change results from a culture change initiative, it is very unlikely to change deeper values. Thus, all that occurs is a cosmetic impression of culture change. An even stronger position is taken by Ray (1986), who argues that one of the main functions of a culture may well be to enable people to resist changes of this type. For this reason it is not surprising to find that unanticipated consequences and backlash effects often occur in cultural change initiatives. For instance, a study of 530 American companies by Gilmore *et al.* (1997) found that while quality, service levels, competency and productivity often improve, climate, employee morale and work enthusiasm decline considerably. Indeed, Woodall (1996) argues that many attempts at cultural change are so badly conducted that they result in degradation of the workforce and raise questions about the ethics of these initiatives.

In the light of this evidence it is important to understand something of the theory of culture change as it is expressed in most of these change programmes. This will be explained in two stages: first, by giving an overview of the methodology itself and, second, by describing some of the techniques that have been advocated to bring about changes.

The Methodology

Almost all culture change models are derived from the four-step process suggested by Silverzweig and Allen (1976), which is summarised below.

Step 1: Analyse Existing Culture

This usually consists of an extensive survey of organisational members to establish specific objectives for cultural change.

Step 2: Experiencing the Culture

Here organisational members are given the opportunity to examine the existing culture, (hopefully to identify its dysfunctions) and then participate in identifying the culture that is required.

Step 3: System Installation

This is where the actual change process occurs, usually by making use of group discussion workshops. The active participation of organisational leaders is said to be vital in this stage, primarily to provide those lower down with something on which to model their own behaviour. It is usually recognised that if the initiative is not completed effectively, all that is likely to result is superficial surface change, for instance people seeking to please those higher up by displaying signs of the behaviour they believe top people want to see.

Step 4: Ongoing Evaluation

Here the degree of actual change is assessed and, as necessary, other methods are used to bring about or reinforce the desired changes.

Techniques

Most of the techniques described here would probably be deployed in stages 3 and 4 of the above methodology. They are also said to be useful ways of reinforcing existing cultures where they are already considered appropriate.

Taking Advantage of Existing Culture

This is sometimes described as 'working around an existing culture', and requires that a comprehensive understanding of the organisational value system is obtained in stage 1 of the methodology. If this is achieved, the picture can be compared with the cultural values that management would like to see in place and, where necessary, discussion and explanation can be used to correct any discrepancies.

When examined closely, some of the best publicised examples of so-called cultural change probably turn out to be little more than working around an existing culture. One example is given in Ackroyd and Crowdy's (1990) study of slaughtermen, which showed how managers hijacked a culture that was already in place and portrayed the results as something that occurred because of their endeavours.

Socialisation

This has been described earlier and consists of a set of processes that enable employees to learn about their firm's culture and pass on their knowledge and understanding to others. While socialisation seldom brings about a radical change in people's values, it can help them to become more aware of any differences between their own values and those of an organisation, and to develop ways of coping with the differences.

Managing Symbols

As noted earlier, a number of authors suggest that a powerful way to understand a culture is to take note of the values communicated through stories and other symbolic events. This being the case, one way to promote cultural change is to introduce stories and myths that spread the new cultural values.

Change Reward Systems

Behavioural psychologists argue that the behavioural elements of a culture are learned and can just as easily be extinguished. Thus cultural change can be encouraged by changing the organisation's system of rewards and punishments. An example of how a behaviourist approach might bring about a stronger customer service orientation is given in Chapter 8, where Organisational Behaviour modification techniques are described.

Add New Members

New values can sometimes be a lot harder to develop than starting from scratch. Therefore, providing they actually have the desired new culture, adding new organisational members can be a powerful strategy. However, if it is to be effective, there must be enough new people to swamp the existing culture, otherwise they will simply be socialised into what is there.

Implement Culture Shock

Culture shock is something that causes an organisation to take a serious look at its own values and behaviour, for example the loss of a key customer, a scandal of some sort, an unsuccessful lawsuit, or something that threatens its existence. When events like these are attributed to something that is lacking in an organisation's culture, it is often the case that drastic changes are made very quickly.

Change the Top People

As well as having a potential shock value, change at the top can have a major impact on an organisation's culture by sending reverberations throughout an organisation. The person at the top often sets the norms of behaviour and when he or she goes, the next level down soon seems to follow, perhaps because these people are seen as key symbols of the old regime, who will have difficulty in adapting to the new one.

Involve Organisational Members

Strictly speaking, changing a culture involves changing its underlying assumptions, values and beliefs. Therefore, top-down culture change can be interpreted by people below as something that forces them to give up assumptions and values that are almost sacred. Therefore, because people are usually more willing to implement decisions they have helped to make, participative techniques can often be more successful.

What, then, are the general conclusions that can be drawn about the ease of cultural change? There are three in particular that are highly significant:

- Cultures are the result of complex social processes that tend to take place over a long period of time, so a programme of cultural change which becomes a 'quick fix' solution to an organisational problem can do more harm than good.
- All cultures are different, and what can be an effective change strategy in one organisation may be far less effective elsewhere.
- The more deeply ingrained a culture, the more difficult it will be to change, and the more an organisation contains multiple sub-cultures, the more complex and time-consuming will be the change process.

Organisations therefore need to consider very carefully whether they should try to interfere with a culture or simply let other changes that have been put in place give rise to an appropriate culture that emerges at its own pace (Hope and Hendry 1995).

A BRIEF NOTE ON NATIONAL CULTURES

At an intuitive level almost everyone is aware that customs, attitudes and values vary between countries. Indeed, the need to adjust our behaviour can sometimes become very obvious if we travel outside our native country. These days, many organisations operate internationally, with branches or subsidiaries abroad, and there is an increasing realisation that people in organisations need to be aware of cultural differences and adjust their behaviour accordingly. For this reason, an important area of study is now that of cross-cultural differences and how these can influence patterns of behaviour (Adler and Bartholomew 1992). Similarly, it is important to note that the culture of an organisation needs to be compatible with the culture of the country or region in which it is located. If this is not the case, people can find that expected patterns of behaviour in the enterprise clash with what they have been brought up to regard as normal and acceptable.

There is a great deal of evidence to show that national cultures vary considerably in terms of beliefs and values that are held sacred, and some of this evidence was presented in Chapter 13. Importantly, it needs to be noted that these cultural effects are what prompt people in different locations to behave in very different ways.

REPLAY

- Culture is one of the less tangible features of organisational life and, while it is hard to define, there is a growing consensus that it consists of a deeply ingrained set of values that provide people in an organisation with a code of acceptable behaviour.

- A number of different perspectives on organisational culture exist, the most pronounced difference being that between integrationists, who view the phenomena as a relatively homogeneous set of values shared by all organisational members, and differentiationists, who hold that there are different sub-cultures in most organisations.

- While the evidence for a universal 'one best culture' is weak, this is the approach adopted by most popular writers in the area, whose descriptions are often taken as a prescription for an ideal culture. An exception to this, however, is the more recent contingency framework of Goffee and Jones (1998).

- Changing an organisation's culture is likely to be tremendously difficult and, if it can be accomplished, the process will probably take a considerable amount of time and effort.

- Organisational culture nearly always contains elements of the culture of the country in which an organisation is located, which means that a culture that is appropriate for a firm in one country may not be appropriate for a branch or division of the same organisation elsewhere.

ORGANISATIONAL CLIMATE

Although the concept of organisational climate is closely allied to culture, it has existed in a developed form for considerably longer and can be traced back to the work of Kurt Lewin (1951). Like culture, it can be difficult to define precisely, and since some academic definitions can be rather obscure, in the interests of simplicity it is defined here as:

> a characteristic ethos or atmosphere within an organisation at a given point in time which is reflected in the way its members perceive, experience and react to the organisational context.

A number of important implications arise from this definition. First, climate is a 'felt' state of affairs, rather than a set of hard, quantifiable attributes. One way to think of it is as the way that people describe relevant features of an organisation to themselves, and interpret what they experience (James and Jones 1974).

Second, climatic conditions can be short-lived (Powell and Butterfield 1978) and this is one of the features that distinguishes climate from culture.

Finally, since climate is experienced by people and affects their attitudes, it gives a basis for the way they will behave (Schneider 1983). This is usually concerned with whether they feel that their membership of an organisation is a psychologically rewarding experience, coupled with the effect this has on their levels of morale, motivation and the desire to remain as organisational members (Litwin and Stringer 1968).

TIME OUT

Carefully consider a group of up to 25 people to which you belong. Preferably this should be a formal group, for instance a section or department at your place of work, or if you choose a group at your university or college, it could be a class or even all the students in your year of the course. You have probably noticed that from time to time there are what seem to be attitude changes in the group. Try to identify some of these that have occurred fairly recently and answer the questions below.

1. What attitudes have you identified? For example, are they attitudes to the organisation as a whole or to a smaller part of it? If you chose an academic location are they attitudes to a course as a whole, a particular subject or class, or towards the institution?

2. What was the nature of these attitude changes? For example, did attitudes become more positive or negative?

3. To what extent do you feel that these attitude changes represent a shift, albeit a temporary one, in climate?

THE NATURE AND ORIGINS OF CLIMATE

The Relation of Climate to Culture

Although there are certain similarities between climate and culture, there are also differences. While both are phenomena that people feel or experience, they tend to be more consciously aware of climate. In addition, although both have effects on behaviour, this occurs in rather different ways. Culture gives people a code of conduct that informs them about the behaviour that is expected, whereas climate tends to result in a set of conditions to which they react. Culture is also more permanent and deeply ingrained. Thus in Smircich's (1983) words it can be regarded as something an organisation '*is*', whereas climate is usually more short-term – a phase that an organisation passes through.

However, one way in which cultures and climates are similar is that both are linked to the value system of organisational members. Values are a fundamental part of a culture and, to some extent, culture itself gives people their values. However, climate is more often a reflection of whether current organisational conditions are in accord with the values that people already hold. Therefore, culture is often a significant background factor to a particular set of climatic conditions.

Before closing this brief contrast, however, it is important to note that this is very much the traditional view of the two concepts. There is another viewpoint that holds that the differences are really much smaller, and that culture and climate may well be the same phenomenon, but measured in different ways (Denison 1996). This is far too important an idea to be ignored or glossed over but, for the present, it is more convenient to use the traditional perspective, and a return to the alternative view will be made at the end of the chapter.

Individual or Group Level Construct?

Although the very expression organisational climate implies that it is an organisation-wide phenomenon, it should be noted that it is something that arises in individual feelings and experiences. This means that it is strongly connected with individual mental processes (Kozlowski and Doherty 1989) and, for this reason, it is necessary to draw a distinction between climate at the individual level and climate at the group level. The individual effect is normally referred to as *psychological climate* (Koys and DeCotis 1991), which reflects how a person experiences and reacts to his or her surroundings. In this book, however, the focus is primarily on *organisational climate*, which is a social phenomenon that affects the behaviour of groups, or even the whole organisation. Nevertheless, there is an important connection between the two levels. Organisational climates are not simply the sum of individual feelings. Rather, when a group of people is exposed to the same organisational conditions, they share their interpretations of the circumstances, and what emerges is a degree of consensus among group members about climate: namely organisational climate.

Psychological climate: how the individual experiences and reacts to his or her surroundings

Organisational climate: how people collectively experience and react to their surroundings

Outcomes or Phenomena?

Climate can have pronounced effects on attitudes and behaviour, but there is sometimes a great deal of confusion about whether it is the phenomenon itself that results

Figure 20.4
Connections between
independent,
intervening and
dependent variables

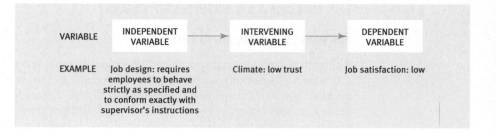

in this effect, or whether what happens is an outcome of something else. Its origins and outcomes will be covered in detail presently, but, for now, it is important to note that most definitions and measures treat climate as something that is both a phenomenon and an outcome; that is, as an intervening variable. This is shown in outline in Figure 20.4.

Note that the independent variable **job design** does not affect the dependent variable **job satisfaction** directly. Rather it influences the climatic dimension of **trust,** which in turn affects **job satisfaction**. The reason for treating climate in this way is largely to provide conceptual clarity; for instance, although we might observe that job satisfaction alters if the design of a job is changed, it is difficult to explain how job design has this effect (cause) on job satisfaction. However, if an intervening variable is placed between the two variables, the causal link is broken down into two stages, and the process can be made much clearer.

TIME OUT

Using the group and its attitude changes that you identified in the previous Time Out exercise, apply the model of cause and effect given in Figure 20.4 and answer the questions below for each attitude.

1. What particular factor (independent variable) prompted the attitude change?
2. What climatic condition (intervening variable) did this create?
3. What was the outcome in terms of attitude?

Hint: You may find it easier to consider matters in the reverse direction; that is, starting with the outcome.

CLIMATE: A MODEL OF ANTECEDENTS AND OUTCOMES

Since climate is usually treated as an intervening variable, it is important to distinguish between the factors that result in climatic conditions and those that are affected by climate. Using some of the results from a diverse range of studies, a model can be constructed which portrays these factors (see Figure 20.5).

Figure 20.5 The origins and outcomes of organisational climate

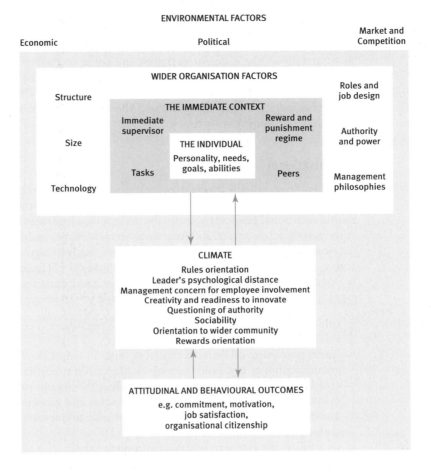

Factors inside and outside an organisation can have an impact on climate. Inside the organisation, influential variables are shown at three levels: the *wider organisation*, the *immediate context* and the *individual*. These can all affect perceptions of climate and, in turn, climate can result in attitudinal and behaviourial outcomes. Before describing the variables in detail it is necessary to emphasise two important points.

- There is an arrow on the model leading from climate to outcomes and another one in the opposite direction. This indicates that climates are often self-reinforcing. That is, poor climatic conditions can result in lowered commitment, motivation and job satisfaction, and these feelings can result in people perceiving that the organisation has a poor climate.

- A similar pair of arrows is shown between climate and the individual. This reflects the idea that some of a person's individual characteristics will shape perceptions of climate, for example needs, goals and personality characteristics. Thus, if there is a poor match between what a person needs or wants and what the organisation provides, there can often be an adverse effect on perceptions of climate. However, people are not totally inflexible, and over a period of time the climatic conditions can sometimes result in them adjusting their aspirations downwards.

In what follows the different variables and some of their effects are all described separately, but in practice most of them are at work together and they can all affect perceptions of climate. For convenience, the explanation starts by describing the dimensions of climate and then its outcomes. The explanation then proceeds by working from the environment inwards.

Organisational Climate

Since people are usually aware of several organisational characteristics or attributes, they experience life in several different ways at the same time. Thus, climate is a multidimensional phenomenon and the most robust measures evaluate it in this way. Although there are several different measurements that can be used to do this, what is given here is a description of the dimensions used in three of the most prominent scales: Litwin and Stringer (1968), Payne and Phesey (1971) and Dastmalchian (1986). Scales of this type are usually pencil-and-paper questionnaires that are completed by employees of an organisation, and they are used to tap perceptions of:

- **rules orientation**: whether behaviour in the organisation is governed by formal rules and regulations
- **leader psychological distance**: whether those in senior positions emphasise their greater authority and hold themselves apart from subordinates
- **creativity and readiness to innovate**: whether the organisation and its management are seen as receptive to new ideas and ways of doing things
- **questioning authority**: whether it is permissible to question the decision of a senior person
- **sociability**: the extent to which a team spirit exists
- **an orientation to wider community**: whether the organisation and its policies are seen to be sensitive to the needs of a wider community
- **rewards orientation**: whether the organisation and its management are seen to encourage effort with rewards, rather than using punishments for lack of effort.

These dimensions are used by people to describe the organisation to themselves and according to what is perceived, they experience membership as being somewhere between psychologically stimulating and rewarding at one extreme, to stultifying at the other. Predictably, the former is more likely to lead to positive attitudinal and behavioural outcomes.

Outcomes

Outcomes shown in the model are both attitudinal and behavioural. Although the list of outcomes is potentially endless, for simplicity, only four examples are shown. These are: *commitment to organisation, motivation, job satisfaction* and *organisational citizenship*.

It is now time to examine some of the factors that influence climate, and the description starts from the outside and works inwards.

The Environmental Context

Economic Factors

The buoyancy and general health of the surrounding economy can result in management feeling optimistic or pessimistic about the future. Where managers are pessimistic costs might be scrutinised or investment curtailed to hoard reserves for hard times ahead. Employees can be remarkably sensitive about these signs, which often promote a climate of insecurity (Dastmalchian 1986).

Political Factors

In Great Britain, central government policies have forced most public sector organisations to make internal adjustments to comply with legislation that requires them to put work that was hitherto performed by their own employees out to tender. Steps such as this can also prompt structural changes that give rise to insecurity, which is quickly reflected in climate.

Market and Competitive Factors

The market for a firm's products can have a dramatic effect on its prosperity, and market conditions can sometimes threaten an organisation's very existence. Where this occurs, the climate of insecurity can prompt a 'rush to the door' as people look for more secure jobs. However, these conditions can sometimes have surprisingly positive effects. Organisational members can perceive that they are all faced with a common threat, which prompts them to pull together to remedy the situation, which has very positive effects on climate (Dastmalchian 1986).

The Organisational Context

Size, Structure and Authority Patterns

One of the important points made in Chapter 18 is that as organisations get larger they tend to become more formal and bureaucratic, which means that size, structure and authority patterns can conveniently be considered together. Bureaucratic organisations usually have a strong rules orientation and a high emphasis on following established procedures. Moreover, size often goes hand in hand with increased job specialisation, lowered interpersonal communication and a greater centralisation of decision making. All of these characteristics tend to result in climatic conditions in which people feel that there is a lack of freedom to use initiative and skills.

Roles and Job Design

This topic is covered in Chapters 7 and 11, where its effects on the way that people experience work are covered in more detail. The work of Hackman and Oldham (1975), for example, clearly demonstrates that certain aspects of job design have psychological effects in terms of whether people feel that work is a stimulating and meaningful experience.

Technology

Technology has an impact on the way that jobs are designed, and there is some suggestion that using automation for repetitive and fragmented jobs can enrich work, enhance feelings of worker control and lower feelings of alienation (Crawley and Spurgeon 1979). Conversely, there is also evidence that computerised clerical work results in lowered feelings of personal control and responsibility. However, much seems to depend on the nature of computerisation and the jobs to which it is applied. In some cases it results in more varied, interesting and responsible work with a more positive impact on climate (Oborne 1994).

Management Philosophies

Philosophy is used here to describe the views that managers hold about the roles and functions of subordinates, which often has an impact on the way they are treated and gives rise to climatic effects. One indication of these philosophies is the payment system used within an organisation – too strong an emphasis on incentive payments can create the impression that managers believe that the only thing which motivates subordinates is money (Dastmalchian and Mansfield 1980).

Authority and Power

The way that authority and power are used can also have climatic repercussions. An organisation that is run in a highly autocratic way by a small, powerful clique of executives can be expected to have a climate lacking in employee collaboration but high in fear.

The Immediate Context

The Immediate Supervisor

A person's immediate supervisor can have a strong effect on climate. While some supervisors can mitigate the effects of frustrating organisational policies and practices, others tend to make these features of working life much worse. Therefore, to the extent that a supervisor shields subordinates from these things, there can be a positive effect on climate. In addition, the interpersonal relationships between a supervisor and subordinates can make the overall work experience more pleasant or unpleasant, and this also has climatic repercussions.

Tasks

Some tasks are inherently more psychologically rewarding than others, and so the nature of the work that a person performs is virtually certain to colour his or her experience of an organisation.

Rewards and Punishments

In order to encourage certain behaviours and discourage those that are considered less desirable, organisations usually have a system of rewards and punishments. Most organisational members are aware of this, if only at a subjective level, and this has an effect on how they experience organisational life.

Peers

While climate is an individually experienced phenomenon, people in the immediate context usually share their experiences and interpretations. This enables them to test their perceptions of reality on others and if these perceptions are confirmed as accurate, what has been perceived becomes the reality of the situation.

The Individual

Chapters 3–10 all deal with individual differences; that is, the ways in which people are unique and have their own **personalities**, **abilities**, **needs** and **goals**. An organisation that provides a facility for individuals to satisfy their needs and achieve cherished goals is more likely to be one where membership is perceived as a rewarding experience, which in turn shapes perceptions of climate at the individual level. Nevertheless, as is pointed out above, group effects are also very powerful. Since groups have some capability to shape the views and perceptions of their members, the ensuing climate is more often manifest as a collective phenomenon.

REPLAY

- Because people in organisations take in information about their surroundings and construct personal realities from what they perceive, organisations always have climates of some sort.
- Thus, climate is an experienced phenomenon and, since people in the workplace share their experiences and interpretations, climate tends to emerge as a collectively experienced state of affairs.
- Climate is influenced by a number of organisational features and conditions and, since these can change, climates can also fluctuate.

OVERVIEW AND CONCLUSIONS

The concepts of organisational culture and organisational climate clearly have some similarities. Both deal with intangible aspects of the way that employees relate to and experience an organisation, and both acknowledge that this results in distinctive patterns of employee behaviour. Nevertheless, the traditional view is that culture and climate are different concepts and deal with different facets of organisational life. There are three ways in which they can be contrasted and these are discussed in what follows.

Culture and Climate as Theoretical Constructs

Culture and climate are both abstract constructs, that are used to explain a state of affairs within an organisation. Of the two, culture describes a more ephemeral and intangible state of affairs – the values that are part of what it is, in much the same way that an individual's personality is fundamental to what he or she is. Climate, on the other hand, is much more explicit and precise. It has no pretence of explaining what an organisation is, but expresses the mental reactions of its members to what they perceive it to be.

Although it has long been recognised that organisations have cultures, serious application of the concept is a fairly recent development. The most penetrating work in the area uses an anthropological frame of reference, the output of which usually produces no more than a description of an organisation's culture, perhaps because many anthropologists see the main role of the discipline as describing and documenting. Climate, however, is largely the preserve of social psychologists, who set out to explain how particular sets of climatic conditions arise, and how these have discernible effects on the behaviour of organisational members. Thus, the way the concepts are defined tends to reflect the views of two very different groups of social scientists about ways in which human behaviour in organisations can best be understood. Needless to say, instead of trying to find ways of reconciling their different points of view, researchers from one school are often dismissive of those from the other. Culturalists criticise climatologists for trying to be too precise about measurement, and those who study climate tend to criticise culturalists for adopting an approach which is too strongly focused on producing one-off descriptions that make it impossible to compare organisations. Commenting on this problem, Denison (1996) argues that it is far from clear that culture and climate are concerned with two distinctly different aspects of organisational life. Both, for example, have similar theoretical foundations and, ultimately, they both address the issue of 'How does this affect behaviour?' Indeed, in Denison's view, the apparent difference has resulted in something of a self-fulfilling prophecy. Since culturalist and climatologists come from different academic backgrounds, they tend to use different methods of investigation, the net result of which is that although they can be studying the same phenomenon, the results they produce create the impression that the two phenomena are totally different.

Culture and Climate as Organisational Phenomena

The conventional view about culture and climate is that they exist at different levels. Culture is usually taken to be deeply embedded in subconsciously held values. Conversely, climate tends to be regarded as more of a surface phenomenon, with easily identifiable effects on behaviour. Although sub-cultures are usually found within organisations, until fairly recently there has been a strong tendency to view culture as a pervasive phenomenon, whereas micro climates tend to be regarded as more inevitable because many of the important factors directly influencing climatic conditions are located in a group's immediate context.

Because cultures are taken to be enduring and slow to change it can be difficult to correct a culture that is considered inappropriate. The antecedents of climates are better understood and it is usually assumed that climates change more quickly than cultures. Although this does not mean that climates are any easier to modify, at a theoretical level it probably means that poor climates are more avoidable.

The Utility of Culture and Climate Concepts to Managers

At the present time it is likely that most managers view culture as a more important topic than climate. The rather naive ideas set out in popular texts on the subject have resulted in something of a managerial love affair with the word, perhaps because managers have been encouraged to believe that a universal set of cultural characteristics can be selected as an off-the-shelf recipe for organisational success. These very simplistic ideas probably mean that the concept has less real utility than appears at first sight. This is not necessarily the fault of managers. They are busy people and if they are encouraged by self-styled gurus (many of whom should know better) to believe that culture is a 'quick-fix' solution, it is probably the self-appointed experts who should be blamed. Nevertheless, the idea that an appropriate culture can make a significant contribution to organisational success is an important one, and as the quality of research in the area improves, it is possible that a more definitive picture that tells which cultures are most appropriate for organisations in different circumstances will emerge. In addition, it seems likely that viable methods to move from one set of cultural characteristics to another can be evolved, and when both of these requirements have been satisfied, culture is likely to come into its own as a highly usable concept. Until then, however, its use can sometimes be nothing more than a blind act of faith.

While it has never caught management's imagination in quite the same way as culture, climate has always been important to organisations. There has long been a recognition that work-related attitudes and behaviour are important for organisational performance. In addition it has been known for some time that structure and immediate contextual factors, such as supervisor style and the influence of workgroups, all play a part in shaping attitudes and behaviour. Climate is also a concept that has been exposed to a more rigorous academic exploration and is less plagued with simplistic ideas than culture, so it is, or should be, a concept that has a great deal of practical utility to managers.

FURTHER READING

Cray, D and GR Mallory (1997) *Making Sense of Managing Culture*, Thomson: London. For those who subscribe to the idea that culture can be easily modified, this book gives an interesting 'how to do it' guide.

Deal, TE and AA Kennedy (1982) *Corporate Culture: The Rites and Rituals of Corporate Life,* Reading, MA: Addison-Wesley. A book by two of the 'founding fathers' of the culture movement. Very firmly located in the application school and in its time highly influential in management circles.

Goffee, R and G Jones (1998) *The Character of a Corporation*, London: HarperCollins. The book gives a full description of the authors' more recent contingency application of the culture concept.

Kanter, RM (1995) *The Change Masters: Corporate Entrepreneurs at Work*, London: Allen and Unwin. A highly influential book, written by a management 'guru'. It more about cultural change than anything else and, because it tends to portray culture change as something that is not too difficult to accomplish, it needs to be taken with a pinch of salt.

Martin, J (1992) *Cultures and Organisations: Three Perspectives*, Beverly Hills, CA: Sage. A penetrating analysis of the concept of culture as applied to organisations.

Moore, JD (1997) *Visions of Culture: An Introduction to Anthropological Theories and Theorists*, London: Sage. A book of readings by 21 major theorists on culture and an analysis of their impact on contemporary thought.

Ouchi, WG (1981) *Theory Z*, Reading, MA: Addison Wesley. The author, who was one of the 'founding fathers' of the excellence movement of the 1980s, compares and distinguishes between American and Japanese company cultures. He draws the conclusion that the superior performance of Japanese firms is attributable to their corporate culture.

Parker, M (2000) *Organisational Culture and Identity*, London: Sage. The book takes a critically symbolic perspective on culture, by exploring how organisations shape the identities of their members. It also addresses the important questions of the ethics of this process.

Peters, TJ and RH Waterman (1982) *In Search of Excellence: Lessons from America's Best Run Companies*, New York: Harper and Row. A book which is also by two of the 'founding fathers' of the 'excellence' movement. More than any other book it established culture as a highly fashionable topic in management circles.

Schein, EH (1992) *Organisational Culture and Leadership*, San Francisco, CA: Jossey-Bass. A thorough exploration of organisational culture from a social psychological perspective.

Sackmann, SA (ed.) (1997) *Cultural Complexity in Organisations*, London: Sage. A book of readings in which different authors deal with culture, sub-cultures, and national cultures.

CASE STUDY 20.1: Coca-Cola

Coca-Cola has never found it easy to convince its critics that it runs an ethical business and the anti-Coke website 'thezeromovement.org' claims that the business model of the world's leading soft drinks group involves waste, pollution and questionable nutrition.

However, Dominique Reiniche, president of Coke's European business, argues that the company is developing a more proactive corporate culture to address such issues. 'We are in a time in which we need to change Coke,' Ms Reiniche says. 'I think we have to do more in terms of the environment, and in terms of climate change we have to go even further. I also think we will probably be pushed further on product reformulations.'

Nevertheless, Coke was among the companies praised publicly by the European Commission last year after it, and other soft drinks groups, agreed voluntarily to restrict marketing to children. Drinks companies have moved faster than food companies in altering their marketing practices, with food groups such as Mars, Unilever and Kellogg's a year behind the soft drinks industry in initiating changes. Ms Reiniche claims Coke is working more closely with regulators and other companies than ever before. 'What we have tried to do this time is to influence the industry agenda and bring others with us,' she says. 'It's the end of everybody doing their own thing and creating solutions to the very urgent challenges we are faced with takes collective action.'

Until May 2007, Ms Reiniche was president of the Union of European Beverages Associations, which negotiated the new marketing agreement with the Commission. Of course, Coke also has self-interest at heart: consumers increasingly care about how and where companies make their products, and what they do with their profits, and a survey on Coke in Europe by a Dutch management school found that more than 40 per cent of people canvassed thought the soft drinks group was not making a positive contribution to society.

Ms Reiniche was appointed to her current job by Neville Isdell, Coke's chief executive, who has also become more critical about the company's role in society. He told the Worldwide Fund for Nature's annual conference in Beijing last month that private and non-profit sectors should work together to find answers to global water needs. 'Arguably, we have seen more focus on environmental issues in the past year than the last 20. This has been driven by heightened public awareness of global climate change, and its impact on water, biodiversity, agriculture and human health,' Mr Isdell said. Coke has now enlisted the help of the WWF to find ways to cut back and replenish the 290bn litres of water it uses annually. The company is also working with Greenpeace to develop environmentally friendly beverage coolers and vending machines to cut the hydro-fluorocarbon greenhouse gases released into the atmosphere, as well as considering the agricultural impact of the expansion of its soft drinks portfolio into tea, coffee and juice drinks, which has led it to source ingredients globally. Ms Reiniche says that Coke also aims to convince consumer groups that it is limiting new media marketing to children in order to address concerns that it will use the web instead of television.

Source: Wiggins, J (2007) Coke develops a thirst for sustainability, *Financial Times*, 2 July

Tasks

Working in small groups of three or four students read the above case material, then answer the questions below.

1. According to Dominique Reiniche, the changes Coke envisages are all aimed at developing a more proactive corporate culture. What does this expression mean; is corporate culture the same thing as organisational culture; if not, what is the difference?

2. In your view, what has prompted Coke to embark on the changes it intends to bring about in its culture in the future?

3. To what extent will the changes it envisages require its employees to adopt different values than hitherto; what will these values need to be?

4. To what other things might Coke need to pay attention to bring about these changes?

REVIEW AND DISCUSSION QUESTIONS

1. Using Schien's (1992) conceptualisation of culture as a layered phenomenon that exists at three levels, analyse the culture of an organisation of your own choice and state what you perceive to be its:
- basic assumptions
- values and beliefs that reflect these basic assumptions
- artifacts and creations that reflect its assumptions and value system.

2. Critically evaluate the idea that a strong culture results in commercial success for an organisation.

3. Describe the assumptions of the 'key variable' (application) and 'root metaphor' conceptualisations of organisational culture and distinguish between the ways in which these two schools view the role of culture in an organisation.

4. In outline, describe a four-stage process that could be used to try to change the culture of an organisation and some of the associated techniques that might be used in these stages.

5. Define organisational climate and compare and contrast culture and climate as:
- theoretical constructs
- organisational phenomena
- constructs that have utility for managers in organisations.

Chapter 21

Organisational Change and Development

LEARNING OUTCOMES

After studying this chapter you should be able to:

- define change, understand its significance for organisations, distinguish between different types of change, and identify external and internal triggers for change

- identify reasons for resistance to change, and describe the tactics that can be used for overcoming resistance

- distinguish between planned and emergent approaches to introducing change, and describe the following methods of bringing about change in employees: the systems approach; the Lewin approach; and the Action Research approach

- define Organisational Development (OD), describe its distinctive characteristics, its underlying philosophies, the role of the change agent and, in outline, describe a model of the OD process, together with techniques that can be used in OD interventions

- explain the concept of the 'learning organisation' and its implications for change in organisations

INTRODUCTION

Although there is nothing new about change in organisations, these days many firms have to face changes of considerable magnitude. To consider this, the chapter starts by defining change, and describes the main external and internal factors that can trigger changes. The next part of the chapter then explores in more detail the types of changes that organisations undertake. Since these changes usually require a degree of adaptation by people within the organisation, and it is widely assumed that humans resist change, the next part of the chapter explores reasons for resistance, and the strategies that can be deployed to overcome it.

The remainder of the chapter deals with the two main approaches to organisational change: planned change and the emergent approach. The first of these is typified by Organisational Development (OD). This defined and its distinctive characteristics explained, together with the values and assumptions underpinning the approach. An outline model of the OD process is given, which is used to trace its different stages, and a description is given of some of the methods used in OD to try to bring about changes in the values, attitudes and behaviour of people in organisations. This is followed by an exploration of the practical utility of OD, which is examined by considering three important issues: whether it delivers what it promises, its relevance for contemporary organisations and whether it is an ethical process.

The final matter to be considered is the emergent approach to organisational change, which also includes a consideration of the so-called 'learning organisation', which theoretically, equips an organisation for continuous change. The chapter concludes with a short overview section.

THE SIGNIFICANCE OF ORGANISATIONAL CHANGE

Organisational change: a move from being in one organisational state to being in another state

As applied to organisations, the word 'change' means that a firm shifts from one state to another (Ford and Ford 1995). In the past, this was usually a matter of making small, gradual adaptations. These days, however, the way that matters were handled in the past is no longer a faithful guide to what is required in the present. Indeed, some authors such as Kanter (1995) argue that to equip themselves for the future many organisations will not only need to completely transform themselves into something radically different, but their very survival will crucially depend on being able to master the process of change. Here, the essential problem is said to be that their environments have become so dynamic and turbulent that they must learn to adapt and respond in a correspondingly dynamic way. This argument is echoed by Peters (1987) who points out that future survival will require firms to radically change the ways in which their core business functions operate, which is shown Table 21.1.

If only a part of what Peters suggests comes true, it is clear that many organisations might need to change considerably; largely by moving away from rigid, bureaucratic structures, which are best suited to coping with stable, relatively unchanging conditions, towards organisational forms that are better able to adapt to rapid environmental change (Kanter *et al.* 1992). Having said this, the ideas of people such as Kanter (1995) and Peters (1987) are only one point of view, and there is an alternative.

For example, both Mintzberg (1994) and Huy and Mintzberg (2003) point out that the current preoccupation with change is probably a serious overstatement, which to

Table 21.1 Forecast changes in the core business functions (adapted from Peters 1987)

Organisational function	Traditional emphasis	New emphasis
Production	Mass production in which capital is more important than people; low-cost efficiency is more strongly emphasised than responsiveness and quality	Short production runs; fast change-over of products; people, quality and responsiveness the most important attributes
Marketing	Mass markets involving extensive advertising, market research and market testing	Fragmented markets with emphasis on market creation; small-scale and short-lived markets
Financial control	Centralised control requiring specialised staff to vet investment proposals and set investment policy	Decentralised control with financial specialists becoming part of business teams and spending authority devolved to local levels
Management information systems	Centralised information control and data processing	Decentralised data processing and information control to suit the needs of local units
Research and development	Centralised with emphasis on large projects and innovation limited to new products and services; technical sophistication is more important than reliability and quality	Innovation not limited to new products and services and speed of development more important; increased emphasis on a wide portfolio of small projects and innovation in the way that the organisation operates become more important

some extent has been brought about by the writings of a small number self-styled gurus and prophets. Here it is worth noting that these prophecies about the necessary characteristics of the 'organisation of the future' have all been heard before, and many of them echo what was being said a few years ago about the inevitable predominance of the 'virtual organisation' (see Chapter 17), which, as yet, has simply not come true. The problem is that the whole idea that constant change is desirable has become one of the foremost mantras of the modern-day manager. Unfortunately it gives rise to a view of the world in which frequent change is seen as both good and necessary, while any resistance to change is perceived as bad and near pathological. However, if we turn-off all the hype about the necessity for change, and recognise it for what it is, we can see that that there is comparatively little in terms of the degree of change and turbulence in the world that is supposed to be there. Thus we have probably all been talked into perceiving the environment as in a state of flux, so we notice only those things that do change, and ignore the vast majority of things that remain stable.

TYPES OF ORGANISATIONAL CHANGE

Change comes in many shapes and sizes. Sometimes it only affects parts of an organisation, while elsewhere the whole of an organisation is affected. It can also vary in depth and involve only small, incremental modifications, while other changes consist of completely abandoning existing ways of doing things. One way to conceptualise these differences is by using a framework provided by Nadler and Tushman (1986), which identifies two dimensions along which change can be categorised:

Figure 21.1 A typology of organisational change (adapted from Nadler and Tushman 1986)

| | SCOPE OF CHANGE | |
	Incremental	Strategic
Reactive	**ADAPTATION** Small, gradual changes, usually in response to changes in the organisation's environment and mostly involving only changes to selected organisational parts Example: adding a customer service department after realising that customers require after-sales service	**RE-CREATION** Usually involves a complete re-think of the organisation's strategy, in order for it to become a different type of organisation, and can affect all of its parts Example: a building society that becomes a public company in order to transform itself into a high street bank
Anticipatory	**FINE-TUNING** Small changes, usually at the operational level of an organisation, in anticipation of future environmental changes Example: retailer of flat-pack, self-assembly furniture realises that customers are losing interest in DIY and offers an assembly service	**RE-ORIENTATION** A change in direction for an organisation that is in anticipation of changes elsewhere and can involve widespread internal changes Example: high street bank that moves from branch services into telephone and internet banking because of anticipated growth in internet shopping

(left margin: TIMING OF CHANGE)

Adaptation: an incremental change that occurs as an organisational reaction to a change in its environment

Fine-tuning: an incremental change that occurs as a result of an organisation's anticipation of changes in its environment

Re-creation: a transformational change that occurs as a result of drastic changes in an organisation's environment

Re-orientation: a transformational change that occurs in anticipation of drastic changes in an organisation's environment

- the scope of change, which can be either incremental or strategic
- the timing of changes; that is, whether change is a reaction to something that has already happened, or is in anticipation of what is expected to happen.

This gives a four-part typology of changes shown in Figure 21.1.

Adaptation is an incremental change that is a reaction to environmental changes. *Fine-tuning*, while still incremental, change occurs when an organisation can foresee a future change in its environment.

The right-hand quadrants in Figure 21.1 are classified by Nadler and Tushman (1986) as 'organisational transformations' and both involve moving an organisation to a completely new state. However, each one is a transformation of a different type. *Re-creation* is a reaction to drastic changes in the environment. It involves a complete re-think of the organisation's strategy and can involve changes throughout the whole enterprise. *Re-orientation* is somewhat different and involves similarly dramatic steps, but these are usually in anticipation of external changes.

Today's turbulent environmental conditions have tended to place an increasing emphasis on strategic change, which involves a major re-focus of the organisation, and can sometimes result in a complete redesign of the firm to do something new, or do what it does in a radically different way. For this reason it is important to consider factors that can trigger changes in an organisation in more depth, and this matter is addressed next.

THE TRIGGERS TO ORGANISATIONAL CHANGE

Most organisations have learned to make minor, incremental changes to adjust to unplanned or unanticipated events. Thus the most problematic changes tend to be those that are of some magnitude, particularly where they are undertaken quickly. Changes

Figure 21.2 Triggers
to change in
organisations

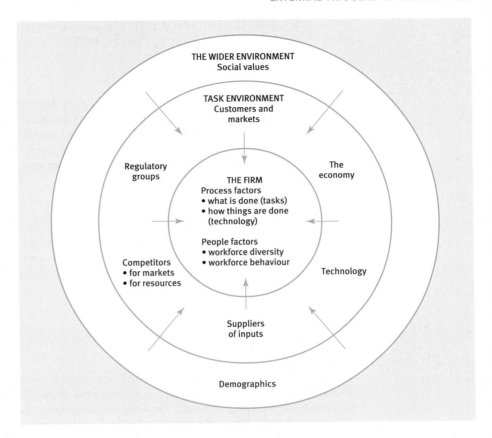

of this nature are not undertaken lightly and usually occur because something forces
the firm to re-evaluate its situation, and these triggers for change, which can emanate
from outside or inside an organisation, are summarised in Figure 21.2.

EXTERNAL TRIGGERS TO CHANGE

Before describing these factors it is important to point-out that environment is not just
'everything out there'; some parts are of considerably more importance to the organisation than others. To distinguish between these, Figure 21.2 is divided into 'task
environment' and 'wider environment' (Dill 1958). Wider environment is one step
removed from the organisation, whereas task environment is that part of the total environment that is most relevant (or potentially relevant) to an organisation in terms of
achieving its goals or objectives. Because its impact is experienced as direct and pressing, this is where firms tend to concentrate most of their attention.

Wider Environmental Triggers

While changes in this part of the environment occur relatively slowly, they can eventually have an impact on one or more of the factors in the task environment, and can

evoke anticipatory change. Two in particular (*demographics* and *social values*) can often be significant.

Demographics

These can ultimately have a significant impact on customers and markets. For instance, young people today have very different lifestyles and purchasing patterns from previous generations. At the opposite end of the age spectrum, people now live longer, are healthier into old age and also expect a lifestyle of their own. Thus both ends of the age spectrum tend to have become separate market segments that require their own products.

Wider Social Values

People now get married later, relationships are probably less permanent, there are many more single households and a far higher proportion of women work than at any time since World War II. Clearly, these trends affect the tastes of consumers and they can alter the characteristics of markets.

Task Environment Triggers

Customers and Markets

Because they have a direct impact on profit, markets are often the strongest triggers to change. These days firms not only face threats from domestic competitors, but many markets have become globalised. Thus organisations often have to adapt to market and competitive changes merely to survive and, to do so, they often look to changes that will make them more flexible and adaptable in the future.

The Economy

Certain changes in wider economic conditions can be very powerful triggers for change. While the industrialised world has slowly pulled itself out of recession since 1995, there have been periodic fears of renewed worldwide recession. Events such as these tend to prompt firms to look for new internal economies to remain competitive.

Technology

Since technology is often seen as a way of keeping pace with (or getting ahead of) the competition, it is strongly related to market triggers. Failure to keep abreast of new technological developments can mean that costs rise relative to those of competitors, and this can have severe consequences. Moreover, because technology advances rapidly, it can result in a never-ending series of changes.

Suppliers of Inputs

On the input side of an organisation there are a number of factors that can be equally important as triggers to change. **Suppliers of capital** such as shareholders and banks usually have expectations about a firm's level of profits and managers can come to feel that the only way to meet these expectations is to reduce costs through greater internal efficiency, which can result in radical alterations to working arrangements and the use of new technologies.

Suppliers of materials are also important and the reliability or stability of suppliers can prompt internal changes, particularly in firms that have a heavy reliance on bought-in components. **Suppliers of labour**, which traditionally means the firm's employees, are also a vital consideration. To serve their markets firms have to acquire the appropriate quantity of human resources of the right quality, and at the right time, which often requires complex, long-term recruitment strategies.

Suppliers of equipment are another important group on the input side. The past decade has been one of fairly rapid technological change. Therefore, in a developed economy, a vital resource in the battle for survival can be up-to-date plant and equipment, together with the knowledge of how to use it.

Competitors

Very few goods and services have no substitutes, and the fact that there are competitors for markets puts severe limitations on a firm's room for manoeuvre. Nothing quite makes a firm sit up and take notice, as much as competitor activity, particularly where it affects profitability. Similarly, competition for resources such as capital, equipment, materials and labour can have knock-on effects that prompt internal changes.

Regulatory groups

Although not involved directly in the input–output chain, this part of task environment contains sources of disturbance that can affect inputs, outputs or internal processes and thus prompt change within the firm.

Consumer groups come in a variety of forms. For example, utilities such as transport, telecommunications, gas, electricity and water are all subject to scrutiny and regulation of prices. Somewhat less powerful in formal terms, but highly influential in terms of media publicity, are bodies such as the Consumers' Association. Almost every industrialised country has an increasingly influential environmental lobby, and anti-pollution legislation can force radical changes in production methods and processes. Thus, all of these groups can exert powerful pressures on a firm's markets or internal processes.

In certain industries **trade and employer associations** can have a huge impact on a firm's conduct and, in some instances, they can be a trigger to change. For example, associations that negotiate with trade unions on behalf of employers influence wage rates. Some associations can also play a part in regulating competition between their members, which clearly has market-related effects.

So far as employee behaviour is concerned, **trade unions** are a prominent regulatory group. Their basic purpose is to limit management's freedom of action *vis-à-vis* employees, and this can also prompt changes, for example to reduce or marginalise the influence of trade unions.

Finally, **government** can influence the firm in many ways. Some of its activities have an effect on commercial matters, such as exporting, which influences the size of a firm's markets. Others, such as employment legislation, can have a more direct impact on employee relations and can be a strong trigger to internal change. A prime example here is the increased amount of legislation that is starting to appear in Great Britain to ensure that the country complies with European social legislation.

INTERNAL TRIGGERS FOR CHANGE

Process Factors

Changes to process factors often occur because of the impact of triggers in the task environment. Some, however, can arise internally and act as a spur for change in their own right. Examples of those that can require internal change are innovations that improve the way that something is manufactured, or allow a service to be delivered at a lower cost, or the development of new products that enable the firm to diversify. When a change to the top management of a firm occurs, there inevitably seems to be an element of 'the new broom sweeping clean', which can often result in structural changes or changes in reporting responsibilities. In a period of expansion, firms sometimes embark on radical structural changes to expand geographically and this can also mean internal change.

People Factors

Although changes to people factors are often prompted by external triggers, there are some that mainly originate inside an organisation. One that has affected many organisations in the last two decades is an increasingly diverse workforce. Large numbers of employees now come from ethnic groups with cultures and norms that are different from those in the traditional British workforce, and to comply with equal opportunities legislation firms have found it necessary to make changes. Many organisations also have workforces that are largely composed of women, and changes can be needed to facilities and patterns of work to allow women to reconcile home and work responsibilities. In addition, some employees only wish to work on a part-time basis, and this can also bring changes in working arrangements.

TIME OUT

Carefully consider the situation of the organisation in which you work. If you have no direct experience of being an employee, use the university or college at which you study. Develop a list of the major changes that the organisation and others in the same industry have undergone over the last three years. Try to discover what prompted these changes and answer the questions below. If necessary, use other people who have been part of the organisation for some time as the source of your information.

1. Were there any forces in the environment of the organisation (and others in the same industry) that triggered the changes and what were these forces?
2. Were there any forces within the organisation that could have triggered some of the changes and what were these forces?

- Organisational change consists of moving an organisation, or one or more of its parts, from one state to another state.
- The different types of change undertaken by organisations can be classified according to their timing and scope. There are four characteristic types: adaptation; fine-tuning; re-creation; and re-orientation.
- The triggers for organisational change can be either external (located in an organisation's wider environment or task environment) or internal (process factors or people factors).

RESISTANCE TO CHANGE

Because change can be rewarding for some people and an unpleasant experience for others, people perceive it differently. The people who propose change are usually those who are most likely to view it in positive terms, but in many cases these are people at the top of an organisation, who are likely to remain untouched by the change. Conversely, those lower down can see matters in a different light, particularly if they perceive that those who advocate the change will not be affected. For these reasons there is a widespread assumption that some resistance to change is inevitable. Nevertheless, there are reservations in some quarters about whether this assumption is universally valid, and a return will be made to this point presently. In the meantime, it is more convenient to consider the potential sources of resistance and, to structure the discussion, the phenomenon will be considered at two levels: the organisational level and the individual level.

Organisational Sources of Resistance

By their very nature organisations have an in-built streak of conservatism (Hall 1987) and so it is hardly surprising that resistance can occur at this level. Katz and Kahn (1978) give six potential reasons for this phenomenon, and these are shown in Figure 21.3.

Figure 21.3
Organisational
sources of resistance
to change

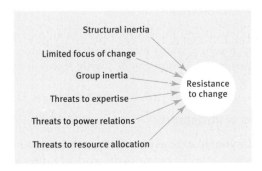

Structural Inertia

The structure of an organisation gives it a strong element of stability, which establishes regular patterns of behaviour that go unquestioned in the minds of organisational members. Thus they often become 'the way that things should be done' (Stephenson 1985). They also give people a feeling that things are predictable and create a strong force to maintain matters as they are.

A Limited Focus of Change

Because many parts of an organisation are interdependent, it can be difficult to change one part in isolation. However, many change initiatives try to do this and people in the changed part find themselves out of step with people in other parts. As a result these people can find it hard to complete their tasks, which results in a degree of hostility to the changed part, and this in turn leads to resistance to change.

Group Inertia

Since groups develop their own norms, which they use to regulate the behaviour of their members, the *status quo* is usually very comfortable. Thus if a proposed change upsets a group's rules and norms, this can result in the group developing a degree of resistance to change.

Perceived Threats to Expertise

One of the most potent sources of a group's power is its expertise. Any change that threatens to reduce the responsibility of a group, or of an individual for exercising this expertise can affect its potential influence, and in these circumstances resistance is only to be expected.

Perceived Threats to Power Relations

Changes often result in new patterns of decision-making responsibility and where a group has previously benefited by making crucial decisions, it can feel that its prestige and standing in the organisation are under threat. In such circumstances, the group will invariably resist the changes.

Perceived Threats to Resource Allocation

The allocation of physical and human resources in an organisation is often taken to be a reflection of prestige, status and influence. Therefore, those who are most satisfied with the current allocation can be highly resistant to a change that upsets the situation.

Individual Sources of Resistance

In addition to organisational sources of resistance, there are a number of personal reasons why people resist change. Drawing on the work of Kotter and Schlesinger (1979),

Figure 21.4 Individual sources of resistance to change

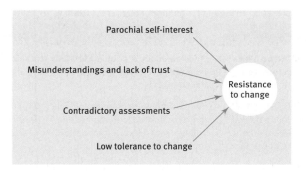

Figure 21.4 Individual sources of resistance to change

Bedeian and Zammuto (1991) gives four generic reasons for resistance, and these are shown in Figure 21.4.

Parochial Self-interest

Almost everybody has something that he or she values about work, for instance income or its substitutes, power over others, prestige, status, security or convenience. People often acquire these things by personal expenditure of time, energy and commitment, and unless things carry on as they are, this is a 'sunk cost' that cannot be recovered. This creates a force for maintaining the *status quo*, and engenders a degree of resistance.

Misunderstandings and Lack of Trust

The less a person knows about the reasons for a change and its impact on him or herself, the more likely it is that the individual will resist the change. This is greatly amplified where there is lack of trust in the proposer of the change because this tends to result in selective perceptions about what the proposer says.

Contradictory Assessments of the Change

People differ in their assessments of the personal costs and benefits of a change. Proposers tend to focus only on what they see as the positive outcomes and they sometimes forget that what they see as a benefit, can be perceived by others as a threat. Where this happens there is a wealth of evidence to suggest that people become resistant to changes long after they have been put in place (Savery *et al*. 1998).

Low Tolerance to Change

People also vary in their capabilities to absorb change. To some extent, this depends on their tolerance to ambiguity, and to someone with a low tolerance a change with unknown consequences can be highly threatening.

Dealing with Resistance to Change

It is so widely assumed that resistance is inevitable that the benchmark of successful change is often taken to be 'overcoming resistance'. However, because resistance can occur for such a wide range of reasons, it is doubtful if there is a single method that

Table 21.2 Tactics for dealing with resistance to change (adapted from Kotter *et al.* 1986)

Tactic	Most appropriately used where	Advantages	Disadvantages
Education and/or communication	Resistance is based on a lack of information or inaccurate information and analysis	Once persuaded, people will often help with the implementation of the change	Can be very time-consuming if large numbers of people are involved
Participation	Initiators do not have all the information needed to design the change and where others have considerable power to resist	People who participate are usually more committed to implementing change. Any relevant information that participants have will be integrated into the change plan	Can be very time-consuming. Participants can design an inappropriate change
Facilitation and support	People resist because of the adjustment problems that are involved	No other tactic works as well where there are adjustment problems	Can be time-consuming, expensive and still fail
Negotiation	Someone or some groups will clearly lose out in a change and where they have considerable power to resist	Sometimes a relatively easy way to avoid major resistance	Can be too expensive in many cases. Can trigger other groups to negotiate
Co-optation	There is a specific situation in which other tactics are too expensive or infeasible	Can help generate support for implementing a change, but less so than participation	Can create problems if other people recognise the co-optation
Manipulation	Other tactics will not work or are too expensive	Can be a relatively quick and inexpensive solution to resistance	Initiators are likely to lose some of their credibility and this can lead to future problems
Coercion	Speed is essential and change initiators possess considerable power	Speed can sometimes overcome a great deal of resistance	Risky: can leave people angry with the initiators

can deal with them all. Thus a contingency approach, in which the method used is centred on the reason for resistance, is likely to be more appropriate. This matter is addressed by Kotter *et al.* (1986) who set out seven ways of overcoming resistance. These can be used singly or in combination and Kotter *et al.* stress the need to choose a tactic that is most appropriate to the circumstances. Their advice on this matter, together with the strengths and weaknesses of the tactics, is summarised in Table 21.2.

Is Resistance Inevitable?

The idea that resistance to change is virtually inevitable is found in almost all textbooks, both in management and Organisational Behaviour, and usually this is accompanied by an assumption that resistance will be an individual level phenomenon. However, it is important to recognise that people are seldom resistant to change *per se*, but because they perceive that the proposed change will have an adverse impact on themselves.

Perhaps more significantly, there is a wealth of evidence to show that individual resistance is comparatively rate. For instance, Kotter (1995) shows that the design of a change initiative may well have an influence on whether resistance is encountered.

In addition, Spreitzer and Quinn (1996) draw attention to the idea that it is people higher up who mostly cling to the *status quo*, which means that resistance can be more of an organisational-level phenomenon than one that exists in lower-level employees.

Some indications as to why this might be the case are provided in a penetrating article by Dent and Goldberg (1999), who note that the idea of individual resistance has been the received wisdom for over 50 years. As such, it has become part of the standard vocabulary adopted by each successive generation of managers in an unthinking way, the net result of which is three important outcomes that perpetuate the myth:

- Since managers are likely to assume that there will be resistance, they can be tempted to use devious strategies such as manipulation or concealment to head off resistance, which then occurs when these strategies are discovered – a self-fulfilling prophecy effect.
- Because resistance is seen as something that only occurs in subordinates, and is then overcome by successful managers, managers have every incentive to maintain the myth because it allows them to present themselves in a very favourable light.
- As a final resort, the widespread assumption that resistance occurs in subordinates allows managers to absolve themselves from blame for the failure of a badly designed change initiative (Krantz 1999).

TIME OUT

Carefully consider any significant changes that have occurred in the last few years that have had an impact on you or on other students at your university or college. These could be changes in grant or fee arrangements, changes to the way your course is delivered or assessed, or even changes in the way your college or university is run. Now answer the questions below.

1. Name these changes, and state who they affect and why.
2. Which of these changes encountered resistance and what form did the resistance take?
3. How was the resistance overcome by the initiator of the change, or was the resistance successful in getting the changes abandoned or modified?

REPLAY

- Resistance can arise at two levels: organisational and individual.
- Seven tactics can be used (singly or in combination) to try to overcome resistance: education and communication; participation; facilitation and support; negotiation; co-optation; manipulation; and coercion.
- While it is widely assumed that resistance to change on the part of individuals is inevitable, there is a stream of research evidence that suggests that this is not the case.

APPROACHES TO INTRODUCING ORGANISATIONAL CHANGE

Planned approach to organisational change: a set of internal actions designed to produce specific outcomes

While organisational change can be introduced in a number of different ways, a fundamental distinction can be made between the planned approach and the emergent approach. The *planned approach to organisational change* (which is closely associated with Organisational Development) has been described by Porras and Silvers (1991) as 'a set of internal actions designed to produce specific outcomes'. This is underpinned by a belief that change is best accomplished through a sequence of predetermined steps, which implies that there is a universal formula for success. While this has the advantage of making the process more understandable, the reader should be aware that the whole approach has been subject to a great deal of criticism. For instance, Huczynski and Buchanan (2001) note that the area is resplendent with what they call 'recipe' models (see Kotter (1995) for an example), which creates an impression that faithfully following the steps enables change to be reduced to a straightforward, linear process. This not only underestimates the complexity of the process, but Buchanan and Storey (1997) argue that it is often misleading in terms of what is actually involved. Indeed they note that change is often a very messy business, which triggers intense political activity because people strive to be the ones that profit by a change, or remain with their empires untouched. For this reason, writers such as Burnes (2000) argue for what they call the *emergent approach*. This rejects the idea that there is any such thing as a universally valid recipe for successful change. Instead, change is viewed as a process that continually unfolds and develops: a process in which the issues that arise cannot be predicted, but have to be tackled as and when they occur. Since this is radically different from the planned approach, discussion will be deferred until later n the chapter and in the meantime some of the models and theories associated with the planned approach will be discussed.

Emergent approach: a contingency perspective that rejects the idea of a universally applicable recipe for organisational change

THE PLANNED CHANGE APPROACH

The Systems Model of Change

Many planned change initiatives use a systemic approach in which an organisation is treated as a set of interacting variables, all of which are likely to need to change together. This idea is shown in Figure 21.5.

The important point about this perspective is its recognition of interdependencies, which has two main implications:

- If arrangements in the pre-change situation work well, all of the five variables are in balance, so that structure is compatible with strategy, technology and so on.
- That if a change is made to one of the variables, this is almost bound to require some degree of adjustment in the others to restore the balance of compatibility.

Here it is worth noting that some of the major difficulties encountered in change initiatives occur because these interconnections are ignored (see Redman and Grieves 1999; Oxman and Smith 2003) and the most neglected variable is often the people. For this reason, much of the effort in planned change is devoted to bringing about change in human behaviour and there are two basic models that underpin these activities: the Lewin model and the Action Research model.

Figure 21.5 The systems model of change

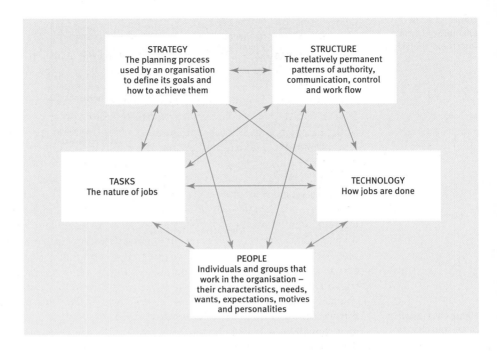

The Lewin Model

Lewin model: a three-stage (unfreeze–move–refreeze) method of bringing about change in human behaviour

Force field analysis: a way of conceptualising a stable situation as forces pushing (in favour of) change balanced by those restraining change

The Lewin Model

Force Field Analysis

Lewin (1951) views change as a dynamic process which takes the form of an ongoing struggle between two sets of forces: one pushing in the direction of change and the other pulling in the opposite direction. This is normally portrayed as a 'force field', where a stable situation consists of a state of equilibrium (balance) between the two sets of forces. To give an example, assume that it has been proposed that a group of employees should change from working in a way in which they all have their own special tasks, to one where they become a multi-skilled team. A simplified force field of 'pushing' and 'restraining' forces for these people is shown in Figure 21.6.

Lewin then argues that the first step in initiating change is to destabilise the current state of equilibrium, which can be done in one or a combination of three basic ways:

- by increasing the strength of the forces pushing for change
- by reducing the strength of the restraining forces
- by changing the direction of a force so that a restraint becomes a push factor.

The most difficult step is usually to get people to abandon their old ways, and Lewin's model gives a basic method of attempting to do this which flows from his force field concept. He views successful change as a three-step process, the essentials of which are shown in Figure 21.7.

Figure 21.6 An example of Lewin's force field analysis

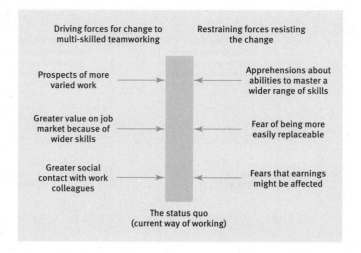

Figure 21.7 Lewin's three-step change process

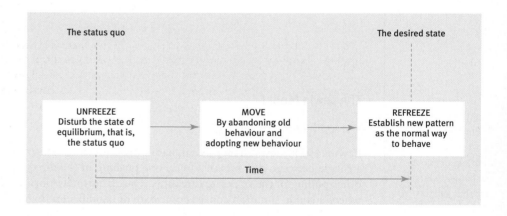

Unfreeze

Here the principles set out earlier in the force field analysis are applied. The aim is to establish a motive for change, which is done up by destabilising the *status quo* situation, usually by a combination of reducing the restraining forces and/or increasing the push forces.

Move (to the new situation)

This is often easier said than done because, when people already have a familiar way of behaving, it can be hard for them to abandon it. However, people have a greater incentive to change if they can see others around them doing the same thing and so some of the Organisational Development (OD) techniques described presently would normally be used.

Refreeze

The aim here is to fix the new pattern of behaviour as 'normal'; often by conditioning people, i.e. by rewarding the new, desired behaviour and discouraging them from regressing to the prior behaviours. Again, because behaviour seems much more normal if it fits in with what others do, peer pressure can be a potent source of reinforcement.

The Action Research Model

Action Research: a participative method of bringing about change in human behaviour that involves stages of data collection, problem diagnosis, action planning, action and re-evaluation

The Lewin model implies that there is a very clear specification for the required, new pattern of behaviour. However, there may only be a vague idea of the ways in which the behaviour itself needs to change. In this situation an incremental approach is required, desirably one that draws on employee ideas about what is needed so that they become the joint authors of the change. This is the province of *Action Research* and an outline five-step method is shown in Figure 21.8.

Problem Identification

The cycle commences when the proposer of change identifies that existing patterns of employee behaviour are incompatible with a changed situation. As an example, assume that a customer service department handles queries and complaints by directing them to specialists, according to the nature of an enquiry. This sometimes leads to customers

Figure 21.8 The Action Research cycle

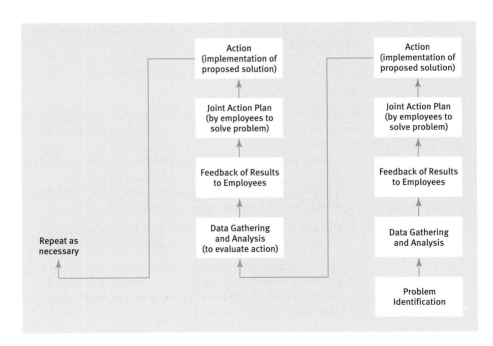

experiencing delay and frustration in getting an answer, which can probably be avoided if all queries are answered promptly in a single call.

Data Gathering and Diagnosis

In Action Research, this is sometimes done by an outside consultant and can be likened to a doctor diagnosing the cause of a patient's illness. Starting with the suspected symptoms (potential customer frustration), data is gathered to reveal its cause, which involves gathering information from customers and also from employees to obtain their version of matters.

Feedback

A fundamental part of the Action Research method is to involve the target of a change (employees) in identifying the extent of a problem and suggesting potential solutions. This is done by a joint exploration of the data that have been gathered by employees and the consultant.

Action Plan

Working together, consultant and employees develop a potential solution to the problem. Since it is hoped that a discussion of this type will lead to a degree of unfreezing of the *status quo*, there is a clear connection with Lewin's three-step model.

Action

The proposed solution is put into practice by employees, who adopt the new patterns of behaviour.

Re-evaluation

Data is gathered to determine whether there is an improvement, how much of an improvement has been made, and how workable the solution is. The cycle is then repeated as necessary.

Clearly the Action Research method has a number of advantages:

- The people who have to implement any changes are involved at an early stage, which can help reduce resistance to change.

- Change is objective-centred and goes far enough to solve the problem but not so far that it creates new, unforeseen problems.

- Because change is introduced in increments, knock-on effects that may become problems in their own right can be identified; for instance, in the example above it might be necessary to re-train employees so that they can answer a wider range of queries.

TIME OUT

Carefully consider the change(s) you identified in the previous Time Out exercise and answer the questions below.

1. What strategy was used to try to introduce the change(s) you identified?
2. Do you feel the strategy was an appropriate way of introducing the change? If not, why not?
3. Identify any other strategies that could have been used and state whether you feel these would have been more or less effective than those used.

REPLAY

- The systems model of change acknowledges interdependence between five main organisational systems; thus a change in one would probably need to be accompanied by changes in the others.
- Lewin's model of change, which is a natural development of his force field analysis, gives a basic, three-step method of unfreeze–move–refreeze, to bring about changes in human behaviour.
- The Action Research model of change gives an incremental approach, in which people who are the target of change become involved in planning and implementing the changes.

ORGANISATIONAL DEVELOPMENT

Organisational Development (OD), which is firmly located within the area of planned change uses the models given in the previous section to underpin its approach. It can be defined as:

> a planned, systematic process in which applied behavioural science principles and practices are introduced into organisations, towards the goal of increasing individual and organisational effectiveness (French and Bell 1999, p 1)

It is concerned with equipping the management of an organisation with a method of bringing about organisational change and has a distinctive approach that lays claim to being much more than just another recipe for change management.

The Distinguishing Characteristics of OD

While OD has some things in common with other approaches, in theory it has a number of unique characteristics, and these are given in what follows.

A Planned, Medium-to Long-term Strategy

OD is not a quick-fix solution to problems. Indeed, it condemns *ad hoc* approaches and, because it deals with fundamental and/or transformational changes, the process can be one that takes years to complete.

A Systematic and Systemic Focus

The basic perspective adopted in OD is that of the organisation as a system of sub-systems, (see Figure 21.5). Therefore, it is strongly concerned with identifying the multitude of simultaneous changes that may need to be made.

Process-orientated focus

Although OD sets out to achieve a better functioning organisation, it is strongly focused on the process of change itself and assumes that how change takes place has a huge impact on whether the objective of a more effective organisation is likely to be realised.

A Normative Re-educative Orientation

OD tends to avoid some of the methods used in other approaches, which sometimes verge on the naked use of power to compel people to change. Most advocates of OD are firmly committed to more persuasive strategies and, for this reason, it draws heavily on the behavioural science disciplines of psychology, sociology, anthropology and political science for its techniques.

The Use of a Change Agent

This role is central to the OD process and is discussed in its own right presently. The *change agent* is an expert who champions, facilitates and guides the change process. While this person can come from inside the organisation, he or she is increasingly imported as a consultant.

Change agent: an expert from either inside or outside an organisation who facilitates and guides an OD intervention

An Orientation to Organisational Self-help

Although OD often involves the use of an outside expert (the change agent), OD practitioners like to think of themselves as somewhat different from other types of management consultant. Many of them would argue that their role is not simply to provide expertise to solve organisational problems, but to improve the organisation's long-term abilities to diagnose and solve its own problems.

In theory, these points mean that OD is a very distinctive way of approaching the matter of change and so it is not surprising that it lays claim to a unique set of philosophies and assumptions. Above all, it adopts a very humanistic approach which contains fundamental assumptions about people in organisations (Porras and Robertson 1992). These are that:

- Effective organisations de-emphasise hierarchical authority and control by involving people in decisions about matters that affect them, which means that OD has anti-bureaucratic values.

- The effectiveness and efficiency of an organisation will increase if work is organised in a way that meets people's needs for responsibility and challenge (Pasmore and Fagans 1992).

- Most people want opportunities for personal growth and achievement, and that, if these needs are met, they will respond positively to opportunities that the organisation offers for increased responsibility and challenge.

- It is normally possible to identify ways in which the design of individual jobs, the tasks of groups and the structure of the organisation can all be modified to meet the needs of the organisation and its human resources.

- While conflict often stands in the way of people accomplishing organisational goals, it is counter-productive to smooth over conflicts, but it is better to bring them out into the open where they can be resolved because this results in a more trusting, supportive climate.

So strongly are these values emphasised by writers on OD that it takes on something of a messianic, evangelical flavour, and recent evidence collected from a survey of over 6,000 American OD practitioners clearly shows that these values are still widely held (Winterberg *et al.* 2004). Indeed, the humanistic agenda, which is paramount in the OD literature, sometimes leaves an uneasy feeling that the pursuit of this is the main aim, and any talk of organisational effectiveness is just attractive packaging. Therefore, 'effectiveness', as OD practitioners define it, can be very different from the meaning that managers and other people attribute to the word. For this reason there are a number of important criticisms of OD. These however, are more appropriately left until later in the chapter.

The Change Agent in OD

Because this person acts as the catalyst for change and assumes the responsibility for steering it through to completion, the change agent occupies a focal role in OD. Broadly speaking, there are three approaches that can be used in this role. The first is what can be called the 'engineering model'. This is similar to the role of a conventional management consultant, in which the change agent plays little part in diagnosing what is needed, probably because the management of an organisation has already decided what it wants. Rather, the main function is to install a new system, for example TQM, and to leave when the new system is up and running.

At the other extreme is what is sometimes called 'the medical model', where the function is to help diagnose an organisation's problems, but not necessarily to play an extensive part in implementing change.

The most widely used approach, however, tends to fall between these two extremes and this is known as the 'process model'. It uses the technique of Process Consultation in which the change agent works in a highly collaborative way with organisational managers, but with a strong emphasis on helping them to decide what changes are necessary, how they can be brought about, and then guiding managers in the early stages of implementation.

Although a change agent often comes from outside an organisation, the person can also be an insider. External change agents are usually employed on a consultancy basis and tend to be people trained in behavioural science techniques. The disadvantages and advantage of employing an outsider are said to be that:

- the person can be viewed by employees as someone who has no understanding of how the firm operates
- he or she can be strongly mistrusted and branded as a management's lapdog
- on the other hand, outsiders usually have the advantage of a fresh and unbiased pair of eyes.

Appointing a change agent from inside also has its inherent advantages and disadvantages:

- Because the person comes from the inside, he or she can be seen as a more plausible advocate of change.
- Set against this, because of his or her prior organisational background, there can be suspicions that the individual will give special favours to his or her own unit, or find ways of exempting it from change.

REPLAY

- Organisational Development (OD) which focuses strongly on the processes of introducing change, is a distinctive approach that has a number of characteristics that distinguish it from other approaches to change: a medium- to long-term focus; a systematic and systemic focus; a focus on processes; a normative re-educative orientation; the use of a change agent; and an organisational self-help orientation.
- OD is underpinned by a humanistic philosophy and a set of assumptions about people in organisations.
- The change agent's role in OD is to act as a catalyst for change and to steer a change initiative through to completion.
- The three main models for the way in which a change agent fulfils this role are: the engineering model; the medical model; and the process model.

For these reasons, and irrespective of whether the person is appointed from inside or outside the organisation, the change agent role can be a difficult one and there are strong suggestions that the person needs to have special aptitudes and competencies. Burke (1987) defines these as:

- a tolerance of ambiguity
- the ability to influence people
- a capability to confront difficult issues
- to be supportive and nurturing with other people
- awareness of his or her own feelings and intuitions
- an ability to teach and coach others
- a sense of humour
- a strong belief in the OD method
- self-confidence
- good conceptual skills
- energy and self-direction.

Organisational Development Interventions

OD intervention: a programme to bring about change in an organisation, or one or more of its parts

An *OD intervention* is a programme used to bring about change in an organisation, or one or more of its parts. It can be focused on problems at one or more of four organisational levels: the whole organisation; the intergroup level; the intragroup level; and the level of the individual. There are many models of the process in the OD literature and these usually divide an intervention into distinct stages. While there are criticisms of this approach, a model that is capable of capturing some of the complexity of what might be involved is provided by Gibson *et al.* (1994). For the purposes of discussion, this is shown in a slightly modified form in Figure 21.9.

Forces for Change

These have already been discussed earlier in the chapter. Note, however, that there is a connection with the box entitled 'Organisational mission and goals' which conveys the idea that there is an interaction between the forces for change and an organisation's goals.

Problem Diagnosis

It is here that problems in the organisation start to be revealed, together with possible remedies and ways of achieving them. This means that diagnosis is one of the most important steps in the OD cycle, which in many cases will be undertaken by an external consultant.

Goals for Change

While these might seem to flow from the previous stage, note that the model contains a box entitled 'Limiting conditions' with arrows going to the 'Goals' box and the 'Select

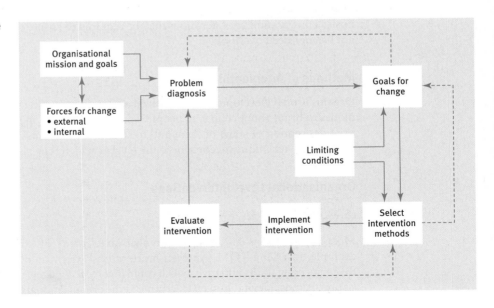

Figure 21.9 An outline of the organisational development process

intervention methods' box. This reflects the idea that the current state of an organ-isation puts limits on what can feasibly be achieved, and in this respect a factor that puts limits on what can be done is 'current management styles'. For instance, TQM only works well if managers have supportive, open styles and if they cannot accept this way of working, severe problems are likely to be encountered (Redman and Grieves 1999). Another limiting factor can be the formal organisation. Structures, policies and systems of control all tend to reflect top management's philosophies about how organ-isations should be run and, if this is not compatible with the changes envisaged lower down, it can be a recipe for disaster (Ziera and Avedisian 1989). Finally, some pro-posed changes run counter to the expectations and attitudes in workgroups, and so the organisation's culture can put strong limits on what is feasible (Harris and Ogbonna 2002).

Intervention Methods

These are the selected ways of delivering the objectives of the intervention, particularly those concerned with bringing about change in people and they will be described in more detail in the next section of the chapter.

Implementation and Evaluation

Depending on the methods employed, this can be a lengthy process. However, in order to determine whether it has achieved its objectives, and if not, to identify further prob-lems that need to be resolved, it is vital to monitor the success of this stage.

Feedback

It is important to note that all the boxes in the model are connected by feedback loops. This reflects the idea that OD is not a precise science, but one in which the choice of appropriate goals and intervention methods depends on the quality of problem diag-nosis. Thus, a number of iterations may be required to ensure that something import-ant has not been overlooked.

Methods of Intervention

Organisational Development has evolved an extremely wide-ranging tool-kit of tech-niques to bring about change in people. Space precludes giving anything other than a brief description of some of them and to structure the discussion, it is convenient to describe the techniques according to the level at which they are normally applied.

Organisational Level Interventions

Organisational Structure

Most interventions at this level involve an element of structural redesign, for example, installing TQM. An even more radical step would be a Business Process Re-engineering (BPR) initiative, which could involve completely restructuring the organ-isation. Almost inevitably, a restructuring at the organisational level also creates a need to address lower-level aspects of structure. Changes of this type can be extremely disruptive for those involved, and they are often the ones that engender a high degree of resistance. However, it is the people lower down who actually make a structure work. Thus when structural redesign is involved, interventions at intergroup, intragroup and individual levels can also be necessary to try to bring about attitude changes. One way of starting this process is described next.

Survey Feedback

It is sometimes important to identify pre-existing patterns of values and attitudes at the diagnosis and planning stage of an intervention. This can be done by conducting a survey of employees in the organisation to tap into their opinions on such matters as management's behavioural style, the quality of communication, levels of motivation, job satisfaction, satisfaction with supervision, or the organisation's culture and climate in a more general way. The results of the survey are then fed back to organisational decision makers and sometimes to employees as well. The information can then be used to identify problems and the techniques that could be deployed to address them.

Intergroup Interventions

Because conflict between groups is fairly common in organisations, interventions at this level usually involve an attempt to change perceptions and attitudes that groups hold about each other.

Intergroup Confrontation

In this method two groups that have a conflictual relationship work with a change agent to resolve the problem. The first step in this process is usually for the groups to meet separately, and each group is asked to come to conclusions about:

- how it views the other group
- what it expects of the other group
- what it believes the other group expects of them.

In the second step, the groups exchange their conclusions, which is followed by a meeting of the two groups to explore their perceptions. This meeting is often designed to be confrontational but in an objective, fact-finding way. Therefore, the change agent needs to firmly control the process, to ensure that the groups move towards collaborative working by exploring similarities and differences, rather than simply exchanging 'blame stories'.

Intragroup Interventions

At this level, the aim is to help a group to work more effectively in terms of its internal processes and a number of techniques can be used.

Process Consultation

This is one of the main techniques used in OD and Schein (1969) who is perhaps its foremost advocate, argues that many groups are riven with dysfunctional behaviour, much of which originates in distortions of reality by group members. In process consultation, the change agent acts as a facilitator or catalyst to help the group diagnose its own problems and generate action plans to remedy the situation. Thus he or she purposely avoids prescribing a remedy for the group, but helps it explore its own processes so that group members become the authors of any changes that are made.

Team Building

OD places a very high value on collaborative behaviour, which is underpinned by a belief that participative working results in a willingness to embrace change (Woodman and Sherwood 1980). The aim is to develop more effective groups by helping them to explore potential shortcomings in their own internal processes. Thus group members work with a change agent to diagnose how well the group works, and to plan changes to improve its functioning, usually by persuading the group to focus on one or more of a number of key activities, such as:

* how it sets its goals and priorities
* how work is allocated within the group
* how it works together
* interpersonal relations within the group.

The group then draws up an action plan of what needs to be done, often by calling on each member to do something specific to improve matters. According to French and Bell (1999) this is the single most important and fastest-growing technique in the OD repertoire. It is said to be particularly useful in global organisations, where groups can have members from very diverse cultural backgrounds, and also with new groups that have come into existence as a result of a re-organisation or a merger.

Sensitivity Training

This is one of the most highly publicised and controversial techniques used in OD (Bramlette and Tucker 1981) and it goes by a number of names, such as T-(training) groups or Encounter groups. It is based on the assumption that poor group performance can often be traced to people's emotional problems, and has the aim of sensitising people to their own behaviour and how this influences relations with others.

T-groups typically work with (but not under) a facilitator and the process often starts with the people seated in a circle facing inwards, with no agenda, no leader and no directions about what to do. Therefore, all the problems encountered in a new group emerge fairly quickly; for example, thrusts for leadership and disagreement about what to do, and how to do it. This tends to result in emotions quickly coming to the surface and it is this that gives rise to the controversial nature of T-groups. People have to expose themselves to a fairly high degree of criticism and take emotional and psychological risks to participate. Not everybody is well equipped to do this and many people are unable to cope with the psychological strains. Thus, there are very mixed reports about the usefulness of the process. Nevertheless, the evidence suggests that participants often learn to take a more realistic view of themselves, develop a clearer understanding of how they view others, and develop enhanced levels of interpersonal sensitivity.

Individual-level Interventions

Because its main focus is on people working together, OD has evolved relatively few techniques that are specifically targeted on individuals. Those that are used tend to be what would normally be considered part of the repertoire of a line manager, or possibly a human resource specialist, for example career planning, or, where stress is encountered, some of the methods described in Chapter 10.

An Evaluation of Organisational Development

Since OD can be an expensive and time-consuming process it is important to examine its utility. From an organisational perspective two questions can be asked: Does OD deliver the benefits that it promises? And is OD relevant in today's conditions? In addition, it is also important to address a third question: Is OD ethical?

Does OD Deliver What it Promises?

The definition of OD given earlier makes it clear that its implicit promise is to deliver two things:

- a more effective organisation
- a happier, more satisfied and more committed workforce.

Unfortunately, it is near impossible to tell whether these aims are achieved. The vast majority of research conducted to assess the success of OD tends to be of dubious methodological soundness (Beer and Walton 1987) and a penetrating study by Porras and Berg (1978) was only able to identify 35 out of 160 published reports that had methodologies sufficiently rigorous to enable them to be included in a meta-analysis. Of these, only nine attempted to evaluate the effects of OD on economic performance, and only half of these reported an improvement. While most of the 35 studies commented on employee variables such as satisfaction and motivation, only 30 per cent of these reported improvements. Clearly, this gives little support for OD's claim to improve performance and human process variables.

The problem is that studies which report improvements tend to reflect what the word 'improvement' means in the eyes of OD practitioners; for instance, greater creativity, more openness and enhanced opportunities for personal development. It is extremely difficult to devise foolproof measures for these attributes, and so improvement can sometimes be little more than a subjective estimate on the part of the researcher, and this gives rise to another problem. French and Bell (1999) note that most OD practitioners have a blind faith in its utility and so they see little need to produce evidence that it actually works. Therefore, much of the so-called evaluation research comes from reports by consultants who undertake interventions, and this gives a clear risk of a 'positive results bias', or self-fulfilling prophecy effects. In addition, while OD has traditionally had a strong emphasis on theory building because a fairly large number of academics (as well as consultants) are active in the area, there now tends to be an increasing separation between theory and practice. This, it has been argued, has resulted in the field becoming increasingly susceptible to fashionable 'fads' (Bunker *et al.* 2004).

As if these things were not enough, there is also some evidence that OD can result in highly dysfunctional outcomes. To start with, change initiatives that aim to develop a strong performance orientation in employees, have a habit of upsetting the psycho-logical contract and this can result in feelings of unfairness and/or a lack of trust (Stiles *et al.* 1997). In addition, culture change initiatives, which are often the pivotal selling feature of an OD intervention, can result in rather unpleasant organisational climates, in which blame stories and a decline in employee commitment and morale can occur (Gilmore *et al.* 1997; Harris and Ogbonna 2002). Moreover, some of the techniques used can have a boomerang effect, for example sensitivity training, which for some people can be such a painful and harrowing process that it results in a great deal of resentment at being forced to undergo the experience for no apparent reason. In sum-mary, therefore, there are grave reservations about whether OD actually delivers what it promises.

The Current Relevance of OD

While OD has a strong focus on matters such as respect for people, trust, egalitarian relationships and participative management, these days, managers' eyes are usually fixed on bottom-line performance. Indeed, many managers would probably argue that organisational changes should desirably be targeted at lowering costs or increasing profits (Van Eynde and Bledsoe 1990). Moreover, many initiatives such as TQM are essentially seen by managers as 'quick-fix, off-the-shelf' solutions, that should have an immediate benefit, rather than being part of a long-term development initiative (Worren *et al.* 1999). In the last two decades managers have found it all too easy to bring about changes of this type without using a persuasive approach. All of this begs the question of whether OD has any relevance to managers, most of whom prefer to concern themselves with hard, tangible features of the organisation such as produc-tivity, quality, continuous improvement and costs, rather than intangibles such as atti-tudes, openness and trust. Perhaps for this reason, although conventional management consulting continues to do well, there is some evidence that OD as a field now tends to be less in demand (Burke 2004).

The Ethics of OD

The great paradox of OD is that while it has a humanistic rationale, it conveniently ignores power differences in organisations (Greenwood *et al.* 1993). Whether this is because it has its origins in America, where academics and consultants are far less reluc-tant to serve the interests of management, or whether it is simply naïve has never been identified. Nevertheless, there is a strong thread in the OD literature which accepts that management's goals are, or should be, sacrosanct. In practice this means that an OD initiative can become little more than an extended exercise in the manipulation of employees, to persuade them that management is right. Nowhere is this more appar-ent than in the aim of changing an organisation's culture. Woodall (1996), for exam-ple, notes that those who advocate the importance of cultural change usually base their argument on four assumptions:

- that successful organisations have strong cultures
- that only management is far-sighted enough to recognise the culture required, and that the rest of the workforce is blind
- that employee values need to be aligned with management's vision
- that employee values can be easily changed.

Setting aside the last of these, which is highly questionable, Woodall also notes that most culture change initiatives implicitly follow Lewin's unfreeze–move–refreeze methodology and this leads to some highly unethical practices. In unfreezing, for example, there are obvious questions about who defines what is wrong with the existing culture and why a new culture is needed. In practice this often amounts to telling employees not only what to think, but how to come up with the right conclusions. This tends to be done by bombarding people with an endless stream of criticism of the existing culture, which is almost bound to induce a sense of psychological insecurity. From then on, because a culture can be highly resistant to change, most of the remainder of the process is devoted to overcoming any resistance. This is not necessarily done in a supportive way, but by trying to induce degradation and shame for holding the values inherent in the old culture. Thus, far from being humanistic, the whole process rests on a set of practices of questionable ethical content.

REPLAY

- An Organisational Development intervention (which can be focused on one or more of four organisational levels) is a programme of steps that is used to bring about changes in an organisation, or one or more of its parts. However, an intervention can be highly iterative and the steps should not be thought of as a sequence that is necessarily completed in a single pass.

- Methods of intervention are normally keyed to the level at which the intervention takes place: whole organisation; intergroup; intragroup; and individual.

- OD is open to some criticism on three grounds: for not delivering what it promises; for not being particularly relevant to current organisational circumstances; and for the questionable ethics of some of its practices.

THE EMERGENT APPROACH TO ORGANISATIONAL CHANGE

Unlike planned change, which is a highly developed approach with its own well understood conventions, the emergent approach to change is nowhere near such a cohesive, highly integrated body of knowledge. Rather, it consists of developments by a disparate group of theorists, who only seem to have one thing in common – their opposition to the tenets of planned change (Burnes 1998). The approach can be labelled 'emergent' for two reasons: first, because it is still emerging as a school of thought and, second, because change is viewed as an emergent process of experimentation and adaptation, in which there is a search for ways of coping with the exigencies of a very uncertain environment that is itself in a constant state of flux.

For this reason, proponents of the approach reject the idea that change can follow a set of pre-planned steps that occur in a neat, fixed way to a set timetable (Senior

1997a). After all, if the environment itself is constantly changing, how can a valid and fixed plan be drawn up in advance? For this reason, it is usually argued that change should be viewed as an ongoing, virtually continuous and open-ended process of transition: something that is usually achieved by a host of small, incremental changes that can eventually add up to a major organisational transformation. Although the approach rejects the idea of a universally applicable strategy that can be specified in advance, a number of workers in the area have developed what could be described as guideline recipes (see, for example, Pettigrew and Whipp (1993) and Kanter *et al.* (1992)). These, however, do not have the status of theoretical models of a change process, but more in the nature of things that need to be achieved along the way. Nevertheless, as Burnes (2000) notes, while most advocates of the emergent approach avoid prescriptive rules, they all draw attention to five organisational features that need to be taken into account in the change process. These are not necessarily targets for change, but are interacting factors that can either facilitate or inhibit proposed changes. They are:

- organisational structures
- organisational culture
- management behaviour
- patterns of power and politics
- organisational learning.

Since the last of these has strong connections with what proponents of the emergent approach would probably regard as an ideal organisational situation for change, it is considered next.

CONTINUOUS CHANGE: THE LEARNING ORGANISATION

Most current ideas about organisational learning argue that a capacity for continuous change is required if an organisation is to survive and prosper in a fast-moving, globalised environment. In organisations of this type, change is said to be a way of life, which means that many of the traditional problems associated with organisational change would largely be absent. This can be seen from the five characteristics of the learning organisation set out by Senge (1991):

- all organisational members have a shared, mutually agreed vision
- people readily disregard old ways of thinking, together with the standard routines that they have used to solve problems and do their jobs in the past
- they are able to conceive of all the organisation's processes, activities, functions and interactions with the environment, as part of a system of interrelationships
- people openly communicate with each other across vertical and horizontal boundaries without fear of criticism or redress
- they subordinate their own personal interests and fragmented departmental interests to work together towards the organisation's shared vision.

So far as can be determined, examples of the fully-fledged learning organisation are extremely rare, and it presents a picture of 'what could be' rather than 'what is' (Pedler *et al.* 1997). Indeed, McGill and Slocum (1993) point out that, to become a learning organisation, a conventional firm probably has to go through a number of intermediate stages. To this end, Koffman and Senge (1993) identify the three main barriers that must be overcome to become a learning organisation.

The Barrier of Fragmentation

The fundamental building block of most organisations is specialisation. Unfortunately this tends to go hand in hand with territorial boundaries that divide different functions into warring kingdoms. Therefore, people lose sight of the interconnected nature of the organisation, which often results in solutions that create a problem for someone else.

The Barrier of Competition rather than Collaboration

In most conventional organisations, competition between sub-units is the dominant mode of behaviour. While there is nothing inherently wrong in this, it tends to result in people competing with those with whom they should collaborate. It also results in a regrettable overemphasis on looking good, which not only reduces collaboration, but also inhibits learning because people have a tendency to conceal what they do not know, or do not understand.

The Barrier of Reactiveness

Life is less stressful for people if they only change as and when it is absolutely necessary. This results in a fire-fighting approach, in which a great deal of attention is devoted to problems, but only when they are known to exist. This in turn promotes risk-avoidance strategies, which are the main enemy of innovation and creativity.

All this begs the question of how a conventional firm can overcome the above barriers. To some authors, such as Kreitner and Kinicki (1995), the answer is 'effective leadership', but this prescription can be little more than American 'management speak' for 'put yourself in the hands of the top person and somehow, his/her god-like presence will make itself felt, and all will be well'. Others, for example Robbins (1998), advocate something that looks remarkably like OD, and from what has been said earlier, there must be some doubt about whether a glib prescription such as this will actually work. In addition, there is another issue of importance which, as yet, nobody seems to have addressed.

The learning organisation is a highly managerialist concept that is intended to benefit the top management of an organisation rather than anyone else. While an organisation of this type probably has a strong capacity to survive and prosper, its top managers are the people who reap the rewards without having to undergo change themselves. As in most prescriptions for change, they will probably be left untouched, and those lower down will have to cope with the radically different patterns of organisational life that are probably more hectic, stressful and insecure. The important question, therefore, is whether anybody has bothered to ask the people lower down whether this is the sort of life that they want?

- The emergent approach to change rejects the idea that change can sensibly be conceptualised as a pre-planned fixed sequence of steps undertaken to a set timetable and, instead, views change as an open-ended process of experimentation and adaptation that tries to achieve a better fit between the organisation and its environment.
- Because it deals with organisations that are equipped for continuous change, a great deal of current attention is focused on the concept of the learning organisation.
- Transforming a conventional organisation into a learning organisation means that a number of important barriers need to be overcome and, as yet, no prescription for doing this has emerged.

OVERVIEW AND CONCLUSIONS

Although organisations have always had to change and adapt, a number of influential authors have argued that the need to do so is now greater than ever. This is often prompted by changes in an organisation's environment, which means that there is a greater tendency for change to occur for strategic reasons.

Although change of some sort can become inevitable, this does not mean that it is welcomed by everyone. For this reason, it is possible that many changes go hand in hand with a measure of resistance and any strategy for dealing with resistance needs to be carefully selected according to the reasons why resistance has appeared.

There are two basic approaches to introducing or implementing organisational change: the planned approach and the emergent approach. The first of these is exemplified by OD, which is strongly focused on changing the human element in an organisation. It is underpinned by a set of philosophies and assumptions about the nature of human behaviour in organisations, uses a systems perspective, and assumes that change in human values and attitudes are necessary if people are to accommodate themselves to a changed situation. However, arguments still rage about whether OD delivers what it promises in terms of a more effective organisation and more satisfied and committed employees. In addition, there are questions about the relevance of OD to contemporary organisations and about the ethics of the approach.

The emergent approach rejects the major tenets of planned change, and in particular the idea that change can be introduced by a universally applicable set of sequenced steps. Instead, change is regarded as an open-ended process in which issues are dealt with as they arise, often by way of a number of small, incremental initiatives that can eventually add up to a major transformation.

A recent concept that is compatible with the emergent approach is that of the learning organisation. This envisages organisations that are continuously ready for change and while this concept attracts a great deal of attention, it is still in its infancy. Thus, although it is clear what a learning organisation will look like, and it may well be the case that this is the direction in which organisations may need to move in the future, there is as yet no definitive prescription about how to become a learning organisation.

FURTHER READING

Argyris, C (1999) *On Organisational Learning*, 2nd edn, Oxford: Blackwell. A classic text, which gives a penetrating exploration of organisational learning and some coverage of organisational development and change.

Burnes, B (2000) *Managing Change: A Strategic Approach to Organisational Dynamics*, 3rd edn, Harlow: Financial Times/Prentice Hall. A comprehensive text that covers a great many approaches to change.

Burnes, B (2004) Kurt Lewin and the planned approach to change: a re-appraisal, *Journal of Management Studies* 41(6): 977–1002. A highly informative article. It reviews the work of one of the founding fathers of the planned approach to change and draws the conclusion that despite criticisms that Lewin's ideas are outdated and redundant, his approach is still highly relevant in the modern world.

Collins, D (1998) *Organisational Change: Sociological Perspectives*, London: Routledge. A penetrating examination of organisational change, which critically discusses many of the myths and populist quick-fix approaches.

Cummings, TG and C Worley (1997) *Organisational Development and Change*, 7th edn, St Paul, MN: West Publishing. A comprehensive text containing many practical examples and case studies.

French, WL and CH Bell (1999) *Organisational Development: Behavioural Science Interventions for Organisational Improvement*, 6th edn, Englewood Cliffs, NJ: Prentice Hall. A classic text that gives comprehensive, if somewhat uncritical, coverage of OD.

Huy QN and H Mintzberg (2003) The rhythm of change, *MIT Sloan Management Review* Summer: 79–84.

Kotter, JP (1995) Leading change: why transformation efforts fail, *Harvard Business Review* March/April: 59–67. An American article illustrating the recipe approach in which the author describes his eight-step process for successful change.

Senior, B (1997) *Organisational Change*, London: Pitman. A well-written text which explores different approaches to managing organisational change.

CASE STUDY 21.1: Dealing with problems at Citigroup

This case deals with a team of 11 highly ambitious, competitive and technically expert, senior bankers at Citigroup, the largest financial services company in America. It operated from both New York and London, and had a highly challenging goal: to take its part of the business from number three in the world to number one, by developing products with international appeal. However, the team faced serious obstacles that threatened its chances of collaborating globally. Relations were difficult between people based in New York, who focused on deals in the Americas, and staff in London, who had responsibility for Europe. The New York-based managers complained of excessive bureaucracy in their London colleagues, who in turn accused them of 'shooting from the hip'. They were unable to resolve these conflicts and often resorted to personal criticism and scapegoating.

'There appeared to be what was a cross-cultural divide between London and New York,' explains Terry Lockhart, senior vice-president for organisational effectiveness. However, this divide did not seem to be related to the merger between Travelers and Citicorp that created Citigroup. Nor was it a simple matter of nationalities but, rather, of working cultures. Indeed, the North Americans who had worked in London for some time reflected more of a European way of working than we might have guessed, says Mr Lockhart. Thus it became clear to Mr Lockhart that intervention of some sort was needed because the internal tensions were distracting the team from concentrating on the competition and developing new clients and more innovative products. For this reason he brought in Elisabeth Marx, a director of Norman Broadbent International, an executive search firm, and with her help, the executives embarked on a programme of personal and team development.

The process began with each executive spending a day being interviewed, completing questionnaires and receiving feedback and coaching from Ms Marx. Her reports and recommendations remained confidential to the individuals, and among characteristics she identified for improvement were: a lack of interpersonal sensitivity; a lack of flexibility; extreme assertiveness; and inattention to networking. This was followed by observation of the team and its sub-groups in action. The results were discussed at a workshop that focused on the qualities of high-performing teams and how to deal with the issues impeding the Citigroup executives. The team then set itself targets and progress was monitored during the following year by Mr Lockhart.

The results were so impressive that Citigroup has now decided to tell the inside story. Not only did internal surveys report an improvement in teamwork, but revenues also rose by 64 per cent, and the team moved up to number two in world rankings.

Interestingly, financial measures were crucial in persuading people to accept the intervention. 'This was a counter-intuitive approach for them,' says Ms Marx. The culture of financial services is not characterised by a deep psychological interest in, or affinity for, softer issues. This was a group of highly individualistic, ambitious and materialistic senior executives and the buy-in for them was money; if they could improve their performance, they could improve their pay. Although there was still some initial scepticism, Mr Lockhart had spent time telling them how they were perceived within the business as being at odds with each other. They knew there were problems and they wanted to tackle them.

Source: Maitland, A. (2002) Citigroup: bridging the culture gap, *Financial Times*, 28 January

Questions

1. Do you feel that the steps taken to resolve the difficulties at Citigroup could be classified as an OD intervention; if so why?

2. At what level in the organisation did the intervention take place: organisational, intergroup, intra-group, or individual?

3. How do you feel that the team and its members might have reacted to being singled-out for treatment in this way?

4. From the point of view of Citigroup, to what extent do you feel that the intervention has been worthwhile?

5. To what extent do you feel that the team members might also feel that the experience was worthwhile?

REVIEW AND DISCUSSION QUESTIONS

1. Describe the main triggers to organisational change that are located in:
- the wider environment
- an organisation's task environment
- the organisation itself.

2. Distinguish between and describe the four types of change identified by Nadler and Tushman (1986).

3. Why do people resist change? Is resistance inevitable and, if so, how can it most appropriately be handled?

4. Describe the systems model of change and trace its implications for the design of an organisational change initiative.

5. Describe Lewin's method for bringing about change in human behaviour.

6. What is Organisational Development (OD)? What distinguishes OD from other approaches to organisational change?

7. Critically evaluate OD in terms of:
- the likelihood of it delivering what it promises
- its relevance to managers in present-day conditions
- its ethics.

Integrating Macro Level Characteristics and Processes and the Macro and Micro Levels of Organisation

INTRODUCTION

This integrative section, which is the final one of the book, has two main tasks. First, it traces links between the topics covered in the six preceding chapters. Some of these chapters deal with organisational characteristics. For example, Chapter 16 (*Goals and Effectiveness*), Chapter 17 (*Structure*), and Chapter 18 (*Organisational Design*) are of this type. Others, notably Chapter 19 (*Organisational Control*), and Chapter 21 (*Change and Development*) deal with organisational processes, and Chapter 20 (*Cultures and Climate*) could be regarded treated as either a characteristic or a process. For convenience, the chapters dealing with characteristics (16, 17 and 18) will be dealt with separately from those that cover processes (19, 20 and 21). In each case the aim will be to explain how the characteristics can have an impact on other characteristics and/ or processes at the same level.

The second task of this integrative section is somewhat more ambitious than the first, and harks back to a point made at the very start of the book, where, in Chapter 1, it was pointed out that it is impossible to understand the complexity of human behaviour in organisations without taking account characteristics, processes and events at two different levels of organisation. These are the *Micro level*, which is covered in Chapters 3–15 and the *Macro level*, covered in Chapters 16–21, and here the task is to trace links between these two levels. Since this involves drawing on material from virtually all chapters in the book, the aim is a somewhat ambitious one and, results in the largest integrative section of all. Therefore, the discussion is split into two integrative sub-sections. The first describes some of the effects that the macro level can have on the micro level, and the second deals with the effects that micro level factors have on the macro level.

As with every other integrative section in the book, space precludes identifying every possible effect, so the discussion is restricted to some of the more prominent and easily identifiable influences. Nevertheless, this brings together important conclusions from all other chapters in the book and, for this reason, unlike prior integrative sections, this one provides short, bulleted lists of 'Replay' points at intervals throughout the text, in order to summarise its main conclusions.

INTEGRATING MACRO LEVEL CHARACTERISTICS AND PROCESSES

Links between Organisational Characteristics

The traditional way of evaluating the effectiveness of an organisation is against the criterion of whether it achieves its goals. This establishes a clear conceptual link between goals and effectiveness and, in theory at least, this link also exists between goals and structure. For example, goals are part and parcel of what an organisation should achieve and its structure is (or should be) a means of achieving its goals (Chandler 1962). Having said this, whether structure actually flows from strategy in this neat linear way is a matter of some debate. For instance, the theory of strategic choice (Child 1997) argues that managers can become so attached to a certain set of structural arrangements that they modify strategies to suit existing structures. However, this in no way negates the potentially strong link between structure and strategy.

In addition, there is an equally strong link between structure and effectiveness. Basic structure (Child 1984) makes provision for an appropriate set of organisational parts to enable an organisation to do what it has to do and, for this reason, a poor basic structure is a barrier to organisational performance and effectiveness (Drucker 1984). A second aspect of structure, the organisation's operating mechanisms (Child 1984) specifies in more detail how things get done, and how operations are coordinated and controlled. Thus, the two essential features of any structure – differentiation and integration – have clear links with goals and effectiveness. Differentiation establishes the necessary parts of an organisation that allow it to achieve its goals, and integration provides for coordination and control of these parts to ensure that goals are achieved. Control, of course, is the actual process that uses these mechanisms.

Links between Organisational Characteristics and Processes

A characteristic that has strong links with structure is an organisation's culture. For example, Harrison's (1972) scheme, given in Chapter 18, shows how certain structural features go hand in hand with patterns of sentiments and values, which points very strongly to a link between culture and structure. It is also likely that there is some connection between culture and effectiveness. For instance, prescriptive writers on organisational culture, such as Peters and Waterman (1982), argue that strong cultures are a vital element in organisational success. While this idea has been criticised as highly simplistic (Thompson and McHugh 1995) and it is now recognised that if it is to be an important factor in success culture must be appropriate as well as strong, this only serves to reinforce the idea that culture, effectiveness and structure are linked.

Culture also has strong links with the process of change. Cultures and structures can be sources of comfort and predictability to those who have lived with them for some time, and to some extent this means that they contain inbuilt forces to resist change (Ray 1986). Thus, where managers are able to bring about cultural change, they exercise the ultimate degree of control over people in an organisation. However, whether an organisation's culture can be easily changed is a highly contentious issue. Cultural pragmatists assume that it is possible, while cultural purists such as Ogbonna (1993) assert that culture is probably too deeply rooted to be easily modified. A more pragmatic, middle-ground proposition is that advanced by advocates of the so-called learning organisation (McGill and Slocum 1993), described in Chapter 21. This explicitly acknowledges a link between culture, change and effectiveness, and seeks to establish cultures that are receptive to continuous change.

Finally, there are also strong connections between goals, effectiveness and change, if only because a strong trigger to change is a perceived reduction in organisational effectiveness, or the failure of an organisation to achieve certain goals.

In summary, therefore, there are very strong links between organisational level characteristics and processes, which will be shown diagrammatically at the end of this integrative section.

INTEGRATING MACRO AND MICRO LEVELS OF ORGANISATION

The Effects of the Macro Level on the Micro Level

Organisational Structure

Structure has a huge effect on individual and group processes, and it is usually intended that this be the case. However, structure does not directly determine behaviour in the same way as an individual's mental processes do; rather, it establishes a set of con-textual circumstances that encourage certain behaviours and inhibit others. There are two fundamental features of an organisation's structure: differentiation, which divides the organisation up into component parts; and integration, which makes provision to control and coordinate the parts to achieve goals. In practice these go hand in hand, but here it is simpler to concentrate on the first and defer discussion of integration until control is considered.

The more an organisation is split up into highly specialised units (the extreme of which is the highly bureaucratised structure), the more likely it is that units come to see themselves as different, which means that people lower down can lose sight of the overall goals for the organisation. To try to overcome these effects, bureaucracies often put limits on the behaviour of individuals by making extensive use of standardised and formalised procedures that specify exactly what should be done. This, however, can have attitudinal and motivational effects, and a number of writers have commented on the way that a highly bureaucratised structure can result in people just following the rules, even if the rules are inappropriate (Merton 1957; Selznick 1966). This, however, is bureaucracy in the extreme, and a more typical example is given in Chapter 18, in Burns and Stalker's (1994) description of the mechanistic organisation. Nevertheless, this still illustrates that structure is likely to affect patterns of behaviour and can also give rise to distinctive attitudes.

The principle of specialisation in the broader structure is often repeated lower down, and this influences the way that jobs are designed. Highly differentiated structures often have jobs with small, restricted task elements, which can result in boredom, low intrin-sic satisfaction, and a stifling of personal initiative, and few opportunities for personal growth (Argyris 1964). In highly specialised structures there is sometimes an attempt to alleviate some of these problems with slight modifications to job design, for instance the job rotation, enlargement or even the enrichment steps described in Chapter 7.

All structural forms have their own strengths and weaknesses, and the current trend towards flatter structures can have its own associated difficulties, albeit of a differ-ent type. Decentralised authority can result in more autonomy and increased job satisfaction, but the structure that results can sometimes be so loose that it gives rise to ambiguity, anxiety and stress. In addition, all structural forms, whether they are mechanistic or organic, establish bases of power, notably the power to reward and/or coerce subordinates that is described in Chapter 14. While the effects of these will be put on one side until control is discussed, there is another phenomenon that must be highlighted. Since sub-units can sometimes come to see themselves as different from others, it is often but a short step from this for sub-units to pursue their own aims at the expense of other groups. Thus structure can establish a tendency for competition between groups, and in some cases this can develop into outright conflict. This is the case even in loose structures and it has been noted, for example, that matrix structures are usually riven with conflict (Davis and Lawrence 1977). Thus, although the effects of structure are not always as adverse as the picture painted here, it can be asserted with some confidence that the differentiation aspect of structure can have effects on work-related attitudes of organisational members, and also on their motivations and tendencies towards intergroup conflict.

Organisational Control

As is explained in Chapter 19, organisational control systems are essentially put in place to monitor progress towards achieving goals or objectives and, where necessary, to set corrective action in motion. This is a process that starts at the macro level, extends downwards, and represents the integrative aspect of structure. For this reason when an organisation is divided up into departments or functions, an important element in the design is to include a facility to coordinate and control the parts. Since control also extends downwards to individuals and groups, the type of control used at this level is often a reflection of the general structural characteristics of an organisation. While a high degree of specialisation usually gives economic efficiency and people know where they stand, if this is reflected too heavily in job design, the associated tedium and monotony sometimes result in higher absenteeism or turnover and a degree of antagonism between the workforce and managers.

Structure also tends to reflect management philosophies about how much control is needed. In general terms, the more an organisation is differentiated, the greater the need for coordination of the parts. Thus structures of this type are often associated with a high degree of standardisation, for example the use of standard operating procedures and tight job specifications, to set out what individuals can or cannot do.

There is little doubt that the nature of control in an organisation can affect attitudes, perceptions and motivations of employees. Therefore, while tight coordination and control might help to head off propensities for intergroup conflict, it has its own pitfalls and Walton (1985) argues that managers have to choose between imposed control and attempting to elicit commitment. In theory, a high degree of employee commitment makes control at the individual level less necessary, and even some degree of commitment probably enables control systems to operate in a way that engenders less hostility. Nevertheless, the desire to obtain employee commitment should be recognised for what it is: an attempt to obtain control by other means.

Culture and Climate

Because people carry a culture in their minds it has a direct and highly pervasive effect on behaviour. Whichever way it is defined, culture provides people with a set of normative rules to regulate certain aspects of their behaviour, and this becomes an invisible force that prompts many of their actions. Therefore, if an organisation has a strong culture and everybody subscribes to the same set of core values, this may well give rise to attitudes, motivations and a sense of shared identity that contributes to its effectiveness, providing, of course, that the culture is appropriate for the goals the organisation seeks to achieve (Luthans 1995). However, it must also be remembered that culture and structure tend to go hand in hand. Harrison's (1972) four-part scheme for classifying cultures shows how structures are associated with value systems that probably result in the existing structure being seen as the most appropriate way for organising and controlling activities. New employees are likely to be socialised into these values and attitudes by those already in the organisation, which in the highly differentiated functional structure is likely to mean that sub-cultures are virtually inevitable (Sackman 1997). Since these represent different value systems, they may well play a part in promoting intergroup conflict, and possibly a level of political activity to pursue conflicts that arise.

Climate tends to have similar, but perhaps more easily identifiable, behavioural effects. While culture provides a code of behaviour that tells people what is appropriate and expected, climate is what they perceive the organisation to be, and is a set of conditions to which they react. Therefore, while both are linked to people's value systems, culture is what the values are, and climate is more a reflection of whether current organisational conditions are concordant with the values that people hold. Where these conditions conflict too heavily with cultural values, a poor climate can arise. For this reason climatic conditions are almost bound to have a huge impact on attitudes, perceptions, motivations and the level of conflict in an organisation.

Returning now to a point that arose when discussing control, as Ray (1986) points out, managers have tried almost every way of controlling employees, only to find that whatever controls they use have limited effect. As such there is now a tendency to try to exercise control in a more subtle way by eliciting commitment or, to put matters differently, by controlling hearts and minds. To some extent this probably occurs of its own accord where culture and structure are compatible, but cultures are extremely slow to change, and if there is an attempt to introduce a radically different and incompatible structure, all sorts of adverse motivational and attitudinal effects can be encountered. There is some evidence that this has happened in recent structural changes made by many organisations, for example in delayering, re-engineering and empowerment initiatives. To work well these changes require attitudes that make cooperation and commitment more likely (Macduffie 1995), but many of these changes have been introduced in organisations that previously had conventional structures and in all likelihood they had developed cultures to match. Thus empowerment often fails to work because managers and supervisors find it hard to let go of the previous way of doing things (Cunningham *et al.* 1996) and people in these organisations often report feelings of demoralisation, demotivation and frustration.

Organisational Change

Many of the points that can be made about change are implicit in what has already been said. As Chapter 21 points out, change can occur at all organisational levels and can be extremely varied in its scope. People come to work for a variety of motives, all of which are usually connected with their self-interests. If someone has learned to play a useful role in an organisation, he or she has almost certainly invested time, energy and brain power into trying to make things work a little better. Thus the person has 'sunk costs' in the organisation that cannot easily be recouped (Patti 1974). For this reason change can be highly threatening to many people and it is not surprising that it can engender emotive feelings such as stress, adverse attitudes, lowered motivations and highly selective perceptions.

Almost any change has different effects on different people – to some it gives more of what they seek to obtain from work, while to others it can take away what they most value. Thus there can be winners and losers. Predictably, those who perceive themselves to be the winners can experience the prospective change as stimulating and motivating and develop more positive attitudes towards the organisation, even to the extent of ignoring any potential drawbacks. For those who see themselves as the losers, however, the change can have the reverse effect.

As well as these effects at the individual level, change can have an impact on group and intergroup processes. It sometimes results in a degree of uncertainty in which goals become more ambiguous, the ground-rules for making decisions are less clear and people become unsure of how resources will be distributed in the future. This is a tremendous spur to political activity as people manoeuvre to retain what power they have, or acquire the levels of power that they desire.

Organisational Communication

Communication has an impact on the downward effects of all the organisational characteristics and processes so far discussed. To some extent, culture is a silent system of communication in its own right, and since this was discussed earlier it needs no further explanation. Moreover, no structure will serve its purpose without effective communication. Control and coordination are crucially dependent on a good flow of accurate information; for instance, people are not really empowered unless information flows freely to them so that they can make appropriate decisions. In addition, change is made much harder without effective communication and people can hardly be expected to welcome a change unless its details and the reasons for the change are clear in their minds. Thus communication affects attitudes, perceptions, motivations and levels of conflict.

Goals and goal achievement have some connection with patterns of communication in organisations. Coordination and control would be impossible without a flow of information, and there is some evidence that different strategies may need different methods of communication. For instance, Kanter (1995) argues that an innovation strategy requires a free flow of information, which implies a greater reliance on informal channels, while cost reduction strategies require more formal arrangements. This tells us that structure can have a huge impact on the process of communication. For example, the long chain of command prevalent in tall structures often results in information exchange being shaped and controlled by those above. Conversely, flat structures, in which power and authority are decentralised, tend to result in less distortion of information because the communication chain is shorter and the decision making process is nearer to the operational level. Communication also has links with culture. Strong cultures often contain powerful ways of communicating the core values to new organisational members, and most cultures have their own methods of communication. This is often what is colloquially referred to as 'the grapevine', which is the organisation's quickest and most effective communication system.

- The differentiation and integration aspects of structure can have implications for patterns of attitudes, motivation and tendencies towards intergroup conflict at lower organisational levels.
- Culture and climate can also have an impact on attitudes and behaviour at lower levels.
- Organisational change is often experienced as disruptive or threatening by people at lower levels, and this can also give rise to attitudinal and motivational effects.
- Communication influences the effectiveness of organisational control mechanisms and has a strong impact on attitudes and motivations lower down, particularly in situations of change.

THE EFFECTS OF THE MICRO LEVEL ON THE MACRO LEVEL

Perhaps because it evokes an image of the use of power and authority, the effects of the macro level of organisation on the micro level are easily appreciated, a corollary of which is that effects in the opposite direction tend to be neglected. Nevertheless, there are many ways in which the micro levels of an organisation have an impact on the macro level, and to structure the explanation, it is convenient to consider three clusters of influence: the effects of individual characteristics; the effects of individual processes; and the effects of group characteristics and processes.

The Effects of Individual Characteristics

Certain individual characteristics are relatively fixed and others are subject to a degree of variation in the light of prevailing organisational circumstances. This gives two sub-clusters of influence and these will be considered in turn.

Dealing first with the relatively permanent characteristics of personality, intelligence and aptitude, their most obvious impact is on the suitability of individuals to occupy specific organisational roles. Since individual performance dovetails into the performance of a group and this feeds into the performance of a whole organisation, individual characteristics can have an impact on goal achievement and hence organisational effectiveness. **Personality** also has an upward impact on employee reactions to change and some change can be so radical that it conflicts with what an individual has come to accept as the reality of how an organisation should function, which gives one reason why change can encounter resistance.

Turning now to the characteristics that can change with organisational circumstances, **perceptions** can have a strong influence on the way that downward communications are interpreted. This is particularly the case when a communication contains an unwelcome message about impending change. Perceptions also have an impact on how methods of control are interpreted. Moreover, perceptions have a profound influence on the way that individuals react to the organisation that surrounds them. For example, in a situation of change, if the organisation fails to show people that the change poses no threat, adverse perceptions can become the first stage in the self-fulfilling prophecy that ultimately leads to resistance.

Attitudes and emotions are also subject to a degree of modification in the light of circumstances, and they can have a huge impact in reactions to change. The more central an attitude is to a person's concept of self, the harder it is to change. Festinger's (1957) theory of cognitive dissonance tells us that unless behaviour and attitude are compatible, the individual experiences some degree of psychological discomfort, tension or even stress. Thus, when a change requires patterns of behaviour that are incompatible with an individual's attitudes, the change tends to be perceived as threatening, the predictable consequence of which is that attitudes harden and the change is resisted. In these circumstances, attitudes can also help to erect perceptual barriers. If an impending change is felt to adversely affect personal freedom, the attitudes this engenders can result in any communication about the change being perceived as one-sided or lacking in credibility (Brehm 1972), and what happens then can depend on how the organisation reacts to this situation. If attitudes have hardened and strong pressure is applied from above, it is likely that pressure will be exerted in return, to give the so-called boomerang effect (Heller *et al.* 1973) in which people do the exact opposite of what they are asked. Finally, work-related attitudes such as job satisfaction and organisational commitment can have a strong impact on the way individuals perform their roles, and clearly this ultimately has implications for organisational goal achievement and effectiveness.

The Effects of Individual Processes

Motivation gives a person the impetus to engage in a course of action that he or she perceives to be rewarding. Therefore, to the extent that an organisation provides conditions that people experience as motivating, there are implications for individual performance which can ultimately have effects on goal achievement and organisational effectiveness. However, motivation is an inner mental state that is not directly under management's control and, because of this, it is difficult to find a set of conditions that are equally motivating for all people. Process theories of motivation, such as expectancy theory (Porter and Lawler 1968; Vroom 1964), tell us that motivation is influenced by expectations about the actual receipt of rewards. Thus if someone was informed in the past that valued rewards were obtainable and this subsequently turned out to be untrue, it is unlikely that a similar promise will have a motivating effect a second time, which has clear implications for the process of communication. Equity theory (Adams 1965) also draws attention to the idea that motivation can be strongly influenced by people's evaluations of the fairness of their rewards compared to those obtained by other people and this has implications for the effectiveness of structures and reward systems throughout an organisation.

Job design, which is often a micro level reflection of the structural design and control system of an organisation, cannot sensibly be considered in isolation from motivation. The design of a job can either make it a stimulating experience, or one that is boring, monotonous and full of drudgery. For this reason, a design that seeks only economic efficiency, and ignores the necessity for satisfaction of intrinsic needs, can actually become a barrier to motivation.

Individual decision making also has important upward effects. Integrating mechanisms embedded in an organisation's structure are unlikely to be effective unless appropriate decisions are made at appropriate times – something that can have a clear effect on achievement of goals and organisational effectiveness. Moreover, in certain circumstances, individual decision making can result in interactions between the macro and micro levels of organisation. If decision making criteria are ambiguous, or decisions have to be taken in conditions of high uncertainty, low-quality decisions can be made and this can result in goals or objectives not being achieved, which in turn creates even more ambiguity down below.

Individual learning processes also have a fairly clear implication for two macro level aspects of organisational functioning. Change almost always involves an element of unlearning the old and learning something new, and the process of adaptation can be dependent on the speed at which this takes place. Thus successful organisational change is strongly influenced by individual learning processes. People seldom restrict themselves to learning only what the organisation wants them to learn and ignore everything else. They also learn to behave in a way that is calculated to maximise their pleasant experiences and minimise unpleasant situations and this has a huge impact on organisational systems of control.

Finally, there is another individual process that has strong implications for organisational functioning. Because it can result in low morale, lowered motivation, decreased performance and lack of job satisfaction, all of which have identifiable economic effects, individual **stress** costs money. Importantly, stress can also have some highly recursive effects. The absenteeism, lowered output and lack of individual effectiveness that result from stress sometimes sound the wrong alarm bells in organisational control systems. Instead of examining whether prevailing stressful conditions have made the organisation the author of its own lack of effectiveness, the result is to increased pressure on those lower down to make up the shortfall, the net result of which is even more widespread stress.

The Effects of Group Processes and Characteristics

Many of the upward individual influences described above are exerted through individuals. However, there are some that are predominantly group-level phenomena that occur only because a group exists. The Homans (1950) model in Chapter 11 shows that important organisational outcomes such as economic efficiency, goal achievement and organisational effectiveness can be strongly influenced by the members of a group. Therefore, unless a clash between the objectives that an organisation has for a group and those that the group has for itself is avoided, the likelihood of achieving these objectives can be poor (Keller 1986).

Groups exert a huge influence on their members that can sometimes extend to the shaping of their perceptions. Thus, information can be subject to a high degree of distortion as it is reinterpreted through a group's communication structure, and this can have a strong impact on an organisation's capability to bring about change.

A group is unlikely to perform its role well unless it has achieved a degree of maturity (Tuckman 1965) and, if it is a temporary one (as is quite common these days), its composition in terms of the complementary skills and abilities of members can be vital (Belbin 1993). While cohesive groups tend to have higher levels of performance, cohesiveness can have its drawbacks, one of which is decision making. What is perhaps more important from an organisation's point of view is that coordination and control through the structure of the organisation can be seriously impaired if groups are too cohesive. Indeed, the more that control is exerted downwards on a highly cohesive group, the greater will be the group's resistance to the control (Buller and Bell 1986).

If an organisation is to function well, groups have to interact with each other, which means that organisational effectiveness can be highly dependent on smooth relations between groups. However, cohesive groups have a higher propensity to view themselves as perfect and others as having nothing but faults, which can result in a situation ripe for intergroup conflict. This not only wastes time and energy, it can also have some highly recursive effects. For instance, conflict can result in winners and losers, with the winners often becoming more self-righteous and complacent, while the losers become tense or demoralised and look for opportunities to regain their honour.

The **headship** role is the most visible one in most groups, and whether this is also a role of leadership is a matter of some importance. Leaders are usually able to exert a degree of influence over followers without recourse to formal authority, which can have implications for willing and committed performance of tasks and ultimately have a bearing on goal achievement and organisational effectiveness. Thus, whether the person in charge is a leader or simply a head, this person's behavioural style has implications for the outcomes of a group's endeavours. Contingency theories of leadership all indicate that high group performance is more easily achieved if the head's behavioural style matches certain contingent circumstances. However, a leader's style is a function of his or her personality and, since this is likely to be relatively unchanging (Fiedler 1965, 1967), there are implications for successful adaptation to change. Moreover, in situations of radical change, it seems likely that very different styles of leader behaviour are required. Bass (1985) points out that the transactional style of behaviour required under steady stable conditions is quite different from the one needed in a dynamic changing situation, where a transformational style is more appropriate.

With respect to **power** in organisations, Chapter 14 points out that a common misconception about power is that is only exercised in a downward direction. However, two of French and Raven's (1959) bases of power are often capable of being exerted upwards. Referent power can establish informal leaders in groups on whom formal heads can become dependent, and the formal head of a group can also be highly dependent on the expert power of subordinates. This is often the case in today's downsized and delayered conditions, where organisations have been so slimmed down that goals can be difficult to achieve without the commitment of the workforce. To achieve this state of affairs employees may well require that managers put limits on the use of formal authority.

As was noted earlier, **political tactics** tend to be used to acquire, maintain or enhance power. Chapter 14 points out that political activity is commonplace in many organisations, and it is probably even more prevalent in today's fast-changing conditions, which are full of ambiguity. This can call into question the reality of formal structures and their associated control mechanisms, and also has an impact on the change process. For example, if people use the change situation to manoeuvre for personal advantage, change will probably take much longer and may even be found to have taken a form that was never intended.

Finally, all organisations seem to have a degree of conflict, either between individuals or groups. The interactionist perspective argues that there is an optimal level of conflict for an organisation and, if there is too much, it absorbs energy that could be devoted to other things, which has implications for macro level matters such as goal achievement, effectiveness and change. However, if there is insufficient conflict, it is argued that the *status quo* is likely to remain unchallenged. Thus the organisation can become characterised by inertia, stagnation and lack of innovation, all of which are likely to have an impact on goal achievement, effectiveness and the willingness to change when necessary.

REPLAY

- The relatively unchanging characteristics of individuals can affect their suitability for roles and also their reactions to prospects of change.
- Characteristics that are more changeable in the light of prevailing organisational circumstances also have a strong impact on reactions to change, while work-related attitudes have an impact on certain aspects of employee performance.
- Individual processes such as motivation, decision making, learning and stress all have upward influences and these in turn are affected by the downward effects of structure and control systems.
- Many of the upward influences are expressed through groups and, in addition, group characteristics and processes have their own impact on the whole organisation.

OVERVIEW AND CONCLUSIONS

Since individuals and groups are all influenced by the context in which they exist, macro level features such as structure, control, goals, culture and communication all have some influence on the behaviour of individuals and groups lower down. In many cases, while these features are largely put in place to try to influence micro level behaviour, people are not just passive recipients of this influence. They experience it with varying degrees of favourability and react to what they experience. Thus there are micro level phenomena that affect those at the macro level, and often in a way that has a bearing on the effectiveness of an organisation's structure, its control mechanisms, its processes of communication and change and the effectiveness of the organisation itself.

For these reasons there are dangers in viewing either the macro or micro levels of organisation in isolation. To obtain a more accurate perspective it is desirable to view a process or characteristic as part of a system of interconnected parts. In this way it is often possible to gain a better understanding of why a phenomenon exists, why it is what it is, how it is affected by other phenomena and how, in turn, it affects them.

With these points in mind, Figure I3, which closed the previous integrative section can now be supplemented with the influences identified above, to give Figure I4.

Figure I4 Interactions within macro and micro level and between different levels of organisation

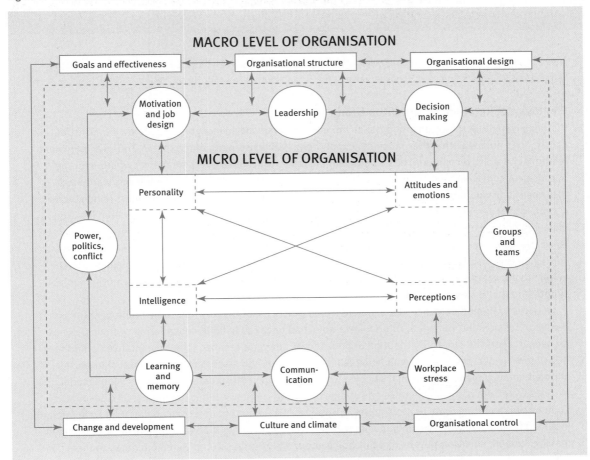

INTEGRATIVE CASE STUDY No. 4: David Orton plc – employment relations

Note To refresh your memory about relevant background details to this case, you are recommended to re-read Case Studies 1, 2 and 3 in this series and, in particular, Case Study No. 3.

Employment Relations at the Orton Group

Historically, neither the Orton group nor its merger partner Costwise recognised trade unions. This, of course does not mean that they failed to acknowledge their existence; rather, that in British employment relations the word 'recognition' has a particular meaning, which effectively means 'recognition for the purposes of collective bargaining'. Thus if either party (company or trade union) felt it was warranted, the other party would be approached to discuss matters on an *ad hoc* basis. Nevertheless, since there was no formal agreement to recognise the trade union, meetings such as this only occurred if it suited management, and not because the trade union was acknowledged as the legitimate voice of the workforce. To all intents and purposes, therefore, Orton was similar to many other companies in the UK. Officially it was a non-unionised firm, even though management freely admitted that many of its employees were union members and, if challenged on the matter, it always denied that it was in any way 'anti-union', but simply said that it saw no need for trade unions.

In terms of Human Resource Management (HRM) practices, both firms had some of the trappings of being 'professionally' managed. Orton for example, had engaged in 'joint consultation' with employees for over 20 years. All stores, distribution depots and its headquarters had Joint Consultative Committees (JCCs), in which employees met with management each month to discuss matters of mutual interest, although management had the final say over what appeared on the agenda and any decisions made. Minutes were kept of these meetings and copies of them were forwarded to Regional Joint Consultative Committees, and from there to headquarters. However, it is important to recognise that JCCs were primarily intended for management to communicate with the workforce, rather than as a vehicle for joint decision making. Indeed, since employees had no choice about sitting on JCCs (and were nominated to them by managers) there were strong suspicions that they existed in order to give a superficial show of participative decision making, rather than to actually share power.

These characteristics of employment relations at the Orton group were typical of those in many other firms in Great Britain where, since 1997, the State's philosophy has been to promote union recognition and voluntary collective bargaining as the preferred way of obtaining good employment relations, but to stop short of endorsing compulsory recognition. However, this situation radically changed in 1999, when the Employment Act introduced provisions for a statutory basis for union recognition. These, which were subsequently incorporated into Schedule A1 of the Trade Union and Labour Relations (Consolidation) Act 1992, gave a procedure in which an employer can agree that one or more trade unions will represent the interests of some or all of the employees in an organisation for the purposes of collective bargaining. Unless otherwise agreed by the parties, the legislation defines collective bargaining as negotiation over hours of work, holidays and pay (the latter including pensions) and in practice, once recognition is obtained, it is also extended to representational rights in individual issues such as grievance and discipline.

Importantly, the legislation allows for recognition rights to be granted in one of three ways:

1. by voluntary agreement with the employer
2. where necessary, by the Central Arbitration Committee of the Advisory, Conciliation and Arbitration Service granting recognition
3. by conducting a ballot to assess the level of employee support for trade union recognition, which if demonstrated would automatically result in compulsory recognition being granted.

The Redundancy Issue

As noted in an earlier case studies in this series, because the Competition Commission required Orton and/or Costwise to divest itself of a number of retail outlets, it took some time for the size and structure of the new Orton group to become clear. Nevertheless, by mid-2005, when the final shape of the new group had emerged, it became clear that a number of distribution depots could be surplus to requirements. Since this could mean that the company might well have to make a substantial number of employees redundant, Orton's Human Resource Manager took two steps. First, he arranged for a preliminary airing of the matter in Joint Consultative Committee meetings at distribution depots, under an agenda item of 'Future Staffing Requirements'. The aim of this was to enable site managers to explain why it had been necessary to conduct a review of distribution depots and stress that while the outcome of the review had not yet been finalised, it was possible that some depots might be involved in a modicum of downsizing.

Second, the HRM manager also made contact with officials of the Retail, Distributive and Allied Workers' Union, and gave the union the same information. He also invited the union to nominate up to three relevant officials to attend a meeting at Orton's headquarters, where they would be brought up-to-date on the matter. Accordingly, a meeting was scheduled to take place in two weeks time and those attending on behalf of Orton were: John Hendry, HRM manager; David Orton, non-executive chairman; and Richard Brewer, Orton's CEO.

The union nominated three regional secretaries (full-time officials of the Union) to attend, who were: Mr Mark Swain, Southern regional secretary; Mr Fred Brown, regional secretary for drivers and warehousing staff; and Mrs Edwina Green, regional secretary for retailing and clerical staffs.

Here it is important to point out that the law establishes a raft of employment rights for employees who are likely to be affected by redundancy, and in the eyes of the law, these rights are treated as sacrosanct. So far as this case is concerned, the most important of these rights are those that establish:

- entitlement to compensation for redundant employees

- protection against unfair dismissal and rights to time off work to search for new jobs

- rights for employee/trade-union consultation with management prior to the occurance of redundancies, for example in the case of 100 or more employees being made redundant at one establishment over a period of 90 days or less, for a 90-day consultation period. This period is designed to provide time for extensive consultation about a host of matters, including avoiding a redundancy situation. In addition, it places an onus on the employer to 'bargain in good faith', and with a view to reaching agreement with employee representatives. Failure to abide by these requirements could lead to a claim for compensation and result in the employer being ordered by the courts to pay a protective award.

The meeting started with a presentation by Mr Brewer, who explained the background to the review of distribution depots, and also stressed that no firm conclusions had yet been reached. Nevertheless, it was highly likely that some depots would be surplus to requirements and thus need to be closed. For this reason a search was now being conducted for potential replacement sites and, when this had been finalised, management would table a further meeting to deal with a more definitive proposal.

However, preliminary soundings of employees had revealed that it was unlikely that any of them would want to be relocated to replacement depots. At this point the company gave notice that, when this stage was reached, the company would want to bring about the changes very quickly in order to avoid excessive and unnecessary transport costs. Therefore, it was looking for a target date of two months hence for completing the move.

In response to this the trade union reserved its position by simply remarking that it noted what management had said, but added that until it had been able to consult with its members, it could not countenance any actual redundancies occurring, and, even then, past experience indicated that there was always a fairly massive agenda to be covered to bring about a successful redundancy exercise. Thus adequate time would be needed for negotiations and, with a redundancy exercise of this potential magnitude, there was a statutory consultation period to be observed, which would be a minimum of 90 days. Thus the idea of getting the whole matter out of the way in only two months was extremely optimistic. He therefore suggested that, as a first step, trade union officials would need to hold workplace meetings at sites likely to be affected, and that this process needed to start immediately.

The trade union official then sought leave to introduce an additional topic onto the agenda: that of Orton's takeover of Costwise in a wider sense. He started by noting that the size and structure of the Orton group now seemed to have been finalised and 'for the record' asked confirmation that the group now consisted of approximately 390 stores, distribution depots, etc., with a total of nearly 120,000 employees. He also asked for confirmation that stores which the Competition Comission had asked Orton to divest itself had nearly all moved, but that there were some that had yet to change ownership, which would be sold to competitors in the near future. It was on these that he wished to focus.

When these stores eventually depart the Orton group, the employees concerned will expect to be able to avail themselves of the protection of statutory legislation: that is, the provisions of the Transfer of Undertakings (Protection of Employment) Regulations. Clearly, when these employees move to a new employer, their conditions of service cease to be a problem for Orton. However, for the union to be able to claim these protective rights on behalf of its members, it could be vital that these employee already work for a firm (i.e. Orton) that recognises a trade union. Therefore, the trade union was desirous of exploring the issue of trade union recognition with the Orton group, with a view to recognition being grated before these changes in employment come into effect. The management side of the meeting agreed to look at this as a matter of some urgency.

In closing the meeting David Orton once again urged the trade union to move quickly in bringing the redundancy issue to a successful conclusion. He reiterated the time limit that management had set on the exercise, and stated that any delay would simply mean that the company would have to go ahead with implementing redundancies. To this the union official stated that he hoped that the chairman's remark was not the lightly veiled threat that it sounded like. 'As a trade union we are here to safeguard our members' interests, not Orton's profits and there is no question of us being railroaded into making precipitate decisions until we have consulted the membership.' He pointed out that the current meeting was the first that the union had been told about the possibility of redundancies; and that is a state of affairs for which Orton itself must bear the responsibility. Therefore, we would formally wish to state again that with the large number that might wind-up being made redundant, a period of 90 days consultation is the minimum we would expect to see; as per the legal entitlement. If this is not forthcoming, it might well be necessary for the union to throw itself at the mercy of the courts and seek an injunction to delay any redundancies by the company.

The Trade Union Consults its Members

Following the meeting between union officials and the Orton management, arrangements were made for large workplace meetings to be held (after working hours) at three distribution depots: Kent; Greater Manchester; and Cheltenham, all of which had originally been part of the Costwise group. Meetings of this nature are never easy to hold because prospective redundancies are a highly emotive matter. Nevertheless, three interesting issues surfaced.

1. The Duplicity of Management

Information emerged at the Kent depot in the form of an internal (Orton) memorandum. This indicated that the company had actually reached a decision some three months earlier about which depots were to be closed, and revealed that plans were well advanced to completely close the Kent depot. Since its activities would be transferred to an (as yet) unopened replacement in Milton Keynes, Buckinghamshire, a very large-scale redundancy exercise would be needed. In the light of this it was considered that there was distinct evidence that the firm had ignored its statutory obligations to consult with the workforce and its union. At the very least, therefore, Orton had deliberately mislead the union, perhaps with the hope that somehow it could be blamed for the delays.

2. Retention Bonuses

In the very early stages of the takeover by the Orton group of Costwise, the management of Costwise had taken the decision to pay retention bonuses to its staff to maintain their morale and head-off any 'rush-for-the-door'. This was a well publicised policy and there was ample proof that it had a happened (internal memoranda, etc.). This, of course, resulted in higher basic pay for Costwise staff, albeit only for the last two years. Nevertheless, staff all anticipated that these bonuses would be reflected in enhanced redundancy payments. However, it now transpired that the chairman of Orton had unilaterally decided that bonus payments should not count for calculation of redundancy payments.

3. Staff Morale in the Orton group

Unsurprisingly, drivers based in distribution depots were a mine of useful information about the disgruntled nature of staff in Orton's retail outlets. While to some extent this could perhaps be expected in ex-Costwise stores, it clearly applied more widely throughout the Orton group. So severe were some of the opinions expressed, which covered everything from poor communication to the autocratic styles of management, that it left a distinct impression that staff felt so 'put upon' that they were on the verge of mutiny. While this had limited relevance to the immediate issue in hand (redundancy), it was considered to be highly germane to the matter of union recognition, because a highly disgruntled workforce can often be one that is ready to take action to improve its own lot.

Immediately following these workplace meetings the trade union officials decided to adopt a somewhat different approach in its next meeting with Orton's management. This would consist of:

- formally confronting management with the written evidence about having already drawn-up detailed plans about which depots will be closed and when
- demanding that management make a full disclosure of these plans and, in furtherance of this, to campaign with its members for a series of short (one day) token strikes to force management's hands
- formally lodge a claim for retention bonuses to be recognised in any redundancy payments made
- press harder for a full recognition agreement with the company, which, if necessary, would involve asking the Advisory, Conciliation and Arbitration Service to organise a recognition ballot.

Task

Working in small groups of three to five students, read the above case scenario and then answer the following questions:

1. What do you feel are the main problems confronting the senior management of David Orton plc at this point in time?

2. Are these problems traceable to issues associated with: the goals and effectiveness of the company; its structure and organisational design; organisational control; the culture and climate of the organisation; organisational change and development?

3. To what extent are any problems that you have identified associated with more than one, or several of these things working in conjunction?

4. To what extent do you feel that the existence of problems such as these are attributable to the way that the top management of the Orton group has conducted itself, or are they mainly attributable to the actions of the trade union or its members?

5. In your view, what is the trade union seeking to achieve as outcomes in this matter, and has it approached achieving them in an appropriate way?

Glossary

A

Achievement tests: tests that assess what a person can currently do

Action Research: a participative method of bringing about change in human behaviour that involves stages of data collection, problem diagnosis, action planning, action and re-evaluation

Actual self: the self as the person currently views him or herself

Actuators: things that adjust the inputs to a process or activity

Adaptation: an incremental change that occurs as an organisational reaction to a change in its environment

Adaptive behaviour: that aimed at removing or circumventing a situation where goal blocking occurs

Adhocracy: a loose, very flexible and constantly evolving set of structural features that dispenses with traditional hierarchies, job titles and rules

Adjourning: the group is disbanded

Adjustment function (of attitude): helps the person adjust to his or her world

Affective component (of attitude): emotional feelings (likes or dislike) about the attitude object

Altercasting: the process of tacit negotiation between a role occupant and senders about behaviour which is acceptable to both

Ambassadors: group members who represent a group with other groups

Analysis by synthesis: a self-adjusting cycle in which an estimate of the identity of an object is derived from incoming sensory data. This is compared with a schema for the object and if the initial inference is confirmed, a search for confirmatory information is made

Anchoring or judgement heuristic: a decision maker arrives at a final judgement by starting at an initial position and then making adjustments to reach the solution that is eventually chosen

Aptitude: the facility or potential to be able to do something (the latent ability)

Aptitude tests: tests that assess what a person will be able to do if given the required training

Assertiveness: a person's desire to satisfy only his or her concerns in a conflict situation

Attention and selection: the tendency to acknowledge some stimuli and ignore or mask out others

Attitudes: a mental state of readiness, organised through experience to behave in a characteristic way towards the object of the attitude

Attributions: imputing a cause for an observed action

Authority: the legitimate power to make decisions in a given area of activity

Authority games: political tactics to resist authority from above or counter resistance to authority from below

Autocratic leaders: those who strongly control subordinates and make all major decisions

Availability heuristic: a rule-of-thumb used by a decision maker to assess the probability of the outcome of a decision

B

Basic structure: expresses the general form of structure and what is expected of organisational members

Behaviour: activity directed at achieving something

Behavioural component: the tendency to act towards the attitude object in a consistent and characteristic way

Behavioural consensus: whether a person's behaviour in a particular situation is typical of other people in the same situation

Behavioural consistency: whether a piece of behaviour is typical of the way that the person normally behaves

Behaviourial distinctiveness: whether a person behaves in the same way in several different circumstances

Behavioural outcomes: the effects of stress on overt behaviour

Behaviourism: the branch of psychology which holds that all human behaviour is determined by factors outside the person

Beliefs: the assumptions that something exists and that it has certain characteristics

Bottom-up goal setting: people set their own goals which are then agreed with their immediate superiors

Bottom-up processing: perceptual processes driven by incoming data imported through sensor organs

Bounded problems: problems that can be more easily defined and treated as separate from the context in which they exist

Bounded rationality: the recoginition that a person's ability to take a position of perfect rationality in decision making is constrained by limited time, limited information, or limited capacity to process information

Bureaucratic control: the use of tight job specifications and standard operating procedures to specify employee behaviour, which becomes the accepted ways of doing things to which employees conform

Burnout: a chronic outcome of stress characterised by a general feeling of complete exhaustion, depersonalisation, disinterest and lack of personal accomplishment

Business process re-engineering: a fundamental re-think and, if necessary, radical redesign of business processes, with the aim of making dramatic improvements to critical aspects of performance, such as cost, quality, service and speed

C

Centralisation: the locus of decision making in an organisation

Change agent: an expert from either inside or outside an organisation who facilitates and guides an OD (organisational development) intervention

Change games: political tactics to bring about or block change

Channels of communication: the carriers of the message

Charismatic authority: that acquired when a person becomes the focus of a particular set of ideals and principles, e.g. Christ

Classical organisation theory: a diverse group of theories which sets out to derive universal rules and guidelines for the design and functioning of organisations

Closed-loop (feedback) control: a method in which the outputs of a process or activity are monitored and, if necessary, inputs are adjusted to achieve the desired outputs

Closure (of messages): the receiver fills in what he or she perceives to be gaps in a message before transmitting it onward

Closure principle: gaps between stimuli are filled in so that discrete stimuli are perceived as connected

Coalition: an alliance of groups and/or individuals who perceive that something they value can be obtained by collaboration

Coercive power: the capability to compel others to behave in a certain way

Cognitive appraisal: a person's perception of a stressor, e.g. whether it is harmful, threatening or challenging

Cognitive complexity: the number of independent dimensions used by a person to evaluate objects and people

Cognitive component: the perceptions and beliefs about an attitude object

Cognitive dissonance: the unpleasant mental feeling that arises when behaviour towards an object is not consistent with the attitude towards the object

Cognitive outcomes: the effects of stress on thought processes

Command groups: permanent groups of people, all under a single manager, who perform like activities

Communal culture: one that is high in sociability and solidarity

Communication: a process in which information and its meaning is conveyed from a sender to receiver(s)

Comparator: something (or someone) that compares the desired attributes of the outputs of a process or activity with those actually achieved

Competing values model: an explanation of how manager values influence the criteria used to evaluate an organisation's effectiveness

Concept of self: a person's view of what he or she is

Condensation (of messages): the extraction of what the receiver of a message perceives to be its key points and transmitting only these onward

Conditioned response: a reflex behaviour elicited by pairing a neutral stimulus with an unconditioned response

Conditioned stimulus: a relatively artificial trigger to the production of a reflex response in an organism

Configuration: the basic arrangements for differentiation and integration in a structure

Consistency principle: that people attempt to maintain consistency between the three components of an attitude: cognitive, affective, behaviourial

Constancy effect: the perceiver is able to make adjustments for distance, etc., so that the object is experienced as the same size irrespective of its distance

Content theories: focus on the needs of people as the prime impetus for motivated behaviour

Context effect: the use of information from the context of the object to infer its identity

Contingency perspective: an approach to problem solving which assumes that there is no universally applicable solution to a particular type of problem and so remedies have to be tailored to the situation in which the problem exists

Contingency theory: that the most appropriate structure for an organisation is the one that matches its particular circumstances

Continuity principle: the existence of missing stimuli is inferred, resulting in a perception of links between unconnected stimuli

Continuous reinforcement: a reward is given each time the desired behaviour occurs

Control model: a symbolic representation of the components necessary for a system of control, how they relate to each other and their functions

Control strategy: a problem-focused attempt to tackle the root cause of stress by changing the nature of the situation, to remove or reduce the impact of stressors

Cooperation: the willingness to satisfy the other party's concerns

Country-focused strategy and structure: primarily geared to serving a wider set of markets by producing goods or services in overseas subsidiaries for sale in local markets

Cultural direction: the extent to which an organisation's culture helps it achieve its goals

Cultural factors: wider social beliefs, values and motives that are absorbed by an individual and guide behaviour towards that which is acceptable within a particular social context

Cultural pervasiveness: the homogeneity of an organisation's culture

Cultural strength: the influence of a culture on the behaviour of organisational members

Cultural systems metaphor: organisations regarded as analogous to cultural systems in which members have common beliefs, values and shared assumptions

Culture change: modification of an existing culture

Culture management: maintaining or making slight modifications to fine-tune an existing culture

Cybernetics: the theoretical study of control processes in electrical, mechanical and biological systems

D

Decision making: the process of making a choice between alternatives

Decoding: a process in which the receiver of a message uses the symbols in which it is conveyed to attribute it with a meaning

Deconstruction: a method used in postmodernist analysis to reveal underlying assumptions in discourse and challenge them with counter-arguments or alternative interpretations

Deep-acting: an antecedent-focused emotion regulation strategy that involves manipulating the components of an emotion before the emotion is fully in progress

Delayering: a reduction of the number of levels in an organisation's hierarchy, usually by removing one or more levels of supervision and/or middle management

Democratic leaders: those who involve followers in decisions

Descriptive approach to leadership: theories that describe leadership in terms of either what a person is, or his or her distinctive style of behaviour

Differentiationist perspective on culture: organisations are made up of different groups with their own sub-cultures

Discourse: the idea that language is more than just a useful tool of communication, because what is said can convey what is seemingly the essential truth about how things are, which has the effect of challenges to an argument, suppressing alternative meanings and supporting particular interpretations or conclusions

Diversity management: a systematic, proactive approach aimed at promoting the positive image of workforce diversity, which usually involves steps to affect the composition of a workforce so that it reflects the degree of diversity in wider society

Domestic organisations: mainly trade within the borders of their country of origin

Downsizing and right sizing: a reduction in the size of an organisation or the scale of its activities, theoretically to attain the appropriate size for its volume of sales

E

Economic context: the overall state of the economy in which an organisation operates, for example whether it is buoyant or recessionary

Effective communication: the extent to which the sender and receiver of a message both attribute it with the same meaning

Efficiency: a measure of resource usage, usually expressed as a ratio of inputs used to produce a given level of outputs

Effort to reward probability: the perceived liklihood that a reward will follow successful task performance

Ego: a component of personality that grows out of the id and which strives to reconcile the demands of the id, superego and the realities of the outside world

Ego-defensive function (of attitude): helps the person to defend his or her self-image

Emergant approach (to change): a contingency perspective that rejects the idea of a universally applicable recipe for organisational change

Emotion: a specific affective experience which is relatively intense and of short duration that occurs in response to a particular event

Emotion amplification: initiating or enhancing public displays of emotion

Emotion regulation: a person's efforts to increase, maintain or decrease one or more of the components of an emotion

Emotion suppression: attempts to reduce or eliminate public displays of emotion

Emotional intelligence: ability or competence in managing one's own feelings and recognising (and dealing effectively with) other people's feelings

Emotional labour: work in which an employee is required to manage his or her own feelings and emotions in the interests of maintaining a sympathetic and friendly relationship with the customer

Employee-centred control: a 'hearts and minds' strategy that involves influencing the way that employees think about themselves and what they do so that they willingly subscribe to management's aims

Empowerment: giving people the authority to make decisions in their own area of operations without the approval of someone above

Enacted environment: management's mental construction of what the environment is, which arises from its selective perceptions of environment

Enacted role problems: inappropriate role behaviour

Encoding: a process in which a message is transformed into a set of symbols that can be conveyed by a channel

Environment: issues, events and pressures that arise externally to an organisation and which present opportunities for it to survive and prosper, but also put constraints on its behaviour and the behaviour of people in a firm

Environmental factors (groups): characteristics of a group's environment that influence its degree of cohesiveness

Environmental stressors: forces external to the organisation that can be potential sources of stress for individuals

Episodic memory: a memory store containing information about episodes and past events in our lives

Epistemology: a branch of philosophy dealing with the nature and origins of knowledge

Equal opportunities: a systematic approach to ensuring there is no unjustifiable discrimination for appointment or promotion on the basis of gender, race, religion, ethnic origin and, more recently, disability

Equity: the fairness of treatment of a person compared to the way that another person is treated

Escalation of commitment to a failing course of action: a decision maker's tendency to persist with a failing course of action, in the face of clear evidence that the decision taken is inappropriate

Escape strategy (stress): an emotion-focused attempt to lower the impact of stressors, but without trying to change the nature of the situation

Espoused theory: the theory of action officially espoused by an organisation

Ethics: an individual's moral beliefs about what is right or wrong, or good and bad, and provides a guide to his or her behaviour

Ethnocentricity: a frame of reference in which members of a cultural group view their culture as superior to all others

European Social Policy: a set of regulations that provides comparable rights for workers across EU member states

Expectations: an anticipation that certain behaviours will result in achieving goals

Expected role problems: a clash between role sender and role occupant about the content of their respective roles

Expert power: the ability to influence others that exists because a person is seen to possess a particular expertise

Explicit knowledge: knowledge available to everybody which is easy to codify, articulate and express

External attribution: the cause of a person's behaviour is assumed to be connected with a factor in his or her environment

Extinction: a decrease in the occurrence of a behaviour arising from its non-reinforcement

Extrinsic rewards: rewards conferred from outside the individual

Extroversion–introversion: one of the two fundamental dimensions of personality used in Eysenck's type theory

F

Feedback: a process in which sender and receiver exchange roles, so that the receiver responds to a message

Figure-to-ground effect (perception): the tendency to organise data so that all figures are seen as existing against a background

Fine-tuning: an incremental change that occurs as a result of an organisation's anticipation of changes in its environment

First-level outcomes (motivation): the immediate results of behaviour

Fixed interval schedule: reinforcement delivered at fixed time intervals

Fixed ratio schedule: reinforcement delivered after a fixed number of desired responses

Flamemail: the use of e-mail to abuse others in the workplace

Flat organisation: a relatively small number of levels in the management hierarchy

Flexible specialisation: the argument that organisational survival now depends upon gaining the economic advantages of specialisation, but being flexible at the same time

Force field analysis: a way of conceptualising a stable situation as forces pushing (in favour of) change balanced by those restraining change

Formal contract: the formally agreed terms of the employment realationship, i.e. the legal concept as reflected in the 'contract of employment'

Formal groups: groups brought into existence by the structure of an organisation

Formalisation: the number of formal rules and procedures governing organisational activities

Forming: the first stage of group development, in which it is essentially a collection of individuals

Fragmentationist perspective on culture: organisations are so full of ambiguities and inconsistencies that frames of reference are individual and constantly changing and so culture is inherently unstable

Fragmented culture: one that is low on both sociability and solidarity

Functional approach: the assumption that attitudes are held because they serve a useful purpose for the holder

Functional approach to leadership: theories that explain leadership in terms of the functions performed by the leader with respect to the followers

Functional flexibility: an organisation's capability to vary what is done and how it is done

Functional significance (perception): the dimensions of evaluation used by a person because they are useful in making sense of the world

Fundamental attribution error: the tendency automatically to attribute internal causes for behaviour

G

General Adaptive Syndrome: a three-stage physiological process that takes place when an organism is subject to a stressor

General intelligence (g): an individual's overall intelligence level as measured by a test

Genetic factors: inherited factors that influence physical and mental characteristics

Glass ceiling: a metaphor for the invisible barrier that seems to exist, which prevents women progressing beyond a certain level in organisations

Global organisation: one that is not tied to a single nation, but operates worldwide as an independent set of subsidiaries coordinated by a headquarters

Globalised economy: the 'one-world' economy, in which large firms compete for business on a worldwide scale

Globally integrated strategy and structure: a diffuse network of highly interdependent subsidiaries, each of which specialises in some degree, but none of which has the capability to operate as a totally independent and autonomous business unit

Goal: a desired state of affairs, which an organisation attempts to realise

Goals (motivation): milestones that are perceived to lead to satisfaction of needs

Goal approach: evaluation of organisational effectiveness against the criterion of the extent to which an organisation achieves its goals

Goal blocking: a state where motivations are aroused but goal attainment is thwarted

Goal difficulty: how challenging and demanding the goal is

Goal displacement: an organisation or one of its sub-units substitutes a goal for which the organisation was not created, or for which resources were not allocated, for its legitimate goal(s)

Goal specificity: how clear and explicit the goal is

Goal succession: the goal(s) of an organisation is deliberately replaced with another one because the orginal goal(s) has been achieved or has become seriously outdated

Grapevine: an informal channel of communication

Group cohesiveness: the attractiveness of a group to its members and their desire to retain membership

Group factors: characteristics of the group and its members that affect its degree of cohesiveness

Group norms: the rules of behaviour adopted by the members of a group

Grouping effects (perception): the tendency to organise data into meaningful groups or patterns

Groupthink: impaired decision making by a group because the desire for unanimity overrides examining the consequences of a decision

Guardians: group members who shield the group from external pressure

H

Halo effect: the assumption that because a person has a certain trait he or she automatically has other traits

Hard goals: those that can be precisely specified in an unambiguous and usually quantifiable way and whose achievement can be measured accurately

Hardiness: a psychological characteristic that helps a person withstand the effects of stressors

Headship: the formal authority over subordinates granted as part of a manager's position

Hegemonic control: control exercised by an elite body whose power is accepted as supreme

Heuristics: rules-of-thumb or simplifying strategies that help a decision maker cope with information overload in the search for solutions

Holistic: the belief that reality is made up of unified wholes that are greater than the simple sum of their parts

Horizontal differentiation: the division of an organisation's overall task into different activities according to a set, organising principle

Horizontal surveillance: a person's actions are monitored by someone at the same level, who is part of the same workgroup

Human relations movement: a view of the employment situation which holds that employees respond primarily to the social context of the workplace, an important part of which is interpersonal relations at work

Hygiene factors: features of the work environment which, if present, help avoid dissatisfaction with work

I

Id: the biologically driven component of personality that consists of inherited drives etc. and which demands immediate gratification of its pleasure-seeking drives

Ideal self: the self as the person would like it to be

Idiographic: theories which describe personality in terms that are unique to the person

Immediate social stressors: features of a person's immediate (social) work context that can be stressful

Impression management: a process in which people seek to control the image that other people have of them

Individual stressors: features of a person's job that can give rise to stress

Influence perspective: an approach to leadership theory which explicitly addresses the issue of 'how' leaders influence follower behaviour

Informal contract: a less formal expression of the employment relationship, which reflects a degree of give and take between the parties

Information richness: the potential information-carrying capacity of a communication medium

In-group members (leadership): those on whom the leader relies to go beyond the minimum level of performance required

Instrumentality (motivation): the perceived strength of the connection between first and second-level outcomes

Integrationist perspective on culture: culture is an organisation-wide phenomenon which consists of shared values to which all or most employees subscribe

Intelligence quotient (IQ): mental age (as indicated by an intelligence test) divided by actual (chronological) age

Intensive technology: all parts contribute together to perform the task

Interactionist perspective (conflict): organisational conflict is seen as neither bad or good but simply inevitable

Interactionist perspective (personality): that hereditary factors and environment interact to determine behaviour

Interactive goal setting: goals are initially set for a particular organisational level by its head, but are then negotiated to a consensus with subordinates at that level

Intermittent reinforcement: a reinforcer is not given every time the desired response occurs

Internal attribution: the cause of a person's behaviour is assumed to be connected with his or her psychological characteristics, e.g. attitudes, personality, etc.

International organisation: one that is primarily located and managed in its country of origin, but also either export to or produce identical or similar goods and services in overseas subsidiaries

International trade strategy and structure: one that is primarily geared to serving a wider set of markets by exporting goods or services from the home country

Interpersonal communication style: the way a person prefers to relate to other people in a communication situation

Intrinsic rewards: psychological rewards that come from inside the person

J

Janus-faced: having two (good and evil) aspects

Job enlargement: horizontal expansion of a job to provide variety for the individual

Job enrichment: enlargement of a job both horizontally and vertically to give the employee more responsibility and control over how the job is performed

Job rotation: the systematic rotation of workers from one job to another to reduce boredom

Job satisfaction: a pleasurable or positive emotional state resulting from a person's appraisal of his or her job or job experience

Job simplification: the breaking down of a job into its simpler constituent elements

Job-related barriers (to motivation): features of the job that remove the likelihood that it can satisfy a person's needs

K

Key results area: areas of activity vital to an organisation's existence

Key variable (application) school (of culture): culture is viewed as an organisational property (something an organisation has) that can be changed at will

Kinaesthetic:motor intelligence (K:M): that part of an intelligence test which assesses practical, mechanical and spatial skills and abilities

Knowledge function (of attitude): helps the person mentally to structure and organise his or her world so that it is more understandable

Knowledge management: a process or practice of creating, acquiring, capturing sharing and using knowledge, wherever it resides, to enhance learning and performance in an organisation

L

Laissez-faire leaders: those who abdicate from the leadership role

Leadership neutralisers: workplace factors that remove the capability of a leader to influence subordinate behaviour

Leadership substitutes: situational factors that enable subordinates to function well without leader guidance

Learning: a relatively permanent change in behaviour, or potential behaviour, that results from experience

Least preferred co-worker (LPC): the subordinate that a supervisor was least able to work with successfully on a prior occasion

Legitimate power: the authority to command the actions of other people that goes with a particular role

Level of stress management: whether dealing with stressors is focused at the level of the individual or the level of the organisation

Levelling of messages: omission of certain details of a message as it is transmitted onward

Lewin model: a three-stage (unfreeze-move-refreeze) method of bringing about change in human behaviour

Libido: the source of all psychological energy, including the sex drive

Long-linked technology: all activities have to be performed in a set sequence

Long-term memory: the relatively permanent store in which information and knowledge is retained

M

Machine metaphor: organisations regarded as analogous to a machine that is designed for a purpose

Manager-directed control: managers specify exactly how and what should be done and closely monitor employee behaviour

Managerial grid: an application of style theories of leadership used for training and development purposes

Means–ends hierarchy: goals at one level in an organisation are the means of achieving the goals of the level immediately above

Means–ends inversion: the method of doing something becomes a goal in its own right, which displaces the end state (goal) that the method was supposed to achieve

Mechanistic organisation: roughly corresponds to a more bureaucratic firm and is best suited to stable environmental conditions

Media: specific ways of conveying a message along a channel

Mediating technology: the parts of an organisation are linked through its centre

Memory: the ability of an organism to retain information internally and demonstrate this retention through behaviour

Mercenary culture: one that is low on sociability and high on solidarity

Meritocracy: a social and economic system in which advancement is based on ability or achievement

Metaphor: a figure of speech in which a term is transferred from an object it ordinarily designates to another object it can designate by implicit analogy

Mission: a statement of an organisation's fundamental reason for existence

Monitoring of outcomes: examining whether the behaviour used has resulted in needs satisfaction

Motivators: features of the job itself that people find enjoyable and that have a motivational effect

Motives and drives: subconscious processes that provide the energy to engage in the goal-directed behaviour

Multinational organisation: one that is primarily located and managed from the country of its origin, but produces goods or services in relatively autonomous overseas subsidiaries to meet the needs of local markets

Multiple constituency (stakeholder) approach (to effectiveness): an evaluation of effectiveness against the criterion of the extent to which an organisation satisfies the interests of its internal and external stakeholders

N

Nature vs. nurture debate: the question of whether hereditary factors or the environment have most effect on behaviour

Need for Achievement (N.Ach): the need to succeed or excel in areas of significance to the person

Need for Affiliation (N.Affil): the need to interact with, and be liked by, other people

Need for Power (N.Pow.): the need to control the activities of other people

Needs: experienced deficiencies between what someone is or has and what he or she wants to be or have, which result in a desire to remove the deficiency

Negative affectivity (NA): a tendency to focus strongly on the negative aspects of work and life

Negative reinforcement: the removal of an aversive stimulus as a result of an organism exhibiting a desired behaviour

Networked culture: one that is high in sociability and low in solidarity

Neuroticism–stability: the second fundamental dimensions of personality used in Eysenck's type theory

Neutral stimulus: a stimulus which does not evoke a reflex response on the part of an organism

Nihilism: a now discredited doctrine that nothing really exists and thus there can be no knowledge of anything and hence knowledge cannot be communicated

Noise: any extraneous signal that interferes with or masks a message

Nomothetic: theories which describe personality in terms of set dimensions that could be applied to all people

Non-adaptive behaviour: that which is directed at shutting out the realisation that goal attainment is blocked

Normative inputs: human values, attitudes, beliefs and motivations

Norming: the third stage of group development, in which ground rules for a group's way of functioning begin to emerge

Number magic: the tendency to replace an important and necessary goal with another one that can be measured, simply because it can be measured

Numeric flexibility: an organisation's capability to vary its number of employees and, in so doing, its level of activity

O

Objective: specific, short-term statement of results that should be achieved

OD intervention: a programme to bring about change in an organisation, or one or more of its parts

Official goals: ideal states that an organisation would wish to achieve

Open system: a system not sealed off from its environment and, therefore, subject to the intrusion of environmental influences

Open-loop (feedforward) control: a method in which the inputs to a process or activity are carefully determined, but with no monitoring of outputs

Operating mechanisms: indicates in greater detail what is expected of individuals in a structure

Operative goals: the actual goals persued by an organisation

Optimise: to seek a solution or decision option that maximises expected utility

Organic organisation: an organisation that has more fluid structural arrangements and is better suited to variable and dynamic environments

Organisational change: a move from being in one organisational state to being in another state

Organisational climate: how people collectively experience and react to their surroundings

Organisational commitment: an attitude towards the organisation as a whole, reflecting the individual's acceptance of its goals and values, his or her willingness to expend effort on its behalf and an intention to remain with the organisation

Organisational factors (groups): organisational features that influence a group's cohesiveness

Organisational slack: the difference between the total resources available to an organisation and those necessary to make side payments to ensure contributions from stakeholders

Organisational stressors: characteristics of the whole organisation that can be potential sources of stress for individuals

Organism metaphor: organisations regarded as analogous to biological organisms

Out-group members: people who give only a basic level of performance

Output control: results to be achieved are specified in terms of outputs, a degree of discretion is permitted in how they are achieved, and outputs are subsequently monitored

P

Perceived role problems: a misinterpretation by a role occupant of a role sender's expectations

Perception: a mental process involving the selection, organisation, structuring and interpretation of information in order to make inferences and give meaning to the information

Perceptual defence: the resistance to acknowledging a stimulus because doing so would contradict a person's deeply held values or what he or she already believes

Perceptual inference: a conclusion about an object is reached on the basis of incomplete evidence

Performing: the final stage of group development, in which the group becomes capable of effective functioning

Physiological outcomes (stress): the effects of stress on a person's bodily health

Planned approach to organisational change: a set of internal actions designed to produce specific outcomes

Pluralist perspective: a management frame of reference in which an organisation is seen as a collection of different groups, all with their own legitimate aims to pursue, and so a degree of conflict is a normal state of affairs

Policy: rules to guide future decision making, if and when certain contingencies arise

Political–legal context: the extent to which the state intervenes in organisations, either directly and/or indirectly

Political systems metaphor: organisations regarded as analogous to a political system composed of diverse groups, all of which have their own objectives

Pooled interdependence: organisational sub-units safeguard each other by contributing discretely to the whole, which safeguards them all

Portfolio approach to control: the use of different strategies for controlling human behaviour accorrding to which one is seen to be most applicable at the time

Positive reinforcement: an outcome occurring after a behaviour that tends to maintain the repetition of the behaviour

Postmodernist: either (i) a new era in which the fundamental nature of organisations will be different from hitherto, or (ii) a philosophical stance which questions current assumptions of the nature of reality

Potential harms and benefits approach: a way of identifying the relevant stakeholders of an organisation as those who potentially benefit or are potentially harmed by its actions

Power base games: political tactics to build or maintain a power base

Predictive validity: whether tests scores are good predictors of behaviour or job performance

Primary factors: the factors which, in Cattell's personality theory, are the fundamental building blocks of personality

Private equity funds: funds put together and raised on the stock exchange by (nominally) private investors, usually to engineer the acquisition or takeover of a large, publicly quoted organisation

Proactive approach (stress): attempts to remove or lessen the influence of stressors before stress occurs

Proactive interference: recall of material learned earlier interferes with recall of material that has been learned later

Problem solving: the process of producing a solution to a recognised problem

Process theories: focus on mental processes which transform the motive force into particular patterns of behaviour

Proctored situation: web-based testing occurs in the presence of a test administrator, usually at a specified location

Productivity: a measure of efficiency consisting of the ratio of inputs to outputs

Proximity principle (perception): objects are perceived as related because of their closeness

Psychological climate: how the individual experiences and reacts to his or her surroundings

Psychological contract: an (unvoiced) set of expectations that the parties have of each other and the obligations that they feel towards each other

Psychological outcomes (stress): the effects of stress on a person's mental health

Punishment: the application of an aversive stimulus (or removal of a positive reinforcement) after a response by an organism that reduces the probability of a repetition of the response

Punishment by application: an aversive stimulus is applied immediately following an act of behaviour that is to be eliminated

Punishment by removal: a positive reinforcement is removed after behaviour which is to be eliminated has occurred

R

Radical perspective: organisational conflicts reflect conflict in wider society between capital and labour

Rational choice: the assumption that decisions are taken with full knowledge of all the relevant facts and that the option chosen maximises expected utility

Rational–legal authority: that which rests on the assumption that rational rules should guide the conduct of society and hence people in high office should command the actions of those below

Reactive approach (stress): attempts to help people better cope with the effects of stress after it has occurred

Receiver (of the message): the person to whom a message is directed

Reciprocal causality (leadership): the idea that followers affect leader behaviour as well as the leader influencing followers

Reciprocal interdependence: the parts are dependent upon each other to perform their respective tasks

Re-creation: a transformational change that occurs as a result of drastic changes in an organisation's environment

Reductionist: the belief that complex systems can be understood completely by understanding their constituent parts

Referent power: the capability to influence others that comes from having attributes or characteristics that make someone a source of reference or role model for other people

Reification: to treat an abstract idea as something that actually exists

Relational conflict: conflict in interpersonal relations

Reliability: whether a test produces the same results when applied to the same person on two separate occasions

Re-orientation: a transformational change that occurs in anticipation of drastic changes in an organisation's environment

Representativeness heuristic: a rule-of-thumb used by a decision maker to judge the likelihood of the outcome of a current decision option by using a stereotyped similarity to something in the past

Resistance through distance: a defensive way of resisting control by psychologically opting out

Resistance through persistence: an aggressive or assertive and overt way of resisting control

Responsibility: the obligation to achieve something

Retrieval: the processes used to recall information or knowledge from the long- (or sometimes short-) term memory store

Retroactive interference: the most recent material learned interferes with recall of material that has been learned earlier

Reward power: the capability to confer rewards on others

Rightsizing: see downsizing

Risky shift: the tendency of groups to make riskier decisions than their members would as individuals

Rivalry games: political tactics to defeat an opponent at the same level

Role: a set of expectations and obligations to act in a specific way in certain contexts

Role ambiguity: the role occupant is unsure of the requirements of his or her role

Role conflict: a clash between the different sets of role expectations

Role expectations: the role occupant's expectations about what the role entails

Role senders: individuals who have behavioural expectations of a role occupant

Role set: the total of all role senders for a given role

Root metaphor school (of culture): culture is assumed to reflect the essence of what an organisation 'is'

Rumour: unverified information of uncertain origin

S

Sampling: the characteristics of the total output of a process or activity is estimated by examining only a proportion of the output

Satisfice: to seek a solution or decision option that is 'good enough' rather than perfect

Scalar chain: a direct line of authority from the top to the bottom of an organisation

Schema: a structured mental representation of what the world is like or what it contains

Scientific management: a set of techniques for organising work methods to give managers greater control over the labour process, i.e. the exchange of effort for rewards

Scouts: group members who maintain contact with their environment and import information

Second-level outcomes (motivation): those that flow in the longer term from first-level outcomes

Self-disclosure: information that people consciously communicate about themselves to others

Self-efficacy: a person's belief in his or her ability to act in a certain way

Self-fulfilling prophecy: a prophecy that comes true solely because it has been made

Self-monitoring: examining one's own behaviour to see whether it has had the desired result

Semantic memory: a memory store recording information of an abstract, conceptual nature

Semi-autonomous work groups: self-managed teams that have a high degree of responsibility for their own work activities

Sensor: something (or someone) that monitors the attributes of the output of a process or activity

Sensor organs: organs that detect information about stimuli in the environment, i.e. the eye for visual information

Sensory registration: the memory stage in which environmental stimuli are first registered for onward transmission into memory

Sequential interdependence: each stage is interdependent with the one before and the one after

Sharpening of messages: selective attention to only part of a message

Short-term (working) memory: the stage in which information from the sensory register enters a short-term memory store

Side payments: inducements that are paid for cooperation or collaboration

Similarity principle (perception): the tendency to infer that two objects alike in some respects are alike in other ways

Situational factors: the effect of a specific experience or situation on a person's feelings and behaviour

Slack: unexploited opportunities or undiscovered economies such as surplus resources

Sociability: the degree of friendliness in the relationships between people

Social control: achieving compliance, conformity or obedience through interpersonal or intergroup processes

Social factors: factors that influence personality that arise from interaction with other people

Social responsibility: an organisation's obligation to contribute to, or protect, the environment of which it is a part

Social rewards: psychological rewards obtained through interaction with other people

Social support (stress): emotional support received through interaction with other people

Socialisation: the process of being taught how to behave and how to feel by other (influential) people within a specific social setting

Socio-emotive or group maintenance leader: the person who ensures that group members have their social needs catered for

Socio-ideological context: the behavioural norms and cultural values prevalent in a society, which can, for example, influence the nature of the relationship between a firm and its employees

Socio-technical systems: an approach to work design in which the people and the technical systems (and the relationship between them) are accorded equal importance

Soft goals: those that are more subjective and qualitative in nature, open to interpretation and whose achievement is much harder to evaluate

Soldiering: working at a much slower pace than the one of which a person is capable

Solidarity: the degree of collectiveness in the relationships between people

Source of message: the person from whom a message originates

Source traits: those that cannot be observed directly and whose existence can only be inferred

Span of control: the number of subordinates reporting to someone

Specialisation: the degree of division of labour and patterns of work organisation at lower organisational levels

Stakeholder: people or groups with an interest in the activities of an organisation and the outcomes of those activities, whether or not the organisation has an interest in them

Stakeholder economy: an economy which is theoretically run for the benefit of all participants who have an interest in the performance of the economy

Stakeholder management perspective: simultaneous attention to the legitimate interests of all the appropriate stakeholders of an organisation

Standardisation: the extent to which formal rules and procedures are applied in all circumstances

Stereotyping: attributing a person with qualities assumed to be typical of members of a particular category (e.g. age, sex, etc.) because the person falls into that category

Stimulus organisation and recognition (perception): the organisation of stimulus information into meaningful patterns that form identifiable wholes

Storming: the second stage of group development, which is characterised by interpersonal conflict

Strategic contingencies: events or activities that are crucial in achieving organisational goals

Strategy: a plan or design to achieve aims, goals or objectives

Stress: an adaptive response to external stimuli that place excessive physical or psychological demands on a person

Stressors: external factors that impinge on a person and potentially result in stress

Strong situations: those where personality characteristics are good predictors of behaviour

Sub-optimisation: sub-unit goals are accorded greater importance (by people in sub-units) than the goals of the organisation as a whole

Superego: a component of personality that reflects the learned rules of society which are absorbed in upbringing

Surface acting: a response-focused emotion regulation strategy that involves manipulating the components of an emotion after it is well into its development

Surface traits: those that are directly observable in behaviour

Symptom-management strategy (stress): an attempt to live with, but mitigate, the effects of stressors

Systems resource (or resource dependency) approach (to effectiveness): evaluation of organisational effectiveness against the criterion of whether the organisation maximises its bargaining position *vis-à-vis* the environment in order to acquire an optimal level of scarce and valued resources

T

Tacit knowledge: individualised personal knowledge and understanding, which although understood by the person, is difficult to describe, articulate and disseminate because it embraces the person's experiences and intuitions

Tall organisation: a relatively large number of different levels in the management hierarchy

Task groups: temporary formal groups formed for a specific short-term purpose

Task leader: the person who occupies the role concerned with ensuring that a group completes its task

Task-related conflict: conflict within a group about how it should complete its task

Team briefing: a cascade system of communication starting at the top of an organisation, in which managers at each level brief their direct subordinates about matters relevant to the subordinates

Teams: strongly task-orientated formal groups

Teamworking: the current name for use of semi-autonomous work groups

Technical complexity: a measure of the ease of coordination and control of a manufacturing technology

Technological context: the choices made by firms about the technology that they use in their activities, which affects employee job tasks, skills and competences

Technological determinism: the belief that technological advances drive changes, e.g. to organisational structures

Teleworker: someone who works at a place other than the one where the results of the work are needed, by using information and communication technology

Theory in use: the theory of action actually implemented by an organisation

Third way: a political ideology in which government charts a path between state regulation and free market forces; its core values include support for: competitive markets, innovation, skills, fairness and equity

Top-down goal setting: goals for a particular organisational level can be imposed from above

Top-down processing (perception): perceptual processes driven by the higher brain

Total Quality Management (TQM): an organisation-wide strategy that focuses on achieving or exceeding customer expectations

Traditional authority: that which rests on the established sanctity of a traditional position, e.g. a king

Trait theory (leadership): the assumption that certain people have inherent characteristics which enable them to be leaders

Traits: individual characteristics of thought or feeling that result in tendencies to behave in specific ways

Transactional leadership: the leadership style that is said to be the most appropriate to stable conditions

Transformational leadership: the approach to leadership which is said to be the most appropriate in times of significant organisational change

Transnational organisation: one that operates simultaneously as an international, multinational and global organisation

Two-factor theory of leadership: that there are two independent dimensions to leader behaviour, that is, initiating structure and consideration

U

Unbounded problems: ambiguous problems that are harder to define and which cannot easily be separated from the context in which they exist

Unconditioned response: a reflex response built into the nervous system of an organism

Unconditioned stimulus: a naturally occurring stimulus to which there is an inbuilt response in an organism's nervous system

Unitarist perspective: a management frame of reference in which an organisation is seen as one large family, all on the same side and pulling in the same direction, and in which conflict is seen as deviant behaviour

Un-proctored situation: web-based testing can occur at any location that has internet access, and without the supervision of a test administrator

V

Valence: the strength of preference for a particular outcome

Values: what a person wants to be true

Value of reward: the extent that a person values a reward

Value-expressive function (of attitude): allows the person to derive satisfaction from expressing attitudes that reflect his or her central values

Variable interval (VI) schedule: reinforcement is delivered at non-uniform time intervals

Variable ratio (VR) schedule: reinforcements which are delivered after a random number of desired responses

Verbal:educational intelligence (V:Ed): that part of an intelligence test which assesses verbal, numeric and educational skills and abilities

Vertical differentiation: the establishment of a hierarchy of authority in the organisation

Vertical surveillance: a person's actions are monitored by someone above him or her in the organisational hierarchy

W

Weak situations: those where personality characteristics are poorer predictors of behaviour

Whistleblowers: people (usually employed by an organisation) who make public unethical or questionable activities of an organisation

Workplace stress: stress that arises from an interaction between people and their jobs

Bibliography

A

Abramson, LY and HA Sackheim (1977) A paradox in depression: uncontrollability and self-blame, *Psychological Bulletin* 84(6): 838–851

Ackers, P, C Smith and P Smith (1996) Against all odds? British trade unions in the new workplace. In P Ackers, C Smith P Smith (eds), *The New Workplace and Trade Unionism: Critical Perspectives on Work Organisation*, London: Routledge

Ackroyd, S and PA Crowdy (1990) Can culture be managed? Working with raw material: the case of English slaughtermen, *Personnel Review* 19(5): 3–13

Ackroyd, S and P Thompson (1999) *Organisational Misbehaviour*, London: Thomson

Adair, J (1979) *Action-centred Leadership*, Aldershot: Gower

Adair, J (1984) *The Skills of Leadership*, Aldershot: Gower

Adair, J (1986) *Effective Team Building*, London: Pan

Adair, J (1998) *The Inspirational Leader*, London: Kogan Page

Adair, J (2004) *Effective Leadership Development*, London: CIPD Publishing

Adam, EC (1972) An analysis of changes in performance quality with operant conditioning procedures, *Journal of Applied Psychology* 56(6): 480–486

Adams, JS (1965) Inequity in social exchange. In L Berkowitz (ed.), *Advances in Experimental Social Psychology*, Vol. 2, New York: Academic Press

Adler, A (1928) *Understanding Human Nature*, London: Allen and Unwin

Adler, NJ (1997) *International Dimensions of Organisational Behaviour*, 3rd edn, London: Thomson

Adler, NJ and S Bartholomew (1992) Academic and professional communities of discourse: generating knowledge on transnational human resource management, *Journal of International Business Studies* 23(3): 551–570

Adler, NJ and GH Ghadar (1990) Strategic human resource management: a global perspective. In R Pieper (ed.), *Human Resource Management: An International Comparison*, Berlin: De Gruyter

Adler, NJ, R Doktor and G Redding (1986) From the Atlantic to the Pacific century, *Journal of Management* Summer: 295–318

Adler, PS and B Borys (1996) Two types of bureaucracy: enabling and coercive, *Administrative Science Quarterly* 41(1): 61–89

Aikin, O (2005) The pressure zone, *People Management* 24 February: 18

Ajzen, I (1988) *Attitudes, Personality and Behaviour*, Milton Keynes: Open University Press

Ajzen, I (1991) The theory of planned behaviour, *Organisational Behaviour and Human Decision Processes* 50(2): 179–211

Alderfer, C (1972) *Existence, Relatedness and Growth: Human Needs in Organisational Settings*, New York: Free Press

Aldrich, H and DA Whetten (1981) Organisation-sets, action-sets and networks: making the most of simplicity. In P Nystrom and WH Starbuck (eds), *Handbook of Organisation Design*, Vol. 1, New York: Oxford University Press

Alford, H (1994) Cellular manufacturing: the development of an idea and its application, *New Technology, Work and Employment* 9(1): 3–18

Algera, JA (1983) Objective and percieved task characteristics as determinants of reactions by task performers, *Journal of Occupational Psychology* 56(2): 95–107

Allen, NJ and MP Meyer (1990) The measurement of antecedents of affective, continuance and normative commitment to the organisation, *Journal of Occupational Psychology* 63(1): 1–18

Allen, TD, DM Freeman, JEA Russell, RC Reizenstein and JO Rentz (2001) Survivor reactions to organisational downsizing: does time ease the pain?, *Journal of Occupational and Organisational Psychology* 74(2): 145–164

Allinson, CW and J Hayes (1988) The learning styles questionnaire: an alternative to Kolb's inventory?, *Journal of Management Studies* 25(3): 269–281

Allinson, ST, AMR Jordan and CE Yeatts (1992) Cluster-analytic approach toward identifying structure and content of human decision making, *Human Relations* 45(1): 49–72

Allport, GW (1954a) Attitudes in the history of social psychology. In G Lindzey and A Aronson (eds), *Handbook of Social Psychology*, Vol. 1, Reading, MA: Addison-Wesley

Allport, GW (1954b) *The Nature of Prejudice*, Reading, MA: Addison-Wesley

Allport, GW (1961) *Pattern and Growth in Personality*, New York: Holt, Rinehart and Winston

Alvesson, M (1995) The meaning and meaninglessness of postmodernism: some ironic remarks, *Organization Studies* 16(6): 1047–1075

Amado, G (1995) Why psychoanalytical knowledge helps us to understand organisations: a discussion with Elliot Jaques, *Human Relations* 48(4): 351–357

Anderson, N and V Shackleton (1993) *Successful Selection Interviewing*, Oxford: Blackwell

Ansoff, IH (1965) *Corporate Strategy*, Harmondsworth: Penguin

Appignanesi, R and C Garratt (1995) *Postmodernism for Beginners*, Cambridge: Icon Books

Argyris, C (1960) *Understanding Organisational Behaviour*, Homewood, IL: Dorsey

Argyris, C (1964) *Integrating the Individual and Organization*, New York: Wiley

Argyris, C (1999) *On Organisational Learning*, 2nd edn, Oxford: Blackwell

Argyris, C and D Schön (1978) *Organisational Learning*, Reading, MA: Addison-Wesley

Arkin, A (1999a) Peak practice, *People Management* 11 November, 57–59

Arkin, A (1999b) Return to the centre, *People Management* 6 May: 34–41

Arlidge, J (2000) Online Britain fails the English test, *The Observer* 16 July: 9

Armitage, CJ and M Conner (1999) The theory of planned behaviour: assessment of predictive validity and perceived control, *British Journal of Social Psychology* 38(1): 35–54

Arnold, J, CL Cooper and IT Robertson (1998) *Work Psychology: Understanding Human Behaviour in the Workplace*, Harlow: Financial Times/Prentice Hall

Arnold, J, IT Robertson and C Cooper (1991) *Work Psychology: Understanding Human Behaviour in the Workplace*, London: Pitman

Arthur, A (2003) A utility theory of truth, *Organisation* 10(2): 205–221

Asch, SE (1946) Forming impressions of personalities, *Journal of Abnormal and Social Psychology* 50(3): 258–290

Asch, SE (1951) Effects of group pressure upon the modification and distortion of judgements. In H Guetzkow (ed.), *Groups, Leadership and Men*, New York: Carnegie Press

Ashford, S (1986) Feedback seeking in individual adaptation: a resource perspective, *Academy of Management Journal* 29(3): 465–487

Ashforth, BE and F Mael (1989) Social identity theory and the organization, *Academy of Management Review* 14(1): 20–39

Astley, WG and RA Braham (1989) Organisational designs for post-industrial strategies. In C Snow (ed.), *Strategy, Organizational Design and Human Resource Management*, Greenwich, CT: JAI Press

Atkinson, J and N Meager (1986) *Changing Work Practices: How Companies Achieve Flexibility to Meet New Needs*, London: National Economic Development Office

Atkinson, RL, RC Atkinson, E Smith and ER Hilgard (1987) *Introduction to Psychology*, 9th edn, Orlando, FL: Harcourt Brace Jovanovich

Austin, JT and P Bobko (1985) Goal-setting theory: unexplored areas and future research needs, *Journal of Occupational Psychology* 58(4): 289–308

B

Baddeley, A (1976) *The Psychology of Memory*, New York: Harper and Row

Bailey, J (1983) *Job Design and Work Organisation*, London: Prentice Hall

Bain, P and P Taylor (2000) Entrapped by the electronic panoptican? Worker resistance in the call centre, *New Technology, Work and Employment* 15(1): 2–18

Bales, RF (1950) *Interaction Process Analysis: A Method for the Study of Small Groups*, Reading, MA: Addison-Wesley

Bamberger, PA and P Bacharach (2006) Abusive supervision and subordinate problem drinking: taking resistance, stress and subordinate personality into account, *Human Relations* 59(6): 723–752

Bammer, K and BH Newberry (eds) (1982) *Stress and Cancer*, Toronto: Hogrefe

Bandura, A (1982) Self-efficacy mechanism in human agency, *American Psychologist* 32(2): 122–147

Bandura, A, D Ross and SA Ross (1961) Transmission of aggression through imitation of aggressive models, *Journal of Abnormal and Social Psychology* 63(3): 575–582

Bandura, A, CB Taylor, SC Williams, IN Medford and JD Barchas (1985) Catecholamine secretion as a function of perceived coping self-efficacy, *Journal of Consulting and Clinical Psychology* 53(3): 406–414

Bandura, A and RH Walters (1963) *Social Learning and Personality Development*, London: Holt, Rinehart and Winston

Bangemann, M (1994) *Europe and the Global Information Society: Recommendations to the European Council*, Brussels: European Commission

Banker, RD, JM Field, RG Schroeder and KK Sinha (1996) The impact of work teams on manufacturing performance: a longitudinal field study, *Academy of Management Journal* 39(4): 867–890

Bannister, D (1970) *Perspectives in Personal Construct Theory*, New York: Academic Press

Barker, J (1993) Tightening the iron cage: Concertive control in self-managed teams *Administrative Science Quarterly* 38(2): 408–437

Barker, RA (2001) The nature of leadership, *Human Relations* 54(4): 469–494

Barnard, CI (1938) *The Functions of the Executive*, Cambridge, MA: Harvard University Press

Barney, JB and RW Griffin (1992) *The Management of Organisations: Strategy, Structure, Behaviour*, Boston, MA: Houghton Mifflin

Baron, RA (1994) The physical environment of work settings: effects on task performance, interpersonal relations and job satisfaction. In BM Staw and LL Cummings (eds), *Research in*

Organisational Behaviour, Vol. 16, Greenwich, CT: JAI Press

Barrick, MR and MK Mount and R Gupta (2003) Meta-analysis of the relationship between the five-factor model of personality and Holland's occupational types, *Personnel Psychology* 56(1): 45–74

Barrick, MR and AM Ryan (eds) (2002) *Personality at Work. Reconsidering the Role of Personality in Organisations*, San Francisco, CA: Josey-Bass

Barron, RA and J Greenberg (1990) *Behaviour in Organisations*, Needham Heights, MA: Allyn and Bacon

Bartlett, CA (1986) Building and managing the transnational: the new organisational challenge. In ME Porter (ed.), *Competition in Global Industries*, Boston, MA: Harvard Business School Press

Bartlett, CA and S Ghoshal (1991) *Managing across Borders*, Boston, MA: Harvard Business School Press

Bartram, D (2005) The changing face of testing, *The Psychologist* 18(11): 666–668

Bartlett, CA and S Ghoshal (1997) *The Individualised Corporation*, London: Random House

Bass, BM (1983) *Organisational Decision Making*, Homewood, IL: Irwin

Bass, BM (1985) *Leadership and Performance beyond Expectations*, New York: Macmillan

Bass, BM and RM Stogdill (1990) *Bass and Stogdill's Handbook of Leadership: Theory, Research and Managerial Application*, New York: Free Press

Bauman, Z (1992) *Intimations of Postmodernity*, London: Routledge

Bavelas, A (1950) Communication patterns in task-oriented groups, *Journal of Acoustical Society of America* 22(4): 725–730

Bazerman, MH (1994) *Judgement in Managerial Decision Making*, 3rd edn, New York: Wiley

Beach, LR (1997) *The Psychology of Decision Making*, London: Sage

Beamish, PW, JP Killing, DJ LeCraw and H Crookell (1991) *International Management: Text and Cases*, Homewood, IL: Irwin

Beck, CE (1999) *Managerial Communication: Bridging Theory and Practice*, London: Prentice Hall

Beck, N and A Kieser (2003) The complexity of rule systems, experience and organisational learning, *Organisation Studies* 24(5): 471–481

Becker, TE, RS Billings, DM Eveleth and NL Gilbert (1996) Foci and bases of employee commitment: implications for job performance, *Academy of Management Journal* 39(2): 464–482

Bedeian, AG (1984) *Organisations: Theory and Application*, New York: Holt-Saunders

Bedeian, AG and RF Zammuto (1991) *Organisations: Theory and Design*, Chicago, IL: Dryden

Beehr, TA (1995) *Psychological Stress in the Workplace*, London: Routledge

Beehr, TA and JE Newman (1978) Job stress, employee health and organisational effectiveness: a factet analysis, model and literature review, *Personnel Psychology* 31(4): 665–699

Beekun, R and WH Glick (2001) Development and test of a contingency framework of coupling: assessing the covariance between structure and culture, *Journal of Applied Behavioural Science* 37(4): 385–407

Beer, M and AL Walton (1987) Organisation change and development, *Annual Review of Psychology* 38: 339–367

Belanger, J, PK Edwards and M Wright (2003) Commitment at work and indipendance from management: a study of advanced teamwork, Work and Occupations 30(2): 234–252

Belbin, RM (1993) *Team Roles at Work*, Oxford: Butterworth-Heinemann

Bell, PA, JD Fisher, A Baum and TE Green (1990) *Environmental Psychology*, 3rd edn, New York: Holt, Rinehart and Winston

Bennis, WG (1959) Leadership theory and administrative behaviour: the problem of authority, *Administrative Science Quarterly* 4(3): 463–476

Benson, H (2005) Are you working too hard? *Harvard Business Review* November: 53–58

Berggren, C (1993) Lean production – the end of history?, *Work, Employment and Society* 7(2): 44–58

Berlo, DK (1960) *The Process of Communication*, New York: Holt, Rinehart and Winston

Bernardin, HJ and K Alvares (1976) The managerial grid as a predictor of conflict resolution and managerial effectiveness, *Administrative Science Quarterly* 21(1): 72–91

Berridge, J, CL Cooper and C Highley-Marchington (1997) *Employee Assistance Programmes and Workplace Counselling*, Chichester: Wiley

Berry, AJ, J Broadbent and D Otley (1995) *Management Control: Themes, Issues and Practices*, London: Macmillan

Berry, JW (1969) On cross-cultural comparability, *International Journal of Psychology* 14(2): 119–128

Bertin, I and A Denbigh (1996) *The Teleworking Handbook: New Ways of Working in the Information Society*, London: The Telecottage Association

Beyer, JM and HM Trice (1987) How an organization's rites reveal its culture, *Organizational Dynamics* Spring: 13–21

Binet, A and T Simon (1908) Le developpement de l'intelligence chez les enfants, *L'Année Psychologique* 14(1): 1–94

Birchall, D and L Lyons (1995) *Creating Tomorrow's Organisation: Unlocking the Benefits of Future Work*, London: Pitman

Black, B (1999) National culture and high commitment management, *Employee Relations* 21(4): 389–404

Blackhurst, C (1996) Whatever happened to Sid?, *Management Today* July: 36–39

Blair, H, SG Taylor and K Randle (1998) A pernicious panacea – a critical appraisal of business re-engineering, *New Technology, Work and Employment* 13(2): 116–128

Blake, RR and AA McCanse (1991) *Leadership Dilemmas: Grid Solutions*, Houston, TX: Gulf

Blake, RR and J Mouton (1964) *The Managerial Grid*, Houston, TX: Gulf

Blau, G and EB Holladay (2006) Testing the discriminant validity of a four-dimensional occupational commitment measure, *Journal of Occupational and Organisational Psychology* 79(4): 691–704

Blau, P (1964) *Exchange and Power in Social Life*, New York: Wiley

Blinkhorn, S and C Johnson (1990) The insignificance of personality testing, *Nature* 34(8): 671–672

Blood, MR and CL Hulin (1967) Job enlargement, worker differences and worker responses, *Journal of Applied Psychology* 51(2): 284–290

Bloom, BS (1956) *Taxonomy of Educational Objectives, Handbook 1: The Cognitive Domain*, London: Longman

Blyton, P and P Turnbull (2004) *The Dynamics of Employer Relations*, 3rd edn, London: Palgrave Macmillan

Boddy, D and N Gunson (1995) *Organisations in the Network Age*, London: Routledge

Bolton, SC (2000) Emotion here, emotion there, emotional organisations everywhere, *Critical Perspectives on Accounting* 11(2): 155–171

Bolton, SC (2004) A simple matter of control? NHS hospital nurses and new management, *Journal of Management Studies* 41(2): 317–333

Boschken, HI (1990) Strategy and structure: reconceiving the relationship, *Journal of Management* March: 135–150

Bottger, P and PW Yetton (1988) An integration of process and decision scheme explanations of group problem solving performance, *Organizational Behaviour and Human Decision Processes* 42(2): 234–249

Bowditch, JL and AF Buono (1985) *A Primer in Organisational Behaviour*, New York: Wiley

Bowen, DE and EE Lawler (1992) The empowerment of service workers: why, how and when?, *Sloan Management Review* Spring: 36–39

Bowen, J and ZL Qui (1992) Satisficing when buying information, *Organisational Behaviour and Human Decision Processes* 60(3): 471–481

Bowers, DG and SE Seashore (1966) Predicting organisational effectiveness with a four-factor theory of leadership, *Administrative Science Quarterly* 11(2): 238–263

Bragganti, N and E Devine (1984) *The Traveler's Guide to European Customs and Manners*, St Paul, MN: Meadowbank

Bramlette, CA and JH Tucker (1981) Encounter groups: positive change or deterioration: more data and a partial replication, *Human Relations* 34(4): 303–314

Breckler, SJ (1984) Empirical validation of affect, behaviour and cognition as distinct components of attitude, *Journal of Personality and Social Psychology* 47(8): 1191–1205

Braverman, M (1974) *Labor and Monopoly Capital: The Degradation of Work in the Twentieth Century*, New York: Monthly Review Press

Brehm, JW (1972) Responses to Loss of Freedom: A Theory of Psychological Reactance, New York: General Learning Press

Brewin, CR and B Andrews (2000) The example of repression, *The Psychologist* 13(12): 615–617

Brewster, C, A Hegewisch, T Lockhart and L Mayne (1993) Flexible working patterns in Europe, *Issues in Personnel Management*, No. 6, London: Institute of Personnel Management

Brief, AP and HK Downey (1983) Cognitive and organisational structures: a conceptual analysis of organising features, *Human Relations* 36(12): 1065–1090

Briner, R (1999) Feeling and smiling, *The Psychologist* 12(1): 16–19

B & Q www.diy.com

Brown, R (2000) *Group Processes*, Oxford: Blackwell

Brown, RH (1990) Rhetoric, textuality and the postmodern turn in sociological theory, *Sociological Theory* 8: 188–197

Brown, SL (2005) Relationship between risk taking behaviour and subsequent perceptions, *British Journal of Psychology* 96(2): 155–164

Brownell, J (1986) *Building Active Listening Skills*, Englewood Cliffs, NJ: Prentice Hall

Bruner, JS (1973) *The Relevance of Education*, New York: Norton

Bruner, JS and L Postman (1947) Emotional selectivity in perception and reaction, *Journal of Personality* 16(1): 69–77

Bryman, A (1992) *Charisma and Leadership in Organisations*, London: Sage

Bryman, A (1996) Leadership in organisations. In SR Clegg, C Hardy and WR Nord (eds), *Handbook of Organisational Studies*, London: Sage

Buchanan, D and J Storey (1997) Role-taking and role-switching in organisational change: the four pluralities. In I McLoughlin and M Harris (eds), *Innovation, Organisational Change and Technology*, London: Thomson

Buitendam, A (1987) The horizontal perspective of organization design and new technology. In JM Pennings and A Buitendam (eds), *New Technology as Organizational Innovation*, Cambridge, MA: Ballinger

Buller, PF and CH Bell Jr (1986) Effects of team building and goal setting on productivity: a field experiment, *Academy of Management Journal* 29(2): 305–328

Bunce, D and MA West (1996) Stress management and innovative interventions at work, *Human Relations* 49(2): 209–232

Bunker, BB, BT Alban and RJ Lewicki (2004) Ideas in currency and OD practice: has the well gone dry?, *The Journal of Applied Behavioural Science* 40(4): 423–431

Burke, WW (1987) *Organisation Development: A Normative View*, Reading, MA: Addison-Wesley

Burke, WW (2004) Internal organisation development practitioners: where do they belong?, *The Journal of Applied Behavioural Science* 40(4): 423–431

Burnes, B (1998) Understanding organisational change. In J Arnold, CL Cooper and IT Robertson (eds), *Work Psychology: Understanding Human Behaviour in the Workplace*, 3rd edn, Harlow: Financial Times/Prentice Hall

Burnes, B (2000) *Managing Change: A Strategic Approach to Organisational Dynamics*, 3rd edn, Harlow: Financial Times/Prentice Hall

Burnes, B (2004) Kurt Lewin and the planned approach to change: a reappraisal, *Journal of Management Studies* 41(6): 977–1002

Burns, JM (1978) *Leadership*, New York: Harper and Row

Burns, T and GM Stalker (1994) *The Management of Innovation*, Oxford: Oxford University Press

Burt, C (1955) The evidence for the concept of intelligence, *British Journal of Educational Psychology* 25(2): 158–177

C

Callaghan, G and P Thompson (2002) We recruit 'attitude': the selection and shaping of routine call centre labour, *Journal of Management Studies* 39(2): 233–254

Callan, VJ (1993) Subordinate–manager communication in different sex dyads: consequences for job satisfaction, *Journal of Occupational and Organisational Psychology* 66(1): 13–27

Callinicos, A (2001) *Against the Third Way*, Cambridge: Polity Press

Campbell, DT (1965) Ethnocentrism and other altruistic motives. In D Levine (ed.), *Nebraska Symposium on Motivation*, Vol. 13, Lincoln, NB: University of Nebraska Press

Cannon, T (1994) *Corporate Responsibility*, London: Pitman

Capelli, P and PD Sherer (1991) The missing role of context in OB: the need for a meso-level approach, *Research in Organisational Behaviour* 13(1): 55–110

Carey, A (1967) The Hawthorne studies: a radical criticism, *American Sociological Review* 32(2): 403–416

Carlisle, YM and DJ Manning (1996) The domain of professional business ethics, *Organization* 3(3): 341–360

Carpenter, L (2006) The exhaustion epidemic, *The Observer 'Women'* No. 12 December: 54–60

Carroll, DT (1983) A disappointing search for excellence, *Harvard Business Review* November/December: 78–88

Cartwright, S and CL Cooper (1996) *Managing Workplace Stress*, London: Sage

Carysforth, C (1998) *Communication for Work*, Oxford: Butterworth-Heinemann

Casey, C (1999) Come join our family: discipline and integration in corporate organisational culture, *Human Relations* 52(2): 155–178

Cassidy, T and R Lynn (1989) A multifactorial approach to achievement motivation: the development of a comprehensive measure, *Journal of Occupational Psychology* 63(4): 301–312

Cattell, RB (1965) *The Scientific Analysis of Personality*, Harmondsworth: Penguin

Caulkin, S (2005) Dial 1 – to take your custom elsewhere, *The Observer* 14 August: 9

Caulkin, S (2006) Rule one: think the worst and it will happen, *The Observer* 5 November: 8

Caulkin, S (2007a) How ICI settled on the wording of its epitaph, *The Observer* 24 June: 8

Caulkin, S (2007b) Watch it, or surveillance will take over our lives, *The Observer* 19 August

Cavanagh, GF, DJ Moberg and M Velasquez (1981) The ethics of organizational politics, *Academy of Management Review* 8(2): 363–374

Cavanaugh, MA, WR Boswell, MV Roehling and JW Boudreau (2000) An empirical examination of self-reported work stress among US managers, *Journal of Applied Psychology* 85(1): 65–74

Chaikin, AL and J Cooper (1973) Evaluation as a function of correspondence and hedonic relevance, *Journal of Experimental Social Psychology* 9(2): 257–264

Chapman, M (2001) Emotional intelligence – critical competence or passing fad? Beyond the rhetoric, *The Occupational Psychologist* 43 August: 3–5

Chandler, AE Jr (1962) *Strategy and Structure: Chapters in the History of the American Enterprise*, Cambridge, MA: MIT Press

Chen, PY and PE Spector (1992) Relationships of work stressors with aggression, withdrawal, theft and substance use: an exploratory study, *Journal of Occupational and Organisational Psychology* 65(3): 177–184

Cherns, A (1987) Principles of socio-technical design revisited, *Human Relations* 40(2): 153–162

Chia, R (1995) From modern to postmodern organisational analysis, *Organization Studies* 16(4): 579–604

Child, J (1972) Organisational structure, environment and performance: the role of strategic choice, *Sociology* 21(1): 1–22

Child, J (1984) *Organization: A Guide to Problems and Practice*, London: Harper and Row

Child, J (1997) Strategic choice in the analysis of action, structure organisations and environment: retrospect and prospect, *Organisation Studies* 18(1): 43–76

Ciborra, C and G Patriotta (1996) Groupware and teamwork in new product development. In C Ciborra (ed.), *Groupware and Teamwork*, Chichester: Wiley

Clark, AE (1996) Job satisfaction in Britain, *British Journal of Industrial Relations* 34(2): 189–217

Clarke, E (2006) Pressure soars, *People Management* 31 August: 31–32

Clark, RD (1971) Group-induced shift towards risk: a critical appraisal, *Psychological Bulletin* 76: 251–270

Claydon, T and M Doyle (1996) Trusting me trusting you? The ethics of employee empowerment, *Personnel Review* 25(6): 13–25

Clear, F and K Dickson (2005) Teleworking practice in small and medium sized firms: managerial style and worker autonomy, *New Technology, Work and Employment* 20(3): 218–233

Clegg, B (2003) Junk that mail, *Professional Manager* March: 22–23

Clegg, SR (1989) *Frameworks of Power*, London: Sage

Cohen, A (2000) The relationship between commitment forms and work outcomes: a comparison of three models, *Human Relations* 53(3): 387–417

Cohen, MD, JG March and JP Olsen (1972) A garbage can model of decision making, *Administrative Science Quarterly* 17(1): 1–25

Cohen, S (1980) After effects of stress on human behaviour and performance: a review of research and theory, *Psychological Bulletin* 88(1): 92–108

Colehart, M, CD Lea and K Thompson (1974) In defense of iconic memory, *Quarterly Journal of Experimental Psychology* 26(4): 633–641

Colenso, M (1997) *High Performing Teams*, London: Butterworth-Heinemann

Collins, AM and MR Quillian (1969) Retrieval time from semantic memory, *Journal of Verbal Learning and Verbal Behaviour* 8(2): 240–247

Collins, D (1998) *Organisational Change: Sociological Perspectives*, London: Routledge

Collins, PD and F Hull (1986) Technology and span of control: Woodward revisited, *Journal of Management Studies* 23(2): 143–164

Collinson, DL (1994) Strategies of resistance: power, knowledge and subjectivity in the workplace. In JM Jermier, D Knights and WR Nord (eds), *Resistance and Power in Organisations*, London: Routledge

Conger, JA (1993) Leadership: the art of empowering others. In JR Gordon (ed.), *A Diagnostic Approach to Organisational Behaviour*, Boston, MA: Allyn and Bacon

Conger, JA and RN Kanugo (1987) Towards a behaviourial theory of charismatic leadership in organisational settings, *Academy of Management Review* 12(4): 637–674

Conner, M and CJ Armitage (1998) Extending the theory of planned behaviour: a review and avenues for further research, *Journal of Applied Social Psychology* 28(6): 1430–1464

Connolly, T, EJ Conlon and SJ Deutsch (1980) Organisational effectiveness: a multiple-constituency approach, *Academy of Management Review* 5(2): 211–217

Conrad, R (1964) Acoustic confusion in immediate memory, *British Journal of Psychology* 55(1): 75–84

Cook, M (1971) *Interpersonal Perception*, Harmondsworth: Penguin

Cook, M and B Cripps (2004) *Psychological Assessment in the Workplace*, Chichester: Wiley

Cook, S (2003) Who cares wins, *Management Today* January: 40–47

Cook, S and H Slack (1991) *Making Management Decisions*, 2nd edn, London: Prentice Hall

Cooley, CH (1964) *Human Nature and the Social Order*, New York: Schocken

Cooper, CL (1996) *Handbook of Stress, Medicine and Health*, Boca Raton, FL: CRC Press

Cooper, CL (1998) Working in a short-term culture, *Management Today* February: 5

Cooper, CL (2005) Another year down?, *People Management* 29 December: 36–37

Cooper, CL and S Cartwright (1994) Healthy mind: healthy organisation – a proactive approach to occupational stress, *Human Relations* 47(4): 455–471

Cooper, CL and MJ Davidson (1991) *The Stress Survivors*, London: Grafton Publishing

Cooper, CL and R Payne (1988) *Causes, Coping and Consequences of Stress at Work*, Chichester: Wiley

Cooper, CL and G Sadri (1991) The impact of stress counselling at work. In PL Perrewe (ed.), *Handbook of Job Stress* (Special Issue), *Journal of Social Behaviour and Personality* 6(7): 411–423

Cooper, CL, J Watts, AJ Baglioni and M Kelly (1988) Stress amongst general practice dentists, *Journal of Occupational Psychology* 61(2): 163–174

Cooper, CL and B White (1995) Organisational behaviour. In S Tyson (ed.), *Strategic Prospects for Human Resource Management*, London: Institute of Personnel and Development

Cooper, R and G Burrell (1988) Modernism, postmodernism and organisational analysis: an introduction, *Organization Studies* 9(1): 91–112

Cordery, JL, WS Mueller and LM Smith (1991) Attitudinal and behavioural outcomes of autonomous group working: a longitudinal field study, *Academy of Management Journal* 31(2): 464–476

Cordes, CL and TW Dougherty (1993) A review and integration of research on job burnout, *Academy of Management Review* 18(3): 621–656

Cosier, RA and DR Dalton (1983) Equity theory and time: a reformulation, *Academy of Management Review* 4(2): 311–319

Costa, P and RR McCrae (1992) *NEO RI-R: Professional Manual*, Psychological Assessment Resources, Odessa: Florida

Covaleski, MA., MW Dirsmith, JB Heian and S Samuel (1998) The calculated and the avowed: techniques of discipline and struggles over identity in the big six accounting firms, *Administrative Science Quarterly* 43(2): 293–327

Cowe R (1996) BT won over by argument for ethical audit, *Guardian* 25 November: 14

Craik, FIM and RS Lockheart (1972) Levels of processing: a framework for memory research, *Journal of Verbal Learning and Verbal Behaviour* 11(5): 671–684

Crawley, R and P Spurgeon (1979) Computer assistance and the air traffic controller's job satisfaction. In RG Sell and P Shipley (eds), *Satisfaction in Work Design: Ergonomics and Other Approaches*, London: Taylor and Francis

Cray, D and GR Mallory (1997) *Making Sense of Managing Culture*, London: Thomson

Cressey, P and P Scott (1992) Employment, technology and industrial relations in the clearing banks: is the honeymoon over?, *New Technology Work and Employment* 7(2): 83–96

Crooks, E (2007) Hayward set his fist BP challenge, *Financial Times* 23 July

Crozier, M (1964) *The Bureaucratic Phenomenon*, Chicago, IL: University of Chicago Press

Cullen, D (1997) Maslow, monkeys and motivation theory, *Organization* 4(3): 355–373

Cully, M, S Woodland, A O'Reilly and G Dix (1999) *Britain at Work: As Depicted by the 1998 Workplace Employee Relations Survey*, London: Routledge

Cummings, TG (1978) Self-regulating work groups: a socio-technical synthesis, *Academy of Management Review* 3(3): 625–634

Cummings, TG and C Worley (1997) *Organisation Development and Change*, 7th edn, St Paul, MN: West Publishing

Cunningham, I and J Hyman (1999) The poverty of empowerment? A critical case study, *Personnel Review* 28(3): 192–207

Cunningham, I, J Hyman and C Baldry (1996) Empowerment: the power to do what?, *Industrial Relations Journal* 27(2): 143–154

Cunningham, JB (1978) A systems-resource approach for evaluating organisational effectiveness, *Human Relations* 31(7): 631–656

Curran, K (2003) Make time for flexibility, *People Management* 24 August: 19

Cyert, RM and JC March (1963) *A Behavioural Theory of the Firm*, Englewood Cliffs, NJ: Prentice Hall

D

Daft, RL (1996) *Organization Theory and Design*, 3rd edn, St Paul, MN: West Publishing

Danford, A (1998) Teamworking and labour regulation in the autocomponents industry, *Work, Employment and Society* 12(3): 409–443

Danserau, FD, G Graen and WJ Haga (1975) A vertical dyad linkage approach to leadership within formal organizations: a longitudinal investigation of the role making process, *Organisational Behaviour and Human Performance* 13(1): 46–78

Darr, W and G Johns (2004) Political decision-making climates: theoretical processes and multi-level antecedents, *Human Relations* 57(2): 169–200

Dastmalchian, A (1986) Environmental characteristics and organizational climate: an exploratory study, *Journal of Management Studies* 23(6): 609–633

Dastmalchian, A and R Mansfield (1980) Payment systems in smaller companies: relationships with size and climate, *Personnel Review* 9(2): 27–32

Datta, DK, JP Guthrie and PM Wright (2005) Management and labour productivity: does industry matter?, *Academy of Management Journal* 48(1): 135–145

Davenport, T (1992) *Process Innovation: Re-engineering Work through Information Technology*, Cambridge, MA: Harvard Business School Press

Davidow, W and T Malone (1992) *The Virtual Organisation*, New York: Harper and Row

Davidson, E (2003) Counter terrorism, *People Management* 26 June: 38–40

Davis, K (1976) Understanding the organisational grapevine and its benefits, *Business and Public Affairs* Spring: 5

Davis, SM and PR Lawrence (1977) *Matrix*, Reading, MA: Addison-Wesley

Deal, TE and AA Kennedy (1982) *Corporate Culture: The Rites and Rituals of Corporate Life*, Reading, MA: Addison-Wesley

Deary, IJ and G Matthews (1993) Personality traits are alive and well, *The Psychologist* July: 299–311

De Brabender, B and C Boone (1990) Sex differences in perceived locus of control, *Journal of Social Psychology* 61(2): 271–276

De Dreu, C and E Van de Vliert (eds) (1997) *Using Conflict in Organisations*, London: Sage

DeFruyt, F and I Merielde (1999) Riasec types and big five traits as predictors of employment status and nature of employment, *Personnel Psychology* 52(3): 701–727

Delbridge, R, J Lowe and N Oliver (2000) Shopfloor responsibilities under lean teamworking, *Human Relations* 53(11): 1549–1579

Denison, DR (1996) What is the difference between organisational culture and organisational climate? A native's point of view on a decade of paradigm wars, *Academy of Management Review* 21(3): 619–654

Dent, EB and SG Goldberg (1999) Challenging resistance to change, *Journal of Applied Behavioural Science* 35(1): 25–41

Dewe, P (1991) Primary appraisal, secondary appraisal and coping: their role in stressful work encounters, *Journal of Occupational Psychology* 64(4): 331–351

Dewe, PJ (1992) Applying the concept of appraisal to work stressors: some exploratory analysis, *Human Relations* 46(2): 143–164

Dewe, P and M O'Driscoll (2002) Stress management interventions: what do managers actually do?, *Personnel Review* 31(2): 143–165

Diehl, C and M Donnelly (2001) *How Did They Manage? Leadership Secrets of History*, London: Spiro Press

Digman, JM (1990) Personality structure: emergence of the five-factor model, *Annual Review of Psychology* 41: 417–446

Dill, W (1958) Environment as an influence on managerial autonomy, *Administrative Science Quarterly* 2(3): 409–433

Dion, KL (1973) Cohesiveness as a determinant of ingroup–outgroup bias, *Journal of Personality and Social Psychology* 28(2): 163–171

Dixon, NM (2000) *Common Knowledge: How Companies Thrive by Sharing What They Know*, Boston, MA: Harvard Business School Press

Doane, D (2003) Lip service brings no solutions, *Guardian* 3 February: 25

Doherty, N and J Horsted (1995) Helping survivors stay on board, *People Management* January: 26–29

Donaldson, L (2001) *The Contingency Theory of Organisations*, Thousand Oaks, CA: Sage

Donaldson, T and LE Preston (1995) The stakeholder theory of the corporation: concepts, evidence and implications, *Academy of Management Review* 20(1): 65–91

Donkin, R (2004) *Financial Times* 24 June

Donkin, R (2005) Appointments: the proper place for psychometric testing, *Financial Times* 25 February

Donnelly, M and D Scholarios (1998) Workers' experiences of redundancy: evidence from Scottish defence-dependent companies, *Personnel Review* 27(4): 325–342

Doward, J (2005) A good sleep is an impossible dream as stress winds-up Britains, *The Observer* 13 March: 15

Doyle, C (2003) *Work and Organisational Psychology: An Introduction With Attitude*, Hove: Psychology Press

Drever, J (1964) *A Dictionary of Psychology*, Harmondsworth: Penguin

Drucker, P (1984) *The Practice of Management*, London: Heinemann

Drucker, P (1988) The coming of the new organisation, *Harvard Business Review*, January–February: 45–53

Drummond, H (1996) *Escalation in Decision Making: The Tragedy of Taurus*, Oxford: Oxford University Press

Duehr, EE and JE Bono (2006) Men and women managers: are stereotypes finally changing?, *Personnel Psychology* 59(4): 815–846

DuGuy, P (2000) *In Praise of Bureaucracy*, London: Sage

Dulewicz, SV and MJ Higgs (1999) Can emotional intelligence be measured and developed?, *Leadership and Organisational Development* 20(5): 242–252

Dunegan, K, D Duchon and M Uhl-Bien (1992) Examining the link between leader–member exchange and subordinate performance: the role of task analyzability and variety as moderators, *Academy of Management Journal* 35(1): 59–76

Dunham, R, JA Grube and MB Castaneda (1994) Organisational commitment: the utility of an integrative definition, *Journal of Applied Psychology* 79(2): 370–380

Dunning, D (2006) Strangers to ourselves, The *Psychologist* 19(10): 600–603

Durkheim, E (1966) *The Division of Labour in Society*, New York: Free Press

E

Eaton, J (2000) *Comparative Employment Relations*, Cambridge: Polity Press

Eaton, SC (2003) If you can use them: flexibility policies, organisational commitment and perceived performance, *Industrial Relations* 42(2): 145–167

EC (1996) *People First: Challenges of Living and Working in the European Information Society*, Brussels: European Commission

Eckman, P and WV Friesen (1975) *Unmasking the Face*, New York: Prentice Hall

Edwards, C (2005) Remote control, *People Management* 16 June: 31–32

Edwards, JE (1997) *How to Conduct Organisational Surveys*, Thousand Oaks, CA: Sage

Edwards, PK (1986) *Conflict at Work*, Oxford: Blackwell

Edwards, R (1979) *Contested Terrain: The Transformation of the Workplace in the Twentieth Century*, London: Heinemann

Ekstrand, BR (1972) To sleep, perchance to dream: about why we forget. In CP Duncan, L Sechrest and AW Melton (eds), *Human Memory*, New York: Appleton Century Crofts

Elkin, AJ and PJ Rosch (1990) Promoting mental health at the workplace: the prevention side of stress management, *Occupational Medicine: State of the Art Review* 5(4): 739–754

Epstein, S (1980) The stability of behaviour: implications for psychological research, *American Psychologist* 35: 790–806

Erdogan, B, RC Linden and ML Kraimer (2006) Justice and leader–member exchange: the moderating role of organisational culture, *Academy of Management Journal* 49(2): 395–406

Erera-Weatherley, PI (1996) Coping with stress: public welfare supervisors doing their best, *Human Relations* 49(2): 157–169

Erez, M (1992) Interpersonal communication systems in organisations and their relationship to cultural values, productivity and innovation: the case of Japanese corporations, *Applied Psychology: An International Review* 41(1): 43–64

Erez, M, C Early and CL Hulin (1985) The impact of participation on goal acceptance and performance: a two-step model, *Academy of Management Journal* 28(1): 50–66

Ericksen, J and L Dyer (2004) Right from the start: explaining the effects of early team events on subsequent project team development and performance, *Administrative Science Quarterly* 49(2): 438–471

Erlenmeyer-Kimling, I and LF Jarvik (1963) Genetics and intelligence: a review, *Science* 142(10): 1477–1479

ESRC (2002) *Britain's World of Work – Myths and Realities*, London: Economic and Social Research Council

Etzioni, A (1964) *Modern Organizations*, Englewood Cliffs, NJ: Prentice Hall

Etzioni, A (1975) *A Comparative Analysis of Complex Organisations: On Power, Involvement and their Correlates*, rev. edn, New York: Free Press

Evans, BK and DG Fischer (1993) The nature of burnout: a study of the three-factor model of burnout in human service and non-human service samples, *Journal of Occupational and Organisational Psychology* 66(1): 29–38

Evans, J (1995) Three-pronged strategy needed to tackle stress, *People Management*, January: 19

Evans, M, H Gunz and M Jalland (1996) The aftermath of downsizing: a cautionary tale about restructuring and careers, *Business Horizons* May–June: 1–5

Eysenck, HJ (1947) *Dimensions of Personality*, London: Routledge and Kegan Paul

Eysenck, HJ (1965) *Fact and Fiction in Psychology*, Harmondsworth: Penguin

Eysenck, HJ (1970) *The Structure of Human Personality*, 3rd edn, London: Methuen

Eysenck, HJ (1991) Dimensions of personality: 16, 5 or 3? – criteria for a taxonomic paradigm, *Personality and Individual Differences* 12(4): 773–790

F

Fagley, NS and PM Miller (1987) The effects of framing on choice of risks vs. certain options,

Organisational Behaviour and Human Decision Processes 39(2): 264–277

Fang, T (1998) Reflection on Hofstede's 5th dimension: a critique of Confucian Dynamism, Paper presented at annual meeting of Academy of Management, San Diego, CA, August

Fayol, H (1916) *General and Industrial Management*, Trans. C Storrs (1946), London: Pitman

Fazio, RH and MP Zanna (1978) On the predictive validity of attitudes, *Journal of Personality* 46(2): 228–243

Feldman, DC (1984) The development and enforcement of group norms, *Academy of Management Review* 9(1): 47–53

Feldman, D and N Klich (1991) Impression management and career strategies. In K Giacalone and P Rosenfeld (eds), *Applied Impression Management: How Image Making Affects Managerial Decisions*, London: Sage

Feldman, DC and HB Thompson (1992) Entry shock, culture shock; socialising the new breed of global managers, *Human Resource Management* Winter: 345–362

Feldman, MS and BT Pentland (2003) Reconceptualising organisational routines as a source of flexibility and change, *Administrative Science Quarterly* 48(1): 94–118

Feldman, MS and A Rafaeli (2002) Organisational routines as sources of connections and understandings, *Journal of Management Studies* 39(3): 309–331

Felfe, J and B Schyns (2006) Personality and the perceptions of transformational leadership: the impact of extraversion, neuroticism, personal need for structure and occupational self-efficacy, *Journal of Applied Social Psychology* 36(3): 708–739

Felstead, A, N Jewson and S Walters (2003) Managerial control of employees working at home, *British Journal of Industrial Relations* 41(2): 241–264

Ferner, A and M Varul (2000) Vanguard subsidiaries and the diffusion of new practices: a case study of German multinationals, *British Journal of Industrial Relations* 38(1): 115–140

Ferris, GR, DD Frink, DC Gilmore, MC Kacmar (1994) Understanding as an antidote for the dysfunctional consequences of organisational politics as a stressor, *Journal of Applied Social Psychology* 24(6): 1204–1220

Festinger, L (1957) *A Theory of Cognitive Dissonance*, Evanston, IL: Row Peterson

Fiedler, FE (1965) Engineering the job to fit the manager, *Harvard Business Review* September–October: 115–122

Fiedler, FE (1967) *A Theory of Leadership Effectiveness*, New York: McGraw-Hill

Fiedler, FE and JE Garcia (1987) *New Approaches to Effective Leadership: Cognitive Resources and Organisational Performance*, New York: Wiley

Fife-Schaw, C., P Sheeran and P Norman (2007) Simulating behaviour change interventions based on the theory of planned behaviour: impacts on intention and action, *British Journal of Social Psychology* 46(1): 43–68

Finholt, T and I Sproull (1990) Electronic groups at work, *Organisation Science* 1(1): 41–64

Finkelstein, S and DC Hambrick (1996) *Strategic Leadership: Top Executives and Their Effects on Organisations*, St Paul, MN: West Publishing

Firth-Cozens, J and GE Hardy (1992) Occupational stress, clinical treatment and changes in job perceptions, *Journal of Occupational and Organisational Psychology* 65(2): 81–88

Fishbein, M and I Ajzen (1975) *Belief, Attitude, Intention and Behaviour*, Reading, MA: Addison-Wesley

Fisher, CD and R Gitelson (1983) A meta-analysis of the correlates of role conflict and ambiguity, *Journal of Applied Psychology* 63(3): 320–333

Fisher, SG, TA Hunter and WDK Macrosson (1998) The structure of Belbin's team roles, *Journal of Occupational and Organisational Psychology* 71(3): 283–288

Fiske, ST (1993) Social cognition and social perception. In LW Porter and MR Rosenweig (eds), *Annual Review of Psychology*, Vol. 4, Palo Alto, CA: Annual Reviews Inc.

Flach, FF (1974) *The Secret Strength of Depression*, Philadelphia, PA: Lippincott

Fleishman, EA (1953) The measurement of leadership attitudes in industry, *Journal of Applied Psychology* 38(1): 153–158

Fontana, D (1990) *Managing Stress*, New York: Routledge

Ford, JD and LW Ford (1995) The role of conversation in producing intentional change in organisations, *Academy of Management Review* 20(2): 541–570

Foster, C and L Harris (2005) Easy to say, difficult to do: diversity management in retail, *Human Resource Management Journal* 15(3): 4–17

Fox, A (1973) Industrial relations: a social critique of pluralist ideology. In J Child (ed.), *Man and Organisation*, New York: Halstead

Fox, ML, DJ Dwyer and DC Ganster (1993) Effects of stressful job demands and control on physiological and attitudinal outcomes in a hospital setting, *Academy of Management Journal* 31(2): 289–318

Foy, N (1983) Networks of the world unite, *Personnel Management* March: 16–19

French, J and B Raven (1959) The bases of social power. In D Cartwright (ed.), *Studies in Social Power*, Ann Arbor, MI: Institute for Social Research

French, JRP and RD Caplan (1973) Organisational stress and individual strain. In AJ Marrow (ed.), *The Failure of Success*, New York: AMACOM

French, WL and CH Bell (1999) *Organisation Development: Behavioural Science Interventions for Organisational Improvement*, 6th edn, Englewood Cliffs, NJ: Prentice Hall

Freud, S (1901a) *The Psychopathology of Everyday Life*, trans. A Tyson (1975), Harmondsworth: Penguin

Freud, S (1901b) *The Ego Mechanisms of Defence*, trans. A Tyson (1975), Harmondsworth: Penguin

Freud, S (1940) *An Outline of Psyhcoanalysis*, trans. J Strachey (1969), London: Hogarth Press

Friedman, A (1977) *Industry and Labour*, London: Macmillan

Friedman, M and R Rosenman (1974) *Type A Behaviour and Your Heart*, New York: Knopf

Fromm, E (1942) *The Fear of Freedom*, London: Routledge and Kegan Paul

Frooman, J (1999) Stakeholder influence strategies, *Academy of Management Review* 24(2): 191–205

Fryer, D and R Payne (1986) Being unemployed: a review of the literature on the psychological experience of unemployment. In CL Cooper and IT Robertson (eds), *International Review of Industrial and Organisational Psychology*, Chichester: Wiley

Furnham, A (1990) Faking personality questionnaires: fabricating different profiles for different purposes, *Current Psychology: Research and Reviews* Spring: 45–55

Furnham, A (2000) Work in 2020: prognostications about the world of work 20 years into the millennium, *Journal of Managerial Psychology* 15(3): 1–10

Furnham, A and T Booth (2005) *Just For the Money? What Really Motivates Us at Work*. London: Cyan Books

Furnham, A, H Steele and D Pendleton (1993) A psychometric assessment of the Belbin team-role self-perception inventory, *Journal of Occupational and Organisational Psychology* 66(3): 245–257

G

Gabriel, Y (1999) Beyond happy families: a critical re-evaluation of the control–resistance–identity triangle, *Human Relations* 52(2): 179–203

Gaines, J and JM Jermier (1983) Emotional exhaustion in high stress organisation, *Academy of Management Journal* 26(3): 567–586

Gallie, D., M White, Y Cheng and M Tomlinson (1998) *Restructuring the Employment Relationship*, Oxford: Oxford University Press

Gandz, J and VV Murray (1980) The experience of workplace politics, *Academy of Management Journal* 15(2): 237–251

Gangé, RM (1974) *Essentials of Learning for Instruction*, Hinsdale, IL: Dryden

Gangon, S and N Cornelius (2000) Re-examining workplace equality: the capabilities approach, *Human Resource Management Journal* 10(4): 68–87

Ganzach, Y (1998) Intelligence and job satisfaction, *Academy of Management Journal* 41(5): 526–539

Garland, H (1990) Throwing good money after bad: the effect of sunk costs on the decision to escalate commitment to an ongoing project, *Journal of Applied Psychology* 74(6): 728–732

Garrett, TM and RJ Klonoski (1992) *Business Ethics*, 3rd edn, Englewood Cliffs, NJ: Prentice Hall

Garten, JE (1992) *A Cold Peace*, New York: Times Books

Garton, L and B Wellman (1995) Social impacts of electronic mail in organisations: a review of the research literature. In B Burleston (ed.), *Communication Yearbook*, Vol. 18, Thousand Oaks, CA: Sage

Geary, JF and A Dobbins (2001) Teamworking: a new dynamic in the pursuit of management control, *Human Resource Management Journal* 11(1): 3–23

Geller, PA and SE Hobfall (1994) Gender differences in job stress, tedium and social support in the workplace, *Journal of Social and Personality Relationships* 11(4): 555–572

Gemmil, GR and WJ Heiser (1972) Machiavellianism as a factor in managerial job strain, job satisfaction and upward mobility, *Academy of Management Journal* 15(1): 53–67

George, JM (1990) Personality, affect and behaviour in groups, *Journal of Applied Psychology* 75(2): 101–117

George JM and GR Jones (1997) Experiencing work: values, attitudes and moods, *Human Relations* 50(4): 393–416

George JM and GR Jones (2001) Towards a process model of individual change in organisations, *Human Relations* 54(1): 419–444

Georgopoulos, BS and AS Tannenbaum (1957) A study of organisational effectiveness, *Sociological Review* 22(4): 534–540

Ghoshal, S (2005) Bad management theories are destroying good management practices, *Academy of Management Learning and Education* 4(1): 75–91

Gibson, CB and ME Zellmer-Bruhn (2001) Metaphors and meanings: an intercultural analysis of the concept of teamwork, *Administrative Science Quarterly* 46(2): 274–303

Gibson, JL, JM Ivancevich and JH Donnelly (1994) *Organisations: Behaviour, Structure, Process*, 8th edn, Boston, MA: Irwin

Giddens, A (2000) *The Third Way and its Critics*, Cambridge: Polity Press

Gilmore, TN, GP Shea and M Useem (1997) Side effects of corporate cultural transformations, *Journal of Applied Behavioural Science* 33(2): 174–189

Ginnett, RC (1990) The airline cockpit crew. In JR Hackman (ed.), *Groups That Work (and Those That Don't)*, San Francisco, CA: Jossey-Bass

Gist, ME (1987) Self-efficacy: implications for organisational behaviour and human resource management, *Academy of Management Review* 12(3): 472–453

Gist, ME and TR Mitchell (1992) Self-efficacy: a theoretical analysis of its determinism and malleability, *Academy of Management Review* 17(2): 183–211

Gleick, J (2003) Get out of my inbox, *Observer Review* 2 March: 1–2

Gleitman, H (1991) *Psychology*, 3rd edn, New York: Norton

Glick, WH, GD Jenkins and N Gupta (1986) Method versus substance: how strong are underlying relationships between job characteristics and attitudinal outcomes, *Academy of Management Journal* 29(3): 441–464

Goffee, R and G Jones (1998) *The Character of a Corporation: How Your Company's Culture Can Make or Break Your Business*, London: HarperCollins

Goffman, I (1971) *The Presentation of Self in Everyday Life*, Harmondsworth: Penguin

Goldberg, LR (1993) The structure of phenotypic personality traits, *American Psychologist* 48(1): 26–34

Goldstein, E (1998) *Sensation and Perception*, San Francisco, CA: Josey-Bass

Goldthorpe, JH, D Lockwood, F Bechofer and J Platt (1968) *The Affluent Worker: Industrial Attitudes and Behaviour*, Cambridge: Cambridge University Press

Goleman, D (1998) *Working With Emotional Intelligence*, London: Bloomsbury

Gordon, IE (1997) *Theories of Visual Perception*, 2nd edn, Chichester: Wiley

Gottesman, II and J Shields (1972) *Schizophrenia and Genetics: A Twin Study Vantage Point*, New York: Academic Press

Gouldner, AW (1954) *Patterns of Industrial Bureaucracy*, New York: Free Press

Grandey, AA, GM Fisk and DD Steiner (2005) Must 'service with a smile be stressful? The moderating role of personal control for American and French employees, *Journal of Applied Psychology* 90(5): 893–904

Graen, GJ, JB Orris and K Alvares (1971) The contingency model of leadership effectiveness: some experimental results, *Journal of Applied Psychology* 55(1): 196–201

Gray, MJ (2003) Personality and performance, *Selection and Development Review* 19(1): 3–5

Green, C (1975) The reciprocal nature of influence between leader and subordinate, *Journal of Applied Psychology* 60(2): 187–193

Green, F (2001) It's been a hard day's night: the concentration and intensification of work in late twentieth century Britain, *British Journal of Industrial Relations* 39(1): 53–80

Green, N (2003) Half of on-the-job training fails, say inspectors, *Financial Times* 18 November

Green, R (2001) Social Europe and the Third Way: the new Labour challenge to European social policy, *Kurwechsel* 3: 43

Greenberg, J (1996) 'Forgive me. I'm new': three experimental demonstrations of the effects of attempts to excuse poor performance, *Organizational Behaviour and Human Decision Processes* 66(2): 167–178

Greenley, GE and GR Foxall (1996) Consumer and nonconsumer stakeholder orientations in UK companies, *Journal of Business Research* 35(1): 105–116

Greenley, GA and GR Foxall (1997) Multiple stakeholder orientation in UK companies and the implications for company performance, *Journal of Management Studies* 34(2): 258–282

Greenwood, DJ, WF Whyte and I Harkavy (1993) Participatory action research as a process and as a goal, *Human Relations* 46(2): 175–192

Grey, C and M Mitev (1995) Re-engineering organisations: a critical appraisal, *Personnel Review* 24(1): 6–18

Griffin, RW and GC McMahan (1994) Motivation through job design. In J Greenberg (ed.), *Organizational Behavior: State of Science*, New York: Lawrence Erlbaum Associates

Grimshaw, D and J Rubery (2003) *The Organisation of Employment*: An International Perspective, London: Palgrave Macmillan

Grint, K (2005) *Leadership: Limits and Possibilities*, Basingstoke: Palgrave Macmillan

Grinyear, PH and M Yasai-Ardekani (1980) Dimensions of organizational structure: a critical replication, *Academy of Management Journal* 22(3): 405–421

Gross, B (1968) *Organizations and their Managing*, New York: Free Press

Gross JJ (1999) Emotion and emotion regulation. In LA Pervin and OP Jehn (eds), *Handbook of Personality: Theory and Research*, 2nd edition, New York: Guilford Press

Guest, D (1992) Employee commitment and control. In JF Hartley and GM Stephenson (eds), *Eemployment Relations*, Oxford: Blackwell

Guest, D and C Conway (2002) Communicating the psychological contract: an employer perspective, *Human Resource Management Journal* 12(2): 22–38

Guzzo, RA and W Dickson (1998) Teams in organisations: recent research on performance and effectiveness, *Annual Review of Psychology* 49: 307–338

Gyngell, E and A Patmore (2006) A vexed question, *People Management* 1 June: 28–30

Gwyther, M (1990) Vocational hell, *Management Today*: 76–77

H

Hackman, JR and GR Oldham (1975) Development of the job diagnostic survey, *Journal of Applied Psychology* 60(2): 159–170

Hackman, JR and GR Oldham (1980) *Work Redesign*, New York: Addison-Wesley

Haddon, L and M Brynin (2005) The character of telework and the characteristics of teleworkers. *New Technology, Work and Employment* 20(1): 34–46

Haire M and WF Grunes (1950) Perceptual defenses: process protection and organised perception of another personality, *Human Relations* 3(3): 403–412

Hakim, K (1990) Core and periphery in employers workforce strategies: evidence from the 1987 ELUS Survey, *Work, Employment and Society* 4(2): 157–188

Halaby, CH (2003) Where job values come from: family and schooling background, cognitive ability and gender, *American Sociological Review* 68(2): 251–278

Hales, C (2005) Rooted in supervision, branching into management: continuity and change in the role of first-line managers, *Journal of Management Studies* 42(3): 471–506

Hall, DT (1987) Careers and socialization, *Journal of Management* 13(3): 291–308

Hall, DT and KE Nougain (1968) An examination of Maslow's need hierarchy in an organisational setting, *Organisational Behaviour and Human Performance* 3(1): 12–35

Hall, E (1966) *The Hidden Dimensions*, New York: Doubleday

Hall, ET and MR Hall (1990) *Understanding Cultural Differences*, Yarmouth, ME: Intercultural Press

Hall, J (1973) Communication revisited, *California Management Review* Fall: 56–67

Hall, RH (1980) Effectiveness theory and organizational effectiveness, *Journal of Applied Behaviourial Science* 16(2): 536–549

Hall, RH (1987) *Organizations: Structures, Processes and Outcomes*, Englewood Cliffs, NJ: Prentice Hall

Hallowell, E (2005) Fast and furious, *People Management* 16 June: 39–40

Hammer, M and J Champey (1993) *Reengineering the Corporation: A Manifesto for Business Transformation*, New York: Brearley

Hammond, TS, RL Keeney and H Raiffa (2006) The hidden traps in decision making, *Harvard Business Review* May: 114–126

Hancock, P (1999) Baudrillard and the metaphysics of motivation: a reappraisal of corporate culturalism in the light of the work and ideas of Jean Baudrillard, *Journal of Management Studies* 36(2): 155–175

Handy, C (1995) Trust and the virtual organisation, *Harvard Business Review* May–June: 40–50

Hansen, M (2002) *Financial Times* 8 August

Hardy, C (ed.) (1995) *Power and Politics in Organisations*, Aldershot: Dartmouth Publishing

Hargie, O and D Tourish (eds) (2000) *Handbook of Communication Audits for Organisations*, London: Routledge

Harley, B (1999) The myth of empowerment: work organisation, hierarchy and employee autonomy in contemporary Australian workplaces, *Work, Employment and Society* 13(1): 41–68

Harris, LC and E Ogbonna (1998) A three perspective approach to understanding culture in retail organisations, *Personnel Review* 27(1/2): 104–123

Harris, LC and E Ogbonna (1999) Developing a market-oriented culture: a critical evaluation, *Journal of Management Studies* 36(2): 177–196

Harris, LC and E Ogbonna (2002) The unintended consequences of culture interventions: a study of unexpected outcomes, *British Journal of Management* 13(1): 31–49

Harrison, EF (1999) *The Managerial Decision-making Process*, 5th edn, Chicago, IL: Houghton Mifflin

Harrison, R (1972) Understanding your organisation's character, *Harvard Business Review* May–June: 119–128

Harrison, R (2000) *Employee Development*, London: Institute of Personnel and Development

Hartog, DND, A Caley and P Dewe (2007) Recruiting leaders: an analysis of advertisements, *Human Resource Management Journal* 17(1): 58–75

Harzing, AW and JV Russeveldt (1995) *International Human Resource Management*, London: Sage

Harzing, AW and A Sorge (2003) The relative impact of country of origin and universal contingencies on internationalisation strategies and corporate control in multinational enterprises: worldwide and European perspectives, *Organisation Studies* 24(2): 187–214

Hatch, MJ (1997) *Organisation Theory: Symbolic and Postmodern Perspectives*, Oxford: Oxford University Press

Hayes, N (1997) *Successful Team Management*, London: Thomson

Hayward, D (2003) *Financial Times* 14 February

Heather, N (1976) *Radical Perspectives in Psychology*, London: Methuen

Heaton, AW and AW Kruglanski (1991) Person perception by introverts and extroverts under time pressure: effects of need for closure, *Personality and Social Psychology Bulletin* 17(2): 161–165

Hebb, DO (1949) *The Organization of Behaviour*, New York: Wiley

Heider, F (1958) *The Psychology of Interpersonal Relations*, New York: Wiley

Heller, JF, MS Pallak and JM Picek (1973) The interactive effects of intent and threat on boomerang attitude change, *Journal of Personality and Social Psychology* 26(2): 273–279

Hellriegal, D, JW Slocum and RW Woodman (1989) *Organizational Behaviour*, South-Western College Publishing

Herbert, IC (1988) How Coke markets to the world: an interview with a marketing executive, *Journal of Business Strategy* September/October: 5–6

Hermalin, B (1998) Towards an economic theory of leadership: leading by example, *American Economic Review* 88: 1188–1206

Hernstein, RJ (1973) *IQ in the Meritocracy*, London: Allen Lane

Hersey, P and KH Blanchard (1988) *Management of Organizational Behaviour: Utilizing Human Resources*, 5th edn, Englewood Cliffs, NJ: Prentice Hall

Herzberg, F (1968) One more time: how do you motivate employees?, *Harvard Business Review* 46(1): 53–62

Herzberg, F (1974) *Work and the Nature of Man*, London: Staples Press

Herzberg, F, B Mausner and B Synderman (1959) *The Motivation to Work*, London: Granada

Hewstone, M (1989) *Causal Attribution: From Cognitive Processes to Collective Beliefs*, Oxford: Blackwell

Hickman, GR (ed.) (1998) *Leading Organisations: Perspectives for a New Era*, Thousand Oaks, CA: Sage

Hickson, DJ, CR Hinings, CA Lee, RE Schneck and JM Pennings (1971) A strategic contingencies theory of intraorganizational power, *Administrative Science Quarterly* 16(2): 216–229

Hickson, DJ and CJ McMillan (1981) *Organisation and Nation: The Aston Programme IV*, Aldershot: Gower

Higgins, ET and JA Bargh (1987) Social cognition and social perception, *Annual Review of Psychology* 38: 369–425

Hill, TP Lewciki, M Czyzewska and G Schuller (1990) The role of learned inferential encoding rules in the perception of faces: effects of non-conscious self-perpetuation of bias, *Journal of Experimental Social Psychology* 26(2): 350–371

Hinings, CR and R Greenwood (2002) Disconnects and consequences in organisation theory, *Administrative Science Quarterly* 47(3): 411–421

Hinings, CR, DJ Hickson, JM Pennings and RE Schneck (1974) Structural conditions of intraorganizational power, *Administrative Science Quarterly* 19(1): 22–44

Hinings, CR, L Thibault, T Slack and LM Kikulis (1996) Values and organisational structure, *Human Relations* 49(7): 885–916

Hirsh, W, C Jackson and M Jackson (1995) *Careers in Organisations: Issues for the Future*, IES Report 287, Brighton: Institute of Employment Studies

Hirst, P and G Thompson (1996) *Globalisation in Question*, Cambridge: Polity Press

Hitt, MA and RD Ireland (1987) Peters and Waterman revisited: the unended quest for excellence, *Academy of Management Executive* 1: 91–98

Hochschild, AR (1983) *The Managed Heart: Commercialization of Human Feelings*, Berkley, CA: University of California Press

Hodgetts, RM (1991) *Organizational Behavior: Theory and Practice*, New York: Macmillan

Hodgetts, RM and F Luthans (1991) *International Management*, New York: McGraw-Hill

Hodson, R and VJ Roscigro (2004) Organisational success and worker dignity: complementary or contradictory, *American Journal of Sociology* 110(3): 672–708

Hofstede, G (1980) *Cultures Consequences: International Differences in Work-related Values*, Beverly Hills, CA: Sage

Hofstede, G (1991) *Cultures and Organisations: Softwares of the Mind*, London: McGraw-Hill

Hofstede, G (1998) Identifying organisational subcultures: an empirical approach, *Journal of Management Studies* 35(1): 1–12

Hofstede, G (2001) *Culture's Consequences: Comparing Values, Behaviours, Institutions and Organisations*, 2nd edn, Thousand Oaks, CA: Sage

Hogg, MA and GM Vaughan (1998*) Social Psychology*, Hemel Hempstead: Prentice Hall

Holbeche, L (1995) Peering into the future of careers, *People Management* May: 26–28

Holbeche, L (1997) *Motivating People in Lean Organisations*, London: Butterworth-Heinemann

Holden, L (1999) The perception gap in employee empowerment: a comparative study of banks in Sweden and Britain, *Personnel Review* 28(3): 222–241

Holder, V (2003) Campaigning to win war of words, *Financial Times* 13 November

Hollyforde, S and S Whiddett (2002) How to nurture motivation, *People Management* 11 July: 52–53

Holmes, TH and RH Rahe (1967) The social readjustment rating scale, *Journal of Psychosomatic Research* 26(2): 213–218

Homans, GC (1950) *The Human Group*, New York: Harcourt Brace and World

Honey, P and A Mumford (1992) *The Manual of Learning Styles*, Maidenhead: Peter Honey

Hope, V and J Hendry (1995) Corporate cultural change – is it relevant for organisations of the 1990s?, *Human Resource Management Journal* 5(1): 61–73

Horner, MS (1970) Femininity and successful achievement: a basic inconsistency. In J Bardwich (ed.), *Feminine Personality and Conflict*, Belmont, CA: Brooks-Cole

Hornsey, MJ, P DeBruijn, T Creed, J Allen, A Ariganto and A Svensson (2005) Keeping it in house: how audience affects responses to group criticism, *European Journal of Social Psychology* 35(2): 291–312

House, RJ and LA Wigdor (1967) Herzberg's dual-factor theory of job satisfaction and motivation: a review of the evidence and a criticism, *Personnel Psychology* 20(4): 369–389

Howell, JP, DE Bowen, PW Dorfman, S Kerr and PM Podsakoff (1990) Substitutes for leadership: effective alternatives to ineffective leadership, *Organizational Dynamics* Summer: 20–38

Hsia, HJ (1977) Redundancy: is it the lost key to better communication?, *AV Communication Review* 25(1): 63–85

Huck, P (2006) Burning questions, *Guardian* 23 August: 8

Huczynski, A and D Buchanan (2001) *Organisational Behaviour: An Introductory Text*, 4th edn, London: Prentice Hall

Hulse, SH, J Deese and N Egeth (1980) *The Psychology of Learning*, 5th edn, New York: McGraw-Hill

Hussein, RT (1989) Informal groups, leadership and productivity, *Leadership and Organization Development Journal* 10(1): 9–16

Hutton, W (1995) *The State We're In*, London: Vintage

Hutton, W (2007) Private equity is casting a plutocratic shadow over British business, *Guardian* 23 February: 39

Huy, QN and A Mintzberg (2003) The rhythm of change, *MIT Sloan Management Review* Summer: 79–84

I

Iffaldo, MT and PM Muchinsky (1985) Job satisfaction and job performance: a meta-analysis, *Psychological Bulletin* 97(3): 251–273

Industrial Society (1994) *Managing Best Practice, the Regular Benchmark: Employee Communications*, London: The Industrial Society.

Ingram, PN (1991) Changes in working practices in British manufacturing in the 1980s: a study of employee concessions made during wage negotiations, *British Journal of Industrial Relations* 29(1): 1–13

IPD (1998) *Stress at Work: Key Facts*, London: Institute of Personnel and Development, October

IRS (2006) *Informing and Consulting Employees in the Workplace*, Industrial Relations Services, 17 November, London: IRS

Ivancevich, JM and JH Donnelly (1975) Relations of organisational structure to job satisfaction, *Administrative Science Quarterly* 20(2): 272–280

Ivancevich, JM and MT Matteson (1993) *Organisational Behaviour and Management*, 3rd edn, Homewood, IL: Irwin

Ivancevich, JM, MT Matteson, SM Freedman and JS Phillips (1990) Worksite stress management interventions, *American Psychologist* 45(2): 252–261

Iverson, RD and DM Buttigieg (1999) Affective, normative and continuance commitment: can the 'right kind' of commitment be managed?, *Journal of Management Studies* 36(3): 307–333

J

Jackson, C (1996) *Understanding Psychological Testing*, Leicester: BPS Books

Jackson, SE (1983) Participation in decision making as a strategy for reducing job-related strain, *Journal of Applied Psychology* 68(1): 3–19

Jago, AG (1982) Leadership: perspectives in theory and research, *Management Science* 28(3): 297–318

James, LR and AP Jones (1974) Organisational climate: a review of theory and research, *Psychological Bulletin* 83(8): 1096–1112

Janis, IL (1972) *Victims of Groupthink*, Boston, MA: Houghton Mifflin

Janis, IL and S Feshback (1953) Effects of fear-arousing communications, *Journal of Abnormal and Social Psychology* 48(1): 78–92

Janssens, M, L Sels and I Van den Brande (2003) Multiple types of psychological contracts: a six-cluster solution, *Human Relations* 56(11): 1344–1378

Jaques, E (1952) *The Changing Culture of a Factory*, London: Tavistock

Jaques, E (1990) In praise of hierarchy, *Harvard Business Review* January–February: 127–133

Jehn, KA (1997) A qualitative analysis of conflict types and dimensions in organisational groups, *Administrative Science Quarterly* 42(3): 530–537

Jermier, JM, D Knights and WR Nord (1994) *Resistance and Power in Organisations*, London: Routledge

Jex, SM, GA Adams, TC Elacqua and DG Bachrach (2002) Type 'A' as a moderator of stressors and job complexity: a comparison of achievement striving and impatience-irritability, *Journal of Applied Social Psychology* 32(5): 977–996

Johnson, G and K Scholes (1999) *Exploring Corporate Strategy: Text and Cases*, 5th edn, Hemel Hempstead: Prentice Hall

Johnson, P and J Gill (1993) *Management Control and Organisational Behaviour*, London: Sage

Jones, EE and RE Nisbett (1972) The actor and the observer: divergent perceptions of the causes of behaviour. In EE Jones, DH Kanouse, HH Kelly, RE Nisbett, S Valins and B Weiner (eds), *Attribution: Perceiving the Causes of Behaviour*, Morristown, NJ: General Learning Press

Jones, F and BC Fletcher (1993) An empirical study of occupational stress transmission in working couples, *Human Relations* 46(7): 881–903

Jones, GR (1995) *Organisation Theory: Text and Cases*, Reading, MA: Addison-Wesley

Jordan, PC (1986) Effects of extrinsic reward on intrinsic motivation: a field experiment, *Academy of Management Journal* 29(2): 405–412

Judge, TA, JE Bono, R Illes and MW Gerhardt (2002) Personality and leadership: a qualitative and quantitative review, *Journal of Applied Psychology* 87(4): 765–780

Judge, TA, CA Higgins, CJ Thoresen and MR Barrick (1999) The Big Five personality traits, general mental ability and career success across life span, *Personnel Psychology* 52(3): 621–652

Jung, CG (1960) The structure and dynamics of the psyche. In H Read (ed.), *The Collected Works of CG Jung*, Vol. 8, London: Routledge and Kegan Paul

Jung, CG (1971) Psychological types. In *The Collected Works of CG Jung*, Vol. 16, Princeton, NJ: Princeton University Press.

K

Kahn, RL, DM Wolfe, RP Quinn, JD Snoek and RA Rosenthal (1964) *Organisational Stress*, New York: Wiley

Kahneman, D and A Tversky (eds) (2000) *Choices, Values and Frames,* Cambridge: Cambridge University Press

Kallenberg, AL (2001) Organising flexibility: the flexible firm in a new century, *British Journal of Industrial Relations* 39(4): 479–504

Kamin, L (1977) *The Science and Politics of IQ,* Harmondsworth: Penguin

Kanfer, R (1992) Work motivation: new directions in theory and research. In I Robertson and CL Cooper (eds), *International Review of Industrial and Organisational Psychology,* Vol. 74, Chichester: Wiley

Kanter, RM (1995) *The Change Masters: Corporate Entrepreneurs at Work,* London: Unwin-Hyman

Kanter, RM, BA Stein and T Jick (1992) *The Challenge of Organisational Change: How Companies Experience It and Leaders Guide It,* New York: Free Press

Katz, D (1960) The functional approach to the study of attitudes, *Public Opinion Quarterly* 24(2): 163–204

Katz, D and RL Kahn (1978) *The Social Psychology of Organisations,* 2nd edn, New York: Wiley

Katzenbach, JR and DK Smith (1993) *The Wisdom of Teams: Creating the High Performance Organization,* Boston, MA: Harvard Business School Press

Kay, J (2007) Heathrow's problems result from a flawed concept, *Financial Times* 25 June

Keeley, M (1984) Impartiality and participant interest theories of organisational effectiveness, *Administrative Science Quarterly* 28(1): 1–23

Keller, RT (1986) Predictors of the performance of project groups in research and development organisations, *Academy of Management Review* 11(4): 715–726

Kelley, HH (1967) Attribution theory in social psychology. In D Levine (ed.), *Nebraska Symposium on Motivation,* Vol. 15, Lincoln, NB: University of Nebraska Press

Kelly, GA (1955) *The Psychology of Personal Constructs,* Vols 1 and 2, New York: Norton

Kelly, J (1992) Does job re-design theory explain job re-design outcomes, *Human Relations* 45(8): 753–774

Kelly, J and N Nicholson (1980) The causation of strikes: a review of theoretical approaches and the potential contribution of social psychology, *Human Relations* 33(12): 853–883

Kenny, DA and SJ Zaccaro (1983) An estimate of variance due to traits in leadership, *Journal of Applied Psychology* 68(4): 678–685

Kenyon, W (2003) How to create a policy for whistle-blowing, *People Management* 20 February: 56–57

Kerr, S and JM Jermier (1978) Substitutes for leadership: their meaning and measurement, *Organisational Behaviour and Human Performance* 22(3): 375–403

Kets de Vries, MF (1998a) Charisma in action: the transformational abilities of Virgin's Richard Branson and ABB's Percy Barnevik, *Organisational Dynamics* 26(3): 7–21

Kets de Vries, MF (1998b) The spirit of despotism: understanding the tyrant within, *Human Relations* 59(2): 195–220

Kets de Vries, MFR and D Miller (1984) *The Neurotic Organisation,* San Francisco, CA: Jossey-Bass

Kets de Vries, MFR and K Balazs (1997) The downside of downsizing, *Human Relations* 50(1): 11–50

Kets de Vries, MFR (2006) The spirit of despotism: understanding the tyrant within, *Human Relations* 59(2): 195–220

Kiecolt-Glaser, J and R Glaser (1987) Psychosocial moderators of immune function, *Annals of Behaviour Medicine* Summer: 16–20

Kiev, A and V Kohn (1979) *Executive Stress: An AMA Survey Report,* New York: American Management Association

Kilmann, RH, MJ Saxton and R Serpa (1985) *Gaining Control of the Corporate Culture,* San Francisco, CA: Josey-Bass

Kinnie, N, S Hutchinson and J Purcell (1998) Downsizing: is it always lean and mean?, *Personnel Review* 27(4): 296–311

Kinnie, N and J Purcell (1998) Side effects, *People Management* April: 34–36

Kipnis, D, SM Schmidt, C Swaffin-Smith and I Wilkinson (1984) Patterns of managerial influence: shotgun managers, tacticians and bystanders, *Organizational Dynamics* Winter: 58–67

Kirkpatrick, SA and EA Locke (1991) Leadership: do traits matter?, *Academy of Management Executive* May: 48–60

Knight, R (2007) *Financial Times* 26 January

Knights, D and D McCabe (2000) Ain't misbehavin'? Opportunities for resistance under new forms of quality management, *Sociology* 34(3): 421–436

Knights, D and F Murray (1994) *Management Divided: Organisational Politics and Information Technology Management*, Chichester: Wiley

Kobasa, SC, SR Maddi and S Kahn (1982) Hardiness and health: a perspective study, *Journal of Personality and Social Psychology* 42(2): 168–177

Koch, R (2002) *The 80/20 Revolution*, London: Nicholas Brealy

Koffman, F and P Senge (1993) Communities of commitment: the heart of learning organisation, *Organisational Dynamics* Autumn: 5–23

Kohlberg, L (1968) The child as a moral philosopher, *Psychology Today* 2(1): 25–30

Kolb, DA and R Fry (1975) Towards an applied theory of experiential learning. In C L Cooper (ed.), *Theories of Group Processes*, Chichester: Wiley (pp. 33–57)

Kolb, DA, JM Rubin and J McIntyre (1974) *Organizational Psychology: An Experimental Approach*, 2nd edn, Englewood Cliffs, NJ: Prentice Hall

Kotter, JP (1990) What do leaders really do?, *Harvard Business Review* 68: 103–111

Kotter, JP (1995) Leading change: why transformation efforts fail, *Harvard Business Review* March/April: 59–67

Kotter, JP and LA Schlesinger (1979) Choosing strategies for change, *Harvard Business Review* March/April: 106–114

Kotter, JP, LA Schlesinger and V Sathe (1986) *Organisation: Text Cases and Readings in Organizational Design and Change*, 2nd edn, Homewood, IL: Irwin

Koys, DJ and TA DeCotis (1991) Inductive measures of psychological climate, *Human Relations* 44(3): 265–285

Koza, MP and JC Thoenig (2003) Rethinking the firm: organisational approaches, *Organisation Studies* 24(8): 1219–1229

Kozlowski, SW, GT Chao, EM Smith and J Hedlund (1993) Organizational downsizing strategies, interventions and research implications. In CL Cooper and IT Robertson (eds), *International Review of Industrial and Organizational Psychology*, New York: Wiley

Kozlowski, SWJ and M Doherty (1989) Integration of climate and leadership: examination of a neglected issue, *Journal of Applied Psychology* 74(5): 546–553

Krantz, J (1999) Comment on challenging resistance to change, *Journal of Applied Behavioural Science* 35(1): 42–44

Kraut, R and R Fish (1997) Prospects for videotelephony. In K Finn, A Sellen and S Wilbur (eds), *Video-mediated Communication*, Mahwah, NJ: Lawrence Erlbaum Associates

Kreitner, R and A Kinicki (1995) *Organizational Behavior*, 3rd edn, Chicago, IL: Irwin

Kren, L (1992) The moderating effect of locus of control on performance incentives and participation, *Human Relations* 45(9): 991–1012

Krueger, J (1991) Accentuation effects and illusory change in exemplar based category learning, *European Journal of Social Psychology* 59(12): 1140–1152

Kvale, S (ed.) (1992) *Psychology and Postmodernism*, London: Sage

L

Laing, RD (1972) *Knots*, Harmondsworth: Penguin

Lambert, LS, JR Edwards and DM Cable (2003) Breach and fulfillment of the psychological contract: a comparison of traditional and expanded views, *Personnel Psychology* 56(3): 985–934

Lang, JR, JE Dittrich and SE White (1978) Management problem-solving models: a review and proposals, *Academy of Management Review* 3(4): 854–865

Larkey, LK (1996) Towards a theory of communicative interactions in culturally diverse workgroups, *Academy of Management Review* 21(2): 463–491

Larwood, L, P Rand and A Der Hovanessian (1979) Sex difference in response to simulated disciplinary cases, *Personnel Psychology* 32(4): 539–550

Latham, GP and EA Locke (1979) Goal-setting: a motivational technique that works, *Organisational Dynamics* Autumn: 68–80

Latham, GP and TP Steele (1983) The motivational effects of participation versus goal setting on performance, *Academy of Management Journal* 26(3): 406–417

Lawrence, PR and JW Lorsch (1969) *Organisation and Environment: Managing Differentiation and Integration*, Homewood, IL: Irwin

Lazarus, RS (1966) *Psychological Stress and the Coping Process*, New York: McGraw-Hill

Lazarus, RS (1971) *Personality*, New York: Prentice Hall

Lazarus, RS (1991) *Emotion and Adaptation*, New York: Oxford University Press

Lazarus, RS and S Folkman (1984) Coping and adaptation. In WD Gentry (ed.), *Handbook of Behavioural Medicine*, New York: Guilford Press

Leavitt, HJ (1951) Some effects of certain patterns on group performance, *Journal of Abnormal and Social Psychology* 46(1): 38–50

Lee, R and P Lawrence (1985) *Organisational Behaviour: Politics at Work*, London: Hutchinson

Lengel, RH and RL Daft (1988) The selection of communication media as an executive skill, *Academy of Management Executive* August: 225–232

Lenway, SA and K Rehbein (1991) Leaders, followers and free riders: an empirical test of variation in corporate political involvement, *Academy of Management Journal* 26(6): 893–905

Leonard, NH, LL Beauvais and RW Scholl (1999) Work motivation: the incorporation of self-based processes, *Human Relations* 52(8): 969–997

LePine, JA, NP Podsakoff and ME LePine (2005) A meta-analytic test of challenge stressor – hindrance stressor framework: an explanation for the inconsistent relationship between stressors and performance, *Academy of Management Journal* 48(5): 764–775

Levitt, B and C Nass (1984) The lid on the garbage can: institutional constraints on decision making in the technical core of college text publishers, *Administrative Science Quarterly* 29(2): 190–207

Lewin, K (1951) *Field Theory in Social Science*, New York: Harper and Row

Lewin, K, R Lippit and RK White (1939) Patterns of aggressive behaviour in experimentally created social climates, *Journal of Social Psychology* 10(2): 271–299

Lewis PS, SH Goodman and PM Fandt (1995) *Management: Challenges in the 21st Century*, St Paul, MN: West Publishing

Lewis, SN and CL Cooper (1987) Stress in two-earner couples and stage in the life cycle, *Journal of Occupational Psychology* 60(4): 289–304

Likert, R (1932) A technique for the measurement of attitudes, *Archives of Psychology* 22(1): 1–55

Likert, R (1961) *New Patterns in Management*, New York: McGraw-Hill

Lim, BC and RE Ployhart (2004) Transformational leadership: relation to the five-factor model and team performance in typical and maximum contexts, *Journal of Applied Psychology* 89(4): 610–621

Lim, VKG (1996) Job insecurity and its outcomes: moderating effects of work-based and nonwork-based social support, *Human Relations* 40(2): 171–194

Lind, JS (1990) Improving process consultation on business and organisations, *International Journal of Technology Management* 5(6): 742–745

Lindsay, C (2003) *A Century of Labour Market Change: 1900–2000. Labour Market Trends (Special Feature)*, London: Office for National Statistics

Lipshitz, R and O Strauss (1997) Coping with uncertainty: a naturalistic decision-making analysis, *Organisational Behaviour and Human Decision Processes* 69(2): 149–163

Little, BR (1969) Sex differences and comparability of three measures of cognitive complexity, *Psychological Reports* 24(5): 607–609

Little, W (2006) *Financial Times* 26 August

Littlefield, D (1996) Oxfam calls on firms to adopt labour code, *People Management* June: 6

Litwin, GH and RA Stringer (1968) *Motivation and Organizational Climate*, Boston, MA: Harvard University Graduate School of Business Administration

Locke, EA (1968) Towards a theory of task performance and incentives, *Organisational Behaviour and Human Performance* 3(2): 157–189

Locke, EA (1976) The nature and cause of job satisfaction. In MD Dunnette (ed.), *Handbook of Industrial and Organizational Psychology*, Chicago, IL: Rand McNally

Locke, EA (1977) The myths of behaviour mod. in organisations, *Academy of Management Review* 2(3): 543–553

Locke, EA and GP Latham (1990) *A Theory of Goal Setting and Task Performance*, Englewood Cliffs, NJ: Prentice Hall

Locke, EA, KN Shaw, LM Saari and GP Latham (1981) Goal setting and task performance 1969–1980, *Psychological Bulletin* 82(2): 127–140

Logie, RH (1999) Working memory, *The Psychologist* 12(4): 174–178

Lord, RG, CL De Valder and GM Allinger (1986) A meta-analysis of the relation between personality traits and leadership perceptions: an application of validity generalisation procedures, *Journal of Applied Psychology* 71(3): 396–419

Lord, W and J Rust (2003) The big five revisited: where are we now?, *Selection and Development Review* 19(4): 15–18

Low Pay Commission (2005) *National Minimum Wage: Annual Report 2005*, London: Low Pay Commission

Lowe, R and P Bennett (2003) Exploring coping reactions to work stress: application of an appraisal theory, *Journal of Occupational and Organisational Psychology* 76(3): 393–400

Lucas, E (2003) The feelgood factor, *Professional Manager* July: 19–20

Lueshy, J (2006) Terrorism: it is perception that counts, *Financial Times* 24 April

Lukes, S (1974) *Power*, London: Macmillan

Luthans, F (1995) *Organizational Behaviour*, 7th edn, New York: McGraw-Hill

Luthans, F and R Kreitner (1985) Organisational Behaviour Modification and Beyond, Glenview, IL: Scott Foresman

Luthans, F and JK Larsen (1986) How managers really communicate, *Human Relations* 39(2): 161–178

M

Maccoby, M (2000) Narcissistic leaders: incredible pros and the inevitable cons, *Harvard Business Review* 78: 69–77

MacCrimmon, KR (1974) Managerial decision making. In JW McGuire (ed.), *Contemporary Management*, Englewood Cliffs, NJ: Prentice Hall

MacCrimmon, KR and D Wehrung (1986) *Taking Risks*, New York: Free Press

Macduffie, JP (1995) Human resource bundles and manufacturing performance: organizational logic and flexible production systems in the world auto industry, *Industrial and Labor Relations Review* 48(2): 107–121

Mackay, C and T Cox (1984) Occupational stress associated with visual display unit operation. In BG Pearce (ed.), *Health Hazards and VDUs*, Chichester: Wiley

MacLachlan, R (1996) Ageism hits one-third of workers, *People Management* January: 11

Madison, DL, RW Allen, LW Porter, PA Renwick and BT Mayes (1980) Organizational politics: an exploration of manager's perceptions, *Human Relations* 33(2): 79–100

Mahoney, TA and PJ Frost (1974) The role of technology in models of organizational effectiveness, *Organizational Behaviour and Human Performance* 11(1): 126–138

Maitland, A (2002) Citigroup: bridging the culture gap, *Financial Times* 28 January

Makin, P, CL Cooper and C Cox (1996) *Organisations and the Psychological Contract*, Leicester: British Psychological Society

Malnight, TW (2001) Emerging structural patterns within multinational corporations: towards process based structures, *Academy of Management Journal* 44(6): 1187–1210

Manstead, T (2005) The social dimension of emotion, *The Psychologist* 18(8): 484–487

Manz, CC and HP Simms (1981) Vicarious learning: the influence of modelling on organisational behaviour, *Academy of Management Review* 6(1): 105–113

March, JG (1982) Theories of choice and making decisions, *Social Science and Modern Society* 20(1): 29–39

March, JG and HA Simon (1958) *Organizations*, New York: Wiley

Marchington, M (2000) Teamwork and employee involvement: terminology, evaluation and context. In S Proctor and F Mueller (eds), *Teamworking*, Basingstoke: Macmillan

Marchington, M and A Wilkinson (1996) *Core Personnel and Development*, London: Institute of Personnel and Development

Marginson, P, P Armstrong, PK Edwards and J Purcell (1995) Extending beyond borders: multinational companies in the international management of labour, *International Journal of Human Resource Management* 6(3): 702–719

Marchington, M, P Parker and A Prestwich (1989) Problems with team briefing in practice, *Employee Relations* 11(4): 21–30

Marshall, A (1891) *Principles of Economics*, 2nd edn, London: Macmillan

Martin, J (1992) *Cultures and Organisations: Three Perspectives*, Oxford: Oxford University Press

Martin, J and M Power (1983) Truth or corporate propaganda: the value of a good war story. In L Pondy, PJ Frost, G Morgan and TC Dandridge (eds), *Organisational Symbolism*, Greenwich, CT: JAI Press

Martin, L (2005) Internal adoption and use in small firms: internal processes, organisational culture and the roles of the owner-manager and key staff, *New Technology, Work and Employment* 20(3): 190–204

Martin, X, A Swaminathan and W Mitchell (1998) Organisational evolution in the international environment: incentives and constraints in international expansion strategy, *Administrative Science Quarterly* 43(3): 566–601

Marx, K (1894/1974) *Capital*, Vol. 3, London: Lawrence Wishart

Maslow, AH (1954) *Motivation and Personality*, New York: Harper and Row

Mathieu, JE and DM Zanjoc (1990) A review and meta-analysis of the antecedents, correlates and consequences of organisational commitment, *Psychological Bulletin* 108(2): 171–199

Mayo, E (1933) *The Human Problems of Industrial Civilization*, New York: Macmillan

McAndrew, FT, A Akande, R Bridgstock, L Mealy, SC Gordon, JE Scheibe, BE Akande-Adetoun, F Odewale, A Morakinyo, P Nyahete and GM Mubavakane (2000) A multicultural study of stereotyping in English speaking countries, *Journal of Social Psychology* 140(4): 487–502

McCabe, D (1996) The best laid schemes O'TQM: strategy, politics and power, *New Technology, Work and Employment* 11(1): 28–38

McCall, GJ and JL Simmons (1966) *Identities and Interactions*, New York: Free Press

McClelland, DC (1967) *The Achieving Society*, New York: Free Press

McClelland, DC (1971) *Motivational Trends in Society*, Morristown, NJ: General Learning Press

McClelland, DC and RE Boyatzis (1982) Leadership motive pattern and long-term success in management, *Journal of Applied Psychology* 67(4): 737–743

McCrae, RR and PT Costa (1990) *Personality in Adulthood*, New York: Guilford Press

McGill, ME and JW Slocum (1993) Unlearning the organisation, *Organisational Dynamics* Autumn: 82–91

McGinnies, E (1949) *Social Behaviour: A Functional Analysis*, Boston, MA: Houghton Mifflin

McLougtin, L and S Gourlay (1994) *Enterprise without Unions: Industrial Relations in the Non-union Firm*, Buckingham: Open University Press

McKenna, C (2006) In the business of consulting: image is everything, *The Observer* 20 November

McNeill, D (2000) *The Face*, London: Penguin

Mehrabian, A (1971) *Silent Messages*, Belmont, CA: Wadsworth

Meindl, JR, SR Ehrlich and JM Dukerich (1987) The romance of leadership and the evaluation of organisational performance, *Academy of Management Review* 12(1): 91–109

Mendenhall, ME, BJ Punnett and D Ricks (1995) *Global Management*, Cambridge, MA: Blackwell

Merrick, N (1997) Business chiefs take to stakeholding ideal, *People Management* May: 12

Merton, RK (1957) *Social Theory and Social Structure*, Glencoe, IL: Free Press

Meyer, JP and NJ Allen (1997) *Commitment in the Workplace: Theory, Research and Application*, London: Sage

Miceli, MP, M Rehg, JP Near and KC Ryan (1999) Can laws protect whistle-blowers? Results of a naturally occurring field experiment, *Work and Occupations* 26(1): 129–151

Michaelsen, LK, WE Watson and RH Black (1989) A realistic test of individual versus group consensus decision making, *Journal of Applied Psychology* 69(4): 834–839

Middleton, R (1983) *A Briefer's Guide to Team Briefing*, London: The Industrial Society

Miles, RE and C Snow (1978) *Organizational Strategy, Structure and Process*, New York: McGraw-Hill

Miles, RE and C Snow (1986) Network organisations: new concepts for new forms, *California Management Review* 28(1): 62–73

Miles, RH (1980) *Macro Organisational Behaviour*, Santa Monica, CA: Goodyear

Miles, RH (1982) *Coffin Nails and Corporate Strategies*, Englewood Cliffs, NJ: Prentice Hall

Miles, TR (1957) Contributions to intelligence testing and the theory of intelligence: on defining intelligence, *British Journal of Educational Psychology* 27(2): 153–165

Milgram, S (1965) Some conditions of obedience and disobedience to authority, *Human Relations* 18(1): 57–76

Miller, D (1994) What happens after success: the perils of excellence, *Journal of Management Studies* 31(3): 325–358

Miller, GA (1956) The magical number seven, plus or minus two: some limits on our capacity for processing information, *Psychological Review* 63(1): 81–97

Millward, N, A Bryson and J Forth (2000) All change at work: British employment relations 1980–1998 as portrayed by the Workplace Industrial Relations Survey Series, London: Routledge

Milne, R (2006) VW – a company that's at war with itself, *Financial Times* 9 November

Miner, FC (1984) Group versus individual decision making: an investigation of performance measures, decision strategies and process losses and gains, *Organisational Behaviour and Human Performance* February: 112–124

Minssen H (2005) Challenges of teamwork in production: demands of communication, *Organisation Studies* 27(1): 103–124

Mintzberg, H (1979a) Organisational power and goals: a skeletal theory. In D Schendel and CW Hofer (eds), *Strategic Manangement: A New View of Business and Policy Planning*, Boston, MA: Little Brown and Co

Mintzberg, H (1979b) *The Structuring of Organizations*, Englewood Cliffs, NJ: Prentice Hall

Mintzberg, H (1983) *Power In and Around Organizations*, Englewood Cliffs, NJ: Prentice Hall

Mintzberg, H (1985) The organisation as political arena, *Journal of Management Studies* 22(2): 133–154

Mintzberg, H (1994) That's not turbulence 'chicken little', it's really opportunity, *Planning Review* 22(6): 7–9

Mischel, W (1977) The interaction of person and situation. In D Magnusson and NS Endler (eds), *Personality at the Crossroads: Current Issues in Interactional Psychology*, Hillsdale, NJ: Lawrence Erlbaum Associates

Mishra, J (1990) Managing the grapevine, *Public Personnel Management* Summer: 213–228

Mitchell, D (1979) *Control without Bureaucracy*, London: McGraw-Hill

Mitchell, TR (1982) Motivation: new directions for theory, research and practice, *Academy of Management Review* 7(1): 80–88

Mitchell, RK, BR Agle and DJ Wood (1997) Toward a theory of stakeholder identification and salience: defining the principles of who and what really counts, *Academy of Management Review* 22(4): 853–886

Mitchell, TR, SG Green and R Wood (1981) An attributional model of leadership and the poor performing subordinate. In LL Cummings and BM Staw (eds), *Research in Organizational Behaviour*, Vol. 3, Greenwich, CT: JAI Press

Mitchell, TR and LS Kalb (1982) Effects of job experience on supervisor's attributions for poor performance, *Journal of Applied Psychology* 62(2): 181–188

Mitchell, TR and RE Wood (1980) Supervisors' responses to subordinate poor performance: a test of an attributional model, *Organisational Behaviour and Human Performance* 25(2): 123–138

Monk, T and D Tepas (1985) Shift work. In CL Cooper and MJ Smith (eds), *Job Stress and Blue-collar Work*, Chichester: Wiley

Monks, J (1999) Ready, willing and able, *People Management* May: 29

Monson, TC, JW Hesley and L Chernick (1982) Specifying when personality traits cannot predict behaviour: an alternative to abandoning the attempt to predict single action criteria, *Journal of Personality and Social Psychology* 43(3): 358–365

Moore, JD (1997) *Visions of Culture: An Introduction to Anthropological Theories and Theorists*, London: Sage

Moorhead, G and RW Griffin (1995) *Organizational Behaviour*, 4th edn, Boston, MA: Houghton Mifflin

Moreland, RL and RB Zajonc (1979) Exposure effects may not depend on stimulus recognition, *Journal of Personality and Social Psychology* 37(5): 1085–1089

Morgan, G (1989) *Creative Organisation Theory: A Resourcebook*, London: Sage

Morgan, G (1997) *Images of Organisation*, London: Sage

Morris, JR, WF Cascio and CE Young (1999) Downsizing after all these years: questions and answers about who did it, how many did it, and who benefited from it, *Organisational Dynamics* Winter: 78–87

Morris, T, H Lydka and M Fenton-O'Creevy (1993) Can commitment be managed? A longitudinal analysis of employee commitment and human resource policies, *Human Resource Management Journal* 3(3): 21–42

Morrison, EW and SL Robinson (1997) When employees feel betrayed: a model of how psychological contract violation develops, *Academy of Management Review* 22(2): 226–256

Moss, L (1981) *Management Stress*, Reading, MA: Addison-Wesley

Mount, MK, MR Barrick, SM Scullen and J Rounds (2005) Higher order dimensions of the big five personality traits and the big six vocational interest types, *Personnel Psychology* 58(2): 447–478

Mount, MK, R Ilies and E Johnson (2006) Relationship of counterproductive work behaviours: the mediating effect of job satisfaction, *Personnel Psychology* 59(3): 591–622

Mowday, RT, RM Steers and LW Porter (1979) The measure of organisational commitment, *Journal of Vocational Behaviour* 14(3): 224–247

Mulholland, K (2002) Gender, emotional labour and teamworking in a call centre, *Personnel Review* 31(3): 283–303

Mulholland, K (2004) Workplace resistance in an Irish call centre: slammin, scammin, smoking and leaving work, *Work, Employment and Society* 15(1): 709–724

Mulinge, MM (2001) Employer control of employees: extending the Lincoln – Kallenberg corporatist model of satisfaction and attachment, *Human Relations* 54(3): 285–318

Mullins, LJ (2002) *Management and Organisational Behaviour*, 6th edn, Harlow: Financial Times/Prentice Hall

Mumford, E and R Hendricks (1996) Business process re-engineering RIP, *People Management* 2 May: 22–29

Muna, FA (1980) *The Arab Executive*, London: St Martin's Press

Murphy, KR, RA Jako and RL Anhalt (1993) Nature and consequences of halo error: a critical analysis, *Journal of Applied Psychology* 77(2): 215–229

Murphy, MG and KM Davey (2002) Ambiguity, ambivalence and indifference in organisational values, *Human Resource Management Journal* 12(1): 3–16

Murray, F and H Willmott (1997) Putting information technology in its place: towards flexible integration in the network age? In B Bloomfield, R Coombs, D Knights and D Littler (eds), *Information Technology and Organisations*, Oxford: Oxford University Press

Murray, S (2000) *Financial Times* 2 May

Myers, IB and MH McCaulley (1985) Manual: a guide to the development and use of the Myers–Briggs Type Indicator, Palto, CA: Consulting Psychological Press

N

Nadler, D and M Tushman (1986) *Managing Strategic Organisational Change: Frame Binding and Frame Breaking*, New York: Delta Consulting Group

Natvany, I (1996) *Putting Pressure to Work*, London: IPD and Pitman

Naughton, J (2000) Any fool can create their own e-commerce site: many do so, *The Observer* 23 July: 10

Naughton, J (2007) You've got mail – all you need is a way to get rid of it, *The Observer Business and Media* 8 July: 12

Nathan, M, G Carpenter and S Roberts (2003) *Getting By, Not Getting On*, London: The Work Foundation

Neck, CP, ML Connerley, CA Zuniga and S Goel (1999) Family therapy meets self-managing teams: explaining self-managing team performance through team member perceptions, *Journal of Applied Behavioural Science* 35(2): 245–259

Negroponte, N (1995) *Being Digital*, London: Hodder and Stoughton

Neisser, U (1976) *Cognition and Reality*, San Francisco, CA: Freeman

Nelson, RE and S Gopalan (2003) Do organisational cultures replicate national cultures? Isomorphism, rejection and reciprocal opposition in the corporate values of three countries, *Organisation Studies* 24(7): 1115–1151

Nemetz, PL and SL Christensen (1996) The challenge of cultural diversity: harnessing a diversity of views to understand multiculturalism, *Academy of Management Review* 21(2): 434–462

Newman, KL and SD Nollen (1996) Culture and congruence: the fit beween management practice and national culture, *Journal of International Business Studies* 27(4): 753–779

Newton, TJ (1994) Discourse and agency: the example of personnel psychology and assessment centres, *Organization Studies* 15(6): 879–902

NICE (2006) *The Depression Report: A New Deal for Depression and Anxiety Disorders*, London: The London School of Economics and Political Science/ESRC

Nichols, N (2005) Objections to evolutionary psychology: reflections, implications and the leadership exemplar, *Human Relations* 58(3): 393–409

Nichols, RG (1962) Listening is good business, *Management of Personnel Quarterly* 1(2): 2–10

Nicholson, N (2005) Objections to evolutionary psychology: reflection, implications and the leadership exemplar, *Human Relations* 58(3): 393–409

Nohria, N and J Berkley (1994) The virtual organisation: bureaucracy, technology and the implosion of control. In C Heckscher and A Donnelon (eds), *The Post-bureaucratic Organisation*, Thousands Oaks, CA: Sage

Nonaka, I and H Takeuchi (1995) *The Knowledge Creating Company*, New York: Oxford University Press

Noon, M and R Delbridge (1993) News from behind my hand: gossip in organisations, *Organisation Studies* 14(1): 23–36

Northouse, PG (1997) *Leadership: Theory and Practice*, London: Sage

Nunamaker, J (1997) Future research in group support systems: needs, some questions and possible directions, *International Journal of Human-Computer Studies* 47(3): 357–385

O'Doherty, D and H Willmott (2001) The question of subjectivity and the labour process, *International Studies of Management and Organisation* 30(4): 112–132

Office for National Statistics (2004) *Inland Revenue: Personal Wealth*, London (www.statistics.gov.uk/cci/nugget.asp)

Ogbonna, E (1993) Managing organisational culture: fantasy or reality?, *Human Resource Management Journal* 3(2): 42–53

O'Leary, A (1990) Stress, emotion and human immune functioning, *Psychological Bulletin* 99(3): 363–382

O'Reilly, CA (1977) Supervisors and peers as information sources, group supportiveness and individual performance, *Journal of Applied Psychology* 62(5): 632–635

O'Reilly, CA and LR Pondy (1979) Organisational communication. In S Kerr (ed.), *Organisational Behaviour*, Columbus, OH: Grid

O'Reilly, CA and KH Roberts (1977) Task group structure, communication and effectiveness in three organisations, *Journal of Applied Psychology* 62(6): 674–681

Orbell, S (2003) Personality systems interaction theory and the theory of planned behaviour: evidence that self-regulatory volitional components enhance enactment of studying behaviour, *British Journal of Social Psychology* 42(1): 95–112

Ott, JS (1989) *The Organizational Culture Perspective*, Pacific Grove, CA: Brooks-Cole

Ouchi, WG (1981) *Theory Z*, Reading, MA: Addison-Wesley

Oxman, JA and BD Smith (2003) The limits of structural change, *MIT Sloan Management Review* Fall: 77–82

O

Oakland, S and A Ostell (1996) Measuring coping: a review and critique, *Human Relations* 49(2): 133–155

Oborne, DJ (1994) *Computers at Work: A Behavioural Approach*, 3rd edn, Chichester: Wiley

O'Connor, ES (1999) The politics of management thought: a case study of the Harvard Business School and the Human Relations School, *Academy of Management Review* 24(1): 117–131

P

Palmer, C (2000) A job old boy? The school ties that still bind, *The Observer* 11 June: 18

Park, SH and GR Ungson (1997) The effect of national culture, organisational complementarity and economic motivation on joint venture dissolution, *Academy of Management Journal* 40(2): 279–307

Parker, M (2000) *Organisational Culture and Identity*, London: Sage

Parker, M (2003) Introduction. Ethics, politics and organizing, *Organisation* 10(2): 187–203

Parker, M and J Slaughter (1988) Management by stress, *Technology Review* October: 27–31

Parker, SM, S Mullarkey and P Jackson (1993) Dimensions of performance effectiveness in high-involvement work organisations, *Human Resource Management Journal* 4(3): 1–21

Parker, S, TD Wall and PR Jackson (1997) 'That's not my job': developing flexible employee work orientations, *Academy of Management Journal* 40(4): 899–929

Parkinson, B (1995) *Ideas and Realities of Emotion*, London: Routledge

Parkinson, B (1996) Emotions are social, *British Journal of Psychology* 87(3): 663–683

Parnell, JA and T Hatem (1999) Cultural antecedents of behavioural differences between American and Egyptian managers, *Journal of Management Studies* 36(3): 399–415

Parry, R (2003) *Enterprise – The Leadership Role*, London: Profile Press

Pascale, R (1985) The paradox of corporate culture: reconciling ourselves to socialisation, *California Management Review* Winter: 120–121

Pascale, R and A Athos (1981) *The Art of Japanese Management*, New York: Simon and Schuster

Pasmore, WA and MR Fagans (1992) Participation, individual development and organisational change: a review and synthesis, *Journal of Management* June: 375–397

Patti, RJ (1974) Organisational resistance and change: the view from below, *Social Science Review* 48(4): 371–372

Pavlov, IP (1927) *Conditioned Reflexes*, Oxford: Oxford University Press

Payne, R and C Cooper (eds) (2001) *Emotions at Work*, Chichester: Wiley

Payne, RL and DC Phesey (1971) GG Stern's organizational climate index: a conceptualization and application to business organizations, *Organizational Behaviour and Human Performance* 6(1): 77–98

Pease, A (1997) *Body Language: How to Read Other's Thoughts by Their Gestures*, 3rd edn, London: Sheldon Press

Pedler, MJ, JG Burgoyne and T Boydell (1997) *The Learning Company: A Strategy for Sustainable Development*, 2nd edn, London: McGraw-Hill

Perkins, DV (1982) The assessment of stress using life events scales. In L Goldberger and S Breznitz (eds), *Handbook of Stress*, New York: Free Press

Perlow, LA, GA Okhuyysen and NP Repenning (2002) The speed trap: exploring the relationship between decision making and temporal context, *Academy of Management Journal* 45(5): 931–955

Perrow, C (1961) The analysis of goals in complex organisations, *American Sociological Review* 26: 55–67

Perrow, C (1972) *Organisational Analysis: A Sociological View*, London: Tavistock

Pervin, A and OP John (1996) *Personality: Theories and Research*, 7th edn, Chichester: Wiley

Pervin, LA (1980) *Personality: Theory, Assessment and Research*, New York: Wiley

Peters, LH, DH Hartke and JT Pohlman (1985) Fiedler's contingency theory of leadership: an application of the meta-analytic procedures of Schmidt and Hunter, *Psychological Bulletin* 97(2): 274–285

Peters, T (1987) A world turned upside down, *Academy of Management Executive* 1: 231–241

Peters, TJ (1985) *Thriving on Chaos: Handbook for a Management Revolution*, Knopf: New York

Peters, TJ and RH Waterman (1982) *In Search of Excellence: Lessons from America's Best-run Companies*, New York: Harper and Row

Petri, HL (1996) *Motivation: Theory, Research and Application*, London: Thomson

Pettigrew, AM (1973) *The Politics of Organizational Decision Making*, London: Tavistock

Pettigrew, AM and R Whipp (1993) Understanding the environment. In C Mabey and B Mayon-White (eds), *Managing Change*, 2nd edn, London: Open University Press/Paul Chapman

Pfeffer, J (1977) The ambiguity of leadership, *Academy of Management Review* 2(1): 104–112

Pfeffer, J (1981) *Power in Organizations*, Marchfield, MA: Pitman

Pfeffer, J (1992) *Managing with Power: Politics and Influence in Organizations*, Boston, MA: Harvard Business School Press

Pfeffer, J (1996) *Competitive Advantage Through People: Unleashing the Power of the Workforce*, Boston, MA: Harvard Business School Press

Pfeffer, J and GR Salanick (1978) *The External Control of Organizations: A Resource–Dependence Perspective*, London: Harper and Row

Pfeffer, J and RI Sutton (2005) *Hard Facts, Dangerous Half-truths and Total Nonsense: Profit From Evidence-Based Management*, Boston, MA: Harvard Business School Press

Phares, EJ (1987) *Introduction to Personality*, 2nd edn, Glenview, IL: Scott Foresman

Phillips, A (2005) *The Penguin Freud Reader*, Harmondsworth: Penguin

Philpott, R (2003) Time to tackle the age-old problem, *People Management* 27 June: 22

Piccolo, RF and JA Colquitt (2006) Transformational leadership and job behaviour: the mediating role of core job characteristics, *Academy of Management Journal* 49(2): 327–340

Pickard, J (1993) The real meaning of empowerment, *Personnel Management* November: 28–33

Pinkley, RL (1990) Dimensions of conflict frame: disputant interpretations of conflict, *Journal of Applied Psychology* 75(1): 117–126

Piore, MJ and CF Sabel (1984) *The Second Industrial Divide: Possibilities for Prosperity*, New York: Basic Books

Piper, WE, M Marrache, R Lacroix, AM Richardson and BD Jones (1983) Cohesion as a basic bond in groups, *Human Relations* 26(2): 93–108

Plomin, R (1994) *Genetics and Experience: The Interplay between Nature and Nurture*, Thousand Oaks, CA: Sage

Ployhart, RE, JA Weekley, BC Holtz and C Kemp (2003) Web-based paper-and-pencil testing of applicants in a proctored setting: are personality, biodata and situational judgment tests comparable?, *Personnel Psychology* 56(3): 733–752

Podsakoff, PM and LJ Williams (1986) The relationship between job performance and job satisfaction. In EA Locke (ed.), *Generalizing from Laboratory to Field Settings*, Lexington, MA: Lexington Books

Polsky, HW (1971) Notes on personal feedback in sensitivity training, *Sociological Enquiry* 41(2): 175–182

Pondy, L (1967) Organisational conflict: concepts and models, *Administrative Science Quarterly* 12(2): 296–320

Poole, M, R Mansfield, J Gould-Williams and P Mendes (2005) British managers' attitudes and behaviour in industrial relations: a twenty year study, *British Journal of Industrial Relations* 43(1): 117–134

Porras, JI and PO Berg (1978) Evaluation methodology in organisational development: analysis and critique, *Journal of Applied Behavioural Science* 14(2): 151–173

Porras, JI and J Robertson (1992) Organisational development: theory, practice and research. In MD Dunnette and CM Hughes (eds), *Handbook of Industrial and Organisational Psychology*, 2nd end, Palo Alto, CA: Consulting Psychologists Press

Porras, JI and R Silvers (1991) Organisation development and transformation, *Annual Review of Psychology* 42: 51–78

Porter, LW (1996) Forty years of organisation studies: reflections from a micro perspective, *Administrative Science Quarterly* 41(2): 262–269

Porter, LW and EE Lawler (1968) *Managerial Attitudes and Performance*, Homewood, IL: Irwin

Porter, ME (1986) Competition in global industries. In ME Porter (ed.), *Competition in Global Industries*, Boston, MA: Harvard Business School Press

Porter, ME (1990) *The Competitive Advantage of Nations*, New York: Free Press

Poster, M (1990) *The Mode of Information: Poststructuralism and Social Context*, Cambridge: Polity Press

Powell, GN and DA Butterfield (1978) The case for sub-system climate in organizations, *Academy of Management Review* 3(2): 151–157

Power, M (2000) Freud and the unconscious, *The Psychologist* 13(12): 612–614

Priestland A and R Hanig (2006) Fuelling the fire, *People Management* 23 February: 4–42

Pritchard, RD and PJ DeLeo (1973) Experimental test of the valence–instrumentality relationships in job performance, *Journal of Applied Psychology* 57(2): 264–279

Proctor, S and F Mueller (eds) (2000) *Teamworking*, London: Macmillan

Pryce, BJ, EJ Donaldson-Fiedler, M Heinz and H Spice (2006) Stress management competencies: integrating stress management into people management. Paper presented to the Occupational Psychology Conference of the British Psychological Society, January

Pugh, DS (ed.) (1971) *Organisation Theory: Selected Readings*, Harmondsworth: Penguin

Pugh, DS and DJ Hickson (1976) *Organizational Structure in its Context: The Aston Programme I*, Aldershot: Gower

Purcell, J (1993) The end of institutional industrial relations, *British Journal of Industrial Relations* 31(1): 6–23

Purcell, J and R Smith (eds) (1979) *The Control of Work*, London: Macmillan

Q

Quinn, JB (1977) Strategic goals: process and politics, *Sloan Management Review* 19: 21–37

Quinn RE (1988) *Beyond Rational Management: Mastering the Paradoxes and Competing Demands of High Performance*, San Francisco, CA: Jossey-Bass

Quinn, RE and J Rohrbaugh (1983) A spatial model of effectiveness criteria, *Management Science* 29: 363–377

R

Raja, V, G Johns and F Ntalianis (2004) The impact of personality characteristics on psychological contracts, *Academy of Management Journal* 47(3): 350–367

Rajan, A, E Lank and K Chapple (1999) *Good Practice in Knowledge Creation and Exchange*, London: Focus/London Training and Enterprise Council

Rathus, SA (1990) *Psychology*, 4th edn, Fort Worth, TX: Holt, Rinehart and Winston

Ray, CA (1986) Corporate culture: the last frontier of control, *Journal of Management Studies* 23(3): 287–297

Redman, T and Grieves (1999) Managing strategic change through TQM: learning from failure, *New Technology, Work and Employment* 14(1): 45–61

Reed, EW and SC Reed (1964) *Mental Retardation: A Family Study*, Philadelphia, PA: Saunders

Reeves, R (2003) Reality bites, *Management Today* May: 37

Reich, R (1985) The executive's new clothes, *The New Republic* 13(1): 23–28

Reichers, AE (1987) An interactionist perspective on newcomer socialisation rates, *Academy of Management Review* 12(3): 278–287

Renn, RW and RJ Vandberg (1995) The critical psychological states; an underrepresented component in job characteristics model research, *Journal of Management* 21(2): 279–303

Revil, J (2003) Life makes you sick, *The Observer* 12 October: 19

Ricardo, D (1817) *The Principles of Political Economy and Taxation*, London: Dent and Son

Robbins, SP (1974) *Managing Organizational Conflict*, New York: Prentice Hall

Robbins, SP (1998) *Organizational Behavior: Concepts, Controversies, Applications*, 8th edn, New York: Prentice Hall

Roberts, J (2003) The manufacture of corporate social responsibility: constructing corporate sensibility, *Organisation* 10(2): 249–265

Roberts, Z (2003) Pressure group, *People Management* 28 August: 1

Robertson, I (2001) Undue diligence, *People Management* 22 November: 42–43

Robertson, I, M Smith and D Cooper (1992) *Motivation: Strategies, Theory and Practice*, 2nd edn, London: Institute of Personnel and Development

Robertson, I, M Smith and D Cooper (1992) *Motivation: Strategies, Theory and Practice*, 2nd edn, London: CIPD

Robinson, AL and AM O'Leary-Kelly (1998) Monkey see, monkey do: the influence of work groups on the antisocial behaviour of employees, *Academy of Management Journal* 41(6): 658–672

Robinson, G and K Dechant (1997) Building a case for diversity, *Academy of Management Executive* 11(3): 21–31

Robinson, O, and A Griffiths (2005) Coping with the stress of transformational change in a government department, *Journal of Applied Behavioural Science* 41(2): 204–221

Roethlisberger, FJ and WJ Dickson (1939) *Management and the Worker*, Cambridge, MA: Harvard University Press

Rogelberg, SG and A Luong (1998) Nonresponse to mailed surveys: a review and guide, *Current Directions in Psychological Science* 7: 60–65

Rogelberg, SG, A Luong, ME Sederburg and DS Cristol (2000) Employee attitude surveys:

examining the attitudes of noncompliant employees, *Journal of Applied Psychology* 85(2): 284–293

Rogers, CR (1961) *On Becoming a Person*, Boston, MA: Houghton Mifflin

Rollinson, DJ, J Handley, C Hook and M Foot (1997) The disciplinary experience and its effects on behaviour: an exploratory study, *Work, Employment and Society* 11(2): 283–311

Romm, C and N Pilskin (1998) Electronic mail as a coalition building information technology, *ACM Transactions on Information Systems* 16(1): 82–100

Ronen, S (1986) *Comparative and Multinational Management*, New York: Wiley

Roney, A and CL Cooper (1997) *Professionals on Workplace Stress*, Chichester: Wiley

Roseman, IJ (2001) A model of appraisal in the emotion system: integrating theory, research and application. In K Scherer and T Johnstone (eds), *Appraisal Processes in Emotion: Theory, Methods and Research*, New York: Oxford University Press

Rosen, B and T Jerdee (1974) Factors influencing disciplinary judgements, *Journal of Applied Psychology* 59(3): 327–331

Rosen, M and J Baroundi (1992) Computer-based technology and the emergence of new forms of control. In A Sturdy, D Knights and H Willmott (eds), *Skill and Consent: Contemporary Studies in the Labour Process*, London: Routledge

Rosenberg, MJ (1960) An analysis of affective-cognitive consistency. In I Hovland and MJ Rosenberg (eds), *Attitude, Organizational and Change*, New Haven, CT: Yale University Press

Rosenfeld, P, RA Gicalone and CA Riorden (1995) *Impression Management in Organisations*, London: Routledge

Rosenthal, R and L Jacobsen (1968) *Pygmalion in the Classroom*, New York: Holt, Rinehart and Winston

Ross, L (1977) The intuitive psychologist and his shortcomings: distortions in the attribution process. In L Berkowitz (ed.), *Advances in Experimental Social Psychology*, New York: Academic Press

Rothschild, J and TD Miethe (1999) Whistleblower disclosures and management retaliation, *Work and Occupations* 26(1): 107–128

Rouillard, LA (1994) *Goals and Goal Setting*, London: Kogan Page

Rousseau, DM (1979) Assessment of technology in organisations: closed versus open systems approaches, *Academy of Management Review* 4(4): 527–541

Rousseau, DM and J Parks (1993) The contracts if individuals and organisations, *Organisational Behaviour* 15(1): 1–43

Rowlinson, S (1996) Low inflation is bringing out ageism in employers, *People Management* 7 March: 19

RSA (1995) *Tomorrow's Company*, London: Royal Society for the Encouragement of Arts, Manufactures and Commerce

Rubens, P (2003) Army tactics are the business, *Financial Times* 26 November

Rubin, DC (1995) *Remembering Our Past: Studies in Autobiographical Memory*, Cambridge: Cambridge University Press

Rubin, RS, DC Munz and WH Bommer (2005) Leading from within: the effects of emotion recognition and personality on transformational leadership behaviour, *Academy of Management Journal* 48(5): 845–858

Runciman, WG (1966) *Relative Deprivation and Social Justice*, London: Routledge and Kegan Paul

S

Sackman, SA (ed.) (1997) *Cultural Complexity in Organisations*, London: Sage

Salaman, G (1978) Management development and organisation theory, *Journal of European Industrial Training* 2(7): 7–11

Salancik, G and J Pfeffer (1977) An examination of need-satisfaction models of job attitudes, *Administrative Science Quarterly* 22(3): 427–456

Sarafino, EP (1997) *Principles of Behaviour Change*, Chichester: Wiley

Sathe, V (1985) *Culture and Related Corporate Realities: Text, Cases and Readings on Organizational Entry, Establishment and Change*, Homewood, IL: Irwin

Savery, LK, A Travaglione and IGJ Firns (1998) The links between absenteeism and commitment during downsizing, *Personnel Review* 27(4): 312–324

Scarborough, H and J Swan (1999) *Case Studies in Knowledge Management*, London: Institute of Personnel and Development

Schaunbroeck, J and DC Ganster (1993) Chronic demands and responsivity to challenge, *Journal of Applied Psychology* 78(1): 73–85

Schaunbroeck, J, DC Ganster and ML Fox (1992) Dispositional affect and work related stress, *Journal of Applied Psychology* 77(4): 322–335

Schein, EH (1969) *Process Consultation: Its Role in Organisational Development*, Reading, MA: Addison-Wesley

Schein, EH (1980) *Organizational Psychology*, 3rd edn, Englewood Cliffs, NJ: Prentice Hall

Schein, EH (1983) The role of the founder in creating organizational culture, *Organizational Dynamics* Summer: 13–28

Schein, EH (1990) Organizational culture, *American Psychologist* 45: 109–119

Schein, EH (1992) *Organizational Culture and Leadership*, San Francisco, CA: Jossey-Bass

Schein, VS (1977) Individual power and political behaviour in organisations: an inadequately explored reality, *Academy of Management Review* 2(1): 64–72

Schemerhorn, JR Jr, JG Hunt and RN Osborn (2000) *Organizational Behaviour*, 7th edn, New York: Wiley

Schick, F (1997) *Making Choices: A Recasting of Decision Theory*, Cambridge: Cambridge University Press

Schmidt, SM and T Kochan (1972) Conflict: towards conceptual clarity, *Administrative Science Quarterly* 17(3): 359–370

Schneider, B (1983) Work climates: an interactionist perspective. In NW Feimer and ES Geller (eds), *Environmental Psychology: Directions and Perspectives*, New York: Praeger

Schneider, L and E Locke (1971) A critique of Herzberg's classification system and a suggested revision, *Organizational Behaviour and Human Performance* 6(3): 441–458

Schneider, SC and JL Barsoux (1997) *Managing across Cultures*, London: Prentice Hall

Schonfeld, IS (1990) Coping with job-related stress: the case of teachers, *Journal of Occupational Psychology* 63(2): 141–190

Schrage, M (2007) Customers want loyalty not perfection, *Financial Times* 1 May

Schweitzer, ME, L Ordonez and B Deuma (2004) Goal setting as a motivator of unethical behaviour, *Academy of Management Journal* 47(3): 422–432

Scott, WE and PM Podsakoff (1982) Leadership supervision and behavioural control: perspectives from an experimental analysis. In LW Fredericksen (ed.), *Handbook of Organizational Behaviour Management*, New York: Wiley

Seashore, S (1954) *Group Cohesiveness in the Industrial Workgroup*, Ann Arbor, MI: University of Michigan

Segall, MW, DT Campbell and MS Herskovits (1966) *The Influence of Culture on Visual Perception*, Indianapolis, IN: Bobbs-Merrill

Seligman, MPP (1975) *Helplessness: On Depression, Development and Death*, San Francisco, CA: Freeman

Selnes, F, BJ Jaworski and AK Kohli (1996) Market orientation in United States and Scandinavian companies: a cross-cultural view, *Scandinavian Journal of Management* 12(2): 139–157

Selye, H (1974) *Stress without Distress*, Philadelphia, PA: Lippincott

Selye, H (1976) *The Stress of Life*, New York: McGraw-Hill

Selye, H (1982) History and present status of the stress concept. In L Goldthorpe and S Brenzitz (eds), *Handbook of Stress*, New York: Free Press

Selznick, P (1957) *Leadership in Administration, a Sociological Interpretation*, New York: Harper and Row

Selznick, P (1966) *TVA and the Grassroots*, New York: Harper and Row

Selznick, P (1984) *Leadership in Administration*, Berkeley, CA: University of California Press

Senge, P (1991) *The Fifth Discipline: The Art and Practice of the Learning Organization*, New York: Random House

Senge, P (1994) The leader's new work: building learning organisations. In C Mabey and P Iles (eds), *Managing Learning*, London: Pitman

Senior, B (1997a) *Organisational Change*, London: Pitman

Senior, B (1997b) Team roles and team performance: is there really a link?, *Journal of Occupational and Organisational Psychology* 70(3): 241–258

Sewell, G (1998) The discipline of teams: the control of team-based industrial work through electronic and peer surveillance, *Administrative Science Quarterly* 43(4): 397–428

Shapira, Z (1997) *Organisational Decision Making*, Cambridge: Cambridge University Press

Shaw, JB and E Barrett-Power (1997) A conceptual framework for assessing organisation, workgroup and individual effectiveness during and after downsizing, *Human Relations* 50(2): 109–127

Shaw, M (1981) *Group Dynamics: The Psychology of Small Group Behaviour*, New York: McGraw-Hill

Sheldon, WH (1954) *A Guide for Somatyping the Adult Male at All Ages*, New York: Harper and Row

Sheeran, P, D Trafimow and CJ Armitage (2003) Predicting behaviour from perceived behavioural control: tests of the accuracy of the theory of planned behaviour, *British Journal of Social Psychology* 42(3): 393–401

Sherif, M (1936) *The Social Psychology of Group Norms*, New York: Harper and Row

Shostak, AB (1980) *Blue Collar Stress*, Reading, MA: Addison-Wesley

Silver, J (1987) The ideology of excellence: management and neo-conservatism, *Studies in Political Economy* 24(1): 5–29

Silverzweig, S and RF Allen (1976) Changing the corporate culture, *Sloan Management Review* 17(3): 33–49

Simon, HA (1957) *Administrative Behaviour*, 2nd edn, New York: Macmillan

Simon, HA (1960) *The New Science of Management Decision*, New York: Harper and Row

Simon, HA (1964) On the concept of organisational goals, *Administrative Science Quarterly* 10(1): 1–22

Simon, HA (1978) Rational decision making in business organisations, *American Economic Review* September: 510–522

Simonson, I and BM Staw (1992) De-escalation strategies: a comparison of techniques for reducing commitment to losing courses of action, *Journal of Applied Psychology* 76(3): 419–426

Sinclair, A (1992) The tyranny of a team ideology, *Organisation Studies* 13(4): 611–626

Singh, JV (1986) Performance, slack and risk-taking in organisational decision making, *Academy of Management Journal* 29(3): 562–583

Skinner, BF (1974) *About Behaviourism*, London: Jonathan Cape

Smethhurst, S (2003) A slice of the cake, *People Management* 6 February: 32–34

Smircich, L (1983) Concepts of culture and organisational analysis, *Administrative Science Quarterly* 28(3): 339–358

Smircich, L and G Morgan (1982) Leadership: the management of meaning, *Journal of Applied Behaviourial Science* 18(2): 2–73

Smith, A (1776) *An Enquiry into the Nature and Causes of the Wealth of Nations*, New York: Modern Library

Smith, M and P Smith (2004) *Testing People at Work*, Oxford: Blackwell

Smith, V (1997) New forms of work organisation, *Annual Review of Sociology*, Vol. 23, Palo Alto, CA: Annual Reviews Inc.

Smith, W (2000) Pity the poor employees, *Guardian* 19 June: 5

Smith, W (2002) Whistling while you work, *Guardian* 21 September: 22

Sonsino S (2007) It's the fault that counts, *People Management* 11 January: 37–38

Sparks, K, CL Cooper, Y Fried and A Shirom (1997) The effects of hours of work on health: a meta-analytic review, *Journal of Occupational and Organisational Psychology* 70(4): 391–408

Sparrowe, RT and RC Linden (2005) Two routes to influence: integrating leader-member exchange and social network perspectives, *Administrative Science Quarterly* 50(3): 505–535

Spearman, CE (1904) General intelligence objectively determined and measured, *American Journal of Psychology* 15(1): 72–101

Spector, P (1982) Behaviour in organisations as a function of employees' locus of control, *Psychological Bulletin* 91(3): 482–497

Spector, P (1995) *Industrial and Organisational Psychology: Research and Practice*, Chichester: Wiley

Sperling, G (1960) The information available in brief visual presentation, *Psychological Monographs* 74, No. 498

Spreitzer, GM and RE Quinn (1996) Empowering middle managers to be transformational leaders, *Journal of Applied Behavioural Science* 32(3): 237–261

Stahl, MJ and AM Harrell (1982) Evolution and validation of a behaviourial decision theory measurement approach to achievement, power and affiliation, *Journal of Applied Psychology* 67(4): 744–751

Stajkovic, AD and F Luthans (1997) A meta-analysis of the effects of organisational behaviour modification on task performance 1975–1995, *Academy of Management Journal* 40(5): 1122–1149

Stanworth, C (1998) Telework and the information age, *New Technology, Work and Employment* 13(1): 51–62

Staw, BM (1975) Attribution of the causes of performance: a new alternative interpretation of cross-sectional research on organisations, *Organisational Behaviour and Human Performance* 13(3): 414–432

Staw, BM (1980) The escalation of commitment to a course of action, *Academy of Management Review* 6(3): 577–587

Staw, BM and SG Barsade (1993) Affect and managerial performance: a test of the sadder-but-wiser vs. happier-and-smarter hypothesis, *Administrative Science Quarterly* 38(3): 304–331

Staw, BM, NE Bell and JA Clausen (1986) The dispositional approach to job attitudes, *Administrative Science Quarterly* 27(1): 49–72

Staw, BM and J Ross (1987) Behaviour in escalation situations: antecedents, prototypes and solutions. In EE Cummings and BM Staw (eds), *Research in Organizational Behavior*, Vol. 9, Greenwich, CT: JAI Press, pp. 39–78

Staw, BM and J Ross (1989) Understanding behaviour in escalation situations, *Science* October: 216–220

Steel, RP and JR Rentsch (1995) Influence of cumulative strategies on the long-range prediction of absenteeism, *Academy of Management Journal* 38(6): 1616–1634

Steers, R and L Porter (1991) *Motivation and Work Behaviour*, New York: McGraw-Hill

Steers, RM and SR Rhodes (1978) Major influences on employee attendance: a process model, *Journal of Applied Psychology* 63(3): 391–407

Stein, H (2001) *Nothing Personal, Just Business: A Guided Journey Into Organisational Darkness*, Westport, CT: Quorum Books

Stephenson, T (1985) *Management: A Political Activity*, Basingstoke: Macmillan

Stern, S (2007) Attitudes to McJobs, *Financial Times* 20 March

Stewart, R (1991) *Managing Today and Tomorrow*, London: Macmillan

Stiles, P, L Gratton, K Truss, V Hope-Hailey and P McGovern (1997) Performance management and the psychological contract, *Human Resource Management Journal* 7(1): 57–66

Stinchcombe, AL (1965) Social structure and organizations. In J March (ed.), *Handbook of Organizations*, Chicago, IL: Rand McNally

Stogdill, RM (1948) Personal factors associated with leadership: a survey of the literature, *Journal of Psychology* 25(1): 35–71

Stogdill, RM (1974) *Handbook of Leadership: A Survey of Theory and Research*, New York: Free Press

Stoner, JAF (1961) A comparison of individual and group decisions involving risk. In R Brown (ed.), *Social Psychology*, New York: Free Press

Stoner, JAF (1968) Risky and cautious shifts in group decisions: the influence of widely held values. *Journal of Experimental and Social Psychology* 4(2): 442–459

Storey, JC, G Salaman and K Platman (2005) Living with enterprise in an enterprise economy: freelance and contract workers in the media, *Human Relations* 58(8): 1033–1054

Strasser, S, JD Eveland, G Cunnins, OL Denitson and JH Romani (1981) Conceptualising the goal and systems models of organisational effectiveness: implications for comparative evaluation research, *Journal of Management Studies* 18(3): 321–340

Symon, G (2000) Information and communication technologies and the networked organisation: a critical analysis, *Journal of Occupational and Organisational Psychology* 73(4): 389–414

Szegedy-Maszak, M (1989) Who becomes an authoritarian?, *Psychology Today* March: 53–67

T

Taggar, S, R Hackett and S Saha (1999) Leadership emergence in autonomous work teams: antecedents and outcomes, *Personnel Psychology* 52(4): 899–926

Tagiuri, R (1969) Person perception. In G Lindzey and E Aronson (eds), *Handbook of Social Psychology*, Vol. 3, Reading, MA: Addison-Wesley

Tajfel, H (1969) Cultural factors in perception. In G Lindzey and E Aronson (eds), *Handbook of Social Psychology*, Vol. 3, Reading, MA: Addison-Wesley

Tajfel, H and JG Turner (1985) The social identity theory of intergroup behaviour. In S Worchel and

WG Austin (eds), *The Psychology of Intergroup Relationships*, 2nd edn, Chicago, Il: Nelson-Hall

Tannenbaum, R (1962) Control in organisations: individual adjustment and performance, *Administrative Science Quarterly* 7(2): 236–257

Tannenbaum, R and WH Schmidt (1958) How to choose a leadership pattern, *Harvard Business Review* March/April: 95–102

Tawney, RH (1931) *Equality*, London: Allen and Unwin

Taylor, A (2005) *Financial Times* 7 June

Taylor, FW (1911) *Scientific Management*, New York: Wiley

Taylor, P (2003) Barclay's University: taking the lead in staff training, *The Financial Times* 23 June

Taylor, P, C Baldry, P Bain and V Ellis (2003) A unique working environment: health, sickness and absence management in UK call centres, *Work, Employment and Society* 17(3): 435–450

Taylor, SW, PT Hertel, MC McCallum and HC Ellis (1979) Cognitive effort and memory, *Human Learning and Memory* 5(3): 607–617

Terborg, J (1981) Interactional psychology and research on human behaviour in organisations, *Academy of Management Review* 6(4): 569–576

Terry, DJ, MA Hogg and KM White (1999) The theory of planned behaviour: self-identity, social identity and group norms, *British Journal of Social Psychology* 38(2): 225–244

Terry, DT (1994) Determinants of coping: the role of stable and situational factors, *Journal of Personality and Social Psychology* 56(4): 895–910

Tett, RP and JP Meyer (1993) Job satisfaction, organisational commitment, turnover intention and turnover: path analyses based on meta-analytic findings, *Personnel Psychology* 46(3): 259–294

Thomas, KW (1976) Conflict and conflict management. In M Dunette (ed.), *Handbook of Industrial and Organizational Psychology*, Chicago, IL: Rand McNally

Thomas, KW (1977) Towards multi-dimensional values in teaching: the example of conflict behaviours, *Academy of Management Review* 2(3): 484–490

Thomas, RR (1990) From affirmative action to affirmative diversity, *Harvard Business Review* March/April: 107–117

Thomas, R and A Davies (2005) Theorising the micro-politics of resistance: new public management and managerial identities in the UK public services, *Organisation Studies* 26(5): 683–706

Thompson, JD (1967) *Organisations in Action*, New York: McGraw-Hill

Thompson, P and S Ackroyd (1995) All quiet on the workplace front? A critique of recent trends in British industrial sociology, *Sociology* 29(4): 615–633

Thompson, P and D McHugh (1995) *Work Organisations: A Critical Introduction*, 2nd edn, Basingstoke: Macmillan

Thorndike, EL (1911) *Animal Intelligence*, New York: Macmillan

Timmins, N (2005) The public sector – still an attractive destination for needs fulfillment, *Financial Times* 14 October

Timmons, S (2003) A failed panopticon: surveillance of nursing practice via new technology, *New Technology, Work and Employment* 18(2): 143–153

Tjosvold, D (1991) *Team Organisation: An Enduring Competitive Advantage*, London: Wiley

Tolman, EC, BE Ritchie and D Kalsh (1946) Studies in spatial learning 1: orientation and shortcut, *Journal of Experimental Psychology* 36(1): 13–24

Toplis, J, V Dulewicz and C Fletcher (2004) *Psychological Testing*, 4th edn, Maidenhead: CIPD Publishing/McGraw-Hill

Tourish, D and A Pinnington (2002) Transformational leadership, corporate cultism and the spirituality paradigm: an unholy trinity in the workplace, *Human Relations* 55(2): 147–172

Townsend, K (2005) Electronic surveillance and cohesive teams: room for resistance in an Australian call centre?, *New Technology, Work and Employment* 20(1): 47–59

Towers, B (2003) Overview: the changing employment relationship. In B Towers (ed.), *Handbook of Employment Relations Law and Preactice*, 4th edn, London: Kogan Page

Tracy, L (1987) Consideration and initiating structure: are they basic dimensions of leader behaviour?, *Social Behaviour and Personality* 15(1): 21–33

Trevino, L and V Bart (1992) Peer reporting of unethical behaviour: a social context perspective, *Academy of Management Journal* 35(1): 38–64

Trist, EL, GW Higgin, H Murray and AB Pollock (1963) *Organisational Choice*, London: Tavistock

Tsui, AS (1989) An empirical examination of the multiple constituency model of organisational effectiveness, *Proceedings of the Academy of Management* April: 188–192

Tuckman, BW (1965) Development sequence in small groups, *Psychological Bulletin* 63(3): 384–399

Tuckman, BW and N Jensen (1977) Stages of group development revisited, *Group and Organisation Studies* 2(3): 419–427

Tulving, E (1974) Theoretical issues in free recall. In TR Dixon and DL Horton (eds), *Verbal Behaviour and General Behaviour Theory*, Englewood Cliffs, NJ: Prentice Hall

Turner, AN and PR Lawrence (1965) *Industrial Jobs and the Worker*, Boston, MA: Harvard School of Business

Turner, D (2003) Stress used as 'excuse to skive', *Financial Times* 21 October

Tversky, A and D Kahneman (1974) Judgement under uncertainty: heuristic and bias, *Science* 185: 1124–1132

V

Vaill, PB (1982) The purpose of high performing systems, *Organizational Dynamics* Autumn: 23–29

Valle, M and PL Perrewe (2000) Do politics perceptions relate to political behaviour? Tests of an implicit assumption and expanded model, *Human Relations* 53(3): 359–386

Van de Vliert, E and C De Dreu (1994) Optimising performance by conflict simulation, *International Journal of Conflict Management* 5(2): 211–222

Van Eynde, DF and JA Bledsoe (1990) The changing practice of organisational development, *Leadership and Organisational Development Journal* 11(2): 25–30

Van Vianen, AEM and AH Fischer (2002) Illuminating the glass ceiling: the role of organisational culture preferences, *Journal of Occupational and Organisational Psychology* 75(3): 315–337

Varey, R (1999) What the world needs now is . . . , *Professional Manager* September: 16–18

Vecchio, R (1987) Situational leadership theory: an examination of a prescriptive theory, *Journal of Applied Psychology* 72(3): 444–451

Vernon, PE (1955) The assessment of children. In *The Bearings of Recent Advances in Psychology on Educational Problems: Studies in Education*, 7, University of London Institute of Education, pp. 189–215

Vernon, PE (1969) *Intelligence and Cultural Environment*, London: Methuen

Vogel, DJ (2005) Is there a market for virtue? The business case for corporate social responsibility, *California Management Review* 47(4): 19–45

Von Neuman, J and O Morgenstern (1947) *Theory of Games and Economic Behaviour*, Princeton, NJ: Princeton University Press

Vroom, VH (1964) *Work and Motivation*, New York: Wiley

W

Wachman, R (2007) How competition ate away Britain's chemicals giant, *The Observer* 24 June: 4–5

Wahaba, MA and LG Bridewell (1976) A review of research on the need hierarchy theory, *Organizational Behaviour and Human Performance* 15(2): 212–240

Walker, CR and RH Guest (1957) *Man on the Assembly Line*, New Haven, CT: Yale University Press

Wallace, C and G Chen (2006) A multi-level integration of personality, climate, self-regulation and performance, *Personnel Psychology* 59(3): 529–557

Walton, CC (1988) *The Moral Manager*, Cambridge, MA: Balinger

Walton, EJ (2005) The persistence of bureaucracy: a meta-analysis of Weber's model of bureaucratic control, *Organisation Studies* 26(4): 569–600

Walton, EJ and S Dawson (2001) Managers' perceptions of criteria of effectiveness, *Journal of Management Studies* 38(2): 173–199

Walton, RE (1977) Work innovations at Topeka: after six years, *Journal of Applied Behavioural Science* 13(4): 422–431

Walton, RE (1985) From control to commitment in the workplace, *Harvard Business Review* March–April: 77–84

Wanous, JP, TL Keon and JC Latack (1983) Expectancy theory and occupational/organisational choices: a review and test, *Organisational Behaviour and Human Performance* 22(1): 66–86

Wanous, JP, AE Reichers and SD Malik (1984) Organisational socialisation and group development: towards an integrated perspective, *Academy of Management Review* 9(4): 670–683

Warr, PB (1996) *Psychology at Work*, 4th edn, Harmondsworth: Penguin

Waters, R (2003) Microsoft offers reward to catch virus writers, *Financial Times* 6 November

Watson, A (2004) Benefits of a different kind, *Financial Times* 4 December

Watson, KM (1982) An analysis of communication patterns: a method for discriminating leader and subordinate roles, *Academy of Management Journal* 25(1): 107–122

Watten, EJ (2005) The persistence of bureaucracy: a meta-analysis of Weber's model of bureaucratic control, *Organisation Studies* 26(4): 569–600

Waugh, HC and DA Norman (1965) Primary memory, *Psychological Review* 72(1): 89–104

Wayne, SJ, LM Shore and RC Linden (1997) Perceived organisational support and leader–member exchange: a social exchange perspective, *Academy of Management Journal* 40(1): 82–111

Webb, TL and P Sheeran (2006) Does changing behavioural intention engender behaviour change? A meta-analysis of experimental evidence, *Psychological Bulletin* 132(2): 249–268

Weber, EU, CJ Anderson and MH Birnbaum (1992) A theory of perceived risk and attractiveness, *Organisational Behaviour and Human Decision Processes* 60(3): 492–523

Weber, M (1947) *The Theory of Social and Economic Organisation*, London: Hodge

Weber, M (1948) *From Max Weber. Essays in Sociology*, Trans., edited and introduction HH Gerth and CW Mills, London: Routledge and Kegan Paul

Webster, J (1996) *Shaping Women's Work: Gender, Employment and Information Technology*, London: Longman

Weick, K (1979) *The Social Psychology of Organizing*, 2nd edn, Reading, MA: Addison-Wesley

Weick, K (2001) *Making Sense of the Organisation*, Oxford: Blackwell

Weick, KE and LD Browning (1986) Argument and narration in organisational communication, *Journal of Management* Summer: 243–259

Weierter, SJM (1997) Who wants to play 'follow the leader'? A theory of charismatic relationships based on routinised charisma and follower characteristics, *Leadership Quarterly* 8(2): 161–186

Weiner, B (1992) *Human Motivation: Metaphors, Theories and Research*, London: Sage

Welch, J (1997) Electronic menaces are a flaming liability, *People Management* 12 June: 24

Welch, J (1999) ROM with a view, *People Management* 17 June: 34–40

Wernimont, P (1966) Intrinsic and extrinsic factors in job satisfaction, *Journal of Applied Psychology* 50(1): 41–50

Wesley, F and H Mintzberg (1989) Visionary leadership and strategic management, *Strategic Management Journal* 10(1): 17–32

West, M (1994) *Effective Teamwork*, Leicester: BPS Books

West, M, D Tjosvold and K Smith (2004) *Teamworking: International Perspectives*, London: Wiley

Whelan, SA (1999) *Creating Effective Work Teams*, London: Sage

White, RP, P Hodgson and S Crainer (1996) *The Future of Leadership: A White Water Revolution*, London: Pitman

Whitehead, AN (1985) *Science and the Modern World*, London: Free Association Books

Whitehead, M (1999) Churning questions, *People Management* 30 September: 46–49

Whitsett, DA and L Yorks (1983) Looking back at Topeka: General Foods and the quality-of-work-life experiment, *California Management Review* 25: 93–100

Whorf, BL (1940) Science and linguistics, *Technology Review* 42(2): 229–248

Wiggins, J (2007) Coke develops a thirst for sustainability, *Financial Times* 2 July

Wilkinson, A (1998) Empowerment: theory and practice, *Personnel Review* 27(1): 40–56

Williams, A (1999) The truth will out, *People Management* May: 23–4

Williams, DR and JS House (1985) Social support and stress reduction. In CL Cooper and MJ Smith (eds), *Job Stress and Blue-collar Work*, Chichester: Wiley

Williams, SD (2002) Self-esteem and the self-censorship of creative ideas, *Personnel Review* 31(4): 495–503

Willmott, H (1993) Strength is ignorance: slavery is freedom: managing culture in modern organisation, *Journal of Management Studies* 30(4): 515–551

Willmott, H (1997) Rethinking managerial work: capitalism, control and subjectivity, *Human Relations* 50(11): 1329–1359

Wilson, DC and RH Rosenfeld (1990) *Managing Organisations: Text, Readings and Cases*, London: McGraw-Hill

Windahl, S, B Signitzer and TJ Olson (1992) *Using Communication Theory: An Introduction to Planned Communication*, London: Sage

Winter, SG (2003) Mistaken perceptions: cases and consequences, *British Journal of Management* 14(1): 39–44

Winterberg, J, L Abrams and C Ott (2004) Assessing the field of organisation development, *The Journal of Applied Behavioural Science* 40(4): 265–279

Wiseman, R and E Greening (2005) It's still bending: verbal suggestion and alleged psychokinetic ability, *British Journal of Psychology* 96(1): 115–127

Wittgenstein, L (1953) *Philosophical Investigations*, Trans. GEM Anscombe (1968), Oxford: Blackwell

Witzel, M (2003) Champion of the individual, *Financial Times* 7 August

Witzel, M (2004) Be principled for a change, *Financial Times* 23 August

Womak, JP, DT Jones and D Roos (1990) *The Machine that Changed the World: The Triumph of Lean Production*, New York: Macmillan

Wood, S and MT Albanese (1995) Can we speak of high commitment management on the shop floor?, *Journal of Management Studies* 32(2): 215–247

Woodall, J (1996) Managing culture change: can it ever be ethical?, *Personnel Review* 25(6): 28–40

Woodman, RW and JJ Sherwood (1980) The role of team development in organisational effectiveness: a critical review, *Psychological Bulletin* 92(2): 166–186

Woodruffe, C (2000) Emotional intelligence: time for time out, *Selection and Development Review* 16(4): 3–9

Woodruffe, C (2001) Promotional intelligence, *People Management* 11 January: 26–29

Woodward, J (1965) *Industrial Organisation: Theory and Practice*, Oxford: Oxford University Press

Word, CO, MP Zanna and J Cooper (1974) The nonverbal mediation of self-fulfilling prophecies in interracial interaction, *Journal of Experimental Social Psychology* 10(1): 109–120

Worren, AM, K Ruddle and K Moor (1999) From organisational development to change management, *Journal of Applied Behavioural Science* 35(3): 273–286

Wren, T, D Hicks and T Price (eds) (2004) *The International Library of Leadership*, Cheltenham: Edward Elgar

Wright, D (1971) *The Psychology of Moral Behaviour*, Harmondsworth: Penguin

Wright, DS, A Taylor, DR Davies, W Sluckin, SG Lee and JT Reason (1970) *Introducing Psychology: An Experimental Approach*, Harmondsworth: Penguin

Wright, P (1995) *Managerial Leadership*, London: Thompson

Wright, PM, TM Gardner, LM Moynihan and MR Allen (2005) The relationship between HR practices and firm performance: examining causal order, *Personnel Psychology* 58(2): 409–446

Y

Yearta, SK, S Maitlis and RB Briner (1995) An exploratory study of goal-setting theory and practice: a motivational technique that works?, *Journal of Occupational and Organisational Psychology* 68(4): 237–252

Yorks, L and DA Whitsett (1985) Hawthorne, Topeka and the issue of science versus advocacy in organisational behaviour, *Academy of Management Review* 10(1): 21–30

Z

Zack, M and J McKenney (1995) Social context and interaction in ongoing computer-supported management groups, *Organisation Science* 6(3): 394–422

Zaremba, A (1988) Working with the organisational grapevine, *Personnel Journal* July: 38–42

Ziera, Y and J Avedisian (1989) Organisational planned change: assessing the chances for success, *Organisational Dynamics* Spring: 31–45

Index of Names

Cunningham, I. 46, 522, 668
Cunningham, J. B. 490
Cunnins, G. 489
Curran, K. 222
Cyert, R. M. 478, 481, 483, 495
Czyzewska, M. 117

D

Daft, R. L. 7, 434, 495
Dalton, D. R. 234
Danford, A. 344
Daniels, K. 307
Danserau, F. D. 353, 463
Darr, W. 424
Dastmalchian, A. 620, 621, 622
Datta, D. K. 42
Davenport, T. 522
Davey, K. M. 136, 475
Davidow, W. 523
Davidson, E. 455
Davidson, M. J. 307
Davies, A. 584
Davies, D. R. 67
Davis, S. M. 509, 667
Dawson, S. 496
De Dreu, C. 424, 427
De Valder, C. L. 360
Deal, T. E. 267, 284, 596, 625
Deary, I. J. 86
DeBrabender, B. 309
DeBruijn, P. 331
Dechant, K. 61
DeCotis, T. A. 617
DeFruyt, F. 94
Delbridge, R. 344, 447
DeLeo, P. J. 230
Denbigh, A. 524
Denison, D. R. 617, 624
Denitson, O. L. 489
Dennelly, M. 366
Dent, E. B. 584, 641
Der Hovanessian, A. 122
Deuma, B. 237
Deutsch, S. J. 492
Devine, E. 443
Dewe, P. 379
Dewe, P. J. 295, 299, 302
Dickson, K. 525
Dickson, W. J. 11, 202, 346
Diehl, D. 366
Digman, J. M. 84

Dill, W. 633
Dion, K. L. 334
Dirsmith, M. W. 578
Dittrich, J. E. 249
Dix, G. 344
Dixon, N. M. 190
Doane, D. 54
Dobbins, A. 585
Doherty, M. 617
Doherty, N. 42
Doktor, R. 213
Donaldson, L. 559
Donaldson, T. 51, 54, 55, 56
Donaldson-Fiedler, E. J. 299
Donnelly, J. H. 502, 511, 651
Donnelly, M. 45
Dougherty, T. W. 290
Doward, J. 284
Downey, H. K. 513
Doyle, C. 62
Doyle, M. 46, 286, 583
Drever, J. 78
Drucker, P. 356, 415, 478, 479, 503, 523, 665
Duchon, D. 353, 463
Duehr, E. E. 117
DuGuy, P. 559
Dukerich, J. M. 356, 380
Dulewicz, V. 93, 94, 100
Dunegan, K. 353, 463
Dunham, R. 144
Dunning, D. 116
Dunning, J. N. 62
Durkheim, E. 607
Dwyer, D. J. 284, 292
Dyer, L. 345

E

Early, C. 236
Eaton, J. 50
Eaton, S. C. 144
Eckman, P. 440
Edwards, J. E. 141, 156
Edwards, J. R. 151
Edwards, P. K. 49, 145, 414
Edwards, R. 580
Ehrlich, S. R. 356, 380
Ekstrand, B. R. 171
Elacqua, T. C. 294
Elkin, A. J. 303
Ellis, H. C. 171
Ellis, V. 584

H

Index of Subjects

References in **bold** indicate that a 'key concept' explanation is included in the margin.

A

ability 94–5
absenteeism, employee 143–4, 291
abstract conceptualisation 184–5
'accommodation' conflict handling 422
achievement test 94, **94**
action-centred leadership 352–3
action research 645–6, **645**
active experimentation 185
activist learning style 186
actuators 570, **570**
adaptation (change) 632, **632**
adaptive behaviour 201, **201**
adaptive learning 183
adhocracy 534, **534**
'adjourning' group development stage 325–6, **325**
adjustment function of attitudes 131–2, **131**
advanced information technologies 518
advanced technology and structure 517–18
affective component of attitudes 131, **131**
affiliation needs 202
aims 472
altercasting 329, **329**
ambassadors 330, **330**
ambiguity, role 329, **329**
analyser strategies 548
analysis by synthesis model 112, **112**
anchoring/judgement heuristic 258, **258**
anxiety, stress and 288–9
application (key variable) school (culture) 602, **602**
appraisal control 575
aptitude 94–5, **94**
aptitude tests 94, **94**
artifacts and creations 592, 593–5
assertiveness 422, **422**
assertiveness training, stress and 301
assessment centre method 87

'attention and selection' perception stage 106–8, **106**
attitudes 131, **131**
  associated constructs 130
  and behaviour 136–9
  case study 157–9, 162–3
  changing 134–5
  formation 132–4
  functions 131–2
  individual processes and 310–11
  measuring 140–1
  OB in action 147
  personality and 160–1
  to risk 265
  timeout 134, 137, 145
  work-related 142–6
attribution leadership theory 380–2
attributions 120–2, **120**
authority 511, **511**
authority games 411, **411**
autocratic leaders 361, **361**
autonomy, and excellence 605
availability heuristic 258, **258**
'avoidance' conflict handling 422

B

Bank Wiring Observation Room studies 11–12
barriers to work motivation 200–1
basic assumptions, culture model 592, 593
basic organisational structure 503, **503**
behaviour 15, 136–7
Behaviour Modification (OB Mod.) 240–4
behavioural component of attitudes 131, **131**
behavioural consensus 121, **121**
behavioural consistency 121, **121**
behavioural control 572–84
behavioural distinctiveness 121, **121**
behavioural outcomes (stress) 291, **291**
behavioural self-control, stress and 301
behaviourism 69, **69**
beliefs 130, **130**, 136

T

two-factor theory
  of leadership 361–2, **361**
  of motivation 206–7
two-store theory of memory 168–72, **168**
type personality theories 81–4

U

unbounded problems 250–2, **250**
uncertainty and decision making 266
uncertainty avoidance 383
unconditioned response 174, **174**
unconditioned stimulus 174, **174**
unconscious (the) 72–3
unitarist perspective on conflict 415, **415**
unproctored situation 87, **87**

V

V/E (valence-expectancy) model 229–30
V:Ed (verbal: educational) intelligence 91, **91**
valence expectancy (V/E) model 229–30
validity 87
value-expressive function of attitudes 132, **132**, 133
'value of reward' concept 231, **231**
values 130, **130**
  and culture 592, 593
  decision making 265

variable interval schedule 178, **178**
variable ratio schedule 178, **178**
VDL (vertical dyadic linkage) model 353–4
verbal (oral) communication 449–53
verbal ability 95
(verbal: educational) intelligence (V:Ed) 91, **91**
vertical differentiation 417, 506, 510–11, **510**
vertical dyadic linkage (VDL) model 353–4
vertical surveillance 584, **584**
virtual organisation 524–6
vision, and leadership 378–79

W

weak situations, and personality 70, **70**
whistleblowers 59, **59**
wider-social culture, leadership and 382
work context
  empowerment and involvement 223
  motivation 221
  physical working environment 221–2
work performance 291
work-related attitudes 142–6
work scheduling 222–3
work space 222
workforce diversity 59–61
workgroup and stress 285
workplace stress 280–1, **280**
written communication 453–4